liberation historiography

Liberation historiography

African American Writers and the Challenge of History, 1794–1861

JOHN ERNEST

The University of North Carolina Press

Chapel Hill and London

© 2004 The University of North Carolina Press
All rights reserved

Designed by Heidi Perov
Set in Berthold Bodoni Light and Cezanne
by Keystone Typesetting, Inc.
Manufactured in the United States of America

The paper in this book meets the guidelines for permanence and durability of
the Committee on Production Guidelines for Book Longevity of the Council on
Library Resources.

Library of Congress Cataloging-in-Publication Data
Ernest, John.
Liberation historiography : African American writers and the challenge of
history, 1794–1861 / by John Ernest.
p. cm.
Includes bibliographical references (p.) and index.
ISBN 0-8078-2853-x (cloth: alk. paper)
ISBN 0-8078-5521-9 (pbk.: alk. paper)
1. African Americans—History—To 1863—Historiography. 2. African American
historians—History—18th century. 3. African American historians—History—
19th century. 4. Historiography—United States—History—18th century.
5. Historiography—United States—History—19th century. I. Title.
E184.65 .E76 2004
973'.0496073—dc22
2003017902

cloth 08 07 06 05 04   5 4 3 2 1
paper 08 07 06 05 04   5 4 3 2 1

Portions of this book have previously appeared, in somewhat different form, in
the following publications:
"Liberation Historiography: African American Historians before the Civil War,"
American Literary History 14, no. 3 (2000): 413–43. Used by permission of Oxford
University Press.
"The Governing Spirit: African American Writers in the Antebellum City on a Hill,"
in *A Mighty Baptism: Race, Gender, and the Creation of American Protestantism*, ed.
Susan Juster and Lisa MacFarlane. Copyright © 1996 by Cornell University. Used by
permission of the publisher, Cornell University Press.
"The Reconstruction of Whiteness: William Wells Brown's *The Escape; or, A Leap for
Freedom*," *PMLA* 113 (1998): 1108–21. Reprinted by permission of the copyright
owner, Modern Language Association of America.

contents

ix • Acknowledgments

1 • Introduction

39 • ONE. The Theater of History

95 • TWO. Scattered Lives, Scattered Documents
Writing Liberation History

155 • THREE. Multiple Lives and Lost Narratives
(Auto)Biography as History

219 • FOUR. The Assembly of History
Orations and Conventions

277 • FIVE. Our Warfare Lies in the Field of Thought
The African American Press and the Work of History

331 • EPILOGUE. William Wells Brown and
the Performance of History

345 • Notes

389 • Bibliography

413 • Index

acknowledgments

It is difficult to map out the course of events that finally led me to this book, but I think it is safe to say that the journey began when I was a graduate student at the University of Virginia, where I wrote a dissertation on white American historians of the nineteenth century. While working on this book, I've often had occasion to realize anew just how well David Levin and Alan Howard prepared me for the work ahead. My debt to these invaluable mentors has only increased over the years.

I started to explore the ideas that developed into *Liberation Historiography* long before I was prepared to write this book, and I have received a great deal of help along the way. Through the years, I've benefited from opportunities to present early findings and often loose ideas to attentive and helpful communities of scholars, both professional and otherwise. This part of my story might begin in 1991 with a talk on nineteenth-century historians for a faculty discussion seminar at Florida International University, where I received warm support and encouragement from my colleagues, and a talk on George Bancroft for the Midwest Modern Language Association Annual Meeting, where members of the audience (as well as the six or seven members of a panel organized by Stephen Carl Arch) offered useful comments.

I began to explore the particular dynamics of African American historiography shortly after those events. *Liberation Historiography* is, in many ways, an extension of the case studies that made up my first book, *Resistance and Reformation in Nineteenth-Century African-American Literature*, and I've benefited greatly from the guidance of my editor at the University Press of Mississippi, Seetha Srinivasan, whose warm support for my work has continued through the years. My work turned more directly to the material I study here when I presented a paper on Jerena Lee and Zilpha Elaw at the 1995 MELUS conference, and then when Lisa MacFarlane—great colleague, intellectual companion, and American Studies czar—asked me to build on my work for the essay that would eventually lead to this book, "The Governing Spirit: African American Writers in the Antebellum City on a Hill." I'm grateful to Lisa and to Susan Juster, coeditors of *A Mighty Baptism: Gender, Race, and the Creation of American Protestantism*, for giving me a chance to try out an early exploration of this material. When I gave a talk on William Wells Brown at the 1996 SENCSA conference, I thought I was adding to the foundation of the book that would follow, a book on African American historians throughout the nineteenth century, unaware that my research would eventually require me to focus on pre–Civil War historical writing for a book in which a version of my talk on Brown would serve as the epilogue rather than the makings of a centerpiece. I was still thinking about that larger project when I gave a talk on nineteenth-century African American historians for the Active Retirement Association in 1997, and I'm grateful to that always engaging group for their patience and interest.

Having entered the project, I discovered time and again that I had much to learn about early African American writing and culture. My work on *Liberation Historiography* began in earnest, as it were, in the spring of 1997, when a Gustafson Junior Faculty Fellowship from the University of New Hampshire gave me the opportunity to complete my initial research and write drafts of the first few chapters. Those chapters laid the groundwork for the project, but they were not adding up to much more than a survey of early African American publications on history. The turning point in this project came later, inspired by numerous conversations with two graduate students who have taught me much through the years: Molly Doyle and Rhondda Thomas. In their own determined quest to understand the specifically religious frameworks and dynamics of nineteenth-century African American literature, Molly and Rhondda helped me refocus this study in important ways. The moral and intellectual integrity they bring to their work has been both an inspiration and a model to me while I've worked on this book. Following the path of that inspiration, I was led to Archie Smith Jr.'s *The Relational Self: Ethics and Therapy from a Black Church Perspective*, which led me, in turn, to the work of James H. Cone as I worked to construct the theoretical framework for this study. A sabbatical semester in 2001 came at just the right time, and was just one of many ways in which the University of New Hampshire has proven to be a very supportive institution.

A path that leads from individual friendships to black theology must finally lead even those of us who value and romanticize solitude and solitary quests to a renewed appreciation of the importance of community—and in this regard, as in others, I have been richly blessed. Even in a longish statement of acknowledgments and debts, I could not possibly list the names of all of the undergraduate and graduate students who have influenced my thinking about African American literature—but if I tried, the list would begin with Lisa Feldman Massey and Avy Trager, both of whom have been essential intellectual companions while I worked on this book. Suffice it to say, though, that I am reminded regularly that the connection between one's teaching and one's scholarship is not just a rhetorical flourish or an institutional convention. I've relied heavily on my students, and I am grateful to them for all that they have helped me understand.

I cannot imagine having come so far in my own work without the encouragement, instruction, and support of my colleagues in the UNH English department. While I owe a great deal to everyone who works or has worked in the English department office, I'm indebted especially to Tory Poulin, who makes all things possible (except for the specific dimensions of the classroom I requested, though I think she's working on this). The American Literature and American Studies faculty at UNH is a vibrant and engaging group of scholar-teachers committed to excellence in teaching, sound and useful scholarship, and community service. David Watters, Briggs Bailey, Sarah Sherman, and Lisa MacFarlane in particular have in various ways both challenged and encouraged me to develop my thinking on the disciplinary integrity of nineteenth-century African American studies. Sarah especially has offered wise counsel on exploring the historical dynamics of literary culture, both in and beyond her comments on my introductory chapter for this book— and she is also one of those relatively rare cultural studies scholars who think carefully about liberation theology and its applications to African American literature. Above all, though, I must acknowledge my debt to Lester Fisher, master of the art of teaching and mentor in the art of thinking. Les's influence on this book is indirect but deep, for I have had the privilege of many conversations in which I was pressed to consider the full range of concerns that a scholar must address, the complex harmonies of thought that an individual must learn to hear, and the play of time and space in which one must learn to live.

Beyond UNH, I've had the good fortune to encounter other scholars who keep me from being cynical about the profession of literary and cultural scholarship. Some of those encounters have been from a distance—a few minutes at a conference, readings of journal articles or book proposals and manuscripts, the occasional email. Others have been close encounters of the professional kind that have developed into important friendships. William Andrews and James A. Miller have been models for me, and my debt to them is deep. Carla Peterson has been warmly supportive and characteristically attentive to things that pass by the notice of many. Bob Levine has been generous through the years, offering me opportunities to present my work before various audiences, engaging me in conversations about the field, and supporting me in ways too numerous to list. Among other things, Bob arranged for me to present a talk drawn from this book at the University of Maryland in 2001—a time when I was finally finding my theoretical feet for the project. The warm welcome I received from the faculty and particularly the graduate students at the University of Maryland has had a remarkably long shelf life and continues to enrich my professional and personal endeavors. Like the list of students who have been important to me, the list of my extended professional community would be quite long if I were to include everyone who has helped me find my way through the material and through the years—but ultimately, all lists and all roads would lead to Gordon Hutner, whose faith in me has been (to me, strangely) unwavering over the years, and who gave me a chance to publish (and, before that, helped me refine) the central essay drawn from this book. As that essay would not have been nearly as strong without Gordon's help (and the wise if challenging advice of the readers for *American Literary History*, to whom I am most grateful), so this book would not be nearly as focused or as purposeful as it is without the guidance I received while preparing that essay for publication. And as the manuscript approached publication, I was aided yet again by the readers for the University of North Carolina Press, and I am deeply grateful to James A. Miller and the anonymous second reader for their attentive readings and impressively thoughtful advice.

In gathering the material for this book, I've relied heavily on the collections and the librarians at some truly great libraries. Alderman Library at the University of Virginia and the Library of Virginia provided me with a number of texts that otherwise would have been difficult to find. The staff at the Maine Historical Society were very generous in helping me locate information about Robert Benjamin Lewis. The Accessible Archives website has connected me quickly to a number of newspaper articles that have been essential to this study. Above all, though, I owe a great debt to the great librarians at the

Dimond Library at the University of New Hampshire. They have helped me in ways too numerous to mention or even to keep track of—and the interlibrary loan staff has been particularly helpful as I looked for texts just off the beaten track of established scholarship.

I might have both started and ended this narrative about the process of thinking about and writing this book by mentioning Sian Hunter, my editor at the University of North Carolina Press, who expressed interest in this project from the beginning and who has continued to do so through the many delays and detours along the way. This book would not be what it is but for Sian's knowledge of the field, her understanding of what makes a book valuable, and her detailed attention to both the style and substance of one's writing. I am grateful also to all of the editorial, production, and marketing staff at the press—particularly to Paul Betz for his strikingly thoughtful and careful work as copyeditor.

As this narrative suggests, my mentors have been many, but I want to note three in particular, all of whom passed away before I finished this book, and to whom this book is dedicated. David Levin got me started on this journey, and I am still working to follow his great and generous example. Willis J. Neal, former boss and oldest friend, was an avid historian of Owego, New York, and he taught me much about the importance of both history and memory. William Bronk, so deeply attentive to the demands of poetry, so richly attuned to the call of the world beyond the worlds we know, taught me much and gave me more than I had any right to expect or hope for. A person would be lucky to encounter one such mentor in life. And I might have included another, who also passed away before I could finish this book, though this is a mentor whom I never met, John Hartford. Actually, I once encountered Mr. Hartford in a bookstore in Charlottesville, Virginia, and spoke to him for all of, I think, ten seconds. I think he was looking for books about steamboats. From a distance, though, I've learned much from John Hartford the historian. I've learned, among other things, that historical understanding involves the responsibility to develop a style of presentation, a mode of thought, an ethical commitment, and a way of living appropriate to and respectful of the subject(s) of one's study. With the great examples of my mentors in mind, I'm still working on meeting these responsibilities.

And that is the work that finally brings this narrative of influences, debts, and community back home. Home, for example, to one of my earliest students and now my great friend and professional companion, Malvina Engelberg. Home to Valerie Cunningham, activist and role model, who carries on the tradition of African American liberation historiography and gives many in New Hampshire reason to believe that fundamental social reform is still possible and that the beloved community is not a distant dream. Home to my closest friend, a most formidable and inspiring model of personal and professional integrity, John Grammer, who somehow managed to meet and marry an equally admirable scholar and person, Elizabeth Elkin Grammer. Home to my young reminder of the importance of history, my pen pal, an attentive reader who actually likes my poetry, a great soul with a large heart, my goddaughter Zoita Elizabeth Grammer. But home, beyond all, to my soul's companion, my closest friend and spiritual guide, Rebecca Mays Ernest, who has contributed more to this book and to my life than she might realize, and certainly more than I can hope to say. If she approves of this book, then the journey has been successful.

liberation historiography

introduction

We pause to think of the Past or dream of the Future and our
Present is already in the Past, our Future in the Present.
— *The Journals of Charlotte Forten Grimké*

In his 1925 essay "The Negro Digs Up His Past," Arthur A. Schomburg characterizes previous publications on African American history as being largely "compendiums of exceptional men and women of African stock" that were "on the whole pathetically over-corrective, ridiculously over-laudatory; it was apologetics turned into biography." Arguing that "a true historical sense develops slowly and with difficulty under such circumstances" as those faced by earlier students of African American achievement, Schomburg celebrated the fact that, by his day, history had become "less a matter of argument and more a matter of record" (231). But whatever a "true historical sense" might be, its development must still be under way, for it has yet to arrive. Indeed, African American history, like all history, remains as much a matter of argument as a matter of record. One might note that "compendiums of exceptional men and women of African stock" still constitute one of the primary popular genres of African American writing; but beyond the work of recovering and publicizing the lives and achievements of African Americans, which is still necessitated by the relative absence of those achievements in the popular media and public consciousness, approaches to the scholarly "matter of record" itself have been and are still today a "matter of argument."[1]

Consider, for example, Wilson Jeremiah Moses's *Afrotopia*, an attempt to recontextualize heated arguments over the nature, validity, and value of Afrocentrism as a scholarly framework. Moses reminds us that "a limitless range of opinion has been attached to the term Afrocentrism by authors across the political spectrum, most of whom are less interested in scholarly investigations of African American cultures and historical traditions than in forwarding myriad self-serving political agendas" (9). Moses here follows Schomburg, and the historical profession generally, in distinguishing between matters of record and of argument, and also in contesting the grounds by which one might claim the authority of "scholarly investigations." Although Moses asserts "that popular conceptions of history among a people are worth understanding," he is clear about what that understanding comes to in the hands of a professional historian: "I am certain, I realize, to offend both the advocates and the opponents of sentimental Afrocentrism and romantic Egyptocentrism by stating my belief that they are usually harmless and inoffensive, if sometimes extravagant, folk traditions. They are whimsical, entertaining, and often charming fantasies developed by nineteenth-century journalists, preachers, novelists, and vernacular storytellers" (17). Moses does an admirable job of historicizing the historical consciousness of the past, but he is never in any danger of believing that the historians of the past pose any significant challenge to current historiographical frameworks and methods.[2]

Between Record and Argument:
The Cultural Dynamics of African American History

Although many today, like Moses, are engaged in the search for a "true historical sense," few seem willing to consider the possibility that African American historians of the past might have something to say about approaches to African American history.[3] In the chapters that follow I argue for a serious assessment of early-nineteenth-century historians who faced the specifically textual challenge of creating an approach to historical representation that could promote the development of a unified African American community. Scholarship on the African American historical consciousness of this period has focused largely on oral culture, and while I recognize the centrality of African American oral culture I am interested here specifically in struggles over written representations of black history and identity. My operating assumption is that, visions of a "true historical sense" or of an objective ideal of scholarship aside, conceptions of historical truth are culturally generated and necessarily reflect struggles for cultural authority—struggles that inform Moses's book as well as those popular or folk historians that he studies and sometimes critiques.[4] As Greg Dening has argued, "One has to understand that 'scientific history' or 'academic history' is as cultural and as social as a dinner-table story or scripture or a political parable. The rhetoric about these logical systems of 'academic histories' and the declatory definition of what they are and are not sometimes hide what disciplines share with everyday cultural phenomena. Indeed the vested interest in making them seem different and above culture is the very quality that makes them the same" (53).[5] Even when they tried to claim the putatively transcultural or "objective" authority of historical writing, early African American writers understood that conceptions of historical scholarship and methodology were deeply implicated in the system of white supremacy that defined every other aspect of American life.

In approaching the work of early African American writers, it is essential to consider their relation to what David Theo Goldberg has called "the racial state," a state built on the ideological foundations that Charles W. Mills outlines so well in his important book *The Racial Contract*. In his study, Mills argues that the Enlightenment "social contract" is underwritten by a "racial contract," a white supremacist ideology that is fundamental to white Western life and thought and to its political and social practice. "White supremacy," Mills argues, "is the unnamed political system that has made the modern world what it is today" (1). According to the terms of the white supremacist "racial contract," "One has an agreement to *mis*interpret the world. One has to learn to see the world wrongly, but with the assurance that this set of mistaken perceptions will be validated by white epistemic authority, whether religious or secular" (18). Clearly, this is connected to white American understandings of what constitutes education. "In effect," Mills argues, "on matters related to race, the Racial Contract prescribes for its signatories an inverted epistemology, an epistemology of ignorance, a particular pattern of localized and global cognitive dysfunctions (which are psychologically and socially functional), producing the ironic outcome that whites will in general be unable to understand the world they themselves have made" (18). Mills continues: "To a significant extent, then, white signatories will live in an inverted delusional world, a racial fantasyland, a 'consensual hallucination.' . . . There will be white mythologies, invented Orients, invented Africans, invented Americas, with a correspondingly fabricated population, countries that never were, inhabited by people who never were—Calibans and Tontos, Man Fridays and Sambos—but who attain a virtual reality through their existence in travelers' tales, folk myth, popular and highbrow fiction, colonial reports, scholarly theory, Hollywood cinema, living in the white imagination and determinedly imposed on their alarmed real-life counterparts" (18–19). "One could say then," Mills explains, "as a general rule, that *white misunderstanding, misrepresentation, evasion, and self-deception on matters related to race* are among the most pervasive mental phenomena of the past few hundred years, a cognitive and moral economy psychically required for conquest, colonization, and enslavement" (19). And this ignorance is not simply an effect of incomplete knowledge or of other *gaps* in the archive; it is, in fact, the *purpose* of a historical understanding shaped by and devoted to white supremacist ideology. As Mills puts it, "These phenomena are in no way *accidental*, but *prescribed* by the terms of the Racial Contract, which requires a certain schedule of structured blindnesses and opacities in order to establish and maintain the white polity" (19).

Writing in the racial state and under the terms of the racial contract, African American historians were and are inevitably metahistorical—for the nature and condition of their subject make the attempt to write history inevitably a task of questioning the terms of history and the politics of historical writing. Even to identify a work of history as an *African American* history is to enter the complex ideological realms of group identity so as to establish the terms by which the history relevant to a dispersed and diverse collective can be gathered and narrated.[6] African American writers, then, long anticipated what historical theorist Alex Callinicos has called "the transformation of philosophy of history into metahistory," focusing on the attempt to "conceptualize" historical inquiry "as a form of writing."[7] Accordingly, I have explored various forms and *forums* of writing in an effort to understand the textual character and uses of African American historical self-consciousness before the Civil War.

The years that I study in this book saw significant shifts and developments in the condition of African Americans, including changes in conceptions of race, increasingly overt measures of white supremacist control, and increasingly militant and independent black activism.[8] While accounting for these shifts and developments, though, I am interested in the largely stable patterns of African American historical theory during these years. David Walker's *Appeal*, published in its three editions from 1829 to 1830, was simply a concentration and amplification of views expressed in earlier publications, and this influential and prophetic work was echoed in both argument and historical method in subsequent publications. Accordingly, after an initial chapter that offers an overview of these patterns of historical thought, I explore specific forms and forums of textualized historical thought—including works identified as historical studies or manifestos (chapter 2), autobiographical writing (chapter 3), orations and convention proceedings (chapter 4), and the historical writing that dominated the black press (chapter 5).

In all forms and forums of historical writing, African Americans necessarily had to contend with and against the developing tradition of white American historical thought as well as the pointed erasure of Africa as a site of history in Enlightenment thought. Included in this struggle was the developing false consciousness fundamental to white American historical thought that made it possible to celebrate liberty in a nation in which slavery influenced every aspect of social life—economic, political, legal, and religious. As anyone who has tried to do even the most basic research in African American history and culture of this time will know, the most readily available documents and sources of historical information either omit African Americans or present African American experience under the slanted white light of the dominant culture. At the end of Octavia Butler's *Kindred*, a 1970s Californian interracial couple are transported to the pre–Civil War South, and when they are finally returned to the twentieth century they travel to Maryland to gather evidence of their strange journey over space and time. They visit the Maryland Historical Society, "itself a converted early mansion," but they find that many of those whom they knew in the past are excluded from the records and that the nineteenth-century newspapers offer partial and slanted accounts. The image of the plantation transformed into a historical society is an apt metaphor for describing the conditions under which African American historical research has long had to function.

Early African American historical writers contended with the cultural dynamics that shaped and limited the preservation of the records of African American experience—and they contended as well with an experience that resisted any conventional mode of recording. James Wilkinson has usefully distinguished between "evidence and the remains of the past." "The remains of the past," in Wilkinson's formulation, "comprise what survives of everything that ever happened; evidence consists of those remains that historians use in making histories. Evidence, in other words, occupies the same relation to remains as history does to the past: it is a tiny subset of a far larger domain. But unlike the past, remains constitute an actual, not a virtual, reality and are thus subject to the effects of time. Not everything in the past has left traces, and not all traces have survived. In the absence of remains, there can be no evidence, and in the absence of evidence, there can be no history" (80). African Americans recognized that much of their history was excluded from or deformed in the official records that served as historical evidence, and they looked to construct a body of historical writing capable of addressing the fragments of history indicated by the evidence while attending also to the story suggested by the "remnants," the fragmented experience of a people struggling to define themselves as a coherent community, the blood on the fields of history. For all of the many advances in the recovery of African American history during the time of legal slavery, as Orlando Patterson has noted, "we know next to nothing about the individual personalities of slaves, or of the way they felt about one another. The data are just not there" (11). Of the lives of nominally free African Americans in the North, or of those who escaped from slavery, we know something more—but those lives, in their contingent relation to those many who were still enslaved, still resisted the best efforts of the historian, and that contingent relation remained central to African American self-definition in the North and to white conceptions of African American identity.

In approaching the challenge of writing (or writing about) history, African Americans engaged in a dynamic mode of composition in which the act and conventions of writing—and the contingencies that shaped the performance of individual and collective identity—were inseparable from any available historical understanding. In approaching this body of writing, then, it is important to think of history as something indicated by the mode of historical writing rather than as a story captured in a historical narrative, reducible to a chronology or to a series of questions for quizzing the historical literacy of hapless schoolchildren. The historical theorist Hans Kellner's reflections on the conventions of historical writing in *Language and Historical Representation* are useful here. "I do not believe," Kellner testifies, "that there are 'stories' out there in the archives or monuments of the past, waiting to be resurrected and told. Neither human activity nor the existing records of such activity take the form of narrative, which is the product of complex cultural forms and deep-seated linguistic conventions deriving from choices that have traditionally been called rhetorical; there is no 'straight' way to invent a history, regardless of the honesty and professionalism of the historian. Indeed, the standards of honesty and professionalism are to be found in precisely those conventions, both in what they permit or mandate and in what they exclude from consideration" (vii). African American writers worked actively to establish their own professionalism while also contending against a white historical tradition that relegated their collective experiences to a singular and containable story, and they were accordingly very much aware of the conventions of historical authority that mandated what could be excluded from consideration. As Dening has noted in his exploration of the performative dynamics of historical study, "The 'theatricality of history-making' involves the notion of viewing in a space so closed around with convention that the audience and actors enter into the conspiracy of their own illusions. The paradox is that self-awareness, performance consciousness, does not disturb the realisms of their understanding" (105). African American writers, working necessarily in the white theater of history, were faced with the challenge of exposing that conspiracy and disrupting the conventions by which the audience and actors alike might identify their roles in the drama of history—and they needed to do this while still claiming the authority of history for their writing. The result was often a fragmented historical narrative that called attention to the reality and limits of its fragmentation, historical studies that explored the politics of historical understanding to shift the focus of the historical story that was vital to the white supremacist system of control.

This mode of historical writing calls also for a corresponding mode of historical reading. I have avoided, throughout this book, any evaluative approach to this writing—for I do not believe that to note that new historical information has been discovered, or to discover errors or other forms of misinformation in any individual text, is to identify a text as irrelevant or even essentially unreliable. The works I study, I assert, have much to teach us about the past, particularly in the mode of apprehending an unrecoverable past that they present. I would apply to these historical texts what Kellner says about reading history—that is, "To read history out of focus . . . in a crooked way that promotes human ways of knowing, at least provisionally, to the status of the 'primary sources' of our understanding of the past is perhaps a sign of the 'deepest respect for reality,' a reality that playfully insists that even reality (the notion of which is always a construction for a purpose) should not control our lives, which must remain in the awkward crookedness of unending examination, re-emplotting, and re-interpretation" (25). Nineteenth-century African Americans, I believe, necessarily read history in this way, and the writing they produced calls upon readers to read historical writing in this way. These writers, both working from and searching for a conception of a collective African American identity, recognized the importance—indeed, the inevitability and, in a white supremacist culture, the *intimacy*—of "unending examination, re-emplotting, and re-interpretation." The texts these writers produced, as becomes clear again and again, are as much readings as writings of history, and they are attempts to teach their readers to become active readers of history as well. In their reflections on history, they try to use the tools of consciousness and the materials of record to liberate consciousness and re-situate their readers in a newly envisioned community of faith and moral duty.

In short, the "struggle against an omnipresent 'white supremacist' social order" (as Clarence Walker has characterized the work of the early historians [*Deromanticizing* 87]) is not merely an unavoidable challenge in this writing; it is a defining condition of African American historical thought. The specific circumstances, contexts, and contingencies of the struggle for collective self-determination are the shaping forces of what I am terming "liberation historiography"—a project not simply of historical recovery but of historical intervention. Early African American historians drew from multiple texts—white scholarship, primary sources, the Bible, classical histories, and oral testimonies—with an interpretative method grounded in the need to address the condition of oppression that defined the African American community. In other words, how the early historians engaged in history "as a form of writing" is of central importance to our understanding of African American history. The work of antebellum African American historians is not simply the prehistory of serious African American historical research; the assumption behind their publications is not simply that the basic terms of the dominant historical narratives are sound but for the omissions in the record. Rather, African American historical representation is both a reading and an unreading, a juxtapositioning of documents, ideology, and individual lives that suspends historical conclusions in favor of a narrative method that joins secular and sacred history. Writing history is an act of moral imagination, and what can be apprehended as historical truth is revealed in the ways in which the narrative *doesn't* add up.

This is a body of writing, in other words, that argues *against* the possibility of a sound historical narrative in a culture shaped by, in Paul Gilroy's formulation, "modernity's protracted ambivalence towards the blacks who haunt its dreams of ordered civilisation" (191)—what Toni Morrison has termed the "pathology" of white Western modernity (qtd. in Gilroy 221). Developing a mode of historical representation capable of responding to and surviving under this pathological ambivalence, African American historians did not operate within a linear conception of time that could work backward toward what we would recognize as Afrocentricity; rather, in early African American writing, Africa stands primarily as a principle of narrative and historical uncertainty, the site of an imaginary order disrupted by profane history that speaks of a destiny resulting from that disruption. The map of that destiny was the map of a kind of historical theology—a theology that required the study of the separation of sacred and profane in the United States. By focusing on this disruption, the historian frames the body of knowledge that one claims as understanding, and the historian works thereby to create a community from the scattered remnants of a largely unknowable past. Matters of argument are, in fact, matters of record—the record of a historical method designed to destabilize the present social order to, in effect, make history possible. The task of the early historians was to write not a continuous narrative but rather a story of disruptions, of fragmentation, so as to identify the contours of a story beyond the reach of representation. Attending to their fragmented stories can enable us to recover the essentially performative nature of the black historians' collective project, for African American history is not what *follows* from the historian's intervention into the "official stories" (to borrow Priscilla Wald's term) of white supremacist ideology; the intervention itself *is* African American history, a performative historiographical mode that supports the shifting performance of individual and collective African American identity necessitated by the containment of blackness within white nationalist history.

Liberation Theology and Liberation Historiography

While researching this study, I benefited from reading Jon Cruz's *Culture on the Margins*, in which Cruz follows the development of the study of black spirituals as an example of what he terms "ethnosympathy," by which he means "the new humanitarian pursuit of the inner world of distinctive and collectively classifiable subjects" (3). "Though rooted in a profound social critique," Cruz notes, "the cultural discovery of black music and the search for cultural authenticity soon began to pivot upon a particular cultural aestheticization of black practices that, in turn, highlighted black religious music over black political and literary voicings. As black culture became aestheticized, a separation emerged between black political claims for a greater social and political inclusion within American civil society and a more acceptable spiritual (and eventually cultural) place for blacks in the hearts and minds of northerners who were championing the new mode of benevolent cultural reception. In essence, a peculiar kind of culturalism triumphed through a cultural eclipse of politics" (6). In focusing on "black political and literary voicings" of the antebellum period, I emphasize the importance of those "argumentative, critical, and elaborate black voices" that were, Cruz argues, "muted, indeed eclipsed" by the "cultural aestheticization of black practices" that, in Cruz's view, influenced the formation of the academic understanding of and approaches to cultural studies.

In early-nineteenth-century African American writing, as in the spirituals, the spiritual, the historical, and the political cannot be separated, and accordingly it is essential that we take seriously the active presence of religious belief in these texts.[9] Clarence Walker has observed that "during the nineteenth century, black and white evangelical Protestants believed that history was progressive and that God was history's prime mover" (*Deromanticizing* 91). For black historians as for white historians like George Bancroft, this belief in providential history was the defining principle of historical investigation and narration. One cannot read David Walker's *Appeal*, Maria Stewart's lectures, the Rev. James W. C. Pennington's *A Text Book of the Origin and History, &c. &c. of the Colored People*, Robert Benjamin Lewis's *Light and Truth*, or any number of other historical works of this period without recognizing the centrality of religious belief to understanding history. Obviously, the grand narrative of Providence in these texts echoes the white national narrative, and if considered solely for its inflated rhetoric of collective destiny this becomes a story we know (or think we do) too well to require any critical response beyond the usual dismissal of religious rhetoric. But just as the Bancroftian vision of national destiny has been influential far beyond any authority granted by its scholarly reputation, so too has African American writing shaped a collective consciousness that should not be either dismissed or underestimated. To note the excessive forms of religious belief is not to undervalue the power of belief any more than noting the excessive rhetoric of professional historians defending their discipline is cause to undervalue the importance of historical understanding.

Working in a religious culture—that is, a culture that identified religion as the foundation of its ideological justification for both domestic and foreign policy—African Americans drew from their own religious beliefs in their attempt to understand and function in their historical situation, and they developed, as a consequence, a distinctive form of Christianity. As Eddie S. Glaude Jr. has argued in his study of African American uses of the Exodus narrative in the early nineteenth century, "the moral identity constituted under the conditions of violence, suffering, and death differentiate in real terms, in spite of the sameness of rhetorical form, black America and white America" (110). Drawing from this insight, I explore the complications African Americans faced in using Christian discourse to struggle against a culture that itself relied heavily on Christian discourse, and accordingly I share Glaude's view that the particular historical dynamics of a collective African American moral identity constitute "a critical point" in the study of this period (110). "The relation of this violence and suffering to notions of solidarity and obligation," Glaude argues, "are critical to the narratives that, to some degree, made antebellum black American practices intelligible. These stories, in particular Exodus, drew on the persistence of violence (that of Pharaoh and Egypt) to shore up the importance of thanksgiving, remembrance, and duty" (110). In other words, the experience of oppression shaped a collective moral identity that allowed African Americans to identify themselves both historically and theologically, as their developing conceptions of a collective identity inspired deeply invested readings of the Bible that, in turn, allowed them to define agency in the world, to conceptualize themselves as theologically identifiable actors on the historical stage.[10]

For the writers I consider, moreover, religion was not simply a generalized framework that defined the basic terms of one's historical vision; rather, beyond the conceptually containable concept "religion" was a dynamic and complex presence in the world, the "truth" of history, but a truth that was complexly both hidden and revealed by human modes of understanding and approaches to social order. These writers examined the available historical records; they considered the implications of law and social practice; they explored the implications of the popular discourses of race, patriotism, and reform; and they drew from the evidence of experience and individual struggle and achievement. The various sources spoke powerfully in their evidence of moral violations and of the white abandonment of the principles that dominated white public discourse. They spoke powerfully as well in their evidence of African American efforts to draw from those principles, and from a religion that was something more than a mode of public discourse, to struggle against oppression and to restore meaning to language. But the message was not always clear, the judgment against oppression was rarely manifest, the condition of the community was not always either conceptually coherent or heroic in its specific manifestations, and there was much that could only be imagined in the physical experience and spiritual condition of those of African origins in the United States. The historical commentator, in short, did not simply work *from* a comforting vision of religious truth; rather, she or he looked *to* a history that variously tested, affirmed, denied, or otherwise complicated one's sense of an overarching divine order.

Even those writers most aggressively certain of the divine basis and endorsement of their historical visions—Robert Benjamin Lewis, for example—emphasized the complicated search for historical understanding not simply as the foreground of their conclusions but as a vital component of the "light and truth" they present. "In the language of scripture," Lewis states in his brief preface to the original 1836 edition of *Light and Truth*, "Christ is often called a *light*, and God is said to *dwell* in light; and light is constantly used as the emblem of *knowledge*. Christ is the author of Truth, and God is a being of infinite truth. Moral Truth is the conformity of words and actions to the thoughts of the heart—as when a man speaks or writes what he thinks, and what is in reality truth." With this as his framework, Lewis notes his own struggle to discern the truth of history and the journey of research that has led finally to the publication of *Light and Truth*. "I have . . . searched diligently," Lewis states, "for fourteen years, in quest of light and truth, in ancient, sacred and profane history, translated by English historians; and have written a History of the Colored and Indian People, from the creation of the world to the present period" (1836 Preface in 1843 edition 3). The history that Lewis wrote is, in fact, a compilation of documents and historical facts that constantly remind the reader of Lewis's fourteen years of research. In lines of verse printed on the title page, the volume advises,

> Search this work with care and candor;
> > Every line and page you read
> Will brighten all the truths of Scripture,
> > Proved by history—plain indeed.

But anyone who has tried to read *Light and Truth* knows that the truth it offers is anything but plain. In fact, the book draws the reader into Lewis's quest and into the terms of understanding, an understanding devoted to the light and truth of sacred history but tied inevitably to the overcast skies of profane historiography and translation.

Lewis's work is representative of antebellum African American historical writing in its dialectical engagement with the forms of worldly understanding and the elusive demands of spiritual truth. Accordingly, in my attempt to understand the historical visions and the historical theorizing of African

Americans thus situated in the antebellum American cultural theater, I have found it useful to draw from black liberation theology, the body of work associated most prominently with James H. Cone that has become a significant presence in theological study and activist theory. Cone's 1969 *Black Theology and Black Power*, inspired in part by the assassination of Martin Luther King Jr., was a powerful and influential call for a theology grounded in black American experience. In 1970, Cone published *A Black Theology of Liberation*, an attempt to develop a theology in which God is identified with the condition of the oppressed and specifically with the black historical experience of oppression and the struggle for liberation. Cone has noted that he developed his approach independently of the liberation theology movement that is more commonly associated with the work of Latin American theologians, work initiated in print (but long before developed in practice) by Gustavo Gutierrez's *Teología de la liberación* in 1971. Over time, though, black theology and various modes of liberation theology have developed in relation to one another, formed coalitions, and have produced a mode of theology influenced by Marxism that constitutes a significant and increasingly influential approach to religious practice and social change.[11]

Cone's *Black Theology and Black Power* was one of many attempts of that time and since to join black religious organizations with the Black Power movement. On July 31, 1966, for example, the National Committee of Negro Churchmen (which later became the National Conference of Black Churchmen) published in the *New York Times* a statement supporting the Black Power movement. These efforts were extended further through the leadership of James Forman, once the executive director of the Student Nonviolent Coordinating Committee and later a leader of the Black Economic Development Conference (BEDC), which was formed in 1968. Forman was the author of the "Black Manifesto," a document presented in 1969 at the Interreligious Foundation for Community Organization, which called for white churches and synagogues of the United States to pay $500 million in reparations to the African American community and explained in detail how the dispersion of that money was to be organized and applied. Shortly after this initial presentation, Forman interrupted the Sunday service at Riverside Church in New York City and read the decidedly revolutionary manifesto. The responses of organized black churches were mixed, and many were critical of the Marxist foundations of the manifesto. Still, Forman's actions, joined with other attempts to attend to the demands of the Black Power movement within the structures of organized black religion, emphasized the need for a religious understanding grounded in and capable of responding to the specific needs of the black community.

Forman addressed the results of a history of oppression; and Cone in his approach to theology tries to do so as well, in part by way of a theological understanding informed by that history. In his 1982 memoir *My Soul Looks Back*, Cone notes his own attempt to determine the appropriate terms of his theological project, in part a matter of understanding, in effect, what makes a black theology *black*. "I have been struggling," Cone states, "to incorporate the experience and culture of the oppressed into the conceptual tools for articulating black theology. For I contend that our rebellion against Europeans should lead to a second step, namely to an affirmation of our own cultural resources as well as those found among other people who have similar experiences of oppression" (103). In part, learning to use those conceptual tools involves the consideration of the black experience as the epistemological foundation of theology, the site at which an appropriate hermeneutical approach to the Bible may be constructed; and, in part, learning to use those conceptual tools involves the recognition of black expressive culture as a significant body of critical theory, not just *expressions from* but *readings of* experience. Central to Cone's theology, then, is the assertion that "theology ... cannot be separated from the community which it represents. It assumes that *truth* has been given to the community at the moment of its birth. Its task is to analyze the implications of that truth, in order to make sure that the community remains committed to that which defines its existence" (*A Black Theology of Liberation* 8). Black liberation theology identifies the black community as a significant source of theological understanding—with *blackness* referring not to skin color but to the historical structures of social order that have been informed over time by various applications of the ideologies of race and by the social technologies of social control that have been both inspired and justified by those shifting ideologies.

While history plays an important role in black liberation theology, assumptions about what constitutes black history, and related assumptions about how to define the black community, deserve more careful consideration than they usually receive. African American collective experience before the Civil War is not simply background or foundation for the present; rather, in this period we begin to see the dynamic and performative response to an unstable but pervasively dominant ideology that is at the heart of both black identity and black history. As Katherine Clay Bassard has suggested in her study of the spiritual work of early African American women's writing, "The study of pre-Emancipation African American culture and literature is significant because it is here that we can trace the beginnings of African American notions of community or 'personhood,' to catch, if you will, African American cultural production in the very act of *performing* community" (20).[12] I am interested in this developing performance, particularly in the various textual forms it took as writers drew from history to craft a theater of consciousness for the developing act(s) of performing community. Cone, Dwight Hopkins, and other theologians have drawn primarily on oral culture for the conceptual tools for articulating a historically informed black theology—with the spirituals, the blues, and the performative tradition of black preaching prominent among the expressive forms they have examined. I draw from liberation theology to understand the written tradition of African American historical commentary, and I suggest that this body of writing offers a theology of historical understanding—that is, an approach to history shaped, on the one hand, by black Christian belief and, on the other, by the pressures of a developing white American historiography that threatened to alienate African Americans from a historically informed understanding of individual and collective identity.

As the perhaps surprising combination of Marxism and theology suggests,[13] liberation theology asserts that institutionally sanctioned religious thought is never politically neutral but rather always functions within a certain sociopolitical theater, and accordingly must always function in a dynamic and contingent relation to the dominant economic and political forces that shape the lives of the people. Accordingly, liberation theology emphasizes the importance of the conditions that shape the lives of the community of faith as well as the historical causes of those conditions. It is considered, indeed, a theological duty to understand what some have called "the structures of sin"— that is, to understand oppression in systemic terms and not simply as isolated and individualized examples of oppression. In black theology, I would suggest, this suggests the limitations of the ideologically convenient concept of *racism*—focusing, as it often does, on a specific action that can be identified in space and time, as something that occurred (in thought or deed) on this day by this person. The recognition of racism is, of course, still essential, but even more important is an understanding of white supremacist ideology as a systemic presence developed historically, the theater within which racism operates—and a theater, not incidentally, in which people who avoid committing identifiable acts of racism can still participate, with no conscious awareness, in a system that distributes education, wealth, opportunity, geographical advantage, and even identity according to a historically informed condition of subjectivity. As liberation theologians in Central or South America would include but look beyond the immediate landowner to understand the economic oppression of their congregations, so black liberation theology would lead one to include but look beyond the immediate representative of racism to discover the systemic operations of racial oppression.

Liberation theology, then, actively seeks an understanding of the systemic conditions that shape individual and communal life, but it does so as part of a central commitment to action *in* the world. That is, liberation theology is a theology of praxis, of an ongoing process of action and reflection, and one that distinguishes between "orthopraxis" and "orthodoxy." A continual engagement in the world, in the lives of the community of the oppressed, is part of an ongoing process of theological reflection, development, and action. A great part of this engagement is the acknowledgment of the interpretive authority of the community of faith—that is, those whose lives have been most intimately and negatively affected by the conditions of the world. Some of the most important work of liberation theologians, as has often been noted, is in the community dialogues that have shaped biblical interpretation according to the experience of the oppressed. Those most in need identify the conditions of their lives in the Bible—for example, the commentary in chapter 18 of Revelation on "the merchants of the earth" who at the fall of Babylon will have occasion to regret their dealings in "slaves, and souls of men." This reading becomes part of a larger process of reading the Bible for moral guidance, returning to the need for moral action in the world—leading, perhaps, to a resistance to a capitalist system that supports those merchants.[14] This emphasis on particular communities—shaped, as they are, by differing historical conditions—has made liberation theology a subject of particular interest to those grappling with the possibility of a coherent theology in a postmodern world, for this is necessarily a fragmented and "polycentric" theology that operates according to significantly different conceptions of community (from those geographically contained by poverty to those communities dispersed but connected by ideologies of race, gender, or sexuality). As one group of religious scholars has argued, "Its many-sided grounding and method of decentering one dominating voice put liberation theology in natural dialogue with postmodern analyses. Postmodern thinking also concerns itself with the limitations and underside of rationality and subjectivity. It is a 'decanonization' of conventional authorities, since it assumes that no thinking is free from time, place, or interest. Much like postmodernity, liberation theology situates itself as a way and language of the 'outposts,' a delegitimizing of the center of knowledge and of power" (Batstone et al. 1). Accordingly, liberation theology (which should, perhaps, be always liberation *theologies*) has increasingly inspired coalitions by which the limitations of vision in any single community of concern can be exposed and reformed in its interactions with other communities.

In presenting the concept of liberation historiography as an approach to understanding the historical theory presented in antebellum African American writing, then, I mean to emphasize the dynamic relation between historical understanding and developing concepts of African American collective identity of this period. African Americans of this time recognized that the narration of history, like the formulation of theology, is never politically neutral. From the availability of the documents of history to the ideological forces that shaped any accessible evidence (and shaped as well the reading of the evidence), history was subject to the needs and assumptions of those closest to the centers of power—whether it be the wealthy gentleman historian William H. Prescott or the Jacksonian secretary of the navy George Bancroft. Accordingly, African American writers looked to history in an attempt to understand and expose "the structures of sin"—and to "thereby compel this guilty nation," as William C. Nell put it in 1841, "to acknowledge the debt she owes her oppressed sons and daughters" ("Speech of Wm. C. Nell"). This is a body of writing that presents historical truth as the intersection of the sacred and secular realms of existence and accordingly looks for *history* in the condition of the oppressed, in the African American communities that exposed white America's abandonment of sacred duty in the service of secular power.

Much of this writing, accordingly, gauges the relation between sacred and secular understandings of historical process so as to identify the terms by which the present could be understood and moral responsibility could be defined. The purpose of historical research and writing was to identify the historical contours of the African American community, and in that way to aid in the ongoing realization of the historical agency of that community. Virtually all of the writers that I discuss in the following chapters recognize that identifying the African American community was itself a challenge. Certainly, one could identify any individual member of that community by placing the individual in the South, or on public transportation in the North, or by trying to send the individual to school, or by any number of means by which white culture controlled and delimited black movement, opportunity, freedom, and identity. The challenge, though, was to work from an African American community of individuals who had been individually and collectively identified and defined by white supremacist ideology and practice—and then from that community to determine the possibility of an imagined community that could exist in positive as well as negative terms. The challenge was to work from an understanding of the historical condition of oppression to a vision of historical agency. Liberation historiography, then, is an attempt to liberate African Americans from an other-defined history so as to provide them with agency in a self-determined understanding of history—and since the ultimate determination of historical authority and agency was God's, these writers read the dual texts of human oppression and biblical destiny to determine their position in a larger and largely unknowable narrative of providential history. Collective self-determination, then, involved gathering together a fragmented people into an equally fragmented and always provisional historical narrative. Historical truth involved the relation of the secular histories that can be known and the sacred history that can be only partially apprehended. Liberation historiography, in short, is a mode of reading history in a way that respects the authority of the fragmented communities of experience, and that arranges those fragments according to the guidance of biblical narratives that themselves become comprehensible through the various experiences of the communities of the oppressed.

But however abstract this might seem in my attempt to condense it to a sentence or paragraph, this is not a body of writing devoted to an abstract ideal of the value of historical understanding. Like liberation theology, what I am terming liberation historiography is a mode of historical investigation devoted to praxis, a dynamic process of action and reflection, of historical discovery in the service of ongoing and concrete systemic reform. That work of reform might involve the recognition that the white supremacist system worked in part by shaping the consciousness of individual readers, and so required active resistance in the form of books that countered that presence. Ann Plato, for example, notes in her 1841 *Essays*, "Some books are injurious to the mind, as well as useful. Books have a silent, but powerful influence on the formation of character" (50). In one of various biographical sketches of the sort that are central to the historical work of African American writing, Plato asserts that her subject "possessed Christian virtue, which often the profound historian does not" (77). In her *Essays*, then, Plato draws readers into various manifestations of history, in the form of the people whose lives she sketches, and in the form of her own reflections on spiritual and worldly matters. What counts as history in her writing is the confluence of the subject, Plato's mode of presenting the subject, and Plato's principles for reading history and evaluating understanding.

Plato here does cultural work similar to that of David Walker in his revolutionary *Appeal* (1829–30), in which Walker similarly discusses the influence of books on the formation of character, and similarly addresses the moral dynamics of reading and writing practices. Indeed, in its attention to the community of the oppressed, the historical causes of that oppression, and the moral responsibility to take action that must follow from historical understanding, Walker's *Appeal* deserves to be recognized as one of the first and still one of the most powerful works of liberation theology and liberation historiography alike. Walker, like most of the writers I discuss in this book, approached historical understanding with an active and demanding Christian faith; as the entry on Walker in the *Encyclopedia of African American Religions* has it, "Walker was intensely religious, and believed that through the action of rising up to claim justice Blacks could play a messianic role in God's plan for the world" (813). Walker's understanding of black power proceeded from his investigation of the historical causes of black powerlessness; and Walker brought to that investigation a biblically informed understanding of God's devotion to the oppressed by which those who were seemingly without power could discover their power. The powerless, Walker argues, become a force in the world by recognizing their place in history, uniting sacred and secular history to understand the grounds and responsibility for militant resistance to the forces of oppression.

In *Liberation Historiography*, I look at various attempts to identify the terms by which African Americans could understand themselves historically, and I look at various corresponding attempts to identify the moral action that must follow that historical understanding. Certainly, there were disagreements over the proper course of action, though it is striking how many of these writers arranged their texts—histories, autobiographies, and orations—so as to lead to a call for physical resistance. Disagreements and principled searches for the proper course of action are a central topic throughout the following chapters. All of these searches, though, involved an understanding of history that was decidedly moral, and an understanding of principle that was inseparable from practice. Identifying the terms by which a fragmented community could understand itself historically, and by which history could be understood so as to identify moral responsibility, and by which moral responsibility could be transformed into concrete action—this was the work of historical research and representation, and these are the characteristics of liberation historiography.

In reading these works, then, my purpose is not to recover an "objective" understanding of the past, nor is it to identify where these writers have their facts right or wrong. I am interested instead in identifying a tradition of historical investigation. Similarly, I am not reading these works in the service of an abstract aesthetic ideal. Rather, I am suggesting that, as the Black Arts movement theorists argued, we need an understanding of literary achievement that is connected to action—and whether that action should be reform, resistance, or revolution seems to me a more useful question to bring to the practice of reading than the questions about aesthetic evaluation and cultural classification we usually entertain. I am interested, in short, in what we now call the cultural work of these texts, but I am interested also in the moral work of these texts—in the moral responsibilities that these texts identified for those who read them in the nineteenth century and that they identify still for those who read them today.

Gathering the Fragments: An Overview

Henry M. Turner, in his introduction to William J. Simmons's 1887 collective biography *Men of Mark: Eminent, Progressive, and Rising*, presents a vision of African American historical work as the foundation for a varied collective cultural mission. "Little as the common observer may regard it," Turner states, "we men who gather up the fragments of our labors, acts, achievements, sayings, songs, oddities, peculiarities, fun, speeches, lectures, poems, war struggles, bravery, degradation and sufferings, and preserve them for the future, now while they are within reach, will stand out as heroes in the day to come." They will be recognized as heroes, Turner suggests, because their work is part of a larger struggle—a struggle not simply to tell the story of the past but to gather the materials necessary for the moral work of the future. "The future orator, statesman, minister, poet, journalist, ethnologist, as well as the historian," Turner asserts, "will from these gather materials to build towers heaven-reaching that will monument the grandeur of our race, and still grander struggles that lifted them from the barren plains of the contempt of the world, to the majestic heights that we are destined to scale in God's Providence" (19). Before the Civil War, African American writers worked to "gather up the fragments" of African American experience and culture, life and thought, with a belief in the sacred framework within which human history functions, and with a belief also that in the relation between sacred and profane could be found the outlines of African American destiny.

As all of these historians demonstrate in their work, gathering the fragments was not a matter of working toward a singular, linear narrative of African American history, for there was no simple story to be told. What I identify as historical theory in these works is a function of historical method—of the process of gathering the fragments of history so as to construct a fragmented historical text, one in which the several parts become significant in their relation to one another, and significant also in their unique and separate manifestations of the untold story of white supremacist oppression and African American experience. In a short "Trifles" piece for the *Anglo-African Magazine* in 1859, Mary A. B. Cary asserts that "words, actions, events, and circumstances become important or trivial in proportion to the relations they sustain, or to the accidents of time and purpose inseparable from their real significance." For the writers here studied, history is defined by such relations, and the work of these writers is accordingly devoted to the belief, as expressed by Cary, that "events small in themselves, become the index to the most stupendous results" (*The Anglo-African Magazine* 55). In these writings, the lives of apparently inconsequential people are placed next to biographies of the most prominent performers on the public stage, seemingly isolated incidents are placed next to grand historical battles, and what can be known is related to an imagined past and an envisioned future. This complex mix of historical focus, moreover, was framed by a social and political environment that was always provisional, shifting, and tested—making it difficult to determine what might eventually emerge as central or marginal, as important or incidental.

In this way, these works often challenge one's notion of history—the stories we tell, the ways in which we tell them, and the reasons for the telling. But in looking back to this period of history, we rarely consult these books beyond the attempt to identify a person or follow the trail of references that might finally lead us to solid evidence about what happened in the past. David Tracy, discussing the implications for black theology of the postmodern concept of the fragment, has noted that "the category of historical context . . . is too often conceived . . . as a kind of totality to disallow the present from experiencing the historical event as a unique fragment of time" (35). Attending to those unique fragments, and attending also to our treatment of them in historical scholarship, we can see that "what happened in the past" has everything to do with our approaches to historical understanding. Even a casual examination of the various explanations of and approaches to the Civil War, or of the various scholarly approaches to slavery over the years, suggests that culturally grounded and ideologically saturated schools of historical study have much more to do with what we call historical understanding than does any concept of objectivity or methodological neutrality we might want to claim. History is never narrated from a disinterested perspective, and every perspective is culturally situated in ways that have everything to do both with the stories we tell and the reasons we tell those stories. Accordingly, in reading African American texts of this period for the historical theory they present—reading them, that is, as interrelated examples of textual modes of historical understanding—I am looking for an understanding of historical contexts that can guide us toward a renewed understanding of African American literary production and a revitalized understanding of the uses of the past.

In chapter 1, "The Theater of History," I present an overview of the challenge of African American historical writing before the Civil War. African Americans recognized that their experience was variously both ignored in and incorporated into white historical writing of the time, and they wrote both to record their experience and to correct the misinformation that extended from and served the white supremacist assumption of the inferiority of those of African origins. Beyond these necessary responses to racist historiography, though, African Americans faced the troubling problem of representing a history that—in its fragmentation and especially in the depth of its moral complexity—resisted representation. How does one tell the story of the Middle Passage, or of slavery? How does one draw from a Christian understanding of the moral violations inherent in this story when the Christian discourse that one wishes to use to speak the truth in the face of falsehood is the same discourse being used in the service of that falsehood? In approaching this challenge, African American writers drew from various sources in a search for the relation between sacred and profane history, and they constructed a mode of historical writing that placed various ideological forces—as represented by the Bible, by various historical sources ancient and modern, by the symbolic presence of Africa as a site of both sacred and profane history—in creative tension with one another.

From the late eighteenth century to the middle of the nineteenth century, African American historical writing was both various and consistent—and the list of publications of works devoted explicitly to a reconsideration of history is impressive. Among the texts that I discuss in the first chapter, for example, are Absalom Jones and Richard Allen's *A Narrative of the Proceedings of the Black People, during the Late Awful Calamity in Philadelphia, in the Year 1793* (1794); *David Walker's Appeal, in Four Articles; Together with a Preamble, to the Coloured Citizens of the World, but in Particular, and Very Expressly, to Those of the United States of America* (1829); Hosea Easton's *A Treatise on the Intellectual Character, and Civil and Political Condition of the Colored People of the U. States* (1837); James W. C. Pennington's *A Text Book of the Origin and History, &c. &c. of the Colored People* (1841); and James Theodore Holly's *A Vindication of the Capacity of the Negro Race for Self-Government, and Civilized Progress, as Demonstrated by Historical Events of the Haytian Revolution; and the Subsequent Acts of That People since Their National Independence* (1857). In addition to the works by Robert Benjamin Lewis, Martin R. Delany, and William C. Nell that I discuss in chapter 2, all of these texts deserve recognition as major historical works of the first half of the nineteenth century; and each of them exemplifies the themes and methods with which I am concerned throughout this book.

Significantly, the writers of these texts were all activists in the related fields of religious reform and cultural reform. Richard Allen, arguably the most influential of the group, was the founding bishop of the African Methodist Episcopal Church. Enslaved at birth, he grew up in Delaware, and eventually served as a Methodist minister and converted his master, who then let him purchase his freedom. As David Walker says so appropriately in the *Appeal*, "When the Lord shall raise up coloured historians in succeeding generations, to present the crimes of this nation, to the then gazing world, the Holy Ghost will make them do justice to the name of Bishop Allen," a man whose name will "stand on the pages of history among the greatest of divines" (58). Absalom Jones, Allen's coauthor, also was enslaved in his youth, and eventually purchased his own and his wife's freedom. Strongly identified with the Free African Society, perhaps the first independent black organization in the United States, Jones like Allen was a minister throughout his life. David Walker, Allen's great admirer, is perhaps the most famous of these men. He was born free, though his life taught him from the first how limited was his freedom. Walker was an important member of Boston's black leadership, a Freemason, and an activist in the transformation of African American organized resistance to a more visible and militant movement. Hosea Easton, rarely mentioned in African American literary or historical scholarship, "was the presiding officer of the Hartford Literary and Religious Institution upon its founding in 1834" (Quarles, *Black Abolitionists* 103). James William

Charles Pennington was, for a time, one of the most important minister-abolitionists of his day, though he lived a troubled life during his later years. Born into slavery, he escaped in 1827 and eventually became a teacher and minister. He audited lectures at the Yale College Divinity School, and was awarded an honorary doctor of divinity degree from the University of Heidelberg. He formed the Union Missionary Society, and for a time taught at the Free African School in Hartford, Connecticut, which led to the writing and publication of *A Text Book*. Holly was an emigrationist. Indeed, Holly, born to free black parents in 1829, advocated emigration throughout his life, and at some personal loss. After establishing a colony in Haiti in 1861 with 110 emigrants, Holly quickly lost his mother, wife, two children, and thirty-nine members of the group to disease, causing others to return to the United States. Still, Holly held to his views and, after having been the first African American to be consecrated a bishop by the Episcopal Church, he became the head of the Orthodox Apostolic Church of Haiti.

In the texts that I examine in the first chapter, the writers return often to familiar stories, pieces of evidence, images of Africa, and biblical verses—familiar tropes that would speak with particular significance to African American readers. Stephen Henderson has identified such recurring tropes in black writing as "mascons," a term he borrowed from the National Aeronautics and Space Administration. "NASA invented the acronym," Henderson explains, "to mean a 'massive concentration' of matter below the lunar surface after it was observed that the gravitational pull on a satellite was stronger in some places than in others. I use it to mean a *massive concentration of Black experiential energy* which powerfully affects the meaning of Black speech, Black song, and Black poetry—if one, indeed, has to make such distinctions" (44). I am obviously applying this term to a different body of writing than that with which Henderson was most immediately interested in his important theoretical work, but I similarly mean it to refer to words, images, biblical passages, historical evidence, and narrative lines that were so often repeated and so similarly contextualized and marshaled in the service of historical understanding as to be particularly significant metanarrative moments in the text. It is not, of course, uncommon for a community to repeat its most revered stories and to invoke continually familiar phrases, to invoke foundation documents both sacred and secular, or to return to the conflicts that originally defined the community's existence. Such are the rituals of community. Nationalist historical understanding, one might say, is a matter of constructing such mascons for identifiable groups of readers. African American writing that both worked against the white nationalist history under construction before the Civil War—and that actively worked as well to construct a black community of historical understanding—similarly participated in a ritualistic invocation of the ideological landmarks of black American identity.

The most direct and sustained examples of historical writing are the subject of chapter 2, "Scattered Lives, Scattered Documents: Writing Liberation History." In this chapter, I examine the work of three major African American historians: Robert Benjamin Lewis, Martin R. Delany, and William C. Nell. Lewis and Nell identified themselves as historians, working to "rescue from oblivion," as Nell puts it, the scattered documents and stories of African American experience; Delany similarly turned to history to establish African American rights to American citizenship and to locate African Americans within the peculiar blend of sacred and profane history that served Freemasonry. Each of these historians responded directly to a developing field of white historical scholarship that omitted African Americans from their rightful presence on the world stage, and each did so by emphasizing the fragmentation of African American history that was the result of totalizing historical narratives informed by white supremacist ideology. Lewis presents a compilation of historical sources that speak of an untold story, a story that Lewis draws out in his arrangement of and commentary on the fragments that he gathers. Delany constructs a collective biography of African American achievement to establish African American claims to the rights of citizenship, but then argues for the futility of this argument and reapplies that collective story of achievement to an argument for an imagined black nationalist community. Nell works from an integrationist perspective but uses the untold stories of African Americans in the American Revolution to shift the terms of both integration and education, placing African Americans at the ideological center of an unfinished revolution and a newly envisioned education that incorporates white history into the developing story of African American progress. These narratives look to the fragmentation of African American history and of the African American community not to transform the fragments into a coherent narrative but rather to suggest a providential narrative veiled by the historical narratives of white nationalism.

The individual stories of a community contained by a white supremacist culture are the subject of chapter 3, "Multiple Lives and Lost Narratives: (Auto)Biography as History." In this chapter I look at the historical theory presented in African American autobiographical writing. Questions about the historical authority of African American autobiography have focused largely on slave narratives, and many of the works I look at are slave narratives. But I am interested in the broader field of African American autobiography and biography, and I am interested as well in the cultural politics that influence how we read these texts as historical authorities. Although these texts can provide a great deal of information about life under the national system of slavery (including northern implications in that system), I do not consider the historical authority of these texts to be simply a function of the information that we can take from them and the extent to which we can "trust" that information to be free of the distortion of a subjective account (the concern that kept historians away from any serious and sophisticated engagement with the slave narratives for so long). Rather, I am interested in the ways in which the historical work of these texts was predetermined by white expectations, whether to serve the needs of the antislavery movement or to provide an exoticized glimpse into African American life. African Americans recognized that their stories were unlikely to find a hearing beyond the conventional expectations of their readers, and that therefore they would serve the needs of the authorized historical narratives of white culture. Accordingly, fundamental to autobiographical writing was the attempt to shift the terms of historical understanding, to tell one's story in such a way as to open a space—of discourse, of ideology—in which an alternate historical vision could be represented. Central to that alternate vision—and central as well to the attempt to liberate individual stories from an overdetermined white historical narrative—was an insistence on the moral framework within which individual life and national history must be understood.

The need to establish different contexts for understanding the significance of individual African American lives was central as well to the collective activism of African American oratory and to the black national convention movement, my subject in chapter 4, "The Assembly of History: Orations and Conventions." Throughout this book, I argue that identity, individual and collective, is performative and that this performance is necessarily multiply contingent—shaped by the complementary or counterperformances of a variety of other individuals, and staged by the cultural scripts of economics, law, politics, and social practice. The performance of identity, in other words, operates in the theater of history, and history is the collection of the various cultural scripts into an ordered drama of human experience. Seen in this light, the performance of orations at public gatherings, often to commemorate significant historical events, and the national convention movement were attempts to create alternate theaters of and for history, to rescript the African American past and present so as to make possible different conceptions of identity, shaped by differently contingent relations.

The proceedings of the national conventions in particular were, I suggest, significant works of history—collecting the African American past but also commenting on the cultural dynamics of historical understanding and of individual and collective agency. In the national convention movement, liberation historiography finds one of its most focused and ambitious forums, the attempt to transform historical understanding into the theater of collective activism. Both individually and together, the proceedings of the national convention movement from the 1830s to the 1860s demonstrate the *process* of liberation historiography, the difficult attempt to maintain an organized structure for collective activism, the equally difficult attempt to draw from the experience of the people the terms by which history should be understood, and the still more difficult attempt to transform that constructed historical understanding into a unified and unifying plan for action.

The contention and multiple perspectives necessary to African American liberation historiography lead me finally to chapter 5, "Our Warfare Lies in the Field of Thought: The African American Press and the Work of History." The convention proceedings are valuable in that they record disagreement and record also the process by which disagreement leads to clear plans for cultural reform. The proceedings indicate also, however, an increasingly troubling attempt to serve the expectations of the culture of white reform, to construct a collective voice that would insist on cultural reform but that would do so without alienating potential white allies. In short, the problem of audience that is central to the narrative and historical dynamics of African American autobiography plays also a prominent role in the national convention movement. Moreover, it is important to remember that, while the national convention movement did include a mix of social classes, it was an almost exclusively male collective performance. It is important to note, then, the continual emphasis in the conventions on the need for a black periodical press, a press that would gather and represent the ideological diversity of the African American community and that would also rescript this performance by changing the dynamics of audience, allowing writers to address directly African American readers and forcing white readers to read from the cultural margins rather than from the center of these publications. The ideological diversity of the African American community as shaped by the diversity of experiences is, throughout the period I consider in this book, one of the great strengths of African American historical writing, the means by which a fragmented community finds the liberating potential in a newly ordered understanding of that fragmentation, a narrative arrangement that allows the fragments to speak with and against one another to suggest the terms of a historical story that resists representation and to identify the grounds for moral activism. Accordingly, a black periodical press is essential to black liberation historiography, establishing as it does an appropriate theater for the collective performance of cultural identity and activism on the historical stage.

In all of these chapters, I have little to say about the many white activists who were similarly working toward cultural reform and historical revision. Some might consider this a serious omission, for white activists influenced not only the course of history but also the trajectories of racial ideology in the United States. Indeed, an important school of historical scholarship has developed in recent years focusing not only on cooperation and alliances across racial lines but also on the resulting transformation of the concept of race itself. Prominent examples of this school of scholarship include, for example, Paul Goodman's *Of One Blood: Abolitionism and the Origins of Racial Equality* (1998), Richard S. Newman's *The Transformation of American Abolitionism: Fighting Slavery in the Early Republic* (2002), and John Stauffer's *The Black Hearts of Men: Radical Abolitionists and the Transformation of Race* (2002). As the titles of their studies indicate, these scholars, along with others, emphasize the transformation of the antislavery movement (focusing particularly on the influence of black abolitionists and radical white abolitionists after 1830), transformations that involved and promoted ideals of racial equality. All three scholars emphasize the ways in which black activists influenced white antislavery thought and social philosophies. Goodman, for example, explores the process by which white abolitionists "conquered their prejudices" by "working together with free blacks" (148). Newman notes that early organized antislavery efforts in Pennsylvania had emphasized the roles to be played by "elite white males," but that during the 1830s Massachusetts abolitionists embraced more egalitarian strategies. Having been denied membership in the Pennsylvania Abolition Society, Newman notes, "black leaders created their own parallel antislavery society." But "in the abolitionist world of the 1830s," Newman continues, "African American reformers quickly became coworkers and allies, bringing with them a protest tradition that emphasized national action, public and often emotional attacks on bondage, and immediate emancipation" (6). Stauffer focuses on the alliances among four important activists, two white and two black: Gerrit Smith, John Brown, Frederick Douglass, and James McCune Smith. In his opening pages, Stauffer quotes from a letter to Gerrit Smith in which black abolitionist James McCune Smith asserted that the work of social reform would require that "the heart of the whites . . . be changed, thoroughly, entirely, permanently changed." "He went on to explain," Stauffer notes, "that whites had to understand what it was like to be black. They had to learn how to view the world as if they were black, shed their 'whiteness' as a sign of superiority, and renounce their belief in skin color as a marker of aptitude and social status. They had to acquire, in effect, a black heart" (1). As the title of his book suggests, Stauffer explores this "moral shift" in the relations among these four important male leaders.

Although I have learned a great deal from these and related studies, readers of *Liberation Historiography* will encounter a more cautionary tale of the ideal of racial cooperation and equality. I have noted important alliances between black and white activists, and I have noted as well the ways in which the African American historical consciousness was shaped by the positive influences of white activism as well as by the negative influences of white racism. However, I have viewed African American writing and activism—and relations between white and black Americans—through the framework established by such studies as Mills's *The Racial Contract* and Goldberg's *The Racial State*, studies that caution us to question, explore, and even re-center (or, perhaps, de-center) the terms of interracial idealism. Accordingly, I would underscore the importance of black communal self-definition and self-determination in any story of racial cooperation. "The modern bi-racial movement," Goodman states, came about because "free blacks . . . convinced a small but prophetic vanguard of white men and women to repudiate colonization and embrace immediate emancipation and racial equality" (3). Indeed, Newman and Stauffer, like Goodman, emphasize the importance of the African American influence on white thought. Obviously, I am interested in exploring that significant influence. My departure from this school of scholarship, then, might be said to be a difference of emphasis—a matter of centering attention on the "prophetic vanguard" not of white men and women but of African American writers and activists—arguably, a relatively slight difference of emphasis, for these scholars have a great deal to say about African American writing and social reform movements. But, as I hope to demonstrate, while African Americans often (and necessarily) attended to their alliances with white activists, the news from the black community on the ideal of racial equality often was not good and always was more complex than the story presented by white reformers.

In *Liberation Historiography*, I address race as a systemic reality and not as a biological entity or simply as a set of social affiliations. In doing so, I do not mean to undervalue the significance of white activists, but I do mean to emphasize that exceptional cases should not distract us from the complex and intricate rule of white supremacist control over fundamental cultural institutions—legal, political, economic, religious, and educational. Goodman, for one, cautions us to remember that "the fact that only a small sector of white opinion proved susceptible to African American persuasion necessarily complicates any explanation of the origins of racial equality in Jacksonian America" (3), and *Of One Blood* is most valuable when read in that light. Stauffer similarly emphasizes that Gerrit Smith and John Brown were exceptional examples of white activists who "transformed themselves and overcame existing social barriers," and in doing so "reimagined their country as a pluralist society in which the standard of excellence depended on righteousness and benevolence rather than on skin color, sex, or material wealth" (2). But if one understands race as something other than skin color, and if one focuses on "the standard of excellence" not as attitudinal but rather as implicit standards that function through the social order regardless of the minds and hearts of individual women and men, then one must note a significant difference between reimagining one's country and changing one's country, or between transforming hearts and transforming the social order.

In other words, if we fail to hold to a systemic understanding of race, we are in danger of replacing what Marcus Wood has called the nineteenth century's "mythology of white abolition martyrdom" with a corresponding mythology of white abolition heroism, a form of idealism—promoted for very worthy ends—that can obscure the complexity of African American historical experience and marginalize the story of African American collective self-determination. This danger is suggested, I believe, in the opening pages of *The Black Hearts of Men*, where Stauffer rather hopefully notes that Gerrit Smith, Brown, Douglass, and McCune Smith met at the inaugural convention of the Radical Abolitionists "in an unprecedented moment of interracial unity" in the same year (1855) that Walt Whitman published his first edition of *Leaves of Grass*. Whitman's "revolutionary poem," Stauffer suggests, "dissolved the boundaries between black and white, rich and poor, sacred and profane, prose and poetry, polite language and slang" (9). "These two vi-

sions," Stauffer notes, "the one political and the other poetic, represent remarkable examples of faith in the possibility of individual and national liberation" (9). Although I do not want to undervalue that faith, perhaps it is
prudent to remember another publication by Whitman, "Prohibition of Colored Persons," an editorial published in the Brooklyn *Daily Times* in 1858,
just a few years after the publication of the original *Leaves of Grass*. In that
editorial, Whitman is clear about the limits of his revolutionary vision: "Who
believes that the Whites and Blacks can ever amalgamate in America? Or who
wishes it to happen? Nature has set an impassable seal against it. Besides, is
not America for the Whites? And is it not better so? As long as the Blacks
remain here, how can they become anything like an independent and heroic
race? There is no chance for it" (qtd. in Levine, Introduction 419). This
editorial, like *Leaves of Grass*, speaks volumes about "the possibility of individual and national liberation" in the antebellum United States, but in a
significantly different way. We are led back to the significance of the conver-
sion of the small vanguard of white activists noted by Goodman who repudi-
ated colonization, but one must then note that Goodman avoids entirely the
subject of African American frustration that led important leaders—Henry
Highland Garnet and Martin R. Delany among them—to actively pursue emigrationist plans, and that led even Douglass to become increasingly pronounced in his criticism of white America, and of white antislavery culture,
over time.

Still, the work of individual white Americans is an important part of the
story of a developing African American historical consciousness; and although I address that work in the chapters that follow, I do not offer a
sustained study of those interracial influences and alliances. Much could and
should be said about the work of Lydia Maria Child, Theodore Weld, William
Goodell, and others in the field of history; about Benjamin Lundy, William
Lloyd Garrison, and others in the press; or about Wendell Phillips, Theodore
Parker, and others on the platform and in the pulpit. These and many other
white writers and activists did important historical work, and their writings
are very much a presence in African American writing at the time (to say
nothing of British writers, who were equally influential and whose presence
in African American writing, like that of white Americans, remains under-
studied). These writers provided much of the research from which African
American writers drew in their own work, and included in their work are
many of the prominent themes, tropes, and other narrative features that I
identify in the African American texts that I discuss. One cannot but note,

though, that the work of these writers and activists has received much more attention than the texts I examine in this study—and I would suggest further that we are not in a position to understand or evaluate their work in relation to African American historical understanding without a correspondingly deep and sustained engagement in the modes of historical writing and theory presented in African American texts of this time.

We need to refocus and re-center the work of understanding what constitutes African American history, for the presentation of African American history is not simply a matter of gathering and recording information to add to the existing historical record. Pioneering work on this has been done by Earl Thorpe, historian of African American historians; Benjamin Quarles, who similarly has studied African American historical thought and who has done more than anyone to place African American thought and experience during this period at the center of our understanding of the abolitionist movement and the Civil War; Clarence Walker, who has presented a forceful challenge to anyone interested in this work in his own approach to the ideological structures of African American historical thought; and Elizabeth Rauh Bethel, whose exploration of "memory and history in antebellum free communities" has established the complexly interwoven strands of an identifiable collective historical consciousness that provided the foundations for African American identity and social activism. Increasingly, this work is being continued, at least indirectly, by a number of scholars determined to question our understanding of that which constitutes the frame and field of African American literary and social activism.[15] What follows from this work, I believe, is the recognition that white supremacist ideology, in all of its multifarious manifestations, and African American experience and collective identity have been shaped by their mutually contingent relation to one another, and African American history is accordingly the product in part of the moral violations inherent in white supremacist social practice. The history of that collective experience, then, must be moral as well as intellectual, culturally centered as well as factually accurate—proceeding, for example, from what Cone identifies as a theological blackness, and working toward what Henderson terms the "saturation" of the text in black experience. There can be no "objective" account that does not participate in what Morrison has called the "pathology" of white Western modernity; and there can be no assumption that the violations of the past are behind us and that they are not replicated and sustained by an academic practice that rides on the unsteady rails of what we recognize as fact.

I focus on African American writers of African American history and historical theory, then, because the cultural position of the individual historical writer and theorist is an important dynamic in this writing. In "Identity and Representation," Bourdieu has argued that "even when he merely states with authority what is already the case, even when he contents himself with asserting what is, the *auctor* produces a change in what is: by virtue of the fact that he states things with authority, that is, in front of and in the name of everyone, publicly and officially, he saves them from their arbitrary nature, he sanctions them, sanctifies them, consecrates them, making them worthy of existing, in conformity with the nature of things, and thus 'natural'" (222). This public ordering and authorization of African American experience, this naturalization of African American history, is very much the point in the writings I study. Indeed, it was important even to establish African American writers as historical authorities—even as writers, as the title of most slave narratives and the prefaces of most African American novels and historical texts of this time attest. Dening reminds us that the presentation of oneself as an author is a significantly conventional cultural performance. "In all of its varied expressions," Dening notes, "narrating is, in Roy Wagner's word, an impersonation— the clustering of signifying actions into recognizable roles, such as bard, novelist, prophet, historian" (104). African American writers, as will become clear in the chapters that follow, worked both with and against the generic conventions in an attempt to reenvision the cultural performances available to them and to rescript the roles that they had been assigned—but the "impersonation" by which individuals are identified by their cultural office, and by which those cultural offices are identified with individuals, was important to all of these writers.[16]

This African American "impersonation" of the historian was, of course, complicated by a culture in which the role of the historian was implicitly reserved for educated white gentlemen, men who created a body of work that is the inevitable frame for the ground of African American historical thought and writing.[17] A frequent presence in this study, in fact, is a white historian who quite successfully identified himself with the cultural office of the historian: George Bancroft, author of the ten-volume *History of the United States*, published from 1834 to 1874. Lincoln is reported to have searched his memory in meeting Bancroft, as politicians often do, to identify the man before him, saying, "Hold on—I know you; you are—History, History of the United States—Mr.—Mr. Bancroft, Mr. George Bancroft" (M. Howe 156). It can be argued that I overemphasize Bancroft's status as representative, similarly

moving from history to Bancroft's history to Bancroft himself, thus transforming him into a virtual manifestation of the white nationalist historical
project. This might be the case—for having read Bancroft's ten volumes, his
two volumes on the history of the Constitution, and his two six-volume revisions of the history, I am determined, I think understandably, to put Bancroft
to work for me whenever possible.

But I've read a number of other histories as well, and I turn to Bancroft so
often because I share the view of Leonard I. Sweet, William L. Van Deburg,
and others that Bancroft is, in fact, particularly important to any attempt to
understand the ideological assumptions that shaped the nineteenth-century
white historical consciousness in the North.[18] As I believe we have much to
learn from reading the narrative modes of history as presented in African
American writing published before the Civil War, so I believe that we have
much to learn from reading white histories that were once quite popular and
influential but now are rarely read. Bancroft offers a particularly prominent
and influential example of an approach to American history—informed by
Bancroft's acquaintance with the work of Herder, Hegel and others, and
shaped by Bancroft's own political involvements as a Jacksonian democrat—
that looked for its authority in a vision of the "folk" and that argued for a
providential design underlying all human history. Most readers would agree
with Susan Mizruchi that Bancroft is an example of "Democratic party ro-
mancers" (43) and that other historians, Richard Hildreth, for example, can
be distinguished from Bancroft in their view that "reliable history is based on
a responsible antiquarianism, combined with a critical responsiveness that
itself constitutes 'historical morality'" (55). However, when one views the
work of various white historians through what Katherine Clay Bassard has
termed the "structures of vision" (5)—that is, modes of reading informed by
Africanist and diasporic experience—these distinctions begin to seem rather
slight, and even the work of Hildreth, for all its antislavery commentary,
seems to have no more claim to "historical morality," methodological or
otherwise, than does Bancroft's. I present Bancroft, then, as a prominent
white historian whose basic assumptions about historical understanding and
narration are in many ways similar to that found in African American historical work of the time, and in this way Bancroft helps me to identify the
established cultural assumptions with and against which African American
historians worked.

The stability of Bancroft's democratic views, I suggest, depended on a
conception of the intellectual method by which the American man of letters

(I use the gender specific term advisedly) could maintain the integrity and security of his public office. An important statement of Bancroft's social and historical philosophy is his essay "The Office of the People," in which Bancroft outlines the tenets of his belief that the United States represents a methodology of perspective—an intellectual procedure guided by moral principles which not only defines the role of the man of letters but which must guide him as well. By aligning social authority with a renewed cultural emphasis on natural rights, Bancroft appropriated the traditional argument for the national aristocracy, in which national ideals are transformed into standards of individual character and character is accordingly understood as at once the necessary achievement of a truly successful writer, the primary focus of that which is written, and the most important critical standard by which books can be judged. To fulfill the ideals that Bancroft identifies in his democratic manifesto "The Necessity, the Reality, and the Promise of the Progress of the Human Race," an example of Bancroft's transcendentalist mode of democratic ideology, the man of letters must find within himself "the ideal man who represents the race" ("Necessity" 485); he must write to reveal within "the actual state of the world . . . the ideal state toward which it should tend" (486); and he must base his endeavors on the conviction that social and political reforms "must flow from internal activity, developed by universal culture," and that "successful revolutions proceed like all other formative processes from inward germs" (515). Bancroft's beliefs led him to historical composition that, though based on detailed research, valued generalizations over close analysis and faith over the sort of analytic scaffoldings that other historians considered essential—for example, William H. Prescott, who was critical of Bancroft's omission of footnotes from his *History*, or Hildreth, who begins his own *History of the United States* with a complaint about histories that read like Fourth of July orations. For Bancroft, the representation of truth must be grounded in but must transcend the processes of the intellect, and it must give voice to a democratic truth that could be discerned in the voice of the People.

Early African American writers employed similar concepts of historical truth and of the grounds for successful revolutions, but they worked from a different understanding of the providential design shaping this history, and a different notion of how the people were to be identified and understood. For Bancroft, "the People" was always a singular concept, and the task of the historian was to extract the voice of the People from the necessarily contentious and even cacophonous voices of the people. It must be said, too, that the people for whom Bancroft assumed to speak were white, and that the relation between the people and the People was, roughly speaking, the relation between white people and ideological whiteness. African American historical theorists and commentators identified the people differently, and that different identification led to a significant revision of the Bancroftian historical vision. Henry Adams, noting that Bancroft's *History of the United States from the Discovery of the American Continent* ended with the American Revolution and the formation of the Constitution, remarked to fellow white historian Francis Parkman in 1884 that Bancroft had "written the History of the United States in a dozen volumes without reaching his subject."[19] African Americans might well have argued that it was entirely appropriate that Bancroft had not reached his subject and that he had concluded his first ten volumes with the American Revolution, for his subject, as understood in Bancroftian terms, did not yet exist in fact. As many black and white Americans alike argued, the American Revolution had yet to be completed, and there was a vast difference between the theoretical United States presented in Bancroft's history and the actual nation gaining power on the world stage. The work of African American historical commentators and theorists was the work of that ongoing revolution.

In my study of that work, I suggest that we need to reenvision the theater of history so as to recognize the historical authority of a wider range of performances, performances designed specifically to promote a liberating application of the past. Paul Gilroy, questioning the stability of such performances, has argued that "the idea of tradition gets understandably invoked to underscore the historical continuities, subcultural conversations, intertextual and intercultural cross-fertilisations which make the notion of a distinctive and self-conscious black culture appear plausible." Serving the needs of "a black political culture locked in a defensive posture against the unjust powers of white supremacy," Gilroy continues, "obsessions with origin and myth can rule contemporary political concerns and the fine grain of history"—and "the idea of tradition," accordingly, "can constitute a refuge" (188). But the conceptual simplification of the "idea of tradition" into an obsession with origin and myth—which themselves are not simply discrete cultural fetishes but rather active principles of the will to narrate untold and untellable stories—also provides a refuge of sorts, for the official "scholarly investigations" sanctioned by the academy are in fact part of the white supremacist culture whose tradition the academy both invokes and represses. The academic mode of continuous history thematizes the story of resistance—and when narrated in this form African American history has always served the needs of a white supremacist culture, making of African American history a bedtime story rather than a call to action. The histories of the early African American historians are, in contrast, artful *untellings* that function always in the context of oppression, containment, and misrepresentations—and they were decidedly both calls to action and attempts to locate the ideological site for that action. Returning to early African American historians, in short, might well be a way of returning African American history to its liberationist roots, approaches to history determined by shifting theaters of oppression and devoted to the world beyond the authorized stage.

chapter one

The Theater of History

On November 14, 1847, William Wells Brown delivered a lecture to the Female Anti-Slavery Society of Salem, Massachusetts, a lecture recorded by Henry M. Parkhurst, "phonographic reporter," and published by the Massachusetts Anti-Slavery Society. In that lecture, Brown announced that his subject would be American slavery "as it is," including "its influence on American character and morals" (*Lecture* 4). Having said that, though, Brown quickly asserted that "Slavery has never been represented; Slavery never can be represented" (4). Any attempt to represent the system of slavery, Brown noted, could only fail; and if he were to try to represent it, he stated, he would need to whisper it to his audience, "one at a time" (4). Brown then goes on to represent slavery in a masterful performance that includes definitions of slavery, examples of its intimate violations (including an early version of the slave auction that would later play so prominent a role in his fictive narrative *Clotel*), commentary on the white press and commercial interests involved in the maintenance of the national system of slavery, remarks on the legal system required by slavery, and observations on the extent to which slavery has corrupted white American character, including the political and religious ideals to which white Americans claimed devotion. It was a system, as Brown's opening remarks indicated, at once so extensive and so

intimate as to both resist and require representation—and the representation
that could only fail would somehow need to be both general and individualized, both a grand dissertation and an intimate communication, whispered
to individual ears but finding the one in the many, the many in the one, in its
approach to the system that provided the underlying but unspeakable unity to
a nation all but lost in its own mythology and its own degradation.

In this lecture Brown captures well the considerable challenges awaiting
those who would represent African American history before the Civil War.
This historical vision would have to include an account of slavery, that fundamental force that shaped the lives of all African Americans, enslaved and
"free." This body of historical scholarship would need to account for the
considerable illusions of white Americans, whose conceptions of black identity were an unavoidable force in the lives of African Americans—and this
scholarship would need to support the sort of social activism capable of
responding to the degrading influences of racial prejudice, what Hosea Easton
(among many others) considered to be "slavery in disguise" (*Treatise* 46).[1]
As part of that program of social reform, African American historical writing would need to support a new branch of education, one capable of addressing the effects of that prejudice, what David Walker called the "ignorance, the mother of treachery and deceit, [that] gnaws into our very vitals"
(*Appeal* 21). Working to serve a largely unformed community, moreover, African American historical writing, even more than national histories written by
white historians in the age of national self-definition, would need to identify
the terms of its own existence—asking what it might mean to write a history of
African Americans, defining the African American community both with and
against the terms used by white Americans by which African Americans found
themselves with common experiences set off from but fundamental to the
white national story. Above all, as Brown's lecture so ably represents, African
American historical understanding would require attention not only to its
matter—historical evidence—but also to its mode. It would necessarily be a
performance on the limited stage available to African Americans in the white
American theater of history.

This would need to be an approach to historical study, indeed, capable of
facing the considerable challenge of defining what history is, how it is to
be presented, and how its authority is to be determined. In so doing, African American writers could not avoid the subject of the concepts of history shaping the lives of white Americans, emerging historical narratives
that largely avoided the fundamental fact of African American life. As David

Walker put it in a passage in his famous *Appeal*, "The preachers and people of the United States form societies against Free Masonry and Intemperance, and write against Sabbath breaking, Sabbath mails, Infidelity, &c. &c. But the fountain head [slavery and oppression], compared to which, all those other evils are comparatively nothing, and from the bloody and murderous head of which, they receive no trifling support, is hardly noticed by the Americans" (40).[2] Addressing this fountainhead, African American historians would need to find reason in madness, historical records in the historical confusion of a nation devoted to both liberty and slavery, and collective promise in a story of a pervasive and fragmenting oppression. They would need to find the terms of a possible community in the story of its negation, heritage in the evidence of its omission, unity in the story of fragmentation, and hope in the story of murderous and multifarious injustice.[3] Walker's presentation of the absence of antislavery collective action in contrast to various reform movements and moral sentiments speaks of a collective denial of history that threatens dire historical effects, for "God suffers some to go on until they are ruined for ever!" (41). Whether and how one understands slavery was, in this way, a test of historical understanding.

In this chapter, I address the various attempts of African American writers to meet the challenge of historical understanding and the identifiable features of an African American *mode* of representing history. In doing so, I am more interested in the continuity of such attempts than in the different contexts that shaped individual historical texts differently over time. For one of the distinctive features of antebellum African American writing is the creation of a tradition of historical writing in which the central conventions (recurring tropes, narrative patterns, central stories, and the like) remained remarkably stable. As Patrick Rael has argued, "Given the broad range of social experiences from which black Americans hailed, the surprise was not that social differences existed among them but that black northerners generally managed to shelter these differences under the umbrella of racial identity and black community activism" (81). In part, the tradition of historical writing that provided the spokes for this unifying umbrella is simply a result of the fact that the fundamental concerns did not change significantly over time. Conceptions of race developed (though they hardly evolved), but the fundamental presence of race as a systemic presence shaping all aspects of American social, political, economic, and religious life did not change. The specific conditions by which citizenship and community could be defined and envisioned changed, but the concept of African American rights to citizenship and of the historically fragmented condition of the African American community did not change. Debates over colonization and African heritage became increasingly complex, but the symbolic status of Africa remained a flexible tool in the construction of a historical vision capable of accounting for slavery and envisioning an African American destiny.

Perhaps another way to put this is simply to say that the conditions of secular history changed, but the demands and promises of sacred history did not. Through adaptations of biblical verses and stories, and through such regular public rituals as antislavery celebrations, antislavery lectures, and annual state and national conventions, African American communities in the North created consistent patterns of communal discourse that spoke of continuity over time and space, an imagined community drawn from biblical pages and involved in providential journeys. This emphasis on the sacred addressed, in part, the inexpressible nature of African American experience. The representation of history, indeed, always ran the risk of diminishing African American experience, individual and collective, by attempting to tell the story that could not be told, a story that becomes conceptually neat and controllable when reduced to a public narrative. But the emphasis on the sacred addressed as well the need to map out the path of African American collective destiny, to give meaning to a world of experiences that defied all reason. For many African American writers, then, the purpose of historical writing was to tell a sacred story about a secular world so as to discover the point of intersection of sacred and secular, the point at which history is defined. What follows is an overview of the work of African Americans who strove to serve that purpose.

"To Publish Our Thoughts": The Textuality of History

Early African American historians had their work cut out for them, sometimes literally. In his 1855 history of African American participation in the American Revolution, William C. Nell tells the story of "Peter Salem, the Colored American, at Bunker Hill," a battle in which Salem is reported to have shot the British major Pitcairn; and in a note on that page, Nell observes that "in some engravings of the battle, this colored soldier occupies a prominent position; but in more recent editions, his figure is *non est inventus*" (21).[4] And this was not the only picture from which African Americans were deleted. As Benjamin Quarles has noted, black intellectuals argued that "it was bad enough . . . for white recorders to misinterpret the historical sources they had ostensibly examined. But this failure of deduction was compounded by a deficiency even more grievous—bias by omission" ("Black History" 90). David Walker, for example, notes in his *Appeal* that white Americans "have newspapers and monthly periodicals, which they receive in continual succession, but on the pages of which, you will scarcely ever find a paragraph respecting slavery" (39). One thinks as well of Hegel's remark that "at this point we leave Africa, not to mention it again. For it is no historical part of the World; it has no movement or development to exhibit" (157). African American historians, accordingly, faced the task of inserting themselves into the historical record.

In this sense, one might say that an early and important phase of African American historical writing is a body of work that would not be recognized as historical writing (though it would certainly be recognized as historical activism): the various petitions to Congress and to state legislative bodies toward the end of the eighteenth century.[5] In a document that Herbert Aptheker identifies as "the earliest extant negro petition to Congress," four black men protested a North Carolina law that called for the capture and reenslavement of those who had been freed. Asserting that laws forbidding the manumission of slaves were "a stretch of power, morally and politically, a Governmental defect," and suggesting that such laws were "a direct violation of the declared fundamental principles of the Constitution," the petitioners asked "for redress of our grievances" (Aptheker 40–44). As Aptheker notes, the congressional debate over whether to accept this petition suggested that this was not the first such case. As Representative William Smith, of South Carolina, argued, "The practice of a former time, in a similar case, was that the petition was sealed up and sent back to the petitioners" (qtd. in Aptheker 40). In addition to avoiding the issues the petitioners addressed, by returning the petitions Congress maintained control over the historical record. Interpretations of law and of events within the framework of the "declared fundamental principles" to which the nation's history could be devoted, the sealed and returned petitions were not allowed a voice, and they speak today of the untold stories, the hidden lives, to which nineteenth-century African American literature is devoted.

Behind the omissions in the historical record were more immediately threatening assumptions that shaped that record—namely, "the belief that blacks, past as well as present, had a genetic predisposition to low aim and lesser achievement, destined indefinitely to lag below the historical horizon"

(Quarles, "Black History" 89). Where black history had not been cut out of the historical record, "what passed for and was accepted as the history of their group was a misrepresentation, a distortion." African Americans faced constantly "the charge that the Afro-American past was inglorious when it was not insignificant, that it was shrouded in mystery when it was not covered with shame" (Quarles, "Black History" 90). Black history was, in effect, viewed as a kind of antihistory that justified its own exclusion from serious historical notice.[6] And so antebellum African American historians, as Quarles argues, necessarily found their work defined for them by the need to respond to open charges and hidden assumptions. And their responses "took two predictable and related forms—a denial of the indictment and the bringing forth of data to refute it" ("Black History" 89).

These responses often were quite direct, and they can seem to reduce African American historical writing to defensive posturing.[7] Certainly, African American historians were regularly and overtly defensive—as is, for example, James Theodore Holly in *A Vindication of the Capacity of the Negro Race for Self-Government, and Civilized Progress, as Demonstrated by Historical Events of the Haytian Revolution; and the Subsequent Acts of That People since Their National Independence* (1857). As the title of this work promises, Holly draws from recent history—"the historical events of the Haytian Revolution" and its aftermath—presenting his own case for "the capacity of the negro race for self-government." The *Vindication* begins with an explanation of its inevitable context—the fact that "the great mass of the Caucasian race still deem the negro as entirely destitute of those qualities, on which they selfishly predicate their own superiority" (21). Holly is very serious about making this case; indeed, the phrase (or variations thereof) *capacity for self government* appears close to twenty times in the forty-eight-page "lecture."[8] Similarly, James W. C. Pennington draws on individual lives to challenge directly the assumption of African inferiority in *A Text Book of the Origin and History, &c. &c. of the Colored People* (1841). Having explored at some length the concept and historical origins of African American identity ("who and whence are the colored people?" [5]), Pennington presents a series of short biographies of native Africans who have established their intellectual abilities beyond all question, noting that he confined his selections to native Africans in response to his "opponents of the Jefferson school" (Pennington refers to Jefferson's argument in *Notes on the State of Virginia*) who answer that African American achievement is the result of white blood intermixed with black.[9]

Like Holly and Pennington, all African American historians of this period worked to refute charges that those of African origins were either inferior or missing from the historical stage; but to frame African American historical writing in this way is to simplify a more complex story, for denial and refutation suggest an ordered theater of historical debate that simply did not exist, and particularly not for African Americans. African American history is defined not as part of a larger story but as a story rather specifically contained by multiple and developing centers of historical authority.[10] Consider, for example, another petition—*To the Honorable Counsel & House of [Representa]tives for the State of Massachusetts Bay in General Court assembled, January 13, 1777.* In this petition, the writers' struggling style emphasizes the extent to which historical experience, ideological frameworks, and racial assumptions are mixed together. Consider the unpunctuated opening paragraph:

> The petition of A Great Number of Blackes detained in a State of slavery in the Bowels of a free & Christian Country Humbly sheweth that your Petitioners apprehend that they have in Common with all other men a Natural and Unaliable Right to that freedom which the Grat Parent of the Unavers hath Bestowed equalley on all menkind and which they have Never forfeited by any Compact or agreement whatever—but that wher Unjustly Dragged by the hand of cruel Power from their Derest friends and sum of them Even torn from the Embraces of their tender Parents—from A populous Pleasant and plentiful country and in violation of Laws of Nature and of Nations and in defiance of all the tender feelings of humanity Brough hear Either to Be sold Like Beast of Burthen & Like them Condemned to Slavery for Life—Among A People Profesing the mild Religion of Jesus A people Not Insensible of the Secrets of Rational Being Nor without spirit to Resent the unjust endeavours of others to Reduce them to a state of Bondage and Subjection your honouer Need not to be informed that A Live of Slavery Like that of your petitioners Deprived of Every social privilege of Every thing Requisit to Render Life Tolable is far worse then Nonexistence. (Aptheker 10)

Notice the mix of discourses here—that of religion, that of natural rights, that of painful experience—and the ways in which the petitioners connect their own experience to the discourse of "Bondage and Subjection" that was so great a presence in the pamphlets, sermons, and essays written to define and justify the American Revolution. Insofar as the American Revolution can be said to have been a war to establish the language and means by which history would be recorded and interpreted, this petition might be considered an attempt to enter the history policed by the authoritative protocols of print discourse—an attempt, in short, to be recognized in history by speaking the language of history.[11]

But the language of this petition works only in a state of great tension—pushing against the contradictions it must invoke in order to make its point, but identifying in those contradictions the systemic logic by which the case was all but decided before the petition was submitted. Can the "slavery" of the white colonists be compared to the slavery of those of African descent in the United States? Can political slavery be invoked as a response to legal slavery? To read this petition today is to remind ourselves that when African American writers could gain access to the available documents, they faced a body of evidence and an attendant discourse of authority that worked against the vision of history they wished to promote. In his monumental *Metahistory*, Hayden White terms the workings of the historian's narrative imagination "prefigurative acts," by which historians determine "as a possible object of knowledge the set of events reported in the documents." "This prefigurative act," White explains, "is *poetic* inasmuch as it is precognitive and precritical in the economy of the historian's own consciousness. It is also poetic insofar as it is constitutive of the structure that will subsequently be imaged in the verbal model offered by the historian as a representation and explanation of 'what *really* happened' in the past" (30–31). Reapplying White's argument, one might say that nineteenth-century African American historical visions were necessarily prefigured, and strongly resisted by the *equally prefiguring* documents.

African American historians understood as well that history was both the written record and the lived memory as shaped by the written record. Indeed, if one begins the story of African American historical writing with Absalom Jones and Richard Allen's *A Narrative of the Proceedings of the Black People, during the Late Awful Calamity in Philadelphia, in the Year 1793*, then one begins with a story of cultural battles fought on the field of literature, of a struggle for historical presence and authority that is specifically *textual*. Jones and Allen wrote the *Narrative* in response to Mathew Carey's *A Short Account of the Malignant Fever, Lately Prevalent in Philadelphia*, in which Carey charged black Philadelphians with taking pecuniary advantage of the outbreak, stating that "some of them were even detected in plundering" (Aptheker 32). Jones and Allen (whose conduct Carey identified as praiseworthy) responded with their own history of the event, but with a strong sense of the limited effects of their efforts. "Mr. Carey's first, second, and third editions, are gone forth into the world," they noted, "and in all probability, have been read by thousands that will never read his fourth—consequently, any alteration he may hereafter make, in the paragraph alluded to, cannot have the desired effect, or atone for the past." "Therefore," they add, with perhaps more faith than hope, "we apprehend it necessary to publish our thoughts of the occasion" (11). Like the headlines in a newspaper, misrepresentations, Jones and Allen knew, can be corrected or revised, but they have a life of their own and are likely to be remembered.[12] African American historical writing begins, in other words, with the recognition that history is not limited to the argument or effect of any single work. Historical consciousness is a more haphazard process, and the vagaries of memory—collective and individual, influenced by works authorized and unauthorized, authoritative and disreputable—will cloud the testimony of any single study. In short, uncovering the "facts" of African American history was only a part of the African American historiographical project, for the assumed inferiority of those of African origins was being written into the dominant historical record.

The *Narrative* is among other things an exercise in historical perspective, one in which readers confront the cultural politics behind the markers *black* and *white* and are led to consider the racial embodiment(s) of historical consciousness in U.S. culture. The narrative closes, significantly, by having readers witness an address to a specific embodiment of public memory—a reprinted letter to Matthew Clarkson, mayor of Philadelphia. Clarkson's response is printed also, lending authority (in somewhat tentative fashion) to the history Jones and Allen have presented. The presence of Clarkson's letter resembles what would become a convention of slave narratives—the testimonies of, most often, prominent whites included in the preface or appendix. I would suggest, though, that it is a mistake to bring a simple reading of cultural politics to the presence of such authenticating documents. As the letters bring authority to the texts, the texts revise the grounds of that authority, shaping the identity or lending weight to the public reputations of those who write the letters. Clarkson seems to be aware of the extent to which his own authority could be influenced by his presence here, for he writes as if a lawyer were advising him—noting the specificity of his connection to African American efforts (Jones, Allen, and "the people employed by them"), and bearing witness to this history "as far as the same came under my notice" (19).

This attention to mutual influences is further exemplified in the documents that conclude the *Narrative*, an address "to those who keep Slaves, and approve the Practice," an appeal "to the People of Colour," and an address "to the Friends of Him who hath no Helper." The first argues that those who endorse or otherwise support slavery give up their right to criticize the behavior of black Americans, as the rationale of slavery "stigmatize[s] us as men, whose baseness is incurable" and therefore in need of patriarchal control. And in this narrative of public aid, the document suggests that white Americans "try the experiment of taking a few black children, and cultivate their minds with the same care, and let them have the same prospect in view, as to living in the world, as you would wish for your own children" (19–20). In their appeal to the people of color, the authors advise African Americans to remember that they are inevitably representatives of the race, and that disreputable conduct can be used to support arguments for slavery. And the closing address expresses gratitude to those who help those in need, and looks for the day when "Ethiopia" shall "stretch out her hand unto God" (23). The documents, in other words, operate as a philosophical gloss on the narrative of events, deconstructing the assumptions that informed Carey's account, addressing practical individual character as a historical development (by which different conditions over time will produce different results), and placing the whole within the sphere of sacred history (implicitly, replacing Carey's judgment with God's).

The textual struggle of and for history is exemplified most notably in David Walker's powerful *Appeal*, a book that makes strong judgments that now as then evoke strong reactions. As Charles M. Wiltse has written, "With the appearance of the *Appeal* a militant antislavery crusade was born" (ix). Copies of the book were distributed secretly to many southern states; and when sixty copies of the book were discovered in Savannah, Georgia, the mayor of that city demanded that the mayor of Boston, where the book was published, suppress it. Whites of both proslavery and antislavery views either denounced the book wholly or expressed disapproval of its radicalism. A price was placed on Walker's head; and when Walker was found dead shortly after the publication of the book's third edition, many suspected foul play, though the evidence suggests that Walker died of consumption.[13] Walker was suspected to be among the inspirations for Nat Turner's rebellion. Walker inspired Maria Stewart and Henry Highland Garnet, among many others; indeed, a writer for the *Colored American* in 1840, who was advocating the formation of reading societies, testified to the book's importance to African American readers, stating, "I have known a small company of individuals patiently listen at one sitting to hear David Walker's 'Appeal to the Free people of Color,' read through" (Beman, "Thoughts—No. III"). The book had, in short, immediate historical power, if uncertain effects. Walker himself recognized this very well, and he built this recognition into the third edition. "Why," he asks in a long footnote, "do the Slave-holders or Tyrants of America and their advocates fight so hard to keep my brethren from receiving and reading my Book of Appeal to them?—Is it because they treat us so well?—Is it because we are satisfied to rest in Slavery to them and their children?" (72). And so the questions continue, as Walker emphasizes that the book has power only insofar as it finds a receptive audience, and as he emphasizes as well the intellectual and moral standards required for a true reception.

While the publication of the book itself, as Walker recognized, was a significant event in history, it was significant also as a work about history and as an important example of an emerging African American historiography. Walker draws from various sources to support his main thesis, presented with considerable emphasis at the beginning of the *Appeal*, that "we Coloured People of these United States, are, the most wretched, degraded and abject set of beings that ever lived since the world began, down to the present day" (xiv). In support of this thesis, and in tacit response to the U.S. Constitution, Walker divides the book into five sections: a "Preamble" and four articles, titled "Our Wretchedness in Consequence of Slavery," "Our Wretchedness in Consequence of Ignorance," "Our Wretchedness in Consequence of the Preachers of the Religion of Jesus Christ," and "Our Wretchedness in Consequence of the Colonizing Plan." As the titles of the articles indicate, the book progresses from the general to the specific, from slavery as a whole to the colonizing plans that extended from slavery. This linear argument simply segments a hectic mode of writing most aptly characterized by Walker's announcement, a third of the way through the seventy-eight-page text, "Oh Heaven! I am full!!! I can hardly move my pen!!!!" (22). The accumulating exclamation points here are representative of the tone throughout, as Walker strains against the boundaries of expression to explain, declare, and denounce the culture of slavery in its various manifestations, including its effect on African American character. As Walker insists on the importance of teaching African American children grammar while breaking every rule himself, so he seems to insist on the power of argument while announcing his frustrations with the task in every sentence. The result is a tension that is, to my mind, a source of the book's considerable power—a seemingly haphazard mode of historical narration that both appeals to and undermines the terms of historical understanding, the effect of Walker's recognition of the cultural politics of historical knowledge.[14]

As both the *Narrative* and the *Appeal* indicate, it is misleading to suggest simply that African American historians faced the task of correcting an inaccurate historical record—for there was no singular record, and the inaccuracies in the record were manifestations of a deeper problem. One of the tasks of African American history, one might then say, was to reposition or recontextualize historical debate—as was the case in Jones and Allen's early history, and as was the case as well with J. Dennis Harris's *A Summer on the Borders of the Caribbean Sea*, published in 1860. More travel narrative than history, *A Summer* nevertheless is an important part of African American historical writing of this period. To be sure, as Howard H. Bell notes in his preface to his edition of Holly's and Harris's books, "For those acquainted with the history of the island [Hispaniola] Harris' kaleidoscopic review can be more than confusing; some of it is quite positively inaccurate" ("Editor's Note," n.p.). The problem is perhaps even greater when the text is read by those *un*acquainted with the history of the island, as most U.S. readers almost certainly were and are. But the history Harris does present, reckless though it is, draws attention to its own recklessness, and questions the nature of historical understanding itself. Harris begins the second chapter—Letter 2—of the book by noting that, beyond what most schoolchildren learn and remember about Columbus landing in the New World, most know little about the history of the island (81). But Harris draws his readers' attention to various levels of historical ignorance. Having presented the island's inhabitants at the arrival of Columbus as "a simple-minded, hospitable, and kind-hearted people" living in a land he twice identifies as Edenic, Harris asserts that "the studious reader of American history will shudder at the bare recollection of the predatory scenes and excessively inhuman and bewildering iniquities of which they fell the victims, and which, if perpetrated now in any part of the world, 'would send a thrill of horror to the heart of universal man'" (84). And Harris indicates that in identifying this as part of American history, he means not only Spanish colonization but also U.S. development, and that scenes much like those he refers to are, in fact, being "perpetrated" as he writes the book.

The history Harris offers is neither comprehensive nor conclusive; rather, it is "homeopathic" (86). That is, Harris offers a small dose of the history created by "inhuman and bewildering iniquities" by way of indicating a cure. In an essay on "the Anglo-African Empire" included as an appendix, Harris quotes extensively from a pamphlet published by "a Philadelphia merchant" who surveys the history of slavery in the Americas and concludes, "*If . . . I were asked what was probably the final purpose of negro slavery, I should answer—To furnish the basis of a free population for the tropics of America*" (178). Throughout *A Summer* Harris suggests, in effect, that the Philadelphia merchant is right, that oppression can create determination, and the historical crimes of the past can be preparation for the destiny revealed in the future. "The history of the escape of slaves in our day," Harris argues, "is as full of heroism as any history in the world" (152). And, as this history might suggest, destiny, once revealed, provides us with a different past. That is, as Harris constructs his vision of the destiny of the "Anglo-African" empire, he deconstructs the moral and even racial foundations of the "Anglo-American" empire. "The meanest thing I have been obliged to do," he states, "and the greatest sin I have committed, has been the registering my name as an American citizen" (90). To identify this as sin is critique enough; but Harris takes it further: "I should like to find out how a man *knows* he is an American citizen! There are members of Congress who can no more tell this than they can tell who are their fathers" (91). Harris refers here to the "colored race" that becomes such a vital part of his vision of empire—and he suggests that this dual empire involves the difference between acknowledging and veiling the collective history. Referring to a politician's "talk about enforcing the laws," Harris suggests, "he may thank Heaven if he is not yet arrested as a fugitive slave" (91). Noting that "the courts of Virginia have decided that an Octoroon is not a negro," Harris wonders, "if an octoroon is not a *negro*, is an octoroon a citizen? And if an octoroon is not a negro, is a quadroon a negro?" (91). The "Anglo-American" realm increasingly makes no sense—or rather makes a world that undermines the sense that it claims. Revealing it in the process of self-deconstruction is as much Harris's historical purpose as is constructing the historical argument for a destined Anglo-African empire. Claiming that "Hayti is a land of historical facts, and the field of unparalleled glory," Harris comes closest to stating his historical method when he asserts, "the history of San Domingo was never completely written, and if it were, would never find a reader" (85).

Unwritten histories that would not find a reader, homeopathic histories designed to cure a historical disease—the antebellum histories were necessarily commentaries on, and events in, a historical story that was very much *about* the writing of history. Dening has noted the ways in which authoritative conceptions of history have been formulated to serve the needs of "government, law, education, bureaucracy—everywhere where the transformation of the past had to be seen to be reliable, measured by the same criteria, true," noting also that "it is not surprising that being accurate became equated with being true and that history became equated with historical facts" (55).[15] While the process that Dening is talking about was emphasized particularly at and following the professionalization of history toward the end of the nineteenth century, his comments are appropriate as well to the early white American historians, many of whom benefited significantly from their ties to the government, and many of whom also stressed the importance of an objective, documented account of history.[16] Bancroft, for example, believed his *History of the United States* to be objective, though readers have had no trouble recognizing that every page of his history, in a well-known characterization, voted for Jackson. Richard Hildreth, competing for authority in white national history, begins his history by asserting, "Of centennial sermons and Fourth-of-July orations, whether professedly such or in the guise of history, there are more than enough" (vii). To say that the (white) national history was being constructed at this time is simply to say that notions of objectivity, of what would count as historical truth or validity in historical interpretation, were themselves under construction.[17]

The antebellum African American historians, from Jones and Allen in 1794 to Harris in 1860, were tasked with responding to constructions of historical truth and not simply to isolated examples of misinformation. To identify the field of history in which their efforts were needed was not simply to identify the facts and documents that would support a story about African American collective experience over time. The cacophony of texts *defining* the field(s) of history was itself the arena in which they had to work. I am following here Dening's argument that

> historical consciousness finds expression in different forms of dramatic unity, that these forms have different conventionalities, that they make the past meaningful both in the conventionality of their textual nature and the conventionality with which they are received and heard. The past is constitutive of the present in the entertainment that histories give. Histories are the theatre of this entertainment. Rather, histories are the varied theatres of this entertainment. That is, histories are not just the content of a story or an interpretation of the past. Histories are not just a message. Histories are the mode of the story's expression, the public occasion of its telling. (48–49)

What joins Jones and Allen's efforts to correct the historical record in 1793 to Harris's wild commentary *on* the historical record in 1860 was the necessity of a certain kind of performance in the developing theater of American history. History, in short, is not the record; it is the heteroglossia of its various recordings. What permits us to describe history as *white* history is not simply the focus on white agents of history but also and more importantly the mode of the story's expression. African American historians, accordingly, could not hope to simply correct the record; they needed to enter into the theater of history, a theater in which they had already been assigned a marginal role, and they needed to shift or disrupt the social rituals of historical propagation that determined the public occasion of the narration of historical stories. They needed a history that defined not just the message or the terms of historical interpretation but also the teller.

"A Mixed Race": Gathering the Community

The rise of the white republic, to borrow Alexander Saxton's phrase, involved the rise of white nationalist history—approaches to history in which developing racial ideologies played a defining role.[18] Involved in this history were the representational protocols fundamental to the establishment of the racial order that—as Benedict Anderson, Mills, Goldberg, and others have demonstrated—was fundamental to the rise of the modern nation-state.[19] Racial otherness was rendered an invisible presence in the national order by way of a spectacular visibility, a performance of the contingencies of group dynamics on the stage of the historical text. The invisibility of the other, in short, is achieved through its constant rendering—as has been so notably the case of the perpetually vanishing Indian, for example, in U.S. history.[20] The developing white nationalist history defined its subject in part through its treatment of racial otherness. Addressing "the inherently homogenizing logic of institutions," Goldberg has argued persuasively that "if the state minimally is a collection of institutions, manifesting and (re-)ordering itself necessarily in and through the logic of such institutional arrangement . . . , then one could say that the state inherently is the institutionalization of homogeneity" (*Racial State*, 30). Similarly, one could say that the historical narratives of the nineteenth century designed to establish the historical foundations of identifiably U.S. institutions were devoted as well to establishing the ideological, historical, and narrative protocols for institutionalizing homogeneity.

The order of the rising white republic involved fundamentally concepts of national embodiment that associated national character with deeply racialized conceptions of what might be called a cognitive order—for culturally specific concepts of reason were, after all, and have remained, the centerpiece of racialist thought. But this strategic idealization of Enlightenment reason was not simply an abstract racial test, for the association of mental character and national citizenship was fundamental to the new nation. As Daniel W. Howe has noted in "The Political Psychology of *The Federalist*," "The analogy between the human mind and the political commonwealth . . . is one of the oldest staples of philosophical discourse" (495) and was prominent in the works of the Scottish moral philosophers by whom many white historians of the nineteenth-century United States were influenced. The analogy between mind and polity was particularly attractive to a nation struggling for order, self-definition, and empire. I am referring to the cultural mode of nationalism that Joel Barlow had in mind when, in his *Advice to the Privileged Orders in the Several States of Europe* (a title that itself views Europe as a potential union of states), he identified a "*habit of thinking*" as "the *only* foundation" for a sociopolitical system. "The *habit of thinking*," Barlow explains, addressing mainly the doctrine of equality, "has so much of nature in it, it is so undistinguishable from the indelible marks of the man, that it is a perfectly safe foundation for any system that we may choose to build upon it." Indeed, "it is the only point of contact by which men communicate as moral associates" (113–14). It is this mode of national self-conception that inspired Bancroft—who once referred to America as an "empire of mind"[21]—to write a history of the United States that begins with the earliest precolonial adventures and ends (in a supplement to the original ten-volume work) with the writing of the Constitution. For Bancroft and others, U.S. history included all that came before—a process of cognitive and philosophical development that eventually led to the United States and to a leader, George Washington, whom Bancroft valorizes for his constitution of mind.[22] Similarly, in a letter to Hezekiah Niles (1818), John Adams asserted that "the real American Revolution" was the "radical change in the principles, opinions, sentiments, and affections of the people," a change that took place "before a drop of blood was shed" (qtd. in Colbourn 3). As Bernard Bailyn, among many others, has reminded us, what was most revolutionary about the American Revolution was "the conceptualization of American life" (20)—or, in Gordon Wood's terms, the creation (and the realization) of "the American Science of Politics."

The institutional ordering of American history—ideological, political, and commercial—brought racial contestation to the center of the American stage, and it is there that African American historians had to confront the dynamic rendering of the African presence in the nation. Alexis de Tocqueville famously explores the mutually contingent relations between the "three races" in *Democracy in America*; in Bancroft's *History of the United States* this exploration becomes a fundamental narrative and ideological principle. In the second of the history's ten volumes, published originally in 1837, Bancroft examines "the three races, the Caucasian, the Ethiopian and the American," whom Providence had brought into the "presence of one another on our soil." Having wondered whether "the red man" would "disappear entirely from the forests" (enabling his *History* gradually to displace their claim to the title of the "American" race), Bancroft turns to "the Ethiopian," and asserts, "The slave-trade united the races by an indissoluble bond; the first ship that brought Africans to America, was a sure pledge, that, in due time, ships from the New World would carry the equal blessings of Christianity to the burning plains of Nigritia, that descendants of Africans would toil for the benefits of European civilization" (2:464). Bancroft presents a developing (white) national identity grounded in the multiple contingencies of racial ideology. African Americans, while demonstrating a complex and sometimes contradictory understanding of the relative benefits of African and European civilizations, questioned the assumption of European achievement behind claims like Bancroft's, but found themselves woven into a complex story.[23] This story was not the "official story" of nationhood, I should emphasize, for such a singular story simply did not exist.[24] White nationalist history instead was a conglomeration of many texts that served to facilitate a developing national imagination. Indeed, the purpose of history was not merely to tell a story of nationhood but also, and more importantly, to negotiate the interrelated stories and the chaos of texts that shaped nationalist imaginations.[25]

Captured in Bancroft's vision of the American past are both the historical misrepresentations to which African American historians needed to respond and the problematic tools they necessarily used in their response. In 1857, Holly would complain that "every thing is done by the enemies of the negro race to vilify and debase them. And the result is, that many of the race themselves, are almost persuaded that they are a brood of inferior beings" (22). The misrepresentations of an undocumented past were being transformed into self-fulfilling prophecies, as a fragmented understanding of a generalized and degraded history reinforced the fragmentation and degradation the African American community suffered in U.S. culture. "Why are things as they are" was linked to the seemingly irrevocable dictates of fate: "They have always been this way." Holly, like all antebellum writers who challenged the ideology of African inferiority, looked to historical writing to counter the effects of both history and white historical texts. As he puts it at the end of his introduction to *A Vindication of the Capacity of the Negro Race*, "I wish, by the undoubted facts of history, to cast back the vile aspersions and foul calumnies that have been heaped upon my race for the last four centuries, by our unprincipled oppressors; whose base interest, at the expense of our blood and our bones, have made them reiterate, from generation to generation, during the long march of ages, every thing that would prop up the impious dogma of our natural and inherent inferiority" (22). Although Holly's invocation of "the undoubted facts of history" might be problematic in the light of the body of work, historical and cultural, to which he was implicitly responding—the "vile aspersions and foul calumnies that have been heaped upon my race for the last four centuries"—his faith in the power of history is instructive here. And, indeed, in *A Vindication* Holly demonstrates a strong sense of what might be called the cultural politics of historical facts. What is important here is Holly's awareness that historical understanding is itself historical, something generated and reinforced "during the long march of ages," reiterated "from generation to generation," as one version of history (oral or written) serves as the foundation for the next.

Like almost all of the writers I discuss in this chapter, and in the chapters that follow, Holly worked to deconstruct one version of history so that he would have the materials he needed to construct a new historical consciousness. And those materials were the same materials used to construct the individual identities of those who were "almost persuaded that they are a brood of inferior beings." As the African American ex-slave, clergyman, and abolitionist James W. C. Pennington argued in his 1859 essay "The Self-Redeeming Power of the Colored Races of the World," "In the economy of God's moral government, no provision is made for waste human materials; and it is not easy to see how the state or church can afford to waste those precious materials which God has committed to their care." Pennington looks, accordingly, for a renewed understanding of human economy in obedience to the laws of "God's moral government," arguing that "Human progress, next to human redemption, must, indeed, enter into the economy of every enlightened state and Christian church" (*The Anglo-African Magazine* 314). Human progress—the use of the materials of history—must be understood as a necessary part of one's moral duty. That is, limited in their ability to draw from a historical record of omissions and distortions, African Americans not only needed to create history as they tried to record it; they also had to create the community that could serve as the visible manifestation of history. As Rael has written, "Religious black nationalism told African American northerners they were part of a special community with a divine mission. It told them *how* to be in that community, and why" (267).[26] Central to the writing of African American history, in short, was the desire to create a vision of history sufficiently complex and extensive to foster a unified sense of community.

However, the narration of a possible black national identity, or of identifiably African American citizenship in a nation within the nation, required more than simply applying the developing African American print culture to the needs of an imagined community—for the black community as both experienced (under the conditions of a white supremacist regime) and imagined (in Benedict Anderson's terms, in white national print culture) was in fact a vital part of the imagined community of the white republic. Moreover, significant differences among black historians—ideological differences, as well as differences shaped by the always shifting conceptions of race—would seem to argue against a coherent historical field capable of ushering into a collective imagination a unified conception of community. But one must note as well that contingency (in relation to white nationalism) and instability (legal, social, economic, and so on) were, in fact, and remain, the defining characteristics of the foundational presence of "race" in American culture. African American history, accordingly, required not a transcendence of these contingencies and instabilities, or an acceptance of race as if it were a stable category of identity, but rather a fluid engagement in an always-shifting ideological site.

Indeed, one of the challenges early African American historians faced was to determine what made their histories African American, and to address the wide spectrum of racial identity within the potential constituents of an African American history. Pertinent here is Benedict Anderson's argument that "nationalism thinks in terms of historical destinies, while racism dreams of eternal contaminations, transmitted from the origins of time through an endless sequence of loathsome copulations: outside history" (136). Did racial mixing make African Americans doubly removed from history—from, say, Hegel's removal to further removals in the United States? Or did such mixing emphasize the contingencies of white and black national history, placing African Americans both inside and outside the pale of white nationalist history, there positioned to transform that history by redefining national destiny?

Henry Highland Garnet, among many others, envisioned a destined mixed race that would transform the white nationalist project; Daniel Coker agreed that mixing was inevitable, but viewed this mixing as a sin; Martin Delany acknowledged the shades of difference in the black community but argued that this only emphasized the centrality of pure African heritage; and David Walker wrote that he "would not give a *pinch of snuff* for white women" (9). One might ask, then, what is African American history? I have in mind Robert F. Reid-Pharr's opening question in *Conjugal Union* of "how one might properly historicize the blackness of Black America, how one might unpack the common sense of that deep tendency within black intellectual life to insist upon black singularity, to conjure that which is pure, unique, that which is decidedly black" (3).

As I've suggested, early African American historians did not recognize a singularity of black identity, though they worked to identify a distinctively black community, recognizing, as does Reid-Pharr, that "racial and national identity exist within history and are thus permeable and dynamic" (3). Certainly, many shared Delany's view that "we are not identical with the Anglo-Saxon," and were sympathetic to Delany's argument that "we have . . . inherent traits, attributes, so to speak, and native characteristics, peculiar to our race, whether pure or mixed blood" ("Political" 334–335). But they shared as well Delany's understanding of the role of white Americans in giving shape to the black community: "The Anglo-American stands preeminent for deeds of injustice and acts of oppression unparalleled, perhaps, in the annals of modern history" (336). Having challenged the essentialized identities imposed by white writers, black historians faced the task of recording the history of the community defined by white oppression without accepting the defining terms of the white oppressors. Blackness was defined, in part, by a common condition of oppression, a condition that informed the historical project, but blackness extended beyond a condition to become a theological nexus, the site for determining the intersection of human and divine history by which a stable historical method could be identified.[27]

Whereas Bancroft envisioned a new people rising in a new world in social, intellectual, and ideological terms, African American historians of this period emphasized the extent to which a people was arising that was physically *new*, though unacknowledged by the dominant culture in its determination to avoid the implications of slavery. Whereas a Bancroftian notion of Providence increasingly meant not seeing the world as it was, African Americans argued with some emphasis that the world, as embodied by the inhabitants of the

United States, was changing. As Garnet argues in his 1848 discourse *The Past and the Present Condition, and the Destiny, of the Colored Race*, "It is a stubborn fact, that it is impossible to separate the pale man and the man of color, and therefore the result which to them is so fearful, is inevitable." Indeed, Garnet continues, "If the colored people should all consent to leave this country, on the day of their departure there would be sore lamentations," for "we would insist upon taking all who have our generous and prolific blood in their veins." "In such an event," Garnet notes, and then names names, "the American church and state would be bereaved" (25). With an eye on a world that the American church and state chooses not to see, Garnet begins this address by apologizing for his use of "some of the improper terms of our times"; specifically, he notes that he will "speak of *races*, when in fact there is but one race, as there was but one Adam" (6).

And what has been, Garnet suggests, shall be, as history unfolds to deconstruct, in effect, the terms of the times, changing what is identified as race into something unaccountable by that term. "*This Western World*," he asserts with emphasis, "*is destined to be filled with a mixed race*" (26). This view was shared even by those who seemed to find the directives of Providence leading elsewhere. In *A Dialogue between a Virginian and an African Minister* (1810), for example, author Daniel Coker has the minister argue that "Divine Providence (as if in order to perpetuate the distinction of colour) has not only placed those different nations at a great distance from each other; but a natural aversion and disgust seems to be implanted in the breast of each" (28). Having said that, though, the minister quickly adds that many have apparently overcome this "natural aversion," and that "it is too late to prevent this evil; the matter is already gone beyond recovery; for it may be proved with mathematical certainty, that if things go on in the present course, the future inhabitants of American will be much checkered" (29). For Coker, these historically re-marked bodies were signs of a sin that would result in divine judgment on the nation; for Garnet and others, this mixing was the result of history and the foreground of national destiny. All involved worked with an understanding of the racial order of the United States and what Leonard Cassuto has identified as the "peculiar disruptive power" of the "racial grotesque"—that is, the "conflicting mixture of signals that intrudes upon the desired order of the world" (8). The African American community embodied cultural conflicts that exposed the ideological grotesque of the white polity.

The largely unacknowledged fact of the development of a mixed race, that is, exposed the concept of race as a cultural fiction, long before that recognition became a commonplace in late twentieth- and twenty-first-century scholarship, thus allowing African American historians the narrative flexibility of a counterperformance, one designed to relocate the theater of history. William Wells Brown, for example, regularly included commentary on his mixed-race status in his lectures, both to emphasize the sexual and familial violations that were common under slavery and to question the stability of the color line. At times, Brown could be rather inventive in his identification of his family line—for example, in his claims that he was the grandson of both Daniel Boone and Simon Lee, a Virginian slave who served in the Revolutionary War. More often, Brown simply referred to his mixed-race identity as a kind of challenge to the expectations of white audiences. In an 1855 lecture in Cincinnati, Ohio, for example, as reported in the *Anti-Slavery Bugle*, Brown began by challenging the ideological foundation of slavery, the social fiction of race, "saying that we were here to comment on the doings of our fathers. If his audience thought he referred to black fathers they were mistaken— neither did he refer to white fathers" (Ripley 4:287). According to the reporter of this speech, Brown then asserted that "we [are] a mixed people." But the reporter himself follows this assertion by offering a parenthetical description of Brown that emphasized the standard categories for identifying racial identity: "Mr. Brown is a light Mulatto, with a broad nose, but except [for] this and the kink in his hair, not of decidedly African features" (Ripley 4:287). While this description defines Brown by the degree of "African features" he both has and lacks, Brown himself insisted on defining himself, for the purposes of this speech, by the degree to which he could and could not claim his white heritage. He asserted that "his white fathers had deprived him of the privilege of appealing to the black race for his ancestry, but he was a type representing both races, and would for the moment throw aside his African ancestry, and appeal to his Anglo-Saxon" (Ripley 4:287). In an 1854 speech, Brown had presented essentially the same point in different terms, asserting, "I speak not now as an Anglo-Saxon, as I have a right to speak, but as an African" (Ripley 4:249).

Brown's shifting performance here, joined with the counterperformance of the reporter of the 1855 lecture, indicates the dynamic, shifting, and unstable nature of racial identity. African American historical writing similarly played off that shifting instability to locate race as a feature *of* historical process, a dynamic narrative principle. In short, histories of African American identity were necessarily histories also of white identity, and historians used the cultural fictions of race to destabilize the assumptions that shaped historical understanding. James W. C. Pennington, for example, concludes his 1841 *Text Book of the Origin and History, &c. &c. of the Colored People* with reflections on the effects of racial mixing. He notes "the history of Vermont, by S. Williams, 1794," in which Williams calculates how long it will take for whites to become black (Williams's inference "from approximative data," Pennington tells us, is that it will take five generations with intermarriage, and four thousand years without). Pennington counters by saying, "I hope it will not be thought too humorous to say, I am sorry that while Mr. Williams was in the way of calculating, he did not give us a guess concerning the prospect of the whites to change *our* complexion to *theirs* on the supposition that *they* had met *us* in Africa" (96). Pennington then notes that Portuguese "who planted themselves on the coast of Africa . . . have been succeeded by descendants blacker than the Africans," and that a colony of Jews are also black (96–97). The past gives Pennington reason to question the vision of collective destiny implicit in commentaries on racial mixing, (re)placing American history in the theater of the African diaspora.

As Pennington's commentary suggests, white Americans were hardly blind to the reality of racial mixing, and the white press responded with dire warnings about the need to police the lines of racial identity—articles then reprinted in the black press, turning the debate over racial identity to different purposes by exposing the instability of white racial identity. In an article first published in the *Charlottesville Jeffersonian* and reprinted in *Frederick Douglass' Paper*, for example, the author asks, "What is a Negro?" and comments on a Philadelphia lecture by "P. A. Browne, Esq. . . . in which he combated the idea that an inferior race could ever be entirely obliterated by breeding toward a superior one." Browne, drawing from a work on natural history, follows the process of mixing from mulatto to quadroon to mestee to white—leading the writer for the *Charlottesville Jeffersonian* to remark that some "may call this white . . . , but we should be very much afraid of marrying such a white for fear of finding ourselves someday blessed with a '*black heir*.'" The writer then tells the story of one such surprise, and suggests a report on the subject that "it would be well for our legislators to investigate, before they make those tainted with Negro blood white men and women" ("What Is a Negro?"). This is, of course, but one of many white public examinations on the subject of maintaining racial boundaries—and one of many examples, as well, of the black press reprinting and thus recontextualizing those examinations.

What is *black* about black historical writing is, to a significant degree, the performative negotiation of the problems and possibilities of racial performance on the public stage. I am thinking here of Saidiya V. Hartman's concept of "performing blackness," in which "blackness is defined . . . in terms of social relationality rather than identity." "Blackness," Hartman argues, "incorporates subjects normatively defined as black, the relations among blacks, whites, and others, and the practices that produce racial difference." With her term "performing blackness," accordingly, Hartman means to convey "both the cross-purposes and the circulation of various modes of performance and performativity that concern the production of racial meaning and subjectivity, the nexus of race, subjection, and spectacle, the forms of racial and race(d) pleasure, enactments of white dominance and power, and the reiteration and/or rearticulation of the conditions of enslavement" (56–57). To speak of African American history, accordingly, is to speak of complex sites of social struggle in which the multifarious relations involved in that struggle are highlighted and dramatically restaged.

Although the flexible discourse of race allowed for creative performances of individual subjectivity, I am suggesting that the realities of race as a systemic presence, a system of control, complicated any attempt to understand the community for which African American history was written. It was simply not enough to note that race was a fiction, for this was a fiction with practical effects in all areas of life. Hosea Easton, for example, begins his *Treatise on the Intellectual Character, and Civil and Political Condition of the Colored People of the U[nited] States* with the "great truth," frequently repeated in nineteenth-century African American writings, that "God hath made of one blood all nations of men"; accordingly, he asserts, "no constitutional difference exists in the children of men, which can be said to be established by hereditary laws" (5). The differences that do exist "are casual or accidental" (5); and as he proceeds, it becomes clear that perceived differences are specifically historical. Easton presents African Americans as a largely degraded people, but he presents this condition as the historical effect of slavery, arguing that as "natural causes produce natural effects, then . . . unnatural causes produce unnatural effects. The slave system is an unnatural cause, and has produced its unnatural effects, as displayed in the deformity of two and a half millions of beings, who have been under its soul-and-body-destroying influence, lineally, for near three hundred years" (24). It is a commonplace to note that prejudice has been shaped historically by the system that relies on it for justification, and that it has also created its subjects over time, sometimes succeeding in shaping their lives to meet the images, the deformed historical body, defined by prejudice. But what is particularly important here is the use of history to imagine a foundation, a starting point missed for the present but still available for the future, a future to be determined by the struggle for natural rights over unnatural violations.

Certainly, that struggle would include a focus on African American achievements. Texts by both black and white abolitionists commonly included collective biographies of men and women of African heritage and of great achievement—as if to accept the fiction that white prejudice is simply the result of a lack of information.[28] In *The Past and the Present Condition*, Garnet argues, either disingenuously or with too much hope, that "the old doctrine of the natural inferiority of the colored race, propagated in America by Mr. Thomas Jefferson, has long been refuted by Dr. John Mason Goode." For those unfamiliar with Goode's good work, Garnet notes that history itself provides "numerous respectable witnesses from among the slandered, both living and dead," among them "Pushkin in Russia, Dumas in France, Toussaint in Hayti, Banaker, Theodore Sedgwick Wright, and a host in America, and a brilliant galaxy in Ancient History" (28). Garnet's list offers a good overview of many of the significant historical subjects pursued by nineteenth-century African American historians—especially in his references to the Haitian Revolution and to ancient history; and Garnet presents here as well one of the recurring methods of African American history, the list of names of prominent people of African lineage.

But African American writers did not rely solely on accounts of African American achievements in their arguments against prejudice; they also looked to history to demonstrate just how deep were the "unnatural" effects of the unnatural system of slavery—and to indicate that the struggle for natural rights, as well as the definition of community, would need to proceed from within as well as from without, from self-determination as well as from corrections of white misinformation. Maria Stewart, for example, was not alone in taking African Americans to task for failing to live up to the demands of history. Noting that "we this day are considered as one of the most degraded races upon the face of the earth," Stewart also looks to history, including the Haitians among the Greeks, the French, and the Poles as examples of "a firmness of character, and independence of spirit." For Stewart, though, this broader text of history leads back to the significant question about the cause of prejudice in the United States, and to a disturbing answer: "And why is it, my friends, that we are despised above all the nations upon the earth? Is it merely because our skins are tinged with a sable hue? No, nor will I ever believe that it is. What then is it; Oh, it is because that we and our fathers have dealt treacherously one with another, and because many of us now possess that envious and malicious disposition, that we had rather die than see each other rise an inch above a beggar" (61). For Stewart, as for Easton, prejudice was formed historically, but its effects had been internalized—and Stewart includes here among the causes of prejudice significant failings in the African American community itself.[29] As Garnet put it when stating his opposition to "those who, either from good or evil motives, plead for the utopian plan of the Colonization of a whole race to the shores of Africa," the project of colonial control was in some ways redundant, for, he argued, "we are now colonized" (25). While colonization schemes sponsored by whites remained a hotly contested concern among African Americans, the great majority of whom expressed stern opposition to their planned removal by whites whose motives were all too transparent, many of the black emigration movements of this period were framed as responses to the internal colonization of which Garnet wrote.

The result of this internal colonization, and the means by which it was perpetuated, was a fragmentation of the community of people of African heritage, and this "scattered" state was by far the primary concern of most writers of the time. One of the earliest and most prominent works in this line is Paul Cuffe's attempt to encourage settlement in Sierra Leone, the English West African colony established for ex-slaves. Cuffe's *A Brief Account of the Settlement and Present Situation of the Colony of Sierra Leone, in Africa* includes an "Address" directed "to my scattered brethren and fellow countrymen at Sierra Leone," recommending "the propriety of assembling yourselves together for the purpose of worshipping the Lord your God" (260). Resisting the white control and deception associated with the American Colonization Society, the African Civilization Society was formed in 1858 and led by Garnet, whose missionary goals were rooted in a similar vision of the multiple fragmentations effected by the history and culture of slavery. In an "apostrophe" to Africa in *The Past and the Present Condition*, Garnet mourns the "children . . . scattered over the whole earth . . . tortured, taunted, and hurried out of life by unprecedented cruelty." And his reflections on the children and their deaths lead to reflections on their conception, as Garnet addresses the violation of the intersection, in nineteenth-century U.S. ideology, of the sacred and the secular realms: womanhood, marriage, and motherhood. "Our sisters ever manifesting the purest kindness, whether in the wilderness of their father-land, or amid the sorrows of the middle passage, or in crowded cities, are unprotected from the lusts of tyrants. They have a regard for virtue, and they possess a sense of honor, but there is no respect paid to these jewels of noble character. Driven into unwilling concubinage, their offspring are sold by their Anglo Saxon fathers. To them the marriage institution is but a name, for their despoilers break down the hymenial alter [*sic*] and scatter its sacred ashes on the winds" (15). From Cuffe's vision of a scattered people to Garnet's vision of the scattered ashes of the marriage institution, the means and effects of internal colonization were both geographical and ideological—and the winds carried not only the ashes of an abandoned cultural institution and moral ideal but also the hope of a people both separated physically and brought together ideologically by the slave trade.

African American writers developed approaches to historical narration, accordingly, capable of accounting for the scattered community—that is, a community that could discover itself *as* a community only by discovering itself as a scattered people joined by a common historical condition. This vision of a community fragmented geographically and psychologically is prominent, for example, in one of the most powerful historical works of the early period, Easton's *Treatise*. Easton notes that "the injury sustained by the colored people, is both national and personal," and again "national in a twofold sense," for not only were they "lineally stolen from their native country" but they also "sustain a national injury by being adopted subjects and citizens, and then be [*sic*] denied their citizenship." Having been "denied birthright in one" and having had their birthright "stolen from them in another," they were then additionally fragmented in the spiritual realm, for "they had lost title to both worlds; for certainly they are denied all title in this, and almost all advantages to prepare for the next." The result is the audience to which all writing of this period is directed: "In this light of the subject, they belong to no people, race, or nation; subjects of no government—citizens of no country—scattered surplus remnants of two races, and of different nations—severed into individuality—rendered a mass of broken fragments, thrown to and fro, by the boisterous passions of this and other ungodly nations" (37). Easton's vision of a scattered community that belongs "to no people, race, or nation"—in effect, a people denied a history *because* of history—reverses the terms of Hegel's proclamation that Africa "is no historical part of the World" because "it has no movement or development to exhibit." Easton's response is that the movement of the slave trade and subsequent developments in the United States are part of a larger project of controlling the terms of history—the means by which people define themselves as a people, the institutional means by which individuals participate in what can be known as history.

The historical narratives written in response to this condition would need to account for the various dimensions of fragmentation—the geographical, the psychological, the moral. But this is hardly the sort of heroic material that one associates with the construction of an imagined nation, and accordingly many writers looked for ways to address the internal divisions, the unnatural effects of which Easton and Stewart wrote, looking for the terms of union in disorder. In his 1813 *Oration on the Abolition of the Slave Trade*, for example, George Lawrence presents a dramatically vivid short history of the slave trade, and then notes that this is a difficult subject for his audience to review. "To harangue you on the sufferings of our ancestors," Lawrence remarks, "I know is excruciating painful, yet bear with me a little; although it rends the tender heart, or forces the silent tear, it is expedient. In reflecting on their situation, our celebration demonstrates itself to be fully sensible of ours" (378). The history of those "pressed down beneath the surface of nature" offers both background and contrast to a group that "soar[s] aloft as the towering eagle to an eminence commanding a view of the world"; and from that eminent perspective, another contrast becomes visible—between a world caught up in "strife and contention" and a community enjoying "the perpetual sunshine of peace and happiness." Lawrence seems to be aware that his contrast is overdrawn, for he addresses the dangers of such strife and contention, and pleads for solidarity, for "union is the foundation of liberty, and its perfection is social love" (378). As I have suggested, this vision of union is a vision shared by many early nineteenth-century African American historians, many of whom, like Lawrence, emphasized the need to face a painful past to understand a possible future. Implicitly, and often explicitly, they argued that this act of understanding would be the central bond of union in the present. Historical understanding was necessary for community, and many African American writers joined Lawrence in envisioning a unified community capable of pressing "undauntedly forward . . . sure of conquest" (Lawrence 378).

These appeals for a beloved community, however, floated on the surface of a turbulent historicity. George Lawrence's vision of communal unity through "social love" was a response to the need for a significant communion, leading him to close his discourse with a call to the scattered community to "let your hearts be linked in the chain that bids defiance to the intrigues of your enemies" (381–82). The chains of oppression would be transformed into the solidarity of defiance through moral union. Nathaniel Paul shared this view, linking it to the significant development of history represented by the abolition of slavery in New York State in an overly—or, perhaps, rhetorically—

optimistic address in 1827. Paul begins the address by claiming communal authority over history not only as a series of events but as a series of documented remembrances: "As the nations which have already passed away, have been careful to select the most important events, peculiar to themselves, and have recorded them for the good of the people that should succeed them, so will we place it upon our history; and we will tell the good story to our children and to our children's children" (3). This acquisition of history signals a more significant development, and an attendant responsibility for "the rising generation" that finds itself, Paul argues, entering into a new age of enlightenment, "a day that our fathers desired to see, but died without the sight: a day in which science, like the sun of the firmament, rising, darting as he advances his beams to every quarter of the globe." And in this new day, the scattered community will rediscover itself: "The mists and darkness scatter at his approach, and all nations and people are blessed with his rays; so the glorious light of science is spreading from east to west, and Afric's sons are catching the glance of its beams as it passes; its enlightening rays scatter the mists of moral darkness and ignorance which have but too long overshadowed their minds; it enlightens the understanding, directs the thoughts of the heart, and is calculated to influence the soul to the performance of every good and virtuous act" (21). In this vision of history, the moral darkness that was both cause and effect of slavery is itself scattered by the "enlightening rays" of an understanding that is the manifestation of historical progress. History becomes the means by which the scattered community will be drawn together, both as a series of events and as a subject to record and pass down from generation to generation.

The need to respond to the imposition of an identity by others shaped not only the developing conception of a collective African American identity but also the historical work required by that vision of identity. The dominant vision of the African American community was of a people scattered, "deformed," and mixed—but therefore inclusive of a larger historical story, the story repressed in official white national narratives. African American historical writing, then, necessarily involved the deconstruction of various narratives and philosophies of history—from Hegel to Bancroft to the rhetoric of Independence Day celebrations. As white history involved the manipulation of racial contingencies and contestation—the ongoing rendering of marginality, the visible spectacle of creating invisibility—so black history necessarily involved an intervention into the ruling narratives of history, a search for the terms of its own existence that involved fundamentally the necessity of responding to the overabundance of defining experiences, and the methods for understanding those experiences, that constructed African Americans as peculiar, overdetermined, and strategically misinterpreted embodiments of history.

"A Just View of Our Origin": Africa and the Recovery of History

Central to the task of reappropriating the terms by which historical presence can be defined was the need to reposition Africa's presence in the African American historical understanding, in part by dramatizing this historical revisionist work through public responses to white characterizations of African history and destiny. Representative in this regard is a document published "in answer to those of the New York Colonization Society," the *Resolutions of the People of Color, at a Meeting Held on the 25th of January, 1831*, the authors of which begin by noting that "a number of gentlemen in this city" have "mistaken views with respect to the wishes and welfare of the people of this State, on the subject of African Colonization" (281). There are two prominent historical issues addressed in this document, both having to do with the nature and terms of the connection between African Americans and Africa. The various white-driven colonization societies operated on the strategic assumption that African Americans were identifiable mainly as Africans, and therefore should be happy to "return." The writers of this document, like many others, asserted in turn that "we claim *this country, the place of our birth, and not Africa*, as our mother country" (282). The other significant assumption underlying white-driven colonization attempts was that those of African origins were a distinct and inferior race. To this, the authors of the resolution responded first by quoting the white Boston diplomat and author Alexander H. Everitt's view that "the blacks must be regarded as the real authors of most of the arts and sciences which give the whites at present the advantages over them," and then by asserting, "the blacks had a long and glorious day: and after what they have been and done, it argues not so much a mistaken theory, as sheer ignorance of the most notorious historical facts, to pretend that they are naturally inferior to the whites" (283–84). Claiming Africa as heritage but not home, claiming racial lineage to dispel the stereotypes and assumptions that supported racial prejudice, African Americans understood racism as a feature in a historical struggle for power that, to be answered, required a complex engagement in history, and an understanding of the complex heritage and dynamic quality of African American identity.

The history of a possible African American community, as this document suggests, was a story in search of its narrative principles, a search that led historians to Africa and the dramatic remembrance of what might be termed an eternal Middle Passage, in which Africa stands as a floating signifier of the "permeable and dynamic" character of racial and national identity.[30] In an 1814 oration, for example, Russell Parrott relies on a dramatic narrative, an emphatically ahistorical representation of a collective history. Noting that the "heart-rending sufferings of the unfortunates who fell within [slavery's] vortex are beyond my feeble description," Parrott calls upon his audience to "fancy yourself on the fertile plains of Africa," and then follows a man abducted and taken on the Middle Passage and finally "placed under a code of laws (if laws they can be called); he is considered as part of the brute creation; the master is invested with a complete control over him" (386). As he guides his audience along this fancied journey, he individualizes the problem of representation: "What language can tell the feelings of his soul? what pen portray the intenseness of his grief?" (385).[31] Thus does the inability to represent the past become the historian's tool, as a past both generalized and individualized is deposited in the reader's imagination, linking that reader to the many who have experienced the Middle Passage. In effect, the historian's task is to reconfigure the historical problem of identity, shaping a community of scattered individuals who claim America as the place of their birth and Africa as the center of their consciousness.

Representative of this mode is Nathaniel Paul, who slips in and out of the present tense as he presents a history of slavery. "On the shores of Africa," Paul begins, "the horror of the scene commences" (6). Paul takes his readers on an imaginative journey and reflects on the moral implications of that journey along the way—presenting slavery as an avoidance of God's determination to counter man's tendency to "usurp undue authority over his fellow," noting that man "should obtain his bread by the sweat of his brow," and suggesting that this avoidance will come back to haunt the enslavers (6–7). The reflections lead back to the eternal crime, as Paul notes, "while I turn my thoughts back and survey what is past, I see our forefathers seized by the hand of the rude ruffian, and torn from their native homes" (9–10). Paul takes his readers through the Middle Passage, inserting himself in the process, as eternal history becomes the history of internalized remembrance: "I view them casting the last and longing look towards the land"; "I view them wafted onward"; "I see the crowd of trafficers in human flesh"; "I view them doomed." Paul's remembrance gives dramatic voice to the historical and moral question posed by this history: "Tell me, ye mighty waters, why did you sustain the ponderous load of misery?"—and as he continues the questions, aimed more directly at God as they progress, he receives the answer: "Be still, and know that I am God!" (11). Paul's narrative of an unknowable past collects the community in his consciousness, as he physically represents that community in the culture of racism, and as his historical narrative leads to the borders of historical understanding.[32]

Much of African American writing might be understood as an ongoing attempt to teach readers to read this eternal Middle Passage, this haunting memory that reminds us that visions of secular history can be all too deceptive and that moral history is still and always present. The challenge, in short, was to trace the correspondence of sacred history and secular history. Noting that "by an almost common consent, the modern world seems determined to pilfer Africa of her glory" (*Past and Present* 6), Garnet, for example, defends the inclusion of Egypt in African American history by referring to historical authorities both sacred and secular. "Moses," he asserts, "is the patriarch of sacred history. The same eminent station is occupied by Herodotus in profane history" (7). Both historians, Garnet argues, lead one back to Egypt in Africa and Africa in Egypt. "Yet in the face of this historical evidence," Garnet complains, "there are those who affirm that the ancient Egyptians were not of the pure African stock," "intellectual resurrectionists" who "dig through a mountain of such evidence, and declare that these people were not negroes" (7). Aside from current debates over the scholarly integrity of either Egypto-centric or Afrocentric interpretations of history, it is important to recognize Garnet's recovery of Egypt and Africa as sites of (lost) memory, and also as sites of possible memory.[33] Insofar as Western historiography is still charac-terized by an imbalance of attention to the full spectrum of human experi-ence, and specifically by a studied neglect of Africa, we must recognize a significant gap between memory and history. Garnet, among many other historians of this period, addresses that gap, and he reminds us to be attentive to how the question of historical foregrounds has been addressed at any given cultural moment. As Garnet and others demonstrate, Africa has served as the shifting framework for studying that gap.

Indeed, in defiance of "intellectual resurrectionists," African Americans found in Africa both an inspiring history of achievements and a vision of an original innocence. Such visions of history were, of course, not African American inventions, for many white writers had presented Africa in similar ways. African American writers simply drew from existing visions of Africa and applied them to the needs of the scattered community. "History informs us that we sprung from one of the most learned nations of the whole earth," Maria Stewart claimed with pride, "from the seat, if not the parent of science; yes, poor, despised Africa was once the resort of sages and legislators of other nations, was esteemed the school for learning, and the most illustrious men in Greece flocked thither for instruction" (65). Others, like William Hamilton, preferred to extend the historical reach still further, and frame it in speculative language, reasoning that "Africa, being situated in the middle of the Globe . . . would make a grand eligible situation for the seat of Authority." Drawing on both geographical speculation and religion's stories of origins, Hamilton further wonders whether Africa would "have made (she lying immediately under the fostering care of the sun) an eligible situation for the growth of man in his first state of existence?" "Let each study the nature of man," Hamilton suggests in response, "and answer the question for himself" ("Oration" 392). Africa can "boast of her antiquity," Hamilton argued, "of her philosophers, her artists, her statesmen, her generals; of her curiosities, her magnificent cities, her stupendous buildings, and of her once widespread commerce" (392–93). But as Hamilton also suggests, Africa served as well as a kind of Edenic myth on which to found African American history, imaged as a state of innocence in dramatic narratives of the slave trade. In an 1809 oration, for example, Henry Sipkins offers "a retrospective view of Africa in its primitive state," a land of "blissful regions . . . almost independent of the arm of husbandry," whose "innocent inhabitants . . . enjoyed with uninterrupted pleasure the state in which, by the beneficent hand of nature, they were placed." The scene changes quickly with the arrival of the slave trade and the "envenomed monster of misery" (367). In his 1814 oration, Parrott similarly presents a vision of a fertile land blessed by Providence but interrupted by the "fiend" of slavery (384–85).[34] As a site of consciousness, Africa served as the mythic origin, the point at which sacred and secular history were originally united and later separated.

With visions of Africa never far in the background, the search for the relation between sacred history and profane history was the central concern of African American historical writing of this period, with a permeable understanding of black nationalism joined to a vision of biblical destiny—and in this, again, black writers were not far different from their white contemporaries. Indeed, African Americans faced the task of working within the historical paradigms defined in part by their white contemporaries and learning to view those paradigms from within where their racial infrastructure was most visible. Many African Americans of the time would agree, for example, with the philosophical perspective so fundamental to Bancroft, who throughout the *History of the United States* rather fervently defines the methods by which the historian of human history becomes the historian of an unfolding providential design: "By comparison of document with document; by an analysis of facts, and the reference of each of them to the laws of the human mind which it illustrates; by separating the idea which inspires combined action from the forms it assumes; by comparing events with the great movement of history,—historic truth may establish itself as a science; and the principles that govern human affairs, extending like a path of light from century to century, become the highest demonstration of the superintending providence of God"[35] (3:398). For African Americans, who had limited access to the documents that themselves spoke of the white control over history, one of the fundamental laws of the human mind was that it was capable of shaping the world to its needs. Comparing the documents, determining what should be accepted as fact, and separating ideas from the forms they assumed became, accordingly, more complex procedures for African Americans than they were for Bancroft. Where Bancroft looked for an underlying unity, African Americans paid particular attention to the signs of a disrupted unity, of a revealing incoherence in the accessible past.

Certainly, there is a historical gulf between the vision of Africa as a primitive Eden and Africa as the seat of civilization, and this gulf itself provided, for many, the key to understanding how African American history could be understood within a Christian providential framework. The historians like Bancroft who constructed the mythology of the United States as a providentially favored nation argued that the "discovery" of the New World had been, in effect, providentially postponed until the world was prepared for new institutions to arise—as Bancroft and others would have it, specifically democratic, Protestant Christian institutions.[36] This preparation included the development of printing presses, the Protestant Reformation, the development of commerce, and the gradual awakening of what Bancroft referred to as the "active classes" or the rising (white) middle class. African American historians of the nineteenth century similarly looked to history for an understanding of an unfolding providential design. But for African American historians, slavery played not a minor but the central role in this providential scheme—not as an evil to be explained away but as a historical eruption that placed

African Americans at the center of the cultural landscape. As Russell Parrott (and others) argued, the "discovery of the new world" was inextricably tied to "the commencement of the sufferings of the Africans" (384). The development of any understanding of providential history, accordingly, would have to extend from a close understanding of historical relation.

Central to that understanding would be a consideration of the relation between European- and African-centered visions of history. A regular feature of African American historical thought, accordingly, was a recovery of the African past that focused particularly on the competing claims of European and African history for the foundations of civilization—often as a means of responding to general views on racial character. Easton, for example, states early in his *Treatise* that "as the intellect of a particular class will be in part the subject of this treatise, I wish in this place to follow the investigation of national difference of intellect, with its cause, by comparing the history of Europe and Africa" (8). The history Easton presents is both sacred and profane, beginning with Ham, "the founder of the African race," and following through from Egypt to Europe. "It is from the Egyptians," Easton asserts, "that many of the arts, both of elegance and ability, have been handed down in an uninterrupted chain, to modern nations of Europe. The Egyptians communicated their arts to the Greeks; the Greeks taught the Romans many improvements, both in the arts of peace and war; and to the Romans, the present inhabitants of Europe are indebted for their civility" (9). In addition to presenting this forward line of progress, Easton presents a retrospective view of racial origins. He notes, that is, the "barbarian" origins of European character, focusing on "the Goths and Vandals, and other fierce tribes," who "made no distinction between what was sacred and what was profane" (11).[37] Easton draws from an unidentified "eminent historian" for support of this view of the origins of Anglo-Saxon character, and notes the irony of the present-day historical contest in this regard: "I would here remark that it is a little singular that modern philosophers, the descendants of this race of savages, should claim for their race a superiority of intellect over those who, at that very time, were enjoying all the real benefits of civilized life" (10).[38]

Working within this framework, Easton reinterprets European history to identify the origins of slavery and prejudice. He notes, for example, that in the sixth century "European slavery was introduced" in the form of the feudal system—and he then extends this and other identified traits of "this same barbarous people" into the seventeenth century—when they "crossed the Atlantic and practiced the same crime their barbarous ancestry had done," bringing with them "the same boasted spirit of enterprise"—and into the nineteenth century, during which the "unholy war with the Indians, and the wicked crusade against the peace of Mexico, are striking illustrations of the nobleness of this race of people" (12). Easton draws from the past to reread the present, presenting "a brief review," in the form of two chronologies, "of the events following each race from their beginning" (12). The African chronology begins "before Christ 2188" with the founding of the "kingdom of Egypt," and follows various military, political, and cultural developments through the ages, concluding with the year 991, at which time, we read, "the figures in arithmetic are brought into Europe by the Saracens from Arabia" (12–13).[39] Easton follows the chronology with a one-paragraph overview of Africa's "several states of eminence" and their eventual downfall, as "Africa has been robbed of her riches and honor, and sons and daughters, to glut the rapacity of the great minds of European bigots" (14). With that as introduction, Easton proceeds with "a short chronological view of the events following the rise of the Europeans," beginning in A.D. 49 when "London is founded by the Romans," and concluding, inexplicably, with "1667, The peace of Breda, which confirms to the English the New Netherlands, now known by names of Pennsylvania, New York, and New Jersey" (14, 18). This work then prepares Easton for later commentary on the American Revolution, the Declaration of Independence, and an argument for the recognition of African American claims to U.S. citizenship.

Using in this way sacred history as the framework for understanding a seemingly inexplicable history of oppression, African American writers looked for a redemption that indicated a deeply conflicted perception of African heritage. Representative is Parrott's vision of Africa's redemption, which he saw as one of the "blessings" of the abolition of the slave trade. It is worth reading this penultimate paragraph of Parrott's 1814 oration in its entirety: "Abolition! already are thy blessings diffusing themselves; already Africa experiences its blessed effects; confidence is again restored between man and man—whole villages are no longer depopulated, to glut that insatiable monster, avarice; mild religion begins to unfold her heavenly truth, through this former land of paganism and error—and over the ruins of the altars that idolatry had reared, the sacred temple points its spire towards heaven. Civilization, with her attending handmaids, agriculture and industry, infuses cheerfulness over the face of nature, and inspires the husbandman with gratitude and joy" (390). The various blessings of civilization listed here were of course all implicated in the development and perpetuation of the slave trade, and African American writers were not always clear on how to separate civilization's blessings from its sins, or how to view Africa as a land to be redeemed without also adopting a colonialist perspective.

As Parrott's example here indicates, those who look back to antebellum African American writers as the prehistory of current debates over the validity of Afrocentrism too often simplify a complex story, for Africa was read variously, and often in the same documents, as both pure and impure, Edenic and sinful, the symbolic site of a significant fall from grace. The vision of a redeemed Africa, of Ethiopia stretching forth her hands, included not only a vision of an Edenic Africa violated by the serpent of the slave trade but also a vision of Africa's own sin in that garden—including recognition of African complicity in the slave trade and a more prominent consideration of, in Maria Stewart's phrase, a "fallen Africa" (60). David Walker, one of the sharpest critics of white America of this time, was equally sharp in his criticism of African Americans, and explained their condition in terms of sacred history. "Ignorance and treachery one against the other," Walker asserted, "a grovelling servile and abject submission to the lash of tyrants, we see plainly, my brethren, are not the natural elements of the blacks, as the Americans try to make us believe; but these are misfortunes which God has suffered our fathers to be enveloped in for many ages, no doubt in consequence of their disobedience to their Maker" (21). The condition of African Americans, including the role that they had come to play in their own oppression, was to be understood historically, so as to identify the terms by which the present was to be understood and by which appropriate action for the future was to be determined. Central to this task was the attempt to understand the violation of the moral imperatives of providential history as revealed not by the continuities in the record but by the record of disruptions, the evidence of incoherence that suggests a possible coherence still not apprehended by humankind. The history of disruptions that reveals the tensions between the profane and the sacred in the United States, antebellum historical writing suggests, is the history of African American experience—and this is the means by which community is defined, and by which historical writing confronts the imperatives of a historical vision capable of encompassing a fragmented community.

Walker's historical evidence, for example, is both sweeping and representative of the eras and issues that dominated African American history through the first half of the nineteenth century. His historical vision is built on the foundation of the African origins of civilization, but also on the progressive constructions on that foundation over time. As he has it in Article 2, "a retrospective view of the arts and sciences" begins with "the sons of Africa or of Ham, among whom learning originated, and was carried thence into Greece, where it was improved upon and refined," eventually spreading further by the Romans "over the then enlightened parts of the world." These developments from African roots have been "enlightening the dark and benighted minds of men from then, down to this day" (19). But the light was mixed with darkness, for included in Walker's historical framework are the Spaniards and the introduction of slavery, a broad history he presents in the Preamble and then returns to in Article 3, at which point he moves quickly from Bartholomew de Las Casas, often associated with the introduction of African slavery into the so-called New World, to "this day, 1829" (35–36). This quick overview of a long historical process emphasizes how deeply embedded slavery is in the United States by reenvisioning the standard historical approach, parodied by Washington Irving, of beginning any history of all or part of the United States with (or before) the story of the discovery of the continent. Included, too, is what might be considered the standard counterhistory to the story of Spanish conquest and the origins of the slave trade: the story of Haiti, "the glory of the blacks and terror of tyrants" (21). But Haiti itself offers a dual lesson—on the one hand, the story of triumph over tyranny and, on the other, an object lesson in dangers of being "dis-united, as the coloured people are now, in the United States of America" (20).[40] Walker draws his readers into this complex representation of sweeping, sometimes contradictory, and often overlapping histories so as to emphasize the need to reread the present as the site of a dangerous historical incoherence, one that requires a historically informed solidarity on the part of the black community.[41]

The attempt to develop historical literacy so that the assumptions of the present can be reinterpreted is formalized in Pennington's *Text Book*. Pennington begins by acknowledging the modest design of the book, "to state facts, points, and arguments, simply, rather than to go extensively into them"; but behind his expressed strategy of simple historical statement is a large goal: "to unembarrass the origin, and show the relative position of the colored people in the different periods among the different nations" (3). Following an opening chapter titled "The Vexed and Vexing Question"—a question he identifies as "who and whence are the colored people?" (5)—and an untitled second chapter that takes "a brief view of the descendants of Cush through the medium of history" (19), the book is organized by a series of questions, statements, assumptions, and goals: "Were the Carthaginians Ethiopians?"; "What can be said to account for the degradation of a people once so highly favored?"; "Slavery on this continent did not originate in the condition of the Africans"; "Are colored Americans, in point of intellect, inferior to white people?"; "American prejudice against color examined, its nature, its tendency and its cure"; and concluding with the deceptively casual question that in many ways underlies the others and returns to the first chapter: "Is there any difficulty in accounting for our complexion?" In addressing these questions and issues, Pennington draws from the Bible, various scholars, and other historians.

Indeed, Pennington's broad scholarly range in the *Text Book* somewhat qualifies in practice his stated goal of relying on simple statements, for the various sources he draws from speak with and against each other, and at varying levels of authority. Included are broad histories—notably, the argument for a relation between Egypt and Ethiopia, and an overview of the Spanish colonies and the introduction of the slave trade—along with anecdotal accounts, a great deal of biblical interpretation, and reference to specific historians and scholars. The book is distinguished by its respect for the office of the historian, as Pennington notes that "no reverential mind would enter upon a historical research to gratify the curious," and also by its acknowledgment of the special problems African Americans face. Addressing "the vexed and vexing question" of the identity of "the colored people," Pennington notes that "every close observer must have seen that we suffer much from the want of a collocation of historical facts as to present a just view of our origin" (5). While Pennington attempts to provide here just such a "collocation," his methods reveal the extent to which his main task is to bring order to scattered documents, drawing from some sources that speak directly and from other sources that reveal beyond their intentions. As one reviewer put it, commenting on a lecture by Pennington drawn from his then-still-forthcoming book, "The lecture clearly showed that the author had investigated thoroughly and ransacked history attentively" ("A Text Book," January 9, 1841). Pennington's *Text Book*, then, is an exercise in bringing order to the fragmented evidence of history, even as his nonnarrative approach emphasizes the fragmentation and his chapter titles reveal the prejudices and ignorance that are the result of that fragmentation. "I have met with not a few colored persons," he notes early in the book, "who held historical views as prejudicial to the truth in our case as the whites do" (7). Such attitudes indicate not only the intended audience for the *Text Book* but also the terms on which it must operate.

The overarching argument under which this organizing task takes place has to do with the nature of historical evidence itself. As Pennington states at the beginning of chapter 2, "Profane, or human history must be valued mainly, in proportion as it has the coincidence of sacred history. In the first period of profane history we have only mist and uncertainty. The facts which we find sufficiently attested to rest our judgment on, are few and far between. Of the ages before the deluge, we know nothing but what the Bible teaches. And as for the first sixteen hundred years after the deluge, there were no regular governments, there were consequently no authentic records" (19). Raised here are two obvious issues that inform Pennington's methods throughout: that profane and sacred history must correspond and that the records of profane history are incomplete. Sacred history, accordingly, provides the framework for reading profane history. That is, one mode of historical evidence becomes the interpretive framework for evaluating the other, and all evidence is read for its ability to address the condition of oppression that marks the occasion for and responsibility of historical research.

Pennington establishes this framework by considering first "the annals of the four universal empires"—the "second Babylonish empire," the "Medo Persian," "the Macedonian," and "the Roman"—which he identifies as "the four great hinges on which the chart of authentic history hangs" (19–20). The histories of these empires have been authenticated, Pennington argues, though the language by which he explains this indicates the tenuousness of historical authenticity: "The developments in the annals of those four empires are, in the main, authentic, because, in general, they have the coincidence of the Sacred Scriptures. These are the four grand theatres on which Divine Providence has controlled a wonderful series of events for his own glory. The sovereigns and subjects of those empires have been seen, as so many agents, acting over scenes of importance from their connection with the redemption system. The sacred writers have been directed to give minutes of those scenes, in a general way, and hence the manifest importance of this coincidence" (20–21). And as did the sacred writers, so Pennington attempts to give the "minutes" of the history that extends in time from these "four grand theatres"—again, "in a general way." The history of the present theater is provisional; the historian's duty is to preserve that provisionality while also drawing from human history to determine the process by which sacred history can be observed from the realm of the profane.

"A Nation within a Nation":
The Black Center of White Nationalist History

To reenvision Africa was to reframe the narrative of Providence, and thus the narrative of American destiny—in effect, establishing African Americans as the agents of providential history, the citizens of a nation imagined but not yet realized. Most African American historians of this period, that is, reframed the narrative of progress to recenter the developing white American narrative of providential history—often using the same tropes for different purposes.[42] In his 1859 essay "The Education of the Colored People," the Reverend Amos Gerry Beman of New Haven asserts that "the colored race is an element of power in the earth, 'like a city set upon a hill it cannot be hid.' Thanks to our friends—and to our foes—and to the providence of God" (337). Beman does not present an alternate vision of national destiny; rather, he presents a vision of what amounts to what Martin R. Delany called in 1852 "a nation within a nation" (*Condition* 209). In fact, Beman suggests that the role of the "colored race" is not only to "contribute their full share to the world's renovation and progress" but also to make visible the moral transgressions and failures of those who resist or restrict this progress (338). As he put it in a March 6, 1841, article for the *Colored American*, "Who ought to speak in trumpet tones to the American nation—to the world? Who ought to thunder in all that is solemn and sublime—all that is powerful in arguments based upon the Rock of Truth—the rights of human nature—in all that is persuasive in eloquence for themselves, and their 'brethren in bonds, as bound with them,' if not colored men?" ("Thoughts, No. IX").

In short, history was not simply documentation but an act of resistance to the systemic apparatus of a developing white supremacist ideology, an attempt to contain that ideology within a different historical vision. The white nationalist narration of an unremembered past in the service of a developing imagined community constituted, for African Americans, a newly formulated estrangement from the terms of a possible collective identity. To imagine a nation within a nation required the use of print culture to counter the false ideal of historical continuity that supported the white national imagination, for the imagined continuity was itself a disruption of a history marked only by pathological discontinuities. As Gilroy has argued, African Americans of both the nineteenth and the twentieth centuries, whatever their differences in other regards, have "shared a sense that the modern world was fragmented along axes constituted by racial conflict and could accommodate nonsynchronous, heterocultural modes of social life in close proximity" (197). Accordingly, "their conceptions of modernity were periodised differently. They were founded on the catastrophic rupture of the middle passage rather than the dream of revolutionary transformation. They were punctuated by the processes of acculturation and terror that followed that catastrophe and by the countercultural aspirations towards freedom, citizenship, and autonomy that developed after it among slaves and their descendants" (197).

This is not to say, of course, that African Americans simply rejected the white nationalist story, for the underlying principles of that story—as expressed, for example, in the Declaration of Independence or in any number of July Fourth celebratory speeches—were principles that the overwhelming majority of African American historical writers honored as the appropriate foundations for a national community. Accordingly, African American historians worked to correct and add to the developing official story of white nationalist history—making of much of their work a collective jeremiad calculated to overrule the white nationalist discourse that Sacvan Bercovitch has termed "the American Jeremiad."[43] In the pages of the early historical texts, one encounters frequently both the history and prehistory of African American contributions to American military and political history—in the form of celebrations of Crispus Attucks; in revisions to the story of the American Revolution and the War of 1812; and generally in readings of the Declaration of Independence, petitions to the federal and state governments, and tales of the American Revolution.[44] Such revisions to the developing white historical record emphasize the extent to which black history was always locked in a contingent relation to white nationalist history, a historical presence embodied in the white readers and writers of African American history.

But African American writers looked for something more than a revised historical record. The glaring discrepancy between the July Fourth orations of white Americans and the realities of life for black Americans were themselves viewed as evidence of the historical mission and destiny of African Americans. The black abolitionist William J. Watkins, responding to Bancroft's 1854 oration "The Necessity, the Reality, and the Promise of the Progress of the Human Race," argued that "our theory is well enough; but our practice is as far removed from it as the east is from the west (Ripley 4:257)." Noting Bancroft's assertion that *our country is bound to allure the world to Liberty by the beauty of its example*," Watkins wondered, "Where has Mr. Bancroft been living that with all his wisdom and erudition he has not found out that the great object of this Government, *as developed in its policy*, is the extension, the consolidation, and the perpetuity of a system of robbery, of plunder, and oppression, aptly characterized the vilest that ever saw the sun" (Ripley 4:256, 257). Emphasizing both the failures and the false consciousness of the dominant culture, African American writers seized the ideals to which Bancroft claimed devotion, but drew from those ideals a fundamentally different view of history. In his expansive view of history, Bancroft outlined the process by which the original reasons for colonization eventually gave way to others, as humankind discovered, by a seemingly natural process, their providential mission, until "at last, the higher design was matured, not to plunder, nor to destroy, nor to enslave; but to found states, to plant permanent Christian colonies, to establish for the oppressed and the enterprising places of refuge and abode, with all the elements of independent national existence" (*History of the United States* 1:118). But this logic was clearly undermined by the failures of principle that marked the resulting nation, and in this way white visions of American history identified the grounds of a peculiarly American version of black nationalism.

Following a line of progress similar to that which Bancroft employed, though with greater emphasis on the horrors committed by the Spanish colonists and the historical effects of these acts, most African American historians claimed the nation's professed ideals, and even its history, as their own. It was, after all, not only their determination to expose the hypocrisy of the dominant culture that led African Americans to quote from and allude to the Declaration of Independence so often in their writing. While some white Americans argued that "the celebration of the *Fourth of July* belongs *exclusively* to the white population of the United States" ("Slaves Have Nothing to Do" 115), black Americans could counter that this very view makes it clear that they in fact have everything to do with the nation's national mythology. In his famous oration "What, to the Slave, Is the Fourth of July?" Frederick Douglass presents a history of the struggle for national liberty to show the extent to which that struggle had been corrupted by slavery. But Douglass is interested in something more than the exposure of "national inconsistencies" in asserting to his white listeners that "the existence of slavery in this country brands your republicanism as a sham, your humanity as a base pretense, and your Christianity as a lie" (265). Indeed, he appeals to his "fellow-citizens" to recognize that they have misapplied their own ideals and misread their own founding documents, arguing that "interpreted, as it *ought* to be interpreted, the Constitution is a glorious liberty document" (266).[45] Hosea Easton, too, examining the debates that preceded the Declaration of Independence and the document itself, asks whether it can be said "from any fair construction of the foregoing extracts, that the colored people are not recognized as citizens" (29). More direct in his vision of the operations of Providence is Peter Williams, who in his 1808 *Oration on the Abolition of the Slave Trade* links the antislavery struggle directly to the American Revolution:

> Oh, God! we thank thee, that thou didst condescend to listen to the cries of Africa's wretched sons; and that thou didst interfere in their behalf. At thy call humanity sprang forth, and espoused the cause of the oppressed: one hand she employed in drawing from their vitals the deadly arrows of injustice; and the other in holding a shield to defend them from fresh assaults: and at that illustrious moment, when the sons of '76 pronounced these United States free and independent; when the spirit of patriotism, erected a temple sacred to liberty; when the inspired voice of Americans first uttered those noble sentiments, "we hold these truths to be self-evident, that all men are created equal; that they are endowed by their Creator with certain unalienable rights; among which are life, liberty, and the pursuit of happiness;" and when the bleeding African, lifting his fetters, exclaimed, "am I not a man and a brother;" then with redoubled efforts, the angel of humanity strove to restore to the African race the inherent rights of man. (350)

With perfect Bancroftian logic, African American historians looked to the past and saw that the preceding generations of white people created more than they understood, that they were only partially self-conscious agents in a grand drama of Providence, and that it remained for the historian to gather events together to interpret them in a true light.

In their response to the Declaration of Independence, African American writers exemplify a major aspect of nineteenth-century African American historiography—the reinterpretation of existing documents to revise and re-center national mythology, using fault lines in the dominant culture's ideological landscape to identify a rising historical narrative in which African Americans could claim a central role. There's a growing body of scholarship that examines the relation between white ideology and black literary production—for example, Russ Castronovo's work on the discourse of citizenship in the nineteenth century, Dwight A. McBride's consideration of what it meant to "tell the truth" about slavery in a world in which the discourse of "truth" was itself implicated in the system of slavery, or Robert E. Washington's argument that, in the twentieth century, "the liberal-left white intelligentsia both fostered and culturally subjugated the dominant black literary schools" (330). Much of this scholarship, both in what it illuminates and in what it quietly overlooks, raises questions about how to understand African American applications or appropriations of the conventions and tropes of the white nationalist discourse of citizenship and liberty. Castronovo, for example, warns of "a political longing . . . to acquire a subjectivity freed from the necessity of grappling with factors that impinge on an 'essential' self," for "freedom is then truly free of all context." "Employed by persons with radically different positions in the social hierarchy such as slave and slaveholder," Castronovo argues, "this nationalized vocabulary traps experiences of freedom and unfreedom in a vague lexicon that expunges signs of systemic injustice, social trauma, private anguish, or any other remainders that refuse to fit a general definition" (*Necro Citizenship* 50). But as I have tried to indicate—and this is, indeed, one of my central points throughout this book—African American writers recognized the impossibility of conceiving of or writing about a liberty free of social context and contingency. As Celeste Michelle Condit and John Louis Lucaites have argued, African American writers recognized the need "to effect a shift in the national public vocabulary that would join the commitment to Equality to the prevailing constitutive values of Liberty and Property," an effort that involved the formation of an "African-American nationality" and a related discourse of rights that "introduced a range of broad and more concrete public usages for the heretofore abstract and minimalist notion of Equality" (69).[46]

Castronovo finds the Frederick Douglass of *My Bondage and My Freedom* to be the great exception to African American writers who fell into the trap of this "vague lexicon" of abstract liberty and citizenship, but I would apply to the great majority of African American writers Castronovo's point about Douglass's discursive and political sophistication—namely, that "in contrast to the range of 'American scholars' including abolitionists, slave narrators, and proslavery pastoralists who propose definitions [of freedom] independent of precedent and culture, Douglass asks us to make sense of political rights by context" (*Necro Citizenship* 61). "To become fluent in freedom," Castronovo argues, "requires archaeological practices—a sort of material etymology of culture—that link present use to past abuse, that reconnect a grammar of citizenship to the difficult semantics of social death" (61). In their attempt to write *as* African Americans *about* African American history, the writers whose texts are the subjects of this chapter and this book worked toward just that kind of fluency in freedom; and in reprinting and recontextualizing the documents and discourse of the developing white nationalist mythology, these writers continually and persistently called upon their readers to attend to context, contingency, and provisionality in the historical understanding they might bring to any conception of the African American community and of the struggle for liberation.[47] As Castronovo argued in an earlier study, for African Americans "subscription to national narrative produced a hybrid narrative in which black rebels resemble white patriots even as they differ from them," a national narrative of "passing" that "exploited and confounded the liberatory identity of the white, enfranchised citizen," "an intervention in the cultural authority of language" (*Fathering* 194).

Particularly representative of this method is the use of two proclamations issued in 1814 by then General Andrew Jackson. The first is a proclamation to "the Free Colored Inhabitants of Louisiana" calling for "every noble-hearted free man of color" to "rally around the standard of the Eagle" by joining "the present contest with Great Britain" (Nell, *Colored Patriots* 286–87); the second is a proclamation that William C. Nell called "one of the highest compliments ever paid by a military chief to his soldiers," in which General Jackson tells the African American troops that they have exceeded his already great expectations. These documents—quoted frequently by Frederick Douglass in various speeches and articles, and quoted in significant historical works by, for example, Hosea Easton in 1837, Robert Benjamin Lewis in 1844, William C. Nell in 1851 and 1855, Martin R. Delany in 1852, William J. Watkins in 1853, William Wells Brown in 1853, 1867, and 1873, and George Washington Williams in 1883—were a staple of African American historical writing. They were important for two reasons. The first and most obvious is that they documented African American service in the defense of United States; the second, and the most significant for most of these writers, is that Jackson addresses the "free" men of color as "fellow citizens," referring to the United States as "*our* country," "*your country*," and "*your native country*" (Nell, 286–88). African American writers seized on this language as authoritative evidence that they should be included in any understanding of national identity and that they should not have to argue for their right to claim citizenship—but this was not simply an abstract or simple application of the evidence of citizenship. That is, it was not incidental to this persistent reprinting of these documents that Jackson could hardly be viewed as a friend to the African American cause. This is the public figure, after all, who stated that publications aimed at the enslaved were "calculated to stimulate them to insurrection, and produce all the horrors of a servile war," and who pronounced the abolitionists' position to be "repugnant to the principles of our national compact, and to the dictates of humanity and religion" (qtd. in Jay, "Leaders of the American Anti-Slavery Society," 121).[48] President Jackson's opposition to the antislavery cause, along with his role as the war-hero representative of white dominance, highlights both the significance and the difficult application of his early proclamations, and his contradictory symbolic roles indicate the fissures in the white nationalist foundation.

This reframing of the documents of white national identity constitutes the central historical work of David Walker's *Appeal* as well. At the end of the *Appeal*, Walker summarizes his historical argument, asking "the candid and unprejudiced of the whole world, to search the pages of historians diligently, and see if the Antideluvians—the Sodomites—the Egyptians—the Babylonians—the Ninevites—the Carthagenians—the Persians—the Macedonians—the Greeks—the Romans—the Mahometans—the Jews—or devils, ever treated a set of human beings, as the white Christians of America do us, the blacks, or Africans." And having brought home his point, Walker then asks for "the attention of the world of mankind to the declaration of these very American people, of the United States." He quotes from the Declaration of Independence and asks Americans, "Do you understand your own language?" (74–75). Comparing this language to the testimony of "cruelties and murders inflicted by your cruel and unmerciful fathers and yourselves on our fathers and on us," Walker essentially compares two historically informed languages: that of the Declaration of Independence and the language of deeds and events in U.S. history. In this way, the historical work of the *Appeal* is to construct a historical framework by which language can be read and evaluated.[49]

Throughout the *Appeal*, Walker reads various documents, including the Bible, the Declaration of Independence, articles in the *Columbian Centinel*, a sermon in South Carolina, and writings by Thomas Jefferson, procolonizationist Henry Clay, and Elias B. Caldwell. Walker reads these texts against a broad cultural omission, noting that white Americans "have newspapers and monthly periodicals, which they receive in continual succession, but on the pages of which, you will scarcely ever find a paragraph respecting slavery" (39). In addition to the Declaration of Independence, Walker reads Jefferson's *Notes on the State of Virginia*, presenting quotations from that work, pausing for commentary, and then presenting additional quotations. At one point he notes to his black readers, "I hope you will try to find out the meaning of this verse—its widest sense and all its bearings: whether you do or not, remember the whites do" (27). And as if to document this interpretive battle, Walker later quotes from speeches by Henry Clay and Elias B. Caldwell at a meeting on colonization, which texts Walker draws from the *National Intelligencer* of December 24, 1816. Again, Walker presents quotations interspersed with commentary. For example, following Clay's reference to Christianity, Walker inserts in brackets, "Here I ask Mr. Clay, what kind of Christianity? Did he mean such as they have among the Americans—distinction, whip, blood and oppression?" (46). At one point, Walker presents a partial quotation, followed by the symbols "&c. *******," noting for his readers, "you know what this means" (46). Walker here teaches his readers a kind of historical literacy, by which statements may be reinterpreted and reapplied. Similarly, Walker reads Caldwell's speech, drawing attention to the possibilities for misreadings: "The last clause of this speech, which was written in a very artful manner, and which will be taken for the speech of a friend, without close examination and deep penetration, I shall now present" (52).

All of the *Appeal* is designed to penetrate such texts and to provide readers with similar interpretive skills—and this is the book's primary historical work. If history is open to interpretation, Walker suggests, history also provides interpretive openings, ways of reading the texts produced in history and the larger text *of* history. Well might Walker insist on the importance of grammar while breaking its rules, for he is viewing a history that has produced an "artful manner" of oppression. He distrusts the art, but knows that he will need to master it if he is to resist it. Throughout the *Appeal*, Walker insists on the importance of education, and draws attention particularly to the withholding of knowledge as the central pillar that supports the system of slavery. He brings a scattered style to the scattered documents that reveal the means by which a disunited and scattered people have been created by history. The purpose of history here is less constructive than deconstructive—that is, it is less Walker's purpose to tell the story of history than to undermine, to untell, the story that has been told. With limited access to documents that in any event would speak against his cause, shaped as they were by the very historical narrative he is trying to resist, Walker draws from a broad and loosely narrated history in an effort to make representative documents speak against themselves.

African American writers, in short, used the failings of the nation's dominant representatives to identify an unfulfilled promise and unfinished revolution.[50] But for African American historians the outlines of a barely discernable providential destiny indicated the great work that remained, work that would begin by recognizing the significance of the history of those with ties to both Africa and the Americas. African American writers, that is, joined their participation in the American Revolution and the development of the favored nation to their African heritage. Embodiments of the true but unfinished American revolution, African Americans were also to become the agents of a biblically grounded mission. As the "western world is destined to be filled with a mixed race," so too, argues Garnet, "this republic, and this continent, are to be the theatre in which the grand drama of our triumphant Destiny is to be enacted" (*Past and Present Condition* 25). Seizing on the contingencies of racial ideology and nationalist history, and emphasizing the creation of an essentially new people in the United States (a people born of the ideological contradictions that undermined the dominant culture's narrative of national destiny) African American historians reframed the terms and implications of national destiny, seeking to relocate, in effect, what Sacvan Bercovitch has termed "the genetics of salvation."[51]

African American destiny, in this body of writing, emerges from the fissures in the (white) national narrative as a sacred presence revealed by secular violations. Garnet, for example, asserts in *The Past and the Present Condition* that "every rood of land in this Union is the grave of a murdered man, and their epitaphs are written upon the monuments of the nation's wealth," epitaphs that speak of a coming judgment, as "deep unearthly voices . . . cry 'We come, we come! for vengeance we come! Tremble, guilty nation, for the God of Justice lives and reigns'" (21). Those familiar with African American writing will pick up here an echo in Garnet's use of the word "tremble," for nearly as important as the Declaration of Independence in African American writing was another declaration by the author of that document. In his *Notes on the State of Virginia*, Jefferson worries about the effects of slavery and writes, "Can the liberties of a nation be thought secure when we have removed their only firm basis, a conviction in the minds of the people that these liberties are of the gift of God? That they are not to be violated but with his wrath? Indeed I tremble for my country when I reflect that God is just: that His justice cannot sleep for ever: that considering numbers, nature and natural means only, a revolution of the wheel of fortune, an exchange of situation, is among possible events: that it may become probable by supernatural interference!" (163).[52] African American historians agreed, and drew conclusions from the historical vision behind Jefferson's fears. In 1815, William Hamilton, noting the opposition to a congressional motion to abolish the slave trade, assumed his audience's familiarity with Jefferson's declaration: "Why they opposed, we know not: except their guilty souls, fearful that it would bring on Mr. Jefferson's doomsday, that made him tremble for the fate of his country, when he reflected that God was just" ("Oration, on the Abolition" 399). William J. Watkins followed the argument still further in his 1853 address *Our Rights as Men*, arguing before a legislative committee on the militia that "if colored men helped achieved [*sic*] *your* liberty as well as mine, if *your* fathers and my fathers found one common revolutionary grave, we ask you in the name of crushed and bleeding humanity, why should you . . . be elevated to heaven, and we be cast down to Hell? No wonder Jefferson 'trembled for his country, when he reflected that God is just, and his justice sleeps not forever.'" And, for Watkins, a significant question followed from this line of reasoning: "Why should *you* be a chosen people more than *we*?" (11).[53]

Why indeed? At the end of his *Dialogue between a Virginian and an African Minister*, Coker quotes the following from 1 Peter 2:9–10, to "show what God is doing for Ethiopia's sons in the United States of America": "But ye are a chosen generation, a royal priesthood, and an holy nation, a peculiar people; that ye should shew forth the praise of him who hath called you out of darkness into his marvelous light: which in time past were not a people, but are now a people of God: which had not obtained mercy, but now have obtained mercy" (39–40). The task of creating a community finds its realization in a reconfiguration of the national mythology and a new vision of a chosen people joining the secular and the sacred in civil practice. Jefferson perceived—in his writings, indeed, embodied—a fissure in the national foundation; African American writers noted that they were both the symbolic sites and the products of that fissure, and found in that position the grounds for a reinterpretation of Providence, a reinterpretation that joined the ideals associated with the American Revolution to African destiny, political ideals with biblical prophecy—the prophecy represented by one of the most frequently repeated phrases in African American writing of the nineteenth century: "Princes shall come out of Egypt; Ethiopia shall soon stretch out her hands unto God" (Psalm 68:31).[54]

Haiti played a significant role in this vision of destiny—sometimes representing the promise of those of African heritage in the United States, and sometimes serving as both the ideological and the symbolic site for a rising black nation.[55] Underlying the whole of Holly's *Vindication*, for example, is a vision of Providence and destiny by which all things can be explained. As Holly states directly at the beginning of the *Vindication*, where he identifies "the revolutionary history of Hayti" as "the basis of this argument," "in this terrible struggle for liberty, the Lord of Hosts directed their arms to be the instruments of His judgment on their oppressors, as the recompense of His violated law of love between man and his fellow, which these tyrants of the new world had been guilty of, in the centuries of blood, wrong, and oppression, which they had perpetrated on the negro race in that isle of the Caribbean Sea" (24). Operating within this framework, Toussaint L'Ouverture, who possessed the qualities of leadership "in a super excellent degree," becomes "another Washington," "the regenerator and savior of his country," a role he played in many African American histories of Haiti (44). Within this framework, too, one can understand Jean-Jacques Dessalines, Toussaint's successor—not only his attempt to massacre all white inhabitants but also his failure to do so by "providential interposition" which "saved the race from a stigma on the pages of history, as foul as that which darkens the moral character of their antagonists" (53). And in this framework, finally, one can see the revolution as a lesson in destiny, a point on which Holly touches throughout, and to which he turns with great emphasis in his concluding paragraphs. Following the vision of the westward movement of empire expressed in verse by Bishop Berkeley and further promoted by Bancroft,[56] Holly argues that "Civilization and Christianity is passing from the East to the West" (65) and that this process will continue until the course returns to the east by way of its global westward course. Within this broad movement, slavery finds its purpose as the Haitian Revolution, Holly argues, is recognized as both a manifestation of Providence and an example of moral duty. "God, therefore in permitting the accursed slave traffic to transplant so many millions of the race, to the New World," Holly argues, "and educing therefrom such a negro nationality as Hayti, indicates thereby, that we have a work now to do here in the Western World, which in his own good time shall shed its orient beams upon the Fatherland of the race" (65). "The responsibility of leading off in this gigantic enterprise," Holly concludes, "Providence seems to have made our peculiar task by the eligibility of our situation in this country, as a point for gaining an easy access to that island" (66).

 This interpretation of the Haitian Revolution became a frequent theme in African American history, and Holly's handling of it is neither original nor otherwise unusual. The *Vindication*, though, is a remarkable document in its elegant insistence and in its brash reconfigurations of its own evidentiary conventions. Appealing to the "undoubted facts of history," Holly also shows how the facts of history are shaped, and can be reshaped, by the perspective of the historian. The question of evidence is particularly important when Holly has a difficult story to tell, as when he must write of Dessalines—for Dessalines might well play into existing stereotypes of the savagery in black identity; in any event, Dessalines certainly complicates Holly's declared thesis that the Haitian Revolution "is one of the noblest, grandest, and most justifiable outbursts against tyrannical oppression that is recorded on the pages of the world's history" (23). But Holly holds to that thesis quite well. I have noted his "providential interposition" argument in this regard, but I would suggest also that Holly actually takes this opportunity to problematize the notion of historical evidence. For example, when he notes that Dessalines "had previously massacred 500 whites," he immediately notes in parentheses, "if any of these treacherous colonists can be called innocent" (52). This is, in fact, a persuasive qualification; but more significant is Holly's sly acknowledgment that Dessalines does not, in fact, fit neatly into his thesis—and thereby fulfills the thesis in another way. First, Holly notes, "we find in this determination of the bloodthirsty man, how well he had learned the lesson of treachery and perfidy from the example of the white man" (53). Dessalines was no worse than the whites, in other words. But more than that, Dessalines was just as bad—and this itself is, for Holly, ironically revealing: "If shocking depravity in perfidiousness and covenant breaking, is needed as another evidence of the negro's equality with the white man, in order to prove his ability to govern himself, then the implacable black chief, Dessalines, furnishes us with that proof" (53). Monstrous himself, Dessalines serves as commentary on the monstrousness of those who argue against the "capacity of the negro race for self-government."

Like Holly's *Vindication*, Harris's *A Summer* is a text designed to promote emigration. There are many similarities in the historical vision of the two works—for example, as Holly speaks of Toussaint as "another Washington," so Harris, noting Napoleon's final victory by deception, presents Toussaint as "the *Washington*, but not '*the Napoleon*,' of Hayti" (141). And as Holly argues that God has allowed the slave trade as part of a larger providential plan, so Harris presents the same vision by ventriloquism—that is, as I noted earlier, by presenting the views of "a retired merchant of Philadelphia, a man of large thought and liberal views" (176). The merchant is quoted presenting a longish discourse on manifest destiny, "a familiar and accepted phrase in the mouths of our politicians" (177). The merchant notes that "pro-slavery adventurers" have their own plans for carrying out this destiny; he then follows a historical pattern by which, he claims with good American historical logic, the persecution of the Puritans in England "really produced New England," and that "the obstinacy of George the Third was as much a cause of the

Declaration of Independence . . . as the perseverance of John Adams" (177). Following this pattern, the merchant reasons, "why should we not begin to look at this, the third great question of the same class, still *un*settled, from the same point of view?" (178). Harris, in turn, suggests that the United States adopt a different policy toward its southern neighbors by understanding that oppression has made Haiti a site of freedom, in part to "forever wipe out the stain which [William] Walker has cast upon the very name of all who boast themselves citizens of this republic," in part to "in some degree recompense the colored race for the services they have rendered to the government," and in part to "lay the foundation of a future empire" (171).[57]

It must be said, however, that if there was wide agreement on the general vision of the destiny of those of African heritage, still the anticipated historical manifestation of that destiny, and the appropriate action that would follow from that vision, was a subject of some debate. Emigration to Haiti was advocated by some but just as vigorously opposed by others. Considerable resistance to the American Colonization Society had been a significant organizing principle of African American political activism, but prominent African Americans—including Cuffe, Jamaican-born John Russwurm, Coker, among many others—had involved themselves in the colonization movement, and other colonization plans were advocated or embraced by such men as Delany and Garnet, though they insisted that their plans were separate from any white-sponsored movements. Preparations for a grand emigration to Canada had inspired the formation of the first national convention of black Americans, but Canadian communities remained in the shadow of U.S. efforts, and revealed that the struggle for survival and against racism would not stop once African Americans crossed the U.S.-Canadian border. While all of these plans for a reorganization of the African American community called upon the past for ideological support, the challenge of representing African American history remained unfulfilled by any clear narrative path. African American destiny was both a story to be told and a story that seemed diminished by the telling.

All of African American historical writing before the Civil War extended from and necessarily returned to the immovable fact of an unrepresentable experience that defined the historical moment in which African American collective identity might be imagined. Involving the cultural politics of textual (mis)representations, the unstable dynamics of racial identity, and strategic manipulations of Africa as a site of collective consciousness, African American destiny was not simply a story to tell but also a way of telling that story. I return, in short, to William Wells Brown's assertion that "Slavery has never been represented; Slavery never can be represented." The problem was that no mere history seemed adequate to account for the multifarious horrors of slavery, and any history written would only emphasize the many unknown lives and unrecorded violations of humanity that the culture of slavery largely omitted from the historical record. As Nathaniel Paul noted, "Its more than detestable picture has been attempted to be portrayed by the learned, and the wise, but all have fallen short, and acknowledged their inadequacy to the task, and have been compelled to submit, by merely giving an imperfect shadow of its reality" (8). Hosea Easton similarly remarks throughout his *Treatise* that "no language capable of being employed by mortal tongue, is sufficiently descriptive to set forth in its true character the effect of that cursed thing, slavery" (23). "Language is lame," Easton exclaims at one point, "in its most successful attempt, to describe [slavery's] enormity; and with all the excite-ment which this country has undergone, in consequence of the discussion of the subject, yet the story is not half told, neither can it be" (26). "I have no language to express what I see, and hear, and feel, on this subject," Easton exclaims at one point; "were I capable of dipping my pen in the deepest dye of crime, and of understanding the science of the bottomless pit, I should then fail in presenting to the intelligence of mortals on earth, the true nature of American deception" (33). Nor does he have the historical documentation he needs, for he notes that "we should without doubt, had not the Europeans destroyed every vestige of history, which fell in their barbarous march, been [sic] favored with an extensive and minute history of the now unknown parts of Africa" (18). Instead, Easton uses the tools of historical narration to speak against themselves. In a wonderful slip noted in a rather long list of "Errata" at the end of the book, Easton notes that, on one page, "instead of 'the superiority'" readers should read "the *pretended* superiority"; and that, on another page, "instead of 'surprising'" we should read "unsurprising" (56). The first refers, of course, to Anglo-Saxon claims of superiority; the second refers to African American self-help. Together, these words capture Easton's primary task, to invert the assumptions we bring to the black and white "races" in the United States by revising the historical background of those assumptions.

History, as Easton suggests, was as much about the cultural desire for historical understanding as it was about the past. I have noted Harris's obser-vation that "the history of San Domingo was never completely written, and if it were, would never find a reader" (85). For Harris, as for all of the historians I have discussed in this chapter, the task was to both tell and not tell the story: to record a history that has never been "completely written," that in many ways could never be *completely* written, and that "would never find a reader." Writing both from and beyond the documents available to them, writing to readers whose modes of understanding have been shaped by the history they need to revise, the early historians struggled both with and against the need to tell the story of the past. The fragmented community, including so many lives unknown and unknowable, that was at the center of the African American historical experience could easily be lost in the methodologies of history; the limited and biased documents could easily speak against the history one tried to construct; any narrative—seductive in its coherence and clarity—might overwhelm the complex stories that remained untold; and the lack of a histor- ical story contributed to the continuing disunity of the African American community. These writers, drawing from history to respond to racism and promote community, devoted themselves to a broad historical vision—one capable of explaining the past, of giving shape to the present, and of defining destiny for the future. But they indicated their awareness that the methods of history cannot be trusted; and that this story can be undermined if it is told too simply. These concerns become particularly visible in the work of the major historians of the period, Robert Benjamin Lewis, Martin R. Delany, and William C. Nell.

chapter two

Scattered Lives, Scattered Documents
Writing Liberation History

illiam C. Nell begins his "Author's Preface" to *The Colored Patriots of the American Revolution* (1855) by quoting from John G. Whittier's "statement of facts relative to the Military Services of Colored Americans in the Revolution of 1776, and the War of 1812" (9). The part of the statement, originally published in the *National Era* in 1847, that Nell quotes is Whittier's overview of the field, in which Whittier notes that "of the services and sufferings of the Colored Soldiers of the Revolution, no attempt has, to our knowledge, been made to preserve a record. They have no historian" (9). Acknowledging his reliance on and gratitude to Whittier and others "who have kindly contributed facts for this work," Nell presents himself as the historian whose task it is to "rescue from oblivion the name and fame of those who, though 'tinged with the hated stain,' yet had warm hearts and active hands in the 'times that tried men's souls'" (9). Nell's task was to gather together the fragments of African American experience in danger of being lost to or ignored by history—which he did by exploring documents and histories, and by way of "journeys . . . made to confer with the living, and even pilgrimages to grave-yards, to save all that may still be gleaned from their fast disappearing records" (9). In his first edition of this work, a twenty-four-page pamphlet published in 1851, Nell had written that he had taken such research journeys to the living and the dead "to glean the shreds and patches for a presentation" (4); in the 396-page book published in 1855, he clearly hoped for something more than a patchwork presentation, though not what we would recognize as narrative history. But his primary concern was to collect and preserve the historical record, inserting the record into historical consciousness while attempting to influence cultural memory.

Significantly, African American historians were not alone in this task. During the first half of the nineteenth century, white America looked actively not only to construct a distinctively American literature but also to collect the documents for an American history. Some of the leading white statesmen worried that such a history would never be written. As John Adams asked both Thomas Jefferson and Thomas McKean, "Who shall write the history of the American Revolution? Who can write it? Who will be able to write it? The most essential documents, the debates and deliberations in Congress, from 1774 to 1783, were all in secret, and are now lost forever" (Cappon 451). According to Michael Kraus, "thirty-five historical societies were founded between 1830 and 1850," though "few of them functioned actively" (176). Perhaps the most notable official effort to collect the materials of the past was that supported by the national government, Peter Force's *American Archives*, published in nine volumes between 1837 and 1853. In an 1838 review of this collection in progress, George Bancroft asserted that "the American Revolution is rightly esteemed one of the greatest events in the history of man; the dawn of a new era. On us, who inherit the benefits of that popular freedom which it generated, devolves the duty of gathering together everything which can illustrate it" (Review of *Documentary History* 484–85). The value of the *American Archives*, in Bancroft's estimation, was that it extended beyond records of public bodies, and that "Mr. Force has gone out into the streets and villages; he has looked for meetings of merchants, for meetings of mechanics; for meetings of planters; has gathered letters from every direction; has entered the halls of petty committees, and has endeavoured to sweep the land for every document of a public nature, that tended to prepare the revolution" (485).

The collection of these documents into a manageable source, Bancroft argued, promised to advance historical knowledge—a process Bancroft, in a characteristic fit of inspiration, believed should be extended still further. Noting his belief that "our independence was the fruit of centuries," and that "the whole previous civilization of the world was the condition, under which the glorious event was possible," Bancroft called for a kind of transcendental documentation of providential history:

> Let us gather up every fragment of its history; let us allow nothing to be lost. Beautiful was the dawn of freedom upon our hills, when the nations of the earth sung for joy at the promise of a new civilization. Let us not allow the light of that morning, as it made the sky brilliant with gladness, to perish from the memory of man. Let us fix indelibly on enduring monuments a fit representation of even the most evanescent hues. Let us count every sunbeam that quickened, every drop of dew that refreshed the immortal tree, which our fathers planted. Let us encourage our own hearts, and cheer our children, by the bright examples of every one among the crowd of messengers, who announced to mankind the glad tidings of the separation of our country from the forms, the superstitions, and the compacts of the Past. (Review of *Documentary History* 487)

As this conclusion to the review makes clear, one's vision of history could very much influence the historical evidence one was likely to collect. And, dew drops and sunbeams aside, the evidence would be shaped by those who had access to and control over the process of cultural documentation—that is, those who had economic, political, legal, religious, and civil power. As Nell and others understood too well, much would be missed by this scrutinizing documentation of the glorious event of the American Revolution.

Certainly, this transformation of the historical evidence was a central feature of Bancroft's *History of the United States*, the first two volumes of which had appeared by the time this review was published. As Nell looked to collect history not only from "facts" that "are all found scattered among the various public documents which repose in the alcoves of our national library" but also from conferences with the living and from the silent testimonies of the graveyard, so Bancroft celebrated a New England tradition devoted to "diligently exploring every form of ancient records, gleaning hints from minutes of trials, extracting a fact from the registry of a will, tracing measures to their primary sources in the journals of our towns, or collecting the inscriptions in grave-yards" (Review of *Documentary History* 482). The historian acquires that vision, one might argue, by means of a kind of literary or archival assertion of manifest destiny, by which all the learning of all the ages is examined and compared in the construction of American identity.

In his celebration of Bancroft as "the prose-Homer of our Republic," published in the *Critic* in 1885, B. G. Lovejoy takes his readers on a revealing tour of Bancroft's home, in which books—"the historian's dumb servants, companions, and friends"—are everywhere as "rooms and nooks . . . have yielded to Literature's rights of squatter sovereignty" (61). Eventually, Bancroft would estimate that he had spent $50,000 to $70,000 on the acquisition of source materials.[1] Not for nothing did John F. Sabin reflect while cataloging Bancroft's library for sale in 1891, "it might be questioned if Mr. Bancroft's residence in Washington were a house with a library, or a library with a few rooms about it to live in" (Sabin 339). In this realm so heavily populated by books, this potential chaos of the textual masses, the historian stands among and above the people, perceiving difference and bringing order to literary government. For, Lovejoy asserts, "in the Republic of Letters, all books are citizens, and one is as good as another in the eyes of the maidservant who kindles the breakfast-room fire, save perhaps the vellum Plautus or illuminated missal." The quality of Bancroft's collection might easily be missed by the uninformed democratic eye, seeing a useless equality when it is best to note differences in value.

And, as Bancroft's view of scientific history suggests, the historian's eye shapes the material which it is his task to bring to order—even at the cost of violating the independent integrity of that material. As Richard C. Vitzthum has documented in his study of Bancroft's use of the wealth of sources available to him, almost all of the quotations presented in the *History of the United States* are thoroughly "Bancroftized" (58)—that is, revised so as to indicate their historical significance from Bancroft's nationalist perspective. "Perhaps unwittingly," Vitzthum suggests, Bancroft "paralleled his argument that Americans gravitated, because of instinctive faith in divine providence and fixed moral law, away from the outer darkness of despotism and anarchy toward the light of unified freedom with a method in which he himself imposed verbal and intellectual unity on the jumble of his historical sources. As God drew Americans inexorably to union, Bancroft drew the documents inexorably to unity" (74).[2] What is American, then, in Bancroft's *History* is not only the providential design that leads to a national vision but also the interpretive method that extends from that vision. Americans, in this way, are defined by their relation to the national text and by their adherence to an interpretive method that revises diversity to constitute a strong narrative of unity.

African Americans saw what that unity usually came to—"you look in vain to Bancroft and other historians for justice to the colored," William Wells Brown complained in 1860 (qtd. in Quarles, "Black History" 91)—though they faced the same task of constructing a coherent historical vision capable of shaping the community. In chapter 1, I offered an overview of the historical narrative that emerges in African American writing of this period—basically, the historical and ideological components of what Wilson Jeremiah Moses has identified as black nationalist thought of the antebellum age. Easton's strategically comparative chronology, Pennington's textbook confrontation of prevailing assumptions, Walker's reading of the discourse of white suprem-acy, and Holly's and Harris's use of history to bring focus to the political grounds for Caribbean emigration—all were attempts to gather history into a coherent response to a community (black, white, and mixed) being es-tablished on unstable historical grounds. These early efforts demonstrated the need for an expansive historical text capable not only of mapping the emerging narrative but also of collecting available documents, of document-ing the untold stories of African American achievement, and of responding to the growing construction of a historical scholarship that, in William Wells Brown's words, "has thrown the colored man out" (qtd. in Quarles, "Black History" 91).

The task of gathering the "disappearing records" of the past into a co-herent and ambitious work of history is my subject in this chapter, which focuses on the work of the three most ambitious African American historians of the antebellum period: Robert Benjamin Lewis, Martin R. Delany, and William C. Nell. All three writers are important in their historical scope and ambition and in the historical methods that support their larger arguments, particularly in what they reveal about the problems of telling a coherent story about African American history in the antebellum United States. "Let us gather up every fragment of its history," Bancroft wrote, referring to the United States; African American historians of the time might have said, in turn, "Let us gather up every fragment of *our* history," but with much greater emphasis on the fragmented nature of that history and on the cultural politics that would necessarily complicate the attempt to gather those materials. The African American community was itself a dynamic of the historical project, a subject continually under construction, continually measured against the multiple contingencies of the historical and cultural forces that gave defini-tive significance to the concept of an African American community. The subject did not precede the fragmented documentation of its history, as the United States (in effect, both a finished story and an unfolding story) essentially preceded the historical project that Bancroft identifies. There was no finished revolution, no identifiable nation, no achievement of independence from the colonial oppressor, and therefore no narrative shell capable of giving shape to the fragments. For African American historians, the fragments themselves were the history, and the only narrative to be constructed *from* the fragments that could represent the history indicated *by* the fragments was itself a fragmented narrative.[3]

In constructing self-consciously fragmented narratives, though, African American historians discovered the liberating potential of an understanding of secular history that did not appropriate the terms by which sacred history could be apprehended. As David Tracy has noted in his meditation on theology's response to the postmodern concept of the fragment, "African American thought, better than any thought even in the last century, succeeded at exposing the pretensions of any modern system of totality and at exposing the contingent and deeply ambiguous cultural character of all claims to universality, including 'whiteness'" (32). Significantly, Tracy notes, African American thought has always involved the use of fragmented forms of representation (in works by Frederick Douglass, W. E. B. Du Bois, Zora Neale Hurston, Toni Morrison, and James H. Cone, in Tracy's genealogy) to understand "the intense, saturated, fragmentary cases of religion." The central insight of African Americans through the years, from before the nineteenth century to the present, Tracy suggests, was that "Christianity as a totality becomes merely christendom. Christendom could not and cannot survive any true experiment with authentic Christianity" (32). As Douglass put it, there is a significant and terrible difference between the Christianity of Christ and the Christianity of this land. White supremacist culture drew together all aspects of social order, including religion, into a totalizing system, but the terms or condition of the totalization, whiteness, remained veiled. African American historians, working to expose this system of totality, turned to the fragments of an unrepresented history, constructing not singular but polycentric narratives, each fragment speaking of a history that could not be fully recovered.[4]

Lewis, Delany, and Nell, no less than Morrison or Cone, approached that history with a reverent understanding of the complex relation between the secular and the sacred. They brought to the project of history deep religious beliefs; but their beliefs, while central to their respective historical visions, did not lead these historians to a grand historical narrative. Rather, the fragmented quality of the historical material available to them seems to have guided these historians to theological visions grounded in history, but visions always under construction, always in process. The fragmented materials of history themselves seem to argue that the sacred resides beyond what can be known; what we can see are the breaks in, the limits of, human understanding. The sacred suggests itself in the discontinuities in and incoherence of the African American collective experience, in the experience of a community enslaved by a community devoted to liberty, in the many discontinuities occasioned by the conflict between Christianity and christendom. The sacred, both revealed and withheld by the fragments of history, thus directs the arrangement of the fragments of human understanding, its artifacts, its isolated examples of the presence of divinity. Exploring the significantly fragmented forms of contemporary writers, Tracy quotes a passage from Toni Morrison's *Beloved* and then turns to the work of James H. Cone, the leader of the movement toward a black theology of liberation. "After his first two more traditionally written theological books," Tracy suggests, "James Cone's theological essays have also adopted a similar use of fragments and fragmentary forms. Thus we see his brilliant forays into fragments that speak for themselves in their singularity, that generate new meaning and new tensions as they work with and against all the other fragments in an ever-new constellation or even into something like the Toni Morrison passage, a phantasmagoric collage of brilliant theological fragments from the African American past" (36). Cone and Morrison, I am suggesting, are simply participating in a tradition deeply embedded in the African American historical experience, a tradition represented most fully in the ambitious historical work of Lewis, Delany, and Nell.

Lewis's *Light and Truth*: Compilation and the Narrative of Destiny

"The first extensive effort of an American Negro to dig into the story of his past," as Vernon Loggins has claimed, is that by Robert Benjamin Lewis in his ambitious history *Light and Truth: Collected from the Bible and Ancient and Modern History, Containing the Universal History of the Colored and the Indian Race, from the Creation of the World to the Present Time*, first copyrighted in 1836 and published in Portland, Maine, by Daniel Clement Colesworthy, a white printer and writer associated with black causes and individuals. The book was published again in 1843, by Severance and Dorr, printers in Augusta, Maine, and a significantly expanded edition was published in

1844 by a "committee of Coloured Gentlemen."[5] Lewis apparently planned to expand the work still further in the 1850s. In a notice published in *Frederick Douglass' Paper* on May 13, 1853, Lewis announced the availability of "a new history," "one of the most valuable works that was ever written for Schools and Families, and intended to remove the prejudices from whites against the Colored and Indian people in the United States." The work, Lewis promised, "will contain four volumes of about four hundred pages each, 12 mo., or about 1600 pages in all," including "two volumes treating of Geography, and two Historical Readers, accompanied with an Atlas of Maps and Charts of all the different nations with capitol cities of each country." Included in the work would be "A Globe Map of the Earth, Sun, Moon and Planets," and "Three Globe Maps of the Earth, that revolve." Lewis reports that he "selected from hundreds of the best authors in Europe, who take the front rank in literature in the world," and that he had included in the work "figures of the ancient historians, with the prophets of Christ and his Apostles, and Bishops who were colored." The notice is an appeal for aid, and Lewis concludes by stating that "if any man or company of men in America or Great Britain wish to do good for themselves and the oppressed people of Israel—proved to be the Indian races—they will do so in assisting to get the work printed." Although Lewis states that "the work is completed for the Press, and the Atlas for the Engraver," the manuscript has yet to be found. What survives is this record of the grandeur of Lewis's ambitions, a truly Bancroftian attempt to locate the African American and American Indian struggle against oppression historically and geographically in global and cosmic order, in secular and sacred history.

The record of Lewis's endeavors that survive, however, is still impressively ambitious in its range. As historian Mia Bay has noted, "Lewis went one step further than the earlier [African American] writers in his discussion of the origins of the races. He maintained that the Garden of Eden was in Ethiopia and that God had created Adam from 'the rich and *black* soil' of the land. Although *Light and Truth* contains no mention of polygenesis, Lewis's account of human origins virtually turned the doctrine of separate creations on its head. Blacks became the first family, and Lewis further insisted that all the early nations were colored: 'Greece, Europe, and NORTH AND SOUTH AMERICA WERE SETTLED BY DESCENDANTS OF EGYPT,' he proclaimed" (45). Further, "Lewis maintained that Plato and Julius Caesar were Ethiopians, and that Moses, Solomon, and many other luminaries were men of color. Moreover, in a section entitled 'The Hair on Men's Heads,' he went further still, arguing that biblical descriptions of the hair of both Christ and God himself showed that the Almighty and his Son were colored also" (45). Joining past to present, Lewis offers extensive commentary on the condition and achievements of African Americans. As Loggins has noted, *Light and Truth* is "the first of the long line of books produced by Negroes which seek to give information about their prominent leaders"—and, indeed, *Light and Truth* has biographical sketches of a number of important writers and leaders, among them Paul Cuffe, David Walker, Hosea Easton, Phillis Wheatley, and Maria Stewart. And as both the title and Lewis's 1853 notice suggest, Lewis is equally interested in American Indians, and he includes a sketch of William Apess and a discussion of Wheatley's correspondence with Samson Occom.

If Lewis's ongoing ambitions made *Light and Truth*, like *Leaves of Grass*, a constantly developing project, Lewis himself was, like Whitman, an energetic promoter of his book. As Bay reports, Lewis "traveled through New England on annual tours" to sell it, and accordingly "*Light and Truth* may well have been the most widely circulated of the nineteenth-century black publications on ethnology" (45–46). Whatever its virtues, though, and in spite of Lewis's best efforts, *Light and Truth* did not raise Lewis into the pantheon of African American writers. Lewis is notably absent from the biographical sketches included in such works as William Wells Brown's histories or William J. Simmons's *Men of Mark* (1887); and he is absent also from the extensive body of reference works on African American history and culture published in recent years. Many of Lewis's views on ancient cultures were echoed in the black press, though some of these arguments, as Bay notes, were presented in *Freedom's Journal* long before Lewis published the first edition of *Light and Truth*.[6] It is, in short, difficult to determine the extent of Lewis's influence.

Biographical information on Lewis is available through a few scattered sources—an unpublished memoir by his daughter, a notice of his marriage in *Freedom's Journal*, and various reports of research that include, for example, word of information available through the Church of Latter-day Saints (for Lewis drew from the Book of Mormon, and his arguments about the American Indians are basically similar to the views of that faith). In the introduction to *Light and Truth*, Lewis is identified as "a descendant of the two races he so ably vindicates" (iii). A notice in the December 5, 1828, issue of the *Freedom's Journal* identifies Lewis as a citizen of Hallowell, Maine; a notice in the *Liberator* identifies him as a Bostonian in the early 1840s; and Lewis's 1853 notice in *Frederick Douglass' Paper* places him in Bath, Maine. Lewis's biographical sketches of Bostonians Walker and Stewart in *Light and Truth* suggest that he knew them personally. Bay, working from a biographical sketch by Lewis's daughter, identifies Lewis as "a jack-of-all-trades" who "made his living painting, papering, and whitewashing houses, cleaning carpets, crafting baskets, caning chairs, and fixing parasols and umbrellas" (44). There is reason to believe that Lewis considered missionary work in Africa, but he continued his work in New England.

If Lewis's views are generally representative of the African American endeavor to recover an Afrocentric understanding of the origins of civilization and the center of sacred history, his zeal in this cause exceeded that of most other writers of the time. One of few lengthy notices of this work in the nineteenth century is that provided by Martin R. Delany in *The Condition, Elevation, Emigration, and Destiny of the Colored People of the United States*. In a lengthy editor's note in the chapter called "Literary and Professional Colored Men and Women" (and one assumes that Delany here serves as "editor"), Delany surveys the field of African American achievement, emphasizing print culture from newspapers to narratives. By far the longest single comment in that note is directed at Lewis's *Light and Truth*. "It may be expected," Delany begins, "that we should say something about a book issued in Boston, purporting to be a history of ancient great men of African descent, by one Mr. Lewis, entitled 'Light and Truth.'" And then Delany quickly gets to the point: "This book is nothing more than a compilation of selected portions of Rollins's, Goldsmith's, Ferguson's, Hume's, and other ancient histories; added to which, is a tissue of historical absurdities and literary blunders, shamefully palpable, for which the author or authors should mantle their faces" (128).[7]

After an initial reading of *Light and Truth*, it is frankly difficult to find fault with Delany's evaluation, for what Lewis presents indeed seems like little more than a compilation (and is, in fact, identified as such), haphazardly organized at best. While one can admire Lewis's attempt to construct an Afrocentric vision of history, one can only regret that he includes in that vision seemingly wild and unsupported interpretations of the Bible and of history. It is difficult to disagree with Bay's view that "*Light and Truth* provides an early example of how easily African-American efforts to rebut white racial doctrine could shade into a black chauvinism that mirrored the very racist logic it opposed" (45). One can share as well Loggins's complaint that "the author accepts as positive truth the legend that the American Indians are descendants of the lost tribes of Israel, and in some way reasons that they are therefore the only true American Christians" (93). Moreover, as both Delany and Loggins suggest, the book does indeed contain many "literary blunders." I am less resistant than Loggins to the fact that "the most homely idiom is placed by the side of a Latin quotation from Seneca, or a French quotation from Voltaire," for reasons that I hope will become clear—but one can hardly avoid noticing that the book was written and produced quickly. In the introduction, the committee of publishers notes that "the author of this compilation has been some years in gathering this information" (iii), and this frank acknowledgment of the book *as* compilation is to the point—but one wonders why the author did not spend more time arranging his materials in a more readable form.

But as we recognize the validity of Delany's criticism of this book, we should attend also to what Delany says next, for Delany is interested not only in standards of literary achievement and historical authority but also in the cultural politics of such standards. Such standards, Delany argues, are violated regularly, and Lewis should be viewed in the context of the distorted culture constructed by such violations. "There is one redeeming quality about 'Light and Truth,'" Delany suggests:

> It is a capital offset to the pitiable literary blunders of Professor George R. Gliddon, late Consul to Egypt, from the United States, Lecturer on Ancient Egyptian Literature, &c., &c., who makes all ancient black men, *white*; and asserts the Egyptians and Ethiopians to have been of the *Caucasian* or white race!—So, also, this colored gentleman, makes all ancient great white men, *black*—as Diogenes, Socrates, Themistocles, Pompey, Caesar, Cato, Cicero, Horace, Virgil, et cetera. Gliddon's idle nonsense has found a capital match in the production of Mr. Lewis' "Light and Truth," and both should be sold together. We may conclude by expressing our thanks to our brother Lewis, as we do not think that Professor Gliddon's learned ignorance, would have ever met an equal but for "Light and Truth."

Delany certainly makes an pointed comparison, for if Gliddon was, as William Stanton has written, "a name-dropper, a sponger, a swinger on the shirttails of the great, a braggart, pretender, and scatologist," he was also "the first to lecture to Americans on Egyptology," and, by 1852, a colleague of Josiah Clark Nott, one of most influential theorists of race traits—and defenders of slavery—of his time. Gliddon's lectures, which ran from 1840 to 1852, attracted great crowds, at times including a "Grand Moving Transparency" (panorama), and eventually leading to the publication of his *Ancient Egypt: A*

Series of Chapters on Early Egyptian History, Archaeology, and Other Subjects Connected with Hieroglyphical Literature (1844), which went through twelve editions and sold 24,000 copies within five years. In his lectures, Gliddon asserted that Egyptians were not what the nineteenth century called Negroes, that the races had been distinct from the beginning and remained so, and that perceived Negroid features in the Sphinx were the result not of design but of physical batterings over time. In this way, Gliddon provided ammunition to the race theorists of the day who promoted the theory of racial distinctions and of polygenesis, theories celebrated particularly by defenders of slavery.

A product of African American and American Indian parents, Lewis was the embodiment of two of the most prominent targets of this developing race "science" in the work of Gliddon, Nott, and Samuel George Morton (a craniologist). Accustomed to being thus targeted, early African American historians recognized that prejudice was itself historical, the product of and framework for historical (mis)understanding and collective action, and Lewis attends to this recognition directly and persistently. Indeed, the title *Light and Truth* reappears toward the end of the book when Lewis is talking about prejudice. In a chapter that offers a scattered collection of commentary on racial types (to which I will return shortly), racial history, and biblical history, Lewis discusses the word "negro," noting that it "is used as an epithet of contempt to the colored people" (342). Lewis suggests that "our friends, the friends of Christ, would do well to consider this, and never write or publish it again to the world" (342). Then, after briefly noting the presence of Africa in the Bible and in Christian history, Lewis presents what is easily the boldest and most definitive assertion in the book: "I am authorized by the word of God to say, whosoever makes use of the word *negro*, applying it to us as a people, after the *light* and *truth* have been proclaimed, are neither friends to God nor man" (342).[8]

Lewis's attention to individual words here and throughout *Light and Truth* is instructive, for in place of Bancroft's union of language Lewis presents a Bakhtinian carnival of documents that speak with and against each other, discovering their relations to one another only loosely. The publishers' claims for the book are fairly straightforward: "We publish this volume of collections from sacred and profane history, with a determination that a correct knowledge of the Colored and Indian people, ancient and modern, may be extended freely, unbiased by any prejudicial effects from descent or station" (iii). The introduction also emphasizes the "descent" of the author of this collection, and the author's identity is central to the vision and mode of history the book presents. The book's primary purpose, indeed, is to locate and respond to prejudice, whereby the two concerns—an unbiased "correct knowledge" and the centrality of the author's identity—come together. But whereas Bancroft's transcendentalist history favors the intuitions of the transcendentalist *reason* over the flawed apprehensions of individual *understanding*, Lewis presents a world in which human constructions and divine revelations are not so easily separated, a world in which the corruptions of human history threaten to overwhelm the "light and truth" that history can reveal. There is creative tension among the various documents Lewis has collected, his arrangement (more often, his apparent lack of arrangement) of the collection, and his own clear assertions of interpretive, ideological, and religious authority. It is a tension that both accounts for and responds to the history of prejudice that has shaped the common understanding of the evidence he presents, and that has at times shaped the evidence itself. Lewis's method emphasizes that historical understanding cannot be separated from the complex testimony of the sources, for the very existence of the sources themselves, giving testimony against prejudice, is central to Lewis's point. What is important is how and why we read these documents: the fact is that they (particularly the Bible) have been there all along, but their testimony has not been attended to since they have been read in other contexts to serve other purposes.

Lewis's sense of this testimony is evident not only in his direct assertions of interpretive and moral authority but also in his arrangement of the documents. *Light and Truth* is divided into fourteen chapters of irregular length. Generally, the chapter arrangement leads from the beginnings of history (the first sentence following the table of contents identifies the historical moment of the Creation, and then argues that Adam and Eve were both Ethiopian and black) to a view of Haiti. But the arrangement is not chronological by any stretch of the imagination. Although "The History of Man" is followed by chapters that explore ancient civilizations, leading eventually to "The Destruction of Jerusalem" (chapter 6) and "The Present State of Judah and Israel" (chapter 7), the organization is broken by a chapter (5) called "Colored Generals and Soldiers," itself divided into sections devoted to individuals (Hannibal, for example) and larger groups ("Colored Soldiers," "The Last American War with Great Britain," and "Proclamation to the Free People of Color," in the last of which Jackson makes his predictable appearance). And the irregularity of the chapters is itself suggestive. Following an eighty-three-page chapter called "Ancient Cities and Kingdoms," and preceding a sixty-five-page chapter titled "Ancient Kings and Wars," is a four-page chapter with the title "Antiquity of America." This brief chapter is devoted to a collection of assertions that various writers through time—including "Plato, an Ethiopian and an eminent Greek historian" (125)—"are supposed to have referred to America in their writings" (124).

This brief chapter is not an anomaly in this sequence that leads finally to "The Present State of Judah and Israel"; rather, it indicates the underlying narrative that informs Lewis's handling of this sequence. The first paragraph of this chapter might be taken as a summary of this underlying narrative and of the interpretive argument that is central to *Light and Truth* as a whole. It is characteristic of both Lewis's mode of argument and his style through most of the text (and the brackets here, I should note, are Lewis's): "America, was first settled by the Israelites—Indians who came out from Egypt. [The View of the Hebrews, by Ethan Smith.] America was discovered by Columbus in 1492, and was peopled by Colonies in A.D., 1620, from Europe. The first settlement in New England was made at Plymouth, in the midst of a fertile country.—The Egyptians were an Ethiopian people. [Herodotus.]" (124). This strange assortment of partial truths and narrative confusion is significant if one is to make sense of *Light and Truth*—that is, if one is to understand the sense that Lewis imposes on history. One should note that Lewis includes his sources in the text itself, and one should note also how little that comes to, as a world of interpretation is whittled down to sharp assertions. Indeed, the narrative is self-contradictory in significant ways, for the distinction between the first settlement and the discovery of the continent is a distinction of historical views, the differing narratives of beginnings that support differing understandings of the historical shape and integrity of the nineteenth century. The dominant culture's narrative—discovery by Columbus and subsequent European colonization—is bracketed by Lewis's narrative of a biblical settlement: that by the Indians-as-Israelites, which develops into that by the Indians-as-Ethiopians.

Central to the story that Lewis suggests here are the relations among American Indians, Israelites, and Ethiopians. The narrative suggested here does not speak well of Lewis's own ability to avoid prejudice, for his vision of biblical history and of a reconfigured Christian destiny includes pointed anti-Jewish commentary. In the section called "The Destruction of Jerusalem," Lewis writes of "the danger of rejecting the Son of God" as a subject "too much neglected and forgotten in the present Christian world." "I design then," Lewis adds, "to give a concise description of the event in which Jesus

Christ came in awful judgment upon the infidel Jews, and vindicated his cause against his persecutors and murderors" (218). And while presenting his vision of what he thinks of as the judgment and its causes, Lewis returns to the lesson for his readers: "Let anti-Christian powers, yea, let all infidels and gospel despisers, consider this and tremble!" (240). "Viewing the destruction of Jerusalem then," he concludes, "as but a type of an event now pending upon antichristian nations, we peruse it with new interest; and it must be viewed in the light of a most impressive warning to this age of the world." The first seven chapters of *Light and Truth* tell the story of origins and of judgment—and throughout Lewis applies the lessons he draws from this story to the contemporary world, suggestive of judgment awaiting those who abandon Christian duty. In this narrative, the presence of the fifth chapter, "Colored Generals and Soldiers," is the presence of a historical militancy in the face of prejudice, of a struggle for rights by those whose rights are left out of the struggle, and thus serves as a reminder of black power and ingenuity throughout history. But how does Lewis reconcile his anti-Jewish sentiments with his identification of Indians as Israelites? And how exactly does the theme of black military achievement fit into the larger narrative suggested by the documents he collects?

These questions are central to *Light and Truth*. The sequence of chapters suggests the biblical foundations of American Indians and of blacks in America, and it indicates that the union of the two races is a sign of a coming destiny. Early in *Light and Truth*, Lewis had marshaled biblical evidence locating "The Red People" in the Bible, and locating also biblical precedent for the mixing of the red and the black (using the *Book of Mormon* as one of his authorities along the way). And in the last of the sequence of chapters I am discussing, "The Present State of Judah and Israel," Lewis presents "Arguments in favor of the native Americans being the descendants of Israel," those who have been "scattered among the nations" (250). Toward the end of chapter 7, before the closing section titled "The True Christians in This Land Are Indians," Lewis presents the vision that I would suggest this sequence of chapters is designed to support: "Surely, then, the natives of the deserts of America must have been a people who once knew God of Israel! They maintained for more than two millenaries, the tradition of him, in many respects correct. What possible account can be given of this, but that they were descendants of Israel, and that the God of Israel has had his merciful eye upon them, with a view in his own time to bring them to light, and effect their restoration?" (267–68). In this vision, African foundations are brought to the site of the lost tribe, there to restore those who, in their actions and principles if not in their beliefs, are "the true Christians," though how they came to be *Christian* remains unexplained. It is significant, though, that Africans were brought to the Americas and that a community of Christian African Americans thus found themselves in the land of the lost biblical tribe. The reunion marks a historical moment that calls for the various talents, including the military skills, of those of African origins to be brought to destined action.

The chapters that follow, I suggest, constitute a second significant sequence, one designed to establish the intellectual, historical, and prophetic foundations for the realization of this destiny, and trace the destined path to its revolutionary manifestation in the final chapter, "St. Domingo or Hayti." These chapters include "The Arts and Sciences," a five-page chapter called "Modern Eminent Colored Men," followed by four historical chapters: "The Great Historical Ages," "The Ancient Arabians," "History of the Prophets," and "Periods, &c."—the last of which includes a chronological table that extends from A.D. 826 to 1791, the final entry being "Insurrection in St. Domingo, in November," which prepares for the concluding chapter. To be sure, there is a great deal of flexibility in this arrangement, as a section on female writers that includes a discussion of Phillis Wheatley and Maria Stewart is part of the chapter called "The Great Historical Ages," which follows a section on modern historians and precedes, with no apparent transition, a section on Alexandria, "Burning of the Libraries." But generally this sequence of chapters extends from scholarly achievements to particular achievers in modern times, to evidence of achievements in history, to a discussion of race by way of the chapter on the "ancient Arabians," to prophetic history, to secular history, and finally to revolution.

One should note, though, that Lewis arranges the documents he presents so as to tell a restrained if suggestive story of Haiti and of revolution, using letters that carry the authority of the revolution to speak to the needs of the community of Lewis's readers. Following an overview of Haiti, Lewis reprints a letter by John Candler from the *Anti-Slavery Reporter* on the rebellion against President Boyer. Lewis writes of the letter in a very brief introduction, "Its comparatively peaceful character reflects much credit on the often calumniated people of that land" (389). The letter ends with a vision of peaceful self-determination and industry: "The Haytiens, however, are not discouraged; they are resolved to exert themselves, and to cultivate the arts of peace; they believe themselves to be on the way to surmount all their difficulties; they write and speak like men who have learned a great deal; they have full reliance on their qualifications for self-government. We trust that the experiment about to be made of forming a new constitution, and of framing laws suited to the present and future exigencies of society, may be entered upon with prudence, and carried through with wisdom" (394). Lewis's rhetoric here places the Haitian "experiment" in the ideological light of what was often referred to as the American experiment—involving the formation of a constitution and the attempt to establish the ideal of representative government.

What follows this letter, somewhat strangely, is another letter that precedes it historically: that of Abbé Grégoire "to the Citizens of Color in the French West Indies, concerning the Decree of the 15th of May, 1791." In Lewis's extracts from this letter, addressed to the slaveholding "people of mixed blood," Grégoire begins by noting, "You were men; you are now citizens," and concludes with an appeal to citizenship:

> Strictly obedient to the laws, teach your children to respect them. By a careful education, instruct them in all the duties of morality; so shall you prepare for the succeeding generation, virtuous citizens, honorable men, enlightened patriots, and defenders of their country!
>
> How will their hearts be affected, when, conducting them to your shores, you direct their looks towards France, telling them, "Beyond those seas is your parent country; it is from thence we have received justice, protection, happiness and liberty. There dwell our fellow citizens, our brethren, and our friends: to them we have sworn an eternal friendship. Heirs of our sentiments, and of our affections, may your hearts and your lips repeat our oaths! Live to love them; and, if necessary, die to defend them." (398)

Grégoire's recognition of his audience as citizens, along with his appeal for active manifestations of citizenship (including military action), echoes the famous proclamation by General Jackson that Lewis, like so many others, cites in his history. In fact, Lewis includes Jackson's comments in the chapter called "Colored Generals and Soldiers," which I have argued constitutes the militant heart of the first sequence of chapters. But as Lewis knew well how little Jackson's recognition of citizenship had come to in succeeding years, so his arrangement of these letters on Haiti extends from a similar recognition.

The historical gap between the two letters is itself intriguing, as is the fact that the earlier letter follows the later one, for Lewis is here interrogating the terms of citizenship and of political unity, an interrogation that collects the various documents and historical narratives of *Light and Truth* under its central concern with prejudice. The years between 1791 and 1843 saw a great deal of violent struggle in Saint Domingue. And this gap, I suggest, is exactly to the point. Grégoire, as I have noted, addresses the mulatto population of Haiti, and includes in his advice to them, "Let the existence of your slaves be no longer their torment; but by your kind treatment of them, expiate the crimes of Europe!" (398). But the divisions of color and caste in Saint Domingue, divisions of condition and of privilege, of alliances formed of distrust and of prejudice, were the divisions that would complicate significantly the turbulent process of national self-definition, problems by no means concluded by the 1840s.

It is significant, then, that this last chapter of the book concludes with "The Scale of Complexion; the Color of the Skin." Lewis offers no transition to this "scale," which he presented in a different form earlier in the book during his discussion of the word "negro," in which he claims divine authority for propagating the light and truth about prejudice to his readers.[9] Here is how the scale is presented:

> Between Black and White is a Mulatto:
> Between Mulatto and White is a Quaderoon.
> Between Quaderoon and White is a Mestizo. (After this the color becomes
>   imperceptible to us.)
> Between Mulatto and Black is a Sambo.
> Between a Sambo and Black is a Mangroon.
> Between a Mangroon and Black the white hue is lost.
> The complexion of the Indian tribes:—Reddish, Copper, Brown, Black,
>   and a white mixed hue. (400)

Delany could have looked to this passage specifically when arguing, however satirically, that *Light and Truth* should be read in combination with Gliddon's work, for Lewis's chart addresses the determination to quantify degrees of racial identity that was supported by the racial "science" of people like Gliddon. But Lewis looks to the divisions to reach for a possible union, though he follows lines that lead in two separate directions, black and white, and includes the multicolor "complexion of the Indian tribes" as a separate category. Following each of the two lines of racial mixture, he calls attention to the point at which differences become imperceptible, and suggests the unity in difference beyond those points. The Indian tribes, intriguingly, remain separate, perhaps suggesting that Lewis's lost tribe plays much the same ideologi-

cal role as Bancroft's or Garnet's vanishing red man—allowing for a triangula-
tion of race relations by which black and white can be oriented in relation to
one another over time.

Lewis's vision of both union and separation speaks of an ongoing historical
struggle rather than a hoped-for reconciliation, a stage in the process of a
larger destiny that he outlines throughout his book, and *Light and Truth*
ultimately is designed to prepare his readers for that struggle. Lewis does not
advocate a simple allegiance of the kind advised by Grégoire or Jackson;
rather, he addresses a people who have been separated by color and by
condition and interprets human history in a way informed by that condition
and addressed to the needs of that community. Concluding with Grégoire's
advice, Lewis draws attention to the limitation of any notion of citizenship
that separates people of color. Lewis would seem to anticipate J. Dennis
Harris's view that "to divide the colored people at this late day by any such
process, would seem to me like *splitting a child in twain*," and would seem to
argue, with Harris, "*I go for a colored nationality*." Following the "scale of
complexion" are the concluding words of *Light and Truth*, both a call for
unity and a warning to those who would disturb that unity: "We are all one,
and oppressed in this land of boasted Liberty and Freedom. 'But wo [*sic*] unto
them by whom it cometh'" (400). Lewis has assembled both the foundations
of and the argument for this warning, a history that speaks of destiny and that
answers to prejudice, and a history that reminds those whom Harris would
later envision as "a colored nationality" that they have a history of militancy
in support of prophecy. Rising through the heteroglossia of the multifarious
documents, chronologies, and declarations that is *Light and Truth* is an argument that constitutes a reapplication of Grégoire's advice to the "Citizens of
Color," calling upon that rising people to look to their ancestors and "live to
love them; and, if necessary, die to defend them."

Martin R. Delany: Destiny's Architect

In spite of his criticism of *Light and Truth*, Martin R. Delany has much in
common with Robert Benjamin Lewis. Like Lewis, Delany looked for the
connection between a biblically informed historical narrative that originated
in African culture and a militant response to the condition of blacks in the
Americas. Indeed, the links among origins, prophecy, and militancy are indicated by the two mottoes Delany printed on the masthead of his Pittsburgh

paper the *Mystery*.[10] The first—"AND MOSES WAS LEARNED IN ALL THE WISDOM OF THE EGYPTIANS"—signaled Delany's assertion of historical and biblical authority, as well as his rootedness in black Freemasonry (which is, no doubt, the source for the paper's title). The second motto, adopted in 1845, following Garnet's "Address to the Slaves," was drawn from Byron's *Childe Harold's Pilgrimage*: "HEREDITARY BONDSMEN! KNOW YE NOT WHO WOULD BE FREE, THEMSELVES MUST STRIKE THE BLOW!"[11] In all of his major works, Delany struggled toward a transformative narrative, one capable of revising the dominant historical narrative developing in the United States, reenvisioning the role of religion as a framework for individual and collective action, deconstructing the arguments for racial oppression and prejudice, and identifying the contours of an imagined black community capable of resisting (ideologically and otherwise) the systemic control of black Americans. It is not for nothing that Delany has been called—in that patriarchal discourse so often used to address intellectual history, a discourse that the very patriarchal Delany would have endorsed—the father of black nationalism.

Delany, though, was more complex than this kind of title would suggest. Like so many nineteenth-century figures—Sojourner Truth, for example, or Abraham Lincoln—Delany has been asked to serve the needs of contemporary cultural politics; and like most other figures, he will be most useful to us when we recognize the full complexity of his life and of the movement with which he is associated. And the complexity of his life cannot be separated from his attempt to write himself, his community, and black history into the cultural consciousness and the historical record of the United States and beyond. Robert S. Levine has said it succinctly and well: "An abolitionist, editor, doctor, novelist, political and racial theorist, inventor, orator, and judge, Delany was a prolific writer who seems to have been unable to conceive of political action apart from writing" (*Martin Delany*, 3). These various social roles often contributed to and shaped one another—as, for example, Delany's inability as a black man to acquire a patent for an invention, joined with his acceptance and then rejection by the Harvard Medical School, contributed inevitably to his political and racial theories; or as his complex editorial relationship with Frederick Douglass helped shape the nature and terms of his role as abolitionist and race representative. As Levine has demonstrated in his excellent study of Delany's and Douglass's relationship, an examination of Delany's life can lead one to a study of the tensions, the competitions, and the ideological disagreements within the culturally restrictive realm of nineteenth-century black male leadership. It is beyond my purpose here, though, to explore Delany's various roles and the cultural politics that shaped those roles; rather, I want to consider Delany as a writer and theorist of history, and examine the ways in which the complexity of his life and world is mirrored not only in his *vision* of history but also in his *narration* of history. For if Delany was unable to conceive of political action apart from writing, he was also unable to conceive of political action apart from a (re)vision of history, a (re)vision that he worked toward in his various texts.

Delany, that is, understood that all writing is a form of political action; as his comments on *Light and Truth* indicate, he had a sharp and satirical sense of the cultural politics of representation. In the text with which I am most concerned in this chapter, *The Condition, Elevation, Emigration, and Destiny of the Colored People of the United States,* Delany asserts that too many African Americans "as a body, . . . have been taught to believe that we must have some person to think for us, instead of thinking for ourselves," to the extent that "the most ordinary white person, is almost revered, while the most qualified colored person is totally neglected" (191). Delany here suggests the frustrations he felt as a self-appointed representative of black America, but he addresses also the practical problem of representing issues concerning black America. As he argues in his preface to *The Condition,* "The colored people are not yet known, even to their most professed friends among the white Americans; for the reason, that politicians, religionists, colonizationists, and abolitionists, have each and all, at different times, presumed to *think* for, dictate to, and *know* better what suited colored people, than they knew for themselves; and consequently, there has been no other knowledge of them obtained than that which has been obtained through these mediums. Their history—past, present, and future, has been written by them, who, for reasons well known, which are named in this volume, are not their representatives, and, therefore, do not properly nor fairly present their wants and claims among their fellows" (10). Delany was not alone in making this point, of course; similar statements were placed at center stage in the black national convention movement and were prominent in the origins of the African American press. But the sharpness and specificity of Delany's critique, including his comments on his abolitionist allies, were unusual, for his published complaints up to this time had remained largely (though not entirely) veiled; and Delany's emphasis on the politics of interpretation and of historical writing is significant as well.

Delany's understanding of the white supremacist control over African American religious and historical consciousness underscores the seriousness behind the second half of his commentary on *Light and Truth*. That is, placing Lewis against Gliddon, Delany addresses how a developing "science" was being used to construct a conceptual framework by which history could be understood and by which actions in history could be justified. As Reginald Horsman has noted in his study of the complex relation between nationalism and theories of race supremacy, "The flowering of the new science of man in the first half of the nineteenth century was ultimately decisive in giving a racial cast to Anglo-Saxonism. Scientists, by mid-century, had provided an abundance of 'proofs' by which English and American Anglo-Saxons could explain their power, progress, governmental stability, and freedom" (43). But as Delany's sharp critique of Lewis indicates, the task was not simply to match false and coercive "proofs" with more of the same; the task was to respond to a world under construction, to question the foundation and design of the construction, and to build there an alternate model of history. As Delany notes in a critique of modes of education that was part of the foreground of Booker T. Washington's methods, "This has been one of our great mistakes— we have gone in advance of ourselves. We have commenced at the superstructure of the building, instead of the foundation—at the top instead of the bottom. We should first be mechanics and common tradesmen, and professions as a matter of course would grow out of the wealth made thereby" (193). In *The Condition*, Delany applies much the same method to the task of reenvisioning history.

As the architectural metaphor of structures and foundations might indicate, Delany's vision of history, like that of other prominent black leaders of the time, was shaped by Freemasonry. Much of nineteenth-century African American historical writing suggests the need to examine more closely than we have the importance of fraternal organizations. In *Light and Truth*, for example, there are hints of the influence of Freemasonry in Lewis's presentation of history. Included in the four names listed as the "publishing committee" for *Light and Truth* is that of Thomas Dalton, who is listed by William H. Grimshaw as the grand master of Prince Hall Grand Lodge from 1831–1832; and Lewis's reliance on the Book of Mormon becomes more interesting still when one considers that Joseph Smith was connected to the Masons.[12] In a chapter called "The Arts and Sciences," moreover, Lewis follows a lengthy section on Egyptian architecture, without transition, with one titled "The Explanation of the Five Virtues." The five virtues that Lewis identifies— "Truth," "Justice," "Temperance," "Prudence," and "Fortitude"—are listed by Grimshaw as Masonic "living stones" or "cardinal virtues."[13] Certainly,

Freemasonry offered Lewis and Delany alike a tradition of historical interpretation that, as they believed, extended back to the Egyptian mysteries, and
it offered as well a framework for understanding the relations among community, historical consciousness, and individual character.

Delany's Masonic ties are explicitly relevant to his historical vision in his
forty-page pamphlet *The Origin and Objects of Ancient Freemasonry: Its Introduction into the United States, and Legitimacy among Colored Men*, published in 1853, shortly following the publication of *The Condition*. The explicit purpose of this treatise, as noted by the committee from the Pittsburgh
St. Cyprian Lodge that solicited it, was to respond to attempts to undermine
the authority of black Freemasons in the United States. Against Masonic
doctrine, blacks had been excluded from the U.S. Freemasons and had therefore formed their own lodges, beginning with the pioneering effort of Prince
Hall in Boston in 1775.[14] In this pamphlet, Delany lists "three distinct periods" in "the history of man's existence from Adam to Solomon": "his origin
in Adam's creation, his preservation in Noah's ark, and his prospects of
redemption from the curse of God's broken laws by the promises held out in
that mysteriously incomprehensible work of building the temple by Solomon" (21). The last, obviously, is of greatest importance to Delany and the
Freemasons; and it is connected to African history, in Delany's view, in that
Africans "were the authors of this mysterious and beautiful Order" which
Solomon transformed into practical government. "Previous to the building"
of Solomon's Temple, Delany explains in a footnote, "Masonry was only
allegorical, consisting of a scientific system of theories, taught through the
medium of Egyptian, Ethiopian, Assyrian, and other oriental hieroglyphics
understood only by the priesthood and a chosen few" (19).

Following a general history, Delany focuses specifically on Freemasonry
"among colored men in the United States"; on prejudice within Freemasonry
(which he finds more prominent in the northern states than in the southern);
and on the African origins of Freemasonry itself. Delany's rhetoric of history
is at times florid, as when he addresses the formation of the National Grand
Lodge of African Americans:

> This perhaps, was the most important period in the history of colored
> Masons in the United States; and had I the power to do so, I would raise
> my voice in tones of thunder, but with the pathetic affections of a
> brother, and thrill the cord of every true Masonic heart throughout the
> country and the world, especially of colored men, in exhortations to sta-

bility and to Union. Without it, satisfied am I that all our efforts, whether as men or Masons, must fail—utterly fail. "A house divided against itself, cannot stand"—the weak divided among themselves in the midst of the mighty, are thrice vanquished—conquered without a blow from the strong; the sturdy hand of the ruthless may shatter in pieces our column guidance, and leave the Virgin of Sympathy to weep through all coming time. (27–28)

But if Delany looks to Freemasonry and to the history it provides to emphasize the dangers of "a house divided," he is equally willing to let that the house *be* divided. "We are either Masons or not Masons," he argues in his preface, "legitimate or illegitimate; if the affirmative, then we *must* be so *acknowledged* and *accepted*—if the negative, we *should* be *rejected*" (12). *The Origin and Objects of Ancient Freemasonry* is devoted to proving that, in fact, "our rights are equal to those of other American Masons, if not better than some," in part by arguing that "to Africa is the world indebted for its knowledge of the mysteries of Ancient Freemasonry. Had Moses or the Israelites never lived in Africa, the mysteries of the wise men of the East never would have been handed down to us" (40). The pamphlet is, in short, both a plea for acceptance and an assertion of Delany's authority over those principles by which acceptance can be argued.

Delany's goals and methods are similar in *The Condition*. He argues for the right of African Americans to be recognized as citizens; he supports that claim by examining the history both before and after the formation of the United States; and he argues that there must be either union or disunion according to the acceptance or rejection of the evidence of history. The publication of *The Condition* follows Delany's frustrations with his own career and with the cumulative career of African American collective self-definition. Moreover, Levine has argued persuasively that *The Condition* arises out of increasingly tense debates with Frederick Douglass over claims to black male leadership generally and the issue of emigration specifically. While the great majority of African Americans, Delany prominent among them, denounced the American Colonization Society as an organization designed to preserve slavery and maintain racial domination, many were, by the early 1850s, exploring the possibility of emigration to Canada, to South and Central America, or to Africa—again, Delany among them. According to his contemporary biographer Frances Rollin, whose account of Delany's life must be approached with caution, Delany was notified by his friend David J. Peck in 1852 that he had

been elected "mayor of Greytown [in Nicaragua], civil governor of the Mos-
quito reservation, and commander-in-chief of the military forces of the province!" (80).[15] Delany did not succeed at convincing other African Americans
to join him in Greytown; and if the mayoral election did in fact take place, it
apparently was to no effect, as Delany did not go to Nicaragua. Instead, Delany
explored the options for emigration in *The Condition*, arguing for the formation of a black nation, with reservations about Canada as a suitable site;
presenting Central and South America as "evidently the ultimate destination
and future home of the colored race on this continent" (178), a point emphasized in his 1854 lecture "The Political Destiny of the Colored Race on the
American Continent"; and including an appendix titled "A Project for an
Expedition of Adventure, to the Eastern Coast of Africa," which, according to
his preface, Delany "laid out at twenty-four years of age" and later "improved."
This last section includes the phrase so often connected with Delany—"We are
a nation within a nation"—a claim of postcolonial identity as Delany identifies
African Americans with "the Poles in Russia, the Hungarians in Austria, the
Welsh, Irish, and Scotch in the British dominions" (209). Following the publication of *The Condition*, Delany continued to lecture, moved to Canada in
1856, became somewhat involved in John Brown's plan for militant resistance
to the slave system, and in 1859 traveled to the Niger Valley in Africa, where he
signed a treaty for land for a proposed colony, the outlines of which he
presented in his *Official Report of the Niger Valley Exploring Party* (1860). The
plan for the colony was abandoned by 1862, at which time Delany turned his
attention to the Civil War in the United States.

As this loose summary of his various ideas and activities over the turbulent
decade of the 1850s indicates, Delany embodied the contradictory tendencies
and historical incoherence of the African American leadership at midcentury.
By "historical incoherence" I do not mean that Delany's understanding of
history was itself incoherent; indeed, he had a sharp sense of the history
that had shaped his life and that continued to define the "condition" of
the "colored people of the United States." Moreover, he had a strong belief in
a providential destiny awaiting those of African origins and spoke sharply
against the view that slavery could be explained by God's displeasure with the
sins of primitive Africa. But the history so clear to him did not yield a clear
narrative, a story that could connect origins and destiny in a secure understanding of one's situation in the present, for the narrative was overwhelmed
by the counternarrative of the dominant culture. To be sure, Delany seems
aggressively assured in "The Political Destiny of the Colored Race on the

American Continent" when he promises that "our object, then, shall be to place before you our true position in this country (the United States), the improbability of realizing our desires, and the sure, practicable, and infallible remedy for the evils we now endure" (327). But his remedy was anything but sure, and *The Condition* is important as an example of historical writing in that it demonstrates Delany's struggle both with and against narrative as he addresses what he calls "a *broken people*" (*The Condition* 209). In *The Origin and Objects of Ancient Freemasonry* Delany constructs a historical narrative designed to establish the institutional authenticity of black Freemasonry while also calling into question the authority of white American Freemasonry. In *The Condition*, that kind of coherence proves elusive.

In part, the problem is that Delany's historical vision in *The Condition* is unavoidably reactive, requiring him to both accept and reject the terms of the dominant culture whose vision of history he is trying to resist. To write about both the condition and the emigration of "the colored people of the United States" required Delany to look to the historical identity of U.S. blacks for an argument to change their identity—to become something other than "the colored people of the United States." Involved in this transformation is a confrontation with the theories of individual and collective destiny that were so closely tied to the developing nationalism of the dominant culture. In *Types of Mankind*, for example, Gliddon and Nott look at what they consider the distinct races or species of humanity and argue that "the Creator has implanted in this group of races an instinct that, in spite of themselves, drives them through all difficulties, to carry out their great mission of civilizing the earth. It is not reason, or philanthropy, which urges them on; but it is destiny." The so-called Caucasian races, by this reasoning, were simply following the path of their destiny by dominating or even "supplanting" others, for "nations and races, like individuals, have each an especial destiny: some are born to rule, and others to be ruled. . . . Some races, moreover, appear destined to live and prosper for a time, until the destroying race comes, which is to exterminate and supplant them" (qtd. in Horsman 136–37). This is the vision of history that shaped Delany's—and he responded with a countervision of destiny.

The vision of black destiny that Delany presents in *The Condition* is various and in some ways contradictory. In a two-paragraph chapter titled "The United States Our Country," Delany seems clear on his position. Noting that "our common country is the United States," he asserts, "We are Americans, having a birthright citizenship—natural claims upon the country—claims common to all others of our fellow citizens—natural rights, which may, by virtue of unjust laws, be obstructed, but can never be annulled. Upon these do we place ourselves, as immovably fixed as the decrees of the living God." Indeed, in the preface, he asserts of "the colored people" that "their feelings, tastes, predilections, wants, demands, and sympathies, are identical, and homogeneous with those of all other Americans" (8). "From here," he asserts with as great authority as Douglass assumes for this issue elsewhere, "will we not be driven by any policy that may be schemed against us" (48). In fact, though, Delany does argue that African Americans have been driven out by policy schemed against them—notably, the Fugitive Slave Law, to which I will return shortly. "The policy is against us," he asserts, and "it is useless to contend against it" (157). He notes, to be sure, that "to advocate the emigration of the colored people of the United States from their native homes, is a new feature in our history, and at first view, may be considered objectionable, as pernicious to our interests" (159–60), but he counters those objections carefully.

But, while doing so, he seems to hold to his original position. In a critical discussion of Liberia, for example, Delany notes that it is "foreign to the designs of the writer of ever making that country or any other out of America, his home" (168).[16] Somewhat later, as he discusses emigration, he asserts, "That the continent of America seems to have been designed by Providence as an asylum for all the various nations of the earth, is very apparent" (171). "Upon the American continent," he states, "we are determined to stay, in spite of every odds against us. What part of the great continent shall our destination be—shall we emigrate to the North or South?" (173). Significantly, of course, Delany extends his vision from the United States to the Americas generally; as Levine has argued, Delany relocates "the black nationalist project of self-help from within the borders of the ever-expanding United States to the larger terrain of the Americas, specifically Central and South America and the Caribbean, . . . emphasizing the ways in which race challenges the very idea of the bordered nation" (*Martin Delany* 63–64). But it should be noted as well that Delany concludes the book with an appendix that presents an argument for leaving not only the United States but the Americas generally, and promoting a colony in Africa. "The land is ours," he asserts in the closing sentences of the book, "there it lies with inexhaustible resources; let us go and possess it. In Eastern Africa must rise up a nation, to whom all the world must pay commercial tribute" (214). To some extent one sees in these various visions of destiny and place the marks of hurried composition, which may explain the inclusion of an appendix from another time in his life, albeit a time to which he would return when embarking on his journey to Africa. But the various visions seem to speak against each other, undermining the very destiny Delany means to define.

Behind these visions of destiny, though, are alternate interpretations of history—which are, at root, different ways of reading the present. And this, I suggest, is Delany's primary concern: to reread the present and thereby guide it toward a different future. As Delany approaches the subject of emigration, he changes the historical grounds for his argument: "That there have been people in all ages under certain circumstances, that may be benefited by emigration, will be admitted" (159). Throughout *The Condition*, though, De-lany demonstrates an awareness that his readers will resist his message on both ideological and practical grounds, as illustrated by one "colored lady of intelligence" who asked, "Do you suppose that I would go in the woods to live for the sake of freedom?" (185). The reviews of the book focused on what the readers took to be Delany's ideological sins—the advocacy of emigrationism, the often sharp criticism of white Americans, northern as well as southern, abolitionist as well as proslavery. In the *Pennsylvania Freeman* of April 29, 1852, Oliver Johnson attacked the book on these grounds, adding, "We could wish that, for his own credit, and that of the colored people, it had never been published" (qtd. in Levine, *Martin Delany* 69). Garrison, less harsh, nev-ertheless was critical of the book's emigrationist stance and particularly of its separatist vision, and argued that Delany was playing into the hands of the American Colonization Society. Garrison worried about the "tone of despon-dency, and an exhibition of the spirit of caste, in the concluding portion of this otherwise instructive and encouraging work"; and he warned that "his arguments for a removal have long since been anticipated by the Colonization Society" (*Liberator*, May 7, 1852, 74). Douglass failed to review the book at all, a decision that Delany found significant in and of itself. Signaling his antici-pation of such responses, Delany set as his task, in effect, to rewrite the historical narrative that placed African Americans where they were in order to argue that they should now go somewhere else. The changing visions of destiny in *The Condition* mark the various stages of this historical revision.

As Delany was critical of Lewis's use of his sources, one might expect to encounter greater methodological integrity in *The Condition*. To some extent, this is the case, but Delany's real complaint against Lewis was his patchwork of sources and his habit of falling into error. *The Condition* is open to some of the same charges, as Garrison's response indicates. Delany occasionally cites his sources—for example, his reliance on David Ramsay's *The History of the*

American Revolution (1789) in one of his early chapters. Generally, though, Delany cites sources for rather uncontroversial information while leaving unsupported his more striking claims. But while acknowledging that *The Condition* quickly grew from the intended pamphlet to a book, and that it was written and published quickly (indeed, he did not even see the proofs before publication, which added to his defensive response to negative reviews), Delany recognizes the need to address the source of his history. In addition to references specifically cited in the text, Delany devotes a paragraph of his preface to a discussion of his sources:

> Many of the distinguished characters referred to in this work, who lived in former days, for which there is no credit given, have been obtained from various sources—as fragments of history, pamphlets, files of newspapers, obsolete American history, and some from Mrs. Child's Collection. Those of modern date, are living facts known to the writer in his travels through the United States, having been from Canada and Maine to Arkansas and Texas. The origin of the breast-works of New Orleans, the writer learned in that city, from old colored men in 1840, and subsequently, from other sources; as well as much useful information concerning that battle, from *Julien Bennoit*, spoken of in the work. He has before referred to it some five or six years ago, through the columns of a paper, of which he was then editor, and not until subsequently to his narrating the same facts in these columns, was he aware that it was ever mentioned in print, when he saw, on the 3d day of March, on looking over the contributions of the "Liberty Bell," a beautiful annual of Boston, the circumstances referred to by DAVID LEE CHILD, Esq., the particulars of which will be found in our version.

What is interesting here is the variety of Delany's sources. The Childs, both involved in the antislavery movement, were nearly as important to Delany in 1852 as Lydia Maria Child would be to William Wells Brown when he included one of Child's stories as a plot line in his fictive narrative *Clotel*. The antislavery movement, like Freemasonry, provided an institutional base for the documentation and reinterpretation of alternate histories. Equally significant is Delany's emphasis on his own travels, and his insistence that he had learned of the "origin of the breast-works of New Orleans" from "old colored men" long before he read about them in the work of David Child. Delany here gives priority to the experience of history, the history carried by the individuals who have lived to see and participate in it.

Individual experience is of tremendous importance to Delany in this work, in which each individual is presented as a representative, an embodiment, of history. Indeed, the heart of *The Condition* as a work of history is Delany's extensive attention to the individual achievement of black Americans—directly to establish the right of citizenship of black Americans, and indirectly to lay the foundation for his argument for emigration. From an overview of the "Claims of Colored Men as Citizens of the United States," in which he examines black invention and labor investment—drawing from many historical sources, which he identifies and quotes with reasonable care—Delany then considers more specific examples of African American contributions to the United States. Beginning with a chapter called "Colored American Warriors," in which he reprints Jackson's proclamation, taken from Nell's original historical pamphlet, Delany then proceeds to list various prominent African Americans in virtually all areas of social life: "Capacity of Colored Men and Women as Citizen Members of Community"; "Practical Utility of Colored People of the Present Day as Members of Society—Business Men and Mechanics"; "Literary and Professional Colored Men and Women"; "Students of Various Professions"; "A Scan at Past Things," a consideration of those "who formerly occupied prominent business positions, and by dint of misfortune or fortune, have withdrawn" (137); "Late Men of Literary, Professional and Artistic Note"; and "Farmers and Herdsmen." Delany's method in these chapters amounts to a collective biography of various men, along with notably few women, of achievement. As I observed in chapter 1, notice of individual achievement was a prominent feature in African American historical writing, a point I will discuss in greater detail in chapter 3. Delany's collective biography is long and includes impressive variety.[17] As Garrison noted in his review of the book, the biographical chapters of *The Condition* are quite effective: "The sketches he has made of several literary and professional colored men and women are not only authentic and highly interesting, but will greatly surprise those, who, having been taught to consider the colored population as a very inferior race, are profoundly ignorant as to all such instances of intellectual power, moral worth, and scientific attainment" ("New Publications" 74). As Delany indicates more than once in *The Condition*, among those "profoundly ignorant" of black American achievement are black Americans themselves.

Certainly, Delany argues that African Americans must battle ignorance with education; more pointedly, though, he contends that black Americans must master the systemic operations of learning, the means by which learning leads to power over history. But Delany's chapters on African American achievements are followed immediately by one titled "National Disfranchisement of Colored People," in which he notes that the various achievements have come to naught, given the effect of the Fugitive Slave Law. Delany begins this chapter simply by reprinting "the Act of Congress, known as the 'Fugitive Slave Law,' for the benefit of the reader, as there are thousands of the American people of all classes, who have never read the provisions of this enactment; and consequently, have no conception of its enormity" (147).[18] He then argues that the Constitution does not recognize the equality of all people and that the Fugitive Slave Law extends this distinction, making all black Americans "slaves in the midst of freedom, waiting patiently, and unconcernedly—indifferently, and stupidly, for masters to come and lay claim to us, trusting to their generosity, whether or not they will own us and carry us into endless bondage" (155). The Fugitive Slave Law, Delany asserts, is the clearest of the many manifestations of a fissure between the expressed ideals of the United States and the political and legal application of those ideals. This is what complicates the historical narrative Delany wants to construct, for having documented the histories of individuals that collectively argue for recognition of citizenship and equality, he draws out the underlying issue, that of power. "By their literary attainments," Delany says earlier in the book, white Americans "are the contributors to, authors and teachers of, literature, science, religion, law, medicine, and all other useful attainments that the world now makes use of." "These," he argues, "are the means by which God intended man to succeed: and this discloses the secret of the white man's success with all of his wickedness, over the head of the colored man, with all of his religion" (45). In effect, white Americans have constructed a history that claims the authority of Providence by appropriating "the means by which God intended man to succeed." Acceptance of that historical narrative by black Americans—for example, the belief that "the Constitution makes no distinction, but includes in its provisions, all the people alike"—would amount to "blind absurdity" (154). As Glenn Hendler has argued, the primary feature of Delany's self-construction as a public figure was "his tendency to push at the limits of the actually existing American public sphere, to transgress and rearticulate hegemonic norms of civility in order to reveal them as merely national norms" (81). But this exposure of the national boundaries of "hegemonic norms of civility" was directed ultimately to the project of giving "public and institutional form to the racialized sentiments at the affective core of his political thought" (Hendler 81), to reestablish those norms on black national grounds. What is needed, Delany argues, are black Americans who can use the same divinely intended "means" toward different ends, a different history. As he put it in an 1852 letter to Frederick Douglass, "I desire that our people have light and information upon the available means of bettering their condition; this they must and shall have. We never have, as heretofore, had any settled and established policy of our own—we have always adopted the policies that white men established for themselves without considering their applicability or adaptedness to us. No people can rise in this way. We must have a position, independent of anything pertaining to white men as nations" (Ripley 4:127–28). The task of establishing a specifically black national policy, however, required black Americans to attend carefully to the racial politics of historical representation—to account, as Delany noted of an article "giving a statistic summary of the five states of CENTRAL AMERICA," for "the peculiar *Anglo-Saxon prejudices* of the writer" and to remember that "wherever found, this same *Anglo-Saxon* race, is the most inveterate enemy of the *colored races*, of whatever origin" (Ripley 4:126).

But although he separates himself from this natural enemy, Delany does not abandon the task of considering the "applicability or adaptedness" of the white American social order to the needs of an envisioned black national polity. Indeed, he goes to great lengths to connect African American history to the historical narrative most immediately available, making the emigration of black Americans to other regions an extension and appropriation of—rather than a break from—the white national mythology. Approaching the subject of emigration, for example, Delany notes that there is historical precedent for such a move, offering as examples "the Exodus of the Jews from Egypt to the land of Judea; . . . the expedition of Dido and her followers from Tyre to Mauritania; and . . . the ever memorable emigration of the Puritans, in 1620, from Great Britain, the land of their birth, to the wilderness of the New World, at which may be fixed the beginning of emigration to this continent as a permanent residence" (159). As his handling of "the ever memorable emigration of the Puritans" indicates, the developing national mythology provides Delany with both a political and a providential framework for African American emigration—the latest type of the biblical exodus from Egypt. Even one of his most assertive and prominent claims—that those of African origin "are a *superior race*"—Delany takes from the argument of "our oppressors," who, "when urging us to go to Africa, tell us that we are better adapted to the climate than they" (202). Indeed, one of Delany's sources for his brief overview of the European colonization of the American continent, David Ramsay's *The History of the American Revolution* (1789), presents this same argument to explain the "imagined necessity" of slavery, the view that "a great part of the low country in several of the provinces must have remained without cultivation, if it had not been cultivated by black men" (23). The reason that the South relied more heavily on slavery than the North, Ramsay asserts, had less to do with "religious principles" than with "climate, and local circumstances." Blacks were simply more capable of working in the southern regions than were whites, according to Ramsay, because "there is a physical difference in the constitution of these varieties of the human species. The latter secrete less by the kidnies, and more by the glands of the skin than the former. This greater degree of transpiration renders the blacks more tolerant of heat, than the whites. The perspirable matter, thrown off by the former, is more foetid than that of the latter. It is perhaps owing to these circumstances, that blacks enjoy better health, in warm and marshy countries, than whites" (23).[19] Delany presents substantially the same argument, noting that "colored people can and do stand warm climates better than whites," but that "they also stand *all other* climates, cold, temperate, and modified, that the white people can stand." In this way blacks are established by "our oppressors own showing" as a superior race "endowed with properties fitting us for *all parts* of the earth." "Of course," Delany concludes, "this proves our right and duty to live wherever we may *choose*; while the white race may only live where they *can*" (202).

Black national destiny, then, involves the choice of the appropriate theater for its realization. Delany's argument for leaving the United States is not a denial of African American claims of citizenship but rather an assertion that the United States is not, in fact, what it claims to be and that therefore the nation's ideals of political economy must be relocated both racially and geographically. The Fugitive Slave Law, Delany argues, "is the law of the land and must be obeyed; and we candidly advise that it is useless for us to contend against it. To suppose its repeal, is to anticipate an overthrow of the Confederate Union; and we must be allowed an expression of opinion, when we say, that candidly we believe, the existence of the Fugitive Slave Law *necessary* to the continuance of the National Compact" (157). But Delany follows immediately by drawing a distinction between the "National Compact" and the national principles to which he expresses devotion. "We say necessary to the continuance of the National Compact," Delany notes, but "certainly we will not be understood as meaning that the enactment of such a Law was *really* necessary, or as favoring in the least this political monstrosity of the THIRTY-

FIRST CONGRESS of the UNITED STATES OF AMERICA—surely not at all; but we speak logically and politically, leaving morality and right out of the question—taking our position on the acknowledged popular basis of American Policy; arguing from premise to conclusion" (157). This distinction between the nation as it is, or the land of "*facts* as they really are" (157), and the nation as it claims to be, or the realm of "morality and right," allows Delany to establish a historical crossroads of sorts, with one path leading to national principles, and one leading to the subversion of those principles—the misuse of "the means by which God intended man to succeed"—in the name of policy. "There are no people who ever lived," Delany asserts, who "love their country and obey their laws as the Americans" (156). This seemingly admirable quality, though, enables the nation to go down the path of policy over principle—basically, to abandon its providential history by falsely ascribing divine authority to its policies: "Their country is their Heaven—their Laws their Scriptures—and the decrees of their Magistrates obeyed as the fiat of God" (156). Heaven reduced to political culture, Scripture supplanted by the laws supporting the system of slavery, God overruled by magistrates—the United States, Delany argues, has confused sacred and profane history.

Delany, then, like other antebellum African American historians, looks to reexamine the relation between sacred and profane history and to thereby construct at once an argument against racism and an argument for African destiny. Consider again Delany's claim that "the continent of America seems to have been designed by Providence as an asylum for all the various nations of the earth," which he presents toward the end of his chapter on the emigration of "colored people of the United States," the chapter that ends with his determination to stay on the American continent. Delany first presents a history of the emigration of the various nations to the continent, "either as adventurers and speculators, or employed seamen and soldiers," "among the earliest and most numerous class" of which "were those of the African race" (171). Delany then extends further back into history with a remarkable claim similar in its way to Lewis's attempt to establish Native Americans as one of the tribes of Israel: "It is now ascertained to our mind, beyond a peradventure, that when the continent was discovered, there were found in Central America, a tribe of the black race, of fine-looking people, having characteristics of color and hair, identifying them originally of the African race—no doubt being a remnant of the Africans who, with the Carthaginian expedition, were adventitiously cast upon this continent, in their memorable excursion to the 'Great Island,' after sailing many miles distant to the West of the Pillars of

Hercules" (172). Delany offers no support for this claim, allowing it to stand as it is, and to serve as the framework for his providential claims:

> We are not inclined to be superstitious, but say, that we can see the "finger of God" in all this; and if the European race may with propriety, boast and claim, that this continent is better adapted to their development, than their own father-land, to claim the superior advantages to the African race, to be derived from this continent. But be that as it may, the world belongs to mankind—his common Father created it for his common good—his temporal destiny is here; and our present warfare, is not upon European rights, nor for European countries; but for the common rights of man, based upon the great principles of common humanity—taking our chance in the world of rights, and claiming to have originally more right to this continent, than the European race. (172)

Here Delany takes the other path of the historical crossroads, arguing for the rights to which the dominant culture claims devotion, having distinguished those rights from U.S. policy, here presented as a political appropriation of universal ideals in the name of European interests. In effect, the American Revolution was the foreground for an appropriation of ideals that now must be reenvisioned in a nation not yet formed.

The *Official Report of the Niger Valley Exploring Party* might be considered the prehistory of this envisioned nation, a nation formed directly in response to the slaveholding United States. In section three of the book, "History of the Project," Delany outlines a history of the political battles in the United States between black abolitionists and white colonizationists. Here Delany explains that, having "formed the design of going to Africa, the land of my ancestry" in his youth, a design he "never abandoned," he had, in concert with "a number of select intelligent gentlemen (of African descent, of course)," avoided the subject of African colonization to avoid compromising black Americans "to the avowed enemies of the race" (32–33). "It was a matter of mere policy" of this group, Delany explains, "to confine their scheme to America (including the West Indies), whilst they were the leading advocates of the regeneration of Africa" (33). That regeneration, as outlined in the *Official Report*, involves an imperialist colonization of Africa and the transformation of the several nations of the continent into a single nation somewhat resembling the United States.[20] "Africa, to be regenerated," Delany argues, "must have a national character, and her position among the existing nations of the earth will depend mainly upon the high standard she may gain compared with them in all her relations, morally, religiously, socially, politically, and commercially" (111). The civilization Delany has in mind is explicitly Christian, for "Christianity certainly is the most advanced civilization that man ever attained to." But Delany means to apply the lessons learned from the failure of the United States: namely, that in order for Christianity, "wherever propagated in its purity, to be effective, law and government must be brought in harmony with it—otherwise it becomes corrupted, and a corresponding degeneracy ensues, placing its votaries even in a worse condition than the primitive" (109). Accordingly, the success of the envisioned African civilization "must be carried out by proper agencies, and these agencies must be a *new element* introduced into their midst, possessing all the attainments, socially and politically, morally and religiously, adequate to so an important an end" (110). The only adequate "agencies," Delany reasons, are "the *descendants of Africa.*" "A part of the most enlightened of that race in America," he therefore asserts, "design to carry out these most desireable measures by the establishment of social and industrial settlements among them [Africans], in order at once to introduce, in an effective manner, all the well-regulated pursuits of civilized life" (110).

Delany's attention to "the most enlightened" of those of African descent in the United States and his colonizationist perspective in general indicate the cracks in his historical edifice. Moreover, Delany is aware of the fact that this scheme for the emigration of the select to colonize Africa can be viewed as an abandonment of U.S. blacks: "The descendants of Africa in North America will doubtless, by the census of 1860, reach five millions; those of Africa may number two hundred millions. I have outgrown, long since, the boundaries of North America, and with them have also outgrown the boundaries of their claims. I, therefore, cannot consent to sacrifice the prospects of two hundred millions, that a fraction of five millions may be benefitted, especially since the measures adopted for the many must necessarily benefit the few" (111). One wonders what has become of the "old colored men" from whom Delany learned in New Orleans, those he includes and claims to embody in the historical record; one wonders about the many lessons he has learned from individuals in his travels throughout the United States. To be sure, he considers the rising African civilization to be a blow against the slaveholding United States, particularly as it develops an agricultural market that includes cotton. But his historical vision, focusing as it does on destiny, leaves many questions unanswered, many lives unaccounted for, in the U.S. present.

In short, Delany looks to Africa to provide narrative closure to African American history, though not without tension. Calling his plan "the grandest prospect for the regeneration of a people that ever was presented in the history of the world," Delany comes to a vision of destiny familiar in African American historical writing: "Princes shall come out of Egypt; Ethiopia shall soon stretch out her hands unto God" (122). But the princes, it seems, have come out of Egypt by way of the United States, perhaps emphasizing the significance of the role of Egypt in Delany's history of Freemasonry. In one of the declarations that have made him an important figure in black nationalist thought, Delany writes, "*Africa for the African race, and black men to rule them*" (121). In the next sentence, he clarifies what should be self-evident: "By black men I mean, men of African descent who claim an identity with the race" (121). Delany's clarification here, along with his emphasis on the most enlightened of the race, serves primarily (regardless of his intentions) to identify the limits of history, limits of which he was very much aware.

In *The Condition* Delany is at once trying to create an ideologically defined community and arguing for the destiny of that community, once formed. Delany tells the story of "a *broken people*," gathering together the pieces of a story that remains to be told, finding in the fragments the materials for a possible vision. Piecing together those fragments was a matter of rejoining modern and ancient history, the developing story of Africans in American history and the largely ignored history of ancient African civilization. As Sterling Stuckey has put it, Delany's "ability to see examples of black genius in the contemporary world was a factor in his conviction that the genius of his people was a reality in ancient history and might again help shape the destiny of humanity" (*Slave Culture* 229), a project that relied on the services of the African American historian.

At the same time that Delany considered this African scheme, he offered another history, in the form of fiction, in his serially published novel *Blake*, in which he presents a different reading of the providential narrative extending from Africa to slavery to regeneration. Fiction provided Delany with the freedom he needed to account for the history beyond the notable lives he could document, even by experience. Through *Blake*, as I have argued elsewhere, Delany could imagine a community not yet realized, and in that way formulate an ideological map of destiny, gathering together a fragmented community under the banner of revolutionary resistance to the mechanisms and assumptions of a white supremacist culture.[21] In *The Condition*, that fragmented community remains beyond the reach of history and can only be recorded in its fragmented state. The imagined community of *The Condition* is accessible only by an argument for collective mission and destiny joined with an argument about the uselessness of any history contextualized and contained by a white supremacist culture. *The Condition* is, in fact, important as an example of historical writing in that it addresses the history embodied by individual lives, looks for a larger narrative capable of accounting for those histories, and struggles with the many untold stories of those beyond documentation and recognizable achievement. Delany *identifies* the fragmentation of black life by exposing the incoherence of the American system, and with this identification Delany then identifies black nationalism as that which results from the fragmentation—indeed, that which resides *in* the fragmentation. He examines, in short, the structures of oppression—revealed as much by the terms of African American achievement as by such actions as the Fugitive Slave Law—so as to locate history in, to borrow Richard Wright's memorable phrase, "the forms of things unknown."

William C. Nell: Sites of Memory and
Liberation Historiography

I have noted that William Wells Brown complained in 1860 that "you look in vain to Bancroft and other historians for justice to the colored." In 1867, though, Brown reprinted in *The Negro in the American Rebellion* a paragraph from the seventh volume of Bancroft's history, published in 1858, where there is the comment that "history" should not "forget to record" the presence of African American soldiers at the battle of Bunker Hill (7:421). One cannot know whether Bancroft was once in danger of forgetting to record this, but the point Brown made in 1860 is well taken: Bancroft and others certainly forgot to record other African American contributions to the establishment and development of the United States. We do know, however, that in 1858 Theodore Parker wrote to Bancroft praising William C. Nell's *The Colored Patriots of the American Revolution* and remarking on the service of African Americans at Bunker Hill. If Nell did inspire Bancroft's brief mention of black soldiers, as Whittier inspired Nell to write his history, then one might note that African American historical writing was in fact having an effect on the dominant historical narrative of the United States then under construction; but one might note as well that Brown chooses to quote Bancroft's brief and rather bland notice rather than Nell's history. Indeed, when Brown performs the usual service of reprinting Jackson's speech to the men of color, the evidence suggests that he takes it not from Nell or other African American sources but from George Livermore's *An Historical Research Respecting the Opinions of the Founders of the Republic on Negroes as Slaves, as Citizens, and as Soldiers*, published in 1862, a work Brown refers to in his preface to *The Negro in the American Rebellion* as "the ablest work ever published on the early history of the negroes of this country."[22] Delany, on the other hand, relies heavily on Nell's original pamphlet in his chapter on "colored American warriors," quoting it at length, and taking Jackson's address directly from *The Colored Patriots* (*The Condition* 76). And Nell notices Delany in turn, mentioning him by name and alluding to *The Condition* in a footnote in his revised 1855 preface.[23] From Whittier to Nell to Parker to Bancroft to Brown, or from Nell to Delany to Nell again, the attempt to (re)shape the historical narrative was in its early stages, though there was hardly a genuinely reciprocal relation between the two historical schools.

The difference between these loosely interwoven strands of historical memory and a genuinely integrated history is a difference Nell characteristically worked to eliminate. Nell's father, William G. Nell, was one of the most prominent members of Boston's black community. One of the founders of the Massachusetts General Colored Association, and a member of the African Baptist Church, the elder Nell knew David Walker and, as James Oliver Horton has written, "was active as a black leader mainly prior to 1830, and was chiefly concerned with separate black action and organization." His son, on the other hand, "assumed a leading role after 1830 and pursued integrationist ends and means" (Horton 46–47). Various commentators have identified as a shaping experience in the younger Nell's life his exclusion from consideration for the Franklin Medal for scholastic achievement, and his exclusion also from the dinner honoring the medal winners, except as a waiter (Horton 47). "As a boy of fourteen in Lyman Beecher's church in 1831," Horton reports, the future historian "was asked by his Sunday school teacher about his plans for adulthood. Nell replied, 'What is the use of my trying to be somebody? I can never be anything but a nigger anyway'" (47). In fact, his accomplishments would prove impressive by any measure. Involved in self-help organizations from an early age,[24] Nell became an apprentice in the *Liberator* office and became one of Garrison's closest African American colleagues. As Roy E. Finkenbine has noted, Nell's contribution to the *Liberator* included "writing articles, supervising the paper's Negro Employment Office, corresponding with other abolitionists, and representing Gar-

rison at various antislavery functions" ("Nell" 1980). He became publisher
(though more a printer than publisher) of the *North Star* when Douglass
started the paper, though eventually he returned to Boston and the *Liberator*
(and tensions between him and Douglass would at one point lead the latter to
refer to Nell as a bitter enemy).[25] He ran (unsuccessfully) for the Massachusetts legislature and devoted many years as a leader in various integration
movements in Boston; he was, by 1855, "instrumental in the integration of
Boston schools" (Horton 49).[26]

As Leonard I. Sweet has noted, Nell was an "indefatigable optimist" who
"crusaded almost as hard against separationist tendencies within the black
community as he did against slavery" (144), but Nell's devotion to integration
was neither naive nor simple. A central feature of his thought, indeed, was the
recognition of the need for the collective effort of an African American community shaped by oppression.[27] Certainly, Nell was capable of great faith in
the natural integration of an educated class, arguing in an 1841 speech that "it
has been a fault with a majority of us, that we have failed to identify ourselves
as members of the one great human family," and suggesting that "it is natural
that persons of like taste should associate with each other; let us, therefore,
prove ourselves men, in literature, philosophy, science, and the arts, and
those who love them will welcome us to their side" ("Speech of Wm. C. Nell").
Nell knew from experience, though, that prejudice could still overrule the
natural associations of taste. In a letter to Garrison published in the *Liberator*
in 1848, Nell told the story of his and Douglass's attempt to attend an anniversary celebration of Franklin's birthday. On arriving, he reports, "we were
called *intruders*, and told, that 'it was a violation of the roles of society for
colored people to associate with whites,' and were threatened ejectment by
the police." Once they were finally admitted, they became "the observed of all
observers," an experience that leads Nell to reflect on the distinctly different
experiences and modes of understanding available to black and white Americans: "It was a painful as well as triumphant hour for Douglass and myself, for
reasons which abolitionists hardly know how to appreciate. None but the
colored man, the immediate recipient of American pro-slavery hate, can fully
testify to the emotions excited by such a development" ("Progress of Justice
and Equality").

Nell was concerned particularly with the effects of prejudice on black
Americans, and his arguments for education were in fact arguments for shap-
ing a distinctive black American perspective into a focused political force.
When trying to secure funding for the publication of *Colored Patriots of the*

American Revolution, Nell wrote to white abolitionist Wendell Phillips: "I never felt more moved to accomplish any object than now to publish my Book and I have abundant reasons for knowing that it is needed and that it will pay for itself amply. Aside from the military facts, the other departments dove-tailed in [are] what will be attractive and instructive to Colored people, and anti-slavery friends. To . . . new converts they will be serviceable in the political campaign now sounding its Battle cry over the country" (Ripley 4:300). The book, Nell noted, would "set forth" "the question of *Colored* antislavery" and in that way contribute "towards general elevation" (301). This was a book in which knowledge was directed toward the needs of the present community, a book founded on the faith that "each name and every past has its use" (301). Nell, in short, worked to create a historical work capable of shaping a community and preparing that community for action. In the same 1841 speech in which he argues for the natural associations of taste, Nell presents also perhaps the central tenet of his thought, the "truth and force of Lord Bacon's sentiment, that 'Knowledge is power' " ("Speech of Wm. C. Nell"). Bancroft once said that "each page of history may begin and end with Great is God and marvelous are his doings among the children of men"; one could say that each page of Nell's history—the history he lived, and the history he wrote—begins and ends with Knowledge is Power.[28] "Knowledge," Nell argued in 1841, "is the foundation of a people's prosperity"; "knowledge will excite in us a spirit of enterprise"; "by the acquisition of knowledge, the people will be prepared for any emergency that may await them"; and, signifi-cantly, the results of knowledge will "thereby compel this guilty nation to acknowledge the debt she owes her oppressed sons and daughters" ("Speech of Wm. C. Nell").[29]

Nell knew that knowledge can give power and it can take it away; accord-ingly, parallel to his view that "we must be a reading people" ("Speech of Wm. C. Nell"), his life was an argument that African Americans must also be a *writing* people. "Let light be shed to dispel the mist of ignorance," Nell argued, "and it will be remembered 'that we are Americans; that we have a claim to the soil for whose independence our fathers struggled by the white man's side, in the contest of '76. The services then rendered, invest us with a right to freedom, in addition to the claims of our common nature' " ("Speech of Wm. C. Nell"). *Colored Patriots* concludes with this argument as well: in that book's penultimate chapter, Nell reprints the Address of the Colored National Convention to the People of the United States, from the Rochester, New York, convention of 1853, an address that insisted on the right of African

Americans to be recognized as citizens, the original of which includes once again Jackson's proclamations among its evidence for recognized citizenship. But Nell knew that "light" would not be "shed to dispel the mist of ignorance" unless African Americans themselves were both enlightened and engaged in writing. Nell concludes his excerpt of the 1853 address with the paragraph in which the convention comments on the cultural politics of representation: "We feel that the imputations cast upon us, for our want of intelligence, morality, and exalted character, may be mainly accounted for by the injustice received at your hands. What stone has been left unturned to degrade us? What hand has refused to fan the flame of popular prejudice against us? What American artist has not caricatured us? What wit has not laughed at us in our wretchedness? What songster has not made merry over our depressed spirits? What press has not ridiculed and contemned us? What pulpit has withheld from our devoted heads its angry lightning, or its sanctimonious hate?" (375–76).[30] The entire address, in fact, is a response to the selective historical memory of white Americans. Driven by the economy of the system of slavery—"the force of fifteen hundred million dollars"—"the *press*, the pulpit, and the platform . . . point their deadly missiles of ridicule, scorn and contempt at us" ("Address of the Colored National Convention"). Any effective response would require a differently constituted and differently motivated press—and it would require as well a determination to consider carefully the perspective by which historical records are kept, examined, and either used or ignored. In his approach to the American Revolution, accordingly, Nell directs his readers to revolutionary actions, and grounds for further action, that are beyond the pale of official history.

Perhaps the most striking example of this is Nell's reporting of a group of refugees who had "taken possession" of the abandoned Blount's Fort "some forty miles below the line of Georgia." "But little is yet known of that persecuted people," Nell says; "their history can only be found in the national archives at Washington. They had been held as slaves in the State referred to; but, during the Revolution, they caught the spirit of liberty,—at that time so prevalent throughout our land,—and fled from their oppressors." (256–57). "During forty years," this group had "effectually eluded or resisted all attempts to reenslave them," and a new generation had grown from the original refugees. The slaveholders finally "called on the president of the United States for assistance." When U.S. forces reach the fort, the community within is naturally "distressed at their situation"; but they are advised to hold firm by "an old patriarch, who had drank the bitter cup of servitude—one who bore on his person the visible marks of the thong, as well as the brand of his master upon his shoulder." The patriarch closes his speech "with the emphatic declaration, 'Give me liberty, or give me death!' " (259). And death is what is received, for the fort is bombed: eventually, a "dreadful explosion overwhelmed them," leaving "two hundred and seventy parents and children in the immediate presence of God, making their appeal for retributive justice upon the government which had murdered them, and the freemen of the North who sustained such unutterable crime" (261).

This reenactment and reconfiguration of the American Revolution leads Nell to his significant vision of community, a biblical vision of gathering together a scattered community that in many ways echoes John Winthrop's lay sermon aboard the *Arbella*, "A Model of Christian Charity." As Stephen Carl Arch has noted, "Winthrop indicates the prophetic nature of his sermon through his repeated use of the image of the 'scattered bones' that will be 'knit' together again in the future" (*Authorizing* 15). The image of scattered bones occurs in the book of Psalms and in Ezekiel, to which Winthrop refers, thus placing the errand into the wilderness within a larger prophetic framework. "Winthrop has cast himself in the role of prophet in this sermon," Arch explains; "an Ezekiel, he must breathe life into the scattered bones of England that stand before him on the deck of the *Arbella*; he must voice the words through which the community can redefine and reshape itself" (15–16). Nell, and African American historians throughout the nineteenth century, faced a similar task, and similarly drew on the image of a scattered community with similar hopes of drawing together the communal body. Indeed, Ezekiel's vision of a people suffering under God's judgment, of a God that operates in history, and of a divine presence that will make itself known to all nations when the scattered people are restored, is perhaps more appropriate to the African American vision of the fact and effects of enslavement and racial domination than it was to the Puritans and their white descendants as they faced the task of surviving (spiritually as well as physically) in what was to them a new world.

Nell's version of the scattered bones, though, is more physical and more horrific than Winthrop's application of the biblical image. As the community within Blount's Fort joins in resistance, they encounter the military force of government and the culture of slavery: "Many were crushed by the falling earth and timbers; many were entirely buried in the ruins. Some were horribly mangled by the fragments of timber and the explosion of charged shells that were in the magazine. Limbs were torn from the bodies to which they had been attached; mothers and babes lay beside each other, wrapped in that sleep which knows no waking" (261). This physical fragmentation is an apt image for the larger fragmentation of the African American community. As the narrative progresses, Nell's image picks up biblical echoes: "Their bones have been bleached in the sun for thirty-seven years, and may yet be seen scattered among the ruins of that ancient fortification" (262). Breathing life into those bones is the task of the historian, who finds the bones displaced in the nation's archives: "These facts are all found scattered among the various public documents which repose in the alcoves of our national library. But no historian has been willing to collect and publish them, in consequence of the deep disgrace which they reflect upon the American arms, and upon those who then controlled the government" (263). In short, Nell here connects metaphorically and methodologically the scattered bones that speak of an unfinished American Revolution and the scattered documents in the library of a nation formed by the false consciousness of that revolution.

Nell recognized that African American history required the revision of what is recognized as *knowledge* in order to shape historical memory into *power*, a cogent collective resistance to a "guilty nation." In an article titled "Pictures of American Slavery," published in the *Liberator* of January 5, 1855, the same year that *Colored Patriots* appeared, Nell presents an image of the power of historical memory. "One noble specimen of a man," Nell observes, "a few weeks since, made good his arrival in Canada. He had twice before escaped from slavery, but had been recaptured. Believing that 'the third time never fails,' he made another attempt, and safely reached Boston, and while walking down State street, over the spot where Attucks fell, and over which Sims and Burns were dragged back to slavery, he exhibited a pistol loaded and capped, declaring that he had resolved to die rather than be again any man's slave" (4). Here the American Revolution, represented by Attucks, joins the antislavery movement, represented by Sims and Burns, in a site of memory that becomes the site of militant resistance. One cannot know whether this "noble specimen of a man" was aware of the historical significance of the spot over which he exhibited his pistol and resolved to fight for his freedom; what is significant here is that Nell remembers, and that he performs the duty of a historian to gather together the events that make this a significant memory, one capable of speaking to the present.

Identifying the historical, ideological, and theological grounds for resistance is the task of African American liberation historiography—a body of work that attends to the scattered bodies and scattered documents that speak

of specific manifestations of dynamic history, history as the struggle for liberation. As Eric Sundquist has noted concerning Frederick Douglass's increasingly open militancy, "If the white postrevolutionary generations remained
paralyzed in the face of the fathers' ambiguous authority on the law of slavery, the black generations were, in fact, not yet *post*revolutionary at all. For
them in particular, the Age of Revolution—not just in the United States but
throughout the slaveholding New World—was far from over" (115). This revolution was tied to the demands of sacred history—an ongoing struggle often
referred to in the black press, as for example in an 1851 article reprinted in
Frederick Douglass' Paper, "The Characteristics of Christian Warriors." Referring to David's struggles as recorded in the Bible, the article states, "We
want just such noble-hearted Christians, men who feel their personal responsibility, men whose piety is fed from God, whose life is hid with Christ in God,
and who do not depend on the church for their ardor, but on Christ the
Savior, having his cause foremost, his love burning, the fire of his grace
carrying them individually onward" ("Characteristics"). The article's author
then takes the lesson to more recent times and the history of Cromwell's
battles, to return to the call for service with historical emphasis: "Now what
we need is Christian soldiers of this stamp; men who fight, not because others
fight, nor because they are in the Church merely, or go forward as the Church
goes forward, but because they are Christ's soldiers; because the great Cap-
tain of their salvation goes forward; because they feel their personal responsibility, and do not try to shirk it, but would walk with Christ, and live upon
Christ, and fight for Christ, and go through the world as Christ's soldiers,
though there were not another Christian living" ("Characteristics").

Working within a similar Christian framework, Nell looks for a moral
revolution that is defined by a history of moral violations. While always arguing against the separation of black and white efforts, Nell creates African
American history not simply in his choice of subjects (which he defends as a
"historical propriety" necessitated by the omission of African Americans
from the official stories) but also and more pointedly in his method, his
intervention into the record, and in his determination to identify "the necessity for a second revolution, no less sublime than that of regenerating public
sentiment in favor of Universal Brotherhood" (380). The invocation of "Universal Brotherhood" in Nell's work operates not as an imagined culmination
of a linear narrative but rather as a concept that finds its foundations in the
complex contingencies of the narrative fragments, and the fragmented narrative, that Nell presents. Distinguishing between the memory of "colored pa-

triots" that will follow from the second revolution and the history of the colored patriots that precedes revolutionary action (379), Nell identifies history as a performance equivalent to the fugitive who stands on the site where Crispus Attucks fell, (re)locating the imperatives of the present on the liberating sites of the past.

Nell presents his history, in fact, as the collaborative effort of an army of historical activists devoted to the cause of Universal Brotherhood. A call for subscribers to the book published in various issues of the *Liberator* in the spring and summer of 1855,[31] for example, presents a rather extensive list of contributors to the research on which Nell relied for the construction of this historical compilation. The call notes that "these facts have been gleaned from military records, State documents, private correspondence, and fireside conversations, confirmed by oral and written testimonies of John Hancock, Governor Eustis, the late Judge Story, Hon. Robert C. Winthrop, Hon. Tristam Burgess, Hon. Charles Pinckney, etc., etc., and by the tributes of Washington, Lafayette, Kosciusko, Thomas Jefferson, and Gen. Jackson." In this, Nell participates in the by now recognizable tradition of antislavery and African American historical writing by drawing on the official records of white America to tell the untold story of African American experience. But Nell extends his list farther still, noting his debt "for further interesting facts and testimonies to John G. Whittier, (the Bard of Freedom); Wendell Phillips, Esq.; J. W. C. Pennington, D.D.; William Howard Day, Esq.; Rev. Theodore Parker, Charles Lenox Remond, Hon. Charles Sumner, Prof. Wm. G. Allen, Lydia Maria Child, James McCune Smith, M.D.; Hon. Henry Wilson, J. Mercer Langston, Esq.; David Lee Child, Esq.; Rev. Daniel A. Payne, Hon. Anson Burlinggame, James M. Whitfield, (the Poet;) Robert Purvis, Esq.; Hon. J. R. Giddings, Rev. Henry Highland Garnet, Prof. Geo. B. Vashon, Edmund Jackson, Esq.; Robert Morris, Esq.; Rev. Amos G. Beman, Dr. M. R. Delany, William Wells Brown, Lewis and Milton Clark, Rev. Henry F. Harrington, the late Henry Bibb, Angelina J. Knox, Rev. John W. Lewis, Hon. Gerrit Smith, Wm. Yates, Esq.; Wm. J. Watkins, Esq.; and several others." Nell here presents a virtual who's who of prominent black and white antislavery activists representing a rather significant ideological range.

And out of the many comes a singular purpose, as Nell takes his readers back to the grounds of revolutionary action. Like the fugitive with loaded pistol in the streets of Boston, Nell in *Colored Patriots* joins the revolutionary past with the revolutionary needs of the present, gathering the historical material that provides a site of memory capable of shaping action—action to which all may contribute, "of every complexion, sect, sex and condition" (380). It is significant, after all, that the first sentences of *Colored Patriots* address not only history but also memory, discussing the petition to the Massachusetts legislature to appropriate funds for "a monument to the memory of CRISPUS ATTUCKS, the first martyr in the Boston Massacre of March 5th, 1770," reprinting both the petition and its signatures (including Nell's); and it is significant also that Nell includes in this discussion the fact that Thomas Sims and Anthony Burns were taken back to slavery from this spot, "both marching over the very ground that ATTUCKS trod" (18).[32] Nell, in effect, begins his history with the same historical memory he uses to mark the significance of the fugitive with loaded pistol vowing his determination to fight to the death. Presenting a history of this unsuccessful 1851 petition, Nell uses the arguments against it as a framework for his history of Attucks and of the Boston Massacre, drawing heavily for support on various historical witnesses (among them, Charles W. Botta, author of *History of the War of Independence of the United States*, originally published in Italian in 1808; a "tea party survivor"; John Adams, "counsel for the soldiers"; the historian David Ramsay; and George Washington). Responding to a defeated memorial, Nell constructs a different memorial in the pages of *Colored Patriots*. The call of this memory, Nell suggests in his conclusion, is particularly resonant for black Americans. "In that degree to which colored Americans may labor to hasten the day," he continues, "they will prove valid their claim to the title, 'Patriots of the Second Revolution'" (380). Defining the original "colored patriots," Nell identifies the ideological contours of the next generation of patriots for the next revolution.[33]

And he supports his case admirably. More than any African American work published before it, *Colored Patriots* is an astonishing achievement of historical research. As a reviewer for the *Kentucky Weekly News* noted, "The compiler of this work, a colored man, seems to have spared no labor in seeking out evidence of the faithfulness with which his people have borne their part, in the perilous periods of our history. He has ransacked Colonial, State and National records, and has succeeded in arraying quite a mass of testimony on the subject" ("Commendatory Notices"). Nell's history is to some extent a history of the historians who have come before, including attention to such figures as Walker and Cuffe and reprinted passages from the work of such figures as Pennington and Easton. By drawing a lengthy sketch of James Forten from a eulogy by Robert Purvis, or another of John B. Vashon from Martin Delany, Nell not only tells the story of history but also tells the story of African American historical writing.

Like Lewis's *Light and Truth, Colored Patriots* is rich with documentation sometimes only loosely knit together, though Nell's sudden transitions are more directed than Lewis's tend to be; like most African American historians, Nell presents biographical sketches of a great number of prominent black Americans, along with significant (and predictable) attention to such close allies as William Lloyd Garrison; like virtually all African American historians, Nell makes his central subject racial prejudice as a product of history. Throughout, he keeps his argument before the reader. He breaks into a biographical sketch of Paul Cuffe, for example, to exclaim, "How gratifying to humanity is this anecdote! and who, that justly appreciates human character, would not prefer Paul Cuffe, the offspring of an African slave, to the proudest statesman that ever dealt out destruction amongst mankind?" (80–81). Similarly, one reads that James Forten was "a *model*, not, as some flippant scribbler asserts, for what are called 'colored men,' but for all men" (181). And the recognized statesmen themselves speak for this cause. Nell inserts a brief anecdote titled "Patriots of the Olden Time" into his chapter on Massachusetts, between a section on the "Marshpee Indians" and one called "Loyalty of an African Benevolent Society." Here he offers a single-paragraph tacit jeremiad focusing on Samuel Adams, who refuses the "present of a female slave," insisting that if she enters his house it will be as a free woman (96).[34] As Paul Cuffe and Samuel Adams speak to one another across the pages, bearing witness to the cause of humanity and liberty, so Nell presents throughout the book a number of documents and incidents that say more together than they say individually, as if to winnow universal principles from the historically specific testaments of history.

But as Nell draws together the various documents that give voice to African American history, he demonstrates his awareness of the extent to which those documents can speak against his purposes. The source of Nell's lengthy sketch of Benjamin Banneker, as he informs the reader *after* presenting the biographical account, "is taken from a Memoir read before the Historical Society of Maryland, by John H. B. Latrobe." This memoir, Nell then remarks, "was undoubtedly published to serve the purposes of the American Colonization Society." But, Nell notes, history can be made to speak against its intended purpose—as in the case of Nell's source for the memoir: "Rev. John T. Raymond, a distinguished colored Baptist clergyman, issued an edition of the pamphlet, in the preface to which he says:—'I have snatched it from their [the colonizationists'] foul purpose, in order to produce a contrary effect. Our people are now too wise to be entangled in their meshes'" (211). Nell was less certain than Raymond that the battle with the colonizationists was wholly won in the minds of African Americans, but he shared Raymond's belief in the power of using historical writing by those who opposed his purposes "to produce a contrary effect."[35] Throughout *Colored Patriots* Nell relies on others to articulate his thesis, selecting his documents carefully, identifying and commenting on the sources, gradually gathering the accumulating effect of the various points made along the way. In all, *Colored Patriots* applies on a grand scale the method behind the frequent quotation of Jackson's proclamation: allowing history to speak for itself, amplifying that voice, and applying the principles of the message. *Colored Patriots* in this way is not only a history of events but also a history of historical understandings, misunderstandings, and distortions. As does Bancroft, Nell looks for the unity in the variety of history; more than Bancroft, Nell makes that search for unity a primary subject of his history.

Readers participate in the search as they read. In the section headed "Condition and Prospects," for example, Nell juxtaposes two significant documents: a passage from Easton's *Treatise* and excerpts from a "memorial" by J. Mercer Langston, presented to the General Assembly of Ohio on April 18, 1854. Born a slave in Virginia, Langston eventually graduated from Oberlin College and theology school (1849 and 1852, respectively) and became Ohio's first black lawyer.[36] From Easton, Nell quotes a passage of frustration over racial prejudice, in which Easton notes that "there can be no appeals made in the name of the laws of the country, or philanthropy, or humanity, or religion, that are capable of drawing forth any thing but the retort,—*you are a negro!*" (*Colored Patriots* 335; Easton 33). The passage is in Easton's highest rhetorical style, using the repeated refrain "*you are a negro*" juxtaposed to a list of achievements, notably in the American Revolution. Later in the *Treatise*, Easton augments this pattern, first in a passage that relies on the repetition of the word "nigger" (41), and later in a passage that rides on the repetition of the word "American" to conclude that "the claims the colored people set up, therefore, are the claims of an American" (49). Together, the three passages guide the reader from the fact of racial identification to Easton's exposure of the racist culture that capitalizes on that identification to, finally, the reapplication of national principles that must follow the exposure.[37] Nell, though, quotes only the first of these passages, thus emphasizing the juxtaposition of

African American contributions to the national struggle and the use of racial difference to deny those contributions.

With no clear transition, Nell follows this with an introduction to Langston's memorial by the Hon. Norton S. Townshend, who, "in submitting to the Senate a bill in accordance with the wish of the petitioners for equal suffrage, remarked, 'That the reasons were so ably set forth in the following memorial of J. Mercer Langston, that nothing further seemed to be required'" (336). The excerpts that follow present a case for citizenship, in many ways echoing that which Easton presents, though Langston focuses his case on a legal interpretation of the Constitution, quoting commentary from Chancellor Kent and the Hon. Mr. Baldwin of the U.S. Senate, and including a character reference from William H. Seward. Langston quotes also a passage from Whittier, the poet whom Nell cites as the inspiration for *Colored Patriots*, in which Whittier refers to those African Americans whose "bones whiten every stricken field of the Revolution" (339). Following the excerpts from the memorial, Nell notes that "Mr. Langston has since had satisfactory proof that colored men are regarded as citizens by a good portion of the Buckeyes," and reprints an "announcement" in which Langston notes his election to "clerk of Brownhelm township, by a very handsome majority, indeed" (341).

The two documents, Easton's and Langston's, speak to each other from across the years, from 1837 to 1854, Langston's serving as a response to Easton's—and as a sign of progress. Together, they echo and reinforce arguments presented elsewhere in *Colored Patriots*.[38] This is not to say that Nell offers a sanguine vision of progress, for Easton's role in this dialogue is as important as is Langston's, if only to place Langston's achievement in perspective. Indeed, in addressing the issue of prejudice, Nell, like Delany before him, is often as hard on black Americans as he is on whites, arguing that black Americans too often simply accept the limited opportunities made available to them and surrender to the expectations of a white supremacist culture. The differences between Nell's and Delany's arguments, though, are significant. In a passage that in some ways reads like a response to Delany's critique of white abolitionists, Nell suggests toward the end of his first chapter that "to those colored friends ... who constantly harp upon real or supposed derelictions of white Abolitionists, it is but seasonable to hint, that some of their own number are very indifferent to practical Anti-Slavery, and that, at the South, there are black, as well as white, slaveholders,—a fact teaching humility to both classes, while, at the same time, it proves the identity of both with the human family" (116). Nell does not here separate the issue of slavery from issues of race, nor does he argue against the prevalence and effects of racial prejudice. Rather, he argues for the necessity of a moral reading of history, one by which universal principles can guide the national community through the labyrinth of racial culture. "These Anti-Slavery tests are presented," he continues, "in the every-day routine of business and social life, and ofttimes prove severe trials, except to those of the genuine radical stamp" (116).

In many ways, *Colored Patriots* is the story of such tests and of the racist culture that shapes such tests. In relating the "interesting account of the trial and execution of a colored man, (said to have been one of the defenders of Fort Moultrie), which took place at Charleston in the year 1817," Nell reviews the evidence and then asserts, "the real proof, no doubt, was written in the color of his skin, and in the harsh and rugged lines of his face. He was found guilty" (239). He follows this by noting, first, that the man's lawyer argued for a new trial, and even tried to take the case beyond the regional courts, and Nell notes as well what this effort came to, and why: "Mr. C[rafts] then forwarded a representation of the case to the President of the United States, through one of the Senators of the State; but the Senator treated with levity the idea of interesting himself in behalf of the life of the negro" (240). This story of both personal and institutional prejudice—the story, as Nell observes, of "the white man's pride"—is the story that informs much of the history presented in *Colored Patriots*. But this story is representative also in that it calls attention to one white man's struggle against racist culture, guided by "motives of humanity," and in that it calls attention to the black prisoner's devotion to his ideals. "Modestly, but firmly" holding to "his proper charac-ter," the black prisoner proceeds to "vindicate not only his own innocence, but the moral equality of his race," forming a religious instruction group in the prison, and thereby representing "the triumph of mental energy over death and unmerited disgrace" (240–41). Noting that this man "had no phi-losophy with which to reason down the natural misgivings which may be supposed to precede a violent and ignominious dissolution of life," Nell compares him favorably with Socrates, and presents him as "a hero and a Christian" (242).[39]

Such stories abound in *Colored Patriots*, and suggest the mode of histori-cal understanding Nell constructs in this work. The philosophy of history in *Colored Patriots* is the philosophy that gradually emerges from several in-stances of individual heroism, often from unnamed historical agents. The various stories of prejudice and partial vision draw into sharper outline the features of a moral understanding of history; and this outline provides the framework for Nell's concluding discussion of "Conditions and Prospects." In his chapter on "elevation" in the "Conditions and Prospects" section, for example, Nell addresses the issue of racial separatism. He notes, for example, that "one argument in favor of Colored Conventions has been, that, in some States, the colored people are so oppressed by local customs, as to be apparently forbidden to have intercourse with the whites," which makes such Conventions necessary (365). Nell admits "that there is some plausibility in this statement," but adds that "it is only a superficial and not an enlarged view of the question" (365). Against such arguments, Nell tells of the success of the "equal school" movement in Massachusetts, which he credits to the existence of other integrated organizations, noting that "associations, like individuals, to a certain extent, are controlled by the surrounding atmosphere" (366). Similarly, Nell argues, the backwardness of an individual state should not be taken as an argument for separate associations: "Instead of their desiring the more advanced to come down to them, they should labor to come up themselves, that Illinois and Indiana, with their Black Laws repealed, and Pennsylvania, with her colored suffrage restored, may stand side by side with the more liberal and liberty-practicing States in other parts of the Union" (365–66). Nell looks for a union of action that is uncompromising in its expectations of the benefits of Universal Brotherhood and the standards by which brotherhood should be defined.

Like many—Delany among them—Nell accepted a conception of civilization largely associated with white America, and was not wholly successful in distinguishing the ideals from the racial ideology. "If colored genius will but imitate the successful examples among the whites," he suggests with more faith than grounds for hope, "the public will surely reward the persevering effort" (368). Like many others of his time and after, Nell could not escape the problem of arguing for advancement for all without implying, to contemporary audiences, the inferiority of some. Nell notes, for example, Henry Clay's pronouncement that God created racial differences, and that Clay argued that "it has been his divine pleasure to make the black man black and the white man white, and to distinguish them by other repulsive constitutional differences." Nell's response to this is that "so far as the conduct of some colored people is concerned, they are constantly strengthening that statement. It is possible so to deport ourselves, that the idea of color shall be forgotten. Do not let it be our fault, that the white people are for ever being reminded of the fact. We need not always give *color* to the idea" (368). Nell seems to accept too much of the argument that he means to denounce, especially as he presents this in a book whose existence is necessary precisely because African American moral actions, achievements, and sacrifices have been ignored.

It is, in fact, Nell's own action, the writing of this history of "patriots" identified in the title and throughout by their color, that brings another dimension to his comments about African American elevation. Indeed, he quotes Clay's comments only to show the source of Rufus Choate's remark that *"though the colored man should win Bunker Hills [sic], the color will cleave to him still"* (368). One of the first subjects covered in *Colored Patriots*, Bunker Hill now returns in a different context, seeming to undermine the argument to which Nell's history is devoted. What is one to make of this development? What is one to make of Nell's earlier observation that "in some engravings of the battle [of Bunker Hill], [Peter Salem] occupies a prominent position; but in more recent editions, his figure is *non est inventus*" (21). As Nell's argument for integration presses on to the ideal of acting in such a way that "the idea of color shall be forgotten," what is one to make of the many places throughout this book in which Nell has noted that the idea of color usually has been remembered in spite of the best efforts of African Americans, and remembered often in murderous ways? One might say that Nell holds to his ideal of a transcendent humanity as tenaciously as does the convicted prisoner whose story he tells—and that that prisoner's execution presses against the history Nell constructs with ominous urgency. Following this line of thought, one can then recast these questions, and begin by noting that the historical story Nell presents is one that demands a moral perspective. Nell strives for objectivity as much as Bancroft does; and his understanding of objectivity is as faulty as Bancroft's, though with greater justice. If one is writing a history about a field of events in which the very existence of the subject has been shaped by moral violations, then how can one approach that subject without the aid of a moral perspective, as shaped by those very events? And how can one hope to escape the circle of interpretation that one finds oneself in? In other words, what is the moral work of history as suggested by Nell's approach, and how does it function?

The answer to this, I suggest, can be found in a passage that is in many ways the ideological and methodological heart of *Colored Patriots*—a section called "The Black Saxons" in Nell's chapter on South Carolina. In a footnote, Nell identifies this section as being "from the writings of Lydia Maria Child" (247). "The Black Saxons" comes from Child's *Fact and Fiction: A Collection of Stories* (1846), the collection that also includes the story "The Quadroons," which William Wells Brown reprints, largely verbatim, in sections interspersed throughout *Clotel*. The story takes place during the War of 1812 and concerns a Mr. Duncan of Charleston, South Carolina, who became suspicious when virtually all of his slaves asked for a pass to attend a Methodist meeting and when he remembers that "the same thing had happened a few days before" (*Fact and Fiction* 192). Mr. Duncan is determined to discover what is going on, and "having purchased a complete suit of negro clothes, and a black mask well fitted to his face," attends the next meeting. There he discovers that the slaves are discussing their possible liberation by the British soldiers. Moreover, the slaves are debating what to do with their masters, with suggestions ranging from mercy to murder to the call to "ravish wives and daughters before their eyes, as they have done to *us!*" In the end, it is decided, "by a considerable majority, that in case the British landed, they would take their freedom *without* murdering their masters" (203). Mr. Duncan, who from the beginning of the story has been reading and thinking about Thierry's *History of the Norman Conquest*, in the end reflects that "a new significance seemed given to Wat Tyler's address to the insurgent labourers of *his* day: an emphatic, and most unwelcome application of *his* indignant question why serfs should toil unpaid, in wind and sun, that lords might sleep on down, and embroider their garments with pearl" (204). While these reflections, Child notes, "did not, so far as I ever heard, lead to the emancipation of his bondmen; . . . they did prevent his revealing a secret, which would have brought hundreds to an immediate and violent death" (204). Instead, he advises "the magistrates to forbid all meetings whatsoever among the coloured people until the war was ended" (204).

This is a fascinating story in many respects, and even more so when Nell makes it part of his history. At the end of the story, Child notes that the protagonist, Mr. Duncan, "visited Boston several years after [the events of the story took place], and told the story to a gentleman, who often repeated it in the circle of his friends. In brief outline it reached my ears" (204).[40] This is a story that, if true, was a part of oral culture before it became a part of written history. Traveling around a circle of friends, and reaching Child only in "brief outline," the story was communicated by gossip and inevitably carried the features of antislavery legend. Indeed, to accept this story as grounded in fact, one must buy the idea of a well-fitted "black mask" that, with the help of "negro clothes," is capable of keeping virtually all of the slaves on Mr. Duncan's plantation from recognizing the master. Constructed from a "brief outline," Child's story is not unlike many works of U.S. historical fiction of the nineteenth century, emphasizing the imaginative investigation of the past, and suggesting the ways in which the moral issues of the past are revealed in the imagination. One thinks of Hawthorne's "Wakefield," or his introduction to *The Scarlet Letter* in "The Custom House." But one should think also, in this case, of the tremendously influential work of Sir Walter Scott. As the title suggests, Child's story emphasizes the similarities between Anglo-Saxon history and African American history—a significant connection, for, as Reginald Horsman has demonstrated so thoroughly, "the concept of a distinct, superior Anglo-Saxon race, with innate endowments enabling it to achieve a perfection of governmental institutions and world dominance, was a product of the first half of the nineteenth century" (9). As Horsman notes, "By the time of the American Revolution Americans were convinced that Anglo-Saxon England before the Norman Conquest had enjoyed freedoms unknown since that date" (9). Duncan is reading the work of Augustin Thierry, who was, Horsman notes, "profoundly influenced" by Scott, and who "believed that the history of England for centuries after the Norman Conquest could be explained as a racial struggle" between Saxon and Norman.

Nell's use of this story is significant, in part because the revised preface that he used for the 1855 edition of *Colored Patriots* ends with an admiring allusion to Sir Walter Scott. "The production of this book," Nell notes in the preface, "like the labors of 'Old Mortality,' rendered immortal by the genius of Scott, I humbly trust will deepen in the heart and conscience of this nation the sense of justice, that will ere long manifest itself in deeds worthy a people who, 'free themselves,' should be 'foremost to make free'" (10). In his reprinting and revision of Child's "The Black Saxons," Nell returns to this sentiment indirectly, joining the history associated with Scott and with Anglo-Saxon nationalism in the United States to that of the enslaved. Nell edits Child's story considerably, though the remaining parts are reprinted largely verbatim, with minor if sometimes intriguing changes. In Nell's version, Mr. Duncan visits the meeting in disguise within the first paragraph, something that takes six pages in Child's version. In Child's second paragraph, Duncan reflects on his reading, observing that the Saxons "tamely submitted to their lot," though he quickly understands that, in fact, "they did not relinquish freedom without a struggle" (190–91). In fact, Duncan understands, one cannot know the full story, since "troubadours rarely sing of the defeated, and conquerors write their own History" (191). But Duncan remembers "Robin Hood and his bold followers, floating in dim and shadowy glory on the outskirts of history," and reflects that "doubtless they had minstrels of their own; unknown in princely halls, untrumpeted by fame, yet singing of their exploits in spirit-stirring tones, to hearts burning with a sense of wrong" (191). Certainly, it is interesting that Nell omits this reflection on the politics of history, particularly as he tries to bring the "outskirts of history" toward the center of attention, recording the history "unknown in princely halls" but preserved nonetheless. This story itself, passed along the circle of friends to reach sources interested in using it for purposes Duncan himself did not, is an example of the shadowy history Nell tries to bring to light. But while Nell omits much of Child's retelling of Anglo Saxon romantic history, the point remains in both versions that Duncan, after witnessing the meeting, "recurred to Saxon history, and remembered how he had thought that troubled must be the sleep of those who rule a conquered people" (Nell, *Colored Patriots* 252; Child, *Fact and Fiction* 203–4).[41]

Presenting a story that is, at best, on the shadowy outskirts of history, reapplying the romantic historical imagination of the dominant culture, Nell here indicates the method that informs much of *Colored Patriots*. Duncan experiences what amounts to a historical revelation when he attends a secret meeting in blackface. Not only does he see the enslaved on his own plantation differently, but he also sees his own history (or what he accepts as history) in a new light. Recognizing the commonality of racial struggle, he finds himself in a somewhat different world, with a somewhat different sense of self. Nell, in his guise as the African American Sir Walter Scott, takes his own readers behind the scenes, and reaches for similar revelations. The history that Nell needs to relate, as "The Black Saxons" indicates, is not a story that can be told directly. Rather, it is a story that must be gathered from the outskirts of the history of the conquerors. But Nell approaches that task in part by reframing the history of the conquerors, and by recasting the cultural politics of race. Nell prints his revision of "The Black Saxons" immediately following a meditation on *intra*racial prejudice, the "complexional distinctions, growing out of the institution of slavery" that "exist, to a great and unhappy extent, even among colored people" (246). Somewhat later, as he speaks against the cause of "exclusive colored action," he notes that William Lloyd Garrison "has, at times, been supposed to be a colored man, because of his long, patient and persevering devotion to our cause" (369). As Child's story indicates on the one hand, and as his presentation of Garrison indicates on the other, Nell presents differences of color as differences of experience, of perspective, of ideological and moral alliances.

Behind his understanding and use of black and white masks, however, is a commitment to a vision of a common history that Duncan, for one, barely begins to indicate. In one of the few places in *Colored Patriots* where Nell breaks into the first person in high style, he notes that many black activists are advocating organizations that would exclude "William Lloyd Garrison, Wendell Phillips, Gerritt [*sic*] Smith, and their fellow-philanthropists," and proclaims, "When my head or heart accepts this theory, I shall be in a fit condition to believe in the Colonization dogma, that our Almighty Father has interposed an insurmountable barrier between the white and colored portion of His children, and that we are, indeed, a peculiar, isolated, distinct race, and always to be so; a state of things in the contemplation of which angels weep, and fiends clap their hands for joy" (369). While Duncan is hardly an example of one who breaks such barriers, he does indicate that the barriers are not divinely sanctioned or insurmountable, and that African American history has the power to place Anglo-Saxon history in a new light. However seemingly frail, this is the hope to which *Colored Patriots* is devoted.

In *Colored Patriots* as in his life in Boston, Nell worked for equal education, challenging both the terms and the center of knowledge in the process. Perhaps the most notable omission from his version of "The Black Saxons" is Child's extended representation of the debate among the slaves, including a long passage about the importance of knowledge. As this story follows Nell's reflection on intraracial prejudice, it is interesting that he retains three paragraphs about one speaker whom Duncan recognizes as "the reputed son of one of his friends," a speaker whose "high, bold forehead, and flashing eye, indicated an intellect too active and daring for servitude" (Nell 251; Child, *Fact and Fiction* 200).[42] This speaker, though, is the one who speaks most urgently and persuasively for violence against the white slaveholders, arguing that "the white men tell us God made them our masters; I say, it was the Devil" (Nell 250; Child 199). One can see why Nell would include a paragraph that makes the product of the two races the strongest voice for the separation of the races. But Nell omits Child's lengthy account of the speaker who follows, a middle-aged man who, unlike the previous speaker, does not use standard English. He notes that, like the previous speaker, he's often reflected on the source of the white man's power, entertaining the notion that "the Devil made white men our masters." "Sometimes," he notes, "I tink one ting, den I tink anoder ting," and "at last, I find it all out." How does the white man do it, he asks? And then he pulls out of his pocket "a crumpled piece of printed paper" and "exclaim[s] triumphantly, 'Dat's de way dey do it! Dey got de *knowledge*'" (201). What follows is a lengthy explanation of the power of knowledge, which one might expect Nell to both include and celebrate, and a description of the process by which the speaker himself acquired literacy, along with a story of how the speaker turned a white man into his unwitting messenger.

But if Nell omits this part of Child's story from his version, he doesn't omit the lesson itself. Indeed, like the last speaker, or as Duncan himself inadvertently does, Nell passes a message on to his readers. In *Colored Patriots* Nell attempts to place his white readers in historical blackface and its black readers at the site of a great historical meeting. Nell gathers together the scattered documents of African American history and scattered lives of the African American communities to identify the terms by which an inclusive Beloved Community may be imagined. While valuing the achievements and institutions of white America and insisting on the importance of integrated efforts, Nell tells the story of prejudice and exclusion in order to relocate the principles and institutions of white America on the revolutionary sites of memory of black America. Working from those revolutionary grounds, education becomes something more than the inclusion of African Americans into the systemic mechanisms of a white supremacist culture; education becomes the mode by which that system is challenged—and it is an education that is needed as much in the white community as in the black.[43]

Nell writes of an unfinished revolution, and *Colored Patriots* accordingly offers no narrative resolution, focusing instead on the fragments of a history as yet beyond the reach of narrative closure, the story of many histories containing the separate seeds that could contribute to an imagined harvest. Each page of *Colored Patriots* speaks of the power of knowledge—a subject that Nell returns to at the end of the "Elevation" section of "Conditions and Prospects," just before his brief conclusion about the necessity of a second revolution. Nell here reprints, with only minor changes, material first published in the *Liberator* of August 24, 1855, under the title "Improvement of Colored People." The material is simply a modest list of achievements, including mention of a poem by Charlotte Forten Grimké (printed in the *Liberator* but omitted from *Colored Patriots*) and mention of "a colored girl in Portsmouth, N.H." recently granted a diploma, Edwin Garrison Draper's graduation from Dartmouth College, and other modest advances. The list, in its brevity and emphasis on very specific and individual achievements, hardly seems the encouraging conclusion to Nell's discourse on "Elevation" that he apparently intends it to be. The list does, though, represent the vision of historical process that Nell addresses in *Colored Patriots*: a story of individual achievements that amount to a collective argument, a story designed to inspire and enable individual efforts, but also a story of fragments of which the value is both relational and contingent. The great and the small, the collective and the individual, the broadly influential and the seemingly local and contained, all exist side by side, as if roughly interchangeable, speaking of a history that is greater than the sum of its parts, a history irreducible to a singular narrative.

The representation of African American history leads, then, to consideration of a history of fragments, and particularly to the fragments embodied by individuals. Lewis, Delany, and Nell followed their respective narratives arguing for the destiny of the black race, or outlining the conditions for unifying the human race, but finally what stands out in each history is a historical method that attends, as indeed it must, to the fact of a fragmented past. They follow the fragments of documentation, finding what they can to address African American history and destiny by searching in other histories, in government records, in the Bible. Ultimately, though, the fragments they find lead to the individual representatives of African American history, those members of the biblically scattered community who have managed to survive with a story to tell. African American liberation historiography, then, leads from the fragmented narratives of Lewis, Delany, and Nell to the histories of individual lives, just as liberation theology leads to renewed attention to the people as a source of interpretation and not just as subjects and objects of interpretation. In their attention to individual experience both within and beyond what historical sources can reveal, in their attention to individual achievement as the foundation for a possible community, and in their use of history to appeal to their readers to work for cultural change and communal self-definition and redefinition, these historians created dynamic texts that awaited the interpretive act of reading, a mode of reading that would be fulfilled only when the histories inspired further action in the theaters of history.

chapter three

Multiple Lives and Lost Narratives
(Auto)Biography as History

o follow the path of African American historical writing to the varying but connected stories of individual experience is to recognize the enormous weight that has been placed on the life stories of individual African Americans, and on the method by which those stories can be told. It is important, then, to consider the status of African American autobiography as history, and to examine the extent to which an individual life can be rendered in print without serving the purposes of the totalizing system that Nell, for one, worked so hard to avoid. African American history is, unavoidably, the history of the cultural construction of identity, the process by which various ideological frameworks and their corresponding institutions determined the set of experiences and the cultural perspectives by which individuals would discover themselves as social beings, and against which those same individuals would need to struggle to define the nature and limits of their potential agency in the world in which they discovered themselves. Such collective self-definitions inevitably required a sophisticated understanding of the concept of race in its various and shifting manifestations. "For three hundred years," as Toni Morrison has argued, "black Americans insisted that 'race' was no usefully distinguishing factor in human relationships. During those same three centuries every academic discipline, including theology, history, and natural science, insisted 'race' was *the* determining factor in human development. When blacks discovered they had shaped or become a culturally formed race, and that it had specific and revered difference, suddenly they were told there is no such thing as 'race,' biological or cultural, that matters and that genuinely intellectual exchange cannot accommodate it" ("Unspeakable" 370). Morrison here points to two important concerns in U.S. (and global) history: (1) the historical and interdisciplinary "creation" of race as a defining category of human identity; and (2) the development of "a culturally formed race" that was the inevitable result of those defining categories. But the culturally formed race does not stand independently, for its ongoing (re)definitions are, in fact, intimately related to both the manipulations of racial categories and the denial of race as a central feature in a white supremacist culture.

Narratives of history, then, might be understood as the grand cultural scripts that define the many roles and the terms of the relations among the roles. The recognized manifestations of historical understanding are communal performances scripted and directed by those who have greatest access to the centers of cultural power—political and social institutions, the economy, the press, and so on. In trying to tell the story of African American history, black historians were trying to put together a different script that would make possible different, and communally coordinated, roles. Indeed, in working against what Mills has termed the "inverted epistemology" of the racial contract (*Racial Contract* 18), African Americans inevitably defined themselves as nonwhite and located themselves outside the social contract while working in the service of ideals largely claimed as the philosophical terrain of the Enlightenment. The embodiment of history, in short, is neither singular nor simple. Each life that is considered as an interesting historical story exists in a complex relation with many other lives, and to complicate or argue against the existing definitions of racial identity is not to escape from the terms of the racial contract or even to revise it significantly.[1]

To explore African American history through the narratives of individual African Americans, then, is to enter into the shifting terrain of racial ideology in which the category of identity is never allowed the luxury of an abstract philosophical consideration. Rather, identity is always located in an unstable relation to those whose lives are governed by the inverted epistemology of the racial contract. Useful here is Archie Smith Jr.'s understanding of the "relational self"—that is, Smith's consideration of "the social, historical, contextual, and, hence, relational character of the self." "The self," Smith argues, "is constituted through a reflexive process with other selves who are implicated in the activity of the actor" (57, 62); as Rajeswari Sunder Rajan has put it, "One's affiliations are multiple, contingent, and frequently contradictory" (5). Recognizing this reflexive process, and these multiple and contingent affiliations, leads one to an understanding of what I have termed "multiply contingent selfhood," by which each act, word, and gesture can be understood as a kind of performance (sometimes habitual, sometimes self-conscious) that is completed or fulfilled only when others, from a variety of cultural positions, respond appropriately. Viewed in this light, one's social identity is always delayed and in danger of being undermined as one's performance awaits verifying responses, reciprocal performances, in the field of social relations, responses that might well contradict one another. In effect, a complex culture provides the many inhabitants of that culture with a variety of roles defined in relation to one another—as, for example, teacher/student, or even parent/child. The culture defines each role in certain ways, but one's performance of that role depends on the extent to which others will respond appropriately.

It is within this framework that I want to consider African American (auto)biographies as modes of historical writing and vehicles for historical study. The separate accounts of individual lives themselves represent the scattered community that were and often remain at the center of African American historical endeavors. They represent as well the embodied experience and perspectives of the complex cultural dynamics that define African American history unavoidably in the context of white U.S. history. Challenging or redefining that context was inherently a part of African American history as embodied in the life stories of individual African Americans. Any attempt to intervene in the white supremacist construction of history, of course, included the need to respond to the image of the savage or "subperson" (as Mills has it), the highly contingent "other," that was so fundamentally a part of white Enlightenment thought. But the challenge extended further still, involving what Velentin Mudimbe has termed the "epistemological ethnocentrism" (qtd. in Mills, *Racial Contract* 44) that characterized white Euro-American cultural theory and practice, a framework that shaped not only white interest in African American life but also the conventions of reading and of understanding that white readers would bring to narratives of African American life. This framework defined the cultural theater within which African Americans, more often than not, had to perform—and the historical theory of and in African American autobiographical writing is a function of the strategies of performance that African American writers developed in that theater.[2]

Interesting Facts and Embodied Histories

In 1792, a pamphlet titled *Copy of a Letter from Benjamin Banneker to the Secretary of State, with His Answer* was printed by Daniel Lawrence of Philadelphia. As the title indicates, the pamphlet reprints Banneker's letter to Thomas Jefferson and Jefferson's reply to Banneker; but it includes as well a three-paragraph biographical sketch of Banneker. The sketch tells the story not only of Banneker's achievements, but also, predictably, of his struggle against the odds, and of Banneker's determination to make use of his limited education: "As some hours of leisure will occur in the most toilsome life, he availed himself of these, not to read and acquire knowledge from writings of genius and discovery, for of such he had none, but to digest and apply, as occasions presented, the few principles of the few rules of arithmetic he had been taught at school" (Porter 328). As a result of such efforts, Banneker "at length attracted the attention of the Messrs. Ellicott," from whom he acquired "books and instruments," the result of which was the almanac that he sent to Jefferson. The sketch concludes by suggesting that the details of Banneker's life "form an interesting fact in the History of Man" (329).

Over sixty years after the publication of *Copy of a Letter from Benjamin Banneker*, a memorial to Thomas L. Jennings was printed in *Frederick Douglass' Paper* and reprinted in the *Anglo-African Magazine*. The purpose of this sketch is also to present facts, specifically in refutation of white abolitionist Gerrit Smith's assertion that "the mass of them [African Americans] are ignorant and thriftless" (*Anglo-African Magazine* 128). This was a particularly serious charge, given Gerrit Smith's devotion to the antislavery cause and his status as a friend to African Americans.[3] Although Smith notes exceptions to his generalizations, this response to Smith moves beyond an exceptionalist approach to African American achievement and presents Thomas L. Jennings as a "representative" of "that large class of earnest, upright colored men who dwell in our large cities," a class "whose noble sacrifices, and unheralded labors are too little known to the public, even to the real friends of freedom" (127). And in its presentation of Jennings's life, this article emphasizes the extent to which individuals embody history:

Mr. Jennings was a native of New York, and in his early youth was one of the bold men of color who, in this then slave state, paraded the streets of the metropolis with a banner inscribed with the figure of a black man, and the words "AM I NOT A MAN AND A BROTHER?" He was one of the colored volunteers who aided in digging trenches on Long Island in the war of 1812. He took a leading part in the celebration of the abolition of slavery in New York in 1827. He was one of the founders of the Wilberforce Society. When in 1830 Wm. Lloyd Garrison came on from Baltimore, Mr. Jennings was among the colored men of New York, Wm. Hamilton, Rev. Peter Williams, Thomas Sipkins, and others, who gave him a cordial welcome and God-speed, and subscribed largely to establish the *Liberator*, and to aid in the publication of "Garrison's Thoughts on Colonization."

He was an actor in the great meeting in Chatham Street Chapel. He was a leading member of the first, second and third of the National Conventions of colored men of the United States, held in New York and Philadelphia in 1831–4. He was one of the originators of the Legal Rights Association in New York city, and President thereof at the time of his death. His suit against the Third Avenue Railroad Company for ejecting his daughter from one of its cars on Sabbath day, led to the abolition of caste in cars in four out of the five city railroads. He was one of the founders, and during many years a trustee of the Abyssinian Baptist Church. (126–27)

This very full life stands—not only in the pages of *Frederick Douglass' Paper* and the *Anglo-African Magazine* but also today—as a monument to lived history; and it stands as well as a reminder of the extent to which issues of class and gender enter history with race. If Gerrit Smith presented the lower classes as representative of African Americans, this article follows suit by presenting a different representative class.

But what is being represented? A people? An argument about the inherent nature of all African Americans? I would suggest that what is being represented is simply the relation between history and individual identity, and the extent to which African Americans could expect that their struggles against political and social oppression would result in an identity that was itself an argument either for or against political and social oppression. The task was to form a community capable of serving as a badge of identity—both by building anew (as in Jennings's work in the Abyssinian Baptist Church) and by deconstructing and reconstructing (as in Jennings's efforts to eliminate segregation in public transportation). But because there was no institution that in itself could serve as a transcendental marker of identity, no institution that was free from the larger struggle against racism, no institution not implicated in the national culture of slavery, each individual stood as a representative of the historical movement toward community, a community formed in resistance, a community constantly trying to forge a collective identity but lacking control over the *terms* of identity. In individuals, one finds both the conditions and the response to conditions that shape and define character; one finds the achievements that are the product of both individual and collective efforts; one finds the ways in which achievements are linked to one's sense of identity; one finds the complex heritage that is both the target of and the response to prejudice; and one sees prejudice itself as a historical dynamic, an ideological and social force that immediately joins one with those who have come before and those who will come after.

It is especially appropriate, then, to consider autobiography and biography as history, but how to understand the ways in which the story of an individual life can be understood as a story about history is hardly a simple matter. In their introduction to *History and Memory*, Geneviève Fabre and Robert O'Meally suggest that "the first black American historians may have been the authors of slave narratives, those whose testimonies comprised not only eyewitness accounts of remembered experience but also a set of world views with interpretations, analyses, and historical judgments." "At these points," they argue, "memory and history come together." Certainly, this chapter is devoted to the assumption that autobiographies, biographies, and collective biographies (books comprised of a number of biographical sketches) are in fact important historical works, but one must note that Fabre and O'Meally here rely on a somewhat idealized understanding of the slave narratives, and of the memory and history that intersect in them. The best-known authors of these narratives—Frederick Douglass and William Wells Brown—wrote numerous autobiographies, and other important (auto)biographies were written or edited by white patrons (most significantly, those of Harriet Tubman and Sojourner Truth). And Josiah Henson's autobiographies were both multiple in number and ghostwritten. Clearly, the intersection of history and memory is a complex matter, and is subject to change over the years, for as history and memory both change, the significance of the intersection itself changes. The changing forms of these (auto)biographies over the years, I will argue, signal ongoing attempts to identify the relationship between individual and national identity, attempts complicated and undermined by U.S. racial culture. Narratives of individual or of multiple lives plot the course of a kind of collective narrative breakdown.

Consider again the examples of Banneker and Jennings. The short sketch of Banneker's life focused on individual character, on the seemingly private achievement of diligence, self-motivation, personal application, intelligence, and so forth—the sort of things one might emphasize in a letter of recommendation. But these qualities become visible in Banneker's engagement with the world around him, a world that makes of his individual qualities a particular kind of representative story. Had Banneker been white, his character would still be significant, but the story told by his efforts would have been differently shaped by his world. The story told about Jennings is almost entirely a public record. After reading the paragraphs that I have quoted, one might feel that one knows very little about Jennings and a great deal about African American history in New York and Philadelphia during Jennings's lifetime. These are the needs that shaped Jennings's potential in certain ways.

One thinks of Clifford Geertz's reminder that "one of the most significant facts about us may finally be that we all begin with the natural equipment to live a thousand kinds of life but end in the end having lived only one" (45). "Our ideas," Geertz argues, "our values, our acts, even our emotions, are, like our nervous system itself, cultural products—products manufactured, indeed, out of tendencies, capacities, and dispositions with which we were born, but manufactured nonetheless" (50). Especially when we recognize that U.S. culture is not monolithic, and that one is a member of many cultures intricately linked—and often at odds with one another—then one can appreciate the lasting value of Geertz's understanding of culture as one approaches the individual life story as a work of history. For "when seen as a set of symbolic devices for controlling behavior," Geertz argues,

> extrasomatic sources of information, culture provides the link between what men are intrinsically capable of becoming and what they actually, one by one, in fact become. Becoming human is becoming individual, and we become individual under the guidance of cultural patterns, historically created systems of meaning in terms of which we give form, order, point, and direction to our lives. And the cultural patterns involved are not general but specific—not just "marriage" but a particular set of notions about what men and women are like, how spouses should treat one another, or who should properly marry whom; not just "reli-

gion" but belief in the wheel of karma, the observance of a month of fasting, or the practice of cattle sacrifice. (52)

One might add to this that religious belief would necessarily include one's position in the cultural grounding of the religious institution—the participation in the African Methodist Episcopal Church that includes a history of prejudice in and separation from "white" churches; the belief in a religion that serves also as a center of social, economic, and political organization; the belief in a religion that includes both the church and, say, Freemasonry.

The representation of history, as suggested by this understanding of culture, cannot be simply the presentation of facts. African American history is defined by conditions and struggles that can only be understood if one accounts for the perspective and the moral understanding that arise from lived experience. How one tells the story of the past, for African Americans, cannot be separated from *what* one includes in that story. History is embodiment—the process of embodiment, the effects of embodiment. This is not to say that African American history does not include information that can be gathered, or that white historians are incapable of presenting a judicious understanding of African American history. But the perspectives and moral understandings born of experience are inseparable from that story, and they make it possible for one to value, say, the white abolitionist Lydia Maria Child's *An Appeal in Favor of That Class of Americans Called Africans* (1833) more than one might value any number of histories written by other white historians afterward, and to value Nell's or Walker's historical vision still more.[4]

The question of embodiment is emphasized by the case of Benjamin Banneker. Banneker presented his almanac and letter to Jefferson as a response to Jefferson's arguments about people of African origins, and as a forceful argument about the fundamental contradiction that someone who could write the words of the Declaration of Independence could yet tolerate slavery. A half century later, in 1845, John H. B. Latrobe presented to the Maryland Historical Society and then published his *Memoir of Benjamin Banneker*. Latrobe was an important figure in the Maryland Colonization Society, and his biography of Banneker turns Banneker's original argument to new purposes.[5] In the third, introductory paragraph of the *Memoir*, Latrobe offers the following reason for considering "a memoir of a free man of colour . . . of sufficient interest to be presented to the Historical Society":

Maryland is the only State in the Union that has clearly indicated her policy in regard to her coloured population. She looks to their gradual and voluntary removal as the only means of solving the difficult problem which their presence involves. To aid in this removal, she appropriated, in 1831, the large sum of $200,000; not in the expectation that this sum would transport them all from this country to Africa; but that, by means of it, a community of freemen capable of self-support and self-government might be established there, that would be so attractive ultimately to the coloured people here, as to produce an emigration, at the proper cost of the emigrants themselves, based on the same motives, and as great in amount as the emigration from Europe to America. This policy and its results must enter largely into the history of Maryland. Its success must mainly depend upon the ability and skill of the emigrants to found such a nation as will accomplish the end in view: and this in its turn depends on the oft mooted question as to the comparative intellect of the two races, the white and the coloured. To decide this, facts are important; and not one more conclusive exists than the abilities and character of Benjamin Banneker.

Banneker still embodies an argument, and that argument is still significant when read in the context of the white American Revolution—but the argument has changed significantly. Latrobe brings Banneker into his vision of Maryland and U.S. history, and makes of Banneker's life a colonizationist argument. Can the facts of Banneker's life be separated from their use? From Banneker's life as an "interesting fact in the History of Man" to his life as and character as "facts" that are important in one's scheme to remove African Americans from the United States, the complexity of historical representation is indicated. Who tells the story, how one tells the story, and why one is telling the story, and what larger vision of history one is serving—these are questions of inescapable implications for the representation of history.

"Formulated Theories and Preconceptions": The White Narration of Black Life

If autobiographical and biographical interventions into the historical record are shaped by the nature of the record, then what counts as historical "fact," as the case of Banneker suggests, can be variously defined. In 1782, for example, one "Belinda, an African" wrote a petition to the legislature of Massachusetts, requesting "such allowance . . . out of the estate of colonel Royall, as will prevent her, and her more infirm daughter, from misery in the greatest extreme, and scatter comfort over the short and downward path of their lives" (Belinda 143). In this petition, Belinda presents a brief history of her capture in Africa, her experience of the Middle Passage, and her years of enslavement in America. This history is the justification for her petition, as her enslavement joins with the story of the American Revolution to form an argument for her portion of the wealth of an enslaver who was "compelled" by the Revolution "to fly, and to breathe away his life in a land, where lawless dominion sits enthroned, pouring blood and vengeance on all who dare to be free" (143). Belinda's petition, reprinted in *The American Museum* in 1787, stands as a historical fact that comments on both the American Revolution and American slavery. Her story, indicated but hardly covered by the petition, remains untold; the "fact" of her existence lies in the contradictions of white U.S. ideology.

Other "facts" spoke differently—as, for example, that of Johnson Green. Published in 1786, and including the engraved image of a hanging, Green's life story is titled *The Life and Confession of Johnson Green, Who Is to Be Executed This Day, August 17th, 1786, for the Atrocious Crime of Burglary; Together with His Last and Dying Words*. This sensationalist account of Green's various crimes can be viewed, as Vincent Carretta has noted, as a kind of spiritual autobiography. Green's parentage (his father was black, his mother Irish), is mentioned at the beginning of the short narrative, but otherwise race plays no explicit role in the account. Rather, Green presents a list of his crimes, with great specificity, and concludes with an appeal to "the great Governour of the Universe, whose Divine Majesty I have offended" (*Life and Confession*, 139). What makes this document significant beyond its time is that it stands, now, as an early document dictated by an African American; indeed, it has been reprinted in a volume that includes the work of Olaudah Equiano and Benjamin Banneker. The recovery of history—and the racialized politics of history—makes for strange bedfellows, as the one common link that joins these figures is their African heritage, however removed that heritage might be from the consciousness of its representatives, such as Green.

What counts as fact, as relevant, as sufficiently interesting to merit publication, was of course determined by the audience—and white curiosity and self-interested benevolence in the story of African American character was a significant and, more often than not, distorting presence. As Saidiya Hartman has argued in a related context, "At issue here is the precariousness of empathy and the uncertain line between witness and spectator" (4). White sympathizers created images of black suffering in their own writing, and one might well say that they also created such images in their reading.[6] What Anna Julia Cooper would later say about white fiction of the closing decades of the century applies equally well to stories about African Americans, in terms of both writing and reading practices, before the Civil War. "Some," wrote Cooper in 1892,

> have taken up the subject with a view to establishing evidences of ready formulated theories and preconceptions; and, blinded by their prejudices and antipathies, have altogether abjured all candid and careful study. Others with flippant indifference have performed a few psychological experiments on their cooks and coachmen, and with astounding egotism, and powers of generalization positively bewildering, forthwith aspire to enlighten the world with dissertations on racial traits of the Negro. A few with really kind intentions and a sincere desire for information have approached the subject as a clumsy microscopist, not quite at home with his instrument, might study a new order of beetle or bug. Not having focused closely enough to obtain a clear-cut view, they begin by telling you that all colored people look exactly alike and end by noting down every chance contortion or idiosyncrasy as a race characteristic. (186–87)

As others have noted, black identity was everywhere and nowhere in the white cultural imagination. The image of the slave could be found in descriptions of the horrors of slavery that looked to the black body primarily to see the *markings*, the text of slavery's physical abuse; the images could be found in engravings, on jewelry, on snuff boxes; they could be found in the story of slavery that stood in for the lives lived under slavery. As Marcus Wood has remarked, "the attempts of Western painters, sculptors, engravers and lithographers to provide European culture with a record of slave experience is . . . a history fraught with irony, paradox, voyeurism and erasure" (8).

The title page of Venture Smith's narrative alone raises questions about what it means to talk about African American history as embodied by individual African Americans: *A Narrative of the Life and Adventures of Venture, a Native of Africa, but Resident above Sixty Years in the United States of America: Related by Himself* (originally published in 1798). This sixty-year "resident" who was brought to America at the age of eight is the subject and voice of what Vincent Carretta has aptly called a "pointedly nonconversion" narrative (9). In an anonymous preface, readers are informed that they are entering into "a relation of simple facts, in which nothing is added in substance to what he related himself" (Smith 3); they are informed as well that "the reader may here see a Franklin and a Washington, in a state of nature, or, rather, in a state of slavery" (3).[7] Indeed, this is a story about a remarkable struggle against a world of obstacles. The narrative begins with the foundations of Venture's life and character in Africa, presenting nearly a landscape of the grounds of character; in the second of its three chapters, Venture tells of his determination to liberate himself; and in the third chapter, Venture presents an account of his liberation (by purchase) of his wife, children, and others who were enslaved (including a very Franklinian accounting of his expenses and losses at each transaction). In this, what is exceptional about Venture's story is simply what is exceptional about Franklin's—the tale of one born low whose life is an ongoing lesson in practical virtues, at the end of which he can say, "It gives me joy to think that I *have* and that I *deserve* so good a character, especially for *truth* and *integrity*" (24). And Venture's life extends beyond Franklin's to tell of the ultimate failure of the representative story one wants to extrapolate from his life—the story of possibility in the new nation. Indeed, Venture tells the story of injustice, contrasting it pointedly with the ethical standards of the African culture he remembers from his youth. He is, in a sense, more Franklinian than Franklin, for Venture tells of a struggle still incomplete, of adages that have yet to enjoy the context of a just nation.[8]

But history was not yet done with Venture—for, in the name of admiration and friendship, a later edition of this narrative included a new section under the title of "Traditions of Venture! Known as Venture Smith. Compiled by H. M. Selden." This added section emphasizes Venture's physical size and feats, and Venture's voice comes across in a manner distinctly different from the narrative proper. Much of the section is presented as a record of an oral tradition about Venture Smith—a mixed-race tradition that carries with it all of the varied and mixed perspectives shaped by U.S. racial culture. Indeed, much of "Traditions" makes of Venture a figure from the kind of tall tales associated with white southwestern humorists. Venture's land, for example, is said to be so fertile that "an old and current tradition says: 'A black snake was once seen moving on and over the heads of the standing rye on one of the fields'" (26). Venture himself is said by "tradition" to have "weighed over three hundred pounds and measured six feet around his waist" (27).[9] One of these accounts, by "Mr. Alex. M. Clark of Haddem Neck, over 82 years of age," includes also this: "Mr. Clark says that Venture called one day on his grandfather, Robert Clark, for him to stack some wheat, saying in disparagement of himself, 'Nigger never know nothing!'" (27). The voice and tone of Venture here are sharply different from what we encountered in the narrative proper. "Traditions," though, also includes a story about Venture that suggests a different perspective and a dramatic determination to draw moral lessons from life: "It is related of Venture that on the occasion of his marriage he threw a rope over the house of his master, where they were living, and had his wife go to the opposite side of the house and pull on the rope hanging there while he remained and pulled on his end of it. After both had tugged at it awhile in vain, he called her to his side of the house and by their unified effort the rope was drawn over to themselves with ease. He then explained the object lesson: "If we pull in life against each other we shall fail, but if we pull together we shall succeed." The success of his later life implies that the lesson was not forgotten by his true and loving wife" (30). Venture lies somewhere behind the Franklinian character and revolutionary challenge to white U.S. culture of the narrative proper, the stereotyped portrait of the massive and primitive black of "Traditions," and the dramatic and conventionally articulate moral instructor of the wedding tradition. What history does he represent? What is the object lesson he would have us draw from his life, and how would he define his representative status to those reading his story?

Venture's own answer is clear, but the answer of Venture's admirers is less so. Venture believed himself to be a model of individual character and achievement, one who succeeded in spite of considerable adversity: "Notwithstanding all the losses I have suffered by fire, by the injustice of knaves, by the cruelty and oppression of false-hearted friends, and the perfidy of my own countrymen whom I have assisted and redeemed from bondage, I am now possessed of more than one hundred acres of land, and three habitable dwelling houses" (24). Even Venture's own sons have failed to follow the model their father established for them: "While I am now looking to the grave as my home, my joy for this world would be full—IF my children, Cuff for whom I paid two hundred dollars when a boy, and Solomon who was born soon after I purchased his mother—If Cuff and Solomon—Oh! that they had walked in the way of their father. But a father's lips are closed in silence and in grief!—Vanity of vanities, all is vanity" (24). These comments, presented in parentheses, are the closing words of Venture's narrative, a narrative that accordingly breaks down, as the sentence gives way to the silence of a father's grief. And the father was silenced further still, for these lines were omitted entirely from later editions of the narrative. Venture's history, in other words, was something of a jeremiad in its original performance, but that history was soon displaced by the story of heroic and decidedly exotic individualism—

including the closing testimonies that emphasize stories of Venture's size and peculiarities. One of those stories tells of the pallbearers at Venture's funeral: "The negroes being behind threw the weight upon themselves, and as they were mounting the long Olmsted hill the darkies complained bitterly. Hanna-well exclaimed, 'Durned great nigger! Ought to have quartered him and gone four times. It makes the gravel stones crack under my feet.'" Venture's life has, indeed, been fragmented, and his larger history reduced to a more containable one and then restaged as a kind of minstrel affair. In the end, history is sacrificed to the fascination over its embodiment.

As with Venture's life, white curiosity about an exoticized black realm of existence emerges most clearly in narratives of northern African Americans whose lives were viewed as a mystery. These northern lives did not fit neatly into the antislavery narrative and so became objects of wonder, commentaries on an envisioned African character that served to define or reconfirm white supremacist assumptions. One thinks, for example, of the white British reformer Harriet Martineau's comments on America as the site of progress in *Society in America*, her three-volume commentary on American theory and practice drawn from her travels through the states in the 1830s. "The Americans possess an advantage in regard to the teaching of manners which they do not yet appreciate," Martineau suggests. "They have before their eyes, in the manners of the coloured race, a perpetual caricature of their own follies; a mirror of conventionalism from which they can never escape. The negroes are the most imitative set of people living. While they are in a degraded condition, with little principle, little knowledge, little independence, they copy the most successfully those things in their superiors which involve the least principle, knowledge, and independence; viz. their conventionalisms" (3:99). For all of her benevolent sympathy for the cause of African Americans north and south, for Martineau the collective term *Americans* was marked white; black Americans were the mirrors of conventionalism that marked the progress and failures of white civilization in the western course of empire.

John W. Blassingame, one of the first historians to consider slave narratives as important and sophisticated sources for the understanding of the system of slavery, has noted that what makes these autobiographies *representative* is not just the experience of the narrator but also the systems of relations she or he describes, the eyewitness account of the experience of slavery, and the subjective perceptions she or he brings to the narration of that experience. One might argue, in turn, that white-narrated biographies and memoirs are themselves representative in what they reveal, in their choice of detail and narrative focus, about white curiosity about African American experience and identity in slavery and beyond. This (white) fascination over the black embodiment of history was, in fact, a controlling force in African American biography and autobiography, a dynamic by which *oppression* and *heroic individualism* became increasingly abstract and *abstracted* categories, making of each individual life a generalized tale of struggle, and making the story safe for the nation by separating it from the legal and cultural institutions and practices that defined national life.[10] Instead of reading from individual life toward an understanding of the larger system, many white narrators and readers read their way from a generalized acknowledgment of the conditions under which African Americans lived toward a sympathetic focus on an individual life—a life that became not an embodiment of a larger historical story to be told but rather a site for a ritualistic affirmation of white sympathy and ethical self-definition.

White curiosity was often quite directly addressed in African American autobiographical or biographical narratives. Perhaps the most blatant example of this is in the gossipy *Memoirs of Elleanor Eldridge* (1843), a narrative *about* the destructive force of gossip that nevertheless engages in gossip about the love life of this Rhode Island woman. Frances Whipple Greene, the white female narrator, notes early in the narrative that "by lending our attention to the lowly fortunes of the indigent and obscure, important principles may be established, valuable truths elicited; and pure, and even lofty examples of virtue may be found" (Greene 14). These lofty virtues lead finally to the familiar path of racial embodiment, as the narrator informs her readers that "Elleanor Eldridge, on the one hand, is the inheritress of African blood, with all its heritage of woe and shame; and the subject of wrong and banishment, by her Indian maternity on the other. Fully, and sadly, have these titles been redeemed. It seems, indeed, as if the wrongs and persecutions of both races had fallen upon Elleanor" (14). Having established the basis of this story (a Bancroftian narrative of three races, with the white commentator acting as mediator, the disembodied voice of justice enforcing the embodiment of injustice), the narrator proceeds to focus increasingly on the untold love story that she is sure must be a part of Eldridge's life—mentioning specifically letters and other private documents to which she does not, at first, have access but to which she eventually gains access.

Turning to those documents, and noting to the reader their primitive character,[11] the narrator then addresses the reader directly: "Let us turn aside, then, for a short time, from the straight-forward path of history, into the

pleasant regions of episode; where, as in a little grotto apart from the high
road, we may indulge in an hour of repose; turning, mean-while, to the simple
story for amusement. Having thus so comfortably established ourselves, with
no evil-minded eaves-dropper to make us afraid; bend now, dear reader, thy
most earnest and delicately adjusted ear; for I am going to tell thee a *secret*"
(38). Engaged in the eavesdropped intimacy of that secret, the story of an
unacknowledged romance in Eldridge's life, the narrator leads the reader
eventually to the unrelated story of Eldridge's loss of her house, finally pleading for white benevolence in the form of the purchase of the *Memoirs*, with
the assurance that "it is pleasant to do good. The very act of generosity is its
own reward" (92).

This story of a comforting white benevolence that transforms white curiosity into a substantial virtue is perhaps *the* fundamental reality shaping the
narration, publication, and marketing of African American life stories, antislavery or otherwise. Henry Trumbull, for example, begins his narration of the
story of "Robert, the Hermit of Massachusetts," by noting that the history of
"this 'strange and mysterious being'" "has until very recently remained a
profound secret!" (Trumbull 5–6). Noting that many, guided by curiosity, had
before visited Robert, Trumbull relates the exchange that led Robert to tell
his story for publication:

> I accosted him in a friendly manner, and he with much civility, bid me
> welcome; and as if willing to permit me to satisfy that curiosity which he
> no doubt supposed had alone prompted me (as it had hundreds of
> others) to visit him, he with much apparent good humour invited me to
> enter, and accept of his seat, when, as he observed, I would have a better
> opportunity to inspect the internal part of his lonely habitation—an
> invitation of which I accepted—and, after making known to him the true
> object of my visit, and with assurances that it was produced by the most
> urgent solicitations of one or more of his friends, who had expressed,
> and I believed sincerely felt an interest in his welfare, so far at least as to
> render his situation more comfortable—I begged that he would gratify
> me with a brief narration of his life, and inform me what powerful cause
> had arose to induce him to quit the pleasures of society, and consign his
> days to voluntary seclusions?—to which, after a considerable pause, and
> with his eyes fixed steadfast upon me, as if to satisfy himself that what I
> had stated was spoken in sincerity, he made the following reply—"that is
> a relation with which I have declined indulging any one, as the enquiry

seemed merely made to gratify idle curiosity; but, as you speak as if you could feel sympathy for distress, I will briefly gratify your request." (Trumbull 9)

What makes the difference, apparently, is the combination of the desire to publish Robert's story as a means of raising funds for Robert joined with, the narrator leads us to assume, the narrator's own transformative benevolence, making of curiosity something more substantial. And, indeed, the narration eventually develops into an antislavery lecture—one that begins with a national failure to live up to professed principles but that becomes a story that establishes "the great honour of the sons of New England," who saw the error of their ways, in sharp contrast to "those who inhabit the southern section of our country" (Trumbull 32). We are given a standard antislavery stump speech by a white New Englander on "the punishments inflicted upon the extreme sufferings of the unhappy slaves of the south" (Trumbull 33). And we are given the opportunity, as well, to join that white northern fraternity by purchasing the book, learning of the story that curiosity wanted to know but that benevolence finally purchased. As Nell Irvin Painter has noted, addressing the relative lack of recognition of the story of Sojourner Truth as a narrative about northern slavery, "as the identification between *slavery* and *the South* tightened during the antebellum era, abolitionists habitually contrasted the open-minded, progressive, free North with the closed-minded, backward, slave-holding South" (Introduction xii). One might ask, with Painter, "How was this possible, with slaves still living in the North well into the nineteenth century?" And one might look to antislavery narratives as an important force in reshaping the white northern self-image. Through these narratives, particularly when narrated by a benevolent white friend of the biographical subject, the story of specifically racial injustice becomes localized, individual, and thereby ready to support the white benevolence necessary to the avoidance of any serious acknowledgment of systemic white supremacy.

Sojourner Truth had, of course, only limited control over her public narrative, but even the stories of highly literate African American autobiographical narrators were similarly transformed into matter of and for white benevolence. That is, many African American narratives are twice-told tales—and in the retelling by white narrators, the story of African American self-determination is resituated and contained. Consider, for example, the brief narrative of James W. C. Pennington's final acquisition of the "deed of manumission" that would provide him with security in the North. The narrative, by

John Hooker of Hartford, Connecticut, appeared in the June 26, 1851, issue of *Frederick Douglass' Paper*, and begins, "It will probably interest most of your readers that the 'chattel personal' generally called Rev. Dr. Pennington, is in a fair way of becoming a man." This sort of light, ironic tone was, of course, common in pieces like this, a signal of enlightened superiority over those degraded enough to find any sense in the system of slavery, and Hooker follows through by narrating the most prominent facts of Pennington's birth in slavery, his escape, and his subsequent career. Hooker then reveals that Pennington came to him, "under the most solemn injunction of secrecy," and told him of his enslavement (unknown even to Pennington's wife). After the passing of the Fugitive Slave Act, money was raised on Pennington's behalf, and a price negotiated with Pennington's former "owner." At this point, our narrator returns to his opening comment and to his ironic voice: "I remarked at the opening of my letter, that. Dr. P. was in 'a fair way of becoming a man.' He is not yet completely one. The title to him still rests with me, and it remains for me, by deed, under my hand and seal, to 'create him a Peer of the Realm.' I shall, however, defer the execution of this instrument for half an hour, till I have walked up and down the whole length of Main street, to see how it seems to be a slaveholder—especially to own a Doctor of Divinity. Possibly during the walk I may change my mind and think it best to send him to a sugar plantation." Hooker then signs the letter, but adds a postscript under his signature: "I have returned from my walk. The deed is executed. John Pembroke [Pennington's name under slavery] is merged into Rev. Pennington. The slave is free—the chattel is a man." Perhaps it is safe to say that some readers would have found this more amusing than others would; in any event, one can only note that the ironic voice that separated North from South at the opening of the letter marks the boundary between white and black by the letter's end, and that white northern benevolence is here described, in effect, as the exercise of restraint in the control one can otherwise claim over the lives of black people. White people giveth life and taketh it away. Hooker's walk was unnecessary; from the moment that Pennington approached him for help in this matter (for legally, Pennington needed a white person for this task), Hooker knew all he needed to know about how it feels to be a slaveholder—as he should have known before.

But even in ways less dramatic than this, white fascination transformed the stories of African American lives, confined slavery to the sins of the white South, and transformed racism into a site for white benevolence. As Marcus Wood has said, "The testimony produced by slaves themselves, which is frequently projected through white creative and economic filters, is . . . complicated in its relation to whatever we understand as historical truth" (8). As Painter notes of Sojourner Truth's first white narrator, Olive Gilbert, "Before Truth had dictated a score of pages, Gilbert began inserting her own commentary. On page 9, Gilbert sharpens Truth's depiction of her parents' situation by appending her own indictment of Southern slavery. Gilbert is addressing Northern abolitionist readers, who, by the 1850s, dissociated *slavery* from *New York*" (Introduction xvii). Later in her career, famous versions of Truth's speeches are presented in conventional black Southern dialect, regardless of the fact that such dialect was unlikely to be an accurate representation of the speech of one born in a Dutch-speaking area of New York.[12] As Carla Peterson has observed, Sojourner Truth "comes to us as always already interpreted by others from their own situated and partial perspectives" (*Doers* 24).[13] Similarly, the life of that other most famous black woman of the nineteenth century, Harriet Tubman, was distorted by the lens of white narration when published in 1869. The first sentence of the first chapter of Sarah Bradford's *Harriet Tubman: The Moses of Her People* identifies Harriet as a child watching the play of "a group of merry little darkies" (13). Later in that narrative, Bradford notes her approval of Tubman's family, adding, "There may be many among the colored race like them; certainly all should not be judged by the idle, miserable darkies who have swarmed about Washington and other cities since the War" (69).[14] Josiah Henson was so transformed by his popular identification as the model for Harriet Beecher Stowe's character Uncle Tom that he becomes, in a highly commercial 1879 version of his life, a rather pathetic caricature of himself.[15]

The white narrator avoids the gaze of the black subject by translating her or his story into a familiar narrative of white ethical self-affirmation and regional self-definition. When other stories are told, they stand on the page like the fragments of an as-yet untold story—as is the case, for example, in Benjamin Drew's 1856 *A North-Side View of Slavery*, a compendium of the stories—some narrated directly, some not—of over 100 former slaves in various communities in Canada. Considered by some to be "the most comprehensive antebellum account of what slavery meant to the Negro," and rivaled only by white abolitionist Theodore Weld's *American Slavery as It Is* (1839) "in documenting slavery's brutality" (Introduction xxii), *A North-Side View of Slavery* is notable as well for what it does not tell. In one of *North-Side*'s narratives, for example, the Reverend Alexander Helmsley proclaims that he has become "a regular Britisher" now that his "American blood has been scourged out of [him]," and adds, "I have lost my American tastes; I am an enemy to tyranny." This is a stance not only of individual resistance but also of historical perspective, for after noting his willingness to fight any white man who would come to Canada, whereas in the United States he would "be afraid of the ghost of a white man after he was dead," Rev. Helmsley states, "I am no scholar, but if some one would refine it, I could give a history of slavery, and show how tyranny operates upon the mind of the slaves" (26).

What *is* narrated in *A North-Side View of Slavery* that is as important to our understanding of African American history as are any number of details about slavery's brutality is the insistence on a kind of narrative truth and on the position from which that truth can be acquired and from which it can be narrated. "What I tell you now," states John Little, "I would tell at the judgment, if I were required. 'Tisn't he who has stood and looked on, that can tell you what slavery is,—'tis he who has endured. I was a slave long enough, and have tasted it all" (142). Little brings this perspective to human terms earlier in the narrative, interrupting a comment about the overseer to note, "I wish he were here now to hear me tell it, to see whether it's the truth—I could look right in his face the whole time" (140). "Historical truth," in these narratives and others, is a function not simply of the information presented but also and more importantly of the moral dynamics of narration.

Never put to the test of having to look in the eyes of the enslaved as he told his story was the author of the book that provoked the publication of *A North-Side View of Slavery*, the Reverend Nehemiah Adams, whose *A South-Side View of Slavery* was published in 1854. Adams, a Boston minister, relates in *A South-Side View of Slavery* that a journey to the South changed his views on slavery. The book surveys the condition of the slaves, as seen from Adams's perspective, from dress to labor to moral instruction. Adams's view of slavery is decided skewed—reminding one of Harriet Jacobs's note in *Incidents in the Life of a Slave Girl* that northern visitors are presented a staged and paternalistic portrait of slavery; indeed, Adams counsels his white Northern readers to hold to racially grounded ideals of national union and "Christian" patience: "Let us feel and act fraternally with regard to the south, defend them against interference, abstain from every thing assuming and dictatorial, leave them to manage their institution in view of their accountability to God ... and we may expect that American slavery will cease to be any thing but a means of good to the African race." Adams's *A South-Side View of Slavery* is a book that adapts and transforms the discourse of antislavery sentiment, applying it now to the combined causes of national union and racial paternalism to promote a kind of providential laissez-faire approach to the problem of slavery.

Adams presents himself as a sentimental subject whose sentiment has been distorted by antislavery representations of the South. As he travels through the South, his actual encounters contradict northern representations of slavery and thereby open the channels of a newly grounded sentiment, free now to speak feelingly about national union and paternalistic hope for "the African race." Indeed, Adams sometimes is quite overtaken by the impulses of sentiment—as, for example, when he notes in the book's penultimate chapter, "The feeling involuntarily arose within me at the south, and especially in the religious meetings of the slaves, Would that all Africa were here!" (206–7). In the concluding chapter, Adams draws together the various observations in the book and calls for faith in God to deal with slavery in time, and faith in Southerners to deal with slaves in the meantime—leading, finally, to the sentimental closing words: "When, at the south, I spent a morning in a burying ground of the colored people, reading the simple, touching inscriptions,—'Their names, their years, spelt by the unlettered muse,'—and saw, all about in the grass, the prickly pear, embryo cactuses, gathering round the graves of the slaves, I felt no need of one to interpret for me. The deep murmur in the tops of the pines overhead, with the birds singing in the branches, comported well with the discovery of this token of present, thorny sorrow, this emblem of Africa in her past history and her coming beauty, and in the love which she is to win from all hearts" (213–4). One imagines that many northerners devoted to sentimental abolitionism might well be attracted to this graveyard vision of "present, thorny sorrow" as the necessary prelude to Africa's "coming beauty," the day when "she is to win" love "from all hearts." One could have one's sentimental opposition to slavery and still maintain one's established system of social and economic relations.[16]

Adams's account of his travels and impressions underscores the unstable nature of an emphasis on "fact" as the foundation of a narrative capable of claiming (or defining) historical truth—and perhaps helps to explain a significant shift toward what William Andrews has called "a new discursive contract" (*To Tell* 183) in African American autobiographies in the 1850s and 1860s. As Andrews argues, "For decades the slave narrator had asked to be believed on the basis, at least in part, of his ability to restrain himself, to keep to the proprieties of discourse that required the ugliest truths of slavery to be veiled. At mid-century, however, the black autobiographer would begin to claim credibility *because* he or she had violated those same proprieties of discourse. The further this new autobiographer placed himself or herself outside the conventions of the standard discourse on slavery, the more truthful this autobiographer claimed to be. I am to be trusted, this new black narrator seemed to be saying, because what I tell you is shocking and ought not to be read" (183). But while I would agree that there is an increasing insistence on the authority of experience toward midcentury, I would emphasize the significance of Andrews's use of the word "contract" here, and I would suggest that white readers assumed that they controlled the terms of the contract. The acceptance of black writers *because* they place themselves outside the conventions of the standard discourse, or *because* they say what ought not to be said, can be an acceptance of narrators who fit white notions of blackness. They become new manifestations of significant facts, new sites of a historical reality that both is and is not what the black narrator claims it to be. It *is* horrible; but this is a horror that African American narrators, to continue the metaphor, were contractually obligated to provide, a horror that identified them as black (that blackness defined by whites) and that reaffirmed the status of white northern readers as benevolent white friends of the oppressed. Adams's account redirects that white benevolence by removing the "blackness" from the representation of slavery. The propriety of the discourse has been reestablished, and the proper response to slavery has been redefined as an effort to be patient about a process that involves the unruly nature of African character.

The problem of white curiosity in the representation of slavery is perhaps nowhere more clear than in those instances where we hear most directly from the voice of authority—when those who have been enslaved are asked direct questions by a white sympathizer. The best known of these narratives of white curiosity is *Louisa Picquet, the Octoroon; or, Inside Views of Southern Domestic Life*. Picquet encountered the white abolitionist Hiram Mattison in Buffalo, New York, while she attempted to raise money for purchasing her mother's freedom. The pamphlet Mattison subsequently published—supposedly but not finally as part of that fund-raising effort[17]—is primarily a series of questions and answers between Mattison and Picquet. Mattison emphasizes Picquet's white appearance, noting that "no one, not apprised of the fact, would suspect that she had a drop of African blood in her veins" (5); what identifies Picquet as black for Mattison are the clear marks of enslavement, including "a certain menial-like diffidence, her plantation expression and pronunciation, her inability to read or write, together with her familiarity with and readiness in describing plantation scenes and sorrows" (5). "Notwithstanding the fair complexion and lady-like bearing of Mrs. Picquet," Mattison adds, "she is of African descent on her mother's side—an octoroon, or eighth blood—and, consequently, one of the four millions in this land of Bibles, and churches, and ministers, and 'liberty,' who 'have *no rights that white men are bound to respect*'" (6).

Here at the beginning of the narrative, Mattison identifies Picquet both with and against the cultural associations of whiteness; but the narrative itself determines Picquet's "blackness" by transforming Picquet into the embodiment of the white abolitionist version of history. Mattison focuses his questions on the whippings (beginning with the first of Mattison's questions recorded in this pamphlet), sexual violations, and familial separations. Indeed, as Anthony G. Barthelemy has noted, Mattison's "self-righteousness imposed a prurient obsession on the interview" (xxxix). Involved in this exchange of questions and answers, then, are contesting versions of the history revealed by the individual life, as Picquet must submit her life to the needs of white antislavery history so as to secure support (at least according to Mattison) for the more complex history she is living—including not only her experience in slavery but also her experience in the North as she tries to raise funds to rescue her mother from slavery. As Barthelemy argues, "Responding to Mattison's questions, Picquet tells us something of her life in slavery and freedom. Mattison, however, was interested in the institution of slavery itself and in its attendant moral corruption. The minister failed to recognize Picquet as an individual; rather, she and her experiences served to substantiate his argument and to justify his self-righteousness and moral indignation" (xxxix). Picquet's history might well be a continuum that connects her former enslavers to her present inquisitor; Mattison's is a continuum that connects the nation as a whole to the slaveholding South.

To be sure, Mattison's outrage seems real, and much of what he says, particularly as he concludes his narrative and draws "morals" from it, might well be found in any antislavery text, regardless of authorship. Mattison argues, for example, that resistance to slavery is a duty and suggests that it is impossible for an American citizen to "hold his peace concerning [slavery], and be innocent" (52)—a recognition that leads to a dramatic vision of a coming divine retribution: "May the Lord arouse this guilty nation to a sense of its deep and unwashed guilt, and bring us to repentance and reformation before the republic shall crumble beneath the weight of our accumulated crimes, and He who led Israel out of Egypt, by his sore judgments, shall arise for the sighing of the millions whom we hold in chains, and shall pour out his fury upon us to our utter confusion and ruin!" (52). One could find the same rhetoric in any number of texts by African American writers. And if one simply skims the surface of this mode of discourse, one *could* find one's way to Russ Castronovo's argument that "disconcerting convergences among white abolitionist, African American, and proslavery writers suggest a conceptual vortex that renders immaterial the difference between various perspectives on black enslavement because all make recourse to an infinitely porous and eternally lifeless political subject" (46).

Finally, though, Mattison's vision of the wrongs of slavery are those abuses necessary for its continuance—the abuses that constitute the blackness of Picquet, who might otherwise be notable simply for her "fair complexion and lady-like bearing." We cannot know the life history Picquet might relate beyond the questions she was asked, but we can sense the collective history she experienced in her cautious answers, avoidances, omissions, and pointed responses. What is black about the history she could provide is not the measure of her blood but rather the moral position she occupies as one who must submit to the considerable exposures of white antislavery outrage in order to work toward an individual salvation. It is useful to return, then, to Hartman's notion of "performing blackness," involving "various modes of performance and performativity that concern the production of racial meaning and subjectivity, the nexus of race, subjection, and spectacle, the forms of racial and race(d) pleasure, enactments of white dominance and power, and the reiteration and/or rearticulation of the conditions of enslavement" (56–57). With this in mind, one might note that Mattison's performance of blackness prior to and in the writing of the text should be distinguished from Picquet's performance of blackness, a performance that speaks through the text, inscribed but unwritten.

Lewis Clarke—like Picquet, light enough to be mistaken for white—had somewhat more control over the story that he dictated to J. C. Lovejoy, but he demonstrates a similarly conflicting historical position in his approach to his narrative. In the edition of his narrative published with that of his brother Milton is included a series of "Questions and Answers," featuring the questions he is most often asked. As in the case of Picquet, many of the questions focus on physical and sexual violations, familial separations, denial of education, distortion of religion, and the like. Lewis Clarke's own narrative is one that emphasizes his *voice*, or at least those features of voice most valued by white audiences. As Andrews has noted, Clarke adapted "the arts of the comic raconteur to the purposes of antislavery propaganda," "trying out stylistic and tonal experiments that could broaden the slave narrator's rhetorical range and emotional appeal while also personalizing the voice of the narrator himself" (139). But one might well wonder about the extent to which broadening the rhetorical range of a literary genre was one of Clarke's concerns; and one might wonder as well about the extent to which his "colloquial style" works to "personalize" the narrative.[18] The terms of historical understanding indicated by the questions and answers that Clarke includes in the narrative are arguably the terms that drive the narrative and determine the voice. As Picquet's authenticity (that is, her status as a black former slave) was tied in part to her own voice, "her plantation expression and pronunciation," and as Douglass reports being urged to bring more of the plantation speech into his lectures (*My Bondage and My Freedom* 367), so Clarke tells his story in a voice that both acknowledges and obscures the presence of his white interlocutor. The questions Clarke is asked point insistently to a significant set of facts that can be recognized as the history of slavery and as the embodiment of that history in the body of the black subject. Blackness becomes a fact to seek out, to identify in the exchange between cruel oppressor and hapless victim by way of white northern intervention in the exchange. The very humanity of the black subject becomes something to establish so as to reestablish that which marks the subject as black—with blackness always under the defining lens of the white eye.

Ultimately, what I am identifying as white antislavery history here is what might be called a *docudramatic* approach to slavery. This notion of history, which assumes the possibility of objectivity and which associates history with fact, did characterize approaches to the history of slavery for many years—years in which the slave narratives were dismissed as possible historical sources. Responding to this habitual omission, Blassingame has noted that "the chief value of the autobiography lies in the fact that it is subjective, that it tells us a great deal about how blacks felt about the conditions under which they lived" (227–28). But as the history of historical approaches to slavery reveal, slave narratives are not alone in being subjective and thus revealing. In the docudramatic understanding of slavery, what matters is one's ability to re-create the conditions of slavery. Individual narratives are reduced to the status of evidence—usually questionable evidence—toward that attempted re-creation. The autobiographical or biographical narrative becomes an individual manifestation and a regional site of slavery.

This docudramatic approach overwhelms one of the most prominent of the narratives filtered through the perspective of a white amanuensis, Solomon Northup's *Twelve Years a Slave*. Northup was kidnaped in 1841, sold into slavery, and finally rescued in 1853; in the year of his rescue, his story was recorded by David Wilson, a lawyer from the upstate New York area to which Northup returned after he was rescued. The book was quite successful and was connected upon publication with the success of Harriet Beecher Stowe's fictional treatment of slavery, *Uncle Tom's Cabin*. Indeed, Stowe mentions Northup, and includes details and excerpts of documents of his experience, in the *Key to Uncle Tom's Cabin*, Stowe's attempt to document, after the fact, the grounds for accepting the reality behind her novel. Harriet Jacobs, famously, refused to allow her story to be reduced to the status of evidence in Stowe's *Key*; *Twelve Years a Slave*, notably, opens with a dedication to Stowe, and presents Northup's narrative as "another *Key to Uncle Tom's Cabin*."[19] Even beyond Stowe's *Key*, Northup's experiences were used to validate Stowe's novel, as Stowe's reputation was used to authenticate Northup's narrative. In an account of Northup's enslavement and eventual return to "liberty" in the North, according to a report in the *Liberator*, the *New York Daily Times* referred to Stowe's novel to describe Northup's experiences, noting that "the condition of this colored man during the nine years that he was in the hands of Eppes, was of a character nearly approaching that described by Mrs. Stowe, as the condition of 'Uncle Tom' while in that region"("Affecting Narration").[20]

The docudramatic approach to history is an exercise in both vision and blindness, for in the attempt to present a full picture of the past, the historian typically ignores, or dismisses as *beyond the subject*, the ideological canvas on which the portrait is constructed and the moral frame that guides the eyes of those who view the image of the past. But as anyone familiar with the misrepresentation of African American history in the U.S. system of education can attest, other images of the past will make themselves known to those who have eyes to see. Northup's narrative, in fact, concludes with a mention of an example of this unintended representation of an alternate story. Northup relates a story told to him by his wife concerning his children's awareness of his possible condition during those years when he was absent: "Elizabeth and Margaret once returned from school—so Anne informed me—weeping bitterly. On inquiring the cause of the children's sorrow, it was found that, while studying geography, their attention had been attracted to the picture of slaves working in the cotton-field, and an overseer following them with his whip. It reminded them of the sufferings their father might be, and as it happened, actually *was*, enduring in the South" (252). These pictures were not intended to make a moral statement about slavery, and one can only expect that for most of the children the pictures simply represent an image of the South in a geography lesson, perhaps with an implicit claim of northern superiority. But the children find themselves living in a fundamentally different world by virtue of their connection to an absent father. This manifestation of the docudramatic approach to history realizes concretely Jacques Derrida's claim that "white mythology . . . has erased within itself the fabulous scene that has produced it, the scene that nevertheless remains active and stirring, inscribed in white ink, an invisible design covered over in the palimpsest" (qtd. in M. Wood 134).

Sadly, *Twelve Years a Slave* largely offers its readers another textbook of the South, a lesson in white political geography that most readers would already know and could only reaffirm, though one that Northup seems to comment on at times. Northup ends by emphasizing that his story "is no fiction, no exaggeration," and adds, "If I have failed in anything, it has been in presenting to the reader too prominently the bright side of the picture" (252). Certainly, *Twelve Years a Slave* includes a number of eloquent denunciations of the system of slavery, though it ends by carefully limiting the book's authority to the region in which Northup was enslaved. But much of the book is a documentary of slavery, including depictions of physical abuse (depictions aided by the book's illustrations) framed by a survey of slave culture. This approach is valuable in that it can emphasize the violence inherent in the commercial and social culture of slavery—the point that Lewis Clarke underscores at the end of his narrative, when he notes that "all of the abuses which I have here related are *necessary*, if slavery must continue to exist" (60). But one can hardly say that this is the unifying principle of Northup's narrative—a claim that one *might* make, for example, with Douglass's 1845 *Narrative*, and that one might make again by noting Douglass's increased emphasis on the culture of slavery in his 1855 *My Bondage and My Freedom*. Northup presents most of his glimpses into southern culture rather incidentally. Toward the beginning of chapter 12, for example, Northup pauses to note of his then master Edwin Epps, "His principal business was raising cotton, and in as much as some may read this book who have never seen a cotton field, a description of the manner of its culture may not be out of place" (123). Later, following a chapter that emphasizes the "tendency" of the system of slavery "to brutalize the humane and finer feelings" of the slaves, Northup pauses to note, "In a previous chapter the mode of cultivating cotton is described. This may be the proper place to speak of the manner of cultivating cane" (159).

Northup offers as well a lengthy description of flirtation, laughter, food, music, and dance during the Christmas holidays. To be sure, he follows this holiday portrait by noting the extent to which it contrasted with everyday life, commenting implicitly on those descriptions of slave life that focus exclusively on such events. "Such is 'southern life as it is,'" Northup states, "*three days in the year*, as I found it—the other three hundred and sixty-two being days of weariness, and fear, and suffering, and unremitting labor" (169). In the end, though, the history of slavery is left behind as Northup returns to life in the North, and he concludes his narrative with a disturbing sense of resolution, as if his story is indeed over. "Chastened and subdued in spirit by the sufferings I have borne," Northup states in the narrative's concluding sentence, "and thankful to that good Being through whose mercy I had been restored to happiness and liberty, I hope henceforward to lead an upright though lowly life, and rest at last in the church yard where my father sleeps" (252). Ultimately, Northup's narrative returns its reader to the safety of the North as the sentimental site for antislavery feeling and as the site in which African American history can be safely contained. In this narrative, that is, the docudramatic tour of slavery disciplines black northern subjectivity.[21]

My point is not, I should emphasize, that knowledge of the daily lives and experiences of the enslaved communities is unimportant; rather, my point is that it is important to question the ways in which this knowledge is framed, and to question as well the implicit or explicit concept of historical understanding that serves as the canvas of such portraits. The limitations of knowledge of slavery's horrors are emphasized by the enormous popular and commercial response to Stowe's *Uncle Tom's Cabin*, which immediately inspired everything from plates to wallpaper to card games. Images of slavery's horrors were everywhere in white American and English culture, but they served the needs of white cultural self-definition and remained only shades away from the various racist images that were regularly featured in books, newspapers, and shopwindows.[22] As Marcus Wood has said, echoing Henry Louis Gates Jr.'s description of the cultural erasure of the reality of slavery, "The black as cultural absentee, the black as blank page for white guilt to inscribe, emerged as a necessary pre-condition for abolitionist polemic against the slave trade" (23). If the guiding assumption of historical study in the past has been that the story of an individual life does not constitute a history of slavery, this assumption now needs to be amended, and we must recognize that detailed descriptions of slavery similarly do not constitute a history of the system of slavery.

To offer an example of this, I need here to present a rather lengthy quotation from the Introduction to the 1968 reprinting of *Twelve Years a Slave*. This is, in fact, a quotation within a quotation, a framework within a framework, as editors Sue Eakin and Joseph Logsdon look back on the introduction of a previous reprinting of Northup's narrative:

> Shortly after the Civil War, Northup's narrative was republished by a Philadelphia firm. The editors made no attempt to ascertain the fate of its author. They felt that such an attempt was unnecessary since Northup's story had blended into the larger panorama of the nation's past.
>
>> To take in or to understand the exact status of such a people in all its bearings, we can pursue no better course than to live among them, to become one of them, to fall from a condition of freedom to one of bondage, to feel the scourge, to bear the marks of the brands, and the outrage of manacles. . . . It can be taken for what it is worth—a personal narrative of personal sufferings and keenly felt and strongly resented wrongs; but in our opinion, the individual will be lost or merged in the general interest and the work will be regarded as a history of an institution which our political economy has now happily superseded, but which, however much its existence may be regretted, should be studied—indeed, must be studied—by everyone whose interest in our country incites him to obtain a correct knowledge of her past existence.
>
> One hundred years later, this still constitutes a valid judgment on the significance of Solomon Northup's life and the importance of his narrative. (xv–xvi)

The assumptions guiding this presentation of Northup's story would be stunning were they not so common. Northup is subsumed by a historical abstraction that stands in for African American history and identity, and the institution of slavery is left safely in the past. What remains for (white) readers of the present (be it 1853, 1869, 1968, or today) is an easy empathy available to those who read Northup's narrative—a kind of historical blackface performance by which an imagined African American identity as shaped by the system of slavery can be known and understood. White readers become "one of them" by reading a narrative of an individual life in which the individual life is "lost or merged in the general interest," a general interest marked by the treatment of slavery as an isolated institution that can be both acknowledged and avoided, opened and contained, by "a correct knowledge" of the past.

The Master Narrative and the Silence of History

White antislavery history, as I am referring to it in this chapter, always reveals its investment in a systemic order that rests on the foundation of white supremacy, and it was this historical framework that defined the contours of African American biography and autobiography before the Civil War. Notwithstanding recent scholarship that has emphasized antislavery alliances across racial lines, African American writers and activists in the North recognized that white supremacy was the unspoken assumption even among those white reformers who were their most fervent allies. As early as 1837, Leon Litwack has observed, "when the *Colored American* reviewed the economic plight of the Negro in the wake of the Panic of 1837, it noted that not one local abolitionist had placed a Negro in any conspicuous position in his business establishment; in fact, it could not even find a Negro in the offices of the New York Anti-Slavery Society" ("Emancipation" 115). And as William H. and Jane H. Pease have noted, much of what white abolitionists said and did "betrayed an implicit and at times explicit belief in [black] racial inferiority" (*They Who Would Be Free* 97). Edmund Quincy, for example, "lashed out in a letter to Caroline Weston in 1846 at 'Wendell's nigger,' whom he held responsible for botching an Antislavery Report," and "as late as 1860 Theodore Parker, a backer of John Brown, observed [in a letter published in 1860] that 'the Anglo-Saxon with common sense does not like this Africanization of America; he wishes the superior race to multiply rather than the inferior'" (97–98).[23]

These were not isolated examples, as Frederick Douglass emphasized in his commentary on a letter from the Reverend Samuel Ringgold Ward published in *Frederick Douglass' Paper* on April 13, 1855. Noting that "we look upon the past as a precedent for the future," Douglass supports Ward's public declaration of frustration with white antislavery allies:

> Our oppressed people are wholly ignored, in one sense, in the generalship of the movement to effect our Redemption. Nothing is done—no, nothing, as our friend Ward asserts, to inspire us with the Idea of our Equality with the whites. We are a poor, pitiful, dependent and servile

class of Negroes, *"unable to keep pace"* with the movement, to which we have adverted—not even capable of *"perceiving what are its demands, or understanding the philosophy of its operations!"* Of course, if we are "unable to keep pace" with our white brethren, in their vivid perception of the demands of our cause, those who assume the leadership of the Anti-Slavery Movement; if it is regarded as having *"transcended our ability,"* we cannot consistently expect to receive from those who indulge in this opinion, a *practical recognition of our Equality.* This is what we are contending for. It is what we have never received. It is what we must receive to inspire us with confidence in the self-appointed generals of the Anti-Slavery host, the Euclids who are *theoretically* working out the almost insoluble problem of our future destiny. (Foner 2:360–61)

Douglass put it even more plainly in 1856, in an article titled "The Unholy Alliance of Negro Hate and Anti-Slavery": "Opposing slavery and hating its victims has come to be a very common form of Abolitionism" ("Unholy Alliance" 387). The selective vision of white antislavery reformers simply did not recognize the systemic implications of black oppression—but this recognition was fundamental to the black historical consciousness from its earliest manifestations in print, motivating the establishment of various institutions devoted to black communal self-determination.

A notable example of this selective vision is the address of the Jamaica Hamic Association, reprinted in the Report of the Committee on Commerce for the 1847 National Convention of Colored People in Troy, New York. (The association was formed with the encouragement of black abolitionist J. W. C. Pennington.) The address calls for economic cooperation and coordination among the scattered community of the African diaspora—noting, in its opening statement, that "by the mysterious providence of God, we find that captivity has dispersed our race far and wide"(Bell, *Minutes,* 1847 proceedings 22). After a description of black progress in Jamaica, the writers of the address note that without significant involvement in and control over commerce, black progress will be strictly limited. "Commerce," the address states, "is the great lever by which modern Europe has been elevated from a state of barbarism and social degradation, whose parallel is only to be found in the present condition of the African race" (23). This parallel, though, the writers of the address argue, has been overlooked by white reformers: "To our white Anti-slavery friends, we would convey our deep and abiding sense of the cordial interests which they have manifested in our advancement. We would at the same time express our regret that in their cursory visits among us, they seem to have quite overlooked the absence of commercial engagements among our class" (23). Increasingly as they approached midcentury, black writers wrote on political economy, commerce, and labor—the systemic context by which individual African American lives could speak of a broader historical story and exert control over the terms of that story.

The systemic structures that determined the contours of the stories that could be told about individual African American lives were quite strong, and the vision of history that black autobiographers could offer was, accordingly, predetermined. As James Olney has argued, "The conventions for slave narratives were so early and so firmly established that one can imagine a sort of master outline"—and Olney notes that "the irony of the phrasing" is "neither unintentional nor insignificant"—"drawn from the great narratives and guiding the lesser ones" (152). This outline would include the presentation of the book, the testimonials or prefaces written by white abolitionists "or by a white amanuensis/editor/author actually responsible for the text" (152); but it would include as well a number of narrative episodes—for example, the struggle for the acquisition of literacy, descriptions of "Christian" slaveholders who were more cruel than others, descriptions of whippings, and a "description of the amounts of food and clothing given to slaves, the work required of them, the pattern of a day, a week, a year" (153). This outline, Olney notes, is largely the result of the focused concern that inspired the writing and publishing of these narratives and that provided an audience for them: "Unlike autobiography in general the narratives are all trained on one and the same objective reality, they have a coherent and defined audience, they have behind them and guiding them an organized group of 'sponsors,' and they are possessed of very specific motives, intentions, and uses understood by narrators, sponsors, and audiences alike: to reveal the truth of slavery and so to bring about its abolition. How, then, could the narratives be anything but very much like one another?" (154).[24] One might revise Olney's question, though, and ask, given the conditions under which they were written, given the organized group of "sponsors" who guided and often edited the writing (or did the writing themselves), and given the cultural forces that shaped the audience for the narratives, what "truth of slavery" could an African American narrator in white America hope to present? What history could be embodied in an individual life story beyond the history expected, even required, by white antislavery sympathizers? What story could be told beyond the story that the antislavery movement told and expected slave narrators to reconfirm?

It is important, in short, to recognize that African American life stories were necessarily performances in the theater of antislavery culture. To say this, though, is not to present African American autobiographies and biographies as exceptional cases of historical writing, but simply to note the conditions under which these life stories can be understood as history—that is, as histories that operate beyond the docudramatic mode. There can be little doubt that readers of slave narratives were interested in something more than the "truth of slavery," for what counted as truth in the docudramatic mode had already been well established. Indeed, Olney's "master outline" emphasizes the extent to which slave narratives provided very predictable "truths." As Frances Smith Foster has argued, "While white abolitionists were eager to privilege the authenticity of black writers' descriptions of slavery, it was only insofar as their descriptions confirmed what white readers had actually accepted as true" (*Witnessing Slavery* 82). The exposure of the abuses under the system of slavery had become a set of conventional and frequent performances—and one can only confirm the wisdom of Dening's observation that "the 'theatricality of history-making' involves the notion of viewing in a space so closed around with convention that the audience and actors enter into the conspiracy of their own illusions" (105).

To recognize the illusions of the antislavery theater of history, illusions variously shared and resisted by African American autobiographical narrators, is to identify the challenges African American writers faced in trying to shift their performances to unauthorized versions of history. Frederick Douglass's 1845 *Narrative of the Life of Frederick Douglass, an American Slave*, so long celebrated as *the* representative narrative not only of life under slavery but of black identity generally, is perhaps most representative in the tensions it reveals between the story Douglass was expected to tell and the history of a life and of a people that called for telling. Robert B. Stepto, for example, has noted that Garrison's preface to Douglass's *Narrative* indicates that, rather than introduce the reader to Douglass's writing, "Garrison is far more interested in writing history . . . and recording his own place in it," and that, accordingly, "we might be tempted to see Garrison's 'Preface' at war with Douglass's tale for authorial control of the narrative as a whole" (*From Behind the Veil* 18). For Stepto, "that tension is stunted by Garrison's enthusiasm for Douglass's tale" (18–19); but for Andrews and others, the tension persists, becoming clear to Douglass himself when later he broke from the Garrisonians and thereby "gained a perspective that allowed him to see signs of 'oppression' in the very 'form' of the fugitive slave narrative that he had written in 1845" (Andrews 217). Douglass's 1855 *My Bondage and My Freedom*, in Andrews's persuasive reading, becomes a declaration of independence not only from the paternal authority of Garrison and the Garrisonian mode of antislavery activism but also from the narrative conventions that determined the history that Douglass could draw from his life in 1845.

Marcus Wood's equally persuasive reading of the 1845 *Narrative*, however, shows Douglass at war with the conventions from the beginning of his autobiographical career. "Douglass challenged the frameworks of the nineteenth-century slave narrative," Wood argues, "and ironised the descriptive and linguistic codes to describe the act of escape," often providing "set pieces that are so perfect in the way they enact the established patterns . . . that they are parodic" (101). "In many ways," Wood argues, "Douglass's *Narrative* gave models of how *not* to give the white Northern abolitionist readers what they wanted or expected" (100)—the most notable being Douglass's sly omission of that part of his narrative in which readers would be most interested, the means of his escape from slavery.[25] Ultimately, though, Wood argues that despite the *Narrative*'s "rhetorical ironising of both Southern and Northern constructions of the fugitive," Douglass's efforts were "finally powerless to resist absorption into the iconographic reductions of the popular print market" (79). As a "final irony," Wood notes, "the free North did everything it could to fill, indeed to obliterate in clamour, the silences which Douglass created around his escape, and his responses to his escape" (102).

But if the clamor persisted, so did the silences—for Douglass's approach is characteristic of the means by which many African American autobiographical narrators relocated the grounds of history in their narratives. The stories told by many autobiographical narrators, that is, address "historical truth" through strategic omissions, indicating the untold stories that resisted representation, stories beyond what white audiences were prepared to hear or were capable of understanding. For example, in an expansion of the narrative he first set out to write, the Reverend G. W. Offley notes that he had been requested by friends to tell a story of a slave woman and her two children that he had mentioned along the way. "I omitted several stories," Offley comments, "because I did not design it as an anti-slavery book, but merely a short sketch of my youthful life, as I am aware that the slave is a hopeless victim in this country" (22). Turning to the larger antislavery story that he was expected to both tell and represent in his life, Offley emphasizes that that larger antislavery narrative remains largely untold, as if to suggest that the hopelessness he feels is a product not only of slavery but also of the controlled narrative of antislavery. "This is not a fictitious tale," Offley cautions, "but a true story. I could write a book of facts more sad than this story, but let this suffice" (28).

That larger book of facts remains uncontained by this story, and the story told is but one of many stories long available to antislavery readers—the story of individual lives victimized by a clearly identifiable manifestation of slavery, the oppressive southern slaveholder. Offley certainly indicates that larger story in much that he relates—for example, his mother's threat to those planning to purchase her children that "they might buy them and welcome, but you had better throw your money in the fire, for if you buy one of my children I will cut all three of their throats while they are asleep, and your money will do you no good" (4). The larger story is indicated as well in Offley's relating his conversation with a slaveholder who wanted Offley to marry his slave girl:

> Here I stopped asking questions and began with my abrupt objections. First objection was because she was almost white; second objection that she might be his illegitimate daughter, and I am utterly opposed to marrying any white man's illegitimate daughter, or otherwise and fur- thermore, I am opposed to the mixing of the two races, and wish the devil had every white man who first originated the system of turning niggers white, for the system has so corrupted our race that you can scarcely tell one race from the other. Then, said he, you think it makes them worse to turn them white, do you? I do, sir; they were not half so devilish in Africa. (39–40)

Offley here and elsewhere indicates the larger, systemic story of slavery that would constitute the "historical truth" within which individual stories of oppression could be understood—a story not simply of individual oppressors but of a system of oppression.

African American writers recognized that identity was multiply contin- gent—defined, that is, not only in the relation of slaveholder and slave or of generalized black and white, but also in those multiple relations shaped by a white supremacist culture. Free of the governing authority over identity in the South, those who escaped found themselves governed again by white anti- slavery assumptions about the meaning of a fugitive identity. African Ameri- cans in the North found themselves defined in relation to a generalized black identity in racist communities and in relation to an unrepresented and unrepresentable black community in the South. Strategic narrative omissions responded to these multiple contingencies by locating the moral authority beyond the sphere of white readers. The dilemma African American auto-biographical narrators faced, then, was to engage in an intricate play of representation from which the voice of historical truth could emerge—a dilemma captured well by Jacqueline Goldsby in her commentary on Harriet Jacobs's narrative approach. "Since, according to Jacobs, 'truth' can be discovered only if it is left 'concealed,'" Goldsby argues, "rules of documentary evidence may not resolve the dilemma that *Incidents*, as a slave narrative, confronts: how to preserve testimony of an experience that is itself beyond representation" (12). Jacobs's response, as I have argued, like that of many autobiographical narrators, is to insist that white northern readers could not understand the story they were being told. "Only by experience," Jacobs asserts in her preface, "can any one realize how deep, and dark, and foul is that pit of abominations," "what Slavery really is" (2). Throughout her narrative, Jacobs confronts her readers with their own lack of experience and their corresponding inability to understand. She asks at one point, "O reader, can you imagine my joy?"; and she answers, "No, you cannot, unless you have been a slave mother" (173). Similarly, Douglass notes toward the end of his narrative that, to understand his situation, "one must needs experience it, or imagine himself in similar circumstances" (*Narrative* 90). Having left open the door of imagination, Douglass then lists the requirements of understanding that clearly keep the white reader from even an imagined empathy, noting at the end of this long list, "I say, let him be placed in this most trying situation,—the situation in which I was placed,—then, and not till then, will he fully appreciate the hardships of, and know how to sympathize with, the toil-worn and whip-scarred fugitive slave" (90).

At the heart of this assertion about the experience that is the foundation for representational authority is an assertion about the moral authority necessary to construct the history of African American life and to determine the contours of African American identity within that history. Accordingly, as African American autobiographical writers depicted the ways in which their lives had been shaped by oppression, and as they underscored the inability of most of their readers to understand the larger picture behind the individual depictions—the full story behind the isolated episodes, the world beyond the incidents—they worked also to represent the development of a different self, one defined not *by* oppression but *against* it, a self uncontainable by the U.S. cultural system. This other life (and the corresponding world of that life) represented in the great majority of African American autobiographical texts emerges in the story of the resistance to oppression but involves more than simply political debates; this other life involves the belief in an overarching realm of order, a divine governing system that gave purpose and direction to lives undervalued or marginalized by the U.S. cultural system. Indeed, most African American autobiographical writing of this period could be viewed less as attempts to represent the evils of the secular realm than as attempts to claim ties to the sacred realm, as is clear particularly in two of the most striking spiritual autobiographies of this period, Jarena Lee's *The Life and Religious Experience of Jarena Lee, a Coloured Lady, Giving an Account of Her Call to Preach the Gospel* (1836) and Zilpha Elaw's *Memoirs of the Life, Religious Experience, Ministerial Travels, and Labours of Mrs. Zilpha Elaw, an American Female of Color* (1846). In Lee's and Elaw's spiritual autobiographies, we see two attempts to establish moral citizenship in both this world and the next—and, indeed, to argue for the necessity of that dual citizenship. Lee and Elaw, that is, present what might be called narratives of sacred national selfhood, ways of reconceptualizing the relation between sacred and secular life, national and individual life, that speak volumes about the challenges of representing African American history to skeptical, condescending, or otherwise resisting readers.

I can best explain what I mean by this by referring to one of the most prominent representations of national selfhood, the figure of George Washington that we encounter in volume 7 of Bancroft's *History of the United States*. Bancroft's Washington is a model of the representative American; indeed, Bancroft presents him as one whose "faculties were so well balanced and combined, that his constitution, free from excess, was tempered evenly with all the elements of activity, and his mind resembled a well ordered commonwealth" (7:396–97).[26] A perfect example of a just correspondence between individual mind and nation, Washington in the pages of Bancroft's *History* embodies the principle *e pluribus unum*, and becomes the site for national balance: "Combining the centripetal and centrifugal forces in their utmost strength and in perfect relations, with creative grandeur of instinct he held ruin in check, and renewed and perfected the institutions of his country. Finding the colonies disconnected and dependent, he left them such a united and well ordered commonwealth as no visionary had believed to be possible" (7:400).[27] Bancroft's message, here and throughout the *History*, is that ideological conflict is necessary, for only through conflict can limited and partial perspectives be combined and balanced to create a new mode of understanding. But the conflict requires a mind attuned to the directives of providence, directives no one—for example, the visionaries Bancroft refers to here—can know with certainty.

And because this intellectual balance must be communicated to others, Washington's voice is as important as his mind. This is, after all, a history in which the narrator at one point bursts forth in Whitmanian rhapsody, "Go forth, then, language of Milton and Hampden, language of my country, take possession of the North American continent!" (4:456). Viewed in this light, Washington becomes representative in his ability to combine and balance not only political forces but discursive ones as well. What we see in Bancroft's presentation of Washington is, in fact, strikingly similar to Mikhail Bakhtin's conception of the complex world of social language. Social language, Bakhtin reminds us, is actually a world of many languages—for example, those of different social stratifications and professions, or those of specialized fields of knowledge—indicating different experiences of and perspectives on life. When one speaks, as Bakhtin argues, one participates in this complex world, to the extent that "every concrete utterance of a speaking subject serves as a point where centrifugal as well as centripetal forces are brought to bear" (272). "The processes of centralization and decentralization, of unification and disunification," Bakhtin contends, "intersect in the utterance" (272). Understanding thus becomes a communal process, something formed when different ways of speaking about the world work with and against one another. In this way, the mythologized Washington that we encounter in the national- ist fantasy of Bancroft's *History* becomes a model not only of leadership but also of judicious speech, balancing the warring factions of the rising nation in a "well ordered commonwealth" of careful utterances.[28]

I say this not in spite of but because of the fact that Bancroft very carefully avoids presenting Washington as a man who lives by and through words. "Washington," Bancroft asserts, "was a man of action, and not of theory or words; his creed appears in his life, not in his professions, which burst from him very rarely, and only at those great moments of crisis in the fortunes of his country, when earth and heaven seemed actually to meet, and his emo- tions became too intense for suppression; but his whole being was one con- tinued act of faith in the eternal, intelligent, moral order of the universe" (7:398). One might say that as the central representative of governing order in the midst of what Washington Irving would later call the American "logocracy or *government of words*" (qtd. in Gustafson 6), George Washington must be a master of discourse. A man of few words, Washington becomes a man of meaningful silences. And when Bancroft's Washington speaks, his voice rises from the intersection of providential and human history, and his utterances embody and transcend conflicting historical and social forces in a new union of national identity.

If we attend to the underlying cultural logic of Bancroft's representation of Washington, then we can follow that logic beyond Bancroft's implicit boundaries and see a correspondence between this white father of the country and those whom Andrews terms "sisters of the spirit." In the autobiographies of Jarena Lee and Zilpha Elaw, one encounters a version of representative selfhood that stands at the intersection of providential and human history and that speaks with the moral authority grounded in but transcending the conflicting forces of human understanding. In these autobiographies the well-constituted Christian is the truly representative self—a self claiming citizenship in both earthly and providential cities; and in these works one's fundamental allegiances are revealed by one's language. When attending the death of her sister, for example, Elaw witnesses her sister's crisis of faith—"I am going to hell," her sister announces from her deathbed—and Elaw witnesses as well her sister's subsequent vision of salvation that rises from this conflict. Commenting on the spiritual victory, Elaw speaks of the "antagonizing conflicts of Christian faith," conflicts that constitute "the natural cause and effect of exercise of Christian faith, in collision with forces asserted by the gospel to be engaged in hostile action to it" (72–73). Noting the universality of this experience, Elaw speaks of Christian conflict and triumph as a "uniformity, like that of the human constitution, admitting of the greatest variety of individual features, yet all governed by the same laws" (73). Like Bancroft's representative of republican selfhood, the Christian self Elaw here describes embodies the complex and conflicted forces of this world and speaks of a possible commonwealth of faith. And out of the spiritual struggle comes a new understanding and a new discourse, for although Elaw's sister is momentarily "to all appearance dead," she revives again, and sings in a language, Elaw reports, "too wonderful for me"; "I could not understand it." The sister then addresses Elaw and informs her that she "must preach the gospel" (73).

While we should recognize that Elaw believes that this possible commonwealth of faith cannot be held within geographical boundaries, it is still important to note her emphasis on its most productive earthly location—for Elaw, like so many others, finds Providence blossoming most fully in the fields of America. Just as many early celebrants of the United States viewed the nation not geographically but ideologically, anticipating the day when all

the world would be America, so Elaw, who believes in the universality of the
Christian faith, believes that America is the ideal site for its development—
and for largely the same reasons as did such literary nationalists as Whitman
and Bancroft. "Human nature must be in every country radically the same,"
Elaw asserts, for "God is the same"; yet, she argues, "the word preached is
generally attended in America with far more powerful and converting results
than in Britain" (144). And although she declines to fully "account for the
cause," she speculates that "the population of the United States have not
been so extensively vitiated by the infidelity and sedition of the press; and
being more thinly spread over an immense territorial space, there is less of
contamination than in the more condensed masses of English society; and
they perhaps possess more honest simplicity of character, and less of the self-
sufficiency of a licentious intellectuality and worldly wisdom" (144). This is a
largely familiar vision of America as a garden of republican virtues thus far
relatively uncorrupted by the temptations of the centralized power and en-
trenched authority that comes with the earthly city.[29] The expansiveness of
the garden itself becomes providential in Elaw's vision, forestalling intellectual and moral contamination simply by making the promotion of worldly
wisdom more difficult.

In this vision of the American city on a hill, as in Bancroft's, the struggle
for faith becomes a battle of conflicting discourses. It is not for nothing that
Elaw warns her readers, "Take heed what you read," and presents the press as
"a tree of knowledge, both of good and evil"—for the press, she warns, is
capable of disrupting and even inverting the relation between words and their
referents, "putting darkness for light, and light for darkness" (52). The press,
Elaw warns, can be "the scavenger of slander, and the harlequin of character;
the masquerade of morals, and the burlesque of religion; the proteus of
sentiment, and the dictionary of licentiousness; the seminary of libertines,
and the hot-bed of sedition" (52). It can so distort moral discourse that the
individual subject of discourse can find herself or himself wandering down a
path that diverges from the providential course. "It is to be deplored," Elaw
laments late in her *Memoirs*, "that there are so many Christians . . . who are of
the world; [who] speak in accordance with its principles and sentiments, and
walk according to its course" (141). Presenting in print her case against the
press, Elaw enters into a struggle not only against those who walk according to
the world's course, but also against the source of the misunderstandings that
encourage such worldly walkers—the misuse of the press and of language
itself.

Like Bancroft's Washington, that is, Lee and Elaw suggest that the representative self must represent discursive governance—a morally driven system of checks and balances capable of transforming limited human utterances into a language capable of speaking transcendent truths. In Lee's and Elaw's spiritual autobiographies, moral self-discovery is not simply a matter of learning one's moral lessons; rather, moral self-discovery is the process of learning how to align the human word with the divine intention. Lee, for example, begins her autobiography and her spiritual journey with a lie; she soon finds herself with a Roman Catholic family that presents her with a novel when she wants to read the Bible; and when she aligns her own words and deeds, once her "heart had believed" and her "tongue had made confession unto salvation," the "first words uttered," she reports, were "a part of that song, which shall fill eternity with its sound": "*glory to God*" (29). From the teller of a lie to a voice in a larger chorus, Lee enters into a moral commonwealth, where language itself is transformed. With sanctification comes her entrance into a new spiritual realm that is also a new realm of discourse: "So great was my joy," she reports, "that it is past description. There is no language that can describe it, except that which was heard by St. Paul, when he was caught up to the third heaven, and heard words which it was not lawful to utter" (34).

Lee's and Elaw's autobiographies point to this realm past description and a discourse "not lawful to utter," but they exist to serve a world governed by other discursive laws; and both authors work to reconstitute the discourse of this world under the governing spirit of the divine realm. They work toward what Elaw calls "a pure language"—and as she explains this concept, it becomes clear that a pure language exists in distinction to human discourse. "A pure language," Elaw explains, "unallowed by the fulsome compliment, the hyperbole, the tautology and circumlocution, the insinuation, double meaning and vagueness, the weakness and poverty, the impurity, bombast, and other defects, with which all human languages are clogged, seems to be essential for the associations of glorified spirits" (74). The language Elaw imagines is, as I have said, *distinct* from human discourse, but it is not *separated* from it; indeed, this pure language rises from the confused mix of social languages. It cannot be known positively, and so must be discerned in negatives, by recognizing "the defects, with which all human languages are clogged." One cannot unclog human language, but if one can recognize the limitations of various forms of human discourse, as Elaw demonstrates here, and recognize also the conflicting varieties of the languages we speak, then one can at least apprehend another language, one expressive of a communal understanding that is something more than the sum of the individual human parts. As Washington's silences spoke eloquently of "one continued act of faith in the eternal, intelligent, moral order of the universe," so Elaw's attention to the noisy defects of human speech points to other possible modes of understanding.

The limitations of language, Elaw suggests, themselves reveal a world of truths just beyond human understanding; to know one's limits is to maintain an awareness of that which lies beyond those limits. Similarly, Jarena Lee looks to such limitations to establish specifically linguistic evidence in support of her vision of hell. Alluding to the biblical descriptions of hell, Lee argues that "this language is too strong and expressive to be applied to any state of suffering in *time*. Were it to be thus applied, the reality could no where be found in human life; the consequence would be, that *this* scripture would be found a false testimony. But when made to apply to an endless state of perdition, in eternity, beyond the bounds of human life, then this language is found not to exceed our views of a state of eternal damnation" (31). Essentially, Lee here measures the inadequacy of any available referents for the biblical signifiers. Descriptions of fire "which burneth with brimstone" and of a "bottomless pit" speak of an unaccountable reality, and its very inapplicability in this world serves as evidence for the existence of another, terrible reality beyond the limits of human understanding and conventional credulity.

In this way, skepticism becomes part of the constitution of faith, for skepticism stands as evidence of the human inability to fully comprehend a reality that Lee and Elaw assert is evident in their lives.[30] Skepticism, that is, identifies the conceptual boundaries of human discourse, a discourse that itself can only promote partial and contested perspectives. And the divine author, working to make those boundaries clear in order to draw humanity to a nearer apprehension of the workings of Providence, finds the best vehicles to be those who will inspire the most skepticism: Lee, a "poor colored female instrument," Elaw, "an American Female of Colour." These instruments of divine authorship are uniquely suited to the task of exposing those whose investment in this world keeps them from recognizing the presence of another. As Elaw notes, "There are many sceptical persons who conceitedly, rashly, and idly scoff at the idea of apparitions and angelic appearances; but they ignorantly do it in the face of the most extensive experience, instinct, belief, and credible testimony of persons of every nation, and of all ages, as well as the inspired statements of the Scriptures" (77). Speaking from the conceptual world of scriptural statements, Elaw sees a world of "facts"—

evidence of "the separate existence of the soul after death"—far more powerful and universal than those on which human governance relies (77–78).
Throughout their spiritual autobiographies, Lee and Elaw anticipate and
even count on the reader's resisting and skeptical response, and build that
response into their texts, there to take part in the ongoing conflicts of human
languages.

Lee's and Elaw's culturally assigned positions—in sharp contrast to their
experience and verbal achievements (they have, after all, become known for
their ability to transform others by words alone)—emphasize that the voice
being resisted is not that of the "poor colored female instrument" but rather
that which sounds through the instrument. As Elaw puts it at the beginning of
her *Memoirs*, she offers in this book "a representation, not, indeed, of the
features of my outward person, drawn and coloured by the skill of the pencil-
ling artist, but of the lineaments of my inward man, as inscribed by the Holy
Ghost" (51). But throughout her spiritual autobiography as throughout Lee's,
Elaw clearly addresses the world that has "drawn and coloured" her outward
person in its own group portrait of the world. Shaping their narratives to
emphasize the presence of a greater artist working through their lives, and
speaking to that world of penciling artists, Lee and Elaw draw together the
various conceptual worlds they encounter into a single system of discursive
governance—making it possible to see the ways in which, as Lee puts it, "our
by-laws of church government and discipline" can "bring into disrepute even
the word of life" (36). And making it possible as well to reconceive what might
seem "fanciful speculations" as "matters of fact" (Elaw 77), a world of revelatory fact and a governing spirit that dominates human life but that human
governance has not yet learned to see.[31]

Revelatory facts indicating a governing spirit are at the heart of Harriet
Jacobs's *Incidents in the Life of a Slave Girl*, as is the task of learning to
interpret those facts and learning one's duty to the spirit. Indeed, one might
say that the story of Linda Brent, the pseudonymous narrator of *Incidents*, is
the story of learning to read anew the divinely authored text of the human
spirit, but that the "human spirit" in this text is not allowed to remain a
disembodied abstraction but rather is presented as an embodied and contingent presence defined by the correspondence between human action and
divine order. This autobiography is striking in a number of respects, but
particularly in its vivid presentation of the sexual crimes committed within
the self-justifying institution of slavery. Jacobs tells of the aggressive sexual
advances of her enslaver, Dr. Flint; of her decision to take a white lover, Mr.

Sands, to avoid Flint's advances; of the children she has through her relations with Mr. Sands; and of her long journey—taken largely to protect her children's future—to the relative freedom of the North. This narrative that begins with an appeal to "the blessing of God" ends with Brent in the North and legally "free," but still without a home of her own—for, she notes, "God so orders circumstance as to keep me with my friend [and employer] Mrs. Bruce" (201). The central question, then, of *Incidents* concerns the relation between Linda Brent's story of moral struggle and the providential narrative—the divinely ordered circumstance—that she invokes at the end.

The paradox of Brent's existence—as a voice for the moral code that she herself has been forced to transgress—is represented at the very beginning of the narrative, on the title page itself. The reader encounters there two epigraphs: the first is a testament, by "a woman of North Carolina," to the degradation inflicted and enforced by the slave system; the second is from the book of Isaiah (32:9): "Rise up, ye women that are at ease! Hear my voice, ye careless daughters! Give ear unto my speech." These epigraphs identify two spheres of existence—northerners who are ignorant and women who are morally "at ease," each capable of a culturally empowered response to this condition—from which the subject of the book, Linda Brent herself, is excluded; they mark the points of a moral journey that she cannot make. Brent's story exists in neither of these two spheres of existence but rather within the world of experience from which each sphere is distanced.[32]

Indeed, Linda Brent's experiences lead her to wonder, even as she identifies herself within the moral sphere, how exactly, by what providential design, her identity and experience as a slave can be possible. She finds herself torn between a paternal model of divinity and a conception of the divine realm that offers otherworldly echoes of politics as usual: "Sometimes I thought God was a compassionate Father, who would forgive my sins for the sake of my sufferings. At other times, it seemed to me there was no justice or mercy in the divine government" (123). "These things," she tells the reader, referring to the existence and perpetuation of "the curse of slavery," "took the shape of mystery, which is to this day not so clear to my soul as I trust it will be hereafter" (123). Lost in the contradictions of the "forms" of human culture, Jacobs sees not a science revealing the great movement of history but rather an inscrutable mystery.

The hope for a renewed awareness of the motive "idea" that informs human history—the means by which Providence finds its human agency—is restricted by the very "forms" used to give shape and meaning to hope. The

model for understanding and maintaining the correspondence between human history and divine history is neither the father nor government, for both
paradigms ultimately invert the relation between the national structure and
its putative foundation. The best model, in effect, would be no model at all—
for all paradigms of the inexpressible are all too human, too eminently ex-
pressible. Like many other African American writers, Jacobs holds determinedly to the theology of Christian mystery as the hermeneutical key to
biblical law. Mystery signifies that which lies beyond human understanding,
and which therefore calls for scrupulous attention to the "forms" of human
history and self-government that obscure the mystery by projecting it on
ideological screens. Mystery signifies as well a mode of understanding and of
communication, an inspired *speaking* not in tongues but rather in the understanding that comes of suspended uncertainty and incomprehension in the
face of revelation—a speaking beyond what one can know, and a speaking that
acknowledges the limits of one's understanding.[33]

Essentially, Brent's struggle is to rediscover the community of mystery
from a disfranchised but therefore morally privileged position. She begins the
struggle for a renewed community when she recognizes that she must engage
in it alone, at the turning point in the narrative, when she refuses Dr. Flint's
"offer" to establish her in a cottage as his mistress. Dr. Flint makes perfectly
clear the restricted terms of this offer: " 'there are,' " he notes rather un-
necessarily, " 'two sides to my proposition; if you reject the bright side, you
will be obliged to take the dark one' " (84). The "bright" side, of course, refers
to Flint's attempt to reposition Brent as a woman (from the site of deferred
desire to the site for sexual exchange) by manipulating her identity as a
mother (offering a "better" life for her children). Adapting Flint's terminology, Brent begins her struggle as a determined and self-determining woman
and mother: "I had my secret hopes; but I must fight my battle alone. I had a
woman's pride, and a mother's love for my children; and I resolved that out of
the darkness of this hour a brighter dawn should rise for them. My master had
power and law on his side; I had a determined will. There is might in each"
(85). This battle is an ideological American civil war, a battle between, on the
one hand, the power and law that claim to both support and depend on
womanhood and motherhood and, on the other, the will of one who is determined to embody the virtues associated with womanhood and motherhood. It is a battle between human and divine law—between human history
and Providence—a battle that can be fought only by one who is a product
of both.[34]

In this struggle lies the hope of a renewed community, the development of an invisible family of the oppressed. For Brent's task is to save her children by first seeming to abandon them and to place her hopes in the reunion of her family in the far dream of self-liberation. With mother and children separated physically, the bonds of this family can be experienced only spiritually, and the experience strengthens Brent's resolve and heightens her spiritual awareness. She begins the struggle against "the doom that awaited my fair baby in slavery" by going to the graves of her parents to vow to save her children "or perish in the attempt" (90). Noting that her own mother's deathbed blessing had been a continuing comfort, she tells the reader that "in many an hour of tribulation I had seemed to hear her voice, sometimes chiding me, sometimes whispering loving words into my wounded heart" (90).[35] While this might seem the conventional voice of motherhood speaking through the heart of memory, a staple of sentimental discourse, Jacobs increasingly makes it clear that she is speaking of a distinctively African American experience of the spirit, of visions and prophecy.[36]

As Brent hears other voices and discovers other bonds, she indicates the revolutionary subtext of the narrative, the threatening presence of the oppressed community endorsed and protected by God. At the graveyard, Brent is reminded of the voice of her mother; as she leaves, she *hears* the voice of her father—significantly, while passing a place associated with either the threat or promise (depending on one's reading of sacred history) of black insurrection: "As I passed the wreck of the old meeting house, where, before Nat Turner's time, the slaves had been allowed to meet for worship, I seemed to hear my father's voice come from it, bidding me not to tarry till I reached freedom or the grave. I rushed on with renovated hopes. My trust in God had been strengthened by that prayer among the graves" (91). The voice signifies the intersection of providential and human history, the manifest sign of one's election as an agent of God.[37] Only when most alone is Brent able to enter into this increasingly visible and imminent community—and the community is increased and strengthened by the threat of oppression that makes it dangerous to acknowledge a common struggle. The bonds of community are forced into literally unspeakable realms, imagined but not known, experienced but not discussed. Referring to her friend Fanny's own seclusion, Jacobs notes the "similar burden[s] of anxiety and fear" experienced by Fanny's mother Aggie and Brent's grandmother—"dangerous secrets [that] deepened the sympathy between the two old persecuted mothers" (149). Similarly, Brent eventually rediscovers her own brother William in one of those coincidences that support the belief in a transcendent, overruling order. Noting that William's "old feelings of affection for me and Ellen were as lively as ever," Brent speaks of the community formed of similar burdens and dangerous secrets when she adds, "There are no bonds so strong as those which are formed by suffering together" (170).

At the beginning of her own long seclusion, Brent has yet another vision, and she emphasizes that this is not to be taken as sentimental figuration but rather as a distinctively spiritual experience:

> And now I will tell you something that happened to me; though you will, perhaps, think it illustrates the superstition of slaves. . . . A band of serenaders were under the window, playing "Home, sweet home." I listened till the sounds did not seem like music, but like the moaning of children. It seemed as if my heart would burst. I rose from my sitting posture, and knelt. A streak of moonlight was on the floor before me, and in the midst of it appeared the forms of my two children. They vanished; but I had seen them distinctly. Some will call it a dream, others a vision. I know not how to account for it, but it made a strong impression on my mind, and I felt certain something had happened to my little ones. (107–8)

In this remarkable account, the evocation of the domestic sphere leads Brent not merely to an instinctual awareness of her children but to a manifest vision. We miss an important dimension of Brent's narrative—and of Jacobs's broader accounting of her world—when we pass by this lightly or try to account for it in ways that Brent herself cannot, for the motive power of a new mode of envisioning lies in the dynamics of individual belief, the unquestioning acceptance of mystifying experience. The point is not to understand it but rather to acknowledge that which lies beyond understanding, and thereby to identify the limitations of culturally authorized ways of knowing. This vision, like the voices of her parents, signals Brent's transition from the labyrinths of the self-contradictory American ideological realm to a defiantly mysterious realm beyond, where the citizens of God's moral government speak beyond what culturally trained ears can hear.[38]

In this way, Jacobs accounts for and capitalizes on her own lack of cultural authority—not just as a woman but as a black woman, and relocates African American history from the slaveholding South to the community of faith that resides between principle and practice, a community homeless but not forsaken. Through her representative Linda Brent, Jacobs can speak of the presence in her life of something absent from her world. The "dream of [her] life . . . not yet realized," and lacking "a hearthstone of [her] own, however humble" (201), Linda Brent embodies the disjunction of the sacred and the secular, which can be rejoined only by realigning human practices with a providential design threatening in its inscrutability. The silence of the mystery that informs Linda Brent's journey to relative freedom and that joins the community of the oppressed is significant precisely because there seem to be no words capable of giving it adequate expression. African American history, in Jacobs's autobiography as in others, is a story waiting to be told but struggling against whatever language might be available for the telling, the language that carries the traces of and is restricted by the contingencies of a white supremacist social order. The history presented in African American autobiographies is a story about a search for community, about the collective need to join principle and practice so as to reframe the language by which one might find one's home and live in a stable community of like-minded believers.

The Community of History and the Site of Liberation

In the revolutionary silence of the unspeakable lies the heart of the historical vision presented in African American autobiographical narratives. Jacobs's significant attention to the community has often been noted as a distinguishing feature of her narrative and, it has been argued, of a woman-centered approach to the narrative of selfhood under slavery—but beyond the concerns of gendered narratives is a larger question raised by Jacobs's representation of a communal resistance to slavery: where, in African American autobiographical narratives, is there any indication of the community of, say, the very black abolitionists who were writing these narratives? It is striking that the authors and subjects of slave narratives and other autobiographies so rarely acknowledge other narrators in their narratives—and, again, we find ourselves with a collective body of work that emphasizes the scattered community, with each individual story called to stand in as a representative tale but with only a generalized or generalizable community represented. African American autobiographical narratives are notable for how much is withheld and for how much might be told were the stories put together.[39] In identifying the silence that waits beyond the borders of the conventions of white constructions of African American history and identity, though, the autobiographical narrators indicated a larger story, spoke to those who could read the history behind those silences, and established a cultural position from which to speak about the systemic history unacknowledged by the official stories of white history. In part, as Stepto has argued, this communal history had to be achieved by shaping the demands of the narrative toward "a ritualized journey into a symbolic South" by which the protagonist can find "new-found balms of group identity" that can "ameliorate, if not obliterate, the conditions imposed by solitude" (qtd. in Andrews 238–39). But the communal identity can be found also in the immersion in northern black life and culture and indicated by an individual voice of historical authority that reiterates the collective vision of the community.

Frederick Douglass's work offers a useful example of this double-voiced historical commentary, for Douglass's 1845 *Narrative* is often viewed as *the* example of a narrative of individual struggle. Andrews, for example, has suggested that the significant shift from the 1845 *Narrative* to the 1855 *My Bondage and My Freedom* can be viewed as a turn from an individual story to a communal narrative. "Although Douglass would not record a literal return to the South until his 1881 *Life and Times*," Andrews argues, "his second autobiography represents his imaginative journey into a South resonant with the symbols of the 'group identity' that Douglass, in 1855, required with a special, poignant need. To create *My Bondage and My Freedom* was to retrace the arc of Frederick Douglass's ascent so that its coordinates became unmistakably communal, not merely individual, so that his apotheosis read immersion in the group identity of Afro-America" (239).[40] But it is important to note that in 1845, too, Douglass carefully places his story of individual struggle within the framework of communal historical understanding—most prominently, by way of his inclusion of an appendix. In the appendix, Douglass returns to his potentially disturbing commentary on religion throughout the narrative proper. "I find," Douglass states at the beginning of the appendix, "since reading over the foregoing Narrative that I have, in several instances, spoken in such a tone and manner, respecting religion, as may possibly lead those unacquainted with my religious views to suppose me an opponent of all religion" (*Narrative* 97). To correct possible misunderstandings, Douglass states directly, "What I have said respecting and against religion, I mean strictly to apply to the *slaveholding religion* of this land, and with no possible reference to Christianity proper; for, between the Christianity of this land, and the Christianity of Christ, I recognize the widest possible difference—so wide, that to receive the one as good, pure, and holy, is of necessity to reject the other as bad, corrupt, and wicked" (97). Douglass clarifies his position even further by emphasizing that he is talking not only about the practice of Christianity in the South but about "the Christianity of America," "north and south" (99, 100).

In making this distinction, the appendix provides the key to understanding the U.S. cultural system and the interpretive key to understanding the *Narrative* itself.[41] It is important to note, therefore, that Douglass here draws heavily from a much-debated resolution passed at the 1843 National Convention of Colored Citizens, held at Buffalo. It was at this convention that Henry Highland Garnet's famous *Address to the Slaves* was presented and hotly debated, with Douglass particularly influential among those who defeated a vote adopting the address as an official statement of the convention. From its initial call to its many debates, the 1843 convention emphasized the need for the black community to organize and work on its own behalf. "Shall we . . . look to the abolitionists," asked Chairman Samuel H. Davis in his opening address, "and wait for them to give us our rights?" Davis's racialization of "the abolitionists" here is, of course, revealing, and perhaps speaks of the larger project that black social reformers envisioned as well as suspicions about the limited sympathy and understanding encouraged by white antislavery activism. The convention joined Davis in asserting the need for black self-determination and in denouncing the systemic oppression of the national system of slavery in resolutions on political parties, on economic independence, and on the nation's so-called Christian churches.

It is the last of these concerns that informs Douglass's appendix to the 1845 *Narrative* in the form of resolutions about U.S. churches, the wording of which concerned Douglass greatly. In their final form, the four resolutions on American churches begin by asserting belief "in the true Church of Christ," which "will stand while time endures." This church, the resolution states, "will evince its spirit by its opposition to all sins, and especially to the sin of slavery, which is a compound of all others." "The great mass of American sects, falsely called churches," the resolution asserts, "which apologize for slavery and prejudice, or practice slaveholding, are in truth no churches, but Synagogues of Satan." The second of the resolutions emphasizes this last point, identifying "slaveholding and prejudice sustaining ministers and churches (falsely so called)" as "the greatest enemies to Christ and to civil and religious liberty in the world." The resolutions that follow call on "the colored people in the free States" to resist these churches, participation in which makes them "guilty of enslaving themselves and others" (15). Echoing these resolutions in the appendix to his *Narrative*, and presenting the case for these resolutions throughout the *Narrative*, Douglass brings a subtext of black-organized resistance to his autobiography that is rarely noted. The black community is in the narrative; its history provides the framework for reading and understanding the story of American slavery and prejudice.[42]

African American autobiographical narrators like Douglass faced the challenge of telling the story of lives shaped not only by the system of slavery but also by the assumptions of the white antislavery movement; and the history that they address is often a direct response to these shaping forces. Entering into the heart of the ideological contradictions of the U.S. social, political, legal, and religious order, these narrators pursued a historiography of liberation that identifies *history* as the response to these systemic fissures. The narrative of the obscured and often unspeakable individual and collective story that operates within those fissures is more suggested than revealed, indicated by what has been omitted or by what has been left behind.

Consider, for example, William G. Allen's *The American Prejudice against Color: An Authentic Narrative, Showing How Easily the Nation Got into an Uproar*, published in London, Edinburgh, and Dublin in 1853. Allen, who identifies himself on the title page as "a refugee from American despotism," begins the narrative by offering a brief introduction to his impressive credentials, and also to his complex identity as viewed through an American lens:

> I am a quadroon, that is, I am of one-fourth African blood, and three-fourths Anglo-Saxon. I graduated at Oneida Institute, in Whitesboro', New York, in 1844; subsequently studied Law with Ellis Gray Loring, Esq., of Boston, Massachusetts; and was thence called to the Professorship of the Greek and German languages, and of Rhetoric and Belles-Lettres of New York Central College, situated in McGrawville, Cortland County,—the only College in America that has ever called a colored man to a Professorship, and one of the very few that receive colored and white students on terms of perfect equality, if, indeed, they receive colored students at all. (3–4)

The story that Allen tells has little to do with his individual achievements and everything to do with his racial status and the cultural politics shaping the antislavery movement, for through his professorship at New York Central College Allen met Mary King, daughter of the Reverend Lyndon King, "a devoted abolitionist,—a fervid preacher of the doctrine, that character is above color,—and . . . one of the ablest advocates of the social, political, and religious rights of the colored man" (4). William and Mary fell in love and became engaged, met with extreme opposition from the family, and eventually were separated by a mob led by a "committee" of prominent gentlemen.

Allen's story, then, becomes a significant episode in "the history of American prejudice against color," and Allen uses the narrative to provide documentation of and commentary on both the episode and the larger history. Indeed, the narrative includes reprintings of several newspaper articles and letters from various people involved in the episode, with Allen noting along the way that different newspapers changed the details of the story "in order to suit its specific locality" (57). By the end of the narrative, the reader encounters a series of these reprintings—and Allen's commentary (in which he often addresses the reader directly) makes it clear that we are being taught how to read the history suggested by the documents, *against* the history that the writers of some of the documents clearly are trying to construct. Some of the documents make for a rather simple interpretive task—as, for example, an article from the *Syracuse Star*, which Allen identifies as "one of the organs of the Fillmore Administration" (52), an article that tells the story of "Rev. Mr. King, Pastor of a regular Wesleyan Methodist, Abolition, Amalgamation Church at Fulton," who "has an interesting and quite pretty daughter, whom, for some three or four years past, he has kept at School at that pink of a 'nigger' Institution" (53). But Allen takes such obvious examples and draws them back to the white antislavery movement itself, noting those few allies that he found, but noting as well the "thousands of men and women calling themselves Abolitionists and Christians" who "were especially rejoiced at my 'defeat'; and expressed themselves to that effect, though using more guarded language than those who made no pretensions to a love of truth, justice, and humanity" (56–57). Ultimately, Allen makes it clear that his history is actually not his but rather the history of those white Americans who opposed his marriage and organized to separate the couple and to murder the professor. "I can assure you," Allen states, "that language has yet to be invented in which to write in its fullness what, when the children of certain parents shall look back fifty years hence, they will regard as the darkest deeds recorded in the history of their ancestors" (51). The public history of Allen's life is the history revealed through his life and the history that remains largely untold. Allen's work as historian is to expose that untold story and to disrupt the story that is being told in its stead. Significantly, Allen echoes Jefferson along the way, though in a different spirit, noting that "it is some consolation to know that 'God is just, and that his justice cannot sleep for-ever'" (71).

The historical grounding of appeals to divine justice is the point of most of the historical work performed by African American autobiographical narrators, and the centerpiece of liberation historiography—as, for example, in *A Narrative of the Life and Travels of Mrs. Nancy Prince,* first published by Prince in Boston in 1850. Prince, whose story includes the rescue of a sister who had fallen under the control of a Boston brothel, offers a reading of history to establish "that God has in all ages of the world punished every nation and people for their sins." "The sins of my beloved country," Prince continues, "are not hid from his notice; his all seeing eye sees and knows the secrets of all hearts; the angels that kept not their first estate but left their own habitations, he hath reserved in everlasting chains unto the great day" (43). Speaking of her visit to Jamaica in *The West Indies,* originally published in 1841 and included in her *Narrative,* Prince tells of a religious gathering in which

> several ministers spoke of the importance of sending the gospel to Africa; they complimented the congregation on their liberality the last year, having given one hundred pounds sterling; they hoped this year they would give five hundred pounds, as there were five thousand members at the present time. There was but one colored minister on the platform. It is generally the policy of these missionaries to have the sanction of colored ministers, to all their assessments and taxes. The colored people give more readily, and are less suspicious of imposition, if one from themselves recommends the measure; this the missionaries understand very well, and know how to take advantage of it. (48–49)

Prince echoes the Jamaica Hamic Association in addressing the commercial control of black culture by white culture and in noting the force of white supremacist ideology in white benevolent efforts.

Prince makes a point of testing the impressions of black Jamaican character she had received prior to her visit—that they were "lazy, and that emancipation has been of no benefit" to them—by observing and talking with the people directly. As Carla Peterson has observed, Prince "combines" what we would recognize as "ethnographic models in novel ways to produce a hybrid text that inscribes both silences and denied knowledges within it," crafting in *The West Indies* "an ethnography that is written backward, presenting us first with its ethnographic conclusions and only belatedly introducing us to the field-worker herself" (91). Prince's approach, significantly, turns her attention to the manipulation of the terms of black history by white commercial interests and to the distinction between the Christianity of Christ and that of the land. "Most of the people of Jamaica are emancipated slaves," Prince notes, "many of them are old, worn out and degraded. Those who are able to work, have yet many obstacles to contend with, and very little to encourage them; every advantage is taken of their ignorance; the same spirit of cruelty is opposed to them that held them for centuries in bondage; even religious teaching is bartered for their hard earnings, while they are allowed but thirty-three cents a day, and are told if they will not work for that they shall not work at all; an extraordinary price is asked of them for every thing they may wish to purchase, even the Bibles are sold to them at a large advance on the first purchase" (50). The history she relates, the narrative of her life in travels, leads to the history of misinformation and of white supremacy as the foundation of the systemic control over black life and identity. History is embodied not by representing facts from which the life can be abstracted; the embodiment of history speaks with its own voice; the autobiographical narrator's voice is the voice of history.

This is the message of Austin Steward in his 1857 autobiography *Twenty-two Years a Slave, and Forty Years a Freeman*, a narrative that proceeds on the faith that " 'Facts are stubborn things,'—and this is the reason why all systems, religious, moral, or social, which are founded in injustice, and supported by fraud and robbery, suffer so much by faithful exposition" (9). Steward asserts at the end of his preface, "In his old age he sends out this history—presenting as it were his *own body*, with the marks and scars of the tender mercies of slave drivers upon it, and asking that these may plead in the name of Justice, Humanity, and Mercy, that those who have the power, may have the magnanimity to strike off the chains from the enslaved, and bid him stand up, a Freeman and a Brother!" But although Steward here pleads for the aid of "those who have the power," his narrative is directed toward the need for a rising black power to resist what he carefully calls "the system of Slavery," "Slavery as an institution" (9–10). Steward's is a life of community service, but, as Jane H. and William H. Pease have noted, Steward is strangely unknown today, his history virtually lost but for his autobiography.[43] "If there was little room for Negroes to exert major leadership within white abolitionist circles," the Peases note, "certainly a man whose greatest contribution was made in the fringe area of organized communities [like Steward's in Wilberforce] had but scant role in the more conventional antislavery channels" (Introduction, xv).

Twenty-two Years a Slave and Forty Years a Freeman is virtually a narra-

tive of the movement from the individual experience of oppression to organized resistance and collective self-definition, as Steward relates his experiences in and out of slavery, gradually leading his readers to the politically
challenging formation and funding of the community in Wilberforce. Along
the way, Steward tells of obstacles in the form of men both white and black; in
the end, Steward turns to the moral of this story for the black community.
"Suffer me then to exhort you, my countrymen," Steward writes in his conclusion, "to cease looking to the white man for example and imitation" (199).
Reviewing slavery as a *national* institution, Steward calls the white North to
task for its acceptance and support of that system; and he reviews as well the
various standard responses to slavery—from the underground railroad to colonization efforts and Liberia. With regard to the future for black Americans,
Steward looks to the possibility of war between Britain and the United States
and argues for the reasonableness of armed resistance to the United States.
With a penultimate chapter that covers the 1847 celebration of the first of
August, commemorating the abolition of slavery in the British Empire, Steward looks in his conclusion toward the possibility of the defense and extension of that empire and to the possibility that blacks, particularly those
gathering in Canada, will participate in that struggle. Steward was, of course,
hardly alone in celebrating the British Empire in comparison with America.
Indeed, a commonplace of abolitionist rhetoric is the application of phrases
like "the land of the free" to Canada and England, and reports of the recognition of one's humanity once one reached British shores were a standard
feature of the antislavery press. Steward, though, extends the logic of that
discursive turn toward England and celebrates Great Britain as the realm
within which black destiny might be achieved.

Working to clear the grounds on which that destiny might be founded,
African American autobiographers presented in their narratives a history of
tensions, and they drew from their experience to comment on the nature and
terms of those tensions. They worked to transform themselves from significant "facts" in a history beyond their control into witnesses of a providential
history yet to be realized, and they worked to transform themselves from
subjects of a degraded U.S. culture to citizens of what Jacobs terms the
"divine government," what Pennington calls "God's moral government," and
what Douglass identifies as the "Christianity of Christ." Their autobiographies speak of a collective African American identity forged in resistance to
its assigned cultural role (even that role which provided many African Americans a publishing forum in white antislavery culture) and a community de-

fined through the exposure of national sins. But if this was an identity with a home in the sacred order, it had yet to be established or secured in the secular realm—and this was, indeed, the fundamental point of most African American autobiographies, that genre devoted to journeys, relocations, and itinerant prophets. In part, the task of (re)envisioning history so as to stabilize the terms of African American identity involved a renegotiation of the contingencies of social life. Accordingly, these autobiographers crafted the act of witnessing into a revolutionary silence—a silence that involved withholding information from the curious (for example, those who expected confirmation of an established story of southern oppression and northern benevolence) or confronting their readers with the degrading spectacle of white curiosity. But this was also a silence that involved an awareness of the cultural politics of discourse, an awareness that testifies to the ultimate authority of the strict laws of the sacred order, and an awareness manifested in the often scrupulous attention to language and to the problem of interpretation that one encounters in these texts. In part, as well, the task of establishing the historical grounds for a reenvisioned African American identity involved shifting the grounds of African American political life—turning, as does Steward, to Great Britain, for example, or looking back at the United States from the shores of the jaded world of England, as does Elaw, or exposing the limits of the "Christianity of this land" by witnessing the tangible effects of its actions, as do Douglass and Prince. The history presented in African American autobiography, in short, is a history related through border crossings—from South to North, from the United States to Canada and England, from the secular realm to the divine order, and from established stories to stories still waiting to be told. The history presented in the autobiographies, in short, is more a history of *mode* than of *matter*.

Autobiography as Liberation Historiography: Samuel Ringgold Ward

One encounters this historical mode in the most fully realized example of liberation historiography: Samuel Ringgold Ward's *Autobiography of a Fugitive Negro: His Anti-Slavery Labours in the United States, Canada, and England*, published in London in 1855. Ward, who pointedly identifies himself in the narrative as both a British subject and a "fugitive negro," and who identifies Toronto as his home on the title page, was born in 1817 on Maryland's Eastern Shore. His family escaped slavery and settled in Greenwich, New Jersey, in 1820, and then in New York City in 1826. Having attended the Free African School with Alexander Crummell and Henry Highland Garnet, Ward became a teacher in Newark, New Jersey, a post he held until 1839. At that time, he was ordained by the New York Congregational Association, after which he served as pastor to a white congregation in South Butler, New York, and, later, to a white congregation in Cortland, New York. Following his involvement in the rescue of captured fugitive slave William "Jerry" Henry (or McHenry) in 1851, Ward had to move to Canada, became an agent of the Anti-Slavery Society of Canada, and in that capacity traveled to England. A clergyman, abolitionist, editor, and author, he was one of the most prominent figures in and commentators on the antislavery movement—and in *Autobiography of a Fugitive Negro* Ward draws from the full range of his experiences, connecting himself to the community of antislavery workers, black and white, whom he mentions by name, and addressing the broad field of antislavery labor (and the racial and cultural politics behind those efforts) throughout his 412-page narrative.

In the end, Ward leaves his readers with a vision of the glories of the British Empire as a moral force in the world. "Coming from a distant colony, as I do," Ward writes in his concluding paragraph,

> and knowing how powerful is the Christian Church of this great country in moulding the religious character of the colonies—knowing, too, how much the colonies have to do with the evangelization of the heathen[44] contiguous to them—it is impossible for me to express how deep and thorough was my gratification to find the religious state of Great Britain what it is, in this respect: indeed, there is no possibility of exaggerating the extent of holy influence which must, of necessity, flow from this all-important fact. The growth of wealth, increase of power, and widening political influence, of Britain, being considered, how thankful ought Britons to be to Britain's God, for the present religious condition of this mighty empire! (411)

Ward's vision of empire is a vision borrowed from American mythology, and in this reapplication of this narrative of a chosen nation, of the reversed course of empire, is the blueprint for the historical narrative that Ward presents through the story of his life.

Ward's is a story of a people scattered and of a history fragmented by other histories. "It is not to be denied," Ward asserts, "that a history of the Negro race is unwritten." The sources for such a history, Ward notes, have been themselves scattered, "interspersed among the annals of other peoples," so that "scraps, patches, anecdotes . . . are all that bear record of us." Like William C. Nell, Ward joins the scattered documents to the scattered lives and finds there the history that resists representation but that is a living presence nonetheless, a history "written in characters of blood." The story of the African diaspora, Ward asserts, has been reduced to the story of the methods and instruments of oppression: "It is a very compact, succinct chronicle: it comprises but one word and its cognate—*slavery, slave trade*." "Our history," Ward concludes, "is that of the chain, the coffle gang, the slave ship, the middle passage, the plantation-hell!" (269–70). In other words, he follows the narrative of the African diaspora to what was and remains the conventional narrative of African American history—a generalized tale of oppression, by which the single fact of the slave trade, represented by the image of the Middle Passage and the spectacle of physical control and abuse, becomes the abstraction that stands in for an untold story.[45]

Taking on the challenge of representative identity, Ward both confronts the facts of this story and examines the insistent ignorance that is veiled by the story's obstinate certainty by tracing the story to its systemic foundations. "It would seem from this fact," Ward notes (referring to the fact of slavery, the fact of the dispersed documentation of African history), "that those who know nothing of the Negro, except as they see him in slavery and menial positions, are quite excusable. But scholars deserve no such extenuation. They know what is written of the ancient Negro—from which they might, if they chose, infer something concerning the modern Negro" (269). Denying the validity of any extenuating circumstances, Ward shapes his narrative into a study not only of African and African American history but also of the determined avoidance of understanding that characterizes white American culture. He addresses black achievement, both ancient and modern; he reviews the biblical history that other African American historians examine as well; and, like those historians, Ward joins sacred and secular history to a vision of black destiny. We encounter Cyprian, Augustine, Tertullian, Euclid, and Terence, presented as "specimens of the *ancient* Negro, exhibiting intellect beyond the ordinary range of modern literati, before the present Anglo-Saxon race had even an origin" (87). "And the schoolmate of Henry Highland Garnet," Ward notes, and of "Alexander Crummell, Thomas Sipkins Sidney, Charles Lewis Reason, Patrick Henry Reason; the friend and associate of Frederic [*sic*] Douglass, James William Charles Pennington, Amos G. Beeman [*sic*], James

McCune Smith, Madison M. Clarke, and others of like high and distinguished attainments, might, perhaps, be deemed excusable, if he simply called the names of these gentlemen as sufficient to contradict any disparaging words concerning the *modern* Negro" (87–88). We encounter Jackson's proclamations as evidence of citizenship and heroism[46] and Madison Washington, Josiah Henson, and the achievements of the Canadian Buxton Settlement as evidence of the nature of modern black character—supporting Ward's case that black character and achievement are "not a matter of speculation" but simply "a matter of history" (214).

But for all of Ward's determination to present the conventional historical evidence to support his case, his listing of black achievements never seems to be the primary point of his historical argument—for he is far more interested in the ideological conditions that make such arguments seem necessary to scholars who "deserve no . . . extenuation." Ward notes early in the narrative that he is, like David Walker, concerned with the unique oppression of blacks in the United States. "It is quite true," Ward states, "that, as a rule, American slaveholders are the worst and most cruel, both to their own mulatto children and to other slaves; it is quite true, that nowhere in the world has the Negro so bitter, so relentless enemies, as are the Americans" (39). This fundamental truth defines the historical problem to which *Autobiography of a Fugitive Negro* is devoted—for this hatred, Ward asserts, "is not because of the existence of slavery, nor of the evil character or the lack of capacity on the part of the Negro" (39). The condition on which this narrative is focused cannot be addressed solely by a presentation of evidence of black achievement, either ancient or modern, nor can it be addressed by the docudramatic mode of representing slavery. "Whatever is or is not the cause of it," Ward states flatly, "there stands the fact; and this feeling is so universal that one almost regards 'American' and 'Negro-hater' as synonymous terms" (39). Noting that "to say the Negro is equal morally to the white man, is to say but very little" (87), Ward similarly remarks that there should be no need to make the case for the intellectual equality of white and black, as the historical evidence is abundant and clear on that score.[47]

Ward makes it clear, too, that this is not a narrative designed to inspire antislavery sympathy in any conventional sense. Speaking of his antislavery efforts, Ward notes that "in pleading the cause of the blacks before the whites, while I tried faithfully to depict the suffering of the enslaved, and the injustice done to the nominally free, I never stooped to ask pity for either. Wronged, outraged, 'scattered, peeled, killed all the day long,' as they are, I never so

compromised my own self-respect, nor ever consented to so deep a degradation of my people, as to condescend to ask pity for them at the hands of their
oppressors" (86). Similarly, Ward's emphasis on oppression in *Autobiography
of a Fugitive Negro* is designed not for sympathy but to insist on fundamental
rights—and, in fact, to comment on the cultural dynamics of white sympathy.
"Those who have done us injury," he notes in a statement that still resonates
today, "think it a virtue to express sympathy with us—a sort of arms'-length,
cold-blooded sympathy; [but those who are prejudiced would not], on any
account, consent to do towards us the commonest justice. What the Negro
needs is, what belongs to him—what has been ruthlessly torn from him—and
what is, by consent of a despotic democracy and a Christless religion, with-
holden from him, guiltily, perseveringly. When he shall have that restored, he
can acquire *pity* enough, and all the sympathy he needs, cheap wares as they
are; but to ask for them instead of his rights was never my calling" (86–87).[48]
As this statement makes clear, Ward's interest in history focuses on his determination to resist "a despotic democracy and a Christless religion," to work
toward a systemic liberation of the oppressed.

The foundation of Ward's approach to history is, in fact, Douglass's and the
National Convention movement's distinction between Christian doctrine and
the practices of U.S. churches. Noting that an Englishman once described
American Christianity as "the Negro-hating Christianity," Ward asserts that
the word *"religion . . .* should be substituted for Christianity; for while a
religion may be from man, and a religion from such an origin may be capable
of *hating*, Christianity is always from God, and, like him, is love" (41). Building on this distinction, Ward argues that racism is not incidental to the religion of America; rather, it is essential to it:

> Surely it is with no pleasure that I say, from experience, deep-wrought
> conviction, that the oppression and the maltreatment of the hapless
> descendant of Africa is not merely an ugly excrescence upon American
> *religion*—not a blot upon it, not even an anomaly, a contradiction, and
> an admitted imperfection, a deplored weakness—a lamented form of
> indwelling, an easily besetting, sin; no, it is a part and parcel of it, a
> cardinal principle, a *sine quâ non*, a cherished defended keystone, a
> corner-stone, of American faith—all the more so as it enters into the
> practice, the everyday practice, of an overwhelming majority (equal to
> ninety-nine hundredths) of its professors, lay and clerical, of all de-
> nominations; not excepting, too, many of the Quakers! (41–42)

Throughout *Autobiography of a Fugitive Slave*, Ward returns again and again to the ideological appropriation of the discourse and authority of Christianity in America, recasting the battle of his life from the culturally localized struggle against slavery and prejudice to the struggle for the philosophical and moral principles to which the nation claims devotion.

Ward sets the stage for his historical analysis of the position of black Americans and for his application of liberation theology to liberation historiography. The oppression of black Americans, viewed through this lens, becomes part of a larger battle and a larger historical tale. Ward accepts the romantic racialist view that those of African origins are more naturally spiritual than Anglo-Saxons, and argues that "when it is considered that . . . the Negroes are, in feeling, the most *religious* people in the world, and that in all they do they are guided, restrained, but made the more ardent, by the religious passion within them, you cannot imagine that this people will or *can* eventually fail in either recovering their rights, or attracting the thunderbolts of divine vengeance upon their oppressors" (98–99). The condition of oppression, in short, becomes the site of history, the nexus of the sacred and secular, and the indication of the larger narrative by which the present and past can be interpreted. "What says all past history," Ward asks, on the subject of the destiny of the oppressed? "When did God cease to hear the cry of the oppressed? What, in history, is the final result of the upward struggles of an oppressed but advancing, praying, God-fearing people? But, to do as our American brethren like to do—leave out all considerations of divine interpositions, or to calculate upon indefinite forbearance of Deity—neither of which is admissible—any one can tell that, left to themselves, these causes must produce one or two important results" (99). The oppression of black Americans becomes the framework by which to interpret the condition of white Americans, and the ideological appropriation of the discourse and forms of Christianity becomes a significant sign. And those who read these signs are faced with an equally significant sense of duty. Ward notes that "the young blacks of the Republic are everywhere acquiring a love for martial pastimes," and asks, "As their fathers fought bravely in the former wars of the Republic, who can deny them the use of arms?" (99).

For Ward, then, a theological reading of history is not simply a matter of abstract morality but of the practical effects of the fundamental hypocrisy required to maintain a white supremacist culture. The white emphasis on material gain and the white acceptance of a superficial culture speak of white character in significant ways. The effects of this falsely founded success are pure republican theory. "The whites have all they want, and are satisfied," Ward notes—but that very satisfaction is becoming dangerous to the character of the white republic, and the oppression of black Americans is, at the same time, shaping the character of a rising republican nation: "They are already most rapidly degenerating: they are given almost solely to the acquisition of money and the pursuit of pleasure. They will therefore become less and less active, more and more lethargic, while in their very midst the blacks will become less lethargic, and more energetic; until the latter, for all practical purposes, will exhibit, and wield too, more of the real American character, its manliness, its enterprise, its love of liberty, than the former. I speak not as a prophet: I only speak of causes now existing and in active operation, already producing some of their inevitable results" (100). The fall of the white republic will meet the rise of the black. Telling the story of a tutor that Ward hired to teach his children, but who eventually fell behind those children in their education, Ward argues that whites and blacks "are now in the relation of teacher and taught, in the matter of liberty and progress; they will reverse positions ere the struggle be over, unless some sudden unforeseen changes occur" (100).

Although the title of Ward's autobiography identifies him as representative in the conventional terms of the white antislavery movement, he draws on this narrative to transform the terms of representative identity, using his life as an entrance into a reenvisionment of the nature and terms of historical study and understanding. Toward the beginning of his narrative, this challenge to conventional assumptions is direct, as Ward asks, "What is antislavery labor?" and argues that it is a mode of endeavor uncontainable by the most visible forms of antislavery activism. Noting the degradation of both religion and the ideal of democracy in America, Ward presents antislavery labor as "the refutation of all this miserable nonsense and heresy—for it is both." And "how is this to be done?" Ward's answer is comprehensive: "Not alone by lecturing, holding anti-slavery conventions, distributing anti-slavery tracts, maintaining anti-slavery societies, and editing anti-slavery journals, much less by making a trade of these, for certain especial pets and favourites to profit by and in which to live in luxury; but, in connection with these labours, right and necessary in themselves, effective as they must be when properly pursued, the cultivation of all the upward tendencies of the coloured man" (42). All of life, every profession occupied by a black American, and the practical efforts to live according to ideals, to live down "the base calumnies of his heartless adversaries" and to demonstrate "his truth and their falsity" is antislavery labor (43). This ideal becomes a standard by which one can measure not only the systemic oppression fundamental to white America but also the systemic effort required of black resistance.

For Ward, the condition of oppression identifies the site of historical study, and the history of a life finds its representative status thereby. Individual African American lives attain their status as significant historical "facts" not simply by representing oppression or by representing a containable notion of individual or collective achievement; rather, individual lives are defined by the condition of oppression and thereby located at the theological nexus of sacred and secular history. The contingencies that define black identity are thus transformed, and the black life stands at the authoritative center of the process of interpretation. Liberation is not the endpoint of this process; liberation is, rather, the process itself, the mode of interpretation that accounts for systemic oppression as the defining *fact* of identity for both oppressors and oppressed. The history of a life is both the story of that systemic oppression as embodied in individual experience and the response to, the intervention in, that story. To read autobiographies as history is to view the process by which scattered lives discover how the unrepresented community can come into being through collective action in resistance to oppression. What is white is not simply the people but the system; what is black is not simply the people but the activist response to the system. Black is a verb, a historically contextualized performance, the process of life.

chapter four

The Assembly of History
Orations and Conventions

On March 5, 1858, African Americans in Boston held a Commemorative Festival at Faneuil Hall, organized primarily by William C. Nell. In her extensive summary and analysis of this event, Elizabeth Rauh Bethel notes that March 5 "marked two important events for African Americans: On March 5, 1770, Crispus Attucks, a fugitive from slavery, had been the first American to die in the Revolution, during the Boston Massacre; and on March 5, 1857, the United States Supreme Court had declared that African Americans had no rights that white Americans were bound to respect when it rendered its decision regarding Dred Scott's freedom suit" (1).[1] Fifth of March celebrations of the Boston Massacre were standard fare in Boston from 1770 until 1783, at which time they were replaced with Fourth of July celebrations. In reviving the day of commemoration, Bethel notes, Nell "transformed the meaning of that eighteenth-century town tradition by redefining the holiday, shrewdly centering Crispus Attucks in the already-popular cultural image of soldier-patriots engaged in an heroic battle. The story told through the symbolism of the Commemorative Festival became a metaphor for the nation's failure to make good the democratic promises of the Revolution to all her citizens" (11). In addition to speakers and musical groups,[2] the event included a display of "Emblems—Relics—Engravings—Documents . . . of Revolutionary and other Historic association" as evidence of African American participation in the American Revolution and the War of 1812, a display that documented as well the ongoing reality of enslavement and political and social oppression. In his opening address, as Bethel notes, "Nell justified the revival of the holiday in blunt language, citing 'the alarming spread of despotism in these United States' in general, and in particular, 'the annihilation of the Citizenship of Colored Americans by the Dred Scott decision'" (19–20).

This event underscores the many dimensions of the office of the African American historian in reminding us of the historian's unavoidable and complex engagement with the popular rituals of white historical memory. Certainly, the Commemorative Festival served the fundamental historical project of providing information, documentary evidence of the troubled but heroic history of African American involvement in the foundational events of the United States; but those same documents also emphasized the importance of access to and selection of the information used to construct national history and the importance of acquiring ownership over the past. Moreover, the documents emphasized the problems of interpretation involved in reading the past—including, as they did, one document written in Arabic and others that authorized the ownership of human beings. In this and other respects, the Commemorative Festival was both a response to and an intervention in the construction of white nationalist history, insisting on the recognition of African American involvement in the wars that secured American nationhood, and insisting also on the recognition of white oppression as a fundamental fact of that nation.

Perhaps most important, the festival itself was a historical event, a collective performance designed to establish and authorize the historical memory of the lived experience of African Americans—in effect, to *historicize* a collective African American voice, a community collecting itself together by collecting its scattered documents and asserting authority over the contingencies of its collective identity. This was not simply celebratory history; as Marcus Wood has stated, Nell's "radical gesture" of constructing "the first African-American historical museum of slavery . . . uses the fetishisation of historical objects within museum culture to problematise the memorial agendas used to recall the War of Independence" (251). The history gathered for the festival and the history manifested in the various performances at the festival were responses to an immediate condition, ones that asserted the duty of the historian (individual and collective) to disrupt the national narrative used to veil oppression, and responses that asserted as well the need to gather the fragments that together would speak of a significant counternarrative, the story of a nation within the nation. White Revolutionary history becomes by this collective historical performance the foundation for an as-yet-unrealized America whose foundational documents—in their ability to identify the ideological contradictions that justify revolutionary resistance—are housed in the imagined museum of African American history. This is, of course, a mode of historical work that extends back to Allen and Jones's response to the false representation of the black community of Philadelphia, to David Walker's rereading of the statements of Jefferson and Clay, to Pennington's response to the assumptions about African history and identity as shaped by a white supremacist culture, and, indeed, to most of the historians I've discussed in this book; it is history as a reading of other narratives, other histories, history as a mode of interpretation, history as the focused response to the contingencies of identity. This is also the mode of history evident in Nell's discovery of the scattered bones of a community fragmented by slavery, and in Nell's tacit assertion of the historian's duty to breathe life into those dry bones by joining the revolutionary with the fugitive in resistance on the battlefields defined by the recovered sites of African American memory.

In referring to the "assembly of history" in the title of this chapter, I mean to emphasize the status of history as collective performance, and to emphasize as well that this performance was directed toward gathering together, assembling, the scattered lives and scattered documents of African American experience to promote a common historical consciousness. African American history is an act of self-conscious intervention, a response that indicates the historical authority of an African American community indicated in but uncontained by the documents of white American history. The history of the Commemorative Festival was a history of harmonies—in the form of glee clubs and of speakers variously shaped by American culture joining together to address common principles under the banner of a coherent ideological community; it was also a history of dissonances—bringing together two martyrs, Crispus Attucks and Dred Scott, to the realities of slavery and the cause of American liberties. This was a history presented as a force that binds together the social body and as a force also capable of fracturing the social body as represented by the decision of the Supreme Court. This was an event that suggested that the narrative of African American history was a patchwork construction of individual voices, a scattered community joined by the active resistance that was the soul and purpose of African American historical endeavor. Drawing from the lessons of this event, one can see the importance of

considering the many collective historical performances of African Americans before the Civil War—in orations devoted to specific commemorative
occasions and in the convention movement by which African Americans tried
to construct a unified social, political, and historical body. It is to these
historical assemblies, and to these assemblings of history, that this chapter
is devoted.[3]

"Orations Worthy the Name": History and the Occasions of Eloquence

In his 1845 *Narrative*, Frederick Douglass famously tells of the process by
which he learned to read—and by which he learned to give voice to his
thoughts about his condition. Gaining basic instruction from schoolchildren,
Douglass eventually acquired a copy of a popular school reader, *The Columbian Orator*, edited and published by a Bostonian with distinct antislavery
sympathies, Caleb Bingham.[4] The readings that Douglass encountered in that
book, as he notes, "gave tongue to interesting thoughts of my own soul, which
had frequently flashed through my mind, and died away for want of utterance." From a dialogue between a slaveholder and a slave Douglass was led to
believe in "the power of truth over the conscience of even a slaveholder";
from an oration by Sheridan Douglass he gained "a bold denunciation of
slavery, and a powerful vindication of human rights." And as the readings
provided Douglass with the tools for self-articulation, self-definition, and self-
defense, they provided him also with a way of understanding those identities
on which his own was contingent: "The more I read, the more I was led to
abhor and detest my enslavers. I could regard them in no other light than a
band of successful robbers, who had left their homes, and gone to Africa, and
stolen us from our homes, and in a strange land reduced us to slavery. I
loathed them as being the meanest as well as the most wicked of men"
(*Narrative* 42). Giving "tongue to interesting thoughts of [his] own soul"
(*Narrative* 42) leads Douglass to the kind of conceptual control over his own
identity that cannot help but extend to the multiple contingencies of identity,
reshaping his conceptual relation to his enslavers, and leading, in turn, to a
rudimentary historical narrative—concerning the "robbers" who had gone to
Africa—capable of accounting for these new conceptual relations. Douglass's
emphasis on the importance of the school reader in the process of his self-
definition and the conceptual reorientation of his historical world under-

scores the irony, of course, in the orientation and title of the book itself, *The Columbian Orator*.

A central if overlooked feature in that irony is the process by which national history is brought into being. In his important consideration of the role of language in the constitution of American nationhood, Christopher Looby focuses on recurring tropes in white discourse of the Revolutionary era of writing or speaking the nation into existence. "These tropes," Looby argues, "at once express a fact about that status and suggest an illusion about it. They represent the troubled, undecidable relation of Americans to the past they sought to detach themselves from even as they were its products, and they condense in a phrase the nation's desire for unconditioned self-fabrication even as they inadvertently concede the nation's utter determination by the chains of circumstance" (26). Language carries its own historical weight, speaking us into existence before we are in a position to envision or transform our surroundings; "The historical world into which, as subjects, we are thrown, is always already represented in the speech of the community." Accordingly, Looby continues, "when we think to change that world, our innovations must operate upon the ready-made linguistic and intersubjective structure which is the form in which we encounter the world the past has prepared for us" (27). Not only the histories written, the texts that represent an imagined coherent community, but also the language in which those histories are written become part of the historical force that rising communities must encounter, resist, and transform if they are to achieve a revolutionary and authoritative self-definition.

In addressing the extensive self-consciousness, in the Revolutionary era, of American nationhood as an effect of language, Looby joins others in recognizing the correspondence between print discourse and the imaginary community essential to the creation of modern nationhood. Looby, though, emphasizes the role of voice in this linguistic act of communal self-creation, indicating by his book's title, *Voicing America*, "the difference between the abstract, alienated, rational polis of print culture and the more passionately attached, quasi-somatically experienced nation for which many Americans longed" (5). In practice, of course, this "voicing" made itself known in print— that is, in the representation of oral performances in print. Importantly, though, Looby's study reveals a persistent determination among the white Revolutionary and early national writers to address this question of oral performance and embodiment. "The question of whether such a linguistically grounded nation is best figured as *written* or *spoken*," Looby notes, "is not, for many writers of the period, a foregone conclusion but, on the contrary, a live issue of some consequence," for "since the United States, by all accounts, manifestly lacked the kind of legitimacy and stability that might be expected of a nation that was grounded in blood loyalty or immemorial facticity—since its legitimacy was explicitly grounded in appeal to rational interest, not visceral passion—*voice* embodied a certain legitimating charisma that print could not" (4). Through voice, the history central to the national self-creation, to the imagined nation, is located in embodied agency—an agency complicated in its involvement in the linguistic communities of the past, and therefore an agency that faces the revolutionary task of joining word and deed in historical revision, reshaping the narrative of the past so as to create the trajectory of a possible narrative of the future. In this way does community, the subject of that narrative, transform the contingencies of its existence, proceeding from a community defined by a common condition to a community defined by a common narrative authority and agency.

To recognize the good sense of Looby's analysis of the foundations of the white imagined nation, though, is only to emphasize the challenge to African Americans interested in telling the story of a different national history, one in which African Americans played a central and defining role. One might question, after all, Looby's assumption that the United States was not "grounded in blood loyalty," and one must note that as voice emphasizes embodiment it emphasizes as well the centrality of the white male body in the Early Republic. Douglass discovered the arguments he needed to respond to his condition in a book that claimed those arguments for the domain of American nationhood, *The Columbian Orator*. Small wonder that his discovery took him to the brink of despair, for the enslaving nation had control not only over his body but also over the arguments for his liberation. Accordingly, the map of African American historical writing before the Civil War leads us inevitably to the print discourse of the spoken word, to the linguistic performances that challenged the white control over African American history in the prison house of language.[5]

That oration was important to African Americans need hardly be said, but it is still worth noting that the orators themselves emphasized the importance of this genre of public communication and that published oratory was perhaps the primary mode of African American publication before the Civil War.[6] Oration emphasized the presence of African American organizations in the U.S. cultural landscape—from various antislavery organizations to religious, fraternal, and political institutions devoted to African American self-determination.

But oration was also a deeply racialized form of address, and to assert African American mastery of this form was to respond forcefully to white supremacist assumptions about African American character and ability. In part, this response took the form of challenges to white celebrations of oratorical power—as one encounters, for example, in an article on Louis Kossuth (leader of the nineteenth-century Hungarian independence movement and a celebrated speaker in the United States) in which the author doubts "whether Kossuth's eloquence would have as great an effect on an *Anglo-Saxon* audience as a Hungarian," suggesting that Kossuth's mode of eloquence "is too tropical almost for our latitude" ("Kossuth"). More often, African Americans responded to the assumption of African American inferiority by emphasizing their oratorical reputations. Douglass noted the presence of racist assumptions even among his allies when he reported that he felt constrained by the expectations of the white abolitionists on the antislavery lecture circuit—that he was asked to perform a conventional role as fugitive slave; and he complains in *My Bondage and My Freedom,* "I was generally introduced as a '*chattel*'—a '*thing*'—a piece of southern '*property*'—the chairman assuring the audience that it could speak" (*My Bondage* 366). Significantly, Douglass included some of his addresses as an appendix to that autobiography. Austin Steward and Samuel Ringgold Ward, among others, similarly integrated samples of their oratorical abilities in their autobiographies.

In part, African American oration was important as a public performance of achievement and intellectual legitimacy in a culture that viewed African American public speaking as part of the antislavery spectacle. African American writing and public speaking alike were viewed condescendingly—often praised and belittled in the same editorial breath. When William Wells Brown published a travel narrative, for example, an article in the *Liberator* stated, against all evidence, that "it is a new thing in this country for a slave to become an author"; and in another article published that same month the *Liberator* noted Brown's presentation of lectures on a variety of subjects and celebrated "the first attempt of a colored man to give a course of Lectures, embracing other topics than the anti-slavery subject."[7] This celebration of what is viewed as Brown's cultural breakthrough reveals the extent to which African American writing and lecturing were set off, contained by the cultural category of race and by white antislavery benevolence.

But African Americans themselves often accepted the basic terms of this containment. In 1809, William Hamilton, for example, responding to the charge that those of African origin "are inferior to white men" in mental ability, displayed for an audience of the Universalist Church in New York City the text of African American orations and offered this commentary on these textualized performances:

> This book contains an introductory address and an oration on the aboli-
> tion of the slave trade, delivered in the African Church, the first of
> January eighteen hundred and eight, by two young men whom you are
> generally acquainted with: the address or frontispiece to the work is a
> flow of tasteful language, that would do credit to the best writers; the
> oration or primary work is not a run of eccentric vagaries, not now a
> sudden gust of passionate exclamation, and then as sudden calm and an
> inertness of expression, but a close adherence to the plane of the subject
> in hand, a warm and animating description of interesting scenes, to-
> gether with an easy graceful style. If we continue to produce specimens
> like these, we shall soon put our enemies to the blush; abashed and
> confounded they shall quit the field, and no longer urge their superi-
> ority of souls. ("Mutual Interest" 83)

Hamilton's defense is revealing, both in his acceptance of the purported rationality of racism (and his corresponding belief that evidence will chase his attackers from the field) and in his defensive description of the oratorical style of the text, a style that resists simple appeals to emotion and follows the dictates of a reasonable understanding of the "plane of the subject." Then as now, African American sermonic styles could be admired with more than a hint of condescension, held up for both praise and caricature.

But whereas Hamilton largely accepts the always implicit white audience of judgment in his understanding of oration, later African American orators would challenge the terms of oratorical valuation, the field of education necessary to prepare one for oratorical accomplishments, and the dictates of the "plane of the subject." African Americans increasingly presented them-selves not simply as able apprentices in the art of oration but as masters of the moral and intellectual core of the art. In doing so, they joined historical interpretation to aesthetics, making of oratory a form that has been shaped by the same historical forces that shape African American identity, and a form that is itself historical, both in the occasion of the address and in the duty to address the occasion of African American public performance.

In thinking about African American oratory, it is important to remember that the lyceum movement was itself shaped by historical and cultural forces. As Mary W. Graham has written, "From 1826 to 1850 most societies [sponsoring speakers in the lyceum movement] depended upon local celebrities ... for their programs," but "rapidly expanding railroads changed this picture in the fifties," a development that helped to "unify northern opinion concerning morals, science, travel, history, and religion" (108). According to Graham, a central feature of this developing regional unity was the exclusion of slavery as a subject acceptable for speakers. "Though such well-known abolitionist lecturers as [Horace] Greeley, [George William] Curtis, [Ralph Waldo] Emerson, [Edward] Everett, [Henry Ward] Beecher, [Carl] Schurz, and [Bayard] Taylor spoke from lyceum platforms in 1860, the lyceum's concern for social unity kept them silent on the sectional controversy," as it had kept them silent on slavery on the lyceum circuit in the past (113).[8] This silence was by no means an unconscious repression; it was a deliberate omission.

There were, of course, many whites who spoke powerfully against slavery, but the cultural control over the lyceum movement indicates the ways in which these speakers were positioned culturally and ideologically—and the speakers positioned themselves further in their approach to their subject. In 1860, as I have noted, Douglass wrote of his support for a reorganization of the abolition movement, noting the ineffectuality of the results of antislavery oration. "The effect of all anti-slavery effort thus far," Douglass observed, "is this: it has filled the whole North with a sentiment opposed to slavery. Sentimental Abolitionism is abundant. It may well be met with in the pulpit, sometimes in the religious newspapers, and more frequently still we meet it in the meetings of the Republican party; yet among them all there is neither will nor purpose to abolish slavery" (Foner, *Life and Writings* 2:522). Beyond the culturally localized goal of abolishing slavery, as Douglass implies, was a larger field of activity that remained unaddressed. Bethel's comments on the white antislavery speakers included in the 1858 Commemorative Festival are instructive here:

> Parker, Phillips, Higginson, and Garrison all condemned slavery as immoral and illegal, and they uniformly called for continued support for the anti-slavery movement. Despite their strong opposition to slavery, however, the white abolitionists set limits on their support for their African-American colleagues. None of the white abolitionists even implicitly supported the claims to full and unconditional citizenship Nell and his colleagues advanced through the martyrdom of Crispus Attucks. To be sure, Parker, Phillips, Higginson, and Garrison were deeply moral men and their anti-slavery politics were not capricious. Yet, like

most white Americans at mid-century, the four were seemingly unable
to countenance the ideas that Nell and his colleagues envisioned: full
and unconditional equality and the eradication of racially set political,
economic, educational, and social barriers. (22)

The white antislavery movement's agenda was implicitly delimited, separated
from the white regional unity of views concerning "morals, science, travel,
history, and religion" that the lyceum movement encouraged and facilitated.
And white antislavery oration, accordingly, operated from that delimited cultural space. Garrison's preface to Douglass's 1845 *Narrative* is representative,
in its condescending praise for Douglass's abilities (given the circumstances
of his birth and the restrictions of his education), while presenting Garrison's
own distinctive style of antislavery rhetoric in implicit contrast—an antislavery speech that both authorizes and contains the narrative that follows.[9]

In the second prefatory letter to Douglass's *Narrative*, white abolitionist
Wendell Phillips, underscoring the importance of a book written by a man
who had been enslaved, begins by noting, "I am glad the time has come when
the 'lions write history'"; for African American orators before the Civil War,
the challenge was to determine what it would *mean* for the lions to write
history and how the relation between historical understanding and oration
was to be conceived. As Marcus Wood has remarked, "There was an unbroken
history of African-American freedom festivals in the Northern free states,
which focused upon dates which had special resonance for those of slave
descent in the Americas," including "1 January, a date commemorating Toussaint l'Ouverture's declaration of the independent state of Hayti, and the
outlawing of the American Atlantic slave trade; 5 July, because of the passage
of 1799 and 1817 gradual abolition legislation; and 1 August, because it com-
memorated British Emancipation in the Caribbean colonies" (250). Wood
argues that the Boston Commemorative Festival was unique among these
dates in reviving a white holiday and joining it to the date of a Supreme Court
authorization of the violations of African American rights, but it is important
to note that each of these dates marks an event fraught with ideological
contradictions. If the date of, say, gradual abolition legislation is a cause for
celebration, it is also a reminder that there should be no need for such
celebration, and it is therefore a cause for renewed and righteous anger, and a
moment to reinforce the importance of black communal organization and
unity. And the orations presented at such events similarly were caught up in
the complex contingencies of history and cultural identity that only empha-

sized the need for the "lions" to determine the terms by which they might present history.

The major statement of a black liberation theory of oration is William G. Allen's "Orators and Oratory," presented on June 22, 1852, to the Dialexian Society of New York Central College, where Allen was a professor. In this remarkable oration, Allen firmly establishes his authority in the field, presenting a survey of the oratorical arts that includes commentary on Demosthenes, Cicero, Julius Caesar, and many others—and a survey of the history associated with oratory that takes his audience and readers from Athens to Ireland, from Rome to the American republic. Allen presents this survey to explore the historical and social conditions of oratorical authority and eloquence, an exploration that leads consistently and firmly to the moral requirements for eloquence and to the role of oratory in the struggle for liberty.

Allen's primary concern is to define the moral demands of oratory, and in that way to identify the primary characteristics of eloquence and persuasive power. Like many other writers of his time, Allen looked for the key to oratorical authority by considering the relation between the sacred and the secular—and accordingly he begins the oration with great idealism, though no greater than we might expect to encounter from, say, Emerson or Thoreau. "He that thinks the largest thought," Allen states, "is the ruler of the world" (230).[10] But Allen immediately uses his assertion of this ideal as a means by which to measure a world given to material standards of progress and power. "Accustomed as the world now is," Allen states, "to regard shadows as substances, and shows as realities, it is unable to recognize its true rulers" (230). With this distinction between, one might say, the actual and the real, Allen offers his fundamental vision of a liberationist model of moral thought: "as [the world] moves onward and upward to God—as the *merely* intellectual shall give place to the moral AND the intellectual, usurpers will be dethroned, rulers attain their proper places, and be known and read of all men" (230). This vision of the power of moral thought is thus joined to a vision of how divine order works through human history—a vision that would be not at all unfamiliar to white theorists of providential history.

For Allen, though, the most pressing fact of secular life was the appropriating power of human systems of order and the ability of men and women within those systems to assume that they were fulfilling a divine directive. Focusing on this cultural chauvinism, Allen argues that the actualities of the present, when examined from the perspective of the oppressed within those communities, reveal underlying intellectual and moral tensions that will eventually prove decisive and divisive. "If Americans had less prejudice," Allen once stated in a public letter, "they could read history more clearly" ("Letter from Wm. G. Allen").[11] A clearer reading, Allen suggests in "Orators and Oratory," would provide insight into the systemic operations of power and the related degradation of public discourse to serve the needs of power. "Is Fillmore the *rightful* ruler of this nation?" asks Allen. "No more necessarily so than I would be a dentist, because all the people of McGrawville should get together and vote me such" (230). The intellectual shortcomings of the world are filtered through the minds that constitute the delimited sphere of representative government in a nation in which "nothing is easier, as, indeed, nothing is more common, than to call both persons and things by improper names" (230). And, so, too, on the global stage: Napoleon figures larger on the historical page, notes Allen, than Toussaint, though "in every element of the *rightful* ruler, Toussaint was the superior" (230–31). "I will not say that Napoleon was less intellectual than Toussaint," Allen states, "I will not say that Toussaint was as intellectual as Napoleon; but I will say that he had character more symmetrical by far, and an ambition more worthy of beings who were made to look upward" (231). Allen begins his oration, in short, with a means by which to read the historical pages written in the present by a standard that measures judgment against an ideal union of the material, the intellectual, and the moral—viewing "our outward world" as "an expression of our interior life" (231).

Allen asserts that oratory is, in fact, necessary only because humankind has fallen—and this belief guides Allen's location of the center of oratorical authority and the heart of oratorical eloquence. "The art of oratory is consequent upon the introduction of sin," he argues; "had there been no disturbing force, all men would have been poets" (231). As liberation theology considers the oppressed community as a significant theological source, a text to be read that guides one's interpretation of the dictates of the Bible, so Allen finds in the condition of oppression both the necessity and the proper subject of oration. For since "the art of oratory is consequent upon the introduction of sin," Allen contends, "and since the sin of sins is the oppression of the weak by the strong, it follows that no other subject can beget the highest efforts of oratory than that of personal or political liberty" (231). Oratory is a response to fundamental conditions of human life and culture; it arises out of oppression and must work toward liberation; accordingly, Allen argues, "it follows . . . that orators worthy the name must originate in the nation that is a transition state, either from slavery to freedom, or freedom to slavery" (232). Allen notes that he nearly claimed "that orators worthy the name, must originate among the oppressed races"; "but in turning to the pages of history," Allen notes, he "was reminded of the fact, that all races, with scarcely an exception, had, at some period of their existence, been in a state of thraldom" (232). Looking back to the Norman Conquest, Allen brings history to the present to state that "in the veins of English and Americans[−]the freest of men−flows the blood of slaves" (232). But while this historical connection to the condition of slavery can account for the eloquence of the "freest of men" in the nineteenth century, it also places them within a historical continuum that allows Allen to state to black Americans, "Take courage, friend, you are only taking your turn" (232).[12]

And it is a significant turn to take, placing African Americans at the front of the march of oratorical responsibility and authority. Allen returns to his central concept, using it to reenvision the relation between oratorical power and historical conditions: "Orations worthy the name must have for their subject personal or political liberty; and orators worthy of the name must necessarily originate in the nation that is on the eve of passing from a state of slavery into freedom, or from a state of freedom into slavery. How could this be otherwise? Where there is no pressure, the highest efforts of genius must lie undeveloped" (232). With this as his framework, Allen examines various examples of oratory, from Demosthenes and Cicero to Kossuth, and then to Frederick Douglass, Samuel Ringgold Ward, and Henry Highland Garnet. He travels from Athens and Rome to the American Revolution and to struggles in Ireland.

Allen's extensive commentary on Kossuth offers a good example of the complexity of Allen's understanding of the historical process that shapes oratory. Finding Kossuth "superior to any orator who has ever spoken," he finds in him also an example of an unfulfilled office of "the world's Apostle of Liberty," for Kossuth was unwilling to devote his gifts to the struggle against American slavery and, in fact, accepted the white American fiction of America as a land of liberty. While Allen is clear about his admiration for Kossuth's abilities, he is also unambiguous in his judgment of Kossuth's application of those abilities. "Before his countrymen," Allen states, "before the world, and before his God, I charge him with the utterance of statements which are not only false; but which he could not, by any possibility, have failed to know were such. 'A great, a glorious, a FREE people,' said he, at the editorial banquet in New York;−'a great word this, gentlemen, but it is LITERALLY (!) true!' LITERALLY true that we are a *free* people! Heavens! was ever irony so severe?"

(237).[13] In his high praise and his sharp judgment of Kossuth, Allen finds a historical process that points to the center of oratorical responsibility. That is, just as David Walker emphasized that black Americans are the most oppressed people in history, so Allen finds in the ignored reality of American slavery the fundamental condition of global oppression, and therefore the appropriate theater for oratory.

Looking at the development of oratory in the United States, then, Allen sees evidence of a national destiny contained within but extending beyond the white nationalist narrative—a destiny that includes significant responsibilities. Ward, Douglass, Charles Lenox Remond, Garrison, and others indicate the rise of oratory, Allen argues—and as their efforts become more effective, positioning the United States as a "nation that is on the eve of passing from a state of slavery into freedom," both oratorical eloquence and oratorical responsibility can be expected to increase. "You live in a great country," Allen tells his audience. "So far as energy, intellect, and activity constitute greatness, the sun has never seen its equal. You not only live in a great country, but a country most remarkable for its spirit of compromise—for calling that which is bitter, sweet, and that which is bad, good. You live in a country where the combat deepens, and still deepens, between the spirit of freedom and the spirit of the pit.—Now, which side will ye choose?" (246). Asserting his faith that their choice is already clear, Allen charges his audience not simply to "cultivate the oratorical" but to "do it diligently, and with purpose; remembering that it is by the exercise of this weapon, perhaps more than any other, that America is to be made a free land, not in name only, but in deed and in truth" (246). Oratorical eloquence, that is, must work to return things to their proper names, return language to meaning, by making of the nation's boasted freedom an accomplishment in both name and deed.[14]

In an address presented in the same year as Allen's "Orators and Oratory," Frederick Douglass demonstrates the implicit challenge in Allen's vision: the need to identify the proper platform of oratory before an audience gathered in the theater of white American false consciousness. The occasion of what is perhaps Douglass's best-known speech was the Fourth of July. Douglass responded to an invitation to speak in Rochester, New York, with an address presented in Corinthian Hall on July 5, 1852—a speech that transforms the Fourth of July from a day for celebrating liberty to a day that reveals to the slave, "more than all other days in the year, the gross injustice and cruelty to which he is the constant victim" ("What, to the Slave" 258). Like Allen, Douglass believed in a necessary "harmony between the speaker and the thing spoken" (qtd. in Blight xxvi). "A good sermon from a bad preacher," Douglass once wrote, and "an exhortation to give liberty to the oppressed by one not inspired by love for the oppressed, are unavailing and worthless" (qtd. in Blight xxvi). In his Fourth of July oration of 1852, as Castronovo has pointed out, "Douglass argues for the centrality of race in any meditation on American nationalism" (*Fathering the Nation* 42). In his position as the raced speaker for this occasion—"the man that was a thing," in Stowe's formulation[15]—Douglass follows the implications of that centrality, exploring the terms of harmony between the speaker and the thing spoken as he constructs a vision of history that repositions both speaker and audience according to the demands of the field of oppression.

Douglass argues that the oration that his audience has come to hear is one of the signs of oppression and manifestations of false consciousness that he has come to challenge. "Why am I called upon to speak here to-day?" Douglass asks. "What have I, or those I represent, to do with your national independence?" (255). Noting that "this Fourth of July is *yours*, not *mine*," Douglass asks, "Do you mean, citizens, to mock me, by asking me to speak to-day?" (255). Emphasizing his status as the manifestation of the ideological contradictions that rule the nation, Douglass refuses to participate in the corruption of language that Allen identified as a prominent trait of both the age and of the nation. Douglass naturally emphasizes his responsibility to be accurate about what the holiday commemorates: to forget the enslaved on this of all days "would be treason most scandalous and shocking, and would make me a reproach before God and the world" (256). Of course, Douglass here accuses his audience of just such treason. At the beginning of his oration, he commented on the distance from the slave plantation of his birth to the lecture platform on which he stood in Rochester; now he tells the audience of another distance, one still uncrossed: "Your high independence only reveals the immeasurable distance between us" (255). Throughout the speech, Douglass reveals that his own experience has prepared him to give voice to the dictates of liberty, and he reveals as well that his audience's "high independence" separates them not only from the speaker but from the cause of liberty.

Douglass asks, in effect, how his position as orator should be understood *historically*; that is, how should one identify this moment and the historical vision it requires? This was, he notes, a central question also at the time of the American Revolution—for as Douglass reminds his audience, although years later it is easy to say that the Revolutionary cause was right and just, it was not clear at the time. He begins by giving, indeed, what seems in virtually all respects a standard Fourth of July address, celebrating the vision of the Revolutionary generation, arguing that they were inspired by and held firm to fundamental principles that forced them to risk all for and to act on "the cause of their country":[16] "They were peace men; but they preferred revolution to peaceful submission to bondage. They were quiet men, but they did not shrink from agitating against oppression. They showed forbearance, but that they knew its limits. They believed in order, but not in the order of tyranny. With them, nothing was 'settled' that was not right. With them, justice, liberty and humanity were 'final,' not slavery and oppression. You may well cherish the memory of such men. They were great in their day and generation. Their solid manhood stands out the more as we contrast it with these degenerate times." Douglass's application of the imagined principles of the Revolutionary generation—that past shaped by and for commemorative rituals—clearly is intended to comment on the abandonment of the Revolutionary struggle for liberty over time, and to apply Revolutionary principles to the antislavery movement at a time when Douglass increasingly was leaving moral suasion behind and embracing more direct resistance to the system of slavery. Concerning those opposed to the colonists, Douglass points out that "their opposition to the then dangerous thought was earnest and powerful; but, amid all their terror and affrighted vociferations against it, the alarming and revolutionary idea moved on, and the country with it" (251). The historical progression of the idea of liberty, Douglass argues—echoing not only Allen but also white nationalist discourse—cannot be stopped, though those who misread history can find themselves left behind.

Indeed, the occasion for his speech, Douglass contends, has become an event devoted to promoting and maintaining just such misreadings. Douglass closes his summary of the history of the American Revolution by noting that this is a subject that he need not address at length, since it has "never lacked for a tongue." The causes and principles of the American Revolution, he remarks, "have all been taught in your common schools, narrated at your firesides, unfolded from your pulpits, and thundered from your legislative halls, and are as familiar to you as household words. They form the staple of your national poetry and eloquence" (253–54). But this cultural saturation of the discourse of false consciousness is exactly the problem Douglass faces in trying to find a language with which to address the subject of liberty and oppression. The language itself is against him, for if he were to speak of liberty and oppression he would be received by an audience well versed in the reapplication of that discourse in support of a nation that can claim that liberty is "literally" true while still sustaining a national system of slavery. Douglass emphasizes this problem by stressing a national characteristic, "I remember also that as a people Americans are remarkably familiar with all facts which make in their own favor. This is esteemed by some as a national trait—perhaps a national weakness. It is a fact that whatever makes for the wealth or for the reputation of Americans and can be had cheap will be found by Americans" (254).

What then was left for Douglass to say? If he were to present history, he would present it to an audience trained in the art of historical reinterpretation—prepared to hear even jeremiads as ritualistic reminders of the fundamental soundness of American institutions. To speak on liberty or oppression would be to tell the audience what they were prepared to hear—perhaps also with the added regional collective self-affirmation facilitated by a former slave invited to present an address against slavery on the Fourth of July in the North. Douglass found himself confined by the discourse of liberty, a discourse filtered through schools, firesides, pulpits, and legislative halls to speak for the delimited resistance to slavery that Douglass could expect from the North.

But the real occasion for this oration, as Douglass recognized, lies exactly in this subtext that shapes both his expected performance and the audience's culturally prepared reception of that performance. Thus it is that Douglass turns the invitation to speak back on his audience and makes his relation to his audience the primary subject of his oration. Announcing that his subject will be and must be American slavery, Douglass announces, "I will use the severest language I can command; and yet not one word shall escape me that any man, whose judgment is not blinded by prejudice, or who is not at heart a slaveholder, shall not confess to be right and just" (256). Douglass here not only indicates his stance on this day but also draws in the cultural politics surrounding the antislavery movement, for he associates his position with Garrison's famous declaration, which Douglass quotes, from the first issue of the *Liberator* (January 1, 1831): "I will not equivocate—I will not excuse" (Garrison, *William Lloyd Garrison* 72; Douglass, "What, to the Slave" 256). Douglass then stages those cultural politics, suggesting, "I fancy I hear some one of my audience say, it is just in this circumstance that you and your brother abolitionists fail to make a favorable impression on the public mind. Would you argue more, and denounce less, would you persuade more, and rebuke less, your cause would be much more likely to succeed" (256). In this way, Douglass addresses the fundamental problem that he faces, that of a cultural discourse that undermines his position by seeming to account for and encompass his position. Douglass asserts in response to this imagined charge from the audience, "I submit, where all is plain there is nothing to be argued" (256). He then goes through the possible arguments he might be expected to present: "Must I undertake to prove that the slave is a man?" "Would you have me argue that man is entitled to liberty?" "Must I argue that a system thus marked with blood, and stained with pollution, is *wrong*?" (256–57). In each case, Douglass demonstrates that white American culture has already answered these questions or revealed the answers through their actions. "What, then," Douglass asks, "remains to be argued?" And he answers that, "at a time like this, scorching irony, not convincing argument, is needed" (257).

In short, facing both a culture and an occasion that appropriate, even at the level of discourse, any possible argument he could make, Douglass responds by refusing to present an argument; facing a culture that controls even the language of liberty, Douglass uses his oration to address just that situation, and then devotes his speech to a significant silence, a refusal to say what should not need be said. What must be done, Douglass suggests, is exactly this sort of act of exposure and provocation. "The feeling of the nation must be quickened," Douglass asserts; "the conscience of the nation must be roused; the propriety of the nation must be startled; the hypocrisy of the nation must be exposed; and its crimes against God and man must be proclaimed and denounced" (258). The responsibility of the orator is to prepare his audiences to hear the eloquence that has been obscured by their *imagined* eloquence, a responsibility that begins by calling things by their proper names: "The existence of slavery in this country brands your republicanism as a sham, your humanity as a base pretense, and your Christianity as a lie" (265). Douglass's task in this speech is to address an event devoted to a ritualized (mis)interpretation of history by encompassing that history within a different historical narrative—and it is hardly surprising, then, that Douglass should end with the representations of both sacred and secular history: the providential narrative of history as indicated by Psalm 68:31 and the secular narrative of antislavery struggle represented by a poem by William Lloyd Garrison. Douglass worked to bring his audience (and, later, his readers) to the crossroads of a historical moment they did not know they had gathered to observe, and in doing so he fulfilled the office of the orator as defined by William G. Allen, oration as informed by liberation historiography.

Although Douglass's eloquence was singular, his argument was not, for

African Americans regularly seized the Fourth of July to distinguish between the Tower of Babel erected by white American displays of patriotism and the temples of liberty to be constructed on the ideological and historical sites of African American experience. An article in the July 13, 1839, issue of the *Colored American*, for example, noted that the prior week had been characterized by "riot and revelry, mirth and merriment, debauchery and dissipation, patriotism and politics." On Independence Day, the article's author states, "we walked forth not for rejoicing, but for observation, and we saw with sorrow, scenes in which we grieve to say civilized man participated. The drunken revelries would have disgraced the Bacchanalian orgies of the Grecian, the discordant yells would shame the war song of the savage." White Western civilization here is reduced to orgy and joined with conventional (and, it must be noted, racist) images of Native American savagery to invert the narrative of white American progress and civilization. "This day," the article states, "is man truly independent: he is independent of order, of law, and even of his God." What remains is the narrative yet to be written, the story by which Independence Day will be associated again with "the sentiments put forth in '76," sentiments "as immutable as truth," which will "overpower and overthrow the false principles" and bring forth the day when "liberty like that first breathed from heaven, will reign triumphant." The article concludes with a vision of the historical perspective from which this prophecy might be understood: "We welcomed the return of the day, for although we are deprived of the full measure of our rights, still the day is ours; to sustain the principles of independence, our fathers fought, bled, and died: they held no office in field nor council; neither are their names blazoned on the page of history, but 'tis well known that, during the eventual period of the war of the revolution 'they fought like brave men long and well,' and the sword of the colored man was as faithfully wielded for the protection of his native land as the noblest white man of them all" ("The Week"). This article is representative of a wide range of commentaries on the Fourth of July regularly presented from the lecture podium and circulated through the African American press.[17] Douglass's argument is, in fact, measured by comparison, and his rhetoric is relatively mild. It is, in fact, Douglass's ritualistic repetition of these arguments, along with his direct address to a white audience, that makes his speech significant. In effect, Douglass brought African American Independence Day celebrations to white America, working less to address history than to (re)make it.

In emphasizing the status of orations as historical moments—significant events in history and significant acts in the (re)construction of historical understanding—I follow Looby and others in noting that while print culture is essential to the creation of nationhood, to the constitution of the imagined nation, oration is essential to the maintenance of that imagined nation, in part by providing a ritualistically renewed and revised framework for interpreting a common history.[18] This is what Douglass comments on in his presentation and *representation* of Fourth of July oratory, nationalist discourse, and selective national memory. Similarly, Robert Purvis, in an 1860 oration before the American Anti-Slavery Society, "The American Government and the Negro," makes a point of his distance from his audience and offers a reinterpretation of the nation. Emphasizing that the government of which he speaks belongs to his audience and not to him, Purvis declares, "Thank God, I have no willing share in a government that deliberately declares one part of its people disfranchised and outlawed" (332). Purvis then proceeds to outline that government, the unofficial story of white American nationhood—listing, for examples, the laws governing slavery, including the Fugitive Slave Act, juxtaposing Justice Taney's decision in the *Dred Scott* case to the actions of Crispus Attucks and to Andrew Jackson's proclamation.

Questions of the ideological implications of interpretation were, of course, central to the antislavery movement, particularly in the increasingly divisive arguments over the relative virtues of moral suasion and political action that focused on the status of the Constitution in relation to slavery. Charles Lenox Remond, in an 1844 address to the New England Anti-Slavery Society, responded to Dr. Walter Channing's defense of the Constitution with a speech that advocated the dissolution of the Union.[19] In that address, Remond states that "it does very well for nine-tenths of the people of the United States, to speak of the awe and reverence they feel as they contemplate the Constitution, but there are those who look upon it with a very different feeling, for they are in a very different position" (206).[20] Remond refers, in effect, to the historical conditions that shape interpretive communities; but he forcefully challenges the false consciousness of those nine-tenths, noting, "What if the word 'slave' is not in [the Constitution]? It does not matter to me nor mine. Slavery was in the understanding that framed it—Slavery is in the will that administers it. If there were nothing but Liberty in it, would there be two and a half millions ground to the dust beneath it this day?" (207).

In an 1860 July Fourth oration, H. Ford Douglas followed the same line of argument as Remond, arguing that "hypocrisy is not a growth peculiar to American soil, but it has reached the most hateful development here" (350).

The Liberty Bell, Douglas asserts, was "more modest than the people" in that it "cracked the first time it was rung, because it had not *brass* enough to tell the lie again!" (350). Like Remond, Douglas viewed the Constitution as a document at the mercy of interpretive communities shaped by history; it was "the Janus of the American Capitol, looking both ways, assuming any color, according as we turn the political kaleidoscope" (351). But, for Douglas, this observation was an entrance into an interpretive method, one shaped by historical reinterpretation: "This is the one redeeming feature in it—that we cannot understand its carefully concealed purpose without the aid of contemporary history" (351). As with Remond, this mode of interpretation leads Douglas to denounce the Constitution as a proslavery document; and Douglas's interpretation, like Remond's, emphasizes slavery as the product of the fundamental orientation of mind of the founding generation and of the generations that followed. "As anti-slavery men," Douglas asserts, "seeking the overthrow of slavery in the shortest possible way, we have to deal with the facts of the government as the fathers made it and construed it, while they lived. I am willing, for one, to accept the unbroken testimony of three-quarters of a century against the anti-slavery character of the American Constitution, and not dodge behind its equivocal phrases for the purpose of cheating the slaveholder, and saving the memory of our dishonest and time-serving fathers from the gibbet of impartial history" (351). What is important to Douglas is the way in which a dialectical reading of the Constitution—drawing, like contemporary black liberation theology, from the evidence of lived experience as a significant *source* of interpretation—reveals the text of history that must be understood before cultural reform can be possible. "I do not believe," Douglas states, "that the fathers wrote that Constitution, intending it to serve the purposes of freedom, and then turned round and construed it on the side of despotism and slavery. If they did, then were they a mean set of contemptible hypocrites, and deserving of the scathing denunciations of every friend of humanity. I do not believe it" (351).[21] The hypocrisy that Douglas sees in American history is not a simple and conscious act of duplicity—the sort of hypocrisy that might allow one to bracket off slavery or racism as a problem to be solved, a scar on the system that can be healed. Rather, Douglas finds, by his interpretive method, a fundamentally different historical text with which to reckon, one in which people can serve the cause of injustice while believing that they are serving the cause of justice, maintaining systems of oppression under the name of liberty. Not incidentally, Douglas's remarks are part of an address devoted to the denunciation of "the antislavery of Abraham Lincoln," and his historical vision is one that connects Lincoln to his apparent proslavery opponents in the South. White antislavery and white proslavery thought are branches of the same historical tree. Significantly, then, Douglas's remarks end with a list of antislavery activists, white and black, and finally with John Brown, the exception that proves the rule of white American history.

The collective performances scripted by the occasion of oration provided African American orators with the means by which to address the multiple contingencies of identity shaped by systemic oppression, and to orchestrate a collective historical memory that could place those multiple contingencies under different frameworks suggesting potentially new scripts of individual and collective identity and action. In his 1860 Fourth of July oration, Douglas juxtaposes his vision of the white supremacist history that usually scripts the celebration of national achievement with a vision of a providential history that has yet to be realized. "Nations who seek success amid the possibilities of the future," Douglas asserts, "are not measured by the accumulation of wealth or by the breadth of territorial domain; for down beneath the glittering splendor which the jeweled hand of Croesus has lifted up to intoxicate the gaze of the unthinking multitude, there will be found a silent and resistless influence working its way beneath the surface of society and shaping the destiny of men" (341). This vision of a gradually revealed providential design was, of course, at this same time being institutionalized in white American history and Fourth of July celebrations, and thus the importance of Douglas's application of liberation historiography—of using the community of the oppressed as the most significant site of interpretation, an interpretation that leads one increasingly to an understanding of the operations of the system of control. "The state lays its iron hand upon the Negro," Douglas notes, "holds him down, and puts the other hand into his pocket and steals his hard earnings, to educate the children of white men; and if we sent our children to school, Abraham Lincoln would kick them out, in the name of Republicanism and antislavery!" (345). Racism is not the primary concern here; Douglas is not simply interested in establishing the abilities of those of African descent. Rather, he is interested in the historical controls that shape collective identity, noting that "man's ability wholly depends upon surrounding circumstances" (347). "What peculiar trait of character do the white men of this country possess," Douglas asks, "as a mark of superiority, either morally or mentally, that is not also manifested by the black man under similar circumstances?" (346). By such a test, indeed, Douglas asserts, white men are found lacking, for "here in this country, under the most favorable circumstances, we have idiots and fools, some in the lunatic asylum, and others, in the high places of government, who essay to be statesmen, who ought to be there" (346).

Addressing the world normalized within the walls of that cultural lunatic asylum, African Americans used the assembly of history occasioned for and by oration to expose the ways in which the construction of history was essential to the maintenance of the system of white supremacy. Frances Ellen Watkins (later Harper), in her 1857 address "Liberty for Slaves," begins by noting the tremendous financial investment in slavery that shapes the lives of all concerned. The sight of the degradations of slavery, Watkins asserts, "should send a thrill of horror through the nerves of civilization and impel the heart of humanity to lofty deeds"—and "so it might," Watkins adds, "if men had not found out a fearful alchemy by which this blood can be transformed into gold" (306). This investment in slavery, while seemingly obvious, was often lost in the sentimental spectacle of oppression—in much the way, one might argue, that Stowe's presentation of the political economy of slavery, so prominent in her treatment of Augustine St. Clare's complex ambivalence in his position as a slaveholder, leads eventually and inevitably to the vision of individualized evil in Simon Legree. We can feel sentimental over a vision of the always already enslaved family of Uncle Tom without examining the terms of his original enslavement or the condition of those left behind as the novel's ethical trajectory travels north to Canada and then across the sea to Liberia.

Different contexts, Watkins says plainly, produce different readings of history. In her 1857 address, Watkins offers an example of a fugitive slave in Boston—and then explains how his situation would be interpreted and acted on if he were "upon the deck of an Austrian ship," "wrecked upon an island or colony of Great Britain," "landed upon the territory of vine-encircled France," "beneath the feebler light which glimmers from the Koran," or "beside the ancient pyramids of Egypt" (306–7). Watkins's historical imagination here draws us through the map of white American ideology, the various ideological and national fields on or against which the white American national vision has been forged—leading back finally to the fugitive slave in Boston. "In its proximity to the plains of Lexington and Concord, Boston [is] almost beneath the shadow of Bunker Hill and almost in sight of Plymouth Rock," and there the fugitive "is thrust back from liberty and manhood and reconverted into a chattel" (307). This imagined restaging of identity in the various ideological theaters of white American historical memory returns

Watkins's audience, then, to the currency of American identity, now relocated in the realm of the "law of God," where it awaits "the requiem of Egypt's ruined hosts and the anthem of the deliverance of Israel's captive people" (307).

This mode of historical restaging is common in African American discourse, often involving strategic comparisons between the United States and Great Britain, with the latter identified as the "land of the brave and the home of the free"; but in their plays on the contingencies of (national) identity, African Americans worked to draw out the underlying history that revealed those national differences as convenient distinctions within a coherent system of political economy. In an 1859 speech at the Athenaeum in Manchester, England, for example, Sarah Parker Remond addresses her audience as a crowd of interested and sympathetic spectators who know little about American slavery. Drawing on popular generalizations of regional differences in the United States, Remond presents the North as a region where "democracy, not what the Americans call democracy, but the true principle of equal rights, prevails" (329). This questionable characterization of the North, along with its interesting distinction between the citizens of the North and the Americans, is set in contrast to a South in which "aristocratic feelings prevail, labor is dishonorable, and five millions of poor whites live in the most degrading ignorance and destitution" (329). Remond here presents a conventional portrait of regional differences, aided considerably by including the analysis of the deeply racist southerner Hinton Helper in *The Impending Crisis,* so as to portray America as a nation in which "for more than thirty years . . . the Slave Power has been dominant," the consequence of which has been that "the slave trade is reopened and all but legitimised in America" (329). But as Remond continues her narrative, the legitimization of the slave trade—domestic and international, commercial and philosophical—extends to encompass the world of her audience. "Here is an incident of slave life for you," Remond states, and then tells the story of "the husband of your own Fanny Kemble" participating in the slave trade. By the end of the speech, Remond returns her audience to their true relation to slavery, noting, "I am met on every hand by the cry 'Cotton!' 'Cotton!'"—which she follows, without explanation, with the assertion that "there is an answer for the cotton cry . . . , and the argument is an unanswerable one" (330).

Perhaps that unspoken argument is suggested by Lucy Stanton in her opening words of a graduation address at Oberlin Collegiate Institute in 1850, of which she was a graduate. "When I forget you, Oh my people," Stanton begins, "may my tongue cleave to the roof of my mouth" (221). Stanton addresses the systemic order of slavery, noting that "the freedom of the slave and the gaining of our rights, social and political, are inseparably connected" (221). But the forgetting of black Americans, unrecognized by many white reformers as "my people," leads Stanton not just to a vision of reformist activism but also to a challenge to apply the discourse of reform to the cause of the enslaved: "Reformers, ye who have labored long to convince man that happiness is found alone in doing good to others, that humanity is a unit, that he who injures one individual wrongs the race,—that to love one's neighbor as one's self is the sum of human virtue—ye that advocate the great principles of Temperance, Peace, and Moral Reform will you not raise your voice in behalf of these stricken ones!—will you not plead the cause of the Slave!" (221). It is, of course, revealing that the question must be asked at all—which I believe is part of Stanton's point. The voice of reformist oratory must discover its connection to the site of oratorical authority, to the cause of the slave—"those who may not plead their own cause" and therefore must inform the voice of those who speak for themselves while pretending to speak for others. Certainly, Stanton does not question the sincerity of the various voices of reform; but in casually noting the established categories of their efforts, the sectionalization of their concerns, under the headings "Temperance," "Peace," and "Moral Reform," Stanton looks to emphasize the fragmentation of the unit of humanity in the fragmentation of its reform efforts. Slavery, Stanton asserts, is in fact "the combination of all crime. It is War." All reform must find its cause in the cause of the enslaved, which encompasses intemperance, war, and sin. And to relocate the center of reform efforts is to place oneself in a historical process that leads to the systemic effects of the system of slavery. "As a people take a step in one reform," Stanton asserts, "the way is prepared for another" (222).

The history presented in orations—histories encouraged by the occasions for oration—suggested that ways had been prepared for reform and that action was required. To speak before a white antislavery crowd was to confront the faces of a white supremacist culture. Regardless of their professed antislavery sentiments, a crowd of white people still willing to celebrate the Fourth of July, or still in need of persuasion about the evils of slavery, or still convinced of the virtue of a detached benevolence—this was a crowd that could not help but shape one's subject, a reminder of the national history constructed for some, a reminder of the difference between a theoretical opposition to, say, the *Dred Scott* case and the personal violation of one's rights. To speak before an

African American crowd, on the other hand, was to imagine the possibilities of community, and perhaps to experience frustration at the lack of organized, collective resistance to the ongoing violations of rights. To speak, say, either on the occasion of the abolition of the Atlantic slave trade or on the Fourth of July was to enter into a history that could only turn celebration back to the common cause that remained.

But the imagined community shaped by African American experience was by no means a comforting vision to many of these lecturers, for the work of building a community of resistance from the community of oppression was still largely ahead, and it was easily stalled or diverted by the illusion of relative freedom and security. In 1840, indeed, one commentator for the *Colored American* complained of the limited power and even the necessity of accomplished oratory when confronting concerns for which no eloquence should be necessary: "Is it true ... that two and a half millions of our kinsmen in these United States are bleeding in bondage, and yet that only about one in ten of the five hundred thousand free colored Americans are abolitionists? And many of these only feel like abolitionists when the subject, is by the highest touches of oratory, forced upon their *feeling*? Slavery, whose enormities written or told in the most ordinary style, no tender-hearted person can read or hear without emotion, are heard with very little interest, unless told in a finished oration by some great champion, and seldom read at all, written in any style!" ("Long Island Scribe"). One might say that if, as Allen argued, "the art of oratory is consequent upon the introduction of sin," then that same fallen condition works to confound the intent of the orator. The need to inspire where no inspiration should be necessary indicates the challenge that confronts the orator, whose very success might be viewed as evidence of a larger failure.

Accordingly, some African American orators worked to provoke their audiences into a disturbing self-consciousness, to move them beyond the occasion and toward the grounds—the condition of oppression—of oratory. In an 1832 lecture in Franklin Hall, Boston, for example, Maria Stewart addressed her audience directly, stating, "Tell us no more of southern slavery; for with few exceptions, although I may be very erroneous in my opinion, yet I consider our condition but little better than that" (51–52). The history that Stewart presents is naturally that history most directly calculated to respond to the present condition of the community—including its inaction. "Did the pilgrims," Stewart asks, "when they first landed on these shores, quietly compose themselves, and say, 'the Britons have all the money and all the

power, and we must continue their servants forever?' Did they sluggishly sigh
and say, 'our lot is hard, the Indians own the soil, and we cannot cultivate it?'
No; they first made powerful efforts to raise themselves, and then God raised
up those illustrious patriots, WASHINGTON AND LAFAYETTE, to assist and defend
them" (56). Stewart draws from history to suggest the means for responding to
present conditions—including the suggestion that African Americans should
be inspired by white colonialists' conquest of Native American land. "And, my
brethren," she asks conclusively, "have you made a powerful effort?" (56).
Similarly, in 1833 Stewart refers to African Americans' historical contributions to the cause of American liberty, noting that "it is true, our fathers bled
and died in the revolutionary war, and others fought bravely under the command of Jackson, in defense of liberty" (64); she adds that "history informs us
that we sprung from one of the most learned nations of the whole earth" (65).
This history only shows, however, the lack of similar resolve in the present,
prompting Stewart to ask, "But where is the man that has distinguished
himself in these modern days by acting wholly in the defense of African rights
and liberty?" (64). A prominent exception is the revolutionary determination
of David Walker. "Although he sleeps," Stewart says, "his memory lives" (64).
The occasion shapes the audience and thereby the subject of history for the
orator who draws from the past to respond to the needs of the present.

Charles Lenox Remond's 1844 address advocating the dissolution of the
Union adds to this pointed memory a certain historical self-consciousness,
claiming the field of history for the field of revolutionary action. Remond asks
what the Union was "to Turner of Southampton, than whom a nobler soul has
never risen upon the human race in all the long line of its prophets and its
heroes!" (206). Remond then joins national allegiances with historical practices: "The Union does not even preserve his name. *He* had no place in life
under its protecting aegis—in history he is only Nat Turner, the miserable
negro" (206). Responding directly to this historical omission and diminution
of Turner, Remond asserts, "*I* will never contemptuously call him *Nat* Turner,
for had he been a white man, Massachusetts and Virginia would have united
to glorify his name and to build his monument; and is it strange, seeing all
these things, that I should feel them too, and act upon the feeling?" (206).
Remond acts on the feeling both in his approach to the historical record and
in his reading of the responsibilities and course of action revealed *by* the historical record, noting that many consider him "wild," "mad," and "a revo-
lutionist"—and following with the significant reapplication of this isolating
discourse: "Sir, in view of all these things, ought not this whole assembly—

this whole nation be revolutionists too?" (206). Remond takes the revolutionary history of a nation to place the white nation at odds with his own history,
and to establish a historical record—including authority over that record and
responsibility to it—that justifies revolutionary action in the present.

Nor was Remond alone in this strategy. As has been, I trust, abundantly
clear throughout this and the previous chapters, African Americans who gave
voice to history reapplied the revolutionary rhetoric of the past to the historical contingencies of the present, and transformed political action into the
need to join word and deed, to restore the word violated in white American
culture. As I mentioned earlier, Sundquist has written of Frederick Douglass's
increasingly open militancy that "if the white postrevolutionary generations
remained paralyzed in the face of the fathers' ambiguous authority on the law
of slavery, the black generations were, in fact, not yet *post*revolutionary at all.
For them in particular, the Age of Revolution—not just in the United States
but throughout the slaveholding New World—was far from over" (115). Despite the nonviolent ideal of the Garrisonian abolitionists, black abolitionists
frequently both predicted and justified slave insurrection by looking back to
the American Revolution and to its historical companion in San Domingo.[22]
As William Wells Brown argued in his 1854 lecture *St. Domingo: Its Revolutions and Its Patriots*, "Toussaint liberated his countrymen; Washington enslaved a portion of his, and aided in giving strength and vitality to an institution that will one day rend asunder the UNION that he helped to form" (37). In
that anticipated struggle, Brown asserts, "the God of Justice will be on the
side of the oppressed blacks . . . and the revolution that was commenced in
1776 would then be finished, and the glorious sentiments of the Declaration
of Independence . . . would be realized" (38). Taking as their foundation a
black liberation theological understanding of God's commitment to the oppressed, black historians found in the site of oppression the occasion for
oration, one from which all other historical investigation would follow—and
it was a vision of history that led increasingly to the need for revolutionary resistance not simply to enslavers but to the enslaving culture of white
supremacy.

The occasion of oratorical history in many ways found its fulfillment in the
most famously militant statement of the time, Henry Highland Garnet's "An
Address to the Slaves of the United States of America," presented at the
National Convention of Negro Citizens in Buffalo, New York, in August 1843.
This address occasioned considerable debate, as the delegates argued over
whether to adopt it as an official statement coming out of the convention. The

convention voted against it—by one vote—with Frederick Douglass prominent among those who argued that the address was too violent and that it would be dangerous to those slaves it might reach, and dangerous to African Americans everywhere when white Americans read it. "Mr. Douglass remarked," the convention's proceedings report, "that there was too much physical force, both in the address and the remarks of the speaker last up. He was for trying the moral means a little longer; that the address, could it reach the slaves, and the advice, either of the address or the gentleman, be followed, while it might not lead the slaves to rise in insurrection for liberty, would, nevertheless, and necessarily be the occasion of an insurrection; and that was what he wished in no way to have any agency in bringing about, and what we were called upon to avoid" (Bell, *Minutes*, 1843 proceedings 13). But if the speech was denied an official endorsement, it remained a vital part of the ideological landscape of the antislavery movement, its status indicated by its association with *David Walker's Appeal* when the two were published together some years later.[23]

Although it was an "address to the slaves," arguably Garnet's speech reached the primary audience for whom it was intended, as he worked to shift the tenor of the assembled black national (male) leadership in Buffalo. Calling his audience his "Brethren and Fellow Citizens," Garnet identifies them historically and politically—asking them to "think of the undying glory that hangs around the ancient name of Africa—and forget not that you are native-born American citizens" (268). Although Garnet addresses his comments to his imagined audience, the slaves in the South, he speaks perhaps more directly still to his northern audience—asserting, for example, "Your condition does not absolve you from your moral obligation," and that "the time has come when you must act for yourselves" (270). African Americans had gathered in Buffalo in part to *regather* the collective energy and will of earlier national convention efforts—and many felt that the time had come to adopt a more deliberate approach. When Garnet proclaims that it is better to *"die freemen than live to be slaves"* (271), he is, of course, calling on the enslaved to resist their enslavers—though perhaps he is saying even more to those who *are* freemen (to the extent that the title was at all accurate in the North) and thus in a position to die as such for the collective cause. Garnet called the slaves to action through the speech; he called his fellow delegates to action in presenting the address at the convention and inspiring debate about its adoption. In an address that emphasizes the connection between the enslaved of the South and the insecurely free of the North ("nor can we be free while you are enslaved," Garnet says), a speech that addresses systemic oppression,

Garnet speaks both directly and indirectly to his northern audience and to the cause of black self-definition and self-determination.

In this address, Garnet draws from history to join word and deed in revolutionary action. Granting that the white North's "opinion of slavery in the abstract is known," he works toward a concrete understanding of the historical moment of which he and his audience are a part—an understanding that focuses on language. Garnet speaks of the Declaration of Independence as "a glorious document," and he says of Patrick Henry's famous "liberty or death" speech, "Oh, what a sentence was that!" (269). But those earlier words have been lost to a corrupting culture that has altered the language of morality. Garnet argues for a different language, noting of the term "slavery," for example, "How much misery is comprehended in that single word!" (269). Reading from that deeply meaningful word, Garnet constructs an extended revolutionary history, saying of Denmark Vesey's organization of "a plan for the liberation of his fellow men" that "many a brave hero fell, but history, faithful to her high trust, will transcribe his name on the same monument with Moses, Hampden, Tell, Bruce and Wallace, Toussaint L'Ouverture, Lafayette and Washington. That tremendous movement shook the whole empire of slavery" (271). Vesey, significantly, was a "freeman," having purchased his liberty, and he was thus an appropriate model for both Garnet's northern and his southern audiences—and he is soon joined by the other revolutionaries Nathaniel Turner, Joseph Cinqué, and Madison Washington in Garnet's history of determined resistance. These leaders responded not only to the system of slavery but also to the system of language that could have justified other approaches or no approach at all. Garnet, in his address, rereads history so as to reread theology, and draws from theology so as to reread history, and draws from both theology and history to identify the duty of facing the choice of "liberty or death." "Tell them in language which they cannot misunderstand," Garnet advises both the slaves in the South and the "freemen" in the North, "of the exceeding sinfulness of slavery" (270). This leads Garnet finally to an emphatic reapplication of language, from abstract opposition to slavery to a language that emphasizes the need for action and can only be fulfilled through action: "Let your motto be resistance! *Resistance*! RESISTANCE!" (272).

In other words, Garnet uses the occasion of oration, this linguistic performance, to call his audiences back to meaning and to the collective effort necessary to restore meaning in a culture in which both revolutionary and Christian rhetoric is used to justify and maintain the system of slavery. Sara Stanley would echo Garnet in 1856 at the State Convention of Colored Men in

Ohio,[24] opening the speech with a rhetorical battle between Truth, Justice, Mercy, Error, and Oppression, guiding her audience toward Freedom, Liberty, and Deity, and leading eventually to "those great, noble words: Liberty and Independence—Free Government—Church and State" ("What, to the Toiling Millions" 285–86). Ultimately this great linguistic struggle for coherence and order leads Stanley to call her audience to just one word. "Intuitively, then," Stanley states, "we search for the panacea for the manifold ills which we suffer. One, and only one, exists; and when each individual among us realizes the absolute impossibility for him to perform any work of supererogation in the common cause, the appliances will prove its own efficacy; it is embodied in one potent word—ACTION" (286–87).

Garnet's argument eventually found an echo, too, in one of its most persuasive opponents in Buffalo in 1843, Frederick Douglass—whose own search for a history capable of responding to the present condition of black America led him to become a more aggressive historian. In his 1857 speech on "West India Emancipation," Douglass notes that "power concedes nothing without a demand," and presents Margaret Garner (over a century later the inspiration for Toni Morrison's *Beloved*) as someone who "should be held and honored as a benefactress" ("If There Is No Struggle" 310). Douglass tells a reconstructed and reframed history, one by which Madison Washington is "more worthy to be remembered than the colored man who shot Pitcairn at Bunker Hill" (311). Comparing the antislavery efforts of Wilberforce to the rebellious resistance of the slaves in the British West Indies, Douglass states, "While one showed that slavery was wrong, the other showed that it was dangerous as well as wrong" (312). And Douglass looks to American history to determine the course of action for the American present, noting, "I am aware that the insurrectionary movements of the slaves were held by many to be prejudicial to their cause. This is said now of such movements at the South. The answer is that abolition followed close on the heels of insurrection in the West Indies, and Virginia was never nearer emancipation than when General Turner kindled the fires of insurrection at Southampton" (312). With a historical perspective shaped in large part by the multiple contingencies of the antislavery lecture circuit, the racial politics of the antislavery movement, and the linguistic demands of maintaining a newspaper directed toward the African American community, Douglass found himself revising the past to account for the changing present—giving voice to a nation increasingly imagined and imaginable, the nation suggested by the collective efforts of African American historians past and present.

White Officers and the Tower of Babel:
The Work of the National Convention Movement

In his 1857 oration "West India Emancipation," Frederick Douglass addressed the racial politics of the antislavery movement and endorsed the organization of black abolitionists into a self-determining political force. "I know, my friends," Douglass stated, "that in some quarters the efforts of colored people meet with very little encouragement. We may fight, but we must fight like the Sepoys of India, under white officers" ("If There Is No Struggle" 309). Douglass referred not only to the authority of black abolitionists but also to the broader cultural organization necessary to promote the solidarity, security, and independence of African American local and national communities. "This class of Abolitionists," Douglass asserted, "don't like colored celebrations, they don't like colored conventions, they don't like colored antislavery fairs for the support of colored newspapers" (309). In part, Douglass suggested, this disdain for black organizations was a product of the white supremacist framework that shaped white abolitionists' understanding of the social problems they were addressing and of the solutions to those problems. "They talk of the proud Anglo-Saxon blood," Douglass complained, "as flippantly as those who profess to believe in the natural inferiority of races" (309). While not dismissing the efforts of the white abolitionists, Douglass did insist on the necessity of organized black efforts, both to define the African American community though common struggle and to address the underlying systemic oppression that infected even the antislavery movement. "I hold it to be no part of gratitude," Douglass argued, "to allow our white friends to do all the work, while we merely hold their coats" (309–10).

Douglass was, not surprisingly, an influential presence in the later phase of the black national convention movement that extended from 1830 to 1864— and in his comments he suggests both the necessity of the black national conventions and their complex and contingent relation to the white community. The first convention, which met in Philadelphia, grew from the suggestion of Hezekiah Grice of Baltimore as a means to discuss emigration to Canada. From the beginning, though, the conventions extended their range to include educational efforts in the United States, various approaches to establishing the African American community as a commercially secure and independent entity, responses to the ongoing work of the American Colonization Society, commentary on the degradation of religion and on American governing ideals, arguments in support of the recognition of the citizenship of African Americans, and debates within the African American community about the proper course of action in the antislavery cause. The conventions became a stage for black male leadership—indeed, in concert with state and local conventions, the national conventions "provided an opportunity for new [male] spokesmen and leaders to emerge," including such prominent figures as James McCune Smith, Martin Delany, J. W. C. Pennington, and Amos Beman (Pease and Pease, *They Who Would Be Free* 123).[25]

They also became a theater for the developing conflicts between white and black abolitionists. In regard to the early conventions, Jane H. and William H. Pease have written, "So strongly influenced were they by white abolitionists, some of whom regularly attended the conventions, that in 1835 they voted to establish the American Moral Reform Society, whose purview would embrace the full sweep of Garrisonian multi-reformism." But this larger focus was an early example of a problem that would plague the conventions—the need to define the black convention movement in its contingent relation to white America. "The absence of a race designation in its sweeping title," the Peases note, suggested the "major flaw" of the American Moral Reform Society: "that its program was so all-embracing that it deflected the group from the convention movement's main purpose, the fostering of race pride and cohesion" (121). Later conflicts between African American organized resistance and expansive ideals of a common humanity were more complex, particularly at those conventions that met close to and during the Civil War, when the promise of a recognized and common citizenship seemed nearer yet tantalizingly out of reach.

The national conventions were clearly important historical events, but what role do they play in a study of early African American historical writing and the development of African American historiography? I present these events as important examples of historical writing because they produced and published documents, the proceedings of the conventions, that should be recognized as historical texts, in that they document historical events, certainly, but also in that they gather and define African American history and provide it with a textual form appropriate to the complex historical situation of African Americans before the Civil War. These documents include narratives of the past—chronologies and documented arguments that most readers would associate with historical texts. But readers familiar with the other African American historical writings that I have surveyed in previous chapters will not encounter in the proceedings of the national conventions any strikingly new information, and they will encounter familiar motifs. Africa is identified as the seat of civilization; slavery interrupts the process of human civilization, forcing renewed attention on the design and demands of providential history; Jackson issues his proclamations recognizing African Americans as citizens; African Americans participate in the American struggle for liberty, long after most white Americans abandon that struggle; and Ethiopia stretches forth her arms, or shall. Individual stories of personal violations, or rights ignored, and of murder join with larger narratives of a scattered community gathering itself at the nexus of sacred and secular history. These are important stories, but what makes their repetition in the various proceedings important is not only their status as stories about the past but also their presence in a complex document that includes committee reports, debates, declarations of sentiment, and addresses to the populations, white and black, beyond the convention.

The various publications that resulted from the conventions are thus important historical texts not simply in content but in their mode of presentation, in their representation of a black historiographical mode that accounts for and responds to the contingencies of a scattered community, that represents the untold stories without attempting to tell more than can be told, and that presents black history as a mode of address, a consideration of history geared toward an intervention in history. That which is recognizable as "history"—information, stories about the past—is presented in broad terms and serves mainly to indicate the dynamic contours of a larger act of historical representation. The conventions were, after all, collective performances designed to be a representative embodiment of an imagined African American community. The history represented in the proceedings of each convention, then, is the story suggested by the gathering: its foreground, the materials and conditions (and conditionality) of that collective embodiment, the individual lives as shaped by national events and the collective gathering that results from the commonalities in those individual histories. The text produced is not simply a textual record of the event, though of course the record of debates and agreements is also important; but we should also attend to the construction of community represented by the text, organized into areas of concern, committees, even lists of professions represented. These various proceedings, the work of the committees and of the debates, are part of an implicit narrative that leads, in each of these texts, to a focused statement, an address to the broad public (sometimes specifically identified, sometimes implicitly). Finally, then, the voice of oratory presented in the proceedings is a collective voice, the result of collective deliberations. That oratorical voice becomes, indeed, a representative voice by virtue of creating the text that claims to speak for the people and voting it into representative authority. The history represented in these documents, then, is not just the information presented but the mode of representation, a mode that must also represent the forum that makes the mode possible—the drawing together of the scattered community into a multifarious but unified voice of historical intervention.[26]

While there are significant changes in focus and tone over the years and in the various conventions, what remains consistent is an emphasis on the basic elements of liberation historiography as I have outlined it in earlier chapters. The conventions identify the terms of oppression that define the African American national community; they distinguish between a corrupt and a pure Christianity; they apply to the African American cause the ideals associated with the American Revolution; they explore the relation between sacred and secular history; and they turn historical commentary to the needs of the community, identifying a course of action sanctioned by history. At the beginning of the 1834 convention in New York, for example, the Declaration of Sentiment notes "the depressed condition of the coloured population of the United States," and notes as well that the convention delegates "in vain searched the history of nations to find a parallel" (Bell, *Minutes*, 1834 proceedings 27). The terms of that condition would change over the years, and the focus of historical understanding and of practical action shifted accordingly from temperance efforts in the early years to education, commercial and agricultural plans, and suffrage in the later years. But the shifts were of emphasis and rarely of substance as each convention addressed in slightly different form an understanding of the systemic oppression of African Americans. The statement of the situation published in 1833 stood virtually unchanged through the years—that "in no country under Heaven have the descendants of an *ancestry* once enrolled in the history of fame; whose glittering monuments stood forth as beacons, disseminating light and knowledge to the uttermost parts of the earth, reduced to such degrading servitude as that under which we labour from the effect of *American slavery* and *American prejudice*" (27–28). Understandings of race changed; antislavery efforts shifted strategies and developed internal divisions; but still the conventions consistently addressed racial identity in its essential form—as a collective effect of the contingent relations among (primarily) free blacks, enslaved blacks, southern slaveholders (and their representatives), and northern whites (and *their* representatives, in the form of both antislavery and proslavery sympathizers). The nature of the problem did not change, nor did the understanding represented in the convention proceedings through the years.

It was oppression that defined the historical African American community, identifying it as a coherent community and connecting it to other oppressed communities throughout history, identifying the historical field to be surveyed and indicating the course of action to be taken. The published call to the most militant of the conventions, the one held in Buffalo in 1843, argued that "the oppressed in all ages of the world have emerged from their condition of degradation and servitude in proportion as they have exerted themselves in their *own cause*, and have convinced the world and their oppressors that they were determined to be free" (Bell, *Minutes*, 1843 proceedings 3). This exertion included, as its foundation, the need to organize the community of oppression into a self-determined collective, one capable of defining itself to the world and to its oppressors on its own terms. "The history of the present and the past establish," the call continued, "the great truth that it is as much impossible for any people to secure the enjoyment of their inalienable rights without organization, as it is to reach an end without means. Acting in accordance with this truth, the oppressed people of England, Ireland and Scotland, have banded themselves together in their respective nations to wage unceasing war against the green-eyed monster, tyranny" (3). In his opening address to that convention, Samuel H. Davis referred back to Jefferson's trembling vision of the future of a nation that sanctioned slavery, and drew as well from the history of oppression, associating the African American struggle with Polish, Irish, and Greek struggles for liberty. "We must profit by the example of our oppressors," Davis argued; "we must act on their principles in resisting tyranny. We must adopt their resolutions in favor of liberty" (6).

The deeply historical character of African American oppression—encompassing both sacred and secular realms—provides the lens through which to read the historical moment and the authority over the principles claimed by the oppressors. The minutes and proceedings of the First Annual Convention of the People of Colour, held in Philadelphia in 1831, begin by noting the recommendation of the Committee of Inquiry "that the Declaration of Independence and Constitution of the United States, be read in our Conventions," arguing that "the truths contained in the former are incontrovertible; and that the latter guarantees in letter and spirit to every freeman born in the country, all the rights and immunities of citizenship" (Bell, *Minutes*, 1831 proceedings 4–5). While there were significant arguments over the years about whether the Constitution should be considered a proslavery or antislavery document, and whether it should play a role in the philosophical and practical definition of antislavery efforts, this invocation of the founding documents remained a fundamental presence over the years—along with the belief that the principles guiding the conventions "are drawn from the book of divine revelation, and are incorporated in the Declaration of Independence" (Bell, *Minutes*, 1833 proceedings 29). That the white citizens of the United States did not apply the sentiments of the Declaration of Independence to African Americans required little argument, though such arguments were of course presented at every convention. More forceful still were the denunciations of American churches—as in the 1843 resolutions that stated, "*Resolved*, That we believe in the true Church of Christ, and that it will stand while time endures, and that it will evince its spirit by its opposition to all sins, and especially to the sin of slavery, which is a compound of all others, and that the great mass of American sects, falsely called churches, which apologize for slavery and prejudice, or practice slaveholding, are in truth no churches, but Synagogues of Satan" (Bell, *Minutes*, 1843 proceedings 15). This understanding of the moral battle they faced identified the terms of the historical story they were to tell—the story of a battle against "the greatest enemies to Christ and to civil and religious liberty in the world" (15).

As in other works of African American history before the Civil War, the historical story to be told was in fact the story of a reading—or a rereading—of the story being told by the oppressors. The reading revealed a national text that lacked coherence; a developing mode of reading, in the service of that text, that failed the test of its own purported hermeneutic principles; and a corresponding degradation of narrative stability that undermined the white national story and that placed African American historical self-definition squarely in the realm of discourse. Particularly revealing are the various commentaries on that persistent concern at all of the conventions, colonization schemes—and particularly those organized by the American Colonization Society (ACS).[27] In 1833, with perhaps too much hope, the Report on African Colonization noted the discursive instability of the ACS and took this as a sign that the organization could not last long: "The investigations that have been made into that society within the past year, justifies us in believing that that great BABEL of oppression and persecution must soon cease to exist. It has been reared so high, that the light of heaven, the benevolence of true philanthropy, and the voice of humanity, forbid its further ascent; and, as in ancient times, the confusion of tongues has already begun, which speedily promises its final consummation—and although it has but recently been classed with the benevolent enterprises of this age, it must shortly be numbered with the ruins of the past" (Bell, *Minutes*, 1833 proceedings 27). The very success of the ACS, in its appeal to white philanthropy, would inevitably make visible the fundamental violation of the organization's announced principles, and would result in a loss of support.

At the next year's convention, however, William Hamilton, in his address as president of the Conventional Board, could only lament the ongoing presence of the ACS and observe that the Babel of oppression had developed into a series of targeted narratives: "That society has spread itself to all places. It is one thing at the south, and another at the north; it blows hot and cold; it sends forth bitter and sweet; it sometimes represents us as the most corrupt, vicious, and abandoned of any class of men in the community. Then again we are kind, meek, and gentle. Here we are ignorant, idle, a nuisance, and a drawback on the resources of the country. But as abandoned as we are, in Africa we shall civilize and christianize all that heathen country" (*Address* 5). By reading the narratives together one could readily observe the internal contradictions, and one could observe as well the unspoken narrative principle that provided this apparent incoherence with an all-too-familiar unifying principle—the white supremacist determination to control or eliminate African Americans in or from the national landscape. As the 1847 Report of the Committee on Abolition put it in characterizing slavery, "Your Committee find this monstrous crime, this stupendous iniquity, closely interwoven with all the great interests, institutions and organizations of the country; pervading and influencing every class and grade of society, securing their support, obtaining their approbation, and commanding their homage" (Bell, *Minutes*, 1847 proceedings 31). In short, African American readings of the national story noted incoherence in order to discern the underlying coherence of white supremacist ideology and a systemic oppression.

Drawing from the difference between the revealed narratives and the official stories of the white body politic, African Americans in the conventions applied the sacred and secular authority of their historically oppressed condition to reposition themselves in relation to their oppressors. In the Declaration of Sentiment of the 1833 convention, the delegates identified their historical oppression, and on that authority declared that "under whatever pretext or authority laws have been promulgated or executed, whether under parliamentary, colonial, or American legislation, *we declare* them in the sight of Heaven wholly *null* and *void*, and should be *immediately abrogated*" (Bell, *Minutes*, 1833 proceedings 28). The "Address to the People of the United

States" of the 1855 convention began by associating the African American community with the dual pillars of the Constitution and Christianity, speaking "in behalf of the Constitution of these United States, during sixty years perverted and misunderstood, so as to read things for persons, and Slavery for Liberty," and speaking also "in behalf of the religion of Jesus Christ, brought into shame and disrepute by the evil constructions and worst practices fastened upon it by the American Church" (Bell, *Minutes*, 1855 proceedings 30). The presentation of the Constitution as an antislavery document was, of course, a radical departure for African Americans allied with Garrison— though, as I have noted, this reading marks also a return to the 1831 convention's belief that the Constitution should be read at every convention.

By 1855, this reading was, in fact, an act of interpretation: the "Address to the People of the United States" guides its readers through an analysis of the Constitution, reading that document from the interpretive framework defined by the condition of the African American community and the operations of the system of slavery. This reading, the address claims, leads to inescapable conclusions, for "to uphold a contrary view of the Constitution, requires that that instrument should contradict itself, and requires also that the idea of personal liberty, as defined by it, and on which you all, fellow-citizens, so confidently rely, shall be entirely erased therefrom" (Bell, *Minutes*, 1855 proceedings 31–32). The misinterpretation of the Constitution, the address asserts to an implied white northern audience, has led to the abrogation of rights of white Americans in the North. "Your local elective franchises are exercised," the address argues; "your very territory occupied, your relations at home and abroad regulated at the bidding of the slave power" (32–33). This lesson in interpretation, in short, is also a lesson in history; and the development of history—as revealed by its interpretive center, the oppressed community—provides the framework by which to arrive at a stable reading of the Constitution:

> During Sixty-eight years you have suffered us to be robbed of these rights and franchises, in the belief that your own continued unimpaired. But now, after the experience of two generations, you find your own rights invaded and your own privileges taken away in like manner with ours. It is now, therefore, demonstrated, by incontrovertible History, that you cannot, by whatever neglect or suffered misinterpretation of the Constitution, imperil or abandon our rights, without, in like manner, imperiling and abandoning your own. It stands forth, in letters of

living light, that there can be not one white free-man while there remains one black slave in the Union. And there can be no higher praise
of the Constitution, than that its workings are absolute—if rightly interpreted, for Freedom—if wrongly, for Slavery—to all. (32)

History is the process by which the human story is either supported or supplanted by the "letters of living light," the events that lead those who can read
to the stable narrative and discursive principles on which a collective history
(itself essential to the stability of the collective) must depend.

But if these readings revealed the principles by which narratives must be
interpreted and evaluated, and if they revealed the dangerous separation of
principle and policy, and of word and deed, they were less clear about the
form of action required in response to the readings. Throughout the conventions, the representatives held to the belief that truth—as revealed by "the
agency of divine truth, and the spirit of American liberty" (Bell, *Minutes*, 1834
proceedings 29)—would do its own work, and that the primary purpose of the
conventions was to promote that truth. "The human voice must supersede
the roar of cannon," the 1847 Report of the Committee on Abolition proclaimed; "truth alone is the legitimate antidote of falsehood. Liberty is always
sufficient to grapple with tyranny" (Bell, *Minutes*, 1847 proceedings 32). One
practical manifestation of this purpose was in the publication, through platform and press, of the condition of African Americans, both free and enslaved, encompassing both the restraints they faced and the progress they
were making. The other primary manifestation of this purpose was in efforts
to improve the condition of the free African American community through
temperance campaigns and through the development of schools and occupa-
tional training and opportunity. Characteristic is the Conventional Address of
the 1832 convention, addressed to "the Free Colored Inhabitants of these
United States," which follows a reference to Jackson's proclamations identifying African Americans as citizens with an admonishment concerning what
such citizenship requires. "You there see that your country expects much
from you," the address proclaimed, "and that you have much to call you into
action, morally, religiously and scientifically. Prepare yourselves to occupy the
several stations to which the wisdom of your country may promote you" (Bell,
Minutes, 1832 proceedings 35).

While these measures sparked debate, the question of how to respond to
the condition of the enslaved was still more difficult. Certainly, all of the
conventions shared the sentiment of the authors of the 1847 Report of the

Committee on Abolition, who said that they had "arrived at the conclusion that the best means of abolishing slavery is proclamation of truth, and that the best means of destroying caste is the mental, moral and industrial improvement of our people" (Bell, *Minutes*, 1847 proceedings 31). But the frustrations that attended this approach became clear in 1843 when the convention in Buffalo debated the acceptance of Garnet's "An Address to the Slaves of the United States of America." In defending his address, Garnet, the proceedings report,

> went into the whole merits of the case. He reviewed the abominable system of slavery, showed its mighty workings, its deeds of darkness and of death—how it robbed parents of children, and children of parents, husbands of wives; how it prostituted the daughters of the slaves; how it murdered the colored man. He referred to the fate of Denmark Vesey and his accomplices—of Nat Turner; to the burning of McIntosh, to the case of Madison Washington, as well as to many other cases—to what had been done to move the slave holders to let go their grasp, and asked what more could be done—if we have not waited long enough—if it were not time to speak louder and longer—to take higher ground and other steps. (Bell, *Minutes*, 1843 proceedings 13)

That Garnet should need to repeat the history that inspired the militancy of his address is, of course, revealing, for this is just the sort of ritualistic repetition of a portrait of African Americans viewed historically to which the conventions were devoted. And while this ritualistic return to the familiar markers of African American citizenship, moral duty, and resistance served as the framework for various attempts at moral and political reform, the conventions suffered continually from an inability to determine or sustain a suitable and effective course of action.[28]

But this ritualistic redefinition of the contours of African American history did serve to promote a stable portrait of an identifiable community in the process of self-definition. The Second Annual Convention, in its report on the condition of the people, begins by relating the history generated by the efforts of the First Annual Convention, offering a "retrospective view of the object for which the Convention was first associated, and the causes which have actuated their deliberations" (Bell, *Minutes*, 1832 proceedings 16). This report returns to the "expulsory laws of Ohio, in 1829, which drove our people to seek a new home in Upper Canada, and their impoverished situation afterwards, excited a general burst of sympathy for their situation" (16). This awakened sympathy led to the convention, which looked to the possibilities of emigration; since that time, though, the committee reports, prejudice in Canada forced the convention to turn "its attention more to the elevation of our people in this, our native home" (17). But that return home is a turn to new problems, following the reactions to the Turner rebellion, which, the committee reports, "have swelled the tide of prejudice until it has almost revolutionized public sentiment, which has given birth to severe legislative enactments in some of the States, and almost ruined our interests and prospects in others, in which, in the opinion of your Committee, our situation is more precarious than it has been at any other period since the Declaration of Independence" (17). In their attempt to discover, promote, and support solutions, in short, the representatives at this and other conventions only found themselves constructing an ever more extensive report on the nature of their situation—taking them back to the relation between American slavery and American prejudice and to the systemic order that defined and sustained that relation.

But there was value in the attempt to report on that complex system of relations, for in doing so the convention presents a history that reinforces the importance of the convention as a source of historical interpretation and of historical intervention. This documentation of the effort to record and resist a history of oppression helped to promote the cause of African American communal self-definition, if only in emphasizing the continuity of conditions that were shaping that community. In response to a continuous oppression, the conventions began to record a continuous resistance, as was emphasized when the 1835 proceedings reprinted, as its Declaration of Sentiments, the declaration published in the 1834 proceedings. In 1843, when the national convention movement was renewed after a hiatus (and after a frustrated attempt to meet in 1841),[29] the call to the convention emphasized what was lost in the absence of the regular yearly gatherings: "Since we have ceased to meet together in National Convention, we have become ignorant of the moral and intellectual strength of our people. We have also been deprived of the councils of our fathers, who have borne the burden and heat of the day—the spirit of virtuous ambition and emulation has died in the bosoms of the young men, and in great degree we have become divided, and the bright rising stars that once shone in our skies, have become partially obscured" (Bell, *Minutes*, 1843 proceedings 3). The loss of the conventions, this call suggests, encouraged the further fragmentation of the community—and to hold a national convention was accordingly important, in part, to preserve the historicity of the community.

This was both a promising and a fragile project, with participants very much aware of their attempt to construct and perform in a public theater devoted to historical intervention. In 1840, responding to efforts to reestablish the national conventions after a lull of over five years, Lewis Woodson noted his support for the efforts, and expressed his belief that a national convention is "one of the most powerful means of our moral elevation" and that "a very large majority of our people are in favor of a national Union, and a National Organization, upon truly national principles." Still, with the possibilities of such a national gathering came risks—particularly the risk that faltering attempts to display national unity would instead demonstrate that no such national union existed. Woodson, in fact, argued against the convention called for in 1840 because he worried about rushed and poor planning. "A small Convention at the present time," Woodson maintained, "would be worse than none. It would have no other tendency than to rouse up and encourage its former enemies; and dishearten, and paralyze its present friends" (Woodson). Many, though, worried about the effects of the ongoing absence of a national theater for African American self-definition and debate. As one commentator stated in 1840, "During the years of '31, '32, and '34, our people were gradually uniting in a measure which was proposed by some of the wisest heads among us, and which I am bold to say, has not been successfully controverted; I mean the convention system." The author of this article, published in the *Colored American*, presents the abandonment of the convention system as both evidence and cause of a kind of historical attention deficit disorder—"the habitual disinclination to put the mind down faithfully to what is worthy of our attention" ("Long Island Scribe")—on the part of African Americans. In promoting the national convention movement, and in orchestrating the conventions themselves, the challenge, in effect, was to gather a community so as to create it and to create a vision of community so as to gather it together.

A primary purpose of the conventions, indeed, was to address the physical, historical, and ideological fragmentation of people of African heritage. The First Annual Convention began by announcing, "Our attention has been called to investigate the political standing of our brethren wherever dispersed, but more particularly the situation of those in this great Republic" (Bell, *Minutes*, 1831 proceedings 12). In 1848, the representatives at the convention emphasized the unity of that community in the Republic, first by offering an overview of the condition of the enslaved that followed standard antislavery rhetoric, but with an emphasis (by way of pronoun) on the collective participation in this oppressed state. "In the Southern States of this Union," the "Address to the Colored People of the United States" stated, "we are held as slaves. All over that wide region our paths are marked with blood. Our backs are yet scarred by the lash, and our souls are yet dark under the pall of slavery. Our sisters are sold for purposes of pollution, and our brethren are sold in the market, with beasts of burden. Shut up in the prison-house of bondage—denied all rights, and deprived of all privileges, we are blotted from the page of human existence, and placed beyond the limits of human regard. DEATH, moral DEATH, has palsied our souls in that quarter, and we are a murdered people" (Bell, *Minutes*, 1848 proceedings 18). This overview emphasizes that the oppression of the enslaved includes their exclusion from the purview of history, "blotted from the page of human existence" and in that way "placed beyond the limits of human regard."

This omission from history emphasizes the historical existence and corresponding responsibilities of African Americans in the North. "In the Northern states," the address continues, "we are not slaves to individuals, not personal slaves, yet in many respects we are the slaves of the community. We are, however, far enough removed from the actual condition of the slaves to make us largely responsible for their continued enslavement, or their speedy deliverance from chains. For in the proportion which we shall rise in the scale of human improvement, in that proportion do we augment the probabilities of a speedy emancipation of our enslaved fellow-countrymen" (18). While this overview of the brethren in the Republic is in many ways simply standard antislavery discourse—"remember them that are in bonds as bound with them"[30]—its particular emphasis in the 1848 convention is still significant in its emphasis on the terms of community and in its consideration of the role of history in shaping that community. "It is more than a mere figure of speech to say," the address concluded, "that we are as a people, chained together. We are one people—one in general complexion, one in a common degradation, one in popular estimation.—As one rises, all must rise, and as one falls all must fall" (18).

The conventions emphasized the necessity of viewing the common oppression historically, and from that perspective to envision and coordinate the rise of the community, efforts that focused increasingly on educational and vocational pursuits. The possibilities of the community as represented at the conventions were encouraging. For example, the 1848 proceedings reported that "on inquiry, it was found that the Convention was composed of Printers, Carpenters, Blacksmiths, Shoemakers, Engineer, Dentist, Gunsmiths, Editors, Tailors, Merchants, Wheelwrights, Painters, Farmers, Physicians, Plasterers, Masons, Students, Clergymen, Barbers and Hair Dressers, Laborers, Coopers, Livery Stable Keepers, Bath House Keepers, Grocery Keepers" (Bell, *Minutes,* 1848 proceedings 12). This was virtually a portrait in the abstract of the various components needed to create a functioning community, and it served as a reminder to the African American community at large that the means for self-determination were in their hands. But this inquiry was necessitated, in part, by tensions at that and other conventions, as some in the leadership—most visibly, Martin Delany—lamented the condition of servitude that many African Americans accepted as their only means of having a livelihood. Delany's formal statements on this led to considerable and heated debate, and to a rhetorical compromise mediated by Frederick Douglass.[31] By 1853, however, the convention's official statements echoed Delany's *The Condition, Elevation, Emigration, and Destiny of the Colored People of the United States* in emphasizing the underlying concern that "as a whole, we constitute, to a very large extent, a body of consumers and non-producers" (Bell, *Minutes,* 1853 proceedings 22) and that without a mutual dependence of all segments of the U.S. population African Americans would have little chance of emerging from or even changing the terms of their systemic oppression. But conflicting resentments of the appropriation of African Americans into a servile class in the North, of African American acceptance of this condition, and of suggestions that some modes of labor were nobler than others continued to plague the attempts by various conventions to address the need for education and vocational training.

The response to these tensions in 1853 was a vision of the professions as, in effect, the scattered bones of a people that would need to be, as in Winthrop's sermon anticipating the challenges awaiting the Puritans, knit together into a community. Identifying the African American community as "a floating people," unmoored from secure professions and home ownership, the 1853 convention offered a vision of an approach to education calculated to breathe life into the community. "As in the human body," the convention's address advised, "the richness of the digested food goes to make up bone, and muscle, and flesh, and the various tissues and vessels of the system—in like manner schools ought so to be fashioned, as to deposit here and there on the surface of society, artisan and merchant, mechanic and farmer, linguist and mathematician—mental powers in every phase, and practical science in as many as may be" (Bell, *Minutes*, 1853 proceedings 30). But, anticipating the split later encouraged by Booker T. Washington's and W. E. B. Du Bois's differing views, the African American community had allowed itself, according to the address, to be divided between intellect and manual skill: "In the past, the misfortune has been that our knowledge has been much distributed. We have had educated *heads* in one large division among us, and educated *hands* in another"— and, "as a consequence, we have grown up to too large an extent—mere scholars on one side and muscular giants on the other. We would equalize these discrepancies. We would produce a harmonious development of character" (32). The convention itself, drawing male representatives from nearly all walks of life, represented the attempt to bring the communal body and mind together by way of a vision of history and a historical assembly determined to identify an approach to historical understanding most directly applicable to the present situation.

It must be emphasized that the representative figure of the communal body delineated at the conventions was decidedly male and leading a patriarchal home. As Howard Holman Bell has remarked, "The national convention had not dealt more gently with women's rights than had most other reform movements of the era. It is true that women had addressed some conventions, but so had men who were considered to be almost enemies" (*Minutes* iv). The 1848 proceedings include a brief excerpt from a speech by a Mrs. Sanford tracing women's historical degradation from Eve and regeneration through Christ, born of a woman; another speech insists on women's right to "co-operate in making the laws we obey," noting that the demand is intended "not to domineer, to dictate or assume. We ask it, for it is a right granted by a higher disposer of human events than man" (Bell, *Minutes*, 1848 proceedings 11). Following the speech, the proceedings report, the delegates resumed discussion "on the indefinite postponement of the Resolution as to Woman's Right" (11). The resolution, ultimately, "was not indefinitely postponed," and the discussion ended with the passing of the resolution and "with three cheers for woman's rights" (12).

But even by 1864, when women were invited to play a greater role in speeches before the convention, women's voices are largely missing from the record. The proceedings note, for example, that at one point the convention president, Frederick Douglass, "introduced Miss Edmonia Highgate, an accomplished young lady of Syracuse" (Bell, *Minutes*, 1864 proceedings 15). The president had sometime before associated Edmonia Highgate with Anna

Dickinson, a Quaker speaker known for her feminist and antislavery views. Apparently addressing a white audience within and beyond the walls of the convention, the president stated, "You have your Anna Dickinsons; and we have ours. We wish to meet you at every point" (14).[32] Apparently, Highgate was indeed valued more as an exhibit than as a speaker, for all that is recorded of her speech is that "Miss Highgate urged the Convention to trust in God and press on, and not abate one jot or tittle until the glorious day of jubilee shall come" (15). Similarly, at that same convention, accomplished activist, speaker, and poet Frances E. W. Harper is treated only briefly. "Mrs. Frances Ellen Watkins Harper was then introduced," the proceedings report, "and spoke feelingly and eloquently of our hopes and prospects in this country" (25). Beyond these few references, women's presence at the conventions, and in the community, can be observed more by implication than by design—in comments, for example, on the home and on the instruction of children, in mentions of the lack of "ownership" of one's wife under slavery, or in mentions of the violations of wives and daughters under slavery. More direct commentary on women's lives and the broader field of women's labor is generally absent from the convention proceedings, and somewhat awkward when included. The 1853 convention's "Report of the Committee on Manual Labor School," for example, offers detailed recommendations for and commentary on the importance of the trades for men, but it seems at a loss when addressing women's labor. "The Department of Industry for Females," the report notes, "the Committee cannot, in the short time given them, intelligently settle upon, except in outline" (Bell, *Minutes*, 1853 proceedings 32). Such outlines and vague traces are all that one can detect of African American women in the black communal body through these conventions.[33]

The male body and the masculine realms of experience remained the official sites on which the historical structures of African American liberation were built. In 1864, for example, deep in the Civil War, and with stories to tell of the African American heroism on the battlefield, convention representatives in Syracuse could with some justice feel that national history and sacred history were coming together to address the condition of the oppressed. A decade earlier William C. Nell told the story of the refugees at Blount's Fort, the story of bones scattered by the cannons of the government forces, the story all but lost in documents scattered in the national archives. In 1864, African Americans in Syracuse saw a time of increasing if reluctant recognition from Washington, and a time when their actions were at the center of the national story—and the story of the lives lost on the battlefield could be, accordingly, read differently. As Dr. P. B. Randolph, of New York, put it in an address to the 1864 convention, "In the heroism displayed at Millikens Bend, Port Hudson, Fort Wagner, Olustee, in the battles now going on before Richmond, and everywhere where our men have faced the foe, they have covered themselves all over with glory. . . . [T]hey have nobly written with their blood the declaration of their right to have their names recorded on the pages of history among the true patriots of the American Revolution for Liberty" (Bell, *Minutes*, 1864 proceedings 24). From one battle to another, all part of the same unfinished American Revolution, African Americans could by 1864 trace the history of their efforts, and they were understandably optimistic in seeing in this history a story of progress, of a shifting position in the national scene.

Indeed, this apparent progress verified the terms of the story African Americans constructed about themselves at the conventions and elsewhere. The 1848 convention's "Address to the Colored People of the United States" reminded the audience, at the convention and on the page, that "the spirit of the age—the voice of inspiration—the deep longings of the human soul—the conflict of right with wrong—the upward tendency of the oppressed throughout the world, abound with evidence, complete and ample, of the final triumph of right over wrong, of freedom over slavery, and equality over caste." "To doubt this," the address continued, "is to forget the past, and blind our eyes to the present, as well as to deny and oppose the great law of progress, written out by the hand of God on the human soul" (Bell, *Minutes*, 1848 proceedings 17). And in fact a review of the past supported this interpretation of the tendency of the age—for "the last ten years," the address noted, "have witnessed a mighty change in the estimate in which we as a people are regarded, both in this and other lands. England has given liberty to nearly one million, and France has emancipated three hundred thousand of our brethren, and our own country shakes with the agitation of our rights" (17–18). This change in international attitudes and law corresponded with a development in the community itself, for "ten or twelve years ago," the address argued, "an educated colored man was regarded as a curiosity, and the thought of a colored man as an author, editor, lawyer or doctor, had scarce been conceived.—Such, thank Heaven, is no longer the case" (18). This shift was viewed as the product of a general development in human history, a time when "truth and light are dispelling the error and darkness of ages" (18), but it was the result as well of African Americans fulfilling their historical duty in the light of such providential change. "Among the colored people," the address declared, "we can point, with pride and hope, to men of education and refinement, who have become such, despite of the most unfavorable influences; we can point to mechanics, farmers, merchants, teachers, ministers, doctors, lawyers, editors, and authors, against whose progress the concentrated energies of American prejudice have proved quite unavailing" (17). It was important not only that African Americans had succeeded, but also that they had done so in the face of considerable resistance—a resistance that defined the contours of the community at large, identifying its position in sacred history.

This story of progress was, however, hardly a naive tale. Indeed, it was clear that the white national history African Americans had known and struggled against was still the ruling story, and one with significant consequences. In 1864, reviewing both the heroism and the suffering of African Americans on the Civil War battlefields, the convention offered a view of a possible history that emphasized the extent to which white supremacist forces still shaped African American experience. "Had . . . the present Administration," the 1864 address argued,

> at the beginning of the war, boldly planted itself upon the doctrine of human equality as taught in the Declaration of Independence; proclaimed liberty to all the slaves in all the Slave States; armed every colored man, previously a slave or a freeman, who would or could fight under the loyal flag; recognized black men as soldiers of the Republic; avenged the first act of violence upon colored prisoners, in contravention of the laws of war; sided with the radical emancipation party in Maryland and Missouri; stood by its antislavery generals, instead of casting them aside,—history would never have had to record the scandalous platform adopted at Chicago, nor the immeasurable horrors at Fort Pillow. (Bell, *Minutes*, 1864 proceedings 48)

The struggle that African Americans found themselves in during the Civil War was not, they recognized, the same struggle in which white Americans, and their government, were engaged. Continued political oppression and new manifestations of a long history of murderous violations were still the order of the day.

Theirs was not simply a story of progress, then, to be noted and celebrated; rather, the story of oppression, and of the responses to that oppression over the years, was a story to read and interpret. As the 1848 address had it, "It is believed that no other nation on the globe could have made more progress in the midst of such an universal and stringent disparagement. It would humble the proudest, crush the energies of the strongest, and retard the progress of the swiftest. In view of our circumstances, we can, without boasting, thank God, and take courage, having placed ourselves where we may fairly challenge comparison with more highly favored men" (Bell, *Minutes*, 1848 proceedings 17). Challenge it, indeed—for this oppression had been the central event in providential history. In the convention's summary of Dr. Randolph's address in 1864, the sacred and the secular come together, making of the African American application of the Exodus story something more than a hopeful vision. "Dr. Randolph opened," the proceedings relate, "by saying that history constantly repeated itself; that an All-wise Providence dictated the paths which men and nations must pursue; and, whenever they willfully forsook those paths, they were certain to be brought back, sooner or later, by the resistless right hand of the Eternal God. The overruling Father brought out the sons of Abraham from Egyptian bondage three thousand years ago, and to-day he leads us—the negro race—with a strong arm from out of the swamps of slavery" (Bell, *Minutes*, 1864 proceedings 20).

This concrete emancipation is part of a larger story, and one to which the history of oppression and of responses to oppression were of central importance. The Red Sea becomes a sea "of human blood," and the land of "promise and plenty" becomes "the glorious highlands of Justice and Freedom" in a story told to provide a historical text by which the meaning and applicability of the divine text might be read and understood (20–21). It was a text grounded in the African American experience, but applicable to all. God's plans, Randolph advised, "are plain. Let the nations take warning!" The purpose of the oppression suffered by African Americans would become clear as the history of their struggles provided the text by which sacred and secular history might, like the African American communal body envisioned in 1853, be maintained in "a harmonious development of character" (32). "Wagner, Hudson, Petersburg, and all the other battles of this war," Randolph reassured his audience, "have not been fought in vain; for the dead heroes of these and other bloody fields are the seeds of mighty harvests of human goodness and greatness, yet to be reaped by the nations and the world, and by Afric's sable descendants on the soil of this, our native land" (21).

With this understanding of history, African Americans could envision a collective identity that extended beyond the immediate contingencies of their condition, explained the purpose of their oppression, and provided the interpretive framework by which future generations might understand not only what liberty is but also how it must be approached in practice. All of the conventions, ultimately, presented an ideal of community similar to that presented in the 1834 Declaration of Sentiment. "Though the blighting hand of time," that declaration announced, "should sweep us from the stage of action; though other generations should pass away, our principles will live for ever; we will teach our children, and our children's children, to hand them down to unborn generations, and to the latest posterity; not merely for the release of the bondman from his chains, nor for the elevation of the free coloured man to the privileges of citizenship; nor for the restoration of the world from infidelity and superstition; but from the more fatal doctrine of *expediency*, without which the true principles of religion can never be established, liberty never secure, or the sacred rights of man remain invisible" (Bell, *Minutes*, 1834 proceedings 29–30). African American history in this way released itself from the documentation of oppression that made the African American community an object of white sentimental benevolence, charity, or pity, and emerged as a mode of understanding liberty not merely as an isolated ideal or condition but as a practical principle of religious and civil governance.

But the more African Americans could measure their progress, the more it became clear that their history could never emerge from its contingent relation to white history or become part of a common history in which race would play no significant role. African American progress, in short, continued to point to the need for a specifically *African American* history, one that would continue to face the necessity of identifying and confronting the systemic presence of white supremacist ideology. In 1864, in an address as president of the convention, the proceedings note, "Mr. Douglass first answered the question, Why need we meet in a National Convention? He showed its necessity from the state of feeling in the country toward the colored man; to answer the question, as we pass to and from this hall, by the men on the streets of Syracuse, 'Where are the d—d niggers going?'" (Bell, *Minutes*, 1864 proceedings 13). At that same convention, Garnet told a still more graphic story. "Mr. Garnet drew a picture," according to the proceedings, "of the shadows which fell upon New-York city in July, 1863, where demoniac hate culminated in that memorable mob. He told us how one man was hung upon a tree; and that then a demon in human form, taking a sharp knife, cut out pieces of the quivering flesh, and offered it to the greedy, blood-thirsty mob, saying, 'Who wants some nigger meat?' and then the reply, 'I!' 'I!' 'I!' as if they were

scrambling for pieces of gold" (20). Such stories were, of course, not unusual, and they were told as particular examples of a larger historical situation
that defined the contours of the African American political and historical
project. In 1848, discussing the need to establish economic independence in
the African American community, the convention's "Address to the Colored
People of the United States" warned its readers, "Understand this, that independence is an essential condition of respectability. To be dependent, is
to be degraded. Men may indeed pity us, but they cannot respect us" (Bell,
Minutes, 1848 proceedings 19). The convention representatives acknowledged that complete independence "of all men . . . would be absurd and
impossible," but they looked to adjust the contingencies of their situation
and become "equally independent with other members of the community,"
achieving a mutual dependence that would secure the means of black self-
determination (19).

So much of African American history, though, was devoted to establishing
a common citizenship with white Americans that the story of a black nation
within the nation became nearly lost at times in the face of the seductions of
white acceptance. As the United States seemed to approach the union of
sacred and secular history through the Civil War, or earlier as African American educational and material progress in the North became more firmly
established, and as increased white sentiment in favor of African American
progress seemed to indicate a brighter coming day just ahead, African Americans continually rediscovered the ongoing tension in their history—a desire to
be part of the nation and a belief that the white nation had abandoned its
principles and that the black nation was destined to embody those principles.
That tension is visible early on in the formation of the American Moral
Reform Society; it was clear again in 1848 when the convention representatives advised the community to "occupy memberships and stations among
white persons, and in white institutions, just so fast as our rights are secured
to us" (Bell, *Minutes*, 1848 proceedings 19). In the same breath, a moment
earlier, the convention representatives had advised devotion to and "careful
study" of the antislavery movement, arguing, "In the careful study of it, you
will learn your own rights, and comprehend your own responsibilities, and,
scan through the vista of coming time, your high, and God-appointed destiny" (18–19). While theoretically these goals were not mutually exclusive,
this and other conventions, and all of African American history, had made
clear that devotion to black liberation and devotion to white institutions often
made for conflicting alliances.

But the promise of inclusion, and the belief in the power of truth published to the world, left African Americans with a hoped-for understanding capable of overbalancing a manifest system of control. In the 1853 "Address of the Colored National Convention to the People of the United States," the convention representatives held to the belief that the oppression of African Americans was a historical consequence of slavery perpetuated primarily by a lack of information among white Americans. "As a people," the address complained just after quoting Jackson's proclamations, "we feel ourselves to be not only deeply injured, but grossly, misunderstood. Our white fellow-countrymen do not know us. They are strangers to our character, ignorant of our capacity, oblivious of our history and progress, and are misinformed as to the principles and ideas that control and guide us as a people. The great mass of American citizens estimate us as being a characterless and purposeless people and hence we hold up our heads, if at all, against the withering influence of a nation's scorn and contempt" (Bell, *Minutes*, 1853 proceedings 16). The answer to this condition, the convention representatives seemed to hope, would be better information, a more encompassing and more widely published history of African and African American achievements.

Behind that hope lurked an acceptance of the terms of white supremacy that coexisted with the various conventions' considerable commentary on the fundamental error of white racial thought, on the systemic character of oppression, and on the particular destiny of African Americans. This was especially the case as the nation approached and then entered a state of civil war, a time during which Douglass's leadership led the conventions to the uneasy balance of moderate appeals for white benevolence and militant warnings of the consequences if African American rights were not recognized. To be sure, many African Americans believed that this tension was the tension of the age, and that the purpose of black organization was to respond to oppression by working with those who opposed such injustice. The 1853 "Call for a Colored National Convention" emphasized the dual and opposing forces, using them to identify the historical moment to which African American organized efforts should respond.[34] "The Fugitive Slave Act," the call stated,

the most cruel, unconstitutional and scandalous outrage of modern times—the proscriptive legislation of several states with a view to drive our people from their border—the exclusion of our children from schools supported by our money—the prohibition of the exercise of the franchise—the exclusion of colored citizens from the jury box—the social barriers erected against our learning trades—the wily and vigorous efforts of the American Colonization Society to employ the arm of government to expel us from our native land—and withal the propitious awakening to the fact of our condition at home and abroad, which has followed the publication of "Uncle Tom's Cabin"—call trumpet-tongued for our union, co-operation and action in the premises. (Bell, *Minutes*, 1853 proceedings 4)

Behind this list, though, was a more complex cultural moment that made it difficult at times to distinguish allies from enemies and difficult to define the tone and substance of a united black voice. Most of the 1853 "Address of the Colored National Convention to the People of the United States" is in fact addressed specifically to white Americans. The writers try to set the tone for the speech by stating, "We shall affect no especial timidity, nor can we pretend to any great boldness. We know our poverty and weakness, and your wealth and greatness. Yet we will not attempt to repress the spirit of liberty within us, or to conceal, in any wise, our sense of the justice and the dignity of our cause" (8). At times, this address does in fact state boldly the case for African American rights—but it is always a case intended to be received by those who have "wealth and greatness." Frederick Douglass, in a letter to Stowe reprinted in the 1853 proceedings, offers a notable example of this approach. Discussing the inappropriateness of colonization efforts, Douglass tells Stowe that "the black man, (*un*-like the Indian,) loves civilization. He does not make very great progress in civilization himself, but he likes to be in the midst of it, and prefers to share its most galling evils, to encountering barbarism" (36). Arguing for Stowe's support of an industrial college, Douglass makes a point of leaving the details of the plan to Stowe and her white friends, asserting that "it is the peculiarity of your favored race that they can always do what they think necessary to be done" (37).

Douglass's conflicted and difficult attempt to establish and adjust, over the course of time, the terms of his own representative identity was, I am suggesting, projected to the convention movement at large. This is not to say that Douglass was solely responsible for these conflicts; he was, in fact, a representative black male leader, both in his ideals and in his conflicts. As Douglass's sequential autobiographies tell the story of a man increasingly groping for the plot and rhetoric of an appropriate narrative embodiment of a life, and for the appropriate terms of a public identity,[35] so the conventions increasingly indicate underlying narrative tensions in the developing history of African Americans. How can one hope to tell this story? Indeed, what is the story that calls for narration? These are the questions that seemed to press with increasing urgency on the authors of the addresses and resolutions of the conventions.

At times, the hope that the brighter day was finally coming, and the cautious appeal for white acceptance and recognition, could even undermine the integrity of black achievement and threaten to silence the voice of African American history. The 1864 "Address of the Colored National Convention to the People of the United States"—again, as in 1853, addressed specifically to a white audience—seems to erase the work of the conventions, the orations, the publications, the petitions, and the acts of physical resistance that have come before. "Considering the number and the generous character of the wrongs and disabilities endured by our race in this country," the address states, "you will bear witness that we have borne with patience our lot, and have seldom troubled the national ear with the burden of complaint. It is true that individuals among us have constantly testified their abhorrence of this injustice; but as a people, we have seldom uttered, as we do this day, our protest and remonstrance against the manifold and needless injustice with which we are upon all sides afflicted" (Bell, *Minutes*, 1864 proceedings 46). And as the address continues, one wonders what became of the ideal of self-determination, for African American rights seemed to be placed entirely in white hands. "We have suffered in silence," the address states,

> trusting that, though long delayed, and perhaps through terrible commotions, the hour would come when justice, honor, and magnanimity would assert their power over the mind and heart of the American people, and restore us to the full exercise and enjoyment of the rights inseparable from human nature. Never having despaired of this consummation so devoutly wished, even in the darkest hours of our history, we are farther than ever from despairing now. Nowhere in the annals of mankind is there recorded an instance of an oppressed people rising more rapidly than ourselves in the favorable estimation of their oppressors. The change is great, and increasing, and is viewed with astonishment and dread by all those who had hoped to stand forever with their heels upon our necks. (46)

To be sure, the conventions never lost sight of the most forceful racists that they were up against; but always, and increasingly over time, they found themselves caught in the complex contingencies of their position—working to define white antislavery benevolence in opposition to proslavery sentiment, and working to define African American identity both with and against the official story of white national character and principles. The 1864 convention produced a "Declaration of Wrongs and Rights," and this effort to locate the united black effort in a history largely determined by a white supremacist culture seemed almost to lead to a silencing of the efforts of the past—in many ways a silencing, indeed, of African American history—for an anticipated future that those at the convention recognized as a delicate opportunity at best.

Clearly working from a belief that the Civil War marked the intersection of sacred and secular history, African Americans knew that they had cause to worry that white Americans facing this crossroads in their history would choose the wrong path. The desire to shape African American history to the concerns at the present involved a recognition that a white unity would still undermine all hope of the integration of the African American story into the pages of white national history. Accordingly, the 1864 convention drew from history in an attempt to define the moment so as to provide white Americans with a clear sense of the choices they faced—and of the consequences of their choices. At the end of the 1864 address, following a long historical argument designed to establish African American claims to citizenship and the recognition of their rights as citizens, the convention representatives turned again to the contingencies of group identity—working to establish an alliance with white northerners in opposition to those with whom they were engaged in civil war. "This kind of government," the address asserted, "must have its foundation in the affections of the people: otherwise the people will hinder, circumvent, and destroy it" (60). With this view of the foundation of representative government, and with an eye on the consequences of war, the address presents a vision of the future as a continuation of the Civil War in other forms. "Now, whoever lives to see this rebellion suppressed at the South," the address states, "as we believe we all shall, will also see the South characterized by a sullen hatred towards the National Government. It will be transmitted from father to son, and will be held by them as 'as sacred animosity.' The treason, mowed down by the armies of Grant and Sherman, will be followed by a strong undergrowth of treason which will go far to disturb the peaceful operation of the hated Government" (61). The convention's representatives here present the African American community as the allies of the national government, allies who will be important to the nation in the future. But they recognize as well—indeed, it is the reason that this argument would need to be presented at all—that white northerners and white southerners could unite, in spite of this inevitable "undergrowth of treason," to the exclusion (or perhaps *by way of* a common exclusion) of African American rights. Accordingly, they warn, "We are among you, and must remain among you; and it is for you to say, whether our presence shall conduce to the general peace and welfare of the country, or be a constant cause of discussion and irritation,—troubles in the State, troubles in the Church, troubles everywhere" (62).

In short, the African American historical work at the conventions led, in the end, to an attempt to read the Civil War and to shape the historical moment. That these assembled historians were prophetic in their reading is a revealing commentary on the enormousness of the task they faced, and on a white national narrative that promoted—indeed, required—historical and moral illiteracy. The great task was to promote the historical and moral literacy of both black and white audiences and readers, to draw these communities into a vision of history that could enable them to locate themselves in the present, identify their relation to sacred order, and then to act accordingly. In the assemblies of history that gave voice to the developing African American oratorical tradition, and in the histories of those assemblies presented in the proceedings of the conventions, African Americans worked to identify history as a complex of relations rather than simply as a series of events. History thus understood called for a reinterpretation or reorientation of the complex of relations that defined U.S. ideological practice, a reorientation from which historical events large and small could be understood.

This task of reorientation was largely the point behind the ongoing drive to establish and maintain an African American press—newspapers and magazines that would view the world's events, past and present, from the perspective afforded by the historical position of the African American community. As Robert S. Levine has argued in his valuable study of the role of David Walker in facilitating the rise of the black press, "Black activists regarded print, rather than oratory, as promising to link together the disparate and scattered black communities of the early republic" ("Circulating" 18). Through the press, African Americans could promote the ongoing circulation of information, particularly the publication and republication of important historical events, necessary for shaping the public dialogue and the common discourse essential to the formation of community. Through the black press, in short, oratory found its voice, history its occasion, and a scattered people their institutional centers. Any understanding of the antebellum African American historical consciousness, accordingly, must attend to the multiform narrative possibilities of the African American periodical press.

chapter five

Our Warfare Lies in the Field of Thought
The African American Press and the Work of History

n his preface to his 1891 publication *The Afro-American Press, and Its Editors*, I. Garland Penn notes that "the object in putting forth this feeble effort is not for the praise of men or for the reaping of money, but to promote the future welfare of Afro-American journalism by telling to its constituents the story of its heroic labors in their behalf" (14). Hardly a feeble effort, Penn's book is a comprehensive and detailed history of the African American press, a work that has served as a foundation for many later studies. Penn's mention of black journalism's "constituents" underscores his sense of the importance of a specifically African American press, one engaged in a battle that requires "heroic labors" on behalf of an imagined community of African American readers. Penn was writing, in fact, to address a long-standing problem that plagued the African American press: the lack of support by its constituency. "I believe," Penn continues, "that the greatest reason why our papers are not better supported is because the Afro-Americans do not sufficiently comprehend the responsibilities and magnitude of the work" (14). The work that Penn tried to record, support, and promote in *The Afro-American Press* is the subject of this chapter, and the magnitude of that work is the reason why it is important to consider what might be called periodical history as the primary vehicle of African American historical theory and practice before the Civil War.[1]

It is not at all unusual, of course, to think of newspapers as histories always in progress, and this was particularly true for newspapers devoted to the ongoing struggle against slavery. In part, this was the case because the press allowed active involvement in the events of the day in the service of a historical vision that looked necessarily to the future. Certainly, that sort of historical vision was the impetus for one of the earliest of the important antislavery newspapers, Benjamin Lundy's *Genius of Universal Emancipation*. In his opening editorial in 1821, Lundy asserted, "That the abomination of abominations, the system of slavery, *must* be abolished, is as clear as the shining of the sun at noonday; the very nature of our government forbids its continuance, and the voice of the ETERNAL has decreed its annihilation." Both promoting and recording that annihilation was the work of the newspaper, recording the seemingly scattered details that could only gradually come together into a coherent narrative—a union, in effect, of human and divine authorship. Noting the full range of concerns and information to which the paper would be devoted, Lundy stated his intentions that "this work shall be a true record of passing events, of the various transactions relative to the enslavement of the Africans; and he hopes it may eventually prove a faithful history of their final emancipation" (Riley 79–80). To read the paper faithfully, one might say, would be to read the unfolding narrative of faith. But the periodical press was important to this narrative also in that it provided a forum for a peaceful negotiation of the inevitable. This case was stated plainly, for example, in a prospectus for a "quarterly anti-slavery magazine" that appeared in the *Colored American* in 1838: "The pen or the sword must soon decide whether or not slavery is to remain one of the elements of our republic. But all those who prefer the mode of argument to that of brute force, it cannot but be deemed important that there should be a periodical in which all questions pertaining to slavery may be settled in the light of thorough investigation" (February 10, 1838).

But while the format and regularity of newspapers and magazines emphasized the daily vigilance and activism required for eventual emancipation, a specifically African American press was essential to the developing African American historiographical tradition. In the pages of African American newspapers and magazines, readers would encounter the subjects and themes (and often the rhetoric) that constitute the conventional narratives and tropes of African American historical self-definition. These periodicals included articles on the history of slavery, the American Revolution, the War of 1812, the Haitian Revolution, and African and European civilization; they ran articles on famous cases of rebellion and rescue, including pieces on Denmark Vesey, Nat Turner, Madison Washington, and John Brown, in addition to prominent rescue efforts like the Oberlin-Wellington rescue; they published biographical sketches that spoke of black achievement from Phillis Wheatley to Richard Allen to Toussaint L'Ouverture; and they included samplings of the records and addresses of organized resistance and communal struggle, from antislavery meetings to local and national black conventions. The history presented in the periodical press was one that included and connected the grand and the small, matters international and local, collective and personal. In other words, the various attempts to establish newspapers and magazines edited by African Americans and directed toward an African American community, only some of which lasted more than a year or two, were essential to the effort to establish a community defined by something other than anti-slavery concerns.[2]

In presenting the periodical press as a form of historical writing, however, I do not mean simply that it is a source of historical information or a locale for a sampling of the rhetoric of history that should ultimately be contained in a historical monograph. Rather, I mean to suggest that the periodical press was uniquely suited to the task of telling the story of African American history—because the story it could tell would be marked by narrative disruption and because, in telling the story, the press could only be multivocal and multi-perspectival. Consider, for example, Carla L. Peterson's study of the racial politics of periodical publication during Reconstruction, in which she examines the many ways in which periodicals shaped the publication, reception, and interpretation of African American writing. Focusing on Frances E. W. Harper's serial publication of her fiction in the pages of the *Christian Recorder*, Peterson applies the work of other scholars of serial fiction to the racial politics encountered by African American writers and readers, and notes importantly that

Nineteenth-century serial composition actively affected both writers and readers. Authors were often influenced by ongoing events, leading them to reshape their narratives and incorporate recent factual occurrences into their fiction. In turn, serial publication encouraged reader participation. This readership was undoubtedly more extensive than that of printed volumes, since newspapers were cheaper and available to

a wider audience. Additionally, . . . newspapers could be passed from
neighbor to neighbor for perusal or even read aloud in groups. As they
read "in parts," readers had time to reread the story at their leisure, to interpret and reinterpret it; installment endings left them thinking as they
waited for the next issue. Furthermore, readers never read the serial fiction in isolation from other "texts"—items in the same newspaper issue,
other novels, or even the readers' own lives and the world they lived in—
but in close conjunction with them. Such an interplay meant that
readers often immediately brought extraneous material to their reading
of serial fiction, or conversely took the fiction into their own lives; at the
extreme, fact and fiction merged in their imaginations. (310–11)

Peterson's point concerns not merely the collective cultural experience of
anticipation and shared excitement that had dominated popular culture at
least since the days of Dickens and *Uncle Tom's Cabin,* for in noting the
interplay of shared and overlapping narratives—among readers and between
texts and the readers' own lives and worlds—Peterson underscores the importance of what and whom we bring to the task of reading. She underscores as
well the fragmented narratives that are simply the result of our reading practices, for we take a story a little at a time, mixing it with other pleasures and
duties, and talking about it with other readers before finishing it on our own.[3]
    I present Peterson's overview of the dynamics of serial publication to sug-
gest the ways in which the periodical press was uniquely suited for what I
have termed liberation historiography—a mode of historical writing that takes
as one of its interpretive sources the condition of the community for which it
is writing, the condition that, indeed, identifies the proper scene of historical
study. It is through the periodical press that the broad outlines and conventional tropes of African American history could connect to the dynamic and
multiple needs (material, cognitive, and theoretical) of the African American
community. The newspaper or magazine itself represented an African American framework, a forum that could allow writers to speak directly to an
African American audience rather than reaching them through the filter of a
white editor. The periodical press provided a forum in which writers and
editors could present the needs and contingencies of African American life
holistically, and not simply as something to be placed under the heading of a
separate racial or antislavery concern.[4] As Todd Vogel has written, the newspaper served "as a stage, where free blacks acted out their views about citizenship and race" (38). Through the periodical press, African American history

became neither a single narrative nor a body of information but a dynamic and communal process that gathered and arranged information to meet the shifting contingencies of African American life, and a form of representation that both told the story and emphasized, through narrative disjuncture and juxtaposition (as articles were placed next to each other, read both separately and together), the extent to which the story remained untold and untellable.

"The Principle of Combination": Periodical History

Throughout the black national conventions, a constant concern was the influence of the press in promoting and maintaining the system of white supremacy by controlling images of African American character and negotiating the cultural politics associated with the system of slavery. The 1843 "Report of Committee upon the Press" is representative in its summary of the influence of the white press. "Your committee entertain the common views entertained of the power and influence of the press," the report noted,

> for good or for evil; they believe that much of the existing good, as well as of the evil in the world, owes itself to the press as an instrumentality, and that most of the peculiar evils to which we of this country are subjected, if not brought into existence, are now sustained by the power and influence of the press; that slaveholding, in this country, finds now, as it ever has found, support and a grand means of defense, in the influence of the newspaper press; that that peculiar and unhallowed sensibility, so prevalent in this country, called prejudice against color, has become wider spread, and firmer fixed, by the views and sentiments which sustain it, having been taken up and palmed off upon the reading public by the press. (Bell, *Minutes*, 1843 proceedings 27)

Simply to report on national or regional politics was to present a social realm in which African Americans were marginalized, rendered invisible, brought to visibility as a problem to be solved, or otherwise degraded. At a time when blackface minstrelsy was the most popular form of entertainment, and (later) when Uncle Tom shows aided in the transformation of Stowe's *Uncle Tom's Cabin* into a warehouse of commercial images of African American identity and experience, the white press brought race into its pages for entertainment, for the purposes of political or ethical self-positioning, and as a commercial necessity.[5]

While the racial presence was sometimes subtle in the white press (the usual assumption of whiteness as the nonracial norm), more often it was direct and even blatant. Readers of the *Democratic Review* could encounter articles that provided models of reflection on and rhetorical engagement in racial concerns—for example, "Do the Various Races of Man Constitute a Single Species?"—that effectively sectioned race off from the mainstream of concerns. A decade later, readers of *Putnam's Monthly* encountered such articles as "Uncle Tomitudes," "Negro Minstrelsy—Ancient and Modern," and "About Niggers." Some publications were more forceful still in their portrayal of African Americans as a separate concern and an inferior race. The *Southern Literary Journal, and Monthly Magazine*, for example, had the following to say under the heading "Natural History of the Negro Race": "It is very questionable whether the abolitionists [sic] in their efforts for the emancipation of the Negro race, are not attempting a thing, physically and morally impossible—if by emancipation be meant, enabling them to be re-publicans. . . . Of this republican liberty in government we believe the black race absolutely incapable" (qtd. in Riley 229n). *DeBow's Review*, one of the most prominent and influential southern periodicals, at first avoided politics but increasingly became one of the primary mouthpieces of proslavery views. Indeed, as Sam G. Riley has noted, "*DeBow's Review* contains probably the most extensive single treatment of this issue to appear in any magazine of the nineteenth century, and DeBow himself became one of the South's most influential exponents of the slavery system" (Riley 47). By contrast, one African American newspaper was launched precisely because of the handling of race concerns in a white publication, the New York *Sun*. As Roland E. Wolseley has noted (drawing from the work of I. Garland Penn), the *Sun* had published in 1846 "editorials proposing the curbing of Negro suffrage in that state." When Willis A. Hodges, an African American, wrote a reply, he found he could get his reply published "only when he agreed to pay fifteen dollars and run it as an advertisement," and, "at that, its sentiments were modified." "Hodges was told by a staff member," Wolseley relates, "when he protested the changes in his reply, that 'the *Sun* shines for all white men, and not for colored men'" (30).

Hodges was told that if he wanted to represent the views of African Americans, he would need to start his own paper—and the representatives at the various national conventions agreed. As the 1843 "Report of Committee upon the Press" argued, "If one class of the people ought to have a press absolutely under their control, it is that class who are the prescribed, and whose rights are cloven down" (Bell, *Minutes*, 1843 proceedings 28). The advantages of establishing an identifiably African American newspaper were many, the report argued, including the ability to establish a community in the way that we have come to associate with Benedict Anderson's views on the role of the press in creating the imagined nation. As the 1843 report argued, an African American press "will . . . have a tendency to unite us in a stronger bond, by teaching us that our cause and our interests are one and common, and that what is for the interest of the one, or a point gained in our common cause in one section of the country, is for the interest of all, or a point gained by all. Besides, being the organ of the whole, it would necessarily chronicle the public measures of the whole, and thus become a medium to enable us to learn about, as well as from each other" (28). In short, an African American press might well be vital in the formation of an African American community—providing a record of the experiences that joined people who might not recognize their common bond, and a forum through which individuals separated geographically, economically, politically, and socially could discover their common cause.

While the conventions debated the practicability of a single, national press for African Americans, the belief in the importance of periodical publications controlled by and directed to African Americans was emphasized again and again.[6] Some sense of the power associated with the press is revealed in the 1847 debates on establishing a national press in which Garnet is reported to have expressed his belief "that the most successful means which can be used for the overthrow of Slavery and Caste in this country, would be found in an able and well-conducted Press, solely under control of the people of color" (Bell, *Minutes*, 1847 proceedings 6). Garnet quoted the lines from Byron's *Childe Harold's Pilgrimage* that were invoked regularly in African American orations and publications (and that Martin R. Delany used on the masthead for his paper the *Mystery*): "Hereditary bondman, know ye not, / Who would be free, themselves must strike the blow?" And, with Byron's brave words behind him, Garnet presses forth in battle, arguing that "the establishment of a National Printing Press would send terror into the ranks of our enemies, and encourage all our friends, whose friendship is greater than their selfishness" (6). Many at the convention agreed. The 1847 "Report of the Committee on a National Press" put forth the position that "we struggle against opinions. Our warfare lies in the field of thought. Glorious struggle! God-like warfare! In training our soldiers for the field, in marshaling our hosts for the fight, in leading the onset, and through the conflict, we need a Printing Press, because a printing press is the vehicle of thought—is a ruler of opinions" (18). The 1848 "Address to the Colored People of the United States" asserted more simply, in commenting on the press, that "it is easy to see that the means which have been used to destroy us, must be used to save us" (Bell, *Minutes*, 1848 proceedings 20). In other words, African American newspapers and magazines were important in the related goals of resisting political oppression, responding to racist representations, and working toward the definition and "uplift" of a community always only tenuously aware of itself as such beyond the common condition imposed by racism, exclusion from citizenship, and the existence and effects of the system of slavery.

There was reason to believe in the power of an African American press, if only because antislavery newspapers inspired such heated response from a public opposed to abolitionist agitation. White antislavery editors, for example, had famously suffered the wrath of the public. William Lloyd Garrison was threatened and paraded in public humiliation by a white mob (including "gentlemen of property and standing") in 1835; another white mob, in 1837, murdered the white abolitionist Elijah Lovejoy in Alton, Illinois, and dragged his printing press into the river. This was evidence of the power of the press in a double sense, for not only were these attempts to silence the antislavery press but they were also viewed as effects of the power of a racist and pro-slavery press. The *Colored American*, for example, reacted strongly to the murder of Lovejoy in an article presented under the dramatic headline "An American Citizen Murdered!! The Press Destroyed!!! The Spirit of Slavery Triumphant!!!" Implicitly connecting this event to Garrison's earlier ordeal, the article asked, "Who are guilty in this matter? Is it the poor ignorant, sunken and abandoned wretches who consummate the work planned out by 'gentlemen of property and standing?' " The people, the article continued, "know not what they do. But the Press, which from the commencement of the Anti-Slavery controversy, has kept alive by base misrepresentation, the worst passions of the human heart, and pointed at abolitionists as fit subjects for the assassin's dagger—the press—Political and Religious, by baptising itself in all manner of abominations, in order to oppose the progress of pure principles, is guilty of this crime" ("An American Citizen Murdered"). Such power must be resisted, of course, and the *Colored American*, like other antislavery publications, regularly reprinted and commented on articles originally published in other papers, noting their misrepresentations and biases.

The evidence of the antislavery press's influence, of course, was positive as well. As Carl Senna has noted, the first African American newspaper, *Free-*

dom's Journal, like David Walker's *Appeal* a short time later, "was considered subversive literature in the South," where "blacks were punished severely for possessing copies." Senna points out that, even so, "the paper's influence reached far beyond its small number of readers." When on July 4, 1827, the New York legislature emancipated slaves in that state, *Freedom's Journal* "on that day . . . received a number of testimonials and toasts to the paper's role in persuading the legislature to free New York's slaves. At one public dinner in Fredericksburg, Virginia, free blacks declared in a toast to *Freedom's Journal* that Virginia, and her sister slave states, ought to show to the people of colour on the 4th of July 1827, that they have approved of the example set them by the legislature of New York" (18–19). Some years later, David Ruggles, the publisher and editor of the *Mirror of Liberty*, announced that the paper "is a free and independent journal—its editor is an unmuzzled man, who goes for freedom of speech and the liberty of the press." As the *Mirror* struggled for survival, "blacks organized public meetings in New York, Hartford, New Bedford, and Boston to raise subscriptions and donations for the *Mirror*" (Senna 27–28). Establishing itself as a clear threat to proslavery forces, and supported philosophically and, to a limited extent, financially by the African American community, the antislavery press was a forceful argument for the importance and effectiveness of an African American press.

This is not to say, however, that the African American press received unqualified support from white allies. To be sure, most of the early African American newspapers and magazines relied heavily on white support and featured writing by whites. The *Ram's Horn* was established by a partnership between Hodges and Thomas Van Rensselaer, a white man. Douglass started the *North Star* and subsequent publications with the help of white European and American supporters, whom he depended on heavily through the years. And whites were as significant a presence on the page as they were behind the scenes. In the *Mirror of Liberty*, Senna notes, "white writers greatly outrepresented black writers" (28). *Frederick Douglass' Monthly*, designed for European circulation, similarly "carried the writings of white abolitionists such as Gerrit Smith, Lewis Tappan, Wendell Phillips, and Charles Sumner" more frequently than it presented writings by black authors, and included as a regular feature a series of "Letters from the Old World," sent from England by Mrs. Julia Griffith Crofts (Bullock 54).[7] But Douglass also encountered significant resistance from the Garrisonians when he formed the *North Star*, who viewed his decision to run his own paper as a betrayal of the Garrisonian cause and its organ, the *Liberator*.[8]

African American newspapers and magazines, then, existed in a necessary but sometimes uneasy alliance with white supporters, and African Americans themselves were sometimes torn by the argument that a specifically African American press would only weaken the alliance necessary to work against the force of the mainstream press. Still, the importance of a specifically African American paper in defining the issues so as to promote the full range of African American rights was regularly reaffirmed—and was emphasized during the Civil War when the 1864 convention found reason to complain about those publications most closely associated with the African American cause. "The weakness of our friends," said the "Address of the Colored National Convention to the People of the United States," "is strength to our foes. When the 'Anti-Slavery Standard' representing the American Anti-Slavery Society, denies that society asks for the enfranchisement of colored men, and the 'Liberator' apologizes for excluding the colored men of Louisiana from the ballot-box, they injure us more vitally than all the ribald jests of the whole proslavery system" (Bell, *Minutes*, 1864 proceedings 48). The collective voice of the African American community was not and could not be, it was clear, fully represented in the pages of publications edited by whites. An article in the *Colored American* stated the case strongly in an appeal to its readers for financial support in 1838: "As to the necessity and importance of our paper;—This point hardly needs an argument. *We* have a place and a part to act in the great contest now waging between liberty and slavery—the powers of light and the powers of darkness. The interests of *three hundred thousand colored freemen*, for themselves, and as the true representatives of the enslaved, not only require, but equal justice to friends and enemies, demands that *we should give our testimony*; and pour our entreaties and rebukes in the ears of this guilty nation" (June 9, 1838).[9] This article was one of many that appeared regularly in appeals for support of the African American press.

As the *Colored American*'s formulation of its journalistic mission and the black community's moral responsibility suggests, African American editors and readers could work through the press to assume authority over white history and over white representations of black history. Steven Mailloux has noted that "an act of reading is precisely the historical intersection of the different cultural rhetorics for reading . . . texts within the social practices of particular historical communities" (3). Far more aware than most of "the social practices of particular historical communities"—and of the associated "cultural rhetorics for reading"—African American editors and writers approached this "historical intersection" with considerable self-consciousness.

Indeed, the periodical press brought those social practices to the forefront of the act of reading, and in that way to the act of understanding history.

The most obvious example of this recontextualization of reading practices was in the common antislavery practice of reprinting information published for the policing and maintenance of the system of slavery—laws, notices about runaway slaves, and the like. This practice was a regular feature of all antislavery publications, and was central to the method of one of the most important and influential of publications by a white abolitionist, Theodore Weld's *American Slavery as It Is*, which presented an antislavery argument based almost entirely on the testimony of the slaveholders.[10] In his introduction to that work, for example, Weld notes the disagreements over the evidence for moral arguments either for or against slavery. "Slaveholders and their apologists," he notes, "are volunteer witnesses in their own cause, and are flooding the world with testimony that their slaves are kindly treated; that they are fed, well clothed, well housed, well lodged, moderately worked, and bountifully provided with all things needful for their comfort" (9). Continuing his legal analogy, Weld promises to present "a multitude of impartial witnesses" for the prosecution, "and then to put slaveholders themselves through a course of cross-questioning which shall draw their condemnation out of their own mouths" (9). Southern testimony was used also to support the antislavery cause more directly, as in the reprinting of an 1828 "Address of the Virginia Convention for the abolition of slavery, to the people of Virginia" in the May 27, 1837, issue of the *Colored American*, a report that, as Henry C. Wright noted to readers of the *Colored American*, "points out the evils of slavery and the remedy." "When slave-holders speak out their unbiased feelings," Wright observes in his prefatory comments, "they generally utter abolition sentiments" ("Important Testimony"). This strategy, the reframing of southern publications, was central to the antislavery press, which regularly reprinted articles from southern papers as well as snippets from the publications of slaveholders, from Thomas Jefferson to lesser-known writers.

Placing this information in a publication edited by African Americans took this rhetorical appropriation to another level still by reframing the systemic mechanisms central to the workings of a white supremacist culture. This practice could be used to reinforce the regional and national distinctions by which the antislavery movement attempted to shape white northern sentiment in the United States and antislavery sentiment in Great Britain. *Douglass' Monthly*, for example, included as a regular feature a column titled "Southern Gems," which "reprinted the announcements of Negroes for sale and rewards for runaway slaves that had appeared in proslavery publications" (Bullock 54). But this practice could be used, further, to emphasize that the system of slavery was a national system, and in this way to challenge the unspoken contingencies of white identity. As Bullock reports, for example, David Ruggles "promised to publish in one issue" of the *Mirror of Liberty* "a slaveholder's directory, 'furnishing the names and residences of all members of the bar, police officers, city marshals, constables, and other persons who lend themselves in the nefarious business of kidnapping; and the names of slaveholders residing in [New York] and in Brooklyn'" (32). Through the periodical press, history could truly become a mirror revealing the features of white national character.

Through the use of that mirror, the African American periodical press could eavesdrop on the presentation of history in white publications and, in that way, follow not only the construction of white national history but also the cracks in the foundation of that developing structure. The *Colored American*, for example, published a series of articles on Tocqueville's *Democracy in America*, collectively "A Review of Those Sections of Chap. XVII Which Relate to the Colored People in the United States," challenging Tocqueville's research and assumptions, and complaining in the third installment, "M. De Tocqueville scarcely admits us to belong to the common family of mankind, calls our physiognomy 'hideous,' &c., &c." ("De Tocqueville's Democracy"). At times, this eavesdropping could be used to suggest the power of the medium in which readers were participating by noting reactions to the African American press or other African American–organized endeavors. The October 26, 1827, issue of *Freedom's Journal*, for example, prints a notice that "the Rev. Dr. Miller of New Jersey, has pronounced, from the pulpit[,] a sentence of eternal condemnation, against the 'Freedom's Journal,' a paper printed in New York, because it exercises the liberty of free speech in favour of the abolition of slavery." The papers sometimes found it necessary to respond to friendly fire as well. In 1837, for example, an editorial in the *Colored American* responded to criticism of the paper and its editor published in William Lloyd Garrison's the *Liberator*, stating strongly that "if the patronage of our brethren of Boston, depends upon our giving circulation to all the injudicious outbreakings of their zeal in our little Journal, we say let their monies perish, ere they come into our coffers, and let our PAPER PERISH too, rather than be sustained at such sacrifices." The editorial concludes by noting that "the trite saying, 'save me from my friends' is as applicable to the present, as to any other period of the world's history" ("Keep Cool, Brethren").[11] Responding to attacks within and without the antislavery community, the African American press recorded the ideological tensions that defined racial politics in the antebellum period—part of the construction of race that went beyond simple racial binaries and simple differentiations of color or of condition.[12]

To take a positive example of this historical eavesdropping, consider an article in the July 13, 1827, issue of *Freedom's Journal* titled "European Colonies in America"—an article that is wholly an excerpt, readers are told, "from an interesting work, entitled 'America, or a General Survey,' &c. &c. By a citizen of the United States." The writer of this historical work considers, in this excerpt, the recent history of Haiti, which then leads him to reflections "in regard to the capacity of the black race." "It would be difficult indeed," the author notes, "to assign any sufficient ground for the supposition of an essential inferiority in this branch of the human family, or in fact of any real inequality among the varieties of the species indicated by their differences of colour, form, or physical structure. If (which may well be doubted) such a prejudice has ever prevailed among enlightened men, it is probably rare at present, and may be expected to become continually more and more so" ("European Colonies in America"). This view, of course, might come as a surprise to many African American readers; but more important are the writer's reflections on "the course of history," by which "each great division of the species has had in its turn the advantage in civilization," has enjoyed a period of considering themselves a favored people, but has passed on, in time, "the sceptre of civilization" into the hands "of some other, before inferior, which claims in its turn, for a while, a similar distinction." The author then explores the, to him, considerable evidence that "the blacks, (whether of African or Asiatic origin) have not only a fair right to be considered as naturally equal to men of any other colour, but are even not without some plausible pretensions to a claim of superiority." The author follows this with a brief overview of the history of Africa, leading to the conclusion that "this race, from the period immediately following the deluge down to the conquest of Assyria and Egypt by the Persians, and the fall of Carthage, enjoyed a decided preponderance throughout the whole ancient western world." While this view of history is important in and of itself, the reprinting of this excerpt adds to historical understanding an implicit argument about the construction and uses of history. The editors of *Freedom's Journal*, that is, apply to the challenge of historical representation the method that Weld and others would later apply to the antislavery movement; they present a history drawn from the testimony of white historians who present the African American historical argument. History in these pages becomes, then, not only a reading of the past but also a reading of the story of the past under construction in the present. It is the construction of history that is central to any understanding of the African American condition under the white supremacist regime, and the periodical press was uniquely suited to represent not only a story about the past but also the dynamics of the construction of the past designed to serve the present.

The immediacy of the periodical press also emphasized that this was a story with a point, that it was to stand side by side with other articles on African American and international life, and that it was applicable to the immediate needs of the community. Again, this was a point only emphasized by the recontextualization of articles from other presses geared toward a white audience. An article from the *Christian Spectator* and reprinted in the *Freedom's Journal* of April 20, 1827, for example, looked back to Jefferson's views on slavery to reflect on the present state of the nation. "It will not do to trust this business to the generosity, or the justice, or the love of liberty, of the slave holders," the writer argued, for "the experiment has been fully tried, and has totally failed" ("People of Colour"). The article quotes from Jefferson's correspondence, noting his view that the revolutionary generation was too deeply involved in the experience of holding slaves to see the problem clearly, and noting also Jefferson's frustrated hopes that rising generations, influenced by the ideal of liberty, would view things differently. Calling Jefferson to task for his own failure to "set himself in earnest" about "the work of emancipation," the author concludes that "the determination to maintain slavery at all hazards, has become exasperated to a sort of desperation, like that of the Holy Alliance in favor of despotism. The enthusiasm of liberty has given place to the enthusiasm of slavery" ("People of Colour"). The author then looks to "the history of Grecian, Roman, British, or even American liberty" to note that "there is not, that I know, a single example of power given up, without constraint. From the days of King John, it has always been abridged by compulsion, and not otherwise." The author then turns to the systemic control of the "lower classes" by the "monarchs of continental Europe" working to guard against the possibility that those classes will "become too sensible of their own power"; "find out the efficacy of the principle of combination, as a political engine"; or "find out their rights and their wrongs, and dare to assert the privilege of rational beings, to think and act for themselves." "The same principle of love of power," the writer asserts, "must be called in to account for conduct among ourselves so strikingly similar" ("People of Colour"). In effect, then, *Freedom's Journal*, in reprinting this piece, anticipates David Walker's warning a few years later, in his commentary on Jefferson's *Notes on the State of Virginia*, that his readers should "try to find out the meaning of this verse—its widest sense and all its bearings," advising them, "whether you do or not, remember the whites do" (*Appeal* 27).

This sort of reading was emphasized, as Peterson and others have noted of later writings, by the publication of serial pieces—for example, on the history of slavery[13]—by which readers became involved in an extended and dynamic process of reading, each new installment presented in the different context provided by that issue's contents. Often, the context was rather direct and telling. The October 2, 1851, issue of *Frederick Douglass' Paper*, for example, included a consideration of "Slavery in 1776" along with a report on the "Free Soil Convention at Cleveland" and the National Convention of the Liberty Party ("Reported"). The *Colored American* published in several installments James McCune Smith's "Lecture on the Haytien Revolutions" in the fall of 1841, thus blending this meditation on the Haitian revolutions with regular reports on daily events, progress reports, and political campaigns of the African American and antislavery communities. Shortly after its formation, the *Colored American* published an article titled "Prejudice against Color in the Light of History," reviewing the evidence of Egyptian and Ethiopian achievement to respond to charges that "the negro . . . is of a degraded race." "All at once," the article notes, "within two or three hundred years, since the enslavement of the African race on the American islands and continent, the wonderful discovery is made, and a discovery, too, confined wholly to countries where the negro has been enslaved—the discovery is made that the Ethiopians, (the tutors of the whole civilized world) are become an inferior race?" ("Prejudice against Color"). Much of the *Colored American* was devoted to supporting, amplifying, and passing on this sense of astonishment by placing the evidence of history against the attitudes and arguments of the present. Indeed, the *Colored American* would later take the Reverend J. W. C. Pennington to task for not similarly contextualizing current concerns historically in his *Text Book*, complaining in its review that "the historical part of the work, giving the origin of the colored people, is most conclusive. And we think, had the author have extended this part of the work more, even had he been forced to have compressed that part on prejudice, &c., it would have materially increased the interest of the book; the historical part being but little understood, while all are more or less familiar with the nature and character of prejudice" ("A Text Book," February 27, 1841). The *Colored*

American, like all African American newspapers and magazines of this time, believed that to report on the present required extensive commentary on the past, and the historical mission of this and other publications was always prominently announced and vigorously argued.

Ultimately, then, the point of the readings of history presented in the periodicals had to do with the reading of history necessary to understand the various forces that combined to determine African American experience and collective identity; and that developing community, involved in this act of discovery and self-definition, was presented also with a collective moral responsibility to respond to those shaping forces. This point—later so forcefully presented by David Walker and by Henry Highland Garnet in their admonishments to the African American free and enslaved communities concerning their moral duty to resist slavery—is presented in numerous ways in the periodical press. It is a point, indeed, only emphasized when it comes from the pen of a white writer. For example, another article reprinted in *Freedom's Journal,* this one from Benjamin Lundy's *Genius of Universal Emancipation,* took the point about the power of the "lower classes" still further. "Who," the writer asks, "were the Generals that commanded the armies of the Republic, in the days of Cromwell? From what grade of society, did France during the Revolution procure her Marshals, was it not from the common people? Who was [*sic*] Toussaint, Dessalines, and a number of other generals who acted so prominent a part in the Revolution of Hayti,—were they not domestic slaves?" ("Slavery"). The reading of history, and the reading in African American periodicals *of* the reading of history, argued for the cause of liberty, for the power of the oppressed when organized and educated, and these readings pointed to the necessity of applying that power to the cause of the day.

The history presented in the pages of *Freedom's Journal* and other periodical publications, as I have noted, was not a singular narrative but a series of narratives juxtaposed against one another and placed within the context of the immediate experiences and needs of the community. This dialectical relation between the "text" of history and the "text" of the African American community, as fundamental to liberation historiography as it is to liberation theology, is realized still further in that the periodical press is itself the voice of the community. There is no single author or narrator of this complex historical text; instead, various voices, from all walks of life, are placed in dynamic relation with one another and with the representatives of the white community that influence African American experience and give shape, both positively and negatively, to the dynamic and contingent dimensions of African American identity. Virtually every prominent figure in the African American community appeared in and wrote for the periodical press; equally important is the fact that the press represented—in the form of letters, biographical pieces, news items, and articles—the active presence of people usually omitted from historical notice. An August 10, 1827, correspondent to *Freedom's Journal* who identifies herself only as "Matilda" could remind the editors of that publication of the importance of "the education of females," noting at the end of her short say, "I merely throw out these hints, in order that some more able pen will take up the subject." Both in her sense that she could influence editorial priorities and in her belief that "some more able pen" would pick up on her "hints," Matilda points to the representative narrative possibilities of the periodical press. These possibilities are suggested time and again in the voice of the press, a voice contextualized and, in part, defined in its relation to the many other voices reprinted from other sources.

Working within that complex locale, both representing and creating a coherent African American community, a writer for *Freedom's Journal* could state, in the February 15, 1828, issue, "We are sure we speak the sentiments of our brethren generally, and especially, the enlightened part, when we say that we are prepared to enlist our means, efforts and influence, in the encouragement of any National Society, whose object is African Education" ([Untitled]). The writer could also suggest the proper balance of power in joint efforts between white and black Americans, asserting that "all coloured men possessing wealth, education or influence would rejoice in the privilege of uniting all their abilities with those of the white population, in any plan, that would raise the standard of education among our colour, reserving to themselves at the same time, the privilege of educating their own children according to their respective views" ([Untitled]). A representative body is achieved, as Jacques Derrida has said of the Declaration of Independence, through its self-creation in the act of signing itself into existence (Warner 104–6); and its representative authority thereby becomes the primary subject presented in the pages of the periodical, as history and community are brought together to define the historical moment announced on the masthead. What is striking in the pages of the African American press from the early days of *Freedom's Journal* to the publications that reported on John Brown and the coming of the Civil War is the continuity of the historical commentary presented. One encounters the same historical information, and usually very similar rhetorical presentations of that information, on Egypt and Africa generally, on Haiti, on Nat Turner and others, on the roots of prejudice and the development and successes of British and American antislavery efforts. One encounters, too, a remarkably stable constellation of leaders and legends, and of writers. Upon these historical foundations the community was defined, its development measured, and the shaping events of the African American experience contextualized and interpreted. The history presented in the African American press, was, in short, a dynamic history, an attempt to join a stable understanding of the past to the shifting contingencies of the present in a definition of a vital community, one that could claim both ideological and moral authority in the theater of U.S. history.[14]

Speaking "Anglo-Africanwise": Periodicals and the Black Historical Community

The history presented in the black periodical press, I've tried to suggest, was not simply the information presented in the pages of the papers; the papers themselves were collective agents of history, reframing not only the events but also the discourse of the past to create a historically (in)formed community of readers. What Robert Levine has said of *Freedom's Journal* can be said of the black press generally: "The material fact of the newspaper itself, circulating county to county and state to state, can be regarded as a synecdoche for the black national body, which the editors imagined as a single body with 'a single voice'" ("Circulating" 22). Levine notes that this "'voice' is very different from the oratorical voice, which simply cannot perform the same circulatory work as a newspaper" (22); I would add that the newspaper included, framed, and circulated the oratorical voice, and that the formation of a single voice depended on the representation (often with a strong editorial hand) of a great diversity of opinions. Rael has rightly noted that "black protest thought as a whole drew its energy less from particular philosophical movements than from a far less formal pattern of discussion, carried out in newspaper debates, the pamphlet press, public speeches and sermons, and the pronouncements of institutions like black conventions" (156). Newspaper editors worked to give shape to this informal discussion, not only by providing a forum for public debates and other disagreements but also by reprinting excerpts from and commenting on pamphlets, speeches, and sermons, and by reporting on black conventions and other political, social, and commercial forums and events. Newspapers worked to create community by representing the circulation of thought and discourse that spoke of a vital community. But further still, the newspapers worked to create community by providing a kind of historical handbook of interpretation in an effort to teach readers the mode of historically informed reading essential to a unified African American community.

Much of the work of the newspapers could be categorized simply as the politics of uplift, the attempt to "elevate" the African American community by inculcating habits of intellectual and moral discipline in the service of bourgeois social values. Certainly, the black press was explicit in its devotion to this work—as, for example, in an article titled "Elevation of Our People" published in the *Colored American* in 1839. But this was hardly simple or unidimensional work, for as the article emphasizes, the work of elevation would need to encompass the various effects, material and psychological, of a history of oppression: "To raise up a people to intellectual, social, and moral life, long having been kept down, oppressed, and proscribed, mentally, socially, and legally; whose education has been entirely neglected, and thought either not proper, or possible by others, and by themselves thought to be out of their power; whose claims have been regarded as though they had none, and against whom has been every man's hand, and whose disposition and habits, social and moral, have been formed under those circumstances, is a work, than which there is none more honorable and God-like" ("Elevation"). This was a project both specific and universal; it was shaped by the "history, and present condition," of African Americans, but it was also inherent in the human condition, for "to occupy the highest possible state of moral elevation, is the true element of man," and thus "to assist in bringing about this object, is to co-operate with God in carrying out his designs" ("Elevation"). The history of the African American people emphasized the importance of collective elevation, but the work of elevation was not simply a response to the condition of oppression.

The *Colored American* editorial is representative of the promotion of reading throughout the African American press, a continual advertisement for the press as both the means to achieve elevation and a manifestation of African American solidarity and communal strength. "The disposition and habits of our people," the *Colored American* editorial observed, "in most cases, are essentially wrong" ("Elevation"). It was essential, the editorial argued, for African Americans to "cultivate a reading disposition" as the foundational step toward a long process of elevation and communal self-determination. "Men must think for themselves," the editorial observed, "and to know what to think about, men must read, and become acquainted with men, with things, and with the world; such is an intelligent man, and has the means for his own elevation, and to direct his children in the proper road, never to be degraded" ("Elevation"). This broad acquaintance with the world will, the editorial asserted, help readers to determine the terms of their present situation (understood relationally) and to enlarge the scope of their influence, for "every man . . . among us, who is a reader, *merely*, and will avail himself of books and papers . . . will not only by contrast know his own condition better, and see its wants, but will have the means for improvement, become conversant with the world, and prepared to lend an influence, to give a right direction and tone, to the habits of all within his reach" ("Elevation").

The problem, though, was not entirely that African American readers lacked "a reading disposition" but also that the reading disposition that did exist was easily turned away from the task at hand. In an editorial titled "Solid Reading," for example, the *Colored American* linked its own faltering fortunes to the growth of a reading industry that undermined the promise of reading. The argument is familiar to those of us living in the computer age: the proliferation of information leads to a increasing loss of focus; the acquisition of knowledge becomes a frivolous entertainment rather than an intellectually "solid" endeavor; and information designed to appeal to a broad audience serves the needs mainly of those interested only in the material rewards of a capitalist market: "Authors and publishers, like men in every kind of business, have gone from the solid and permanent, to the fanciful and imaginative, to please the eye, and tickle the ear, until they have created entire new dispositions, and established new tastes, so that now, it is almost impossible to secure the reading of a book like the Bible, or books upon the theology of the Bible, or books illustrating great principles, or detailing great moral events, or giving the history of the triumphs of moral principle—in a word, upon anything really vital to human happiness, or almost to human existence" ("Solid Reading"). The result is a transformation of what counts as knowledge, for "if an author would write or publish a book, he must hardly consult the subject, but rather the public taste" ("Solid Reading"). Transformed, too, is the ethical application of knowledge, for that same author "must not look to see what will do the most good, but what will secure the most extensive reading, almost without regard to the good, or the evil, which might ensue" ("Solid Reading"). Under such circumstances, this editorial lamented, the press could not lead but could only follow—and a press dedicated to social reform was faced with the task of representing a community conditioned to resist that representation. "It is upon this principle mainly," the editorial concluded, "that we can account why most of the religious periodicals—the temperance papers—the anti-slavery papers, and papers devoted more directly to the interests and improvement of the colored people show to be wanting in support: they are [not] suited to the popular will!—they do not gratify the vitiated taste of the public" ("Solid Reading").

Behind the challenge, then, of creating an African American press was the challenge of creating an appropriate audience for the press.[15] In part, of course, this involved the promotion of an "imagined community"—and Rael, among other scholars, has noted the importance of the African American press in appropriating the discourse of nationhood for the purposes of defining the nation within the nation, the black community. "Through public media like newspapers," Rael observes, "African American elites gained access to the discourse of nation; by constructing those media themselves, they found the capacity to appropriate and reformulate ideas of nation in their own defense" (216). But these reformulated ideas of nation required the support of a reformulated "reading disposition." Promoting a black "imagined community" involved promoting a black community of readers—a community shaped not simply by a common discourse and body of texts but also by reading practices, modes of interpretation, determined by and capable of responding to the same historical conditions that joined the diverse people of African origins into an identifiably common situation, a possible community. As I have argued throughout this book, transforming that possible, that always immanent, community into a realized social and political entity required the promotion of a specifically African American approach to historical understanding. Similarly, the African American press faced the challenge of training its readers in the art of liberation historiography.

Creating the "voice" of the African American press, accordingly, involved the promotion of an African American mode of reading and historical interpretation. Often, and with increasing frequency in the 1850s, the voice published in the press was satirical, a humorous (though deadly serious) representation of a white national voice speaking in defense of the historical disruptions—the break between principle and practice—fundamental to the white supremacist order. In a short piece published in the *Weekly Anglo-African* of October 1, 1859, for example, the writer represents the implicit white national voice so as to distinguish between an "American" mode of discourse and an "Anglo-African" mode: "Truly we are a great people! Whatsoever we do is right. We have a high notion of ourselves. We can do anything. We can make wrong right, and can right wrongs. We take special interest in toleration, if in that toleration a wrong is involved. Wrongs smartly executed or inflicted please us far more than right doing. Of course, in all this we speak nationally, and not Anglo-Africanwise. We Americans are, so we think, singularly fortunate in having instructors and instruction that lead to these results, and that make us in these days conquer our prejudices, and throw aside old-fashioned notions of right and wrong" ("Whither Are We Tending?"). Both in the title of this short piece—"Whither Are We Tending?"—and in its reference to "old-fashioned notions of right and wrong," the *Weekly Anglo-African* warned of a destructive historical process that was shaping the national consciousness. As an article in the *Colored American* put it years earlier, "One of the most unfavorable signs of the times, is the little respect paid to establish truths, independent of external things; the delusion in our day so general, that principles external and immutable, can be modified or destroyed by circumstances" ("The General Theological Seminary"). To follow the course of circumstance was to speak an American discourse; to speak "Anglo-Africanwise," in contrast, was to adopt a mode of reasoning—and of discourse—which did not abandon the lessons of history.

The promotion of an African American mode of discourse was particularly prominent in the regular attention in the press to religion and the "sin of slavery," a phrase repeated so regularly as to be a fundamental principle of historical understanding, a standard entrance into a wide range of articles on U.S. culture.[16] As Stowe's Augustine St. Clare observed, understanding, interpretation, and even discourse had been warped and bent by the system of slavery; in the pages of the antislavery press, to ignore this fundamental sin made any talk of elevation wishful thinking at best, for "the great sin of slavery and caste as they exist in this country, do more to neutralize the means of grace, and block up the way of salvation, than all other things combined" ("The Church in Fault"). "Slavery," this *Colored American* editorial continues, "is THE SIN of the nation and caste, THE SIN of the Church; and if these sins need not to be prayed and wept over—if they need not to be repented of and removed, then may all sin be tolerated" ("The Church in Fault"). This vision of slavery, of course, shaped visions of U.S. national history, leading to apocalyptic visions that were seemingly justified, years later, by the Civil War. Commenting on regional tensions, for example, the *Colored American* opined that "the very day in which the South, in any of her high-handed measures, succeeds in separating herself from the North, she casts her NATIONAL DIE, and may sing her FUNERAL DIRGE. Nothing but her connection with the North shields her from HIGH HEAVEN'S CURSE, and from the REVENGE OF BLOOD GUILTINESS. Leave the South to herself, and her patriotic slave system would soon work out its own redemption, through rivers of blood!" ("Meeting of Congress").

But this moral reading of history—in effect, of the secular corruption of sacred history—led as well to readings of racial divisions in the North. The *Colored American* in particular followed closely the historical process by which the Church had been corrupted, drawing from but recontextualizing articles in the antislavery press generally. An article provided by "one of the agents of the Anti-Slavery Society," for example, followed the history of Methodism, noting that in its early days "the cord of caste set" only "loosely on the church." "But as members increased—(and wealth and pride also)," the writer continues, "as the Society gradually emerged from obscurity, the colored brethren began to find their situation more and more uncomfortable, until at length a circumstance occurred which broke the bonds of christian fraternity between them, and ultimately led to a final separation" ("Prejudice in the Church"). The article presents a history of the formation of the African Methodist Episcopal Church, but it ultimately concludes that the separation has been damaging to the cause of African American spiritual guidance. "Being without schools," the author concludes, "without the means of systematic education, and especially that which is preparatory to usefulness as a minister," African American ministers "are of course much less qualified to do good, than they would have been, had they had the advantages of regular training, or had they only the same models of disciplined mind and popular preaching before them which the junior class of white ministers have, to improve themselves by" ("Prejudice in the Church"). Certainly, both white and black religious leaders expressed concern about the preparation of black ministers, but in the pages of the *Colored American* one is more likely to encounter criticism of white theological training than of black religious practices.[17] Indeed, one article (not originally written for the black press) surveys a number of theological institutes that had attempted to restrict or suppress antislavery activity—including Lane Seminary, Western Reserve College, Marion College and Theological Seminary of Missouri, Hanover College and Theological Seminary, and Princeton Seminary—and notes that all of the institutions suffered severe problems (ranging from institutional breakdown to acts of God, in the form of punishing storms). "We ask our readers to say," the article concluded, "if it would not be well, seriously to inquire whether the sin which brought upon Israel a chastisement of 70 years' captivity, may not be one of the grounds of his controversy with our churches, and our theological institutions? One thing is certain—the sure word of prophecy informs us that the day is to come when the whole church militant and triumphant, will sing for joy over the destruction of every institution which stands in the way of the glory of God, and the liberty and salvation of souls" ("Facts respecting Pro-Slavery Colleges and Theological Seminaries"). African Americans, whose identity as a group was chained to the history of the system of slavery, had much to learn from the educational institutions from which they were excluded—but these lessons included an understanding of the corruption of those institutions and of the consequences of moral complacency.

In article after article, the African American press emphasized the need to attend to moral instruction and to search secular history for evidence of sacred history. Readers were guided through history (usually, beginning with biblical history) so as to be reminded that "the impress of change and decay is deeply, indelibly stamped upon all terrestrial things" (Beman, "Thoughts for the Season"). An 1840 *Colored American* article, representative of the historical overviews regularly published in the African American press, called upon readers to observe, "since the destruction of Sodom, how many wrecks have been scattered on the shores of time—how many nations have flourished and fallen—how many of the high places of population, commerce, and wealth have become desolate—how many empires have passed away, whose mighty shadows haunt the present time, to warn their successors in conquest and power, who, pressing forward in the same career of pride, are destined to the same doom" ("Nation Warned"). At times, these surveys of history seem designed to offer comfort to the powerless—drawing from the "awful pages in the records of time" to observe again and again, *"How are the mighty fallen!"* ("The Destruction of Babylon"). At times, too, these stories of changing fortunes were geared toward inspiring or provoking a spiritual renewal, reminding readers that "as it is with nations and empires, so it is with individuals," that life is temporal but the soul is eternal (Beman, "Thoughts for the Season"). Together, these familiar admonitions located the African American spiritual condition, and the responsibilities resulting from that condition, historically, suggesting that African Americans particularly should recognize and understand the need to determine the lessons of history so as to determine that which is unchanging. Because it was shaped by the break between eternal principle and temporal practice, African American identity was a secular key to sacred history.

An African American mode of discourse, this vision of history implied, would be one that attended to the "sin of slavery" and to the responsibilities of principles uncorrupted by circumstance. As Amos Gerry Beman put it in one of his meditations serialized in the *Colored American*, "Man cannot create truth: truth is eternal like its glorious AUTHOR" ("Thoughts, No. IX"). To speak "Anglo-Africanwise" was, in effect, to address the eternal by speaking historically—to give voice to principles sounded throughout history by people of various backgrounds. What made the discourse "black" was not a simple understanding of race (that is, a discourse drawn only from other black speakers) but an understanding of race as a systemic construction. African Americans had become, in effect, African Americans through a series of laws, practices, and modes of (mis)representation that involved increasingly corrupted and contorted principles, violations against sacred history. To speak Anglo-Africanwise was to speak from an understanding of those successive and layered violations, to speak from or toward eternal principles—*from* those that can be discerned and *toward* those that can be but vaguely apprehended.

Benedict Anderson has noted that, in creating "languages-of-power," the discursive modes of "print-capitalism" "laid the bases for national consciousness" (44–45). One might follow by saying that African Americans similarly worked to establish the foundation for a black national consciousness by appropriating established "languages-of-power," in part by way of the deconstruction of the white national discourse, and in part by a reapplication of print discourse from the past. Of course, it was hardly difficult to deconstruct the white national discourse; doing so was simply a matter of quoting from the authorizing texts of white national identity—the Bible, the Declaration of Independence, and the like—and noting the obvious contradictions between principle and practice. As proslavery writers regularly demonstrated, the burden of creative interpretation was all on the side of those defending slavery and racial dominance. Of course, this work was still necessary, and, as I have noted, "readings" of the founding texts of the white national consciousness were a regular and prominent feature of African American publications before the Civil War. But African American writers seemed to recognize the truth of another of Anderson's points—that "print-capitalism gave a new fixity to language, which in the long run helped to build that image of antiquity so central to the subjective idea of the nation" (44). In the pages of the African American press, the reprinting of texts from the past takes on a particular significance, one not available in a newspaper headed by a white editor, for the language of antiquity enters into the forum of African American communal elevation, and both the process of elevation and the historical process that created the need for elevation are redefined through the lens provided by the wisdom of the ages, a field of discourse that finds its present forum in the African American communal struggle. Something so simple, for example, as the reprinting of various statements on the subject of slavery—by Pope Leo X, William Penn, Alexander Pope, Jonathan Edwards, Adam Smith, Thomas Jefferson, John Wesley, and many others—in the pages of *Frederick Douglass' Paper* was a significant recontextualization of the language of power or, to borrow from Jefferson, "the language of truth."[18]

In claiming the authority of a "fixity of language," the continuity of the African American press was itself important—asserting not only that African Americans had an identifiable "voice" but also that the voice was stable over time. Although many African American papers lasted only a short time, their editors pressed the case for continuity by referring to previous publications, in much the same way that each national convention presented itself both as a singular achievement and as part of a larger, and continuous, historical movement. Samuel Cornish, for example, sometimes referred back to his work with *Freedom's Journal* to emphasize that his views—and his editorial practices—had not changed over time, a continuity that he then asserted was representative of the imagined community that the *Colored American* represented. In a May 13, 1837, editorial on colonization, for example, Cornish reprinted an editorial from the June 8, 1827, issue of *Freedom's Journal*, asserting that "our object in republishing the article at this time is, to show that intelligent colored people never had but one view of Colonization. They have always been opposed to it, as being at war with all their sacred rights, and interests. The article further shows, that there is no change in respect to our rights in this country. We have, for ages, been unwavering in the opinion, that we should some day possess in our native land, a perfect equality, in all respects, with our white brethren."[19] "This doctrine," Cornish noted at the close of the editorial, "is neither Tappan nor Garrisonian. It is Bibleism, and we claim some instrumentality in teaching it to both of these good men (Tappan and Garrison)" ("Colored People Always Opposed to Colonization"). This editorial, in short, asserts a singular view held over time by "intelligent colored people" concerning colonization as well as a singular purpose "for ages" concerning the African American struggle for civil rights and social equality. In its opposition to those in favor of emigrationist schemes (a frequent concern in the *Colored American*), it creates an image of a stable community while responding to evidence of the contrary. Not incidentally, it concludes by distinguishing its position from the positions identified with prominent white abolitionists, while asserting that the latter were influenced by an unwavering black press.

Considered in isolation, Cornish's presentation of the continuity of thought by "intelligent colored people" can seem, at best, disingenuous, an assertion of a singular position against a world of disagreement. To be sure, Cornish used the *Colored American* as a mouthpiece, and the absence of his former joint editor, John Browne Russwurm, allowed Cornish to be even more assertive about his anticolonizationist position (at the same time that Russwurm became editor of a paper in Liberia) while also glossing over the differences of opinion on the subject that had been a concern during the publication of *Freedom's Journal*. But beyond Cornish's editorial assertions on specific subjects was a more fundamental claim to continuity of thought, a determination to promote historically informed critical reading that, Cornish believed, could only support his positions in the end. The *Colored American*, like all African American periodicals of the time, provided a forum for debate and disagreements, and used these forums to instruct readers on the mode of reading essential to the development and stability of the African American community. The *Colored American* regularly published articles from or summarized identifiable tendencies in the white press—calling readers' attention to articles claiming that "abolition" is "dying away" ("Abolition Dying Away"), or instructing readers on principles of misrepresentation fundamental to proslavery or racist arguments. One editorial, for example, warned readers of the "specious and false kind of reasoning which attempts to prove things right by what we would here call *comparative detraction*," a process of reasoning in which one searches for "some defect, real or apparent, in morals or government, so that attention may be drawn off from their deficiencies or ill conduct," so that, "by changing its bent, they may be able to mistify observation, as to the actual hollowness of their own professions" (untitled editorial, August 14, 1841). The African American press generally, like Cornish in the *Colored American*, worked to link the lively exchanges characteristic of the press at the time to the specific principles associated with the cause of African American "elevation," making of elevation not the attempt to attain the status of white Americans but rather the attempt to learn from observing white American culture how to distinguish between true and false elevation. Placing a historically informed mode of critical reading at the center of its concerns, African American discourse presented itself as the discourse of a universal humanity by distinguishing itself from the deceptive and blatantly exclusionary universalism of white American discourse. African American experience, understood through the correspondence of sacred and secular history, became the entrance to an inclusive vision of society.

But the press continued to struggle against the reality that its "imagined community" remained all too imaginary and fragile. Editors faced an uphill battle to acquire both readers and financial security—and their most fervent assertions of the importance of an African American press were usually presented in desperate articles calling for financial support. In an 1839 editorial in the *Colored Americans* addressed to "brethren and friends," the case for the press was again presented. "It is now nearly three years," the editorial noted, "since the publication of the Colored American was commenced as the mouth piece to our people, through which to meet together and compare views, have a free interchange of opinion, and strike upon some plan, for the correction of our own errors, the improvement of our social condition, the procurement of civil rights, and to help on the holy cause of universal freedom, in our country and throughout the world." Having linked the existence of the paper to the existence of the community—and of the ideals that, the paper argued, define the community—the paper joined implicitly the fortunes of the paper to the fortunes of the community, and asserted, "We have now arrived at the darkest point yet, in the history of the COLORED AMERICAN" ("Appeal to the Friends of the Colored American").

The link between the paper and the community, between the *Colored American* and colored Americans, was presented more directly still in another article relating to subscriptions, a report by subscription agent W. P. Johnson concerning his experiences with "our people in Schenectady." "I saw a great many instances," Johnson reported, "where the whites had cheated and fooled the poor colored people of their property. I at one sight [*sic*] saw 13 houses and lots that had a few years ago belonged to colored people, and they are all gone now but one, and they have tried hard to get that one." Sounding the *Colored American*'s familiar call, Johnson added, "We should be as careful then to educate our children as we are to give them bread." "Touching our paper," Johnson continued, "I found very few who seem to appreciate the great good that is being produced, or its claims on them. What few I did find, plead poverty. In fact, I am sorry to say that Schenectady is the only place where I have been and failed to please the people generally in the discharge of my duties as a professing Christian, and as agent for our journal; and it is the only place where I have been and labored so hard with so little success." Johnson's blending of concerns—the loss of property with the complacency about education and religious instruction, his own failure to make an impression as both "a professing Christian" and "as agent for our journal"—is appropriate to the claims of the *Colored American* as well as other African American papers. "They have all the means in their hands to do great things," Johnson noted at the end, "and my prayer to God is that he will bind them together in love and religion, so that their labors may be crowned with success" ("The Fourth and Fifth of July in the City of Schenectady"). The challenge of binding the community together was linked with the challenge of putting "all the means in their hands to do great things" by way of an African American press capable of instructing "our people" in those arts of reading that would protect them from being "fooled and cheated" not only of their property but of their existence as a self-determined community.

The Gallery of History: The *Anglo-African Monthly*

I have focused primarily on *Freedom's Journal* and the *Colored American* to outline the ways in which the forum of the periodical press shaped the presentation of history in the earliest of African American newspapers. In the remaining pages of this chapter I will focus on a periodical that arrived toward the end of the antebellum period, the *Anglo-African Magazine* (1859–60), arguably one of the most important African American publications before the Civil War, and decidedly a monumental achievement in African American historical writing. The publisher and editor, Thomas Hamilton, was, in Bullock's words, "a member of a pioneering family of journalists and civil rights activists" (55); and in 1859 Hamilton added significantly to African American political and literary history in launching two publications, the monthly *Anglo-African Magazine* and the *Weekly Anglo-African* newspaper. It is in the *Anglo-African Magazine* that chapters of Martin R. Delany's novel *Blake* first appeared; it is there, too, that Frances E. W. Harper's short story "The Two Offers" first appeared. The magazine was, as it was intended to be, a showcase and forum for black intellectuals and literary artists. As Bullock has noted, "The roster of contributors to the *Anglo-African Magazine* was a veritable roll call of the black scholars of that day" (60). Besides Delany and Harper, readers of the magazine would encounter writings by Amos Gerry Beman, Edward Wilmot Blyden, Robert Campbell, Mary Ann Shadd Cary, Frederick Douglass, Sarah M. Douglass, James Theodore Holly, John Mercer Langston, J. Sella Martin, William C. Nell, Daniel Alexander Payne, James

W. C. Pennington, Charles B. Ray, James McCune Smith, George B. Vashon, and William J. Wilson. When Hamilton issued a bound edition of the first volume of the magazine, he could claim with considerable justice, as an advertisement had it, that the *Anglo-African Magazine* "contains more facts and statistics of the colored race than any other publication extant" (qtd. in Bullock 62).

It is this bound volume that I wish to present as the culminating work of history in this study, the one that encompasses all of the principles of African American historiographical method that I have outlined in the previous chapters and sections. Certainly, the volume was important, as Hamilton himself recognized, as a collection of "facts and statistics," and therefore it is an important record of information, an archive of sorts, on African American history. But beyond its status as a record of information, the *Anglo-African Magazine* is a dazzling collective performance, an assembly of history in the double sense of being a multivocal, multiperspectival presentation of history as well as a careful assembly of the many dimensions of the African American experience that must be accounted for if one is to try to represent African American history. In an article titled "Civilization," James McCune Smith argued, "If we look into the institutions of mankind, we find that wherever these institutions favor a free admixture of human thought, there, civilization advances; but, wherever human institutions isolate human thought, keep soul from communion with its fellow soul, there progress ceases" (15).[20] This is the principle that animates the *Anglo-African Magazine*. Indeed, this magazine is an assembly that calls attention to itself as such—an assembly in which the seams show, in which the views work with and against one another, in which the partial view offered by each article or series of articles, placed in juxtaposition with other partial views, emphasizes the untold stories just beyond the act of representation, just beyond understanding. It is, finally, a representation of the past that is always firmly grounded in the needs of the present, a representation of the community that is also an attempt to discover, define, and address the needs of the community. "Our work here," wrote Hamilton for the magazine's opening "Apology," "is, to purify the State, and purify Christianity from the foul blot which here rests upon them" (4). This is history with a mission, but also a history that examines and questions the terms of its mission.

The *Anglo-African Magazine*'s historical mission begins, simply enough, by representing a large range of concerns—many of them culturally associated with African American experience and identity, and some of them not.

Readers would encounter articles by Robert Campbell on Jamaica ("Struggles for Freedom in Jamaica" and "Effects of Emancipation in Jamaica") and ones by Martin R. Delany on outer space ("The Attraction of Planets" and "Comets"). Mary A. B. Cary's "Trifles" followed the theme "Tall oaks from little acorns grow," noting the importance of apparently small acts; Edward W. Blyden, addressing the effects of international politics on the situation in Liberia, contributed "A Chapter in the History of the Slave Trade." A. J. R. Connor provided the words and music to "My Cherished Hope, My Fondest Dream"; another of James McCune Smith's articles was "On the Four-teenth Query of Thomas Jefferson's Notes on Virginia." George B. Vashon's "The Successive Advances of Astronomy" might be complemented by James Field's "The Shadows of Intemperance," which would be related to but of a different philosophical tone than Robert Gordon's "In the Constitution of Man There Exists a Religious Element," in which Gordon supports the theme of his article's subtitle, "Theology Is the Only Science That Meets It." An article simply titled "Chess" touches on the Egyptian roots of the game; it would be followed later by a review of *The Book of the First American Chess Congress.*

Woven throughout the various issues of the *Anglo-African Magazine* were serialized features that provided focus and continuity. The importance of Delany's fictional work *Blake* to a collective work that I am identifying as written history should not be underestimated, for Delany's novel itself winds its way through various political and cultural concerns in both national and international settings, presenting history as a collective strategy, a deliberate manipulation of the contingencies of the African American condition and the politics of conspiracy and paranoia.[21] The novel is perhaps more forceful still in this context, interwoven with, for example, the running feature "A Statisti-cal View of the Colored Population of the United States—from 1790–1850," a series of articles and statistical tables that addresses the cultural politics and inaccuracies of census data, and that responds also to assertions that black Americans thrive under slavery and wither under the light of liberty. In "The German Invasion," an extensive consideration of migration, James McCune Smith studies the "invasion" of the American continent by various groups—including Spanish, English, African, and Irish peoples—in order to explore "the composite genius of the American people" (46). J. Theodore Holly's series, "Thoughts on Hayti," accepts this understanding of the values of mi-gration but applies them to a careful argument that black Americans should emigrate to Haiti to establish a black nationalist force capable of addressing the international pressures that play such a significant role in Delany's novel and Blyden's commentary on the present state of Liberia. Writing under the pen name "Ethiop," William J. Wilson contributed a remarkable series of fictional sketches entitled the "Afric-American Picture Gallery," which comments not only on African American history but also on representation and understanding of that history, about which I will have more to say later.

Although I am emphasizing the *assembly* of history in the pages of the *Anglo-African Magazine*, mode over matter, it is important to stress that the great majority of the articles present careful readings of history in which sound scholarship is clearly a priority—always, though, with an eye toward applying the lessons of the past to the immediate needs of the present. In many cases, the primary purpose of the history is to monumentalize the struggle for African American liberty and rights. Representative is John Mercer Langston's "The Oberlin Wellington Rescue," which offers a sound history of the rescue so as to identity that event as a "glorious exhibition" of Oberlin's "purpose to stand firm in favor of Justice and Christianity, the Declaration and the Constitution, Law and Order, and against Injustice and Atheism, Despotism and Slavery, Mob-violence and Misrule" (209). But even such monumentalizing efforts are directed finally to a central concern of the present. An article titled "The First Colored Convention," for example, proudly exclaims, "We had giants in those days!" (305). The article covers the events leading to the convention's planning and conception, and it covers the concerns debated at the convention, but much of the article's purpose is simply to celebrate and record those giants—listing the names of Bishop Allen, Bell, Cornish, Forten, Peck, Paul, Rush, Steward, Williams, Hamilton, Watkins, Whipper, and Woodson, while constructing an extensive verbal monument to the efforts of Hezekiah Grice. Ultimately, though, this article turns to present concerns, using the history of the early convention to argue against emigration—noting, for example, of Grice himself, "where, in the wide world, in what region, or under what sun, could he so effectually have labored to elevate the black man, as on this soil and under American institutions?" (310). Indeed, the article leads to a stunningly strong statement opposing the colonizationists. "So profoundly are we opposed," the writer states, "to the favorite doctrine of the Puritans and their co-workers, the colonizationists—*Ubi Libertas, ibi Patria*—that we could almost beseech Divine Providence to reverse some past events, and to fling back into the heart of Virginia and Maryland their Sam. Wards, Highland Garnets, J. W. Penningtons, Frederick

Douglasses, and the twenty thousand who now shout hosannas in Canada—
and we would soon see some stirring in the direction of *Ubi Patria, ibi Libertas!*" (310). History here is used to establish the path of African American
success, and thereby to identify and evaluate the relative value of the often
deceptive paths available in the present.

At the foundation of all of the historical commentary presented in the
Anglo-African Magazine is an ongoing attempt to identify and apply the theological principles by which historical understanding might proceed. J. W. C.
Pennington's three-part "A Review of Slavery and the Slave Trade," for example, begins by looking back to the introduction of slavery in the Americas, a
glance back that includes a discussion of Bartholomew de Las Casas among
others, and then turns to such important early antislavery leaders as Thomas
Clarkson, John Woolman, and Granville Sharp. But this is only a prelude to a
still more comprehensive overview in Pennington's history—in which, he
notes, "it will appear" that the slave trade "has existed in civilized as well
as barbarous nations, through a long succession of ages, and from the re-
motest antiquity" (94). In his study of slavery, Pennington consults a range of
writers from Aesop, Terence, and Plutarch to Gibbon and Adam Smith—
continually comparing historical forms of slavery with that practiced in the
United States. "The celebrated Adam Smith," Pennington notes, for example,
"in his 'Wealth of Nations,' says, that 'the condition of a slave is better under
an *arbitrary* than under a free government,' and this, we believe, is supported
by the history of all ages and nations" (125). This study leads Pennington to
his consideration of the effects of the system of slavery in the United States,
including the effects on Africans who participated in the slave trade, but
particularly on the white citizens of the nation. "When men once consent to
be unjust," Pennington concludes, "they lose at the same instant with their
virtue, a considerable portion of that sense of shame, which, till then had
been found a successful protector against the allies of vice. Such was the
situation of the despotic sovereigns of Africa, and such is the situation of *some*
of the Slave-holders in a land, the first article of whose national creed we have
quoted before" (125). Presenting Christianity as the force that will lead to the
abolition of slavery, a case that he supports historically, Pennington leads his
readers to a vision of the developing Southern confederacy that looks beyond
the front of unity to underlying divisions. "However united for some political
purposes," Pennington argues, "they are divided on this subject [Christian
duty]; and yet they all profess to be under the influence of Christianity—it

reminds us of the story of an itinerant player who announced the play of *Hamlet*, with the part of Hamlet left out. So it would really seem that in the Slave States, it was Christianity with the part of the *Christian* left out" (156).

Comments like these were not incidental, of course, to the larger purpose of the *Anglo-African Magazine*, for this is a mode of history drawn from and devoted to a dynamic conception of community—an approach to history that emphasizes the dialectical relationship between the condition of the oppressed and the responsibilities of historical understanding. In 1827, an editorial from the first issue of *Freedom's Journal* announced the central mission of the newspaper—to be the voice of the community, and to thereby exercise some influence in the representation of African American character. "We wish to plead our own cause," the editorial stated; "too long have others spoken for us. Too long has the public been deceived by misrepresentations, in things which concern us dearly, though in the estimation of some mere trifles; for though there are many in society who exercise towards us benevolent feelings; still (with sorrow we confess it) there are others who make it their business to enlarge upon the least trifle, which tends to the discredit of any person of color; and pronounce anathemas and denounce our whole body for the misconduct of this guilty one" ("To Our Patrons"). In 1859, Hamilton continued this cause in his opening "Apology" for the *Anglo-African Magazine*, emphasizing the systemic nature of those misrepresentations. "The wealth, the intellect, the Legislation, (State and Federal,) the pulpit, and the science of America," Hamilton asserted, "have concentrated on no one point so heartily as in the endeavor to write down the negro as something less than a man" (1). Like the editors of *Freedom's Journal*, Hamilton recognized the importance not only of responding to these misrepresentations but also of establishing, as part of that response, the presence and power of an African American communal voice. Hamilton anticipates many of the writers for the *Anglo-African Magazine* in considering the oppressed community as the central concern of the day, the practical and ideological site where the relation between sacred and secular history was to be determined. The story to be told of that relation, and of the responsibilities and possibilities it would reveal, was a story in which African Americans must participate, for their history could be related by no one else. As Hamilton puts it in his "Apology," "Frederick Douglass has said that 'the twelve millions of blacks in the United States and its environs must occupy the notice and the care of the Almighty;' these millions, in order to assert and maintain their rank as men among men, must speak for themselves; no outside tongue, however gifted with eloquence, can tell their story; no outside eye, however penetrating, can see their wants; no outside organization, however benevolently intended, nor however cunningly contrived, can develop the energies and aspirations which make up their mission" (1). Central to the mission of the *Anglo-African Magazine*, then, and central also to the construction of history in its pages, was the attempt to provide a vibrant and diverse black community with the forum by which it could determine itself *as* a community. "The negro," Hamilton argued, "is something more than endurance; he is a force." The question was how this force would be embodied in action, how it would acquire definition as a community—which, for Hamilton and others, involved the transition from a resisting force, shaped by the actions of others, to a self-determined one. "When the energies which now inbrute him," Hamilton asserted, "exhaust themselves—as they inevitably must—the force which he now expounds in resistance will cause him to rise: his force can hardly be measured to-day; the opinions regarding him are excessive; his foes estimate him too low—his friends, perhaps, too high: besides, there is not a-wanting among these latter, in spite of their own good feelings, that 'tribe idolatry' which regards him as 'not quite us'" (2).

But how should the embodiment of that force be understood? Many of the writers for the *Anglo-African Magazine* address this question both directly and indirectly, often and necessarily addressing the concepts of race administered by the dominant culture. An article titled "A Word to Our People," for example, begins, "The other day, in the Senate of the United States, a senator pronounced Americans of African descent, inferior to Americans of Caucasian origin" (293). The writer, as one might expect, proceeds to refute this view, asking his readers, "Suppose a million of people, from Mount Caucasius itself, carried to the coast of Guinea, whipped, scourged, crushed beneath the iron hands and the superior civilization of the African River Kings, would they increase and multiply?" (293–94). But the writer then descends from his imagined survey of Mount Caucasius to consider what claims those of African origin might have to a peculiar character. He considers the claims of those, black and white, who argued for what George Fredrickson has termed "romantic racialism," the belief that Africans were more spiritual, more benevolent than Anglo-Saxons. Our writer, though, rejects these claims on the evidence he surveys, and asks finally, "But if not in love, nor in benevolence, nor in education, is there any other direction in which we manifest force of character?" (295). Indeed, the writer ridicules the whole enterprise of identifying an inherent quality by which "the African race" might claim superiority.

"I believe that we are strong in the gastronomic line," he states; "we are remarkably good eaters"—and accordingly he suggests that "a society for the demolition of broiled turkeys would be wonderfully popular among us" (295). But as these comments indicate, the writer has little to contribute to this line of argument, concluding that "in no direction can we be said to manifest force of character equal to the whites. And this lack on our part is, in reality, the source of our degradation" (295). This sort of sharp, and even sarcastic, criticism of the community was, as I have noted, somewhat rare but hardly absent from African American writing of this period. "A Word to Our People," then, works to explore what it might mean to say "our people," and suggests that the response to systemic oppression has been a corresponding systemic imitation of white America's principles and values. This, the writer proposes, is the source of the problem, and he is led to the conclusion that "we cannot equal the whites, so long as we strive to equal them. The ideal is too low. It is not an original, inherent, self-propelling power. It is, therefore, and we are, therefore, *deficient in force of character*" (296).

While few are as sharp as the author of "A Word to Our People," many writers agreed that the terms for understanding African American character, and for asserting the rights of African Americans as citizens, were themselves distorted and distorting presences in the struggle for African American self-determination. Writers responded to this problem in various ways. Some, like "S. S. N.," the author of "Anglo-Saxons, and Anglo-Africans," looked to the fictions of race as the site of the instability in the present struggle. "We are always amused with certain Reform Orators of the country," S. S. N. states, "who are forever curing the wounds they themselves inflict on the 'Apostate American People,' by fulsome laudations of what they call 'THE GREAT ANGLO-SAXON RACE.'—There is such refreshing self-exaltation in the thing—such an indirect, 'We thank Thee, Lord, that thou hast made us of better stuff, than the poor negro, for whom we plead,'—and withal such poetic license used with the facts of history, that we wonder they don't feel ashamed of the romance they so often repeat" (247). The writer, drawing from history, quickly undermines any such claims to greatness, and asks finally, "What is to prevent *our* taking rank with them, seeing that we have a common history in misfortune!" (248). But the writer brings the same wit to what he views as the pretensions of the black American community, asserting, "as equally amusing it is, that we ourselves have become by some mysterious process—'Anglo-Africans.'—We have searched History for the union of the Angles and the Africans, and have failed to find it.—Nevertheless, the fact must be patent, for are we not writing for an Anglo-African Magazine?" (249). In this funhouse mirror world of discourse, this and other writers for the *Anglo-African Magazine* seem to ask, how is the community to acquire a faithful likeness of itself?

James McCune Smith, among others, argued that the likeness was to be drawn from history and from a reconsideration and revitalization of language itself. Smith's most direct commentary along these lines comes in his remarks on the Dred Scot decision in his article "Citizenship," which begins by deconstructing the logic behind the most famous words of Judge Roger Taney's opinion in that decision, that blacks in America "have no rights that white men are bound to respect." But while he dismisses the value of the statement as authoritative (arguing that the Court's acceptance of the Dred Scot case contradicted Taney's words), Smith still bemoans "the easy rapidity with which this atrocious sentiment passed from tongue to tongue, and the sudden possession which it took of the public mind" (145). In searching for the terms of a possible citizenship, Smith looks back to Aristotle and to the Roman Republic for an understanding of the word "citizen," and then considers U.S. history before concluding that "the free blacks are citizens of the United States, under the Constitution thereof; it is, for us, a most excellent Constitution, 'a better one,' as Frederick Douglas [*sic*] has well said 'than would be framed by a Convention held to-day in the United States'" (149). Smith's reflections become, in short, a sort of linguistic jeremiad, turning to the ancient meaning of words so as to return to a nation apparently unable to read its own Constitution.

Through the multivocal forum of the *Anglo-African Magazine*, writers could respond to the ideological incoherence of the dominant culture more fully than if they were to rely solely on the discourse of scholarship and reason. They could, in fact, simply mirror that incoherence so as to open the space in which scholarship could operate. Consider, for example, another piece by William J. Wilson (writing as "Ethiop"), titled "The Anglo-African and the African Slave Trade." Wilson begins by simply remarking that it is virtually impossible to address, in white America, the issue of slavery as a moral concern. "The sinfulness of slavery and the slave trade in any and every form," Wilson says, "no disinterested, no honest man will deny; nevertheless, it is utterly useless, worse than folly, to call it up to the attention of the Anglo-American, for his serious consideration." The problem, Wilson asserts, is that economic expediency is the guiding passion of white America. Accordingly, for the white American, "whatever is free from personal danger, and free from apparent encroachment on a strong power, and will pay, is not *sinful*, but lawful and right. Whatever is fraught with danger, and whatever encroaches individually, and will not pay, why that may be regarded as sinful. *Right and wrong, heart and conscience*, with the Anglo-American, are only relative terms, ponderous ambiguities, glittering generalities, words of doubtful meaning, or of no meaning" (283).

Wilson follows many others—from David Walker in the *Appeal* to Harriet Beecher Stowe in *Uncle Tom's Cabin*—in pointing out that an inevitable consequence of the maintenance of the system of slavery is the corruption of discourse, and that a necessary consequence of the values encouraged by the system of slavery is the corruption of character. And, like both Walker and Stowe before him, Wilson turns these consequences back to those who refuse to recognize them, applying with a vengeance the underlying logic of the system of slavery:

> We earnestly beg the timid christian slave-propagandist, to banish his fears, if he have any; and the more subtle, to no longer carry two faces; and let the trade be free, untrammeled, general: for at present it will not only pay, but is safe, and moreover, truly democratic. Why should a few be permitted to monopolize this grand scheme of rapid promotion of American slavery, to the detriment of the many? Why should we foster any privileged class in this wonderfully democratic country of ours. Let us be consistent, even in the working of our accursed system of oppression. Let us be free. Free to buy slaves, free to sell slaves. Free to import, free to export. Free to bind, free to loose, free to flog, free to kill. We love freedom. (285)

Drawing his readers into the carnivalesque world of the United States under the system of slavery, Wilson indulges them in a fantasy of force-feeding proslavery America the candied discourse of its own desires. He expands the possibilities of representation by identifying its enslavement; he frees language by showing its imprisonment in the house of bondage. And in this way he helps to prepare for a community that will need to reclaim the discourse of liberty for its own use.

The forum provided by a periodical publication, though, allowed for a larger representation of the community than did most of the national conventions or public speaking platforms—and accordingly provided for a larger version of the discursive disarray of the arguments that were to shape the community and provide it with its connection to the past. While women do not constitute by any means a significant presence in the *Anglo-African Mag-*

azine in numbers of articles or even range of subjects, their presence is strong nonetheless, and their writing often responds to the pretensions just beneath the surface of work by other contributors to the magazine, those whose self-defined purpose seems to be the exposure of such pretensions. In a serial feature, "Town and Country, or Fancy Sketches," a writer working under the pen name "Jane Rustic" uses a wedding as a setting for a series of reflections on the underrepresented concerns of the women of the community. At one point, the narrator visits a convention in progress, and "as I went in," she tells her readers,

> a rather pompous looking man was on the floor, reading a string of resolutions that he had written for the occasion.
>
> "Resolved, That this convention form a society called the Anti-sunshine Society.
>
> Resolved, that it shall be the duty of this convention to send out lecturers, and circulate documents and tracts, to show the superiority of gaslight over sunshine.
>
> Resolved, That no woman shall hold any office in our Society, unless it be to collect funds.
>
> Resolved, That the sun is a bore, because it freckles our faces and tans our complexions.
>
> Resolved, That we will petition the man in the moon to weave a curtain of clouds, or a shroud of mist to bar the rising of the sun." (384)

I will leave it to others to consider the full range of concerns embodied in this rich passage, noting only that Jane Rustic calls attention to both the form and substance of the patriarchal assumptions that black women faced beyond the concerns discussed throughout the *Anglo-African Magazine.* In discourse and in public organization, African American men were creating for themselves a forum for public performances of leadership, but our narrator suggests that the leadership precludes the concerns and participation of many who were expected to be led, and in the process creates another forum for pompous pretensions and unstable discourse.[22]

The various attempts to define the nature and terms of a possible African American community were all directed toward a similar sense of a historical crossroads just ahead, a point at which the definition would determine the fate of the community that was, in any event, identifiable in its common delineation by a controlling white culture. Amos Gerry Beman viewed this historical situation as the culmination of a long history of God's identification with the oppressed. Echoing John Winthrop, and relocating the center of the American experiment, Beman asserted, "The colored race is an element of power in the earth, 'like a city set upon a hill it cannot be hid.' Thanks to our friends—and to our foes—and to the providence of God" (337). Beman identifies this unique position of "the colored race" in providential history in part by looking to African American history, noting that "in the darkest night of our history in this land, a few stars of hope and promise have shone forth, like Phillis Wheatley, and Benjamin Banneker—minds which stirred up thought for the race in Washington and Jefferson. The past has given, as a people, a Richard Allen, an Absalom Jones and a John Gloucester, a Theodore S. Wright, a David Walker, to say nothing of a Denmark Vesey, of a Nathaniel Turner—names significant, and inspiring all" (338). But this is, for Beman, not just a story to tell, but rather a text to interpret; and the text reveals the stories still untold, lost in the oppression to which these significant names draw our attention. Now, " 'mute and inglorious,' " Beman exclaims, "what a multitude of Penningtons, Delanys, Crummells, McCune Smiths, Whippers, Douglasses, Garnets, Robert Morrises, W. J. Wilsons, Rocks, and Rogers, there are now held and crushed in the withering chains of slavery" (338). Extending that reading, Beman sees African American history in much the same light that some white Americans viewed the significance of the American Revolution, as an event that would mark a new epoch in the world.

It is in this way that black identity can be read as embodiment; it is in this way that the concerns of race and condition can be brought into their proper theological light—for, argues Beman of the black man, "crushed, embruted and oppressed he may be, ignorant and debased, all unconscious of what he *is*, of the race to which he belongs, he is, nevertheless, the *representative* of millions in this land—of millions on the earth" (337–38). The African American struggle in this way becomes a global struggle, not by a simple universalism, but in the particularity of the oppression that defines that struggle. "Around" the African American, Beman asserts, returning to the city on the hill, "the central thought of the world is revolving; on his brow the gaze of civilized man and Christianized philanthropy is burning; he is thus the centre of a deep and mighty, of a far-reaching and living, THOUGHT" (337). This sense of a providential mission, of course, naturally raises questions about the degree to which that far-reaching and living thought was reaching the African American community itself, and it is accordingly appropriate that Beman presents this vision in an essay on education.

Concerns over education were naturally at the center of the attempt to define an African American (or Anglo-African) community, and they are fundamental also to the *Anglo-African Magazine*'s status as a work of history. The magazine addressed the historical concern over education most directly by exposing the conditions under which many African Americans were being educated. In an article titled "American Caste, and Common Schools," for example, J. Holland Townsend looks back to record the resistance to the white Quaker Prudence Crandall's attempt to educate African American children in her Connecticut school, and to the remarkable response to the Noyes Academy in Canaan, New Hampshire, at which Henry Highland Garnet, Alexander Crummell, Thomas Paul, and others were enrolled. A Canaan town meeting resulted in the decision to "abolish the school in 'the *interest* of the town, the *honor* of the State, and the *good* of the whole community, (both black and white)'"; following through on this decision, the town's appointed committee "enlisted the assistance of men from neighboring towns and nearly one hundred yoke of oxen, and removed the school building from its foundations to 'the common near the Baptist meeting-house'" (Litwack, *North of Slavery* 119). Crandall's boarding school for girls met with similar, if less spectacular, resistance from the town of Canterbury, Connecticut, when Crandall admitted a black student. Canterbury, like Canaan, held a town meeting, and "appointed a committee to persuade Miss Crandall to abandon her project in view of 'the injurious effects, and incalculable evils' that would follow" (Litwack, *North of Slavery* 128). Crandall, with abolitionist support, refused to yield, and accordingly Connecticut's state legislators "formally agreed that an increase of the Negro population would not serve the best interests of the state and thus adopted a law which prohibited the establishment of 'any school, academy, or literary institution, for the instruction or education of colored persons who are not inhabitants of this state' and which forbade anyone to instruct, harbor, or board such persons without the approval of local authorities," thus depriving Crandall of a significant portion of her student base and dealing a "mortal blow" to her school (Litwack, *North of Slavery* 129). Townsend references these well-known instances but devotes most of his article to schools in the West, with a particular focus on California, where he finds the situation all too familiar. The situation back east was covered by another item in the *Anglo-African Magazine*, a reprinting of a report, "Communication from the New York Society for the Promotion of Education among Colored Children," which was, Hamilton noted at the end of the report, "of intrinsic value as a record of what Caste Schools are" (224). These and other records of the state of education naturally raised the

question of how to educate African American children, and on what principles. Various writers in the *Anglo-African Magazine* agreed that the situation required an approach to education particularly suited for African American children. "We are too apt to take the precepts that are taught to the ruling
race in this country," argued M. H. Freeman, "and apply them to ourselves
without considering that different traits in our character, either natural or
acquired by our different circumstances, require an entirely different treatment" (118). But what would that different treatment be—or, as Freeman
asked, "What then is an education?" "It is certainly not," Freeman continued,
"as many seem to suppose, merely a large collection of facts laid up in the
store-house of memory, whence may be brought forth at any time and in any
quantity things new and old. Nor is it a mere knowledge of languages, mathe-
matics, histories and philosophies. The various sciences, each and all, may be
used as a means of education, but they are not the education itself. Education
is the harmonious development of the physical, mental, and moral powers of
man" (115). For Freeman, what followed from this quite reasonable conception of education was the equally reasonable conclusion that education is part
of a larger system, and that African Americans need to play a role in every part
of that system if their children are to be properly educated—in part, by being
properly inspired by the opportunities for which they were preparing and
reassured as to their chances of claiming those opportunities. "We need the
educating power of wealth," Freeman argued, "of civil and political honors
and offices for our children, for these are the means that first develop in the
children of the other race, that due self-respect and self-reliance which must
lie at the foundation of any just and harmonious development of mind" (116).

Freeman's article, however, was followed almost immediately by one from
clergyman Daniel Alexander Payne in which Payne insisted that "knowledge
is more to be desired, and really more valuable than gold" (119). "Give your
child gold without knowledge," Payne argued, "and this will be the self-
evident proof that you wish to curse him." Payne was, indeed, as impatient
with alternative priorities as Freeman, exclaiming at one point, "Don't tell us
that you have educated him as well as enriched him. For there is many an
educated fool. Give him *first of all*, that *knowledge* which will *qualify* him to
make a *right proper* and *beneficent* use of gold, or give him no gold at all"
(120). Frances Ellen Watkins, in her well-known essay "Our Greatest Want,"
somewhat later echoed Payne, arguing that "our greatest want is not gold or
silver, talent or genius, but true men and true women" (160). For Watkins, to
accept the belief that wealth was the primary source of power and public

status was to miss the point of the historical moment in which African Americans, and the nation generally, found themselves, for "leading ideas impress themselves upon communities and countries" (160), and the nation but needed a "Moses in freedom" who could guide the nation through to a new understanding of the character and responsibilities of liberty.

Underlying these differences of opinion concerning the relative value of wealth as a guiding goal was a common understanding that African American children faced a systemic challenge that required an approach to education capable of addressing something more than the acquisition of knowledge and vocational training—one that addressed, indeed, the systemic mechanisms of racial discrimination. What was needed, in short, was a pedagogy of liberation, and one that, like the periodical press itself, could speak *from* the experience of African Americans *to* the experience of African Americans. As Beman argued, "We need teachers for our youth who can, aside from their prescribed text-books, speak to them of their condition, and inspire them with noble ideas of self-respect, development, and enterprise" (339). This approach to education would involve discussions of "all the great questions of humanity, which now agitate the world," and would include "the science of political economy" so as to "show the people how to secure their highest welfare" (339–40). For Freeman, addressing "the educational wants of the free colored people," such an approach would be secure in its principles and revolutionary in its results. "Teach your child to look upon slavery and prejudice," Freeman argued, "in the light of reason and revolution, and you at once strip this boasted land and its landed institutions of its grandeur and its glory, and reveal at a glance its true character. Its flaunted freedom and equality, a stupid failure—its high sounding republicanism, a pitiful oligarchy of men-stealers and women-whippers, its religion a shameless inconsistency, and an arrant hypocrisy, lifting its hand red with a brother's blood to Heaven, and mouthing its impious prayers in the face of the great Jehovah, while it tramples on God's image, and traffics in the souls of men" (119). Exposing the American system for what it is, Freeman and others argued, would clear the ideological, discursive, and practical space for African American children to imagine a nation conceived but not yet born, and one in which "the colored race," as Beman had it, could realize its position as "an element of power in the earth, 'like a city set upon a hill.'" Educational reform would amount to a revision of history, replacing the nation's myths drawn from Puritan origins with the nation's reality as embodied in the African American community.

Then as now, though, to imagine such an approach to education was to rediscover that race was not biological but systemic, not a matter of individual attitudes but rather of historical practices that had been institutionalized in virtually every realm of society. To imagine such an approach to education, indeed, was to be reminded that educational ideals continually faced an entrance exam administered by market forces. It was, in short, to rediscover the significant difference between racism (examples of which can be isolated in space and time, individualized, *located*) and white supremacy—social, legal, economic, philosophical, and religious practices flexible enough to underwrite the antislavery movement as well as proslavery apologists, thriving on both the denunciation of racism and the perpetuation of social inequality. James McCune Smith, in his reflections on citizenship, spoke for both his own time and ours in commenting on the state of education:

> Young America, as instructed in the Ward Schools of the City of New York, and we fear throughout the land, is forced to *cram*, into the *dates* of every sanguinary conflict of the Revolution, the *numbers* slain, and the *event* of the battle; it is pitiful to hear school boys complain of their inability to remember these dates; thus filling the young mind with the *dates* instead of the *principles* of the Revolution, generally a hatred instead of a reverence for that great event. A School History, sound on the principles of liberty which lay at the root, and culminated in the result of the American Revolution, would be entirely too Anti-slavery to command *the market*. So the South not only buys our goods, but saps the principles of our youth, and gains command of the next generation. WILLIAM GOODELL owes it to the cause to write and print, a "Constitution of the United States with questions and answers for the use of schools." (146)[23]

One is reminded of the regular news features in our own time that sound alarms about the decaying state of education because students cannot identify a president or a Civil War general or recognize other facts dredged up from our nation's past. But one need not look far to see a systemic ignorance about "the *principles* of the Revolution" or to see the alliance of market forces and what we call the educational system. Such were the concerns of many nineteenth-century African Americans who could see all too well the ways in which their children were being prepared for their position in the American system. Central to the vision of history presented in the pages of the *Anglo-African Magazine*, accordingly, was a vision of education capable of liberating children from the dominant culture's educational priorities.[24]

Education, history, philosophy, and social science came together in the pages of the *Anglo-African Magazine* to both reflect and create community—reflect it in its present condition, and create it on the principles that would lead to its liberation from a system of oppression. What James McCune Smith wrote about the social changes occasioned by immigration can be applied to the magazine's mission itself—that "revolutions are not the noisy things historians describe them to be. In their beginning, progress and completion, there is a quiet, stealthy march and the final explosion is seldom more than the astonished exclamations, or the useless struggles of the old fogey institutions when they find they must ROTATE" (49–50). The *Anglo-African Magazine* worked to promote, facilitate, and prepare the people for that rotation. But if it was devoted to such revolutionary rotations, the magazine was devoted also to igniting and directing the final explosion. Representative of the editorial bent of the *Anglo-African Magazine* is J. Holland Townsend's argument in "The Policy That We Should Pursue," that "instead of fostering the false teachings that have led to such disastrous consequences, and made us the servile tools of the white man, by submitting to every indignity that he chooses to inflict upon us, we should adopt that noble sentiment, and inscribe it on our banners in characters of living light, 'better die than suffer our liberties to be taken away'" (325). Echoing Garnet here, though applying the admonishment to the free black population in the North, Townsend located his own sense of duty historically, arguing that "we should be admonished to act upon this important subject in view of the enlightened spirit of the age, and the grandeur of that revolution which at present is overturning the dynasties of oppression upon the continent of Europe" (325). As the historical moment became increasingly defined, so African American history came into focus, joining the responsibilities of education to the duties of theology. "In behalf of the genius of our youth," Townsend concluded, "and the sublimity lingering around the history of our forefathers, we should swear by the altars of our God, that our country shall be free" (325). History was coming to a point, and it was incumbent on the African American community to see the point and apply it in their lives.

This revolutionary vision is the core of the history presented in the pages of the *Anglo-African Magazine*, but what makes this publication such a masterful example of collective history is the inclusion of a series of fictional sketches by William J. Wilson (again writing under the pen name "Ethiop"), "The Afric-American Picture Gallery," which has been strangely neglected in American literary criticism. In the series, Ethiop takes his readers on a tour through an "almost unknown Gallery" of paintings, sketches, and statues relating to black history. The pictures are numbered and arranged appropriately. The picture titled "The Slave Ship," for example, is in the Gallery's south end, a portrait of Crispus Attucks is in the northeast end, two pictures representing the underground railroad are at either side of the Gallery, and an encounter with a slaveholder and a slave catcher "in search of runaways" is listed as "Two Portraits That Ought to Be Hung Up." The pictures cover a range of concerns from a sunset in Africa to a portrait of Toussaint L'Ouverture to a depiction of Mount Vernon. Indeed, if one wants a quick overview of the conventional features of African American history from the early slave trade to the brink of the Civil War, one could get more from these fictional sketches than from most of the textbooks used in K–12 schools. For each picture, our narrator provides a verbal depiction, on which effort he often comments—and, in the process, the narrator relates to his readers the most prominent and familiar features of African American history (for, despite the inclusion of Toussaint L'Ouverture, the sketches are devoted almost exclusively to African America). As Ethiop writes of the portrait of Toussaint L'Ouverture, "a picture of a great man with whose acts we are familiar, calls up the whole history of his times. Our minds thus become reimpressed with the events and we arrive at the philosophy of them" (87). Ethiop calls up the historical events for his readers and suggests the philosophy they embody, as if to follow James McCune's Smith's admonishment to teach the principles behind the facts.[25]

As might be expected, that philosophy offers extensive commentary on the character of white America. Included in the series is a trip to the Black Forest, first viewed through a portrait, after the narrator receives a letter from someone who has been following the sketches in the *Anglo-African Magazine*. Once in the Black Forest, Ethiop encounters the old man who summoned him, Bernice, an artist who has in his collection duplicates and originals of many of the artistic pieces in the Gallery itself. But this visit to the Black Forest is particularly interesting for two encounters that our narrator has there. The first is a discovery of "a *Tablet* of stone which mine host informed me was dug out of the mountain peak of the *Black Forest*," engraved on one side with words that were "curiously spelt by the aid of 41 singular, new and beautiful characters, or letters, each representing a distinct sound; and so many only are employed as are necessary to make up each word." This text bridging oral and print cultures requires careful decoding, which our narrator manages, and is revealed to be a historical document, listed from the year

"4,000," on "the Amecans, or milk white race." The text is a message left to future generations relating the history of the fall of a race that has since "disappeared from among the children of men" (176). Included in that message is the story of slavery—from the Middle Passage to the increasing reliance on slave labor and the abandonment of Christianity—leading eventually to a race of people who fell victim to the temptations of luxury and the subsequent failings of character that, as virtually every American publication of the time noted, were threats to a republic.[26] After reading this tablet, our narrator has his second significant encounter in the Black Forest—the discovery of a white man held in chains by Bernice. The man, we learn, is a former slaveholder who killed Bernice's son, and now is forced to pay for his crimes by living out his days in Bernice's cavern in the Black Forest, though Bernice will not harm him physically. When our narrator asks Bernice why he did not turn to the law, Bernice replies, "*Laws!!* what laws, what justice is there for the oppressed of our *class?*" (176). We are told, in fact, that the man appealed to Bernice "earnestly for his rights," and that Bernice told him, in turn, that he had no rights that Bernice was bound to respect.

In contrast to this vision of the future of white America (historical and eschatological) is a vision of black America, rendered in various ways but most notably through the commentary on the Gallery's tenth picture, titled simply "A New Picture," a picture of a boy. "This boy," the narrator explains, "*Thomas Onward* (I call him *Tom* for shortness,) though he has seen all of life—yea more, is not an *Old Tom* by any means; nor an *Uncle Tom*, nor a *Saintly Tom*, nor even what is commonly deemed a good Tom; but a shrewd little rogue, a real live *Young Tom*, up to all considerable mischief and equal to all emergencies" (100). I need not comment on the choice of names, but it is worth emphasizing that the narrator is presenting a figure that has not been represented, as if to direct us back to Thomas Hamilton's opening editorial for the *Anglo-African Magazine*, in which he argues that "the negro is something more than endurance; he is a force," a force that "can hardly be measured to-day"—for "the opinions regarding him are excessive; his foes estimate him too low—his friends, perhaps, too high: besides, there is not a-wanting among these latter, in spite of their own good feelings, that 'tribe idolatry' which regards him as 'not quite us'" (2). Ethiop says of Tom that "one would scarcely conclude that this boy has come down to us through nearly three hundred years of hard trial." "And yet," the narrator continues, "it is true. Such is his history. He was almost whipped into childhood, whipped up to boyhood. He has been whipped up to manhood, whipped down to old age, whipped out of existence. He was toiled into life; he has been toiled through life; toiled out of life. He has been robbed of his toil, robbed of his body, robbed of all but his soul" (100). Thus shaped, though, the boy, as revealed by the discerning eye of the portrait's artist and translated by Ethiop, maintains something that has not been touched. "The American Nation," Ethiop suggests, "if it can, may try its hardened hand yet a few centuries longer upon our live little Tom; but it will hardly mould him to their lik-ing" (101). The portrait of Tom stands as a portrait of the promise of Afri-can America, in sharp contrast to "the hard, grave, iron, half savage and half barbarous faces of Washington and Jefferson, of Clay, Webster and Cal-houn" (101).

Negotiating the historical process revealed by that contrast is the collective effort represented by the *Anglo-African Magazine* itself, for what is perhaps most notable about "The Afric-American Picture Gallery" is that it brings a self-reflexive principle to the history presented in the magazine's pages. The second picture is titled "The First and the Last Colored Editor" (placed at the north end of the Gallery). Ethiop's description reads, in part, as follows: "The Last Colored Editor, quite a young man, with a finely formed head and ample brow—thoughtful, earnest, resolute—sits in chair editorial, with the first number of the Freedom's Journal, the first journal ever edited by, and devoted to the cause of the colored man in America, held in one hand and outspread before him, while the other, as though expressive of his resolve, is firmly clenched." Surrounding the "Last Colored Editor" are "piles of all the journals edited by colored men from the commencement up till the present, among which the Freedom's Journal, Colored American, People's Press, North Star, and Frederick Douglass's paper are the more prominent" (53). The picture, clearly, is intended to define the historical moment of the *Anglo-African Magazine*, "linking together . . . our once scarcely hopeful past with the now bright present" (54). But the commentary continues later in Ethiop's sketches when a white gentleman appears at the Gallery and an-nounces, "I read your Picture Sketches in the last number of the Anglo-African Magazine and have sought out your Gallery" (89). But while he is a fan of the Picture Sketches, the white gentleman is hardly a fan of the magazine itself. Identifying himself as a friend to the African race, the gentleman tells Ethiop that the *Anglo-African Magazine* "is uncalled for" (89), and he sug-gests that if there are African American writers who "had capacity" then they "might write for our anti-slavery journals and other ably conducted magazines in the country, such as Harper's or the Atlantic Monthly. It would be more credible. You don't want a separate magazine and pen up your thoughts there" (89). The narrator responds that the *Anglo-African Magazine* "is simply headed by colored men, but excludes no man on account of his color from its pages, and it were unfortunate . . . that since colored men are the oppressed, it were unfortunate that every *anti-slavery* journal in the country is not edited by colored men" (89). In this exchange—which leaves the white gentleman, already "colored" by a previous remark of Ethiop's, now "colored more deeply than before" (89)—Ethiop accounts for the racial politics of the periodical press, relocates the claims for authority over those politics, and reminds his readers of the significance of the magazine they are reading. From its opening editorial to its concluding pages, the *Anglo-African Magazine* was hardly a transparent medium; and in these sketches Ethiop addresses the necessity of a practice of reading that is self-conscious in its cultural groundings.

The importance of that self-consciousness is underscored as Ethiop includes in his tour of the Gallery a variety of visitors. Early in the sketches, we are introduced to "a colored lady" who is critical of the artistic merit of the artifacts in the Gallery. Our narrator, in the early days of what has turned into a long struggle over the understanding of aesthetics that rules those academic departments in which the teaching of African American expressive culture is often tenuously housed, delivers what has often been the standard defense of African American art. He tells his visiting critic that "these pictures, as a whole, make no claim to the high artistic merit you look for in them, though I think some of them rather clever as works of *art*; but they serve as simple reminders of what the people of color were, now are, and will yet be. What they have gone through, are going through, and have yet to go through" (89). But Ethiop does not give up the fight entirely, for as the sketches continue it becomes clear that the representation of history through these artistic productions is an accomplishment of considerable artistry and craft, and that the sketches gesture toward an understanding of aesthetics capable of accounting for the dynamic relations among artistry, history, and community. As the sketches develop, in short, they seem both testaments to and examples of an aesthetics of liberation.

Central to the aesthetic principle underlying the "Afric-American Picture Gallery"—which is, itself, a serialized, dynamic artistic performance that comments on its own creation as it proceeds—is careful attention to and commentary on the community it is designed to serve. The Gallery is visited at one point by a group including individuals both black and white, male and female, representing a number of social positions from the clergy to the medical professions to various forms of social service; some are identified as being of "respectable" social standing. As the visitors tour the Gallery, they are drawn into the history behind the art, and the conditions resulting from that history, and they engage in often lively discussions about what should be done to remedy those conditions. Through these conversations, Ethiop presents a wide range of opinions on education, politics, antislavery and uplift organizations, and theology. At one point, for example, the "Doctor" in the group is asked his opinion about a picture titled "Condition," a depiction of "a *colored youth*" clearly struggling with poverty. The Doctor responds, "You may improve the condition, if you change the nature" (244). "An opinion," our narrator continues, "from so high an authority, and so deliberately given, was not without its weight; and the 'Skeptic' shook his head doubtingly; while the 'Philosopher' with thumb and finger, and outstretched hand, launched out on hair-splitting subtleties, to prove the amount of labor necessary to make even the 'Doctor's' proposition good. He also entered upon a learned dissertation, upon the nature of the world in general, and our *poor little 'Condition' in particular*; and wound up by saying that 'whatever is, is right.'" This discussion, along with others included in the sketches, extends the reach of Ethiop's satirical eye to the community of his readers, and even to the pages of the *Anglo-African Magazine* itself.

Ethiop's representation of such conversations serves as a reminder that debates over the proper course of reform—and employment in the cause of reform—can become self-serving and self-perpetuating endeavors, and the "Picture Gallery" sketches press increasingly toward the need for action while also suggesting the role of art in that revolutionary responsibility. In a set of pictures titled "Preaching" and "After Preaching," Ethiop addresses the use of religion as a form of social control in the "sunny South," "among the best of the good old plantations" (216). The second of the pictures represents the congregation's "faithful leaders, who, being men carefully selected by the white piety of the sunny South, are of course, all of the Uncle Tom school" (217). However, "in the back-ground," Ethiop notes, "may also be seen a few young, determined-looking faces, on which are expressed disbelief in, and detestation of, the whole affair" (217). "These faces," Ethiop continues, "in contrast with the others of the congregation, give a most striking effect to the picture. They are the unruly, the skeptical, the worthless of the block—the wicked ones, who would rather run the risk than be bound up in the religious love so feelingly and so faithfully proclaimed to them—the religious love of the land" (217). By this point in the sketches, though, and in the *Anglo-*

African Magazine generally, one wants to know the terms of this description—that is, wicked by whose standards? Ethiop continues: "It is of this class comes our Nat Turners, who laid a scheme for redemption, and the *man* in Georgia who received nine hundred and ninety-nine lashes by way of gentle 'compulsion,' and then would not so much as reveal one particle of the *plan* laid by and for the uprising of his oppressed brethren" (217). From this class, we are told, come the Margaret Garners, the Douglasses, and the Browns. The portrait of piety and of religious contentment and peace gives way, through Ethiop's description, to a portrait that "may be studied with profit by any Southern Preacher, master or monster who will take the trouble to visit the Afric-American Picture Gallery" (217). African American history offers its own lessons for those who will trouble themselves to study it.

But the dynamics of artistic representation become an essential element in the representation of that history, if only because the culture in which that representation must function is so endlessly capable of controlling the terms of understanding, and even the language itself, so as to turn the lessons of history into yet another feature in the culture of control. It is appropriate, then, that the last of the episodes of the "Afric-American Picture Gallery" presented in the first volume of the *Anglo-African Magazine* features another visitor to the Gallery, a fugitive from slavery, whose story Ethiop relates. The story is detailed, and at one point refers the reader to the newspapers of various towns in Maine for verification, much as Harriet Jacobs refers the reader to the records of New York City for her manumission papers.[27] Bill, the fugitive, had once escaped from slavery but was betrayed by a white northerner. "Alas, poor fellow!" our narrator exclaims; "little did he think that a betrayer almost invariably lurks under a white skin; and that the same who seemed more civil than the ferocious Southerner, would be the one to send him back to his chains and to the prison-house of bondage for a little more than a mess of pottage" (322). Bill seems to learn his lesson, though, returning to slavery as if happy for the chance to escape the burdens of life in the North. Back in the South, Bill becomes, for the slaveholders, a model spokesman for the virtues of slavery and, for the slaves, a model informant and guide—as becomes clear when a number of slaves escape the following summer. This piece reminds readers of the important heritage of African American tricksterism, and of the ways in which one's position in U.S. culture is never independent, never secure. The artistry of "The Afric-American Picture Gallery" is, I would suggest, a vital element in the representation, understanding, and negotiation of African American history—reminding us that this is not a singular story but a gallery of many stories, connected by a complex narrative of experience and by significant silences that push against and through that collective experience. The dynamic and flexible perspectives available through fiction, as Toni Morrison would later realize so brilliantly, are vital to the representation and understanding of the African American past.

It seems appropriate, then, that the first volume of the *Anglo-African Magazine* leads to and concludes with texts not authored for the magazine— texts that require interpretation, that are both readings and writings of the dominant culture, and that suggest the inevitability of revolutionary action. A two-part piece titled "The Outbreak in Virginia" is about John Brown's actions at Harpers Ferry. The piece, the editor notes, is a collection of articles "from the daily papers, for future reference" and is presented as "an account of this unhappy event, which, though deeply deplored by many friends of freedom, only foreshadows the beginning of a state of affairs that will yet make Old Virginia regret her apostasy to the liberty-loving, tyranny-hating principles of her Washington, her Jefferson, and her Patrick Henry." "That we may not be charged with impartiality in making up the history," the editor comments, "we collate from Southern papers and papers of the North upholding the damnable institution" (347). The other piece is a reprinting of Nat Turner's *Confessions*, which is presented, the accompanying editorial comment explains, for "two reasons": "First, to place upon record this most remarkable episode in the history of human slavery, which proves to the philosophic observer, that in the midst of the most perfectly contrived and apparently secure systems of slavery, humanity will out, and engender from its bosom, forces, that will contend against oppression, however unsuccessfully; and secondly, that the two methods of Nat Turner and of John Brown may be compared. The one is the mode in which the slave seeks for freedom for his fellows, and the other, the mode in which the white man seeks to set the slave free" (386). Following through on this comparison, the editor argues that "had the order of events been reversed—had Nat Turner been in John Brown's place, at the head of these twenty one men, governed by his inexorable logic and cool daring, the soil of Virginia and Maryland and the far South, would by this time be drenched in blood, and the wild and sanguinary course of these men, no earthly power then could stay" (386). Noting that the South's present course "will engender in its bosom and nurse into maturity a hundred Nat Turners," the editor brings the comparison to a point: "These two narratives present a fearful choice to the slaveholders, nay, to this great nation—which of the two modes of emancipation shall take place?" (386). Leaving its readers to reflect on this question, the first volume of the *Anglo-African Magazine* concludes with a short article titled "The Execution of John Brown."

What is particularly interesting here, of course, is that the *Anglo-African Magazine* asks a question that was unlikely to find its identified audience—those to whom this choice is primarily directed—among the magazine's readers. Few slaveholders would have, I trust, paused over these articles. Of course, the magazine wanted its white northern readers to ponder the question, and leaves them, at the end, with a white martyr to the cause. But I would suggest that the question is directed toward a black northern audience just as Garnet's address to the slaves was directed as much to African American leaders in the North as it was to slaves in the South. In addressing white Americans, the *Anglo-African Magazine* addresses an ideological fixture in American culture on which African American identity was locked in a mutually contingent relation. African American history must, of necessity, account for that contingency—including the ways in which African American historical texts can be transformed by white readers into documentaries of exotic suffering, occasions for benevolent self-affirmation. The representation of history required a careful accounting for and negotiation with the same cultural forces that have influenced and continue to influence the course of African American experience. This history must be, accordingly, a reading as well as a writing—a series of texts like those presented in the closing pages of the *Anglo-African Magazine* that are important in the information they present but important also in their implicit commentary on the source of that history, the white newspapers and narrators who assume control over the concerns central to the collective African American experience. To read the account of John Brown presented in this magazine, or to reread Nat Turner's *Confessions* in this context, is to be aware of the challenge of representation and to reread the productions of a white supremacist culture so as to turn them to the needs of the African American historical community and, through that community, to the revitalization of American culture—its ideals, its institutions, and its language.

William Wells Brown and
the Performance of History

I began chapter 1 with a discussion of William Wells Brown, and it seems only fitting to end this study by returning to Brown's work. Indeed, those familiar with African American literature published before the Civil War might think that the historical work of William Wells Brown has been conspicuously missing from this study, though I have referred to his work frequently along the way. He is an obvious candidate for extensive commentary in a book like this, and those who do write or comment on the tradition of African American historical scholarship generally mention Brown along with George Washington Williams and William C. Nell as the pioneers in the field. Moreover, the concerns I have focused on in this study—among others, fragmented and strategically juxtaposed narratives, appropriations of white nationalist and philosophical discourse, and a studied reorientation of biblical hermeneutics in accordance with the terms and condition of oppressed communities—are all concerns central to Brown's greatest achievement, *Clotel; or, The President's Daughter: A Narrative of Slave Life in the United States* (1853). One might well expect Brown to be a more prominent figure in this book, but I have limited myself to a field of concerns that kept me from a sustained discussion of Brown's work. I have not included *Clotel*, for example, because of my decision to focus primarily on nonfictional narratives, and I have not included Brown's major histories because they were published following the start of the Civil War, after the period I have been concerned with in this study. Still, there is reason to return to Brown here at the end of this book.

Originally, I had planned to discuss African American historical writing throughout the nineteenth century, but I have focused, in the end, on African American writing before the Civil War because I see the war as both marking and inspiring a turning point—a not entirely positive one—in African American historical writing. African American historical scholarship changed significantly after the Civil War; indeed, much of the work published from the end of the Civil War into the beginnings of the twentieth century is more recognizable as historical scholarship. George Washington Williams (sometimes called "the black Bancroft") is considered the great historian of this period, and he is at times the only earlier historian mentioned in studies that move quickly to W. E. B. Du Bois and the beginnings of African American historical scholarship. Williams's majestic *History of the Negro Race in America from 1619 to 1880* is impressive in its documentation of the African American past, and Williams understood the need to establish his credentials as an authoritative historian, noting that "while men with the reputation of Bancroft and Hildreth could pass unchallenged when disregarding largely the use of documents and the citation of authorities, I would find myself challenged by a large number of critics" (1:vii). Other African American historians, also attending to the cultural politics of disciplinary credentials, emphasized as well another realm of authority. Many of the histories written during the years following the Civil War, that is, focus on what might be called the institutional presence of African Americans in the nineteenth century. Toward the end of the century, African Americans wrote histories of religious denominations, individual churches, the Underground Railroad, black military units, and other significant institutions and events that marked the achievements of African American collective self-determination.[1] These histories, in both method and subject matter, implicitly argue that a crossroads had been reached in the Civil War, and a great transformation accomplished. African American experience and concerns had come to the center of the U.S. public historical stage; secular history had been forced to confront the imperatives of sacred history; and the African American historical presence had been accordingly transformed.

There were, of course, many transformations to follow as white Americans adopted, in effect, new skin for old ceremonies, reinstituting the system of racial control under different names and methods; and William Wells Brown, one of the best of scholars educated in the school of slavery and white supremacist culture, most certainly understood the need to be shifty in the "new" postwar country. I'd like to present Brown, then, as a transitional historian, working to bring African American identity and experience into the theater of authoritative history but still very much a practitioner of the poetics of the discourse of distrust. Brown, like Nell before him and Williams after him, worked to gather the materials that would demonstrate African American achievement, promote African American collective self-definition, and establish people of African origins as historical agents throughout history and in the United States. But like Nell and others before him and somewhat unlike Williams after, Brown adopted a narrative method that both responded to and challenged the epistemological assumptions of the white supremacist culture that contained and defined African American identity and experience. After the Civil War, most African American historians proceeded as if confident of the possibilities of representation; before the Civil War, questions about the possibility of representation collectively constituted the dominant shaping principle of African American historical writing. As I noted in chapter 1, Brown once asserted that "Slavery has never been represented" and that "Slavery never can be represented" (*Lecture* 4); Brown followed through on this by recognizing that if slavery could not be represented, neither could what was called "freedom" for African Americans, and that African American history more broadly presented formidable challenges to the historian's method and art.

Those familiar with Brown's work might wonder *how* to understand Brown as a historian—and, certainly, how far to trust Brown's representation of history. Brown's contemporaries sometimes had the same problem. Consider, for example, Charlotte Forten Grimké, the nineteenth-century African American essayist and educator, who often had an opportunity to socialize with Brown. Reflecting back on one such evening, Grimké wrote in her journal, "He tells such ridiculous stories, that although I believe as little as I please—I can't help being amused" (330). This seems to me a fairly apt description not only of Brown but of his many publications. Born in Kentucky, probably in 1814, Brown was best known as a former slave who lent a powerful voice to the antislavery movement.[2] Over the course of his career, Brown published more than a dozen books—including poetry, fiction, memoirs, travel narratives, and historical studies—beyond the nine editions of his 1847 *Narrative* that had established his reputation. Still, those who have read all or even some of

Brown's work might well come back to Grimké's comment, for, strangely, Brown uses the same material again and again. Stories from his autobiographies turn up in his fiction; stories in the autobiographies themselves change; novels are reshaped; episodes from his autobiographies become episodes in his plays, where Brown plays a minstrel version of himself, with the name changed; stories from his fiction turn up again in his histories; and material from earlier historical works reappears in later historical works, in different contexts, serving different historical purposes. Ridiculous stories, indeed; and someone like myself, an earnest student of the past, often cannot know what to believe and what to take as amusement.

But this, it seems to me, is Brown's point—for Brown was a trickster narrator from the very beginning of his writing career, and a master at making ridiculous stories impart a kind of discomforting truth. For Brown, it seems to me, literary genres were less conventions to be followed or even reshaped than they were codes of cultural authority and modes of performance. It seems to me entirely appropriate, for example, that Brown's work has been associated with recent performance art, as in Harry J. Elam Jr.'s consideration of Brown's only published play, *The Escape; or, A Leap for Freedom*.[3] Brown's plays were written for performance on the antislavery lecture circuit, where he challenged his audiences' expectations concerning what a black antislavery lecturer might present.[4] In his travel narratives, as I have argued elsewhere, Brown transforms himself into a "fugitive tourist," presenting a strategic cultural critique and challenging readers' assumptions while seeming to imitate the behavior and attitudes of a conventional type of cultured American tourist in Europe.[5] In all his work, Brown worked both with and against expectations and conventions. As Robert S. Levine has justly written, "A deadly serious moralist, Brown was also something of a confidence man and trickster whose views on such explosive subjects as race and gender can be difficult to pin down. An artist who challenges the culture's 'official' stories, Brown can seem to be suspicious of any kind of coherent or definitive narrative" (Introduction 4).

What I wish to present here is a somewhat sketchy overview of Brown's textual performance as historical confidence man, hopefully without losing sight of the William Wells Brown who was, in fact, "a deadly serious moralist." Brown's three major historical works are *The Black Man, His Antecedents, His Genius, and His Achievements* (1863), *The Negro in the American Rebellion: His Heroism and His Fidelity* (1867), and *The Rising Son; or, The Antecedents and Advancement of the Colored Race* (1873). Each is, to some extent, a regrouping, reinvention, and recontextualization of the material from the preceding work; and what is new in each work is shaped, in turn, by the recycled material. *The Black Man* includes an opening autobiographical "Memoir of the Author," followed by a historical essay, "The Black Man and His Antecedents," which is followed by what is commonly termed a collective biography—a series of fifty-three (in a later edition, fifty-seven) individual biographical sketches. *The Negro in the American Rebellion* was the first treatment of black Americans in the Civil War, though it begins by looking back to African Americans in the Revolutionary War and the War of 1812, and ends (or nearly so, anyway) with a meditation on class and race in the postwar United States. *The Rising Son*, in many ways the most ambitious of the three works, begins with a "Memoir of the Author," followed by various chapters that, among other things, trace the history of the African diaspora in the New World back to Egypt and into the post–Civil War United States—and concluding with a collective biography under the general chapter heading "Representative Men and Women," in which the sketches presented in *The Black Man* are considerably expanded and revised.

In all of these works, Brown had designs on the present that he approached by challenging the codes and modes, the ideological design, of the American past, and thereby of historical understanding itself. Historical theory and visions of historical progress were linked inexorably in Brown's time to racialist assumptions and devoted to visions of Anglo-Saxon superiority and, increasingly, to a more general but aggressive program of white supremacy.[6] One could not write a history without somehow becoming entangled in this web of racialist ideology; one could not construct a narrative of black progress without becoming implicated in the narrative of white progress, a narrative that shaped not only conceptions of social order and purpose but also the very documents the black historian would need to construct a history.

In his creation and revision of history in these texts, accordingly, Brown attempts to create a vision of history capable of defining the contours of an African American community and a field of experience that is at once transhistorical and antihistorical. His histories are *transhistorical* in that they address a field of experience unacknowledged by historical understanding—a community that, by the logic of racialist understanding, should not exist as it does. And in this way his histories are *antihistorical*, challenging the terms of historical understanding, gesturing to a history unaccountable in the ruling narratives of progress, a field of experience unknown, waiting outside the realm of the ruling evidentiary discourse, beyond the purview of authorized epistemological methods and assumptions.

Without a shared understanding of history there can be no community—and so it is hardly surprising that Brown published his first extended work of history, *The Black Man*, in 1863, at a time when the emancipation of the enslaved was a subject of considerable debate, and at a time generally in which the capacity of black Americans as a national presence and as an intellectual force was being questioned with renewed vigor. In his opening essay, "The Black Man and His Antecedents," Brown challenges the narrative of white racial superiority by way of an Afrocentric interpretation of history, an interpretation supported by strategic readings of, among others, Macaulay, Hume, and even Caesar. Brown then applies the same evidentiary strategy to his own time, quoting unsympathetic white northerners and southerners out of their contexts and into his to show not only that African Americans have proven their ability and potential but also that white Americans are very much aware of that potential. And this is the point of the collective biography that follows, a series of success stories, from every field of human endeavor—representative embodiments of republican citizenry. There is no clear organizational structure to the biographical sketches, and no clear standard of length, as if the lives still await an organizing cultural framework.

But as he presents this biographical evidence of the achievements of the black race, Brown also plays with the evidence—though in ways that many of his readers might well not notice. Included in the biographies, for example, are sketches of Joseph Jenkins—which Brown's biographer locates "in the shadowland between the real and the imaginary"—and a sketch titled "A Man without a Name." Brown's sketch of Jenkins is a portrait of a native African in England, a man of many professions, and a man who occupies many of the cultural roles expected of a black man in white culture, assuming authority over each role but contained by none. Jenkins, indeed, is a type of Brown's own performative approach to his public life, and Brown's description of Jenkins constitutes an ideological portrait of Brown within the constellation of black male leadership of the time, providing him with a veiled way of distinguishing himself from Frederick Douglass, Samuel Ringgold Ward, Henry Highland Garnet, Martin Robison Delany, and Charles Lenox Remond.[7]

Brown's "A Man without a Name" is worth noting as well, if only because this sketch of the nameless man is a fictionalized account of Brown's own life. The story is a version of Brown's own escape from slavery, though now pre-

sented to one Colonel Rice and set in December 1852. The title of the story
and its dramatic conclusion come from the story Brown had told before about
being forced to change his name when the slaveholder's nephew, also named
William, arrives on the scene. In his 1847 *Narrative*, Brown tells this story
with some emphasis, and one would imagine that any reader of *The Black
Man* at all familiar with Brown's *Narrative* would recognize it.

This story is expanded in *The Negro in the American Rebellion*, this time
completing the fictional revision of Brown's life by having the character in the
story take on the name of his white benefactor, as Brown himself reports in
his *Narrative* to have taken on the name of the Quaker Wells Brown, who
helped Brown in his escape to the North. But the name here is not Wells
Brown, and the story is not presented, and could not be, as Brown's own;
rather, we are again engaged with a fugitive slave William who encounters the
white Colonel Rice, who is this time accompanied by one Squire Loomis.
When these fictional stand-ins for history encounter what was in *The Black
Man* the end of the story—that is, the moment when the fugitive announces,
"So, sir, for once, you have a man standing before you without a name"—this
time one of them replies, blurting to the nameless fugitive, "I will name you
George Loomis," a name the fugitive happily accepts.

Not only do these stories violate the historical integrity of the text, but they
also violate the integrity of Brown's original story, the one he told about
himself in his 1847 *Narrative*. For at that time, he had placed great value on
maintaining his original first name, William, and had only accepted the addition of Wells Brown. The William in *The Negro in the American Rebellion*
changes from William to George without hesitation, and then this fictional
version of Brown goes on to rediscover his long-lost mother, something Brown
himself never did.

If readers of my summary are confused by now, they have reason to be, for
Brown's intertwined and transformed stories force one to locate all of Brown's
work where Brown's biographer locates the other biographical sketch I mentioned, the one on Joseph Jenkins—namely, "in the shadowland between the
real and the imaginary." And we travel deeper into that shadowland when we
notice, for example, a bit of historical reporting in chapter 35 of *The Negro in
the American Rebellion* adapted from Brown's 1853 fictional narrative *Clotel*.
And one can hardly fail to notice that the same chapter, titled "Wit and
Humor of the War," reads like blackface minstrelsy, with the performance
now significantly recontextualized, played out on a stage in which some of the
black performers carry guns and wear the uniforms of military authority.

The Negro in the American Rebellion, which ultimately is concerned less with the Civil War itself than with the racial politics of its aftermath, is in fact directed toward the shadowland between the real and the imaginary—not the shadowland of Brown's creative genius but rather the more ominous shadowland of U.S. history and culture—and in this way it anticipates Brown's major historical achievement, a book that combines and recontextualizes material from the previous two historical works, *The Rising Son; or, The Antecedents and Advancement of the Colored Race*. Brown published this ambitious work in 1873, during Reconstruction, the hope and almost inevitable failure of which Brown had outlined in the closing chapters of *The Negro in the American Rebellion*. As in that earlier text, *The Rising Son* builds up to a chapter on caste, though now four-fifths of the text is devoted to just that subject, the closing fifth being a collection of biographical sketches—reprinted, revised, and expanded from *The Black Man*—that again serve as testimony to the success of black individuals and, implicitly, to the failure of the larger collective biography, that of the nation itself.

In *The Rising Son* the chapter titled "Caste" from the earlier text is now called "Caste and Progress," thus joining the problem with its source, the racialist ideology fundamental to the national narratives of progress. Although the two chapters on caste begin in the same way, and although both explore the cultural politics of race and prejudice, they are significantly different in many respects. Particularly significant is how they end. In the 1867 volume, the chapter concludes with the story of a "prominent member" of "a fashionable church" who is outraged when a merchant brings a black man to sit with him in his pew. He insists that the black man be expelled immediately until he discovers that the black man is a businessman worth five million dollars, at which point he asks to be introduced. In the 1873 volume, the chapter called "Caste and Progress" ends not with the economics of race relations but rather with the politics of racial advancement, represented by a list of various black men either elected or appointed to political offices. And, significantly, this chapter is followed by an anachronistic chapter on the abolitionists that focuses on antebellum white politicians and public figures who risked their positions and their economic security by working for the antislavery cause.

Of the two conclusions to Brown's meditations on race, the "five million dollar" tale is the better story, and might well seem the more convincing response to U.S. racialist ideology. But although Brown offers a less dramatic and more tenuously hopeful story in *The Rising Son*, he also looks for a more substantial rewriting of the national narrative of progress, as if to gesture

toward a more conventional mode of historical understanding than that presented in his previous works. The national narrative of progress need not be
abandoned, he seems to say, only revised and enlarged.

Of course, Brown was no fool; if he worked toward a vision of history
capable of entering into the national narrative, he also kept his distance from
that field. In *The Rising Son*, the last sentence we encounter before we begin
the long section called "Representative Men and Women" states simply, "God
helps those who help themselves" (417). Brown follows his advice carefully,
helping himself by constructing a narrative of history that allows him to
remain, to borrow a phrase from Whitman, "both in and out of the game." In
The Negro in the American Rebellion we discover Brown as trickster narrator
indirectly in those chapters in which he offers us either thinly veiled minstrelsy or fictionalized autobiography presented as historical reporting; in *The
Black Man* and *The Rising Son* we encounter the trickster narrator more directly, in the memoirs that open the two books. The autobiographical memoir
at the beginning of *The Black Man*, aside from offering significant revisions of
Brown's life story (for example, the revelation that he is related to Daniel
Boone), and aside from adapting portions of Brown's 1858 drama *The Escape*
under the guise of autobiography, also ends rather strangely with what seems
a somewhat incidental story of unfair treatment—an episode that originally
appeared in Brown's travel narrative *Three Years in Europe* in which Brown,
staying at a hotel during his tour of Great Britain, is given wet sheets for his
bed. By Brown's accounting, this seems less a story of racial prejudice than of
poor hotel service—a problem he solves by throwing the wet sheets out the
window. When he is told that he will have to pay for the sheets, he agrees, and
promises to publish the bill in the newspaper—upon which promise he is, of
course, given dry sheets and good service. Similarly, *The Rising Son* opens
with a memoir, purportedly by Alonzo D. Moore of Ohio, which focuses on
incidents both grand and, well, *incidental*. We have again the story of the wet
sheets. We have also a story—not so incidental, though Brown nearly makes
its seem so—about Brown's encounter with the Ku Klux Klan. Brown escapes
by appearing to save the life of one of the Klan; fortunately, the sometimes Dr.
Brown had with him a syringe and a supply of "a solution of the acetate of
morphia," which he injected into the ailing man while pretending to perform
a kind of conjuring ritual. But this memoir ends with a story of Brown on the
antislavery lecture circuit. In the story, the hostile audience has prepared to
drop a bag of flour on Brown's head, as if to transform his lecture into a kind
of whiteface performance; but one of the conspirators is so moved by Brown's

speech that he tells Brown of his plan. Brown then positions himself, cries out the given signal, "Let it slide," and watches the flour drop on the conspirators.

In these stories, we see the one consistent version of Brown that appears in every book that he wrote—the trickster who knows something about turning the tables on an apparently hostile audience. In *The Rising Son*, the trickster is there to respond to economic injustice, to violent threats, to racial markings. The trickster works by publishing the evidence of wrongs, evidence written in the offender's own hand; he works by injecting the enemy with the drug of his own stereotypes; and he works by positioning himself and letting it slide, whatever "it" might be. The memoirs do indeed introduce these histories, and they present what is, finally, the best portrait of Brown the historian. Working against historical understanding, playing with evidentiary conventions, telling stories that serve as conceptual loopholes in the larger narrative of his historical argument, Brown performs his role as a historian not by writing a stable history but rather by disrupting the national narrative, undermining the white nationalist fantasy, and gesturing toward a history still unknown and, by all cultural standards, still unknowable. In his histories, I am suggesting, Brown attempted not to write history but rather to make history possible—helping those, both white and black, who had not yet learned to help themselves.

African American writers from the late eighteenth century to the Civil War similarly worked to create possibilities, to create openings for new national and global historical narratives. At times, these openings involved innocent or hopeful visions of a brighter day coming in the secular world; more often, these writers worked with a past and present that could be neither comprehended nor represented, and the future promised by these historical visions was a future of continuing cultural negotiation and struggle. One might say that the great majority of African American historical writers recognized the validity of a point that Foucault would articulate more than a century later, that "to imagine another system is to extend our participation in the present system" ("Intellectuals and Power" 230). Certainly, these writers understood that power could not be located in "a unique source of sovereignty," and that power was instead "the moving substrate of force relations which, by virtue of their inequality, constantly engender states of power," states that "are always local and unstable." They recognized, that is, "the omnipresence of power," an omnipresence that exists "not because it has the privilege of consolidating everything under its invincible unity, but because it is produced from one moment to the next, at every point" (Foucault, *History of Sexuality* 93). Racial concepts and practices (in their various economic, political, and legal guises) were among the most prominent and fundamental of the "force relations" that defined what these writers worked to identify as African American experience. In writing as raced historians addressing a racially marked field of experience, these writers devoted themselves to strategic interventions into dynamic (re)productions of power. As African American history was effectively created by white supremacist ideology and practice, the strategic representation of African American history became the means for breaking into the mechanisms of power.

This was, of necessity, a dynamic approach to historical understanding and representation, one that involved shifting the terms of its defining conditions, its focus, and its mythical foundations to address the always shifting, shifty, and unstable "force relations" that constituted the reality of race—the cultural constructs as realized in the lived experience—in the United States. African American historical thought, almost by definition, could not operate on some imagined objective and abstract plane of research and representation; it necessarily involved a constant reworking of modes of discourse and required historical writers to play the contingencies of institutional and narrative order, for those contingencies constituted what was African American about history. African American historical writers, to be sure, both imagined and promoted what might be termed a textual nation—a performative synthesis of the elements of black experience—but that synthesis was always unstable, always threatened by textual control through the very "force relations" that defined its possibilities and constituted its challenges.

African American historical writing, that is, operated in the theater of print discourse identified by Absalom Jones and Richard Allen's *A Narrative of the Proceedings of the Black People, during the Late Awful Calamity in Philadelphia, in the Year 1793*, in which the authors note that they are responding to an error in a text by Mathew Carey that has already gone through three editions. Their corrective narrative is, in effect, appended to a text that already has a life of its own. As with African American additions to the traditional literary canon, we are left with a cultural process of supplements, an expanded anthology of notice but not a history, literary or otherwise, that is fundamentally reconceived. Similarly, African Americans wrote in a culture willing, at best, to accept narrative supplements. The white national narrative operated along the lines of its prototypical representative life, Benjamin Franklin's story of his rise to prominence. In his self-biography, Franklin acknowledged that which would threaten to expose the incoherence of the official narrative of his life by presenting certain aspects of his character as *errata*. Beyond the supplemental notices of error—indeed, *because* some aspects of his character are restricted to episodes that can be ascribed to errors of judgment—Franklin's narrative (along with the character the narrative represents) is allowed to maintain its veil of coherence. The editor speaks for the author; the author crafts the narrator; the narrator performs the role of the autobiographical subject—and to notice these layers of the controlled performance of public self-presentation is simply to remind oneself that, whatever might have happened, history belongs to those who control the text and manipulate its instabilities.

Liberation historiography, like liberation theology, begins by recognizing that historiography, like theology, is always culturally situated, always implicated in complexly intertwined systems of power. It does not promise liberation from those systems of power to some imagined outside, some fundamentally new order, for there is no outside. Rather, liberation historiography envisions liberation as a manipulation of the instabilities of power in the service of empowering reinterpretations of the authoritative, and the authorizing, text of "history" (that presence so often evoked in the abstract). Standards of research and of evidence are not relaxed by this process; rather, this process begins by recognizing that such standards have always been relaxed, most often in the form of selective focus in ruling assumptions about what should constitute the subject worthy of research and what stories stand in need of additional study or revision. Liberation historiography looks to the condition of oppression to determine the need and goals for historical research. In the community defined by the experience of overwhelming inequalities of power, one is forced to acknowledge that things are not what some people say they are, that the nation's official narrative of community is incapable of explaining, accounting for, or even acknowledging its subject.

African American writers before the Civil War recognized that the clear incoherence and sheer chaos of African American experience exposed the instabilities of the white nationalist "text" of history, indicating a history uncontained and unaccountable by the existing narratives. The liberation suggested by their approach to history was not conclusion but rather process, a dynamic reconstitution of the terms of social process and governance. The collective historical representation they constructed mirrored their primary guiding text, the Bible, itself a fragmented narrative in which the fragments speak of identifiable historical individuals, communities, and episodes, each fragment both appealing to and claiming the authority of a realm of order beyond the representative powers of any single human author or any single historical subject. African American writers pieced together their own fragmented narratives, addressing a world of experience best viewed through the cracks and gaps between secular and sacred history. To be sure, these writers recognized the discourse of religion to be a discourse of mystification—one capable, for example, of serving the needs of the system of slavery. But they recognized it also to be a discourse of mystery, one capable of serving the needs of historical representation while also addressing realms of experience beyond the possibility of representation. They apprehended their subject most powerfully when they found ways to foreground the fragmentation of the story they were trying to tell, and thereby to represent multiple perspectives representing multiple subjects. As the multiple authors of the Bible speak for and speak of an authorship unknown and unknowable, so African American historical writing before the Civil War addresses, in its very fragmentation, the limits of historical understanding and the presence of a realm of existence uncontainable by the systems of order we construct. These writers worked to apprehend visions of that brighter coming day not to counsel patience but rather to provoke righteous action, a sense of that moral responsibility that follows the recognition of clear moral violations and disorder. In their texts, African American identity emerges not simply as the product of history or the subset of a national community but rather as a response to the challenge of history, something one does as well as someone one is. A terrible beauty is born in the pages they wrote, a vision not of a world to be realized but of a process to be continued.

notes

Introduction

1. From William Wells Brown's *The Black Man: His Antecedents, His Genius, and His Achievements* to such recent works as Kareem Abdul-Jabbar's *Black Profiles in Courage: A Legacy of African American Achievement*, collective biographies have been a staple of African American publishing—though the popularity of the genre is by no means limited to African American readers. For a good overview of this genre, see Elizabeth Grammer.

The most prominent arguments over the record, of course, concern Afrocentrism—as in Wilson Jeremiah Moses's *Afrotopia: The Roots of African American Popular History*, Stephen Howe's *Afrocentrism: Mythical Pasts and Imagined Homes*, and Clarence E. Walker's *We Can't Go Home Again: An Argument about Afrocentrism*. In my discussion of Moses's book, I focus on attacks on Afrocentrism, but in doing so I am not presenting a defense of either specific Afrocentric scholars (against, for example, Howe's critique of one scholar's "shoddy ideas") nor a defense of Afrocentrism as a scholarly perspective and methodology, for such a defense is not the purpose of this book. I am, however, interested in historical writing as the reflection, definition, and embodiment of lived perspectives—and I believe that academically "respectable" historical writing generally veils its own messy and contingent relation to the lived perspectives shaped by the "Racial Contract" that Charles W. Mills has identified as the guiding framework of white Western thought. Accordingly, I'm interested here in the ways in which attacks on the scholarship associated with Afrocentrism constitute dismissals of a much wider range of concerns. Howe, for example, begins *Afrocentrism* by quoting African American pianist and composer Anthony Davis's complaint that "if somebody uses tradition as a way of limiting your choices, in a way that's as racist as saying you have to sit at the back of the bus" (qtd. in Howe 1). Davis acquires unusual authority here as a historical theorist, for Howe suggests that "his complaint applies powerfully to important modern currents in Afro-American thought. For a mystical, essentialist, irrationalist and often, in the end, racist set of doctrines has arisen, out of the cultural nationalist milieu, to occupy centre ground of media attention in relation to black American thinking. The self-ascribed or preferred label for these doctrines is Afrocentricity, or Afrocentrism" (Howe 1). Aside from being a very poor opening definition of Afrocentrism (and Howe improves on this definition considerably beyond this introductory move), the process by which a number of cultural practices are brought under a single label so quickly here is worth noting. One must note, in response, that somehow a great number of academic disciplines—history among them—have managed to survive their own histories of shoddy ideas, crackpot theories, and racist frameworks; and white America has certainly relied rather heavily on mystical, essentialist, irrationalist, and racist set of doctrines, but somehow manages to preserve its sense of the integrity of its project. It is simply insufficient to contrast Afrocentrism with an imagined scholarly perspective that relies on "sound" or "objective" scholarship. The tradition of white historical scholarship on the U.S. system of slavery, Reconstruction, and any number of other concerns relating to race suggests the need for a more complex engagement with U.S. Afrocentrism as a complexly contingent *and therefore* problematic scholarly framework, just as the ideal of a race-neutral mode of historical understanding—based on a superficial understanding of race or, as in Davis's comment, on a naive understanding of tradition and of choices without limits—is itself a complexly contingent and problematic framework.

2. Moses is concerned specifically with "historiographies of progress and decline that have surfaced in African American consciousness—from the end of the eighteenth to the middle of the twentieth century," and his broad scope forces him to paint at times with broad stokes. But while I have benefited from *Afrotopia*, surely an essential work for anyone engaged in these concerns, I am not persuaded that one can categorize early African American historiography quite so neatly. I am, instead, interested in the ways in which historiographies of liberation utilized narratives of both progress and decline (at times simultaneously) to reframe the historical situation of the present so as to both justify and guide communal action.

3. The early historians have received surprisingly little attention. As Earl E. Thorpe has noted, "literature on American historiography has had almost nothing to say about black historians," and this remains true of the early historians. Most commentators on African American historians assume, with John Hope Franklin, that "the first generation began auspiciously with the publication of the two-volume *History of the Negro Race in America* by George Washington Williams" (13); Bethel is a notable and recent exception to this rule. Thorpe's work remains the pioneering and indispensable study of these historians, though it is largely an introduction to the individual historians and their work. Quarles's essay is an essential companion to Thorpe's work. Important as well are Bethel, Loggins, and C. Walker, *Deromanticizing* and *We Can't Go Home Again*. Increasingly, this body of writing is gaining recognition as an important if problematic reflection of African American communal self-definition, requiring an increasingly fine-tuned understanding of class concerns (as in Rael's work, for example) and apparent ideological inconsistencies (as in Bay's work).

4. In his introduction, Moses critiques the many sides of debates over Afrocentrism and Egyptocentrism, sometimes reducing the debate to academic politics in contrast

to the work of "professional historians." In his extended response to Mary Lefkowitz's *Not Out of Africa*, for example, Moses asserts that "demagogues like Maulana Karenga leap at the chance to debate her, thereby enhancing their notoriety and appealing to their constituencies as defenders of the 'stolen legacy' of African peoples. In the process, they assist Mary Lefkowitz, once an obscure drudge in the academic back-waters of a classics department, in her quest for status as a 'public intellectual' " (8). By this formulation of academic culture, it becomes possible to refer to "racial polemicists of the Lefkowitz-Karenga ilk" (9). It is important to consider the issues Moses discusses as presented within a different, and African-centered, framework—particularly that of Magubane in *The Ties that Bind*.

5. On the institutionalization of the American historical profession, see Novick and, for related concerns, Peter Hall.

6. The development of scholarship on the construction of whiteness and on the enforcement of the United States as a white supremacist nation helps to clarify the process by which African Americans faced ideological minefields in trying to construct a history of African Americans, for that history could not simply be about the experience of those who were identified as black but would also necessarily have to confront the process by which and the reasons for which they were identified as black and the ways in which that "blackness" was both maintained and policed. For legal background, see Franklin and McNeil; Higginbotham; and Rogers Smith. For scientific background, see W. Stanton. For general cultural background on the United States as a "racial state," see Fredrickson; Gossett, *Race*; Horsman; Jacobson; Roediger; Saxton; and Takaki. For general philosophical and theoretical frameworks that are especially relevant in this regard, see Goldberg and Mills.

7. The focus on history "as a form of writing" itself has a long history, but I am thinking particularly of the scholarship of the 1980s. In 1989, debates over the ways in which the writing of history problematized any possible understanding of history were the subject of a special forum in the *American Historical Review*, in which David Harlan, identifying the current forces in the field, announced "the return of literature," which "has plunged historical studies into an extended epistemological crisis" ("Intellectual History" 581). Of course, "literature" never left the historical field, and the "epistemological crisis" has been less an occasional anxiety than a defining characteristic of the historical profession. One measure of the variety within this ongoing crisis is the fact that most debates concerning the relationship between literature and history include, rather prominently, summaries of the story thus far. Naturally, one's position in the debate influences the story one tells. Accordingly, the forum in the *American Historical Review* provides a useful introduction to the dynamics and agendas involved in the debate. For a more general introduction, see *The Writing of History: Literary Form and Historical Understanding*, edited by Robert H. Canary and Henry Kozicki; Canary and Kozicki offer a selective but useful bibliography. See also the first chapter of Dominick LaCapra's *History and Criticism*.

What might be called the "returnings of literature" has been a succession of new roles for an established player—a sort of literary Rambo who began as a defensive veteran fighting for respect, became an avenging soldier representing a wounded nation, and was transformed, finally, into something more deliberately offensive. The presence of "literature" as a field for reflection has had various and distinct implications, but one might say that the most prominent concerns have included considerations of the role of literary craft *in* historical accounts, considerations of historical accounts *as* literature, and, later, considerations of historical knowledge itself as a kind of unwritten or prewritten literature (reflecting the entrance, most prominently, of structuralism and poststructuralism, according to which what Harlan calls an "epistemological crisis" might be more properly understood as what Barthes calls a "crisis of commentary" [*Criticism and Truth* 64]). Naturally, each of these "returnings" (in my own reductive history) has been influenced by and has contributed to scholarly discourse on the others: in making claims about how to read historical works one of course makes claims about how to write historical works; and in making claims about how one thinks about history one of course is talking about conventions of writing and reading histories.

F. R. Ankersmit has distinguished between a "traditional historiography" and a "new historiography," the latter of which is "text-oriented" and has accordingly "marginalized the problem of the biotope of both traditional historiography and traditional critical philosophy of history." As Ankersmit notes, "The critical philosopher of history might ask what is to be understood by historical reality if the way of thinking which underlies the new historiography is accepted" (9–10). Some of Ankersmit's work is directed toward drawing practical analogies between historical writing and the visual arts; in his essay, he argues for a reconceptualization of the evolution of historical theory, one in which each identifiable stage becomes a new effort to expand the historian's conceptual framework. Each stage represents not a deeper "penetration" of the past but rather a "step taken from the space of the past in the direction of the space of the reader, i.e., of the present" (26).

As is probably clear, my views on the historical profession have been shaped by the significant body of writing on the "linguistic turn" in historiographical theory. Beginning with a strong grounding in the careful work of David Levin, I've since strayed into works that extend Levin's study of the relation between literary methods and historical scholarship to more overtly theoretical realms, but also including many that attend to Levin's concern for the ethical integrity of historical writing. I cannot represent that full field of scholarship here, but particularly important for my present concerns are Gossman, Harlan, Hollinger, Kellner, LaCapra, Mink, Novick, and White.

8. Aside from the obvious centrality of such events as the Compromise of 1850 and the *Dred Scott* case, the changing cultural climate might be best indicated by developments and shifts (of loyalty, of ideology, of practice, of focus) in the antislavery movement and corresponding shifts in black leadership. On the antislavery movement, see A. Adams; Dillon; Filler; Harrold; Jeffrey; Kraditor; Pease and Pease, *They Who Would Be Free*; Perry; Quarles, *Black Abolitionists*; and Walters. On black leadership, see Bell, *A Survey*; Horton and Horton, *In Hope of Liberty* and *Black Bostonians*; and Rael.

9. In saying this, I join a growing number of scholars, particularly in African

American studies, who are critical of the generally reductivist approach to religious belief often presented in literary scholarship. For a representative sampling of this work, see, for example, V. Anderson; Bassard; Cruz; G. Davis; Glaude; Haynes; Howard-Pittney; Juster and MacFarlane; Mizruchi; Moody, *Sentimental Confessions*; and T. Smith. Consider also the established and developing scholarship on the role of religion in antislavery ideology and culture; particularly Lesick; McKivigan; Perry; Stauffer; and Strong. See also the introduction to Ernest, *Resistance and Reformation*.

10. For a study and critique of the centrality of the Exodus story in liberation theology, see Aichele et al., 282–93.

11. For useful introductions to black liberation theology, see Cone, Hayes, Hopkins, and Wilmore. Liberation theology is not limited to the black experience, though I would argue for the importance of remembering that specific communities shape theological methods and assumptions in specific ways. For an introduction to the broader field of liberation theology, see Batstone et al. and Planas. For examples of liberation theology applied to African American culture and literary history, see especially Wimbush, *African Americans and the Bible*, a collection of essays organized by the interpretive categories of liberation theology; and Connor's *Imagining Grace: Liberating Theologies in the Slave Narrative Tradition*.

12. Later in *Spiritual Interrogations* Bassard continues this line of argument usefully:

> My argument is this: the forms and practices we designate African American culture are active and constitutive of African American community rather than passive indicators of race/group identity. Seen in this light, Judith Butler's conceptualization of gender as "performance" is particularly helpful. Yet while pre-Emancipation African Americans cannot be said to be performing "race" (read: "blackness") . . . we can say that they are *performing community*, engaging in and (re)producing cultural forms and practices whose central function is community building and the production of the terms by which African Americans come to identify themselves as "a people." (128)

13. The best commentary on Marxist thought and liberation theology, both a critique and an attempted theological renewal, is Alistair Kee's *Marx and the Failure of Liberation Theology*.

14. I am grateful to the Allen Dwight Callahan for this example, included in his workshop presentation, "Liberation Theology and The New Testament." Following that workshop, I began to appreciate anew allusions to Revelation 18 in various texts—among them, *Narrative of the Life of Frederick Douglass, An American Slave* and *A Narrative of the Life and Travels of Mrs. Nancy Prince*.

15. With only a few and notable exceptions, scholars of African American literature over the last few decades have not attended to the wide field of literature that one encounters in Vernon Loggins's *The Negro Author* (1931). Blyden Jackson's magnificent *A History of Afro-American Literature* (1989) is, of course, one of the great exceptions, as is Dickson D. Bruce Jr.'s rich and encompassing study *The Origins of African American Literature* (2001).

16. As Bassard argues, responding to Foucault's interrogative, "What matter who's speaking?": "The women who signed themselves as authors of poetry, fiction, autobiography, essays, and political speeches of this era in African American literary history gather as a collective witness to the importance of the author not just as a function of textuality but as a specific embodiment (of 'real people . . . in real time,' to quote Ortner) of a subjectivity that comes into being by virtue of its investment in authorship as a position of agency and empowerment" (21).

17. As David Levin has noted, "The New England man of letters was a gentleman of letters, trained for some other, more 'useful' profession and usually practicing it" (4). One need hardly add that this "gentleman of letters" was white.

18. Sweet, for example, devotes a full chapter to Bancroft in *Black Images of America*. See also Van Deburg, 26-30. Among white historians, Hoggan's is an extreme example of an open appreciation for Bancroft's particular form of ideological narrative. Hoggan argues that "the specifically American system consists of a Christian constitutional system of limitations in politics and a free market along scriptural lines in economics. These values alone are conducive to the fulfillment of the American genius" (1). More characteristic are those historians, by far the majority, who view Bancroft as a practitioner of a historical method that was clearly subjective and overtly ideological, in contrast to the professional historians who followed Bancroft toward the end of the nineteenth century. The best studies of Bancroft remain Callcott; Nye, *George Bancroft*; Bassett; Levin; and Canary.

19. Henry Adams, 562-63. To the original ten volumes of Bancroft's *History of the United States*, Adams adds Bancroft's two-volume *History of the Formation of the Constitution of the United States of America*, which Bancroft later incorporated into his final revision of the six-volume edition of the work. On Bancroft and the conceptions of the nation that inform nineteenth-century American histories generally, see Levin; Callcott; and Vitzthum.

Chapter One

1. As Patrick Rael has put it, "throughout the diaspora white oppressors' categorization of people of African descent also determined the fate of black identities, but black people themselves, in how they reacted to their situations, conditioned the emergence of black identities" (14). Many African American writers pressed the relation between prejudice and enslavement—as, for example, in a June 5, 1841, article in the *Colored American* critical of the white abolitionist Thomas Van Rensellaer that noted that Van Rensellaer "has not only proved himself to be a larger man in theory than in practice—but also a covert upholder of northern prejudice, and consequently of southern slavery" ("Theory and Practice"). I will discuss, in chapter 3, the presence of racial prejudice among white antislavery activists; the best study of abolitionists, white and black, who confronted and "transformed" race as part of the work of antislavery activism is John Stauffer's *The Black Hearts of Men*. See also Goodman's *Of One Blood*.

2. This passage was later repeated verbatim but without acknowledgment in another historical pamphlet, William Paul Quinn's *The Origin, Horrors, and Results of Slavery* (1834). The passage is inserted in Quinn's pamphlet as an "Addition," in the style of Walker's dynamic mode of presentation, in which additions are highlighted, emphasizing the layered writing of the text.

3. In addressing the need to identify "unity in the story of fragmentation," I am not trying to simplify the complex understanding of what Homi Bhabha terms "national memory," "the site of hybridity of histories and the displacement of narratives" (qtd. in Castronovo, *Fathering* 6). I agree with Russ Castronovo's analysis in which "national narrative, once assumed as the site of cohesion, can be seen to fissure into sites of contestation" (*Fathering* 6). I am concerned, though, with the African American attempt to identify an internal cohesion in various sites of contestation and to gather various sites of history and memory into a mode of historiographical intervention. That the unity defined by the gathering of stories of fragmentation was a tenuous and unstable unity will be clear to anyone familiar with African American history. But I am interested in the ways in which that instability was built into and accounted for in African American historical writing, locating collective unity in historical method rather than in a singular narrative of collective experience.

4. On the cultural politics of white visual representations of the black American presence, see especially Boime, chap. 1; and Reilly.

5. For commentary on the petitions, see Kaplan and Kaplan, chap. 1; Bradley, 101–3; and Nash, chap. 3.

6. There were, of course, exceptions; see, for example, Child, *An Appeal in Favor of That Class of Americans Called Africans*; Grégoire; and Livermore. Some commentators on U.S. culture were generally insightful on issues of race and slavery. One thinks particularly of Martineau and Tocqueville. Finally, Bancroft and Hildreth, the major early white historians (the latter also the author of one of the first antislavery novels), both attended to slavery, though often in problematic ways.

On misrepresentations of African and African American identity, consider, for example, works informed by theories of polygenesis, such as John Campbell's *Negromania* (1851); or Nott and Gliddon's *Types of Mankind* (1854). Concerning biblical arguments in support of slavery and white supremacy, see, for example, Stringfellow's *Scriptural and Statistical Views* (1856). On the representation of African American history, see Huggins; Hine, *State*; J. Anderson; and C. Walker, *Deromanticizing*. For general background on nineteenth-century U.S. racialist thought, see Bay; Fredrickson; Gossett, *Race*; W. Stanton, 54–143; Takaki; and Tise.

7. Responses to prejudice were a regular feature in the African American press, and did not change much over the years. Usually, the responses were dressed in scientific or scholarly garb, as in a piece by "Augustine" for the *Colored American* on June 2, 1838, which distinguishes between different kinds of prejudice—based on family, nation, and caste ("Augustine"). But often these responses were both edgy and sarcastic, and the articles were frequently addressed to an imagined white interlocutor, as in the March 18, 1837, article in the *Colored American*: "The negro, you say, is of a degraded race. But who are you?" The article goes on to trace American

identity to Europe, identifying Europeans as formerly "hordes of naked barbarians," and tracing back further to "the Greeks, the Romans, the Hebrews" and then back to the Egyptians and Ethiopians—regularly addressing the white interlocutor in the process in this representative example of print performance for African American readers ("Prejudice against Color"). Through this representation of white ignorance, writers accounted not only for the factual-historical challenge of racial prejudice but also for the racial dynamics involved. One of the best examples of this strategic representation of white interlocutors is Daniel Coker's *A Dialogue between a Virginian and an African Minister* (1810).

8. Holly's publication began as lecture for "a Literary Society of Colored Young Men, in the City of New Haven, Ct.," after Holly returned from Haiti in the fall of 1855. Holly reports also that he presented the lecture during the summer of 1856 in "Ohio, Michigan, and Canada West" (19).

9. In a review of the *Text Book* published in the February 27, 1841, issue of the *Colored American*, Pennington was criticized for focusing too much on prejudice. "The historical part of the work, giving the origin of the colored people," the review asserted, "is most conclusive. And we think, had the author have extended this part of the work more, even had he been forced to have compressed that part on prejudice, &c., it would have materially increased the interest of the book; the historical part being but little understood, while all are more or less familiar with the nature and character of prejudice" ("A Text Book," February 27, 1841). See also "A Text Book," January 9, 1841.

10. Lionel Gossman's commentary on white historians of the period is useful here. "The role the Romantic historian attributed to himself," Gossman explains,

> was similar to that for the Romantic poet. If the poet, according to Baudelaire, was the interpreter of "le langage des fleurs et des choses muettes," the historian was to recover and read the lost languages of the mute past. . . . By making the past speak and restoring communication with it, it was believed, the historian could ward off the potentially destructive conflicts produced by repression and exclusion; by revealing the continuity between remotest origins and the present . . . he could ground the social and political order and demonstrate that the antagonisms and ruptures—notably the persistent social antagonisms—that seemed to threaten its legitimacy and stability were not absolute or beyond all mediation. Understandably . . . the historical imagination of the nineteenth century was drawn to what was remote, hidden, or inaccessible: to beginnings and ends, to the archive, the tomb, the womb, the so-called mute peoples. (*Between History and Literature* 258–59)

11. As Rael has argued, even the discourse of elevation—speaking, as it did, of a range of concerns from individual character to notions of historical progress—provided only a problematic and unstable tool for African American collective self-definition. On the one hand, "elevation offered a common, though hardly fixed, vocabulary, a conceptual lingua franca through which Americans in the antebellum North of both races expressed their values and concerns. Precisely because it was

vague, diffuse, and flexible, the language of elevation provided a loose network of words and understandings through which a wide array of ideas could be comprehended, manipulated, and expressed" (125). On the other hand, however, "because it was shared," the ideology of elevation "expressed a very general and latent consensus, held by most Americans, not about specific issues or platforms, but about the broadest elements in the northern worldview—many of which Americans took so much for granted that they would have been hard pressed even to elucidate them. In this way— by marking the bounds of public speech—the ideology of elevation and uplift served to constrain the range of possible ideological options while it simultaneously permitted the expression of ideas by providing a comprehensive vocabulary that could frame them for an ever-broadening public sphere" (125). For background on the language of (white) American history and constitutional order, see Gustafson; Looby; and Simpson.

12. Interestingly, Parrott, in an 1814 address, tells this story to focus on a white hero, presenting Benjamin Rush as the "guardian angel" of Philadelphia during the time of the "pale disease" (388).

13. See Hinks, *To Awaken*, appendix E: "David Walker's Death and the History of His Family." Hinks adds that "certainly there were numerous Southerners who wanted Walker dead, and neither the possibility of murder nor the possibility that he was stalked can be discounted" (269–70).

14. On Walker's style and his use of the jeremiad sermonic form, see Peterson, *Doers*, 64–66; see also Baker's discussion of the various "roles" that Walker plays in the *Appeal* in *Long Black Song*, 60–67, and of Walker's style, 68–71.

15. Dening, of course, is hardly alone or innovative in questioning the assumptions that govern the historical profession. For a good overview of the history of history as a discipline, see Novick.

16. William H. Prescott, for example, though concerned never to break the interest of the narrative with extraneous details, was equally concerned with the substance, and even the placement, of the notes, the omission of which he considered to be an "evil" ("Bancroft" 302). The narrative, Prescott believed, is not to be encumbered by "scaffolding or learning"—qualifications and verifications. Prescott's attitude was to "go right on, & explain in the notes" (*Literary Memoranda* 1:121). The narrative is, in effect, an interpretation of the notes, which the reader, drawn along by his emotional involvement in the story, takes on faith; but the notes are essential as a substantiation and even examination of that faith:

> We want to see the grounds of his conclusions, the scaffolding by which he has raised his structure; to estimate the true value of his authorities; to know something of their characters, positions in society, and the probable influences to which they were exposed. Where there is contradiction, we want to see it stated; the *pros* and *cons*, and the grounds for rejecting this and admitting that. We want to have a reason for our faith, otherwise we are merely led blindfold. Our guide may be an excellent guide; he may have travelled over the path till it has become a beaten track to him; but we like to use our own eyesight too, to

observe somewhat for ourselves, and to know, if possible, why he has taken this particular road in preference to that which his predecessors have travelled. ("Bancroft" 303)

The purpose, the desired effect, of the notes is to lead readers through the process that the historian has undergone, to present to them not only the documentation for this vision of history but also the complex dynamics of that vision.

17. On the construction of and debates about possible approaches to American history, see Kraus, 163–83. On the significance of Hildreth's implicit commentary on Bancroft and other historians, see Kelly. On the influence of New England historians' cultural environment on their approaches to history, see Levin, 3–23. In the chapters that follow his consideration of "the historian as Romantic man of letters," Levin presents the primary assumptions that shaped nineteenth-century American historical thought, including concepts of "Nature, Progress, and Moral Judgment" (chap. 2), "Representative Men" (chap. 3), "Teutonic Germs" (chap. 4), "Priestcraft and Catholicism" (chap. 5), and "The Infidel: Vanishing Races" (chap. 6).

18. On the role of race in the white American historical consciousness of this period, see Fredrickson, 1–42; Gossett, *Race*, 84–122; Horsman, 81–97; Levin, 74–92; Litwack, *North of Slavery*; Norton; Saxton; Sweet, 7–22; and C. Walker, *Deromanticizing*, 87–107.

19. I'm thinking, of course, of B. Anderson's chapter, "Patriotism and Racism." Goldberg's best statement in this regard is in his chapter called "Racialized Discourse" in *Racist Culture*, though his commentary on "representational exceptionalism" (23) in *The Racial State* is pertinent as well. Mills addresses issues of representation throughout *The Racial Contract*, following his argument that whites create for themselves an

inverted delusional world, a racial fantasyland, a "consensual hallucination," to quote William Gibson's famous characterization of cyberspace, though this particular hallucination is located in real space. There will be white mythologies, invented Orients, invented Africans, invented Americas, with a correspondingly fabricated population, countries that never were, inhabited by people who never were—Calibans and Tontos, Man Fridays and Sambos—but who attain a virtual reality through their existence in travelers' tales, folk myth, popular and highbrow fiction, colonial reports, scholarly theory, Hollywood cinema, living in the white imagination and determinedly imposed on their alarmed real-life counterparts. (18–19)

20. A particularly intriguing example of this is Bancroft's one-volume *History of the Colonization of the United States* (1885), abridged from the first two volumes of his *History of the United States* and apparently designed for home and school use. Unlike his original volumes, the *History of the Colonization* is illustrated, and this history of racial contestation features throughout, and almost exclusively, illustrations of American Indians—beginning with the cover and the frontispiece, the latter a sketch of Pocahontas in European garb.

21. George Bancroft to Evert Duyckinck, May 26, 1855. Quoted in McWilliams, 7.

22. See my discussion of this in chapter 3.

23. Garnet, for example, echoes and seems to answer Bancroft's vision of race and new world destiny in *The Past and the Present Condition*, asserting that "the Red men of North America are retreating from the approach of the white man. They have fallen like trees on the ground in which they first took root, and on the soil which their foliage once shaded. But the Colored race, although they have been transplanted in a foreign land, have clung to and grown with their oppressors, as the wild ivy entwines around the trees of the forest, nor can they be torn thence" (25). As does Bancroft, Garnet largely sacrifices the "Red men of North America" in his exploration of the contingencies of racial destiny; unlike Bancroft, Garnet's vision of this competitive racial theater is one that calls into question the stability of the concept of race. As Garnet argues, "It is a stubborn fact, that it is impossible to separate the pale man and the man of color, and therefore the result which to them is so fearful, is inevitable."

The black press, however, was more than capable of restabilizing the concept of race through its treatment of "the red men"—as in, for example, an article, "History of the Red Race," printed in the December 4, 1841, issue of the *Colored American*, in which a biblical explanation of the presence of "the Red Race" in the Americas leads to a rejection of the notion that physical differences are the result of climate in favor of the notion of the essential racial divisions of "white, red and black" "soon after the flood."

24. On the national narrative as an "official story" that extends from and shapes concepts and practices of "social unacceptability and political censorship, personal prohibitions and cultural conventions, the literary market and language," see Wald (1); see also Castronovo's study of the ways in which the "national narrative, once assumed as the site of cohesion, can be seen to fissure into sites of contestation, exclusion, and repression" (*Fathering the Nation* 6). As Castronovo emphasizes, it is important to note that the white national narrative was not as monolithic, as neatly constituted, or as consensual a conceptual structure as is sometimes suggested. For commentary on this, see, for example, Shaffer's *The Politics of History*. In his study of white nineteenth-century American historians, Callcott reports a significant example of the ways in which disagreements about "the" national narrative were tied directly to regional divisions and perceived racial alliances. Callcott addresses the famous story of the caning of Sumner in Congress: "The first important sectional outburst among historians came in 1847 when New England historian Lorenzo Sabine cast aspersion on Southern efforts in the Revolution, and Southern critics angrily replied that he had abused the facts. Senator Charles Sumner's citation from Sabine was part of the incendiary speech that led to Sumner's caning by Preston Brooks" (217). The South was, like the North, attracted to systems of (and for) history and society, to laws of history and to sociology—an attraction inseparable from debates about race and slavery, as is demonstrated by historical articles in the proslavery organ *DeBow's Review* and such publications as J. K. Paulding's *Slavery in the United States* (1836), Edmund Ruffin's *The Political Economy of Slavery* (1853), Henry Hughes's *A Treatise on Sociology* (1854), George Fitzhugh's *Sociology for the South* (1854), and J. H. Van Evrie's *White Supremacy and Negro Subordination* (1868).

25. On the tensions in the developing white nationalist historical imagination, see especially Wertheimer.

26. Rael follows through on this point, from the abstract ideological level to the cultural level, considering the ways in which the African American leadership in the North worked to instruct or control the African American community according to developing standards of white middle-class respectability. At times, one can see in this instruction an attempt to police the boundaries of the community—for example, in "A Chapter on Locks," an article published in the *Colored American* on March 2, 1839, the writer joins "a remarkable deficiency in the locks on the doors of '*our people*'" with a similar deficiency in "the mouths of 'our people.'" "We have been worried, tormented and exasperated," the editorial continues, "to find that too generally 'where the locks on the doors are deficient' the locks on the lips are in a similar condition." But black writers could be even more harsh in their criticism of the African American community—as was, for example, the "Long Island Scribe" who wrote a series of essays collectively called "The Reflector" for the *Colored American*. In the fifth article of that series, in the March 28, 1840, issue, the "Scribe" addresses the topic of *attention*, and complains of the lack of political and historical understanding fundamental to the African American community. Taking as his example "the 'Amistad' affair," the "Scribe" asserts, "In the short period of a few months, God has, in the history of this matter, presented as a theme of a reflection more commanding than the history of the slave trade has furnished since the days of Wilberforce; and yet I hazard the prediction, that this case will go through our courts, and that our people will fail through sheer inattention to record in their minds a correct outline, even of the facts" ("Long Island Scribe").

27. Pertinent here is Houston Baker Jr.'s discussion of "whether a way of life known as black American culture is distinct and separate from a way of life known as white culture. The relevance of historical information in arriving at an answer," Baker emphasizes, "cannot be overrated. If, as proposed here, the history of a people is the culture, then the history of the black American is black American culture, and the only way to arrive at an understanding of black American culture is to comprehend fully the history of the black American. Moreover, to survey the evolution of his way of life is to analyze why *culture* came to be defined in America as something spiritual, transcendental, and white" (*Long Black Song* 1–2). I am suggesting that early African American historians worked from a similar conception of the challenge of identifying black American culture, but perhaps with a more complex understanding of the challenge of gathering and constructing "the history of the black American."

28. Consider, for example, H. G. Adams, *God's Image in Ebony*, and Grégoire, *On the Cultural Achievements of Negroes*.

29. On Stewart's "reconfiguration of the black jeremiad as articulated by Walker," see Peterson, *Doers*, 66–73; see also Logan, 23–43.

30. This vision of Africa was regularly represented in dramatic historical narratives that slipped in and out of the present tense. See, for example, Paul, 6–11; P. Williams, *An Oration*, 348; Hamilton, "Oration on the Abolition," 394–96; Lawrence, 376; also Sipkins, 367–70.

31. Similarly, Sipkins concludes his imagined narration of the slave trade with this comment: "But why attempt to portray, in their true colours, scenes of oppression, which language the most descriptive is inadequate to delineate: or why any longer expatiate on a subject of such complicated misery" (370).

32. See also P. Williams, *An Oration*, 348; Hamilton, "Oration on the Abolition," 394–96; Lawrence, 376–78; and Sipkins, 367–70.

33. Against Moses's general anatomy of Egyptocentrism in *Afrotopia*, which does not include a significant discussion of Garnet's views (whom Moses does discuss in *The Golden Age of Black Nationalism*, primarily in regard to Garnet's changing views on emigration), one should read Glaude's nuanced reading of Garnet's use of the Exodus story in African American thought, particularly chap. 8. Moses also says relatively little in *Afrotopia* about contemporary debates over Egypt and Africa, about which see Quarles, "Black History," 101–3. On the role of Egypt in the white American symbolic imagination, Irwin's study still remains invaluable. For an example of a white historian whose views on Egypt corresponded with those of African American writers of the time, see Child, *An Appeal in Favor*, 141–43.

34. On the complex story of African American images of Africa, see Adeleke; Magubane; Moses, *Afrotopia*; and Skinner.

35. As C. Walker has stated, "the idealist tradition of writing by black historians" of this period (and later) "was very Bancroftian in its analysis of the race problem in that it placed great emphasis upon the role of Providence as a force of historical causation" (*Deromanticizing* 87). See also Sweet, who argues that "in a unique way, Bancroft's immensely popular writings summed up the major nineteenth-century intellectual themes of the ideal image of America and the mission and destiny of America in the world" (1–2). For the best overview of the role of Providence in the work of the white American historians of this period, see Levin. On white American theories of history during this period, see Levin, Callcott, and Vitzthum. See also Dekker on the "stadialist model of progress," which divided human history into "four main stages of society resulting from four basic modes of subsistence: (1) a 'savage' stage based on hunting and fishing; (2) a 'barbarian' stage based on herding; (3) a stage considered 'civilized' and based mainly on agriculture; (4) a stage based on commerce and manufacturing which was sometimes considered over-civilized" (75). For commentary on the racial ideology implicit in white Euro-American theories of progress, see especially C. Walker, *Deromanticizing*; and Mills, *The Racial Contract*.

36. Consider Bancroft's explanation in his *History of the United States*:

The period of success in planting colonies in Virginia had arrived; yet not till changes had occurred, affecting the character of European politics and society, and moulding the forms of colonization. The reformation had interrupted the harmony of religious opinion in the west of Europe; and differences in the church began to constitute the basis of political parties. Commercial intercourse equally sustained a revolution. It had been conducted on the narrow seas by land; it now launched out upon the broadest waters; and, after the East Indies had been reached by doubling the southern promontory of Africa, the great commerce of the world was performed upon the ocean. The art of printing had become known; and the press diffused intelligence and multiplied the facilities of instruction. The feudal institutions which had been reared in the middle ages, were already undermined by the current of time and events, and, swaying from their base, threatened to fall. Productive industry had, on the one side, built up the fortunes and extended the influence of the active classes; while habits of indolence and of expense had impaired the estates and diminished the power of the nobility. These changes also produced corresponding results in the institutions which were to rise in America. (117)

Bancroft presents, here, several historically discrete revolutions—in "religious opinion," in "commercial intercourse," in communications, and in social organization. Of course, these various revolutions were interrelated, each influenced by and influencing the others. The Reformation led to a restructuring of political activity, which "interrupted" European homogeneity; the significance of that interruption was heightened by the broadening base of commerce; the broadening base of commerce corresponded to the broadened commerce of the mind facilitated by the developing press; and all of these changes undermined traditional social structures, as the "active classes" gained the knowledge and the opportunity to improve their lot. And whereas these changes worked against tradition in Europe, in the New World they were free to influence the initiation of new traditions, "the institutions which were to rise in America."

37. The recasting of white Euro-American history was one of the most frequently used strategies in African American historical writing of this period, and something that appeared in the African American periodical press with great regularity. I have noted the March 18, 1837, article, "Prejudice against Color in the Light of History," in the *Colored American*. In that newspaper, see also the "Correspondence" from "Sigma" (July 15, 1837).

38. Interest in and constructions of Anglo-Saxon history were developing during this time—at times with the aim of establishing the barbaric roots of British and American civilization, on which see, for example, Child's thirty-sixth letter in her *Letters from New-York* (164) and her somewhat later *Appeal for the Indians* (8–10, 16). More often, however, Anglo-Saxon history was constructed to distinguish a core tradition in a culture that was, at that time, expanding the boundaries of whiteness to include immigrant populations. The best study on the developing mythology and cultural presence of Anglo-Saxon history is Horsman's *Race and Manifest Destiny*.

39. Easton adds a parenthetical comment here: "Poor negroes, I wonder where they got learning. These are the race of people who are charged with an inferiority of intellect" (13–14).

40. In the passage I quote from here, Walker asserts that Carthage failed to give "good support" to Hannibal, "that mighty son of Africa" (20). The disunity of the people of Carthage, Walker suggests, restricted Hannibal's success, and a similar disunity in the United States is "the reason our natural enemies are enabled to keep their feet on our throats" (20).

41. This incoherence was, of course, read as a commentary on the white United States—and even the vision of a primitive Africa could in this way serve the needs of those bringing the historical record to bear on the system of slavery in the land of liberty. In an article titled "Immediate Emancipation" in the March 9, 1839, issue of the *Colored American*, for example, the author, "Justica," offers her or his own vision of this historical moment of incoherence: "When a country, the foundation of whose laws begins with the declaration of the equality of the rights of men, and ends the code of her jurisprudence, by enslaving a part of her inhabitants, there is reason to doubt her sincerity! to suspect the boasted democracy of unlawful intentions! and to scorn her vaunted republic. Such an anomaly were better fitted for the barbarous days of Greece and Rome than the enlightened reign of the gospel; for heathen darkness than civilized intelligence! for Africa than America." The author goes on to suggest that America should learn to recognize its dangerous incoherence in the present by careful attention to the past: "But if America: having forgot her first love of liberty, be unmindful of consistency, regardless of justice as declared by the divine law, and reckless even of expediency, let her at least hear the warning voice of history" (Justica).

42. An important part of this project, of course, were regular reminders of the dominant culture's own belief in the centrality of Protestant Christianity and in the United States as the product of providential history. It is worth noting that the African American press would often use white representatives—sometimes ironically, sometimes not—to promote the importance of Christianity, and in that way open the door to an argument focusing on national duties when viewed in that religious framework. The *Colored American*, for example, reprinted a piece by John Quincy Adams in which Adams presented the Bible as "the first and almost the only book deserving universal recommendation" (John Quincy Adams). A month earlier the *Colored American* had published an article on the Bible that argued "a nation must be truly blessed if it were governed by no other laws than those of this blessed book; it is so complete a system that nothing can be added to it or taken from it" ("The Bible"). Often, the *Colored American* would reprint articles that applied biblical study to the issues of the day, while also presenting the dominant culture in the act of working through (or around) those issues. Consider, for example, "Was Abraham a Slaveholder?"

43. On African American jeremiads, see Moses, *Black Messiahs*, chap. 3; Howard-Pittney; and Sale, 9–19.

44. As Sale has noted, "The revolutionary period, a defining moment in the history of the nation, has long been evoked and valued by many African American writers and activists as a moment of promise. . . . Virtually every document of political protest written by African American men—and some by white and African American women—between the Revolutionary and the Civil Wars laid claim to the authorizing notion that 'all men are born equally free'" (11). I have noted some of the most significant books and pamphlets on this subject, and I will discuss others in subsequent chapters. For examples from the African American press (and the examples are too numerous to allow me to offer anything more than a sampling), see the *Colored American*'s reprint of Dr. Blake's speech for a "young men's convention," in which Blake attacks prejudice from different angles—factual, historical, moral, and natural—

asserting at one point, "that he [someone of African heritage] possesses patriotism, let those white men who fought by him in the battles of the American revolution, answer, Yes! in fighting for that liberty which is the inalienable right of every son of Adam—but which, after he had fought and bled to achieve it, was denied him, even in this land of boasted freedom" ("Remarks of Dr. Blake"). The African American press also worked to recontextualize the American Revolution so as to highlight the racial politics obscured by the developing white national mythology—for example, Nell's commentary on the deletion of African Americans from the portrait of American history, or the listing of "the slave population of each colony" in 1776 in the October 2, 1851, issue of *Frederick Douglass' Paper*. This article notes that, since that time, seven of these colonies "have effected the abolition of slavery in their borders," but it notes as well that "the history of these States warrants the conclusion that its abolition was not owing to any prejudice in the minds of the people against slaves" but rather because slavery was unprofitable in the economy of those states ("Slavery in 1776"). For additional examples (though this is only a sampling) of strategic references to the Declaration of Independence and to African American participation in the American Revolution, see *The Minutes and Proceedings of the First Annual Meeting of the American Moral Reform Society*, 202; the 1831 *Resolutions of the People of Color*, 283–85; P. Williams, "Discourse," 295; M. Stewart, 56; Easton, 28; Parrott, 390; and "Speech of H. H. Garnet."

   On the role of antislavery thought and African American resistance in the formation of American Revolution ideology and mythology, see Linebaugh and Rediker, chap. 7; Nash, chap. 1; Kaplan and Kaplan, chaps. 2–3; Bradley, chap. 1; and Frey.

   45. This view, of course, signals Douglass's departure from Garrisonian abolitionism, and this departure was no doubt one of his reasons for emphasizing the Constitution as an antislavery document.

   46. Castronovo's argument should be balanced as well by Sale's discussion of the African American appropriation of white liberal theory. Sale suggests the need "to think of liberal theory as a *discourse of natural rights*, and its incarnation in the United States in the period between the Revolutionary War and the Civil War as a *discourse of national identity*, in the Foucaultian sense of discourse" (18). Sale argues that "statements such as 'all men are created equal' and 'all men have a natural right to Life, Liberty, and Estates,' which were produced by the discourse of natural rights, were not *intrinsically* attached to a particular political agenda or class." Rather, Sale continues, "such discursive statements . . . may be mobilized and deployed for different and often opposed ideological purposes. At issue then is not the *unity* of an ideology . . . but rather the way in which discourse *disperses* the series of statements associated with it, thereby producing differently authorized subject-positions" (18–19).

   47. I am aware of the limitations, here and throughout this book, of my terminology, and although I've tried to use the terms "African American" and "black" in specific ways to indicate specific ideological positions, the lines between one usage and the other blur at times, and at times neither term is entirely appropriate to describe writers still in the process of describing community, and often at odds in

their sense of the ideological field and the appropriate naming practices for the community they imagine. I reference the debates over the collective naming practices in chapter 5. On the "names controversy," see Rael, chap. 3; and Stuckey, *Slave Culture*, chap. 4.

On the contingent discourses of race, rights, and citizenship, see especially McBride, chap. 2; and Crane, chap. 1.

48. Jay, 121–30.

49. I am not suggesting that this was unique to Walker's work but rather that Walker (whose work should be read in part as a founding example of black literary and cultural theory) represents and develops a general tendency in the writing of the antebellum period. Many writers wondered, indeed, whether white Americans understood their own language. As a writer for the *Colored American*, put it, "How can America, remembering that her very capital is the depth of slavery, unblushing read, boast and proclaim, the declaration of independence, the assertion of the equal and unalienable rights of men?" ("Justica").

50. Relevant here and throughout is Lionel Gossman's observation that "hidden mediating links had to be disclosed between forces that were visibly in conflict: man and nature, man and his own nature, male and female, the West and the East, the postrevolutionary bourgeoisie and the people, the scholarly historian and common people to whom he owed his existence and whose history was in many cases the preferred object of his study. This could only be done, however, by bringing to light, naming, and acknowledging what the historical record had so often tried to suppress— the injustices of the past, the acts of violence by which the distinctions and discriminations (such as property, the family, and the state) that the historian himself accepted as the condition of civilization and progress had been established, and which had been repeated at each successive stage in human development" (*Between History and Literature* 259).

51. Bercovitch writes, "The genetics of salvation . . . confirms the Puritan mission from within—adds to the assurance of Scripture prophecy the 'internal evidence' of generational succession"; "it blends the heterogeneous covenants of community and grace; and it adapts the rhetoric to new conditions without abandoning the founders' vision" (65).

52. This passage from Jefferson's *Notes on the State of Virginia* was often reprinted or alluded to in antebellum African American publications—for example, in the article "Slavery and the Slave Trade" in *Frederick Douglass' Paper* (November 20, 1851) and again in a longer excerpt with commentary under the title "Jefferson and Slavery" (*Frederick Douglass' Paper*, April 1, 1852), first printed in the *New York Tribune*; and the passage was put to very prominent use by William Wells Brown in *Clotel* (1853).

53. Wilson Jeremiah Moses, following the presence of this vision of African Americans as, in effect, a *more* chosen people than their white compatriots, explains, "If the bondage of the Colonies to England was similar to the enslavement of Israel in Egypt, was not the bondage of blacks in America an even more perfect analogy? If Americans, by virtue of the ideals of their revolution, were in fact a covenanted people and entrusted with the mission to safeguard the divine and natural laws of human rights,

was there not a danger to the covenant in perpetuating slavery?" (*Black Messiahs* 31). Small wonder, then, that "early black writers in America often referred to themselves as a chosen people. Their enslavement did not necessarily symbolize a curse or a mark of God's disfavor; it boded rather that He had some great plan in store for them" (*Black Messiahs* 32).

54. This phrase appears regularly in African American writing of this time (and since), working as a kind of touchstone but also as a narrative gesture toward the sacred context by which to understand shifting secular events. One encounters this phrase, for example, in Jones and Allen's *Narrative*, at the end of which the coauthors include "A Short Address to the Friends of Him Who Hath No Helper," which concludes, "May he, who hath arisen to plead our cause, and engaged you as volunteers in the service, add to your numbers until the princes shall come forth from Egypt, and Ethiopia stretch out her hand unto God" (23). Similarly, Cuffe includes at the end of his *Brief Account* an address to "my scattered brethren," calling them to "walk together in the light of the Lord," in the hope that "Ethiopia may stretch out her hand unto God" (260). In 1808 orations on the abolition of the slave trade, Absalom Jones and Peter Williams Jr. both conclude their historical survey of slavery and tyranny by looking toward the day when "Ethiopia shall stretch forth her hands" (P. Williams, *Oration* 353; see also Jones, 341). And Maria Stewart, weaving in and out of historical, social, and religious observations, quotes this verse repeatedly.

For examples of the use of this biblical prophecy in African American historical writing (though only a sampling of its many occurrences), see Coker, 23; Delany, *Official Report*, 122; Garnet, 11; Jones and Allen, 23; M. Stewart, 5, 11, 54, 60; and Jones, 341. For commentary on this passage, particularly as marshaled by Stewart, see Logan, 23–43.

55. On the Haitian Revolution, see Fick; and Ott. On the Haitian Revolution in African American thought and literature, see Hunt, *Haiti's Influence*; and Sundquist, *To Wake the Nations*, pt. 1.

56. Bancroft's application of this figure of national destiny is worth emphasizing, in part to underscore the importance of written history and the textual battles that African Americans faced. At the beginning of a review of Bancroft's *History of the United States*, written after the publication of volume 3, Prescott chides Bancroft for misquoting "the celebrated line of Bishop Berkeley, 'Westward the *course* of empire takes its way'" ("Bancroft" 272, Prescott's emphasis). Bancroft had replaced "course" with "star." Prescott is characteristically cautious about applying the line to the United States. The line, he notes, "is too gratifying to national vanity not to be often quoted (though not always quoted right); and if we look on it in the nature of a prediction, the completion of it not being limited to any particular time, it will not be easy to disprove it. Had the bishop substituted 'freedom' for 'empire,' it would be already fully justified by experience" ("Bancroft" 272).

Significantly, the misquotation appears not in but on Bancroft's *History*, in a circular emblem on the binding itself, and it remained there uncorrected even after Prescott, Edward Everett, and, presumably, others, pointed out the error (see M. Howe, 2:323 n). Indeed, Bancroft used the same emblem, with the same misquotation, on the binding of his *History of the Constitution*, published in 1882. Either Bancroft was unconcerned about the error, or he deliberately revised the line. In either case, the "misquotation" is a useful emblem of the historical task Bancroft pursued, and the historical role he wished to play, in writing the *History of the United States*. The word "star" in this context corresponds nicely with Bancroft's conception of the United States within the scheme of providential history. In the figure of the star, the two nations, the United States as providentially favored nation and as philosophical/ moral example to the world, come together, much as the moral identity and the historical identity of the American Puritan community came together in the figure of "a city on a hill."

It is particularly fitting that the misquoted line appear on the binding of the *History*, for the *History* itself is an emblem of the dual significance of this use of the word "star." The dual identity of the nation, as political/social community and as idea, corresponds to the dual identity of the *History* as "book" (a cultural product, an object for consumption and promotion) and as a portal to a "text" (in one of Barthes's definitions, "a methodological field" [*Rustle* 57]). As the reader "progresses" through the *History*, book and text come together. The reader is not merely offered a view of the past; she or he is trained to view the past (and, accordingly, the present) in accordance with the ideological framework the historian draws from the field of history, the historian's "methodological field." That is, the reader learns to apply (or submit to) the methodology of perspective by which the ideal and the actual can be related. Thus might the masses become the "People," in Bancroft's terminology—and thus, in turn, might the "work" that is the United States more nearly approximate the transcendental text for which, Bancroft believed, it stands.

57. Harris is, of course, referring to William Walker's overthrow of the Nicaraguan government in 1855. Walker made himself president in 1856 before being overthrown in 1857.

Chapter Two

1. See W. Stewart, 15; and M. Howe, 2:261.

2. Historians of this time would often copy and/or alter, as Richard C. Vitzthum has noted, "ideas, phrases, and even whole sentences and paragraphs" (8)—indeed, even whole chapters—from other works. In his study of historical writings in the nineteenth-century United States, George H. Callcott has demonstrated the prevalence and legitimacy of this practice, noting that "the early nineteenth-century historian felt no need to argue for originality, and he would not have understood why he should make a fetish of reworking material when what he wanted to say already had been better said by another" (136). "As contemporary critics understood the altering of quotations," Callcott notes, "they also understood and approved what the plagiarizers were doing. Critics were aware of having seen the same words before and frequently compared the later account with its source, remarking on the improvement that had been made over the earlier account but seldom considering it a matter of

dishonesty in the use of phraseology" (137). As I have argued in *Resistance and Reformation*, by this practice old passages were placed in new contexts to serve new ideas and to create new applications of familiar knowledge and new arrangements of accepted truths (24–25).

3. As Lionel Gossman has argued, "The role of history in the political programs of the first half of the nineteenth century was crucial. By discovering the hidden anonymous history of the nation beneath the outmoded histories of its rules and its narrow ruling class, histories were expected to provide the legitimation of a new political order, a new state, and at the same time to impose the idea of this state on the consciousness of its citizens. Since history's objective was at once revolutionary (to furnish a basis for a new political order) and conservative (to found and authorize that order by revealing it to be the culmination of a continuous historical development, albeit a long-concealed, underground one), part of its aim was to achieve in itself a reconciliation of the investigative and disruptive practice of historical criticism and scholarship with the narrative art that establishes connections and asserts continuities" (153).

4. The term "polycentric" is from David Tracy, who notes that "pluralism is no longer adequate to describe our situation" and that "we need a word like polycentrism—a word that tries to articulate the reality of the many centers that are now present in our culture" (30).

5. The 1843 edition, apparently the same as the 1836 edition, is ninety-six pages long and includes most of the material of the first two chapters of the 1844 edition. Mia Bay notes that *Light and Truth* was "initially published in four installments by Lewis himself" and "republished in a one-volume edition in 1844 by a 'Committee of Colored Men'" which "also issued a second edition" (45).

6. See, for example, "Observations on the Early History of the Negro Race" in the December 5, 1828, issue of *Freedom's Journal*.

7. Delany notes that he is not alone in his response to *Light and Truth*, for "Reverends D. A. Payne, M. M. Clark, and other learned colored gentlemen, agree with us in the disapproval of this book" (129). Having noted Lewis's failures, Delany goes on to question the value and wisdom of even the attempt itself:

> If viewed in the light of a "Yankee trick," simply by which to make money, it may, peradventure, be a very clever trick; but the publisher should have recollected, that the ostensible object of his work was, the edification and enlightenment of the public in general and the colored people in particular, upon a great and important subject of truth; and that those who must be the most injured by it, will be the very class of people, whom he professes a desire to benefit. We much regret the fact, that there are but too many of our brethren, who undertake to dabble in literary matters, in the shape of newspaper and book-making, who are wholly unqualified for the important work. This, however, seems to be called forth by the palpable neglect, and indifference of those who have had the educational advantages, but neglected to make such use of them. (*The Condition* 128–29)

I cannot agree with Delany's views on Lewis's motivations for publishing the book, for Lewis is clearly addressing issues to which he is deeply committed, and he is not doing so in a fashion designed to attract a broad audience. And it is worth noting that, as I will discuss in the next section of this chapter, many found fault with *The Condition* itself on grounds similar to Delany's criticism of Lewis's text.

8. Lewis then immediately supports his claim by quoting Matthew 25:40: "I say unto you, inasmuch as ye have done it unto one of the least of these, my brethren, ye have done it unto *me*" (342).

9. The somewhat different version of the list that Lewis presents earlier in *Light and Truth* reads as follows:

Mangroon, is all black, a full blood, (a whole negro.)
Sambo, is three quarters blood, (three quarters negro.)
Mulatto, is one half blood, (one half negro.)
Quadroon, is one quarter blood, (one quarter negro.)
Mestizo, is a half quarter blood, (a half quarter negro.)
Niger, a Latin word, was formerly used by the Moors—the old Romans, to
    designate any black, inferior object, &c., a plant, a marsh, flat, moist ground,
    bog, or animal. (340)

10. Delany founded the *Mystery* and served as editor from 1843 to 1847. The paper later became the *Christian Herald* and then the *Christian Recorder*, both of the latter organs of the African Methodist Episcopal Church.

11. See Ullman, 60–61; see also Levine, *Martin Delany*, 27.

12. See L. Williams, 92. Horton notes that Thomas Dalton joined the African Lodge in 1825, and that "he became senior warden in 1827, was co-secretary with David Walker, author of *Walker's Appeal*, and remained an active member until at least 1876, when he was eighty-three years old" (46). Lewis includes Walker among his few biographical sketches, identifying him as "a distinguished Friend" (329). On the importance of Freemasonry in the construction of black masculinity, and specifically on the role of Freemasonry in the construction of Delany as a representative man, see Wallace, chap. 2.

13. Early in his *Official History of Freemasonry*, Grimshaw refers to "the living stones of brotherly love, relief, truth, fortitude, prudence, temperance and justice"; later he lists as "our cardinal virtues" "Temperance, Fortitude, Prudence and Justice, as well as the fundamental principles, Brotherly Love, Friendship and Truth." Later still, he includes among the symbolic rungs on Jacobs's ladder temperance, fortitude, and prudence (9, 101, 334).

14. See L. Williams, 12–17.

15. Levine rightly notes that "the account of Nicaraguan politics Delany offered to Rollin, however truthful, has an air of wish-fulfillment fantasy in the way it places him at center stage of a government at odds with the United States during a time when he felt especially disempowered in the nation of his birth"; that "there is a fundamental elitism underlying his plans for governance"; and that "a colonizing, or imperial, desire guides his Central American vision" (*Martin Delany* 63).

16. Delany notes that had the announced plans for establishing educational and religious institutions in Liberia been achieved, "and honorably maintained, the Republic of Liberia would have met with words of encouragement, not only from himself . . . but . . . from the leading spirits among, if not from the whole colored population of the United States" (168–69). Instead, Delany asserts, "Liberia in Africa, is a mere dependency of Southern slaveholders, and American Colonizationists, and unworthy of any respectful consideration from us" (170).

17. Important here is Robert F. Reid-Pharr's argument that Delany promotes a bourgeois conception of black achievement and community—that, indeed, "the figure of the bourgeois was absolutely necessary to the project of Black American cultural production if only because it stood so firmly against the figures of master and slave. That is to say, the bourgeois's presence counterbalanced the grotesque and erotically charged interdependency of the master/slave dyad, an interdependency that posed a serious threat to the economic, political, familial, and emotional independence thought necessary for the proper functioning of a 'free' nation" (112).

18. Delany notes that he had intended to print the 1793 act, but that "since this Bill includes all the provisions of that Act, in fact, although called a 'supplement,' is a substitute, *de facto*," reprinting the 1793 act "would be superfluous" (147).

19. While Ramsay here justifies slavery, he goes on to present the conventional argument against it—that "the political evils of slavery do not so much arise from the distresses it occasions to slaves, as from its diminishing the incitements to industry, and from its unhappy influence on the general state of society" (24).

20. As Delany testifies, "I have determined to leave to my children the inheritance of a country, the possession of territorial domain, the blessings of a national education, and the indisputable right of self-government; that they may not succeed to the servility and degradation bequeathed to us by our fathers" (110).

21. See Ernest, *Resistance and Reformation*, chap. 4; see also Levine, *Martin Delany*, chap. 5.

22. In Livermore and in Brown, the passage includes reference to a source, "Niles's Register, vol. vii, p. 205," and the speech begins, "Soldiers! From the shores of Mobile I collected you to arms . . ."; in Nell, the source is not cited, and the address begins, "SOLDIERS!—When, on the banks of the Mobile, I called you to take up arms . . ." Brown takes some of his history verbatim from Livermore. In *The Black Man* Brown refers to Nell's *Colored Patriots* as "a book filled with interesting incidents connected with the history of the blacks of this country, past and present" (240). Brown's commentary on Nell's *Colored Patriots* is repeated and somewhat foregrounded (by default, as other material is largely deleted) in *Rising Son* (485).

23. Nell also notes his debt to Delany for a biographical sketch of John B. Vashon (181).

24. As James Oliver Horton notes, "At age of sixteen [Nell] was secretary of the Juvenile Garrison Independent Society, a group of black youths organized for education, community service, and self-help" (47).

25. In a letter published in *Frederick Douglass' Paper*, "Douglass condemned Nell, Robert Purvis, and Charles L. Remond 'as my bitterest enemies, and the *practical*

enemies of the colored people' " (Ripley 4:181). In a public letter, Nell responded by documenting his exchange with Douglass and the remarks to which Douglass himself had responded, adding that, "as to your holding me up as a practical enemy of the colored people, my pen smiles at the idea" (Ripley 4:176). See also R. P. Smith, "William Cooper Nell."

26. Nell's campaign was regularly covered in the *Liberator*. See, for example, "Equal School Rights," April 7, 1854; "Equal School Rights–The Boston Smith School," August 18, 1854; "Equal School Rights–The Smith School," (18 August 18, 1854; "Equal School Rights in Boston," November 10, 1854; "Equal School Rights," April 6, 1855; and "Abolition of Caste Schools," August 31, 1855). See also Wesley, "Integration versus Separatism."

27. As Sweet notes, in 1859 "Nell joined William Wells Brown in organizing a convention to consider 'the Moral, Social, and Political Elevation' of blacks," though Nell apologized "at the convention for its exclusive nature but [justified] it on the grounds that such conventions helped to shape a sorely diseased public opinion" (146). For the best study of Nell's integrationist activism, see Wesley, "Integration versus Separatism."

28. In the advertisements for the self-help Adelphic Union Library Association printed in the *Liberator*, the phrase "Knowledge is Power" is presented as the association's motto.

29. Nell's linking of knowledge and power was hardly unique, of course. For a similar application of the maxim "knowledge is power"–that is, one that identifies knowledge with white British and U.S. power, calls upon African Americans for a dedicated commitment to the acquisition of knowledge while warning them of the dangers of superficial applications of knowledge, and then turns finally to racial prejudice as a systemic obstacle to African American education–see "Means of Elevation.–No. IV."

30. This address was published also in the August 5, 1853, issue of the *Liberator*.

31. See "Colored Patriots of the American Revolution." The notice was reprinted in the *Liberator* on June 1, 1855, July 6, 1855, and August 3, 1855. On Nell's efforts to secure funding for the enlarged edition of *Colored Patriots*, see also his July 8, 1855, letter to Wendell Phillips (Ripley 4:298–303).

32. As Wesley has noted, Nell was frustrated by the Massachusetts legislature's rejection of his first petition for funding of the envisioned Attucks monument, and he complained that "the rejection of this petition was to be expected if we accept the axiom that a colored man never gets justice in the United States, except by mistake" (qtd. in Wesley 220).

33. Color has everything to do with this next battle, Nell suggests. "Let it be recorded," he notes in the midst of his history of Attucks's right to a memorial, "the same session of the Legislature which had refused the ATTUCKS monument, granted one to ISAAC DAVIS, of Concord. Both were promoters of the American Revolution, but one was white, the other was *black*; and this is the only solution to the problem *why* justice was not fairly meted out" (18). In his preface, Nell refers to another monument–one that guides his historical vision: "I was born on Beacon Hill, and from early childhood, have loved to visit the Eastern wing of the State House, and

read the four stones taken from the monument that once towered from its summit. One contains the following inscription:—

'Americans, while from this eminence scenes of luxuriant fertility, of flourishing commerce, and the abodes of social happiness, meet your view, forget not those who by their exertions have secured to you these blessings.'" (10)

34. Nell adds, "The woman took up her abode with the family of this champion of liberty; and there she lived free and died free" (96).

35. Nell, for example, continued to face colonization debates in 1859, in a public dispute with Henry Highland Garnet over Garnet's promotion of the African Civilization Society. In a letter to the *Weekly Anglo-African*, Nell asserted that "facts can be piled Olympus high in proof that the African Civilization movement is accepted by Colonizationists as but another channel for their own cherished operations to remove colored Americans from their homes to Africa." The foundation of the African Civilization Society's argument for emigration, Nell noted, was that "the colored American has no reason to hope for equality in the United States," a view that Nell argued did not hold up when viewed historically: "In view of my observation and experience of the anti-slavery progress within the last twenty-five years, I must be most jolly green to accept any such unphilosophical and fallacious presentation" ("Letter from Wm. C. Nell" 2). Nell was also one of many prominent black male leaders who wrote letters on the African Civilization Society for the April 21, 1860, issue of the *Weekly Anglo-African*; in his, Nell asserted that "money and energy solicited for the African civilization movement could be better appropriated towards civilizing white and colored Americans here at home" ("The Colored Citizens of New York").

36. This is only part of a long and distinguished career. Langston was also the first president of Virginia State College and Virginia's first black congressman. He became dean of the law department of Howard University in 1869. President Hayes appointed him minister resident and consul general to Haiti and chargé d'affaires to Santo Domingo. Langston University in Langston, Oklahoma, takes its name from John Mercer Langston.

37. I use the term "capitalize" advisedly. Easton notes that racist culture markets racism in the form of images in bookstores and public houses (*Treatise* 41–42).

38. For example, Nell notes that "distinctions of color are not recognized in the letter of the United States Constitution," though he adds that "that instrument leaves it in the power of the Congress and individual States to trample on or acknowledge, as tyranny may dictate, the rights of colored citizens" (315). Later in *Colored Patriots*, Nell reprints excerpts from a memorial to Langston "presented to the General Assembly of the State of Ohio, April 18, 1854," which echoes Nell's earlier point, noting that "the Constitution of the United States makes no distinction of color. There is no word 'white' to be found in that instrument" (339).

39. Nell extends his point about Christian character on the next page, dealing with the execution, where he remarks that the man said that "he truly forgave all those who had taken any part in his condemnation" (243).

40. Nell leaves out Child's comments about the manner in which the story reached her ears; he also makes minor changes in the dialect used in the story.

41. In Child's version, Duncan first has this thought at the beginning of the story (191).

42. In both Child's and Nell's versions of the story, an attempt is made to indicate that this "superiority" is not inherent but rather due to advantages of education. See Nell, 251; Child, 200.

43. I am underscoring Nell's own emphasis on a revolution of consciousness, but, as I've suggested, Nell also turned his history directly to the need for more immediate and physical resistance to white oppression as organized by the system of slavery. As the Hortons have noted, "At a community meeting in Boston in 1850, William Cooper Nell cautioned African Americans to be watchful for kidnappers. If confronted, he urged them to defend themselves, acting as they would to 'rid themselves of any wild beast'" ("Affirmation of Manhood" 146).

Chapter Three

1. I have in mind here David Theo Goldberg's argument that "liberalism's response to matters of race in the face of the fact that race matters amounts to denying or ignoring race, paternalistically effacing a self-determined social subjectivity from those who would define themselves thus without imposing it on others" (*The Racial State* 70). "This erasure in the name of non-racialism," Goldberg explains, "rubs out at once the history of racist invisibility, domination, and exploitation, replacing the memory of an infantilized past with the denial of responsibility for radically unequal and only superficially deracialized presents. Racelessness is the legacy. Divested of a historically located responsibility, the relatively powerful in the society alongside and indeed through state rule are readily able to reinstate the invisibility of the subject positions of the presently marginalized" (70). Applying a similar perspective to U.S. antislavery culture, and to the situation of Frederick Douglass specifically, Russ Castronovo has argued that "the abstract thinking of abolitionists, however enlightened, foists amnesia on the fugitive slave, insisting that he forget his mother's legacy and African heritage. A specific existence is no more encouraging: U.S. society fixates on racial inheritance in order to deny Douglass the rights accorded to citizens blessed with complexions that seemingly have no history" (*Necro Citizenship* 60). See also Lewis R. Gordon on the "problem of biography in Africana thought," and his consideration of "Frederick Douglass as an existentialist" (22–61).

2. Useful here is Dwight A. McBride's concept of the "discursive reader, which the slave implies in his or her testimony," a reader that is not "a particular person or even . . . a particular community of persons" but rather is "a confluence of political, moral, and social discursive concerns that animate, necessitate, and indeed make possible slave testimony itself." McBride associates this discursive reader with Benedict Anderson's "imagined communities," noting that "the discursive reader, for

the slave witness, is the imagined horizon wherein the pro-slavery advocates (and their arguments for slavery), the abolitionists (from the sentimental moralists to the staunchly political Garrisonians), and the ongoing debates between these two over slavery (which are characterized by such discursive sites as black humanity, natural rights, the Christian morality of slavery, the treatment of slaves under slavery, etc.) come together as an entity that will be the recipient of the slave's testimony" (151). As I will suggest, one needs to extend this "imagined horizon" still farther, for there were no monolithic communities of proslavery advocates or abolitionists, and African American narrators found themselves working within complex and unstable cultural and discursive categories even among their self-proclaimed allies.

3. On Gerrit Smith's significant devotion not only to abolitionism but also to racial equality, and on the trust that he earned, see Stauffer, 14–20, 139–44, and 265–75.

4. I should note here that I view much of Diana Fuss's attempt "to break or in some way to weaken the hold which the essentialist/constructionist binarism has on feminist theory" (1)—and to weaken its hold as well on related theories concerning group identities—as a new simplification of the cultural and historical dynamics of individual and collective identity. I think also that Fuss's dismissal of the authority of experience is dangerously tidy. However, I do agree with her sense of the value of experience viewed as "itself a product of ideological practices, as Althusser insists," which, accordingly, "might function as a window onto the complicated workings of ideology." "Experience," Fuss continues, "would itself then become 'evidence' of a sort for the productions of ideology, but evidence which is obviously constructed and clearly knowledge-dependent" (118).

5. John Hazlehurst Boneval Latrobe—lawyer and inventor of the popular Latrobe stove—helped found the Maryland State Colonization Society and in 1853 succeeded Henry Clay as the president of the national society, a post Latrobe held for thirty-seven years. In 1840, John Brown Russwurm, the governor of the colony of Maryland in Liberia purchased for the colony (for business ventures) a ship he named the *Latrobe*, though it immediately had to be repaired, and was soon sold. For the history of this colony and of Latrobe's involvement in it, see P. Campbell. In *The Condition*, 91, Delany mentions Latrobe's role as the biographer of Benjamin Banneker. See also Griffith, 109.

6. For useful commentary on the figure of black suffering in white abolitionist discourse, see McBride, 42–84.

7. Smith's amanuensis has been identified as Connecticut schoolmaster Elisha Niles.

8. Along these lines, consider Rafia Zafar's observation that "Franklin's life can be viewed as parallel and progenitor to many slave narratives," particularly in Franklin's "emphasis," in his account of his life, "on personal freedom, espousal of hard work and industriousness, and announcement of lowly origins" (90); see also Zafar's mention of Smith's narrative (91, 186–87). In *After Franklin*, Stephen Carl Arch usefully complicates prevailing assumptions about how we understand the history of "self-life-writing" (4), and he distinguishes between "self-biographies" and autobiographies in his study of the conceptual shift in understanding the self and notions of

individual agency from the eighteenth to the early nineteenth century. See especially Arch's commentary on *The Life of William Grimes, the Runaway Slave, Written by Himself* (180–84), which he associates with Smith's narrative.

9. The narrative notes that "the tradition of the waist measure was received by the compiler from two sources," and it cites "Mr. Orville Percival of Moodus, in 1894" (27).

10. Again, I have in mind here the developing scholarship on race and citizenship, especially Goldberg; Mills; Castronovo; Crane, chap. 1; and Sale.

11. The narrator compares herself to the Editor of *Sartor Resartus*, and then adds, "It may be hinted . . . that Elleanor's documents want the pith and marrow contained in those of Teufelsdroch; but of this I am not bound to speak, since my province is not criticism, but narration" (38).

12. For biographies that challenge our received image of Sojourner Truth, see Carleton Mabee's *Sojourner Truth: Slave, Prophet, Legend* and Nell Irvin Painter's *Sojourner Truth: A Life, a Symbol*.

13. Peterson observes further that "to define their role as white amanuenses offering a testimonial of Truth's life, both Olive Gilbert and Frances Titus chose to portray themselves as women who have 'achieved' Culture writing on behalf of a child of Nature whose attributes are chiefly physical and thus 'ascribed' " (*Doers* 30).

14. It must be noted as well that the expanded second edition of Tubman's biography, published in 1886, omits the "Essay on Woman-Whipping" included after the appendix in the first edition.

15. Even the titles of the successive versions of Henson's narrative are revealing, indicating his transformation and the increasingly elaborate production of his life story: *The Life of Josiah Henson, Formerly a Slave, Now an Inhabitant of Canada: As Narrated by Himself* (1849); *Truth Stranger Than Fiction: Father Henson's Story of His Own Life, with an Introduction by Mrs. H. B. Stowe* (1858); *"Truth Is Stranger than Fiction": An Autobiography of the Rev. Josiah Henson* (1879); and John Lobb, ed., *An Autobiography of the Rev. Josiah Henson ("Uncle Tom"), from 1789 to 1881, with a Preface by Mrs. Harriet Beecher Stowe and Introductory Notes by George Sturge, S. Morley, Esq., M.P., Wendell Phillips, and John G. Whittier* (1881).

16. Adams's reconsideration of slavery was sufficiently threatening to the antislavery movement to inspire an extended and heated series of responses in Garrison's antislavery paper the *Liberator* from September 1854 to July 1856. Adams's book inspired also black abolitionist William Wells Brown's turn to dramatic writing, about which see Ernest, "The Reconstruction of Whiteness."

17. As Foreman notes, Mattison reprints in the book Picquet's own public notice that she has succeeded in raising the money and securing her mother's freedom. "Picquet's announcement," Foreman points out, "renders null and void her interest in the yet-to-be-published narrative and undermines Mattison's legitimacy as the freedom facilitator he purports to be, placing his other interests in fuller relief" (516).

18. Andrews comments that Lovejoy's presence makes it difficult to determine how much Lewis is the author of this voice; but beyond that are questions about how to understand the voice in relation to the audience (139–40).

19. For an important reconsideration of the cultural politics involved in Stowe's *A Key to "Uncle Tom's Cabin,"* see Levine, *Martin Delany*, 147–53.

20. The article was reprinted in the January 28, 1853, issue of *Frederick Douglass' Paper*, which is my source. That same article builds to the story of Northup being forced to whip a woman who has been "stripped naked," a typical example of the emphasis on the physical abuse of women that characterized northern commentaries on slavery. A condensed account of this article was published in the February 18, 1853, issue of the *Liberator*. In its publication of extracts from Northup's *Twelve Years a Slave* later that year (September 9, 1853), the *Liberator* stated in its prefatory comments, "We have no doubt that it [the narrative] will obtain a wide circulation, and deepen the sympathy already existing for the 'Uncle Toms' and 'Elizas' ground into the dust beneath the heel of oppression, in this 'land of the free, and home of the brave.'"

21. It is only fair to note that Northup's experiences were invoked to support more radical visions of social reform as well. In a letter published in the March 23, 1855, issue of the *Liberator*, for example, Henry C. Wright (one of the more radical of Garrisonian abolitionists) remarks that *Twelve Years a Slave* "has been widely read in New England" and that "no narrative of man's experience as a slave, a chattel, is more touching, or better calculated to expose the true character and designs of slaveholders." While respecting the power of the published narrative, however, Wright recommends seeing Northup in person: "But it is far more potent to see the man, and hear him, in his clear, manly, straight-forward way, speak of slavery as he experienced it, and as he saw it in others. Those who have read his Narrative can scarce fail to desire to see the man, thus kidnapped and tortured in body and soul, for twelve years, and to hear his story from his own lips." Noting the legal proceedings following Northup's rescue, and the arguments presented by his kidnappers, Wright asks, "What is this Union to Solomon Northup? Literally a confederacy of kidnappers." But the limits of Wright's invocation of Northup's story in support of radical social reform are perhaps suggested by the actual responses to the questions he raises at the end of his letter: "Where is the Church or political party that will refuse to open the way to give this victim of slavery a hearing, and repay him for the suffering this Union has inflicted on him? But there are 4,000,000 of kidnapped men, women and children still under the *American* lash. Who will help to redeem them, and pay for their sufferings?"

22. On the commercial culture inspired by *Uncle Tom's Cabin*, see Gossett, *Uncle Tom's Cabin and American Culture*; and M. Wood, chap. 4.

23. Parker's letter was published as *John Brown's Expedition Reviewed in a Letter from Theodore Parker, at Rome, to Francis Jackson, Boston* (Boston, 1860); the Peases take the quotation from page 14 of that pamphlet.

24. I should note here that Olney is not simply saying that all slave narratives look alike; rather, he is arguing that the narratives, by and large, were written under similar circumstances and within a restricted social forum, and that "all the mixed, heterogeneous, heterogeneric elements in slave narratives come to be so regular, so con-

stant, so indispensable to the mode that they finally establish a set of conventions" (152).

25. For a slightly different take on Douglass's conspicuous omissions, see McBride, 154-56.

26. The seventh volume of Bancroft's *History* was first published in 1858.

27. In using the words "centripetal" and "centrifugal," Bancroft draws on a tradition of using Newtonian physics to explain the U.S. form of government. See, for example, *The Federalist Papers*, no. 9. As Bloomfield has noted, "The analogy between federalism and Newtonian physics became a popular theme in early American oratory" (58 n. 15). On the presence and influence of Newtonian physics in American literature, see Martin; and Limon.

28. On the concept of a representative republican language, capable of bonding the government, the people, and the nation's founding principle, see Gustafson, especially chap. 10, "Corrupt Language and a Corrupt Body Politic, or the Disunion of Words and Things." On nineteenth-century concepts of and debates over the role of language, see Cmiel; Rodgers; and Simpson.

29. I am thinking of the vision of an American republican tradition influenced heavily by the libertarian thought of English commonwealthmen, of the kind presented in Bailyn; Pocock; and G. Wood.

30. Relevant here is Peterson's argument that Lee "adopted a geographic self-marginalization whose power lay both in constant mobility and in the habitation of those liminal spaces opened up by the Second Great Awakening" (*Doers* 75).

31. Peterson has noted that historical scholarship has found that marginalized groups responded to the negative effects of "the industrial advances of the early nineteenth century" by turning to the "socially and geographically liminal spaces and experiences of the Second Great Awakening in which the carnivalesque flourished," a space in which "hierarchies of class, race, and gender are deconstructed, [and] the individual self loses its boundaries to merge with the other congregants and with the Godhead" (*Doers* 76). Addressing Lee in this context, Peterson argues that the camp meeting space "is structured not according to a capitalist economy of exchange but rather following what Luce Irigaray has called an alternative economy of mysticism—a transgressive libidinal economy that exists outside the labor market and its symbolic linguistic order and is characterized by the nonrational, the sensual, the oral, the carnivalesque" (76). I would add that Lee, Elaw, Jacobs, and others worked to bring "this space of the clearing" (76) to print, and thereby to resituate the terms by which history can be narrated and understood.

32. On Brent's transgressions, see Andrews, 247-53.; on Jacobs's call for a careful readership, see Foster, "Harriet Jacobs's *Incidents*."

33. I have in mind here Paul Ricoeur's presentation of "a Christian interpretation of the mystery of history" and his conception of the "false problem" of "the clash between Christian eschatology and the concept of progress" (81). Asserting that "the subject of the natural and uninterrupted progress of mankind is the aftermath of a secularization and . . . rationalist corruption of Christian eschatology," Ricoeur argues

that "nothing is more misleading than to oppose progress and hope or progress and mystery" (81). Ricoeur's narrative of "a Christian interpretation of the mystery of history" involves "three stages in the flux of history, three ways of understanding and recovering meaning, and three levels of interpretation: the abstract level of progress, the existential level of ambiguity, and the mysterious level of hope" (81, 82). For Ricoeur, what is commonly called progress is simply the ongoing *"accumulation of acquirements,"* the development of human tools of production and understanding. By acquirements, that is, Ricoeur means "tools in the broadest sense of the term: material or cultural tools, tools of knowledge, and even tools of consciousness and of the spirit" (81). The "level of ambiguity," Ricoeur argues, begins with the recognition of "the inadequacy of knowing about the equipment (even in the broadest sense) of a civilization in order to understand it." It is at this level of historical interpretation, Ricoeur suggests, that one can recognize that the significance of a culture's "equipment does not lie within the equipment itself; it depends upon the fundamental attitudes taken by the men of a given civilization in respect to their own technical possibilities" (87). "The tool," Ricoeur observes, "is not even useful unless it is valued" (87)—and, being a tool, it cannot be adequately valued unless its function is itself recognized and valued. The last stage of Ricoeur's "Christian interpretation of the mystery of history" is the "level of hope." This level, Ricoeur explains, can be "summarized in two words"—"meaning and mystery"—that "in some way nullify each other but are nevertheless the contrasted language of hope" (93). And one might say that Ricoeur's conception of these terms is the same conception that we discover at the center of nineteenth-century African American literature: "Meaning: there is a unity of meaning; it is the fundamental source of the courage to live in history. Mystery: but this meaning is hidden; no one can *say* it, rely upon it, or draw an assurance from it which would be a counter-assurance against the dangers of history. One must risk it on signs" (93). On the application of this mode of understanding to nineteenth-century African American literature, see the introduction to Ernest, *Resistance and Reformation.*

34. On the terms and significance of Brent's struggle with Flint, see Nelson, chap. 7.

35. It is important to remember that Jacobs worries about her own presence as mother in her children's lives, for they "cannot remember me with such entire satisfaction as I remembered my mother" (90). Like her mother, though, Jacobs hopes to give them a voice to remember.

36. Baker argues in *Workings of the Spirit* that "a primary component of what might be termed 'classical' Afro-American discourse is 'soul.' In more sacral dimensions, this component is labeled 'spirit.' Soul motivates; spirit moves. The generative source of style in Afro-America is soul; the impetus for salvation is spirit" (75). I would suggest that Jacobs here makes a point of writing from the soul in the name of the spirit. On Jacobs's related response to white patriarchal sentimental culture and the domestication of blackness, see Merish, chap. 4.

37. Nat Turner's presence here is, of course, significant. Indeed, Turner was a

prominent presence in nineteenth-century African American publications. See Sund-quist, chap. 1. On Turner's presence in American literature generally, see M. Davis.

38. Clearly, I depart from Russ Castronovo in his reading of *Incidents* in *Necro Citizenship*. Castronovo argues that "Linda refuses to see the soul as an alternative to the culturally bound and determined body. To exist as a soul is to reap the rewards of a generic personhood, but it is also to incur prohibitions that authorize the unequal distribution of disembodiment, social transparency, and other resources associated with the public sphere. *Incidents* fuses materiality and spirituality to lay bare the repressive effects of having a soul" (157). But African American understandings of the soul in relation to the contingencies of race were not nearly so simplistic as Castro-novo suggests, and African American discourses of spirituality did not simply follow the pattern of the dominant culture, in which the ideological imperatives of whiteness rendered citizenship, in both this world and the next, an unstable fiction of law. Castronovo seems to view Linda's turn "from the body's materiality to the soul's immortality" as a backward tendency, noting that Linda "chats with her dead father, sees her children as ghosts, and longs for death as a final freedom, yet instead of overcoming the institutional conditions that circumscribe her mortal being, each of these spiritual encounters intensifies slavery's despair as social death" (157). Surely, though, this is a misrepresentation of Jacobs's presentation of her visions and her understanding of her spiritual state, which carry her through her experiences and are central to the civic activism, and to her revision of the terms of civil authority, throughout her narration of her life's history.

More satisfying is Castronovo's return, later in *Necro Citizenship*, to Jacobs's spiri-tual visions—and in this second phase of his argument Castronovo articulates bril-liantly the argument I am presenting in a (perhaps significantly) different context. Here, Castronovo notes that Jacobs associates Nat Turner with her father's communi-cation from beyond the grave and argues that "her allusion to Nat Turner suggests that ghostly thoughts, while often hierarchical and dispossessive, can also foment defiance. Her stance that the spiritual—if it can be rematerialized—carries liberatory potential pits her against one of the most cited authorities on revolutionary struggle, Frantz Fanon. Unlike Fanon's estimation of the occult as a backward tendency, Jacobs portrays slavery's hauntings as tangible vestiges of a radical legacy that have been suppressed" (196). "In pursuing a revolutionary memory as fragile as a ruin," Castro-novo explains, "*Incidents* recuperates black liberation theology from its subvention under white spiritualism" (196). Addressing Linda's vision of her children, Castro-novo argues that "historically weighted, [Linda's] spirit vision falls short of tran-scending contestation and discord. Unlike the sleepwalking medium who achieves liberatory insensibility of her surroundings, the 'slave girl' become slave mother experiences second sight as the recognition of contingency.... In Brent's case ... the actual and imaginary more than meet; they articulate a deep interconnectedness that challenges fantasies of liberal individualism. Rewritten as the slave superstition from whence it derived, the occult secures not independence but contingency, not auton-omy but community" (199–200).

39. I have in mind here Moody's important commentary on her experience teaching graduate seminars, and her disagreements with her students concerning what constitutes "history" and historical context and theoretical frameworks for literary study ("Personal Places" 23–27).

40. Levine has emphasized the complexity and cultural reach of Douglass's communal vision in *My Bondage and My Freedom* in his important reading of Douglass's promotion of the dual and sometime incompatible ideals of "temperate self-help" and "revolutionary social change." See *Martin Delany*, 112–43.

41. For my reading of the *Narrative* in this regard, see *Resistance and Reformation*, 156–57.

42. Sadly, a recent anthology of African American literature, *Call and Response*, omits Douglass's appendix from the *Narrative*. Though this is an anthology devoted, admirably so, to a literary history informed by the Black Aesthetic, in this case it omits the black aesthetic framework from Douglass's narrative.

43. There is no entry on Steward, for example, in the *Oxford Companion to African American Literature*. Steward became a successful grocer in Rochester, New York, was active for a while in the Canadian community of Wilberforce, taught school in Canandaigua, New York, served as agent for the *National Anti-Slavery Standard*, was actively involved in the 1830 Annual Convention for the Improvement of Colored People, and was president of the New York Convention of Colored Men in 1840.

44. Ward has a footnote here: "I am among those who believe that the British colonies are both the agency by which, and the medium through which, the gospel can, ought, *must*, be given to the heathen world. The situation, origin, growth, progress, language, and relations, of those colonies, all seem, to me, to point in that direction."

45. As Boime has noted, "The one component of slavery upon which conservatives, radicals, and liberals could always agree was the inhumane condition under which the slaves existed. Early abolitionists stressed the moral issue and took pains to enumerate the instances of sadistic treatment, the application of instruments of torture, and the expressions of discrimination in colonial policy" (47). Marcus Wood notes further that "the representation of slave torture in the art and literature of the West focused around a fairly consistent set of signs and rituals" (216). "The pain of slaves," Wood observes, "when translated into imagery and visual narrative, is most commonly related to, and imparted through, a series of objects." In these representations, Wood argues, "the slave emerges predominantly as an object afflicted, not as a subject capable of describing his or her affliction" (216). On visual representations of the torture and suffering of the enslaved, see Boime, chap. 3; Wood, chap. 5; and Reilly.

46. Ward also offers a sly reference to "Old Hickory," as Jackson was called, in his narration of an episode in the life of an enslaved man, also named Andrew Jackson, who fought off five slave-catchers with a hickory stick (176).

47. Ward accounts for the difference between British and American views on race by noting "the very low origin of early American settlers, and the very deficient cultivation as compared with other nations" (40). It is important to note Ward's own

problematic views on race and national character—for example, his anti-Catholicism in his consideration of what he takes to be the inferiority of the Irish (whom he compares unfavorably with the Welsh), about which see 370–84.

48. Ward here echoes a familiar complaint about the limitations of antislavery sympathy. As Rael has observed, "The market revolution in the North inculcated an ideology that excoriated slaveholding but stood mute on the rights of those freed. This left free blacks huddling under the weak shelter of humanitarian sentiment and revolutionary logic against the maelstrom of economic imperative, centuries-long prejudice, and an emerging racial science that found it increasingly easy to write blacks out of the brotherhood of man" (26). In the pages of *Frederick Douglass' Monthly* in 1860, Douglass announced his support of efforts to reorganize the abolition movement, a movement that had been damaged greatly by internal divisions and philosophical differences. Noting the great need for reorganization, Douglass suggested that the movement was stalled, in effect, by its own success in promoting antislavery sentiment in the North: "The effect of all anti-slavery effort thus far is this: It has filled the whole North with a sentiment opposed to slavery. Sentimental Abolitionism is abundant. It may well be met with in the pulpit, sometimes in the religious newspapers, and more frequently still we meet it in the meetings of the Republican party; yet among them all there is neither will nor purpose to abolish slavery" (Foner, *Life and Writings* 2:522). The problem was not that antislavery sentiments were not being promoted; the problem was that they *were* being both promoted and normalized among white Northerners who supported the cause but resisted the implications of the message. In a call for the establishment of a national African American press, a committee of black abolitionists argued that "the amount of hatred against us has been conventional antipathy; and of the favorable feeling has been human sympathy. Our friends sorrow with us, because they say we are unfortunate! We must batter down those antipathies, we must command something manlier than sympathies" (Ripley 4:9).

Chapter Four

1. I am deeply indebted to Bethel's thorough commentary on this event. See also M. Wood, 250–51.

2. William Lloyd Garrison, Theodore Parker, Wendell Phillips, John S. Rock, and Charles Remond shared the platform with the Attucks Glee Club, the Bards of Freedom, and the Northern Singers. Bethel notes as well that "in addition to the two most well-known female participants at the 1858 Festival, Frances Ellen Watkins and Charlotte Forten, women appeared throughout the program and were publicly visible on the stage at Faneuil Hall" (9). Watkins had composed "Freedom's Battle" for the event, a song performed by the Attucks Glee Club, and the Northern Vocalists performed a song composed by Forten (Bethel 10).

3. On the importance of antislavery celebrations in formulating black activism, see Rael, chap. 2. As Rael demonstrates, "The antislavery celebration was a key com-

ponent in the process through which black leaders submerged difference and presented to white America a unified racial front" (81).

4. For background and commentary on *The Columbian Orator*, see David W. Blight's introduction to his edition of the work. See also Fishkin and Peterson, 190–98; and Mailloux, 14–15.

5. In his commentary on David Walker's "view of language as the means of empowerment," Warren offers a useful example of the cultural control over language (121): "letters from the anonymous 'V.' concerning the *Appeal*," published in the *Liberator*, that "mix approval and disapproval" (122). Warren observes that in these letters "V. effectively rewrites Walker's *Appeal*, sanitizing its indignant call for immediate emancipation and secularizing its tone of Old Testament prophecy" (122). "By rewording Walker," Warren argues, "V. makes an appeal to the spirit of liberal humanism, but his gradualist language silences the *Appeal* more effectively than Southern legislatures were able to do" (122).

6. Noting that "black leaders relied overwhelmingly on the power of public speech to sway their audiences," Rael argues that "northern free blacks . . . constructed black identity through self-conscious acts of public political speech. They thus built a notion, prepared specifically for the public sphere, of their shared interests as an oppressed race" (45).

7. "A Fugitive Slave Turned Author," 5; "William Wells Brown at Philadelphia," 14.

8. Warren (13–14) notes the controversy that followed Wendell Phillips's determination to lecture on slavery at the Concord Lyceum. When the subject was put to a vote, Phillips was invited to give the lecture again—leading to the resignation of two curators and the president of the lyceum.

9. Interestingly, Garrison compares Douglass with Patrick Henry, about whom see Looby—though in telling this story, Garrison emphasizes his own role in this drama, his ability to identify the significance of this moment in the context of the larger national narrative. In effect, whereas Douglass gave voice to the evils of slavery, Garrison gives voice to the achievement behind the act of giving voice, emphasizing Douglass's *speaking* over the content of his speech, including in his remarks an account of his call-and-response approach to his comments that followed Douglass's address.

10. For another, related, commentary on oration, see William Whipper's 1828 *Address Delivered in Wesley Church*. Among other things, Whipper comments on oration and fashion, the duty of the scholar, and the applications of Scotch philosophy.

11. *Frederick Douglass' Paper*, May 20, 1852.

12. That turn involved for Allen still more mixtures of blood circulating through the nation's veins. He dismissed the notion of "African nationality . . . if, by African nationality is meant, a nation composed entirely of pure Africans." He argued that "nations worthy of the name, are only produced by a fusion of races" ("Letter from Wm. G. Allen," May 20, 1852). Responding to the controversy that followed this and other public statements, Allen emphasized his point later that year: *"No truly great nation composed of a* SINGLE *race had ever yet written its name on any page of human*

history, nor never can, if there be any virtue in science, philosophy and religion." The "'single-race theory,' as the theory for the upbuilding of nations," Allen concluded, "is anti-Christian–atheistical. It is the legitimate theory of the pro-slavery and the prejudiced, and underlies the whole project of the abomination of abominations– Liberia Colonization" ("Letter from Wm. G. Allen," July 30, 1852).

13. Allen's frustration concerning the public's embracing of Kossuth extended to the African American community as well. In a letter to *Frederick Douglass' Paper* (January 1, 1852), Allen attacked a public statement of support for Kossuth from the black community of New York City: "You have seen the address of the colored people of New York City to Kossuth. What a stupendously foolish thing! Not a word of their own wrongs–their sufferings–their enslavement;–no point, no directness, no nothing except the mere rhetoric." Allen notes that the community promises Kossuth financial support that would better be devoted to "the benefit of the four millions in our own land who are ground to the dust in chains and slavery, and the tens of thousands of others who, by cruel laws and customs are kept in poverty and degradation" ("Letter from William G. Allen").

14. An 1852 speech by Wilbur M. Hayward, titled "American Eloquence," is akin to Allen's "Orators and Oratory" in many respects, following the path of oratorical power through history and finally locating the rise of eloquence in the United States; then associating eloquence with liberty, responsibility, and national destiny; and finally turning this overview of national eloquence to the cause of antislavery (after praising Douglass along the way, as well as the usual suspects of white oratorical power, and the trinity of "Calhoun, Clay and Webster").

15. *Uncle Tom's Cabin* was serialized in the *National Era* in 1851–1852 with the subtitle *The Man That Was a Thing*.

16. As Ericson has argued, "Douglass's speech is really two speeches in one. The first 'speech' is a fairly typical antebellum Fourth of July oration," one that "could well have been delivered by any contemporary American orator, black or white, abolitionist or not" (55). But Douglass's "second 'speech,'" Ericson notes, is distinctly an antislavery jeremiad (55–60).

17. See, for example, W. P. Johnson, "The Fourth and Fifth of July in the City of Schenectady."

18. The historicity of African American oration was a sign of the Africanist sensibility on the U.S. public stages, as Peterson suggests in her commentary on Sojourner Truth. "Truth's links to African and African-American oral cultures," Peterson speculates, "may be located . . . in her belief in the primacy of the spoken word, its importance as a mode of action rather than simply an articulation of thought, its magical power to create events, to make the past present, and vision reality" (48).

19. The address was published in the *National Anti-Slavery Standard*, July 18, 1844.

20. Remond begins by noting that he cannot expect his "humble views . . . to make much impression upon the many–upon the body of this nation, for whose benefit the Constitution was made; but they will meet a response from the few whom it entirely

overlooks, or sees but to trample upon, and the fewer still, who identify themselves with the outcast, by occupying this position, of a dissolution of their union with Slaveholders" (206).

21. Douglas here echoes a resolution from the 1847 National Convention, which stated that "the Declaration of American Independence is not a lie, and, if the fathers of the Revolution were not base and shameless hypocrites, it is evident that all men are created equal, and are endowed by their Creator with certain inalienable rights, among which are life, liberty, and the pursuit of happiness" (Bell, *Minutes*, 1847 proceedings 16).

22. For commentary on the San Domingo Revolution in the U.S. imagination, see Hunt; and Sundquist.

23. For useful commentary on Garnet's speech, its possible Africanist roots, and the politics of the responses to (and attempts to contain) the speech, see Stuckey, 154–60. Stauffer (108–9) speculates that Garnet might have been influenced by a speech presented a year earlier by white abolitionist Gerrit Smith, titled "Address to the Slaves of the United States" and published in the February 24, 1842, issue of the *National Anti-Slavery Standard*.

24. Stanley was a member of the Ladies Anti-Slavery Society of Delaware, Ohio. Her remarks were read by William Harris.

25. On conventioneers' efforts to adopt and maintain methods for ensuring a philosophically just approach to (male) representation at the conventions, see Rael, 30–44.

26. Rael is particularly instructive on the effort to promote a unified communal identity in the convention movement. To be sure, as Rael emphasizes, a black elite, male leadership worked to shape the movement, but "rather than suggesting the hegemony of a small class of black elites," Rael concludes, "the convention movement illustrated themes of conflict and contention. While cadres of prominent national figures dominated the movement, they hardly suppressed debate. Instead, movement stalwarts exerted what authority they had in less direct ways, largely through their steadfast presence, and through the control of the movement's larger agenda, which their ubiquity conferred" (35). "For every gesture conventioneers made that revealed an elite, exclusionary social perspective," Rael notes, "they set forth another in the opposite direction" (37).

27. Concerns about the ACS remained a part of the concerns addressed by the national convention movement. The 1834 proceedings asserted that "as long at least as the Colonization Society exists, will a Convention of coloured people be highly necessary" (Bell, *Minutes*, 1834 proceedings 5). Later conventions included heated debates on related concerns—for example, on Garnet's support of an emigration movement. For commentary on the complex politics surrounding the ACS, within and beyond the black community, see Bruce, "Black and White Voices."

28. Characteristic were the various attempts to encourage a turn to agriculture, supported by republican theory about the character, individual and collective, shaped by agricultural pursuits. These attempts were aided by testimonials from successful African American farmers, and later by grants of land to various African American

leaders by white abolitionist Gerrit Smith. By the 1853 convention, Douglass could state flatly to Harriet Beecher Stowe, in a letter reprinted in the convention proceedings, that agriculture was not the answer to the question of how to uplift the African American community (35).

29. Bell says that between 1835 and 1843 "there were numerous attempts to revive the national assemblies," but that "it was not . . . until the autumn of 1841 that a sizeable number of men set their names to a call for such an assembly" (*A Survey* 69). On that failed attempt, see Bell, *A Survey*, 69–71.

30. The phrase is from Hebrews 13:3. It was included in the engraving for the title page of Lydia Maria Child's *Authentic Anecdotes of American Slavery* (1838), a reprint of a British antislavery emblem with a different motto. The British version quoted Psalm 2:3: "Let us break their bands asunder, and cast away their cords from us." For commentary on this transformed antislavery emblem and motto, see Yellin, 17–23.

31. The debate concerned the fourth resolution of the 1848 national convention in Cleveland, Ohio. The resolution reads as follows: "Resolved, That the occupation of domestics and servants among our people is degrading to us as a class, and we deem it our bounden duty to discountenance such pursuits, except where necessity compels the person to resort thereto as a means of livelihood" (Bell, *Minutes*, 1848 proceedings 13). When the resolution was read and discussed, some in the assembly were offended. J. D. Patterson is recorded as arguing "that those who were in the editorial chair and others, not in places of servants, must not cast slurs upon those, who were in such places from necessity" (5). Douglass is reported to have said that "he wished not that it should stand thus:–White Lawyer–Black Chimney-sweep; but White Lawyer, Black Lawyer, as in Massachusetts; White Domestic, Black Domestic. He said: Let us say what is necessary to be done, is honorable to do; and leave situations in which we are considered degraded, as soon as necessity ceases" (6). The resolution was voted on without amendment and "was adopted with but one dissenting vote" (6). For commentary, see Bell, *A Survey*, 102–3; and Rael, 35–36.

32. On Dickinson, see Callaghan.

33. Women's omission from the records of the convention proceedings underscores the importance of Peterson's observation that African American women orators manipulated the "socially and geographically liminal spaces" of evangelical movements, though a few worked in officially sanctioned cultural forums–notably, Frances E. W. Harper in her early career as an antislavery lecturer. Some, like Maria Stewart, insisted on a hearing but faced significant resistance. Peterson's *"Doers of the Word"* and Logan's *"We Are Coming"* offer excellent surveys of and commentaries on the forums for and strategies of nineteenth-century women orators.

34. The call stated that "both reason and feeling have assigned to us a place in the conflict now going on in our land between liberty and equality on the one hand, and slavery and caste on the other–a place which we cannot fail to occupy without branding ourselves as unworthy of our natural post, and recreant to the cause we profess to love" (Bell, *Minutes*, 1853 proceedings 3).

35. I am drawing from my reading of Douglass's autobiographies in chapter 5 of *Resistance and Reformation.*

Chapter Five

1. For useful background on the African American and antislavery press of this period, see Hutton; Rhodes; Senna; and Wolseley. Bruce rightly weaves history and commentary of the African American press, the *Liberator*, and the American press generally through *The Origins of African American Literature*; see especially chaps. 5–7.

2. The press, its editors realized, was important as well in responding to the vision of a biblically scattered community central to African American historical thought. As Samuel Cornish put it in his opening editorial for the *Colored American* (March 4, 1837), an African American press was necessary "because our afflicted population in the free states, are scattered in handfuls over nearly 5000 towns, and can only be reached by the Press—a public journal must therefore be sent down, at least weekly, to rouse them up. To call all their energies into action—and where they have been down trodden, paralyzed and worn out, to create new energies for them, that such dry bones may live" (Ripley 3:216).

3. This dynamic reading practice is, of course, characteristic of all periodicals, and African American editors would, like other editors, turn this dynamic to serve their editorial purposes. For an excellent consideration of the *Liberator* in this regard, see Rohrbach.

4. In contemporary terms, this would be the difference between a newsweekly that offers a special issue or article on "race" and a black newsmonthly that approaches all news from the perspective provided by African American experience; and it would be the difference between a "unit on race" in a classroom or the "race chapter" in a scholarly book and an approach to teaching and to scholarship that begins by recognizing the systemic presence of race, and therefore recognizes that race cannot, in fact, be set off from other concerns. On African Americans' views concerning the problems and possibilities of the press, see Rael, 213–16.

5. Verbal and visual caricatures of African American identity and assemblies were of course common. As Reilly has noted, "The print shops of Boston, New York, and Philadelphia were wellsprings of antiblack pictures" (52). Beyond racist "entertainment," Marcus Wood writes, "the seamless integration of the slave into the day-to-day economic transactions of the North and South is represented with a terrible graphic finality in the sheets of trade icons which concluded Northern printers' stock books. These books provided the basic visual vocabulary for trade and product advertisement in mid-nineteenth-century America" (89). "The significance of advertising for the print culture of America in the first half of the nineteenth century is difficult to overestimate" (89), Wood remarks, and the iconic representation of commerce in and control over the enslaved (for example, the well-known icon of the runaway slave) was an important part of advertising at the time.

6. On the debates over the role of the black press and the need for an official paper (*Frederick Douglass' Paper* was endorsed by the national convention of 1855), see Levine, *Martin Delany*, 22–32; on Douglass's vision of his work as editor as a repre-

sentative example of attempts to define an African American press, official or unofficial, see Fanuzzi.

7. Bullock notes that "another white friend who assisted Douglass was Abram Pryne of Williamson and McGrawville, New York," who "served as editor during a six-month period that Douglass spent in England during 1859–60" (54).

8. For an important reconsideration of how to read the tension between Douglass and Garrison, see Fanuzzi, who argues that it is a mistake to read their conflict either as personal or as part of what we would today call identity politics—though the conflict, Fanuzzi acknowledges, was certainly "bitter," "inflammatory," and "undoubtedly racial" (56). He sees their public conflicts as part of "a conventional weapon in a newspaper war, used for the strategic purpose of positioning. For both Douglass and Garrison, the authenticity of identity in fact mattered less than the thrusts and counterthrusts of what Gramsci would call a 'war of position' over what mattered most for both combatants in the antislavery struggle: the historic title of a people" (56).

9. Cornish here echoes the case he made for a specifically African American press in his editorial for the *Colored American*'s inaugural issue of March 4, 1837. An African American press was necessary, Cornish argued, "because no class of men, however pious and benevolent, can take our place in the great work of redeeming our character and removing our disabilities. They may identify themselves with us, and enter into our sympathies. Still it is ours to will and do" (Ripley 3:217).

10. *American Slavery As It Is* included "evidence" gathered by Theodore Weld, Angelina Grimké Weld, and Angelina's sister Sarah Grimké. Material (excerpts from southern papers, for example) and commentary from this book were often referred to or reprinted—most prominently in William Wells Brown's *Clotel*, which incorporates passages verbatim.

11. Similarly, Benjamin F. Roberts, the black editor of the *Anti-Slavery Herald*, complained of white criticism of and interference in his efforts, asserting that "there has been and *now is*, a combined effort on the part of certain *professed* abolitionists to muzzle, exterminate and put down the efforts of certain colored individuals effecting the welfare of their colored brethren" (Ripley 3:269).

12. The *Colored American* of course supported Garrison, and Garrison was sometimes a prominent presence in the paper—as, for example, when the *Colored American* printed Garrison's "Address Delivered at the Broadway Tabernacle, N.Y. on the First of August, 1838, by Request of the People of Color in That City . . ." during August and September 1838. But it is important to note that the paper's identity allowed its editor to contextualize Garrison's work within a black national framework. The *Colored American*, which regularly distinguished between "friends" and "brethren" of the black community, sometimes presented Garrison and other white friends as people coming along in their understanding of issues central to African Americans. In an article titled "The Emigration Scheme," for example, the *Colored American* comments on a notice of Nancy Prince's pamphlet *The West Indies*. "The editor of the Liberator," the piece states, "who, in relation to this scheme, has always been wanting in that usual sagacity with which he generally sees matters as they

associate themselves with our cause, now thus expresses himself in the conclusion of his remarks upon the little work here referred to" ("The Emigration Scheme"). The *Colored American* notes with approval that the *Liberator* now advises its black readers against emigration to Jamaica or Trinidad.

While African American support of Garrison remained strong, the *Colored American* was representative in its attempts to keep the achievements of white abolitionists from obscuring the history of black activism. The year before Garrison presented his address at the Broadway Tabernacle, for example, black abolitionist Rev. Charles W. Gardner spoke in the same forum and noted that "William Lloyd Garrison has been branded as the individual who turned the people of color against the colonization scheme. But I can tell you, sir, that when William Lloyd Garrison was a schoolboy, the people of color in different parts of the country were holding extensive meetings, which always agreed in declaring that they regarded the scheme as visionary in itself, and calculated only to rivet the chains of those who remain in slavery" (Ripley 3:210).

13. See, for example, the series "History of Slavery" in *Freedom's Journal* of July 13, 1827; July 27, 1827; and August 3, 1827.

14. This definition of community, I should emphasize, was as often sternly patriarchal as it was traditionally republican. The *Colored American*, for example, included a statement on gender roles, asserting that "men are made to be their own masters.–The great concerns of the active world are intended to be carried on by men; and among bodies of men who have no agency in them, human nature is not developed." "A man is intended by nature," the article continues, "to be not only the lord of his own household, but a part of the governing body of society." On the other hand, the article asserts,

> the nature of women . . . may be perfectly developed within the domestic circle alone. Her character is not incomplete because she has no voice in public affairs. In times of tranquillity and enjoyment, the duties of public life and the various excellencies which are called into play for dispensing happiness within the social circle, abroad, afford ample scope for every amiable and elegant accomplishment. When the frown of fortune is upon us–the convulsions and reverses that attend the private history of every family; poverty–sickness– danger and difficulty–give opportunity to those attributes of fortitude, energy, tenderness, and moral heroism, which elevate the character of woman to that of a ministering angel.–Enough is left to her, therefore, even where political liberty is unknown, for the display of private excellence. ("A Fragment")

These views are characteristic of the views expressed, explicitly or implicitly, in the great majority of articles found in the African American press of this time. In this chapter as throughout this book, I am focusing on activities in the public print sphere and trying to identify dominant patterns, and I am well aware of the limitations of this approach. The terms of that dominance will have to be studied, and the findings will necessarily revise much of what I am presenting here. Still, I write with the faith that the process of identification and revision is worthwhile, and that it is a process that will continue as we look for a balanced understanding of what community leaders tried to accomplish and of the ways in which their efforts were deeply flawed, repeating many of the injustices, blindnesses, and violations they worked to address.

15. Encouraging and facilitating reading was a constant concern among African American activists, and they created numerous libraries and literary societies through the years. The *Colored American*, like other papers, looked to link the paper with organized efforts to promote reading. In an editorial published in the June 10, 1838, issue of the *Colored American*, for example, Cornish promoted the establishment of "a *Reading Room*, in connection with this Paper," noting that "our large exchange list, together with the pamphlets and other literary productions, which are presented and furnished us, weekly, will give great facilities to such an enterprise; and there is nothing so much needed by all classes of our people, as a well-furnished and well-selected reading establishment" (Ripley 3:261). "The reason why we have so many empty minds and idle hands," Cornish asserted, sounding what was a continual theme in his paper, "is our deficiency of literary and scientific institutions. Where the acquirement of knowledge, mental and moral, is neglected, there the vices grow and luxuriate" (Ripley 3:261).

16. See, for example, the "Declaration of Sentiments, on the Sin of Slavery" and "The Church in Fault," both published in the *Colored American*; "The Anglo-African and the African Slave Trade" in the *Anglo-African Magazine*; the *Minutes of the Fourth Annual Convention, for the Improvement of the Free People of Colour, in the United States* (1834), 30, in Bell, *Minutes*; and the *Minutes of the National Convention of Colored Citizens* (1843), 15, in Bell, *Minutes*.

17. As this article demonstrates, the *Colored American* did, however, publish articles critical of black ministers. Similarly, the paper published a letter from black leader William Watkins, who argued, "There is . . . at the fountainhead of our colored communities, a most serious obstacle to the improvement of our people; an obstacle which cannot, for many years, be wholly obviated, but which should, so far as it is practicable, be removed, and such incipient measures adopted as will check, for the future, the evil to which we have alluded. But what is this evil? It is in unequivocal terms, *the incompetency of the colored ministry, in general, to supply the intellectual wants of the colored population of the country*" (Ripley 3:233). Consider also Mary Ann Shadd's letter of January 25, 1849, to the *North Star*, in which she asserts that "the influence of a corrupt clergy among us, sapping our every means, and, as a compensation, inculcating ignorance as a duty, superstition as true religion—in short, hanging like millstones about our necks, should be faithfully proclaimed" (Ripley 4:32).

18. The phrase comes from *A Summary View of the Rights of British America*. For Jefferson, the "language of truth" is a narrative "divested of those expressions of servility which would persuade his majesty that we are asking favors, and not rights" (5). For the reprinting of remarks on slavery by various writers throughout history, see "Slavery and the Slave Trade."

19. The original editorial addresses the American Colonization Society, asserting that the journal has never tried "to prejudice the minds of our brethren against the society, or render them suspicious of its motives," but that the journal has in-

stead consistently published its opposition "to colonization in PRINCIPLE, OBJECT, AND TENDENCY."

20. Page citations for articles published in the *Anglo-American Magazine* are from the reprint of the bound edition of the magazine's volume 1 (1859).

21. On *Blake* in this regard, see especially Sundquist, 183–221; Ernest, *Resistance and Reformation*, 109–39; and Levine, *Martin Delany*, 177–223.

22. The central concern of this sketch is, here and elsewhere, quite clear: "When I was a girl, we used to call the days when the boys made their speeches and the girls showed their copy-books and samples, exhibitions. I shall never get the run of these new-fangled words. Miranda, she knows all about these things; you can't puzzle her with the big words. Sometimes she tells me about these new ideas about woman's rights, and woman's mission, and gives me good satisfaction. I once asked my old man what he thought of woman's rights and woman's mission. He said that it was to keep the house clean and stay home and take care of her husband and children. But, said I, suppose she has not got a husband. Well, then, he said, she ought to get one" (385).

23. William Goodell (1792–1878), an active New York abolitionist and editor of various reformist papers, was the author of a highly influential study of the legal structures of the system of slavery, *The American Slave Code in Theory and Practice: Its Distinctive Features Shown by Its Statutes, Judicial Decisions, and Illustrative Facts* (1853).

24. Though based on the immediate requirements of liberation, the vision of education was broad and encompassing. Among the articles published in the *Anglo-African Magazine*, for example, is an essay on poetry by a student, identified as "May." The piece includes an editorial note stating that "the following is the production of a pupil of one of our Grammar schools, and as we have now opened a Youth's Department, we would be glad to receive contributions from similar sources" (122).

25. Wilson follows Smith in other ways as well, for Smith wrote a series of ten sketches titled the "Republic of Letters," depicting African Americans of various professions—from bootblack to inventor, from whitewasher to schoolmaster. As Stauffer has noted, Smith's "sketches are word paintings, really—impressionistic and at times abstract portraits done in an experimental style. In both form and content they are, like so many of his other writings, far ahead of their time. He employs a rich array of wordplay and parody, irony and humor. And he creates a narrator who subjectively participates in the consciousness of his characters while objectively analyzing the culture in which they live" (118).

26. Lydia Maria Child, for example, presents good republican philosophy in *The American Frugal Housewife* when in demonstrating her sense of the extent of the mother's responsibilities she remarks: "Nations do not plunge *at once* into ruin—governments do not change *suddenly*—the causes which bring about the final blow, are scarcely perceptible in the beginning; but they increase in numbers, and in power; they press harder and harder upon the energies and virtue of a people; and the last steps only are alarmingly hurried and irregular" (91). Ethiop puts a racial spin on this philosophy, in some ways echoing Samuel Ringgold Ward's vision of the declining educational achievements of the white race. "And they wrapped themselves up in

their ease and luxury in hopeful security," Ethiop writes; "and their hand slackened; and great physical and mental weakness came over them; and many changes came in among them; so much so, that your forefathers looked upon them with much concern." The transformation leads to a new racial era: "Yea their hair darkened, so also did their eyes and their skins; and they said unto your forefathers let us come in among you and be of you and partake of your substance" (175).

27. Brent/Jacobs responds to the news that her freedom has been secured by a "bill of sale," and comments on this bill: "Those words struck me like a blow. So I was *sold* at last! A human being *sold* in the free city of New York! The bill of sale is on record, and future generations will learn from it that women were articles of traffic in New York, late in the nineteenth century of the Christian religion. It may hereafter prove a useful document to antiquaries, who are seeking to measure the progress of civilization in the United States" (200).

Epilogue

1. In addition to William Still's well-known *The Underground Rail Road* (1872), I am thinking, for example, of Joseph T. Wilson's *Emancipation* (1882); B. T. Tanner's *An Outline of the History and Government for African Methodist Churchmen, Ministerial and Lay* (1884); Rev. James M. Simms's *The First Colored Baptist Church in North America* (1888); Charles Henry Phillips's *The History of the Colored Methodist Episcopal Church in America* (1898); Edward A. Johnson's *History of Negro Soldiers in the Spanish-American War* (1899); Rt. Rev. Wesley J. Gaines's *African Methodism in the South* (1890); and Rev. L. M. Hagood's *The Colored Man in the Methodist Episcopal Church* (1890).

2. An untiring advocate of antislavery, temperance, and other reform causes, Brown received mixed reviews as a lecturer. Farrison cites many reviews that praise Brown's abilities, and certainly Brown's reputation suggests a certain power. But concerning the 1844 American Anti-Slavery meeting, Farrison notes, "This being Brown's first speech at a national antislavery convention and in the presence of a large number of talented thinkers and orators, it probably did not lift the audience to great heights. The *National Anti-Slavery Standard* reported his words very briefly; the *Liberator* did not report them at all" (87). Both papers, it should be noted, reported extensively on Brown's lectures in the years that followed. Still, Charlotte Forten Grimké had this to say in her diary in 1854: "This evening went to Mr. Brown's lecture. I thought that he spoke much better than he usually does. His manner was more animated. But although in private conversation he has greatly improved, I do not think he is a very good lecturer." "As a writer," Grimké (then Forten) adds kindly, "he is very highly spoken of by some of the leading English journals" (111); one should add that Brown prominently featured the favorable reviews in some of his published work.

3. See Elam, "The Black Performer and the Performance of Blackness."

4. See Ernest, "The Reconstruction of Whiteness."

5. See Ernest, "Fugitive Performances."

6. On the relation between theories of racial supremacy and theories of the progress of civilization, see especially Horsman. See also Levin; and Callcott.

7. Jenkins, Brown writes, is "too black for Douglass, not black enough for Ward, not tall enough for Garnet, too calm for Delany, [and] figure, though fine, not genteel enough for Remond" (*The Black Man* 261). See Ernest, "The Reconstruction of Whiteness," 1108–10; and Ernest, "Fugitive Performances," 162.

Bibliography

All articles from the *Colored American, Frederick Douglass' Paper*, and *Freedom's Journal* were obtained from the Accessible Archives Database.

Abdul-Jabbar, Kareem, with Alan Steinberg. *Black Profiles in Courage: A Legacy of African American Achievement.* New York: William Morrow, 1996.

"Abolition Dying Away." *Colored American*, May 8, 1841.

"Abolition of Caste Schools." *Liberator*, August 31, 1855, 138.

"About Niggers." *Putnam's Monthly* 6, no. 36 (December 1855): 608–12.

Adams, Alice Dana. *The Neglected Period of Anti-Slavery in America, 1808–1831.* 1908. Williamstown, Mass.: Corner House, 1973.

Adams, Henry. *The Letters of Henry Adams.* Vol. 2. Edited by J. C. Levenson, Ernest Samuels, Charles Vandersee, and Viola Hopkins Winner. Cambridge, Mass.: Harvard University Press, 1982.

Adams, H. G., ed. *God's Image in Ebony: Being a Series of Biographical Sketches, Facts, Anecdotes, etc., Demonstrative of the Mental Powers and Intellectual Capacities of the Negro Race. With a Brief Sketch of the Anti-Slavery Movement in America, by F. W. Chesson; and a Concluding Chapter of Additional Evidence, Communicated by Wilson Armistead, ESQ.* London: Partridge and Oakey, 1854.

Adams, John Quincy. "The Holy Bible." *Colored American*, December 22, 1838.

Adams, Nehemiah. *A South-Side View of Slavery; or, Three Months at the South, in 1854.* 1854. New York: Negro Universities Press, 1969.

"Address of the Colored National Convention to the People of the United States." *Liberator*, August 5, 1853, 121.

"Address of the New York State Convention to Their Colored Fellow Citizens." *Colored American*, November 21, 1840.

Adeleke, Tunde. *UnAfrican Americans: Nineteenth-Century Black Nationalists and the Civilizing Mission.* Lexington: University Press of Kentucky, 1998.

"Affecting Narration." *Liberator*, February 18, 1853, 28.

Aichele, George, Fred W. Burnett, Elizabeth A. Castelli, Robert M. Fowler, David Jobling, Stephen D. Moore, Gary A. Phillips, Rina Pippin, Regina M. Schwartz, and

Wilhelm Wellner [The Bible and Culture Collective]. *The Postmodern Bible*. New Haven: Yale University Press, 1995.

Allen, William G. *The American Prejudice against Color: An Authentic Narrative, Showing How Easily the Nation Got into an Uproar*. 1853. New York: Arno Press and the New York Times, 1969.

——. "Letter from William G. Allen." *Frederick Douglass' Paper*, January 1, 1852.

——. "Letter from Wm. G. Allen." *Frederick Douglass' Paper*, May 20, 1852.

——. "Letter from Wm. G. Allen." *Frederick Douglass' Paper*, July 30, 1852.

——. "Orators and Oratory." 1852. In Foner and Branham, *Lift Every Voice*, 229–46.

"An American Citizen Murdered!! The Press Destroyed!!! The Spirit of Slavery Triumphant!!!!" *Colored American*, November 25, 1837.

Anderson, Benedict. *Imagined Communities: Reflections on the Origin and Spread of Nationalism*. London: Verso, 1983.

Anderson, James D. "Secondary School History Textbooks and the Treatment of Black History." In Hine, *The State of Afro-American History*, 253–74.

Anderson, Victor. *Beyond Ontological Blackness: An Essay on African American Religious and Cultural Criticism*. New York: Continuum, 1995.

Andrews, William L. *To Tell a Free Story: The First Century of Afro-American Autobiography, 1760–1865*. Urbana: University of Illinois Press, 1986.

The Anglo-African Magazine. Vol. 1, *1859*. Edited by William Loren Katz. New York: Arno Press and the New York Times, 1968.

Ankersmit, F. R. "The Reality Effect in the Writing of History: The Dynamics of Historiographical Topology." *Mededelingen van de Afdeling Letterkunde*, n.s., 52, no. 1 (1989): 5–37.

"Appeal to the Friends of the Colored American." *Colored American*, November 23, 1839.

Aptheker, Herbert, ed. *A Documentary History of the Negro People in the United States*. Vol. 1, *From the Colonial Times through the Civil War*. 1979. New York: Carol Publishing Group, 1990.

Arch, Stephen Carl. *After Franklin: The Emergence of Autobiography in Post-Revolutionary America, 1780–1830*. Hanover, N.H.: University Press of New England, 2001.

——. *Authorizing the Past: The Rhetoric of History in Seventeenth-Century New England*. DeKalb: Northern Illinois University Press, 1994.

"Augustine." "For the Colored American." *Colored American*, June 2, 1838.

Bailyn, Bernard. *The Ideological Origins of the American Revolution*. Cambridge, Mass.: Harvard University Press, 1967.

Baker, Houston A., Jr. *Long Black Song: Essays in Black American Literature and Culture*. Charlottesville: University Press of Virginia, 1972.

——. *Workings of the Spirit: The Poetics of Afro-American Women's Writing*. Chicago: University of Chicago Press, 1991.

Bakhtin, Mikhail. *The Dialogic Imagination*. Edited by Michael Holquist. Translated by Caryl Emerson and Michael Holquist. Austin: University of Texas Press, 1981.

Bancroft, George. *History of the Colonization of the United States*. New York: Julius Hart, 1885.

——. *History of the Formation of the Constitution of the United States of America*. 2 vols. New York: D. Appleton, 1882.

——. *History of the United States from the Discovery of the American Continent.* 10 vols. Boston: Little, Brown, 1872–74.

——. *Literary and Historical Miscellanies.* New York: Harper and Brothers, 1855.

——. "The Necessity, the Reality, and the Promise of the Progress of the Human Race." In Bancroft, *Literary and Historical Miscellanies,* 481–517.

——. "The Office of the People in Art, Government and Religion." In Bancroft, *Literary and Historical Miscellanies,* 408–35.

——. Review of *Documentary History of the American Revolution: Published in Conformity to an Act of Congress,* by Matthew St. Clair Clarke and Peter Force. *North American Review,* April 1838, 475–87.

Barlow, Joel. *Advice to the Privileged Orders, in the Several States of Europe, Resulting from the Necessity and Propriety of a General Revolution in the Principle of Government.* In *The Works of Joel Barlow,* edited by William K. Bottorff and Arthur L. Ford, 91–311. Gainesville, Fla.: Scholars Facsimiles and Reprints, 1970.

Barthelemy, Anthony G. Introduction to *Collected Black Women's Narratives.* New York: Oxford University Press, 1988.

Barthes, Roland. *Criticism and Truth.* Translated by Katrine Pilcher Keuneman. Minneapolis: University of Minnesota Press, 1987.

——. *The Rustle of Language.* Translated by Richard Howard. Berkeley: University of California Press, 1986.

Bassard, Katherine Clay. *Spiritual Interrogations: Culture, Gender, and Community in Early African American Women's Writing.* Princeton: Princeton University Press, 1999.

Bassett, John Spencer. *The Middle Group of American Historians.* New York: Macmillan, 1917.

Batstone, David, Eduardo Mendieta, Lois Ann Lorentzen, and Dwight N. Hopkins, eds. *Liberation Theologies, Postmodernity, and the Americas.* London: Routledge, 1997.

Bay, Mia. *The White Image in the Black Mind: African-American Ideas about White People, 1830–1925.* New York: Oxford University Press, 2000.

Belinda. "Petition of an African Slave, to the Legislature of Massachusetts." 1782. In Carretta, *Unchained Voices,* 142–44.

Bell, Howard Holman. "Editor's Note." In *Search for a Place: Black Separatism and Africa, 1860,* ed. Howard H. Bell. Ann Arbor: University of Michigan Press, 1971.

——. *A Survey of the Negro Convention Movement, 1830–1861.* New York: Arno Press and the New York Times, 1969.

——, ed. *Black Separatism and the Caribbean, 1860.* Ann Arbor: University of Michigan Press, 1970.

——, ed. *Minutes of the Proceedings of the National Negro Conventions, 1830–1864.* New York: Arno Press and the New York Times, 1969.

Beman, Amos Gerry. "The Education of the Colored People." 1859. In *The Anglo-African Magazine,* 1:337–40.

——. "Thoughts–No. III." *Colored American,* December 5, 1840.

——. "Thoughts, No. IX." *Colored American,* March 6, 1841.

——. "Thoughts for the Season." *Colored American,* January 16, 1841.

Bercovitch, Sacvan. *The American Jeremiad.* Madison: University of Wisconsin Press, 1978.

Bethel, Elizabeth Rauh. *The Roots of African-American Identity: Memory and History in Antebellum Free Communities.* New York: St. Martin's Press, 1997.

"The Bible." *Colored American*, November 17, 1838.

Bingham, Caleb. *The Columbian Orator, Containing a Variety of Original and Selected Pieces Together with Rules, Which Are Calculated to Improve Youth and Others, in the Ornamental and Useful Art of Eloquence.* Edited by David W. Blight. New York: New York University Press, 1998.

Blassingame, John W. *The Slave Community: Plantation Life in the Antebellum South.* New York: Oxford University Press, 1972.

Blight, David W. Introduction to *The Columbian Orator*, by Caleb Bingham. New York: New York University Press, 1998.

Bloomfield, Maxwell. "Constitutional Values and the Literature of the Early Republic." *Journal of American Culture* 11, no. 4 (Winter 1988): 53–58.

Boime, Albert. *The Art of Exclusion: Representing Blacks in the Nineteenth Century.* London: Thames and Hudson, 1990.

Bourdieu, Pierre. "Identity and Representation." 1982. In *Language and Symbolic Power*, edited by John B. Thompson, translated by Gino Raymond and Matthew Adamson, 220–28. Cambridge, Mass.: Harvard University Press, 1991.

Bradford, Sarah. *Harriet Tubman: The Moses of Her People.* 2d ed. 1886. New York: Citadel Press, 1991.

Bradley, Patricia. *Slavery, Propaganda, and the American Revolution.* Jackson: University Press of Mississippi, 1998.

Brown, William Wells. *The Black Man, His Antecedents, His Genius, and His Achievements.* 4th ed. 1865. Salem, N.H.: Ayer, 1992.

——. *Clotel; or, The President's Daughter: A Narrative of Slave Life in the United States.* 1853. Edited by Robert S. Levine. Boston: Bedford/St. Martin's, 2000.

——. *A Lecture Delivered before the Female Anti-Slavery Society of Salem, at Lyceum Hall, Nov. 14, 1847.* Boston: Massachusetts Anti-Slavery Society, 1847.

——. *Narrative of William W. Brown, a Fugitive Slave.* 1847. In *From Fugitive Slave to Free Man: The Autobiographies of William Wells Brown.* Edited by William L. Andrews. New York: Mentor, 1993.

——. *The Negro in the American Rebellion: His Heroism and His Fidelity.* 1867. New York: Kraus Reprint, 1969.

——. *The Rising Son; or, The Antecedents and Advancement of the Colored Race.* 1874. New York: Negro Universities Press, 1970.

——. *St. Domingo: Its Revolutions and Its Patriots: A Lecture, Delivered before the Metropolitan Athenaeum, London, May 16, and at St. Thomas' Church, Philadelphia, December 20, 1854.* Boston: Marsh, 1855.

——. *Three Years in Europe; or, Places I Have Seen and People I Have Met.* London: Charles Gilpin, 1852.

Bruce, Dickson D., Jr. "Black and White Voices in an Early African-American Colonization Narrative: Problems of Genre and Emergence." In *Criticism and the Color Line: Desegregating American Literary Studies*, edited by Henry B. Wonham, 112–25. New Brunswick, N.J.: Rutgers University Press, 1996.

——. *The Origins of African American Literature, 1680–1865.* Charlottesville: University Press of Virginia, 2001.

Bullock, Penelope L. *The Afro-American Periodical Press, 1838–1909.* Baton Rouge: Louisiana State University Press, 1981.

Butler, Octavia E. *Kindred*. Boston: Beacon Press, 1979.

Callaghan, J. Calvin. "The Annual Meeting of the Pennsylvania Anti-Slavery Society, 1860." In *Antislavery and Disunion, 1858–1861: Studies in the Rhetoric of Compromise and Conflict*, edited by J. Jeffery Auer, 242–61. Gloucester, Mass.: Peter Smith, 1968.

Callcott, George H. *History in the United States, 1800–1860: Its Practice and Purpose*. Baltimore: Johns Hopkins Press, 1970.

Callinicos, Alex. *Theories and Narratives: Reflections on the Philosophy of History*. Durham, N.C.: Duke University Press, 1995.

Campbell, John. *Negro-mania: Being an Examination of the Falsely Assumed Equality of the Various Races of Man . . .* Philadelphia, 1851.

Campbell, Penelope. *Maryland in Africa: The Maryland State Colonization Society, 1831–1857*. Urbana: University of Illinois Press, 1971.

Canary, Robert H. *George Bancroft*. New York: Twayne, 1974.

Canary, Robert H., and Henry Kozicki. *The Writing of History: Literary Form and Historical Understanding*. Madison: University of Wisconsin Press, 1978.

Cappon, Lester J., ed. *The Adams-Jefferson Letters: The Complete Correspondence between Thomas Jefferson and Abigail and John Adams*. Vol. 2. Chapel Hill: University of North Carolina Press, 1959.

Carretta, Vincent, ed. *Unchained Voices: An Anthology of Black Authors in the English-Speaking World of the Eighteenth Century*. Lexington: University of Kentucky Press, 1996.

Cassuto, Leonard. *The Inhuman Race: The Racial Grotesque in American Literature and Culture*. New York: Columbia University Press, 1997.

Castronovo, Russ. *Fathering the Nation: American Genealogies of Slavery and Freedom*. Berkeley: University of California Press, 1995.

———. *Necro Citizenship: Death, Eroticism, and the Public Sphere in the Nineteenth-Century United States*. Durham, N.C.: Duke University Press, 2001.

"A Chapter on Locks." *Colored American*, March 2, 1839.

"The Characteristics of Christian Warriors." *Frederick Douglass' Paper*, December 25, 1851.

Child, L. Maria. *The American Frugal Housewife: Dedicated to Those Who Are Not Ashamed of Economy*. Boston, 1832.

———. *An Appeal for the Indians*. New York, 1868.

———. *An Appeal in Favor of That Class of Americans Called Africans*. 1833. Amherst: University of Massachusetts Press, 1996.

———. *Fact and Fiction: A Collection of Stories*. New York, Boston, 1846.

———. *Letters from New-York*. 1843. Edited by Bruce Mills. Athens: University of Georgia Press, 1998.

"The Church in Fault." *Colored American*, February 3, 1838.

Clarke, Lewis, and Milton Clarke. *Narratives of the Sufferings of Lewis and Milton Clarke, Sons of a Soldier of the Revolution, during a Captivity of More Than Twenty Years among the Slaveholders of Kentucky, One of the So Called Christian States of North America: Dictated by Themselves*. Boston, 1846.

Cmiel, Kenneth. *Democratic Eloquence: The Fight over Popular Speech in Nineteenth-Century America*. New York: William Morrow, 1990.

Coker, Daniel. *A Dialogue between a Virginian and an African Minister.* 1810. New York: Arno Press and the New York Times, 1969.

Colbourn, H. Trevor. *The Lamp of Experience: Whig History and the Intellectual Origins of the American Revolution.* Chapel Hill: University of North Carolina Press, 1965.

"The Colored Citizens of New York and the African Civilization Society." *Weekly Anglo-African.* April 21, 1860. 2.

"Colored Patriots of the American Revolution." *Liberator*, May 25, 1855, 83.

"Colored People Always Opposed to Colonization." *Colored American*, May 13, 1837.

"Commendatory Notices." *Liberator*, January 11, 1856, 7.

Condit, Celeste Michelle, and John Louis Lucaites. *Crafting Equality: America's Anglo-African Word.* Chicago: University of Chicago Press, 1993.

Cone, James H. *Black Theology and Black Power.* New York: Seabury, 1969.

———. *A Black Theology of Liberation.* 2d ed. Maryknoll, N.Y.: Orbis, 1990.

———. *My Soul Looks Back.* Nashville: Abingdon, 1982.

Connor, Kimberly Rae. *Imagining Grace: Liberating Theologies in the Slave Narrative Tradition.* Urbana: University of Illinois Press, 2000.

Cooper, Anna Julia. *A Voice from the South by a Black Woman of the South.* 1892. New York: Oxford University Press, 1988.

Crane, Gregg D. *Race, Citizenship, and Law in American Literature.* Cambridge: Cambridge University Press, 2002.

Cruz, Jon. *Culture on the Margins: The Black Spiritual and the Rise of American Cultural Interpretation.* Princeton: Princeton University Press, 1999.

Cuffe, Paul. *A Brief Account of the Settlement and Present Situation of the Colony of Sierra Leone, in Africa; as Communicated by Paul Cuffe (a Man of Colour) to His Friend in New York: Also, an Explanation of the Object of His Visit, and Some Advice to the People of Colour in the United States. To Which is Subjoined, an Address to the People of Colour, from the Convention of Delegates from the Abolition Societies in the United States.* 1812. In Porter, *Early Negro Writing*, 256–64.

Davis, Gerald L. *I Got the Word in Me and I Can Sing It, You Know: A Study of the Performed African-American Sermon.* Philadelphia: University of Pennsylvania Press, 1985.

Davis, Mary Kemp. *Nat Turner before the Bar of Judgment: Fictional Treatments of the Southampton Slave Insurrection.* Baton Rouge: Louisiana State University Press, 1999.

"Declaration of Sentiments, on the Sin of Slavery." *Colored American*, June 17, 1837.

Dekker, George. *The American Historical Romance.* Cambridge: Cambridge University Press, 1987.

Delany, Martin Robison. *The Condition, Elevation, Emigration, and Destiny of the Colored People of the United States.* 1852. New York: Arno Press and the New York Times, 1968.

———. *Official Report of the Niger Valley Exploring Party.* 1860. In Bell, *Search for a Place*, 23–148. Ann Arbor: University of Michigan Press, 1971.

———. *The Origin and Objects of Ancient Freemasonry: Its Introduction into the United States, and Legitimacy among Colored Men.* Pittsburgh, 1853.

———. "Political Destiny of the Colored Race on the American Continent." 1854. In *Two*

Biographies by African-American Women, edited by William L. Andrews, 327–67. New York: Oxford University Press, 1991.

Dening, Greg. *Performances.* Chicago: University of Chicago Press, 1996.

"The Destruction of Babylon: Sacred Geography and Antiquities: Number V." *Colored American,* June 20, 1840.

"De Tocqueville's Democracy in America: A Review of Those Sections of Chapter XVII Which Relate to the Colored People in the United States: No. III." *Colored American,* February 6, 1841.

Dillon, Merton. *The Abolitionists: The Growth of a Dissenting Minority.* 1974. New York: Norton, 1979.

"Do the Various Races of Man Constitute a Single Species?" *Democratic Review* 11, no. 50 (August 1842): 113–39.

Douglas, H. Ford. "I Do Not Believe in the Antislavery of Abraham Lincoln." 1860. In Foner and Branham, *Lift Every Voice,* 340–54.

Douglass, Frederick. "If There Is No Struggle, There Is No Progress." 1857. In Foner and Branham, *Lift Every Voice,* 308–12.

———. *Life and Times of Frederick Douglass.* 1881. In *Frederick Douglass: Autobiographies,* edited by Henry Louis Gates Jr. New York: Library of America, 1994.

———. *My Bondage and My Freedom.* 1855. In *Frederick Douglass: Autobiographies,* edited by Henry Louis Gates Jr. New York: Library of America, 1994.

———. *Narrative of the Life of Frederick Douglass, an American Slave.* 1845. In *Frederick Douglass: Autobiographies,* edited by Henry Louis Gates Jr. New York: Library of America, 1994.

———. "The Unholy Alliance of Negro Hate and Anti-Slavery." 1856. In Foner, *The Life and Writings of Frederick Douglass,* 2:385–87.

———. "What, to the Slave, Is the Fourth of July?" 1852. In Foner and Branham, *Lift Every Voice,* 246–68.

Drew, Benjamin. *A North-Side View of Slavery: The Refugee; or, The Narratives of Fugitive Slaves in Canada, Related by Themselves with an Account of the History and Condition of the Colored Population of Upper Canada.* 1856. Reading, Mass.: Addison-Wesley, 1969.

Eakin, Sue, and Joseph Logsdon. Introduction to *Twelve Years a Slave: Narrative of Solomon Northup, a Citizen of New-York, Kidnapped in Washington City in 1841, and Rescued in 1853, from a Cotton Plantation near the Red River, in Louisiana.* Baton Rouge: Louisiana State University Press, 1968.

Easton, Hosea. *A Treatise on the Intellectual Character, and Civil and Political Condition of the Colored People of the U. States; and the Prejudice Exercised towards Them: With a Sermon on the Duty of the Church to Them.* 1837. New York: Arno Press and the New York Times, 1969.

Elam, Harry J., Jr. "The Black Performer and the Performance of Blackness: *The Escape; or, A Leap for Freedom* by William Wells Brown and *No Place to Be Somebody* by Charles Gordone." In *African American Performance and Theater History: A Critical Reader,* edited by Harry J. Elam Jr. and David Krasner, 288–305. New York: Oxford University Press, 2001.

Elaw, Zilpha. *Memoirs of the Life, Religious Experience, Ministerial Travels, and Labours of Mrs. Zilpha Elaw, an American Female of Colour; Together with Some Account of* the Great Religious Revivals in America. 1846. In *Sisters of the Spirit: Three Black Women's Autobiographies of the Nineteenth Century*, edited by William L. Andrews, 49–160. Bloomington: Indiana University Press, 1986.

"Elevation of Our People." *Colored American*, November 23, 1839.

"The Emigration Scheme." *Colored American*, November 13, 1841.

Ericson, David F. *The Debate over Slavery: Antislavery and Proslavery Liberalism in Antebellum America*. New York: New York University Press, 2000.

Ernest, John. "Fugitive Performances: William Wells Brown's *Three Years in Europe* and Harriet Martineau's *Society in America*." In *Literature on the Move: Comparing Diasporic Ethnicities in Europe and the Americas*, edited by Dominique Marçais, Mark Niemeyer, Bernard Vincent, and Cathy Waegner, 159–68. Heidelberg: C. Winter, 2002.

——. "The Reconstruction of Whiteness: William Wells Brown's *The Escape; or, A Leap for Freedom*." *PMLA* 113 (1998): 1108–21.

——. *Resistance and Reformation in Nineteenth-Century African-American Literature: Brown, Wilson, Jacobs, Delany, Douglass, and Harper*. Jackson: University Press of Mississippi, 1995.

"European Colonies in America." *Freedom's Journal*, July 13, 1827.

Fabre, Geneviève, and Robert O'Meally, eds. *History and Memory in African-American Culture*. New York: Oxford University Press, 1994.

"Facts respecting Pro-Slavery Colleges and Theological Seminaries." *Colored American*, October 13, 1838.

Fanuzzi, Robert. "Frederick Douglass's 'Colored Newspaper': Identity Politics in Black and White." In *The Black Press: New Literary and Historical Essays*, edited by Todd Vogel, 55–70. New Brunswick, N.J.: Rutgers University Press, 2001.

Farrison, William Edward. *William Wells Brown: Author and Reformer*. Chicago: University of Chicago Press, 1969.

Fick, Carolyn E. *The Making of Haiti: The Saint Domingue Revolution from Below*. Knoxville: University of Tennessee Press, 1990.

Filler, Louis. *Crusade against Slavery: Friends, Foes, and Reforms, 1820–1860*. Algonac, Mich.: Reference Publications, 1986.

Finkenbine, Roy E. "Nell, William Cooper." In *Encyclopedia of African-American Culture and History*, edited by Jack Salzman, David Lionel Smith, and Cornel West, 4:1980. New York: Macmillan Library Reference USA, 1996.

Fishkin, Shelley Fisher, and Carla Peterson. "'We Hold These Truths to Be Self-Evident': The Rhetoric of Frederic Douglass's Journalism." In *Frederick Douglass: New Literary and Historical Essays*, edited by Eric J. Sundquist, 189–204. Cambridge: Cambridge University Press, 1990.

Fitzhugh, George. *Sociology for the South; or, the Failure of Free Society*. Richmond, 1854.

Foner, Philip S. *The Life and Writings of Frederick Douglass*. 5 vols. New York: International Publishers. 1950.

Foner, Philip S., and Robert James Branham, eds. *Lift Every Voice: African American Oratory, 1787–1900*. Tuscaloosa: University of Alabama Press, 1998.

Foreman, P. Gabrielle. "Who's Your Mama? 'White' Mulatta Genealogies, Early Photography, and Anti-Passing Narratives of Slavery and Freedom." *American Literary History* 14, no. 3 (Fall 2002): 505–39.

Foster, Frances Smith. "Harriet Jacobs's *Incidents* and the 'Careless Daughters' (and Sons) Who Read It." In *The (Other) American Traditions: Nineteenth-Century Women Writers*, edited by Joyce W. Warren, 92–107. New Brunswick, N.J.: Rutgers University Press, 1993.

——. *Witnessing Slavery: The Development of Ante-Bellum Slave Narratives*. 1979. 2d ed. Madison: University of Wisconsin Press, 1994.

Foucault, Michel. *The History of Sexuality*. Vol. 1, *Introduction*. Translated by Robert Hurley. New York: Vintage, 1978.

——. "Intellectuals and Power." In *Language, Counter-Memory, Practice: Selected Essays and Interviews*, edited by Donald Bouchard, translated by Donald Bouchard and Sherry Simon, 205–17. Ithaca, N.Y.: Cornell University Press, 1977.

"A Fragment." *Colored American*, August 17, 1839.

Franklin, John Hope. "On the Evolution of Scholarship in Afro-American History." In Hine, *The State of Afro-American History*, 13–22.

Franklin, John Hope, and Genna Rae McNeil, eds. *African Americans and the Living Constitution*. Washington: Smithsonian Institution Press, 1995.

Fredrickson, George M. *The Black Image in the White Mind: The Debate on Afro-American Character and Destiny, 1817–1914*. New York: Harper and Row, 1971.

"The Free Soil Convention at Cleveland." *Frederick Douglass' Paper*, October 2, 1851.

Frey, Sylvia R. *Water from the Rock: Black Resistance in a Revolutionary Age*. Princeton: Princeton University Press, 1991.

"A Fugitive Slave Turned Author." *Liberator*, January 12, 1855, 5.

Fuss, Diana. *Essentially Speaking: Feminism, Nature and Difference*. New York: Routledge, 1989.

Gaines, Rt. Rev. Wesley J. *African Methodism in the South; or, Twenty-five Years of Freedom*. 1890. Chicago: Afro-Am Press, 1969.

Garnet, Henry Highland. "An Address to the Slaves of the United States of America." 1843. In *Call and Response: The Riverside Anthology of the African American Literary Tradition*, edited by Patricia Liggins Hill, Bernard W. Bell, Trudier Harris, William J. Harris, R. Baxter Miller, and Sondra A. O'Neale, 268–72. Boston: Houghton Mifflin, 1998.

——. *The Past and the Present Condition, and the Destiny, of the Colored Race: A Discourse Delivered at the Fifteenth Anniversary of the Female Benevolent Society of Troy, N.Y., Feb. 14, 1848*. Troy, N.Y.: 1848.

Garrison, William Lloyd. "Address Delivered at the Broadway Tabernacle, N.Y., on the First of August, 1838, by Request of the People of Color of That City, in Commemoration of the Complete Emancipation of 600,000 Slaves on That Day in the British West Indies." *Colored American*, August 18, 1838; August 25, 1838; September 1, 1838.

——. "To the Public." 1831. In *William Lloyd Garrison and the Fight against Slavery: Selections from The Liberator*, edited by William E. Cain, 70–72. Boston: Bedford, 1995.

Geertz, Clifford. *The Interpretation of Cultures: Selected Essays*. New York: Basic Books, 1973.

"The General Theological Seminary of the Protestant Episcopal Church in the U.S." *Colored American*, September 7, 1839.

Gilroy, Paul. *The Black Atlantic: Modernity and Double Consciousness*. Cambridge, Mass.: Harvard University Press, 1993.

Glaude, Eddie S., Jr. *Exodus! Religion, Race, and Nation in Early-Nineteenth-Century Black America*. Chicago: University of Chicago Press, 2000.

Gliddon, George R. *Ancient Egypt: A Series of Chapters on Early Egyptian History, Archaeology, and Other Subjects Connected with Hieroglyphical Literature*. New York, 1844.

Goldberg, David Theo. *The Racial State*. Malden, Mass.: Blackwell, 2002.

——. *Racist Culture: Philosophy and the Politics of Meaning*. Cambridge, Mass.: Blackwell, 1993.

Goldsby, Jacqueline. " 'I Disguised My Hand': Writing Versions of the Truth in Harriet Jacobs's *Incidents in the Life of a Slave Girl* and John Jacobs's 'A True Tale of Slavery.' " In *Harriet Jacobs and Incidents in the Life of a Slave Girl: New Critical Essays*, edited by Deborah M. Garfield and Rafia Zafar, 11–43. Cambridge: Cambridge University Press, 1996.

Goodman, Paul. *Of One Blood: Abolitionism and the Origins of Racial Equality*. Berkeley: University of California Press, 1998.

Gordon, Lewis R. *Existentia Africana: Understanding Africana Existential Thought*. New York: Routledge, 2000.

Gossett, Thomas F. *Race: The History of an Idea in America*. 1963. New York: Schocken, 1965.

——. *Uncle Tom's Cabin and American Culture*. Dallas: Southern Methodist University Press, 1985.

Gossman, Lionel. *Between History and Literature*. Cambridge, Mass.: Harvard University Press, 1990.

——. "History and Literature: Reproduction or Signification." In Canary and Kozicki, *The Writing of History*, 3–39.

Graham, Mary W. "The Lyceum Movement and Sectional Controversy, 1860." In *Antislavery and Disunion, 1858–1861: Studies in the Rhetoric of Compromise and Conflict*, edited by J. Jeffery Auer, 108–13. Gloucester, Mass.: Peter Smith, 1968.

Grammer, Elizabeth Elkin. "Collective Biography." In *The Oxford Companion to African American Literature*, edited by William L. Andrews, Frances Smith Foster, and Trudier Harris, 161–62. New York: Oxford University Press, 1997.

Green, Johnson. *The Life and Confession of Johnson Green, Who Is to Be Executed This Day, August 17th, 1786, for the Atrocious Crime of Burglary; Together with His Last and Dying Words*. In Carretta, *Unchained Voices*, 134–41.

Greene, Frances Whipple. *Memoirs of Elleanor Eldridge*. 2d ed. 1843. Salem, N.H.: Ayer, 1971.

Grégoire, Henri. *On the Cultural Achievements of Negroes*. 1808. Translated by Thomas Cassirer and Jean-François Brière. Amherst: University of Massachusetts Press, 1996.

Griffith, Cyril E. *The African Dream: Martin R. Delany and the Emergence of Pan-African Thought*. University Park: Pennsylvania State University Press, 1975.

Grimké, Charlotte Forten. *The Journals of Charlotte Forten Grimké*. Edited by Brenda Stevenson. New York: Oxford University Press, 1988.

Grimshaw, William H. *Official History of Freemasonry among the Colored People in North America*. 1903. New York: Negro Universities Press, 1969.

Gustafson, Thomas. *Representative Words: Politics, Literature, and the American Language, 1776–1865*. Cambridge: Cambridge University Press, 1992.

Gutierrez, Gustavo. *A Theology of Liberation*. Rev. ed. Translated and edited by Sister Caridad Inda and John Eagleson. Maryknoll, N.Y.: Orbis, 1988.

Hagood, Rev. L. M. *The Colored Man in the Methodist Episcopal Church*. 1890. Westport, Conn.: Negro Universities Press, 1970.

Hall, Peter Dobkin. *The Organization of American Culture, 1700–1900: Private Institutions, Elites, and the Origins of American Nationality*. New York: New York University Press, 1984.

Hamilton, William. *Address to the Fourth Annual Convention of the Free People of Color of the United States: Delivered at the Opening of Their Session in the City of New-York, June 2, 1834*. 1834. New York: Arno Press and the New York Times, 1969.

——. "Mutual Interest, Mutual Benefit, and Mutual Relief." 1809. In Foner and Branham, *Lift Every Voice*, 80–86.

——. "An Oration, on the Abolition of the Slave Trade, Delivered in the Episcopal Asbury African Church, in Elizabeth St., New York, January 2, 1815." In Porter, *Early Negro Writing*, 391–99.

Harlan, David. *The Degradation of American History*. Chicago: University of Chicago Press, 1997.

——. "Intellectual History and the Return of Literature." *American Historical Review* 94 (1989): 581–609.

Harris, J. Dennis. *A Summer on the Borders of the Caribbean Sea*. 1860. In Bell, *Black Separatism and the Caribbean*, 67–184.

Harrold, Stanley. *The Abolitionists and the South, 1831–1861*. Lexington: University of Kentucky Press, 1995.

Hartman, Saidiya V. *Scenes of Subjection: Terror, Slavery, and Self-Making in Nineteenth-Century America*. New York: Oxford University Press, 1997.

Hayes, Diana L. *And Still We Rise: An Introduction to Black Liberation Theology*. New York: Paulist Press, 1996.

Haynes, Carolyn A. *Divine Destiny: Gender and Race in Nineteenth-Century Protestantism*. Jackson: University Press of Mississippi, 1998.

Hayward, Wilbur M. "American Eloquence." *Frederick Douglass' Paper*, September 3, 1852.

Hegel, G. W. F. *Philosophy of History*. Translated by J. Sibree. Vol. 12 of *A Library of Universal Literature, in Four Parts, Comprising Science, Biography, Fiction and the Great Orations: Part One—Science*. New York: Collier, 1901.

Helper, Hinton Rowan. *The Impending Crisis of the South: How to Meet It*. 1857. Cambridge, Mass.: Belknap Press of Harvard University Press, 1968.

Henderson, Stephen. "Introduction: The Forms of Things Unknown." In *Understanding the New Black Poetry: Black Speech and Black Music as Poetic References*, 3–69. New York: William Morrow, 1973.

Hendler, Glenn. *Public Sentiments: Structures of Feeling in Nineteenth-Century American Literature*. Chapel Hill: University of North Carolina Press, 2001.

Henson, Josiah. *An Autobiography of the Rev. Josiah Henson ("Uncle Tom"), from 1789 to 1881, with a Preface by Mrs. Harriet Beecher Stowe and Introductory Notes by George Sturge, S. Morley, Esq., M.P., Wendell Phillips, and John G. Whittier.* Edited by John Lobb. London, Ont., 1881.

———. *The Life of Josiah Henson, Formerly a Slave, Now an Inhabitant of Canada: As Narrated by Himself.* Boston, 1849.

———. *"Truth Is Stranger Than Fiction": An Autobiography of the Rev. Josiah Henson (Mrs. Harriet Beecher Stowe's "Uncle Tom"), from 1789 to 1879; with a Preface by Mrs. Harriet Beecher Stowe, Introductory Notes by Wendell Phillips and John G. Whittier, and an Appendix on the Exodus by Bishop Gilbert Haven.* Boston, 1879.

———. *Truth Stranger Than Fiction: Father Henson's Story of His Own Life, with an Introduction by Mrs. H. B. Stowe.* 1858. Williamstown, Mass.: Corner House, 1973.

Higginbotham, A. Leon, Jr. *Shades of Freedom: Racial Politics and Presumptions of the American Legal Process.* New York: Oxford University Press, 1996.

Hildreth, Richard. *The History of the United States of America.* Rev. ed. 6 vols. New York: Harper and Brothers, 1848–51.

Hine, Darlene Clark. "Lifting the Veil, Shattering the Silence: Black Women's History in Slavery and Freedom." In Hine, *The State of Afro-American History,* 223–49.

———, ed. *The State of Afro-American History: Past, Present, and Future.* Baton Rouge: Louisiana State University Press, 1986.

Hinks, Peter P. *To Awaken My Afflicted Brethren: David Walker and the Problem of Antebellum Slave Resistance.* University Park: Pennsylvania State University Press, 1997.

"History of Slavery." *Freedom's Journal,* July 13, 1827; July 27, 1827; August 3, 1827.

"History of the Red Race." *Colored American,* December 4, 1841.

Hoggan, David L. *The Myth of the "New History": The Techniques and Tactics of the New Mythologists of American History.* Nutley, N.J.: Craig Press, 1965.

Hollinger, David A. *In the American Province: Studies in the History and Historiography of Ideas.* Baltimore: Johns Hopkins University Press, 1985.

Holly, James Theodore. *A Vindication of the Capacity of the Negro Race for Self-Government, and Civilized Progress, as Demonstrated by Historical Events of the Haytian Revolution; and the Subsequent Acts of That People since Their National Independence.* 1857. In Bell, *Black Separatism and the Caribbean,* 17–66.

Hopkins, Dwight N. *Introducing Black Theology of Liberation.* Maryknoll, N.Y.: Orbis, 1999.

Horsman, Reginald. *Race and Manifest Destiny: The Origins of American Racial Anglo-Saxonism.* Cambridge, Mass.: Harvard University Press, 1981.

Horton, James Oliver. *Free People of Color: Inside the African American Community.* Washington: Smithsonian Institution Press, 1993.

Horton, James Oliver, and Lois E. Horton. "The Affirmation of Manhood: Black Garrisonians in Antebellum Boston." In Donald M. Jacobs, *Courage and Conscience,* 127–53.

———. *Black Bostonians: Family Life and Community Struggle in the Antebellum North.* New York: Holmes and Meier, 1979.

———. *In Hope of Liberty: Culture, Community, and Protest among Northern Free Blacks, 1700–1860.* New York: Oxford University Press, 1997.

Howard-Pittney, David. *The Afro-American Jeremiad: Appeals for Justice in America.* Philadelphia: Temple University Press, 1990.

Howe, Daniel Walker. "The Political Psychology of *The Federalist.*" *William and Mary Quarterly* 44 (1987): 485–509.

Howe, Mark Antony DeWolfe. *The Life and Letters of George Bancroft.* 2 vols. New York: Scribner's, 1908.

Howe, Stephen. *Afrocentrism: Mythical Pasts and Imagined Homes.* London: Verso, 1999.

Huggins, Nathan I. "Integrating Afro-American History into American History." In Hine, *The State of Afro-American History,* 157–68.

Hughes, Henry. "A Treatise on Sociology." 1854. In *Slavery Defended: The Views of the Old South,* edited by Eric L. McKitrick, 51–56. Englewood Cliffs, N.J.: Prentice-Hall, 1963.

Hunt, Alfred N. *Haiti's Influence on Antebellum America: Slumbering Volcano in the Caribbean.* Baton Rouge: Louisiana State University Press, 1988.

Hutton, Frankie. *The Early Black Press in America, 1827 to 1860.* Westport, Conn.: Greenwood Press, 1993.

Irwin, John T. *American Hieroglyphics: The Symbol of the Egyptian Hieroglyphics in the American Renaissance.* Baltimore: Johns Hopkins University Press, 1980.

Jackson, Blyden. *A History of Afro-American Literature.* Vol. 1, *The Long Beginning, 1746–1895.* Baton Rouge: Louisiana State University Press, 1989.

Jacobs, Donald M., ed. *Courage and Conscience: Black and White Abolitionists in Boston.* Bloomington: Indiana University Press, 1993.

Jacobs, Harriet. *Incidents in the Life of a Slave Girl, Written by Herself.* 1861. Cambridge, Mass.: Harvard University Press, 1987.

Jacobson, Matthew Frye. *Whiteness of a Different Color: European Immigrants and the Alchemy of Race.* Cambridge, Mass.: Harvard University Press, 1998.

Jay, William. "Leaders of the American Anti-Slavery Society Reply to an Attack by President Andrew Jackson." 1855. In *The Abolitionists: A Collection of Their Writings,* edited by Louis Ruchames, 121–30. New York: G. P. Putnam's Sons, 1963.

Jefferson, Thomas. *Notes on the State of Virginia.* 1787. Chapel Hill: University of North Carolina Press, 1982.

———. *A Summary View of the Rights of British America.* 1774. In *Writings,* by Thomas Jefferson, 103–22. New York: Library of America, 1984.

"Jefferson and Slavery." *Frederick Douglass' Paper,* April 1, 1852.

Jeffrey, Julie Roy. *The Great Silent Army of Abolitionism: Ordinary Women in the Antislavery Movement.* Chapel Hill: University of North Carolina Press, 1998.

Johnson, Edward A. *History of Negro Soldiers in the Spanish-American War, and Other Items of Interest.* Raleigh, 1899.

Johnson, W. P. "The Fourth and Fifth of July in the City of Schenectady." *Colored American,* July 24, 1841.

Jones, Absalom. *A Thanksgiving Sermon, Preached January 1, 1808, in St. Thomas's, or the African Episcopal, Church, Philadelphia: On Account of the Abolition of the African Slave Trade, on That Day, by the Congress of the United States.* In Porter, *Early Negro Writing,* 335–42.

Jones, Absalom, and Richard Allen. *A Narrative of the Proceedings of the Black People, during the Late Awful Calamity in Philadelphia, in the Year 1793: And a Refutation of Some Censures, Thrown upon Them in Some Late Publications*. 1794. New York: Arno Press and the New York Times, 1969.

Juster, Susan, and Lisa MacFarlane, eds. *A Mighty Baptism: Race, Gender, and the Creation of American Protestantism*. Ithaca, N.Y.: Cornell University Press, 1996.

"Justica." "Immediate Emancipation." *Colored American*, March 9, 1839.

Kaplan, Sidney, and Emma Nogrady Kaplan. *The Black Presence in the Era of the American Revolution*. Rev. ed. Amherst: University of Massachusetts Press, 1989.

Kee, Alistair. *Marx and the Failure of Liberation Theology*. Philadelphia: Trinity Press International, 1990.

"Keep Cool, Brethren." *Colored American*, October 14, 1837.

Kellner, Hans. *Language and Historical Representation: Getting the Story Crooked*. Madison: University of Wisconsin Press, 1989.

Kelly, Alfred H. "Richard Hildreth." In *The Marcus W. Jernegan Essays in American Historiography*, edited by William T. Hutchinson, 25–42. Chicago: University of Chicago Press, 1937.

"Kossuth." *Frederick Douglass' Paper*, October 9, 1851.

Kraditor, Aileen S. *Means and Ends in American Abolitionism: Garrison and His Critics in Strategy and Tactics, 1834–1850*. New York: Vintage, 1970.

Kraus, Michael. *A History of American History*. New York: Farrar and Rinehart, 1937.

LaCapra, Dominick. *History and Criticism*. Ithaca, N.Y.: Cornell University Press, 1985.

Latrobe, John H. B. *Memoir of Benjamin Banneker, Read before the Maryland Historical Society, at the Monthly Meeting, May 1, 1845*. Baltimore, 1845.

Lawrence, George. *Oration on the Abolition of the Slave Trade, Delivered on the First Day of January, 1813, in The African Methodist Episcopal Church, 1813*. In Porter, *Early Negro Writing*. 374–82.

Lee, Jarena. *The Life and Religious Experience of Jarena Lee, a Coloured Lady, Giving an Account of Her Call to Preach the Gospel: Revised and Corrected from the Original Manuscript, Written By Herself*. 1836. In *Sisters of the Spirit: Three Black Women's Autobiographies of the Nineteenth Century*, edited by William L. Andrews, 25–52. Bloomington: Indiana University Press, 1986.

Lesick, Lawrence Thomas. *The Lane Rebels: Evangelicalism and Antislavery in Antebellum America*. Metuchen, N.J.: Scarecrow, 1980.

Levin, David. *History as Romantic Art: Bancroft, Prescott, Motley, and Parkman*. Stanford: Stanford University Press, 1959.

Levine, Robert S. "Circulating the Nation: David Walker, the Missouri Compromise, and the Rise of the Black Press." In *The Black Press: New Literary and Historical Essays*, edited by Todd Vogel, 17–36. New Brunswick, N.J.: Rutgers University Press, 2001.

———. Introduction and notes to *Clotel; or, The President's Daughter: A Narrative of Slave Life in the United States*, by William Wells Brown. Boston: Bedford/St. Martin's, 2000.

———. *Martin Delany, Frederick Douglass, and the Politics of Representative Identity*. Chapel Hill: University of North Carolina Press, 1997.

Lewis, Robert Benjamin. *Light and Truth: Collected from the Bible and Ancient and Modern History, Containing the Universal History of the Colored and the Indian Race, from the Creation of the World to the Present Time*. Boston, 1844.

——. *Light and Truth, from Ancient and Sacred History.* Augusta, Me., 1843.

Limon, John. *The Place of Fiction in the Time of Science: A Disciplinary History of American Writing.* Cambridge: Cambridge University Press, 1990.

Linebaugh, Peter, and Marcus Rediker. *The Many-Headed Hydra: Sailors, Slaves, Commoners, and the Hidden History of the Revolutionary Atlantic.* Boston: Beacon, 2000.

Litwack, Leon F. "The Emancipation of the Negro Abolitionist." In *The Abolitionists,* edited by Richard O. Curry, 112–21. Hinsdale, Ill.: Dryden Press, 1973.

——. *North of Slavery: The Negro in the Free States, 1790–1860.* Chicago: University of Chicago Press, 1961.

Livermore, George. *An Historical Research Respecting the Opinions of the Founders of the Republic on Negroes as Slaves, as Citizens, and as Soldiers.* 4th ed. 1863. New York: Burt Franklin, 1968.

Logan, Shirley Wilson. *"We Are Coming": The Persuasive Discourse of Nineteenth-Century Black Women.* Carbondale: Southern Illinois University Press, 1999.

Loggins, Vernon. *The Negro Author: His Development in America.* New York: Columbia University Press, 1931.

"Long Island Scribe." "The Reflector: No. V." *Colored American,* March 28, 1840.

Looby, Christopher. *Voicing America: Language, Literary Form, and the Origins of the United States.* Chicago: University of Chicago Press, 1996.

Lovejoy, B. G. "Authors at Home: VI. George Bancroft at Washington." *Critic,* February 7, 1885, 61–62.

Mabee, Carleton, with Susan Mabee Newhouse. *Sojourner Truth: Slave, Prophet, Legend.* New York: New York University Press, 1993.

Magubane, Bernard Makhosezwe. *The Ties That Bind: African-American Consciousness of Africa.* Trenton, N.J.: Africa World Press, 1987.

Mailloux, Steven. "Misreading as a Historical Act: Cultural Rhetoric, Bible Politics, and Fuller's 1845 Review of Douglass's *Narrative.*" In *Readers in History: Nineteenth-Century American Literature and the Contexts of Response,* 3–31. Baltimore: Johns Hopkins University Press, 1993.

Martin, Ronald E. *American Literature and the Universe of Force.* Durham, N.C.: Duke University Press, 1981.

Martineau, Harriet. *Society in America.* 3 vols. London: Saunders and Otley, 1837.

Mattison, H. *Louisa Picquet, the Octoroon; or, Inside Views of Southern Domestic Life.* 1861. In *Collected Black Women's Narratives.* New York: Oxford University Press, 1988.

McBride, Dwight A. *Impossible Witnesses: Truth, Abolitionism, and Slave Testimony.* New York: New York University Press, 2001.

McKivigan, John R. *The War against Proslavery Religion: Abolitionism and the Northern Churches, 1830–1865.* Ithaca, N.Y.: Cornell University Press, 1984.

McWilliams, John P., Jr. *Hawthorne, Melville, and the American Character: A Looking-Glass Business.* Cambridge: Cambridge University Press, 1985.

"Means of Elevation.—No. IV." *Colored American,* August 3, 1839.

"Meeting of Congress." *Colored American,* September 2, 1837.

Merish, Lori. *Sentimental Materialism: Gender, Commodity Culture, and Nineteenth-Century American Literature.* Durham, N.C.: Duke University Press, 2000.

Mills, Charles W. *Blackness Visible: Essays on Philosophy and Race*. Ithaca, N.Y.: Cornell University Press, 1998.
——. *The Racial Contract*. Ithaca, N.Y.: Cornell University Press, 1997.
Mink, Louis O. "Narrative Form as a Cognitive Instrument." In Canary and Kozicki, *The Writing of History*, 129–49.
The Minutes and Proceedings of the First Annual Meeting of the American Moral Reform Society, Held at Philadelphia in the Presbyterian Church in Seventh Street, below Shippen, from the 14th to the 19th of August, 1837. In Porter, *Early Negro Writing*, 200–248.
Mizruchi, Susan L. *The Power of Historical Knowledge: Narrating the Past in Hawthorne, James, and Dreiser*. Princeton: Princeton University Press, 1988.
Moody, Joycelyn K. "Personal Places: Slavery and Mission in Graduate Seminars." In *Approaches to Teaching Narrative of the Life of Frederick Douglass*, edited by James C. Hall, 19–30. New York: Modern Language Association of America, 1999.
——. *Sentimental Confessions: Spiritual Narratives of Nineteenth-Century African American Women*. Athens: University of Georgia Press, 2001.
Morrison, Toni. "Unspeakable Things Unspoken: The Afro-American Presence in American Literature." In *Within the Circle: An Anthology of African American Literary Criticism from the Harlem Renaissance to the Present*, edited by Angelyn Mitchell, 368–98. Durham, N.C.: Duke University Press, 1994.
Moses, Wilson Jeremiah. *Afrotopia: The Roots of African American Popular History*. Cambridge: Cambridge University Press, 1998.
——. *Black Messiahs and Uncle Toms: Social and Literary Manipulations of a Religious Myth*. Rev. ed. University Park: Pennsylvania State University Press, 1993.
——. *The Golden Age of Black Nationalism, 1850–1925*. New York: Oxford University Press, 1978.
Nash, Gary B. *Race and Revolution*. Madison, Wis.: Madison House, 1990.
"Nation Warned." *Colored American*, March 14, 1840.
"Negro Minstrelsy—Ancient and Modern." *Putnam's Monthly* 5, no. 25 (January 1855): 72–79.
Nell, William C. *The Colored Patriots of the American Revolution, with Sketches of Several Distinguished Colored Persons: To Which Is Added a Brief Survey of the Condition and Prospects of Colored Americans*. 1855. Salem, N.H.: Ayer, 1986.
——. "Letter from William C. Nell." *Weekly Anglo-American*, April 21, 1860, 2.
——. "Letter from Wm. C. Nell." *Weekly Anglo-African*, September 17, 1859, 2.
——. "Pictures of American Slavery." *Liberator*, January 5, 1855, 4.
——. "Progress of Justice and Equality." *Liberator*, February 11, 1848, 21.
——. *Services of Colored Americans, in the Wars of 1776 and 1812*. 1851. New York: AMS, 1976.
——. "Speech of Wm. C. Nell." *Liberator*, November 12, 1841, 184.
Nelson, Dana D. *The Word in Black and White: Reading "Race" in American Literature, 1638–1867*. New York: Oxford University Press, 1993.
Newman, Richard S. *The Transformation of American Abolitionism: Fighting Slavery in the Early Republic*. Chapel Hill: University of North Carolina Press, 2002.
"New Publications." *Liberator*, May 7, 1852, 74.

Northup, Solomon. *Twelve Years a Slave: Narrative of Solomon Northup, a Citizen of New York, Kidnapped in Washington City in 1841, and Rescued in 1853, from a Cotton Plantation near the Red River, in Louisiana.* Baton Rouge: Louisiana State University Press, 1968.

Norton, Anne. *Alternative Americas: A Reading of Antebellum Political Culture.* Chicago: University of Chicago Press, 1986.

Nott, Josiah Clark, and George R. Gliddon. *Types of Mankind; or, Ethnological Researches, Based upon the Ancient Monuments, Paintings, Sculptures, and Crania of Races, and upon Their Natural, Geographical, Philological, and Biblical History* . . . Philadelphia, 1854.

Novick, Peter. *That Noble Dream: The "Objectivity Question" and the Historical Profession.* Cambridge: Cambridge University Press, 1988.

Nye, Russel B. *Fettered Freedom: Civil Liberties and the Slavery Controversy, 1830–1860.* 1963. Urbana: University of Illinois Press, 1972.

——. *George Bancroft, Brahmin Rebel.* New York: Knopf, 1944.

"Observations on the Early History of the Negro Race." *Freedom's Journal,* December 5, 1828.

Offley, Rev. G. W. *A Narrative of the Life and Labors of the Rev. G. W. Offley, a Colored Man, and Local Preacher.* Hartford, Conn., 1860.

Olney, James. "'I Was Born': Slave Narratives, Their Status as Autobiography and as Literature." In *The Slave's Narrative,* edited by Charles T. Davis and Henry Louis Gates Jr., 148–75. Oxford: Oxford University Press, 1985.

Ott, Thomas O. *The Haitian Revolution, 1789–1804.* Knoxville: University of Tennessee Press, 1973.

Painter, Nell Irvin. Introduction to *Narrative of Sojourner Truth: A Bondswoman of Olden Time, with a History of Her Labors and Correspondence Drawn from Her "Book of Life"; also, a Memorial Chapter,* edited by Nell Irvin Painter. New York: Penguin, 1998.

——. *Sojourner Truth: A Life, a Symbol.* New York: Norton, 1996.

Parrott, Russell. *An Oration of the Abolition of the Slave Trade . . . Delivered on the First of January, 1814, at the African Church of St. Thomas.* In Porter, *Early Negro Writing,* 383–90.

Patterson, Orlando. *Slavery and Social Death: A Comparative Study.* Cambridge, Mass.: Harvard University Press, 1982.

Paul, Nathaniel. *An Address, Delivered on the Celebration of the Abolition of Slavery, in the State of New York, July 5, 1827.* 1827. New York: Arno Press and the New York Times, 1969.

Paulding, James Kirke. *Slavery in the United States.* New York, 1836.

Pease, Jane H., and William H. Pease. Introduction to *Twenty-two Years a Slave and Forty Years a Freeman,* by Austin Steward. Reading, Mass.: Addison-Wesley, 1969.

——. *They Who Would Be Free: Blacks' Search for Freedom, 1830–1861.* New York: Atheneum, 1974.

Penn, I. Garland. *The Afro-American Press, and Its Editors.* 1891. Salem, N.H.: Ayer, 1988.

Pennington, James W. C. *A Text Book of the Origin and History, &c. &c. of the Colored People.* Hartford, 1841.

"People of Colour." *Freedom's Journal*, April 20, 1827.

Perry, Lewis. *Radical Abolitionism: Anarchy and the Government of God in Antislavery Thought*. 1973. Knoxville: University of Tennessee Press, 1995.

Peterson, Carla L. *"Doers of the Word": African-American Women Speakers and Writers in the North (1830–1880)*. New York: Oxford University Press, 1995.

———. *Reconstructing the Nation: Frances Harper, Charlotte Forten, and the Racial Politics of Periodical Publication*. Worcester, Mass.: American Antiquarian Society, 1998.

Phillips, Charles Henry. *The History of the Colored Methodist Episcopal Church in America: Comprising Its Organization, Subsequent Development, and Present Status*. 1898. 3d ed. Jackson, Tenn., 1925.

Planas, Ricardo. *Liberation Theology: The Political Expression of Religion*. Kansas City, Mo.: Sheed and Ward, 1986.

Plato, Ann. *Essays: Including Biographies and Miscellaneous Pieces, in Prose and Poetry*. 1841. New York: Oxford University Press, 1988.

Pocock, J. G. A. *The Machiavellian Moment: Florentine Political Thought and the Atlantic Republican Tradition*. Cambridge: Cambridge University Press, 1975.

Porter, Dorothy, ed. *Early Negro Writing, 1760–1837*. Baltimore: Black Classic Press, 1995.

"Prejudice against Color in the Light of History." *Colored American*, March 18, 1837.

"Prejudice in the Church." *Colored American*, October 14, 1837.

Prescott, William H. "Bancroft's United States." In *Biographical and Critical Miscellanies*, 272–314. Philadelphia: Lippincott, 1875.

———. *Literary Memoranda*. 2 vols. Norman: University of Oklahoma Press, 1961.

Pride, Armisted S., and Clint C. Wilson II. *A History of the Black Press*. Washington, D.C.: Howard University Press, 1997.

Prince, Nancy. *A Narrative of the Life and Travels of Mrs. Nancy Prince, Written by Herself*. 2d ed. 1853. In *Collected Black Women's Narratives*. New York: Oxford University Press, 1988.

Purvis, Robert. "The American Government and the Negro." 1860. In Foner and Branham, *Lift Every Voice*, 331–39.

Quarles, Benjamin. *Black Abolitionists*. New York: Oxford University Press, 1969.

———. "Black History's Antebellum Origins." *Proceedings of the American Antiquarian Society* 89 (1979): 89–122.

Quinn, William Paul. *The Origin, Horrors, and Results of Slavery, Faithfully and Minutely Described, in a Series of Facts, and its Advocates Pathetically Addressed*. 1834. In Porter, *Early Negro Writing*, 614–36.

Rael, Patrick. *Black Identity and Black Protest in the Antebellum North*. Chapel Hill: University of North Carolina Press, 2002.

Ramsay, David. *The History of the American Revolution*. 1789. Edited by Lester H. Cohen, Indianapolis: Liberty Classics, 1990.

Reid-Pharr, Robert F. *Conjugal Union: The Body, the House, and the Black American*. New York: Oxford University Press, 1999.

Reilly, Bernard F. "The Art of the Antislavery Movement." In Donald M. Jacobs, *Courage and Conscience*, 47–73.

"Remarks of Dr. Blake." *Colored American*, September 16, 1837.

Remond, Charles Lenox. "For the Dissolution of the Union." 1844. In Foner and Branham, *Lift Every Voice*, 205–8.

Remond, Sarah Parker. "Why Slavery Is Still Rampant." 1859. In Foner and Branham, *Lift Every Voice*, 328–31.

"Reported for Frederick Douglass Paper." *Frederick Douglass' Paper*, October 2, 1851.

Resolutions of the People of Color, at a Meeting Held on the 25th of January, 1831; with an Address to the Citizens of New York, in Answer to Those of the New York Colonization Society. In Porter, *Early Negro Writing*, 281–85.

Rhodes, Jane. *Mary Ann Shadd Cary: The Black Press and Protest in the Nineteenth Century*. Bloomington: Indiana University Press, 1998.

Ricoeur, Paul. "Christianity and the Meaning of History." In *History and Truth*, translated by Charles A. Kelbley, 81–97. Evanston: Northwestern University Press, 1965.

Riley, Sam G. *Magazines of the American South*. New York: Greenwood Press, 1986.

Ripley, C. Peter, ed. *The Black Abolitionist Papers*. 5 vols. Chapel Hill: University of North Carolina Press, 1985–92.

Rodgers, Daniel T. *Contested Truths: Keywords in American Politics since Independence*. New York: Basic Books, 1987.

Roediger, David R. *The Wages of Whiteness: Race and the Making of the American Working Class*. London: Verso, 1991.

Rohrbach, Augusta. " 'Truth Stronger and Stranger Than Fiction': Reexamining William Lloyd Garrison's *Liberator*." *American Literature* 73, no. 4 (2001): 727–55.

Rollin, Frank [Frances] A. *Life and Public Services of Martin R. Delany, Sub-Assistant Commissioner Bureau Relief of Refugees, Freedmen, and of Abandoned Lands, and Late Major 104th U.S. Colored Troops*. 1883. In *Two Biographies by African-American Women*, edited by William L. Andrews. New York: Oxford University Press, 1991.

Ruffin, Edmund. *The Political Economy of Slavery; or, The Institution Considered in Regard to Its Influence on Public Wealth and the General Welfare*. Washington, D.C., 1853.

Sabin, John F. "George Bancroft's Library." *Critic*, December 12, 1891, 339–40.

Sale, Maggie Montesinos. *The Slumbering Volcano: American Slave Ship Revolts and the Production of Rebellious Masculinity*. Durham, N.C.: Duke University Press, 1997.

Saxton, Alexander. *The Rise and Fall of the White Republic: Class Politics and Mass Culture in Nineteenth-Century America*. London: Verso, 1990.

Schomburg, Arthur A. "The Negro Digs Up His Past." In *The New Negro: An Interpretation* [1925], edited by Alain Locke, 231–37. New York: Arno Press and the New York Times, 1968.

Segal, Ronald. *The Black Diaspora: Five Centuries of the Black Experience outside Africa*. New York: Noonday Press, 1995.

Senna, Carl. *The Black Press and the Struggle for Civil Rights*. New York: Franklin Watts, 1993.

Shaffer, Arthur H. *The Politics of History*. Chicago: Precedent Publishing, 1975.

"Sigma." "Correspondence." *Colored American*, July 15, 1837.

Simmons, William J. *Men of Mark: Eminent, Progressive, and Rising*. 1887. Chicago: Johnson Publishing, 1970.

Simms, Rev. James M. *The First Colored Baptist Church in North America: Constituted at Savannah, Georgia, January 20, A.D. 1788: With Biographical Sketches of the Pastors.* 1888. New York: Negro Universities Press, 1969.

Simpson, David. *The Politics of American English, 1776–1850.* New York: Oxford University Press, 1986.

Sipkins, Henry. *An Oration on the Abolition of the Slave Trade: Delivered in the African Church, in the City of New York, January 2, 1809.* In Porter, *Early Negro Writing,* 365–73.

Skinner, Elliott P. *African Americans and U.S. Policy toward Africa, 1850–1924.* Washington, D.C.: Howard University Press, 1992.

"Slavery." *Freedom's Journal,* November 30, 1827.

"Slavery and the Slave Trade." *Frederick Douglass' Paper,* November 20, 1851.

"Slavery in 1776." *Frederick Douglass' Paper,* October 2, 1851.

"Slaves Have Nothing to Do with the Fourth of July." *Anti-Slavery Record* 1, no. 10 (October 1835): 115.

Smith, Archie, Jr. *The Relational Self: Ethics and Therapy from a Black Church Perspective.* Nashville: Abingdon, 1982.

Smith, Robert P. "William Cooper Nell: Crusading Black Abolitionist." *Journal of Negro History* 55, no. 3 (July 1970): 182–99.

Smith, Rogers M. *Civic Ideals: Conflicting Visions of Citizenship in U.S. History.* New Haven: Yale University Press, 1997.

Smith, Theophus H. *Conjuring Culture: Biblical Formations of Black America.* New York: Oxford University Press, 1994.

Smith, Venture. *A Narrative of the Life and Adventures of Venture, a Native of Africa, but Resident above Sixty Years in the United States of America: Related by Himself.* 1798. In *Five Black Lives: The Autobiographies of Venture Smith, James Mars, William Grimes, The Rev. G. W. Offley, James L. Smith,* edited by Arna Bontemps, 1–34. Middletown, Conn.: Wesleyan University Press, 1971.

"Solid Reading." *Colored American,* July 20, 1839.

"Speech of H. H. Garnet." *Colored American,* May 30, 1840.

Stanley, Sara G. "What, to the Toiling Millions There, Is This Boasted Liberty?" 1856. In Foner and Branham, *Lift Every Voice,* 284–87.

Stanton, Lucy. "A Plea for the Oppressed." 1850. In Foner and Branham, *Lift Every Voice,* 220–23.

Stanton, William. *The Leopard's Spots: Scientific Attitudes toward Race in America, 1815–59.* Chicago: University of Chicago Press, 1960.

Stauffer, John. *The Black Hearts of Men: Radical Abolitionists and the Transformation of Race.* Cambridge, Mass.: Harvard University Press, 2002.

Stepto, Robert B. "Distrust of the Reader in Afro-American Narratives." In *Reconstructing American Literary History,* ed. Sacvan Bercovitch, 300–322. Cambridge, Mass.: Harvard University Press, 1986.

——. *From Behind the Veil: A Study of Afro-American Narrative.* 2d ed. Urbana: University of Illinois Press, 1991.

Steward, Austin. *Twenty-two Years a Slave, and Forty Years a Freeman: Embracing a Correspondence of Several Years, while President of Wilberforce Colony, London, Canada West.* 1857. Reading, Mass.: Addison-Wesley, 1969.

Stewart, Maria W. *Productions of Mrs. Maria W. Stewart*. 1835. In *Spiritual Narratives*. New York: Oxford University Press, 1988.

Stewart, Watt. "George Bancroft." In *The Marcus J. Jernegan Essays in American Historiography*, edited by William T. Hutchinson, 1–24. Chicago: University of Chicago Press, 1937.

Still, William. *The Underground Rail Road: A Record of Facts, Authentic Narratives, Letters, &c., Narrating the Hardships Hair-breadth Escapes and Death Struggles of the Slaves in Their Efforts for Freedom, as Related by Themselves and Others, or Witnessed by the Author; Together with Sketches of Some of the Largest Stockholders, and Most Liberal Aiders and Advisers, of the Road*. 1871. Chicago: Johnson Publishing Co., 1970.

Stowe, Harriet Beecher. *A Key to Uncle Tom's Cabin: Presenting the Original Facts and Documents upon Which the Story Is Founded, Together with Corroborative Statements Verifying the Truth of the Work*. 1853. Bedford, Mass.: Applewood Books, 1998.

——. *Uncle Tom's Cabin; or, Life among the Lowly*. 1852. New York: Vintage Books/Library of America, 1991.

Stringfellow, Thornton. *Scriptural and Statistical Views in Favor of Slavery*. Richmond, 1856.

Strong, Douglas M. *Perfectionist Politics: Abolitionism and the Religious Tensions of American Democracy*. Syracuse: Syracuse University Press, 1999.

Stuckey, Sterling. *Slave Culture: Nationalist Theory and the Foundations of Black America*. New York: Oxford University Press, 1987.

Sunder Rajan, Rajeswari. *Real and Imagined Women: Gender, Culture, and Postcolonialism*. New York: Routledge, 1993.

Sundquist, Eric J. *To Wake the Nations: Race in the Making of American Literature*. Cambridge, Mass: Belknap Press of Harvard University Press, 1993.

Sweet, Leonard I. *Black Images of America, 1784–1870*. New York: Norton, 1976.

Takaki, Ronald. *Iron Cages: Race and Culture in Nineteenth-Century America*. New York: Oxford University Press, 1990.

Tanner, B. T. *An Outline of the History and Government for African Methodist Churchmen, Ministerial and Lay: In Catechetical Form*. 1884.

"A Text Book of the Origin and History, &c., &c., of the Colored People." *Colored American*, January 9, 1841.

"A Text Book of the Origin and History, &c., &c., of the Colored People." *Colored American*, February 27, 1841.

"Theory and Practice." *Colored American*, June 5, 1841.

Thorpe, Earl E. *Black Historians: A Critique*. New York: William Morrow, 1971.

Tise, Larry E. *Proslavery: A History of the Defense of Slavery in America, 1701–1840*. Athens: University of Georgia Press, 1987.

"To Our Patrons." *Freedom's Journal*, March 16, 1827.

Tracy, David. "African American Thought: The Discovery of Fragments." In *Black Faith and Public Talk: Critical Essays on James H. Cone's Black Theology and Black Power*, edited by Dwight N. Hopkins, 29–38. Maryknoll, N.Y.: Orbis, 1999.

Trumbull, Henry. *Life and Adventures of Robert, the Hermit of Massachusetts, Who has lived 14 Years in a Cave, secluded from human society. Comprising, An account of his Birth, Parentage, Sufferings, and providential escape from unjust and cruel Bondage in early life—and his reasons for becoming a Recluse. Taken from his own mouth, and published for his benefit.* Providence, 1829.

Turner, Henry M. "Introduction, Accompanied by a Sketch of the Life of Rev. W. J. Simmons, A.B., A.M., D.D." In *Men of Mark: Eminent, Progressive, and Rising,* by William J. Simmons. 1887. Chicago: Johnson Publishing, 1970.

Ullman, Victor. *Martin R. Delany: The Beginnings of Black Nationalism.* Boston: Beacon Press, 1971.

"Uncle Tomitudes." *Putnam's Monthly* 1, no. 1 (January 1853): 97–102.

[Untitled]. *Freedom's Journal,* February 15, 1828.

Van Deburg, William L. *Slavery and Race in American Popular Culture.* Madison: University of Wisconsin Press, 1984.

Van Evrie, J. H. *White Supremacy and Negro Subordination; or, Negroes a Subordinate Race, and (So-called) Slavery Its Normal Condition, with an Appendix Showing the Past and Present Condition of the Countries South of Us.* New York, 1868.

Vitzthum, Richard C. *The American Compromise: Theme and Method in the Histories of Bancroft, Parkman, and Adams.* Norman: University of Oklahoma Press, 1974.

Vogel, Todd. "The New Face of Black Labor." In *The Black Press: New Literary and Historical Essays,* edited by Todd Vogel, 37–54. New Brunswick, N.J.: Rutgers University Press, 2001.

Wald, Priscilla. *Constituting Americans: Cultural Anxiety and Narrative Form.* Durham, N.C.: Duke University Press, 1995.

Walker, Clarence E. *Deromanticizing Black History: Critical Essays and Reappraisals.* Knoxville: University of Tennessee Press, 1991.

——. *We Can't Go Home Again: An Argument about Afrocentrism.* Oxford: Oxford University Press, 2001.

Walker, David. *David Walker's Appeal, in Four Articles; Together with a Preamble, to the Coloured Citizens of the World, but in Particular, and Very Expressly, to Those of The United States of America.* 3d ed. 1830. New York: Hill and Wang, 1965.

"Walker, David." In *Encyclopedia of African American Religions,* edited by Larry G. Murphy, J. Gordon Melton, and Gary L. Ward, 812–13. New York: Garland, 1993.

Wallace, Maurice O. *Constructing the Black Masculine: Identity and Ideality in African American Men's Literature and Culture, 1775–1995.* Durham, N.C.: Duke University Press, 2002.

Walters, Ronald G. *The Antislavery Appeal: American Abolitionism after 1830.* Baltimore: Johns Hopkins Press, 1976.

Ward, Samuel Ringgold. *Autobiography of a Fugitive Negro: His Anti-Slavery Labours in the United States, Canada, and England.* 1855. New York: Arno Press and the New York Times, 1968.

Warner, Michael. *The Letters of the Republic: Publication and the Public Sphere in Eighteenth-Century America.* Cambridge, Mass.: Harvard University Press, 1990.

Warren, James Perrin. *Culture of Eloquence: Oratory and Reform in Antebellum America.* University Park: Pennsylvania State University Press, 1999.

"Was Abraham a Slaveholder?" *Colored American,* February 2, 1839.

Washington, Robert E. *The Ideologies of African American Literature: From the Harlem*

Renaissance to the Black Nationalist Revolt. Lanham, Md.: Rowman and
Littlefield, 2001.

Watkins, Frances Ellen. "Liberty for Slaves." 1857. In Foner and Branham, *Lift Every Voice*, 305–7.

Watkins, William J. *Our Rights as Men: An Address Delivered in Boston, before the Legislative Committee on the Militia, February 24, 1853.* 1853. New York: Arno Press and the New York Times, 1969.

"The Week." *Colored American*, June 13, 1839.

Weld, Theodore Dwight. *American Slavery as It Is: Testimony of a Thousand Witnesses.* 1839. New York: Arno Press and the New York Times, 1968.

Wertheimer, Eric. *Imagined Empires: Incas, Aztecs, and the New World of American Literature, 1771–1876.* Cambridge: Cambridge University Press, 1999.

Wesley, Dorothy Porter. "Integration versus Separatism: William Cooper Nell's Role in the Struggle for Equality." In *Courage and Conscience*, edited by Donald M. Jacobs, 207–24.

"What Is a Negro?" *Frederick Douglass' Paper*, February 10, 1854.

Whipper, William. *An Address Delivered in Wesley Church on the Evening of June 12, before the Colored Reading Society of Philadelphia, for Mental Improvement.* 1828. In Porter, *Early Negro Writing*, 105–19.

White, Hayden. *Metahistory: The Historical Imagination in Nineteenth-Century Europe.* Baltimore: Johns Hopkins University Press, 1973.

"Whither Are We Tending?" *Weekly Anglo-African*, October 1, 1859, 2.

Wilkinson, James. "A Choice of Fictions: Historians, Memory, and Evidence." *PMLA* 111 (1996): 80–92.

"William Wells Brown at Philadelphia." *Liberator*, January 26, 1855, 14.

Williams, George W. *History of the Negro Race in America from 1619 to 1880: Negroes as Slaves, as Soldiers, and as Citizens; Together with a Preliminary Consideration of the Unity of the Human Family, an Historical Sketch of Africa, and an Account of the Negro Governments of Sierra Leone and Liberia.* 1883. Salem, N.H.: Ayer, 1989.

Williams, Loretta J. *Black Freemasonry and Middle-Class Realities.* Columbia: University of Missouri Press, 1980.

Williams, Peter. *A Discourse Delivered in St. Philip's Church, for the Benefit of the Coloured Community of Wilberforce, in Upper Canada, on the Fourth of July, 1830.* In Porter, *Early Negro Writing*, 294–302.

——. *An Oration on the Abolition of the Slave Trade: Delivered in the African Church, in The City of New York, January 1, 1808.* In Porter, *Early Negro Writing*, 343–54.

"William Wells Brown at Philadelphia." *Liberator*, January 26, 1855, 14.

Wilmore, Gayraud S. *Black Religion and Black Radicalism: An Interpretation of the Religious History of African Americans.* 3d ed. Maryknoll, N.Y.: Orbis, 1998.

Wilson, Joseph T. *Emancipation: Its Course and Progress, from 1491 B.C. to A.D. 1875, with a Review of President Lincoln's Proclamations, the XIII Amendment, and the Progress of the Freed People since Emancipation, with a History of the Emancipation Monument.* Hampton, Va., 1882.

Wiltse, Charles M. Introduction to *David Walker's Appeal, in Four Articles; Together with a Preamble, to the Coloured Citizens of the World, but in Particular, and Very Expressly, to Those of the United States of America.* New York: Hill and Wang, 1965.

Wimbush, Vincent L., ed. *African Americans and the Bible: Sacred Texts and Social Textures.* New York: Continuum, 2000.

Wolseley, Roland E. *The Black Press, U.S.A.* 2d ed. Ames: Iowa State University Press, 1990.

Wood, Gordon S. *The Creation of the American Republic, 1776–1787.* 1969. New York: Norton, 1972.

Wood, Marcus. *Blind Memory: Visual Representations of Slavery in England and America, 1780–1865.* New York: Routledge, 2000.

Woodson, Lewis. "To David Ruggles, John N. Still, Reuben Ruby, Samuel Hardenburg, and Others." *Colored American,* August 15, 1840.

Wright, Henry C. "Important Testimony." *Colored American,* May 27, 1837.

Yellin, Jean Fagan. *Women and Sisters: The Antislavery Feminists in American Culture.* New Haven: Yale University Press, 1989.

Zafar, Rafia. *We Wear the Mask: African Americans Write American Literature, 1760–1870.* New York: Columbia University Press, 1997.

index

Abyssinian Baptist Church, 159
Adams, Henry, 36
Adams, John, 54, 91, 96, 141
Adams, John Quincy, 359 (n. 42)
Adams, Nehemiah, 174–75, 371 (n. 16)
Adams, Samuel, 142
"Address of the Virginia Convention for the abolition of slavery," 287
Adelphic Union Library Association, 367
Aesop, 309
Africa, 87, 106, 293, 309, 322; in Enlightenment thought, 5; as symbolic site, 9, 22, 69, 91; and effects of the slave trade, 64–65, 73, 74–75, 164, 309; regeneration of, 67, 129–30; in African American historical imagination, 68–78, 92, 252, 289; and biblical prophecy and Providence, 71, 72–73, 74–75, 79, 119, 131; and Freemasonry, 117, 118; and colonization, 119, 129–30; Henry Highland Garnet on, 247
African American conventions. See Conventions, African American
African Baptist Church, 133
African Benevolent Society, 142
African Civilization Society, 64–65
African Methodist Episcopal Church, 23, 162, 299
Afrocentricism, 2, 9, 70, 75, 104, 336
Allen, Richard, 23, 50, 52–53, 221, 279, 308, 316. See also A Narrative of the Proceedings of the Black People, during the Late Awful Calamity in Philadelphia, in the Year 1793
Allen, William G., 140, 244, 234, 236; on prejudice, 230
—works: The American Prejudice against Color, 205–6; "Letter from William G. Allen," 379 (n. 13); "Letter from Wm. G. Allen," 230, 378 (n. 12); "Orators and Oratory," 229–32
American Anti-Slavery Society, 238, 286
American Colonization Society, 64–65, 91, 118, 122, 142, 250, 255, 256
American Moral Reform Society, 270
American Museum, 164
American Revolution, 60, 231, 279; African Americans in, 25; George Bancroft on, 36; and resistance to slavery, 45–46, 136–38, 163–64, 233–36, 239, 246; and American discourse, 45–46, 223–24, 234–35; as philosophical event, 54, 234, 320; and African American rights, 74, 143, 219–20; African American appropriations of, 80, 129, 234, 253; as unfinished, 87, 136, 138; African American service in, 95, 135, 266, 335; historical recording of, 96–97; African American jeremiads and, 134, 237, 238; Frederick Douglass on, 233–34; Maria Stewart on, 245. See also Attucks, Crispus; Boston Massacre; Bunker Hill, battle of; Fourth of July

Anderson, Benedict, 53, 57, 283, 301

Andrews, William L., 175–76, 178–79, 187–88, 371 (n. 18)

Anglo-African Magazine, 21, 138, 158, 159, 305–29

Ankersmit, F. R., 348 (n. 7)

Anti-Slavery Bugle, 60

Anti-Slavery Herald, 383 (n. 11)

Anti-Slavery Reporter, 110

Anti-Slavery Society of Canada, 211

Apess, William, 103

Aptheker, Herbert, 43

Arch, Stephen Carl, 137

Aristotle, 313

Atlantic Monthly, 324

Attucks, Crispus, 80, 140, 219, 221, 227, 238, 322

Augustine, 212

Autobiography (and memoirs), 26; as mode of historical writing, 157, 160, 208–10, 212–13, 214–17; and representative identity, 159–60, 190–91, 212, 216; multiple versions of, 160–61; and white curiosity, 164–65, 169–71, 176–79; white narration of, 164–84; as historical source, 168–69; slave narratives as form of, 168–69, 186–87; and docudramatic presentation, 179–84; and white readers, 188–90, 205–6; and struggles with discourse, 194–97; and spiritual community, 194–202

Bacon, Francis, 135

Bailyn, Bernard, 54

Baker, Houston A., Jr., 356 (n. 27), 374 (n. 36)

Bakhtin, Mikhail, 106, 192

Bancroft, George, 17, 67–68, 89, 133, 194, 373 (n. 27); and Providence, 10, 72, 81, 135, 357 (n. 36), 362 (n. 56); as representative historian, 34; on United States as philosophical achievement, 35, 54; and representative identity, 35, 191–93, 195, 196; on race, 35–36, 55; historical method of, 36, 52, 72, 96–97, 98–99, 99–100, 350 (n. 18), 362 (n. 56); on African American history, 98–99, 132; compared to Robert Ben-

jamin Lewis, 106–7, 113; compared to William C. Nell, 143, 147; on George Washington, 191–93; compared to George Washington Williams, 332

—works: *History of the United States*, 33, 35, 36, 52, 54–55, 72, 81, 97, 98, 357 (n. 36), 362 (n. 56); "The Necessity, the Reality, and the Promise of the Progress of the Human Race," 35, 80; "The Office of the People in Art, Government and Religion," 35; review of *Documentary History of the American Revolution*, 96–97

Banneker, Benjamin, 63, 142, 158, 161, 162–63, 164, 316

Barlow, Joel, 54

Barthelemy, Anthony G., 177

Barthes, Roland, 348 (n. 7), 363 (n. 56)

Bassard, Katherine Clay, 14–15, 34, 349 (n. 12), 350 (n. 16)

Bay, Mia, 102, 103, 104, 364 (n. 5)

Beecher, Henry Ward, 227

Beecher, Lyman, 133

Belinda, 163–64

Bell, Howard Helman, 50, 264, 381 (n. 29)

Beman, Amos Gerry, 140, 212, 251, 305, 315–16, 319

—works: "The Education of the Colored People," 79; "Thoughts for the Season," 300; "Thoughts—No. III," 48–49; "Thoughts, No. IX," 301

Bercovitch, Sacvan, 80, 87, 361 (n. 51)

Berkeley, George, 89, 362 (n. 56)

Bethel, Elizabeth Rauh, 32, 219, 220, 227–28, 377 (n. 2)

Bibb, Henry, 140

Bible: as historical source, 8, 77, 78, 85, 153; and Exodus narrative, 10–11, 126, 177, 242, 268; as framework for African American history, 11, 12; and black theology, 14, 16, 107, 230, 342–43; and Africa as symbolic site, 22; and African American imagined community, 42, 139, 301; and African American destiny, 71, 109–10; as response to racism, 106; and Christian responsibility, 139; as governing text, 359 (n. 42)

—books and citations of: Ezekiel, 137; Hebrews, 381 (n. 30); Isaiah, 198; Matthew, 365 (n. 8); 1 Peter, 88; Psalm 68:31, 48, 75, 88, 131, 236, 362 (n. 54); Psalms, 137; Revelation (chap. 18), 16, 349 (n. 14)
    See also Christianity; Moses; Providence
Bingham, Caleb, 222
Black Arts movement, 20
Black conventions. *See* Conventions, African American
Black Economic Development Conference, 13
Blackface minstrelsy, 281
"Black Manifesto," 13
Blassingame, John W., 179
Bloomfield, Maxwell, 373 (n. 27)
Blyden, Edward Wilmot, 305, 308; "A Chapter in the History of the Slave Trade," 307
Boime, Albert, 376 (n. 45)
Bonaparte, Napoleon, 230
Book of Mormon, 103, 109, 116
Book of the First American Chess Congress, 307
Boone, Daniel, 60, 339
Boston Massacre, 141, 219
Botta, Charles W., 141
Bourdieu, Pierre, 33
Bradford, Sarah, 173
Brooklyn *Daily Times*, 31
Brown, John, 29, 119, 184, 240, 279, 293, 328, 329
Brown, William Wells, 84, 103, 123, 140, 160, 331–40; on representation of slavery, 39–40, 92, 333; on race, 60, 335, 338; on misrepresentation of African American history, 98–99; and African American authorship, 225; narrative method of, 333, 334; biographical background of, 333–34; historical method of, 335–36, 337–40; and social performance, 336–37, 339–40
—works: *The Black Man*, 334–39, 388 (n. 7); *Clotel*, 148, 331, 337; *The Escape*, 334, 339; *A Lecture Delivered*

before the Female Anti-Slavery Society of Salem, 39, 333; *Narrative of William W. Brown*, 333, 337; *The Negro in the American Rebellion*, 132, 133, 334–39; *The Rising Son*, 338–40, 334–35; *St. Domingo*, 246; *Three Years in Europe*, 339
Bullock, Penelope L., 288, 305, 388 (n. 7)
Bunker Hill, battle of, 42, 132, 147, 241, 249
Burgess, Tristam, 140
Burlinggame, Anson, 140
Burns, Anthony, 138, 141
Butler, Octavia, 5
Byron, George Gordon, Lord, 114, 283

Caesar, Gaius Julius, 102, 105, 229, 336
Caldwell, Elias B., 85, 86
Calhoun, John, 324
Callahan, Allen Dwight, 349 (n. 14)
Callcott, George H., 363 (n. 2)
Callinicos, Alex, 4
Campbell, Robert, 305, 307
Candler, John, 110
Carey, Matthew, 46–47, 341
Carretta, Vincent, 164, 165
Cary, Mary A. B., 21, 305
Cary, Mary Ann Shadd, 305, 385 (n. 17)
Cassuto, Leonard, 59
Castronovo, Russ, 82, 83, 178, 233, 351 (n. 3), 355 (n. 24), 369 (n. 1), 375 (n. 38)
Cato, Marcus Porcius, 105
Celebrations, African American, 209, 219, 228; Commemorative Festival at Faneuil Hall, 219–21, 227–28. *See also* Fourth of July
Channing, Walter, 238
Charlottesville Jeffersonian, 61
Child, David Lee, 123, 140
Child, Lydia Maria, 31, 123, 140
—works: *The American Frugal House-wife*, 386 (n. 26); *An Appeal in Favor of That Class of Americans Called Africans*, 162; *Fact and Fiction*, 147–52
Christianity: African American approaches to, 10–11, 15; David Walker on, 86; corruption of, 86, 100, 101, 128,

203–4, 214–15, 253, 255, 298–300;
Frederick Douglass on, 100, 236; African American approaches to, 100–101;
Martin R. Delany on, 128–29, 130, 131;
and sense of responsibility in, 139,
300, 309–10; William C. Nell on, 145;
and justifications of slavery, 174–75;
and antislavery discourse, 177, 298;
Jarena Lee on, 193, 195, 197; Zilpha
Elaw on, 193–97; Harriet Jacobs on,
198–202; Nancy Prince on, 207–8;
Samuel Ringgold Ward on, 211, 214–
15; William G. Allen on, 230; effects
of slavery on theology of, 299–300;
James W. C. Pennington on, 309–10;
William J. Wilson on, 313–14. *See also*
Bible; Moses; Providence (Christian)
Christian Recorder, 279
Christian Spectator, 290
Church of Jesus Christ of Latter-day
Saints, 103
Cicero, Marcus Tullius, 105, 229, 231
Cinqué, Joseph, 248
Civil War, 32, 119, 270; and historical
methodology, 22; and African American historical agency, 265–66; and
white supremacy, 267, 274, 286; as
result of moral transgressions, 298; as
turning point in African American historiography, 333
Clark, Alex M., 166
Clarke, Lewis, 140, 178–79, 181
Clarke, Madison M., 213
Clarke, Milton, 140, 178
Clarkson, Matthew, 47
Clarkson, Thomas, 309
Clay, Henry, 85, 86, 146, 147, 221, 324
Coker, Daniel, 58; *A Dialogue between a
Virginian and an African Minister*, 59,
88, 91
Colbourn, H. Trevor, 54
Colesworthy, Daniel Clement, 101
Colonization, 129, 302. *See also*
Emigration
Colored American, 184, 278, 286, 296–
97, 301, 324
–articles in: "Abolition Dying Away,"
303; "An American Citizen Mur-

dered," 284; "Appeal to the Friends of
the Colored American," 304; "The
Church in Fault," 298; "Colored People Always Opposed to Colonization,"
302; "The Destruction of Babylon,"
300; "De Tocqueville's Democracy in
America," 288; "Elevation of Our People," 295; "The Emigration Scheme,"
383 (n. 12); "Facts respecting Pro-
Slavery Colleges," 299–300; "For the
Colored American" (Augustine), 351
(n. 7); "The Fourth and Fifth of July in
the City of Schenectady," 305; "A
Fragment," 384 (n. 14); "The General
Theological Seminary," 298; "Important Testimony," 287; "Lecture on the
Haytien Revolutions," 291; "Nation
Warned," 300; "Prejudice against
Color in the Light of History," 291, 352
(n. 7); "Prejudice in the Church," 299;
"The Reflector: No. V. ("Long Island
Scribe"), 244, 261, 356 (n. 26);
"Remarks of Dr. Blake," 369 (n. 44);
"Solid Reading," 296; "A Text Book,"
291; "Theory and Practice," 350 (n. 1);
"Thoughts—No. III," 48–49;
"Thoughts, No. IX," 79, 301;
"Thoughts for the Season," 300; "The
Week," 237;
Columbian Centinel, 85
Columbian Orator, The (Bingham), 222–
23, 224
Columbus, Christopher, 50, 108
"Communication from the New York
Society for the Promotion of Education among Colored Children," 317
Community, 62–63, 66, 69; problem of
defining, 14, 17, 40–42, 57, 69, 99;
scattered or fragmented, 18, 19, 28, 55,
64–65, 66, 67, 93, 131–32, 137–38,
152, 157, 202, 211, 221, 252–53, 260–
62, 275–76; role of African American
press in, 27, 293–95, 297; and African
American self-definition, 29, 30, 118,
155, 294, 311–13; and education, 40,
79, 86, 135–36, 151, 317–20; Bible and
imagined community, 42, 139, 301;
and citizenship, 51, 65, 74, 84, 120–21,

124, 247, 313; as shaped by the system
of slavery, 62–63; and biblical destiny,
48, 71, 75, 87, 88, 109–10, 119, 121–22,
125, 126, 127, 128, 129, 130, 131, 236,
316, 362 (n. 54); and occupations, 116,
124, 263–64, 381 (n. 31); and uplift,
116, 272, 295–96, 301–2, 303, 352
(n. 11); and African American identity
as contingent, 157, 189–90, 217, 222,
240, 253; and representative identity,
159–60, 168–69, 212, 216; and discourse, 301–2
Condit, Celeste Michelle, 83
Cone, James H., 15, 32, 100, 101,
—works: *Black Theology and Black
Power*, 13; *A Black Theology of Liberation*, 13, 14; *My Soul Looks Back*, 14
Confessions of Nat Turner, 328, 329
Congress, U.S., 43–46
Connor, A. J. R., 307
Constitution, U.S., 34, 36, 54, 239; as
antislavery document, 43, 81, 257,
308; David Walker and, 49; as white
supremacist document, 125, 238; and
African American rights, 144, 254–55,
257, 308, 313; as proslavery document,
238–39
Conventions, African American, 146;
Address of the Colored National Convention to the People of the United
States, 135–36; State Convention of
Colored Men in Ohio (1856), 248–49;
debates on occupations, 263–64, 381
(n. 31); and women, 264–65; and Civil
War, 265–66, 267, 270, 274–75; on
racism, 269–70; on Fugitive Slave
Law, 271–72
—national conventions, 26–27, 91, 115,
159, 302, 314; of 1831, 154, 250, 257,
261, 308; of 1832, 258, 259–60; of
1833, 255–56; of 1834, 256, 258, 260,
269, 380 (n. 27); of 1835, 260; of 1843,
204, 214, 246, 254, 255, 259, 260, 281,
282–83; of 1847, 185, 256, 258–59,
283–84, 380 (n. 21); of 1848, 261–62,
263, 264, 266–68, 270, 284, 381
(n. 31); of 1853, 135–36, 263–64, 265,
268, 271–72, 381 (nn. 28, 34); of 1855,

257–58; of 1864, 264–66, 267, 268,
273, 274, 286
Cooper, Anna Julia, 165
*Copy of a Letter from Benjamin Ban-
neker to the Secretary of State*, 158
Cornish, Samuel, 302, 303, 308, 382
(n. 2), 383 (n. 9), 385 (n. 15)
Crandall, Prudence, 317
Critic, 98
Crofts, Julia Griffith, 285
Cromwell, Oliver, 139, 292
Crummell, Alexander, 211, 212, 316, 317
Cruz, Jon, 9, 10
Cuffe, Paul, 65, 91, 103, 141, 142; *A Brief
Account*, 64–65, 362 (n. 54)
Curtis, George William, 227
Cyprian, 212

Dalton, Thomas, 116
Davis, Samuel H., 204, 254
Day, William Howard, 140
DeBow's Review, 282
Declaration of Independence, 74, 87, 91,
162; African American appropriations
of, 80, 81, 82, 85, 248, 301, 308; William Wells Brown on, 246; Henry
Highland Garnet on, 248; and African
American national conventions, 254–
55, 260, 267; and representative
authority, 293. *See also* Fourth of July
Dekker, George, 357 (n. 35)
Delany, Martin R., 23, 25, 84, 93, 99, 100,
101, 113–32, 140, 142, 153, 251, 283,
308, 316, 336, 366 (n. 20); on emigration, 31, 91, 118–19, 120, 122, 126–27,
366 (n. 16); on race and prejudice, 58,
116, 126, 127; and black nationalism,
79, 114, 131, 132; on Robert Benjamin
Lewis's *Light and Truth*, 104–5, 112,
116, 364 (n. 7); historical philosophy
of, 114; relationship with Frederick
Douglass, 114, 118; biographical background of, 114–15; on black self-
reliance, 115; on white supremacy,
115–16; on black uplift, 116; and Freemasonry, 116–18, 120; on Africa, 118,
121–22, 131; on Providence and black
destiny, 119, 121–22, 125, 126, 127, 128,

129, 130, 131; on African American citizenship, 120–21, 124; and historical
sources, 122–23; on Christianity, 128,
130; and William C. Nell, 133, 142, 144;
on Fugitive Slave Law, 366 (n. 18)
—works: "The Attraction of Planets,"
307; *Blake*, 131, 305, 307; "Comets,"
307; *The Condition*, 104, 115, 116, 117,
118, 119, 120–29, 131, 132, 263; *Official
Report of the Niger Valley Exploring
Party*, 119, 129; *The Origin and Objects
of Ancient Freemasonry*, 117–18, 120;
"Political Destiny of the Colored Race
on the American Continent," 119–20
Democratic Review, 282
Demosthenes, 229, 231
Dening, Greg, 3, 7, 33, 51–52, 187
Derrida, Jacques, 181, 293
Dessalines, Jean-Jacques, 89, 90, 292
Dickens, Charles, 280
Dickinson, Anna, 264–65
Diogenes, 105
Douglas, H. Ford, 238–40
Douglass, Frederick, 29, 30, 84, 100, 121,
160, 209, 210, 212, 214, 231, 263, 305–
16 passim, 327, 336; on white Ameri-
cans, 31, 139, 184–85, 227, 246, 269;
on antislavery movement, 31, 184–85,
225, 227, 250, 377 (n. 48); and Martin
R. Delany, 114, 122, 126, 263; and
William C. Nell, 134, 366 (n. 25); and
Samuel Ringgold Ward, 184–85; on
corruption of Christianity, 203–4, 236;
and *The Columbian Orator*, 222, 223,
224; and William Lloyd Garrison, 228;
and Wendell Phillips, 228; on American Revolution, 233–34; and African
American activism, 246–47; and
national conventions, 246–47, 264–
65, 269, 272–73; and black uplift, 272;
and *North Star*, 285
—works: *Life and Times of Frederick
Douglass*, 203; *My Bondage and My
Freedom*, 83, 179, 181, 187–88, 203,
225; *Narrative of the Life of Frederick
Douglass*, 181, 190, 203–5, 222; "The
Unholy Alliance of Negro Hate and
Anti-Slavery," 185; "West India Eman-

cipation," 249, 250; "What, to the
Slave, Is the Fourth of July?," 81, 232–
37
Douglass, Sarah M., 305
Douglass, Sheridan, 222
Douglass' Monthly, 287
Dred Scott decision, 219, 220, 221, 238,
243, 313
Drew, Benjamin: *A North-Side View of
Slavery*, 173–74
Du Bois, W. E. B., 100, 264, 332
Dumas, Alexandre, 63

Eakin, Sue, 183
Easton, Hosea, 23, 64, 66, 81–82, 84, 99,
103, 141; *Treatise*, 23, 40, 62–63, 65,
73–74, 92, 143, 144, 368 (n. 37)
Edwards, Jonathan, 302
Egyptocentrism, 70
Elam, Henry J., Jr., 334
Elaw, Zilpha, 191, 210; *Memoirs of the
Life*, 193–97
Eldridge, Elleanor, 169–70
Emerson, Ralph Waldo, 227, 229
Emigration, 91, 122, 384 (n. 12); and the
Caribbean, 99; and South and Central
America, 118; and Africa, 118, 119, 121,
129–30; and Canada, 119, 259–60;
and black national conventions, 250
Episcopal Church, 24
Epps, Edwin, 181
Equiano, Olaudah, 164
Ericson, David F., 379 (n. 16)
Ethiop. *See* Wilson, William J.
Euclid, 212
Everett, Edward, 227
Everitt, Alexander H., 68

Fabre, Geneviève, 160
Fanuzzi, Robert, 383 (n. 8)
Farrison, William Edward, 387 (n. 2)
Female Anti-Slavery Society (Salem,
Mass.), 39
Ferguson, Adam, 104
Field, James, 307
Finkenbine, Roy E., 133
Force, Peter, 96
Foreman, P. Gabrielle, 371 (n. 17)

Forman, James, 13, 14, 142

Forten, James, 308

Foster, Frances Smith, 187

Foucault, Michel, 340

Fourth of July, 67–68, 80, 81, 219; Frederick Douglass on, 232–37; H. Ford Douglass on, 238–40; *See also* American Revolution; Celebrations, African American; Declaration of Independence

Franklin, Benjamin, 166, 341, 342

Franklin, John Hope, 346 (n. 3)

Frederick Douglass' Monthly, 285

Frederick Douglass' Paper, 102, 103, 158, 159, 172, 184, 302, 324

–articles in: "The Characteristics of Christian Warriors," 139; "Slavery in 1776," 291, 360 (n. 44); "What Is a Negro?," 61

Fredrickson, George, 311

Free African School, 24, 211

Free African Society, 23

Freedom's Journal, 103, 284, 285, 302, 303, 305, 324; reframing white culture, 288–91; as multivocal text, 292–93; and imagined community, 293–94; and African American self-representation, 310

–articles in: "European Colonies in America," 289; "People of Colour," 290–91

Freeman, M. H., 318, 319

Freemasonry, 23, 114, 116–18, 120, 131, 162; David Walker on, 41; and Prince Hall Grand Lodge, 116; and Egypt, 116–17; and St. Cyprian Lodge (Pittsburgh), 117; and Africa, 117, 118; and prejudice, 117–18; Martin R. Delany on, 117–18, 120

French Revolution, 292

Fugitive Slave Law, 121, 125, 127, 132, 172, 238, 271–72

Fuss, Diana, 370 (n. 4)

Garner, Margaret, 249, 327

Garnet, Henry Highland, 91, 140, 231, 249, 283, 308, 316, 317, 321, 329, 336; and emigration, 31; and David Walker, 48; on race, 58, 59, 64, 113, 269–70, 355 (n. 23); and black achievement, 63; and effects of slavery, 64–65; and Africa, 70; and African American destiny, 87; and Samuel Ringgold Ward, 211, 212; and African American activism, 247–48, 259, 292; and power of the press, 283

–works: *Address to the Slaves of the United States of America,* 114, 204, 246–48, 259; *The Past and the Present Condition,* 59, 63, 64–65, 70, 87, 355 (n. 23)

Garrison, William Lloyd, 31, 159, 232, 302; on Martin R. Delany's *Condition,* 122, 124; and William C. Nell, 133–34, 142, 150, 151; preface to Frederick Douglass's *Narrative,* 187–88, 228, 378 (n. 9); and 1858 Commemorative Festival at Faneuil Hall, 227–28; and Frederick Douglass, 235, 236; threatened by mob, 284; criticized in *Colored American,* 288; and African American community, 383 (n. 12)

Gates, Henry Louis, Jr., 182

Geertz, Clifford, 161–62

Genius of Universal Emancipation, 278, 292

Gibbon, Edward, 309

Giddings, J. R., 140

Gilbert, Olive, 173

Gilroy, Paul, 8, 36, 79

Glaude, Eddie S., 10–11

Gliddon, George R., 105–6, 112, 116, 120

Gloucester, John, 316

Goldberg, David Theo, 3, 29, 53, 369 (n. 1)

Goldsby, Jacqueline, 190

Goldsmith, Oliver, 104

Goode, John Mason, 63

Goodell, William, 31

Goodman, Paul, 28, 29, 30, 31

Gordon, Robert, 307

Gossman, Lionel, 352 (n. 10), 361 (n. 50), 364 (n. 3)

Graham, Mary W., 226–27

Grant, Ulysses S., 274

Greeley, Horace, 227

Green, Johnson, 164
Greene, Frances Whipple, 169
Grégoire, Abbé, 111, 112, 113
Grice, Hezekiah, 250, 308
Grimké, Charlotte Forten, 152, 333–34
Grimshaw, William H., 116, 365 (n. 13)
Gutierrez, Gustavo, 13

Haiti, 24, 63–64, 76, 88–91, 107, 110,
    289, 293; and revolution in, 44, 63,
    89–90, 110, 279, 291, 292; James The-
    odore Holly on, 88–90; Robert Ben-
    jamin Lewis on, 110–12
Hall, Prince, 117
Hamilton, Thomas, 305, 306, 310, 311,
    323
Hamilton, William, 71, 87–88, 159, 225–
    26, 256
Hamlet, Prince of Denmark (Shake-
    speare), 310
Hampden, John, 248
Hancock, John, 140
Hanover College and Theological Semi-
    nary, 299
Harlan, David, 347 (n. 7)
Harper, Frances Ellen Watkins, 265, 279,
    318, 324; "Liberty for Slaves," 241–42;
    "The Two Offers," 305
Harpers Ferry, Va., 328
Harrington, Henry F., 140
Harris, J. Dennis, 50–51, 52–53, 90–91,
    92–93, 99, 113
Hartford Literary and Religious Institu-
    tion, 23
Hartman, Saidiya V., 62, 164, 178
Harvard Medical School, 114
Hayward, Wilbur M., 379 (n. 14)
Hegel, Georg Wilhelm Friedrich, 34, 43,
    57, 63, 67–68
Heidelberg, University of, 24
Helmsley, Alexander, 173–74
Helper, Hinton, 242
Henderson, Stephen, 24, 32
Hendler, Glenn, 125
Henry, Patrick, 248, 328
Henry, William "Jerry," 211
Henson, Josiah, 160, 173, 213
Herder, Johann Gottfried von, 34

Herodotus, 70, 108
Higginson, Thomas Wentworth, 227
Highgate, Edmonia, 264–65
Hildreth, Richard, 34, 35, 52, 332
Hinks, Peter P., 353 (n. 13)
Hodges, Willis A., 282, 285
Hoggan, David L., 350 (n. 18)
Holly, James Theodore, 24, 45, 50, 53,
    99, 305; *A Vindication*, 23, 44, 56, 88–
    90; "Thoughts on Hayti," 307–8
Hooker, John, 172
Hopkins, Dwight, 15
Horace, 105
Horsman, Reginald, 116, 149
Horton, James Oliver, 133, 365 (n. 12),
    366 (n. 24), 369 (n. 43)
Horton, Lois E., 369 (n. 43)
Howe, Daniel W., 54
Howe, Stephen, 345 (n. 1)
Hume, David, 104, 336
Hurston, Zora Neale, 100

Independence Day. *See* Fourth of July
Interreligious Foundation for Commu-
    nity Organization, 13
Irving, Washington, 76, 192

Jackson, Andrew, 52, 84–85, 113, 245;
    proclamations to black soldiers (1814),
    84, 107, 111, 124, 133, 136, 143, 213,
    238, 252, 271, 366 (n. 22)
Jackson, Edmund, 140
Jacobs, Harriet, 174, 180, 209, 374
    (n. 35); *Incidents in the Life of a Slave
    Girl*, 190, 197–202, 387 (n. 27)
Jamaica Hamic Association, 185–86, 207
Jefferson, Thomas, 96, 140, 162, 221, 287,
    302, 316, 324, 328; as representative of
    white supremacist thought, 44, 63;
    Notes on the State of Virginia, 44, 85,
    87–88, 291, 361 (n. 52); in David
    Walker's *Appeal*, 85; on slavery as
    immoral, 87–88, 206, 254, 290, 361
    (n. 52); and Benjamin Banneker, 162;
    and the "language of truth," 385
    (n. 18)
Jennings, Thomas L., 158–59, 160, 161
Johnson, Oliver, 122

Johnson, W. P., 304–5
Jones, Absalom, 23, 50, 52–53, 221, 316. See also *A Narrative of the Proceedings of the Black People*
July Fourth. *See* Fourth of July
Justica (in *Colored American*), 359 (n. 41), 361 (n. 49)

Kellner, Hans, 6, 7
Kemble, Fanny, 242
Kentucky Weekly News, 141
King, Lyndon, 205–6
King, Martin Luther, Jr., 13
King, Mary, 205–6
Knox, Angelina J., 140
Kosciusko, Thaddeus, 140
Kossuth, Louis, 225, 231
Kraus, Michael, 96
Ku Klux Klan, 339

Lafayette, Marquis de, 140, 245, 248
Lane Seminary, 299
Langston, John Mercer, 140, 143, 144, 305, 308, 368 (n. 36)
Las Casas, Bartholomew de, 76, 309
Latrobe, John H. B., 142, 162–63; *Memoir of Benjamin Banneker*, 162–63, 370 (n. 5)
Lawrence, George, 66
Lee, Jarena, 191, 193; *The Life and Religious Experience of Jarena Lee*, 193, 195–97
Lee, Simon, 60
Leo X (pope), 302
Levin, David, 350 (n. 17), 354 (n. 17)
Levine, Robert S., 114, 118, 194, 275, 334, 365 (n. 15), 376 (n. 40)
Lewis, John W., 140
Lewis, Robert Benjamin, 12, 23, 25, 84, 93, 99, 100, 122, 128, 153; *Light and Truth*, 10, 101–13, 115, 116, 142; and race, 106, 112–13, 365 (n. 9)
Liberation theology, 13–17, 18, 19, 153, 215, 230, 239, 342
Liberator, 159, 235, and William C. Nell, 133–34, 138, 140, 152; and Solomon Northup, 180; and African American authorship, 225; and Frederick Doug-

lass, 285; African American criticism of, 286, 288
—articles in: "Affecting Narration," 180; "Improvement of Colored People," 152; "Pictures of American Slavery," 138
Liberia, 121, 209, 303, 307, 308
Life and Adventures of Robert, the Hermit of Massachusetts, 170–71
Lincoln, Abraham, 33, 114, 240
Little, John, 174
Litwack, Leon, 184
Livermore, George, 133
Loggins, Vernon, 101, 103, 104, 105
Logsdon, Joseph, 183
Looby, Christopher, 223–24, 238
Lovejoy, B. G., 98
Lovejoy, Elijah, 284
Lovejoy, J. C., 178
Lucaites, John Louis, 83
Lundy, Benjamin, 31, 278, 292

Macaulay, Thomas Babington, 336
Mailloux, Steven, 286
Marion College, 299
Martin, J. Sella, 305
Martineau, Harriet, 168
Marxism, 13, 15
Maryland Colonization Society, 162
Massachusetts Anti-Slavery Society, 39
Massachusetts General Colored Association, 133
Mattison, Hiram, 176–78
McBride, Dwight A., 82, 369 (n. 2)
McHenry, William "Jerry." *See* Henry, William "Jerry"
McKean, Thomas, 96
Memoirs. *See* Autobiography
Memoirs of Elleanor Eldridge, 169–70
Methodism, 299
Middle Passage, 22, 69–70, 80, 164, 292
Mills, Charles W., 3, 4, 29, 53, 156, 157, 354 (n. 19)
Mirror of Liberty, 285, 288
Mizruchi, Susan, 34
Moody, Joycelyn K., 376 (n. 39)
Moore, Alonzo D., 339

Mormons. *See* Church of Jesus Christ of Latter-day Saints

Morris, Robert, 140, 316

Morrison, Toni, 8, 32, 100, 101, 155–56, 249, 328

Morton, Samuel George, 106

Moses, 70, 102, 114, 118, 248, 319

Moses, Wilson Jeremiah, 2, 3, 99, 345 (n. 1), 346 (nn. 2, 4), 361 (n. 53)

Mudimbe, Velentin, 157

Mystery, 114, 283, 365 (n. 10)

Narrative of the Proceedings of the Black People, during the Late Awful Calamity in Philadelphia, in the Year 1793, 23, 46–48, 50, 341, 362 (n. 54)

National Anti-Slavery Standard, 286

National Committee of Negro Churchmen, 13

National Conference of Black Churchmen, 13

National Era, 95

National Intelligencer, 86

Native Americans, 53, 128, 237; Robert Benjamin Lewis on, 102, 103, 104, 106, 108, 109–10, 112; William C. Nell on, 142; Maria Stewart on, 245; Frederick Douglass on, 272; George Bancroft and, 354 (n. 20); Henry Highland Garnet on, 355 (n. 23)

Nell, William C., 23, 25, 84, 93, 99, 100, 101, 124, 132–53, 155, 162, 265, 305, 331, 333; on misrepresentation of the American Revolution, 42; on documentation and recording of history, 95, 97, 219, 221; and Martin R. Delany, 124, 144; and racial prejudice, 133, 134–35, 142, 143, 144, 145, 146, 147, 150; and the *Liberator*, 133–34; and racial cooperation, 134, 139–41, 147, 151–52; and Frederick Douglass, 134, 367 (n. 25); on education, 135–36, 151; on scattered community, 137–38; on African American activism, 138–40; and philosophy of history, 145–46; use of Lydia Maria Child's "The Black Saxons," 147–52; on colonization and emigration, 151; and 1858 Commem-

orative Festival at Faneuil Hall, 219–21, 227–28; on Crispus Attucks monument, 367 (n. 33); and Henry Highland Garnet, 368 (n. 35)

–works: "The Colored Citizens of New York and the African Civilization Society," 368 (n. 35); *The Colored Patriots of the American Revolution*, 95, 132, 133, 135–38, 139–53, 368 (nn. 38, 39); "Letter from Wm. C. Nell" (1859), 368 (n. 35); "Pictures of American Slavery," 138; "Speech of Wm. C. Nell," 17, 134, 135

Nell, William G., 133

Newman, Richard S., 28–29

New York Anti-Slavery Society, 184

New York Colonization Society, 68–69

New York Congregational Association, 211

New York Daily Times, 180

New York *Sun*, 282

New York Times, 13

Niles, Hezekiah, 54

North Star, 134, 285, 324

Northup, Solomon: *Twelve Years a Slave*, 180–84

Nott, Josiah Clark, 105, 106, 120

Oberlin-Wellington rescue, 279

Occom, Samson, 103

Offley, G. W., 188–89

Olney, James, 186, 187, 372 (n. 24)

O'Meally, Robert, 160

Orthodox Apostolic Church, 24

Painter, Nell Irvin, 171, 173

Panic of 1837, 184

Parker, Theodore, 31, 132, 133, 140, 184, 227

Parkhurst, Henry M., 39

Parkman, Francis, 36

Parrott, Russell, 69, 71, 73, 353 (n. 12); on Africa's redemption, 74–75

Patterson, Orlando, 6

Paul, Nathaniel, 66–67, 69–70, 92

Paul, Thomas, 317

Payne, Daniel Alexander, 140, 305, 318

Pease, Jane H., 184, 251

Pease, William H., 184, 251
Peck, David J., 118
Penn, I. Garland, 277, 282
Penn, William, 302
Pennington, James W. C., 23–24, 45, 99, 140, 185, 209, 212, 221, 251, 305–6, 308, 316; on race and racism, 44, 61, 77–78; on African American origins, 77–78; on Providence, 78; on the Bible as historical source, 78; historical method of, 78; and William C. Nell, 141; freedom purchased, 171–72 —works: "A Review of Slavery and the Slave Trade," 309; "The Self-Redeeming Power of the Colored Races of the World," 56; *A Text Book*, 10, 23, 24, 44, 61, 76–78, 291, 352 (n. 9)
Pennsylvania Abolition Society, 28
Pennsylvania Freeman, 122
Peterson, Carla L., 173, 207, 279–80, 291, 356 (n. 29), 371 (n. 13), 373 (nn. 30, 31); *"Doers of the Word,"* 379 (n. 18), 381 (n. 33)
Phillips, Wendell, 31, 135, 140, 151, 227, 228, 285
Picquet, Louisa, 176–78, 179
Pinckney, Charles, 140
Plato, Ann, 18–19, 102, 108
Pompey, 105
Pope, Alexander, 302
Prescott, William H., 17, 35, 353 (n. 16), 362 (n. 56)
Prince, Nancy, 207–8, 210
Princeton Seminary, 299
Protestant Reformation, 72
Providence (Christian), 10, 58, 98, 128, 308; and Africa, 71, 72–73, 74–75, 79, 119, 131, 185; James W. C. Pennington on, 78; Peter Williams on, 82; and U.S. mythology, 88; James Theodore Holly on, 89–90; George Bancroft on, 97; and African destiny, 119, 316; Martin R. Delany on, 121, 126, 129; Zilpha Elaw on, 193–94, 196; Jarena Lee on, 196; Harriet Jacobs on, 198–99; William G. Allen on, 229; and white national history, 357 (nn. 35, 36)

Purvis, Robert, 140, 142, 238; "The American Government and the Negro," 238
Putnam's Monthly, 282

Quarles, Benjamin, 32, 42–43, 43–44
Quincy, Edmund, 184
Quinn, William Paul, 351 (n. 2)

Race, 54, 55, 114, 120; and white supremacy, 15–16, 18, 21, 25, 30, 32, 36, 57, 116, 171–75, 333, 335, 341; racial cooperation, 29; definitions of, 30, 57, 62, 382 (n. 4); George Bancroft on, 35–36, 55; and prejudice, 40, 62–64, 68, 77, 106, 107, 117, 126, 134–35, 142, 143, 144, 160, 162, 213–14, 230, 269–70, 291, 311, 338, 339; David Walker on, 41, 58; James W. C. Pennington on, 44, 61, 77–78; and imagined community, 57–64, 155–56; Henry Highland Garnet on, 58, 59, 64, 113, 269–70, 355 (n. 23); Martin R. Delany on, 58, 116, 126, 127; William Wells Brown on, 60, 335, 338; and polygenesis, 102; Robert Benjamin Lewis on, 106, 112–13, 365 (n. 9); and discourse, 301; and romantic racialism, 311; and education, 317–20; as systemic, 319–20
Rael, Patrick, 41, 57, 294, 297, 350 (n. 1), 352 (n. 11), 356 (n. 26), 377 (nn. 48, 3), 378 (n. 6), 380 (n. 26)
Rajan, Rajeswari Sunder, 157
Ramsay, David, 122–23, 126–27, 141, 366 (n. 19)
Ram's Horn, 285
Randolph, P. B., 266, 268
Ray, Charles B., 306
Raymond, John T., 142–43
Reason, Charles Lewis, 212
Reason, Patrick Henry, 212
Reconstruction, 338
Reid-Pharr, Robert F., 58, 366 (n. 17)
Reilly, Bernard F., 382 (n. 5)
Remond, Charles Lenox, 140, 232, 238, 239, 245–46, 336, 379 (n. 20)
Remond, Sarah Parker, 242

Ricoeur, Paul, 373 (n. 33)
Riley, Sam G., 282
Roberts, Benjamin F., 383 (n. 11)
Rollin, Frank (Frances) A., 118
Ruggles, David, 285, 288
Russwurm, John Browne, 91, 303

Sabin, John F., 98
Sale, Maggie Montesinos, 359 (n. 44), 360 (n. 46)
Salem, Peter, 42
San Domingo, 51, 92–93, 110, 112, 246
Saxton, Alexander, 53
Schomburg, Arthur A., 1, 2
Schurz, Carl, 227
Scott, Sir Walter, 149, 150
Selden, H. M., 166
Seneca, Lucius Annaeus, 105
Senna, Carl, 284–85
Seward, William H., 144
Shakespeare, William. See *Hamlet, Prince of Denmark*
Sharp, Granville, 309
Sidney, Thomas Sipkins, 212
Simmons, William J., 20, 103
Sims, Thomas, 138, 141,
Sipkins, Henry, 71, 357 (n. 31)
Sipkins, Thomas, 159
Slave narratives. *See* Autobiography
Smith, Adam, 302, 309
Smith, Archie, Jr., 156–57
Smith, Gerrit, 29, 30, 140, 151, 158, 159, 285
Smith, James McCune, 29, 30, 140, 212–13, 251, 291, 313, 320
—works: "Civilization," 306, 313, 316, 321, 322; "The German Invasion," 307; "On the Fourteenth Query of Thomas Jefferson's Notes on Virginia," 307; "Republic of Letters," 386 (n. 25)
Smith, Joseph, 116
Smith, Venture, 165–68
Smith, William, 43
Socrates, 105, 145
Solomon, 102
Southern Literary Journal, and Monthly Magazine, 282
Stanley, Sara G., 248–49

Stanton, Lucy, 242–43
Stanton, William, 105
"Statistical View of the Colored Population of the United States—from 1790–1850," 307
Stauffer, John, 28, 29, 30–31
Stepto, Robert B., 187, 203
Steward, Austin, 208–9, 210, 225, 308, 376 (n. 43)
Stewart, Maria, 10, 48, 63–64, 66, 71, 75, 103, 110, 244–45
Story, Joseph, 140
Stowe, Harriet Beecher, 173, 233, 241, 272; *A Key to Uncle Tom's Cabin*, 180; *Uncle Tom's Cabin*, 180, 182, 280, 281, 298, 314
Stuckey, Sterling, 131
Student Nonviolent Coordinating Committee, 13
Sumner, Charles, 140, 285
Sundquist, Eric J., 139, 246
Sweet, Leonard I., 34, 134, 357 (n. 35), 367 (n. 27)

Taney, Roger, 238, 313
Tappan, Lewis, 285, 302
Taylor, Bayard, 227
Tell, William, 248
Terence, 212, 309
Tertullian, 212
Themistocles, 105
Theological Seminary of Missouri, 299
Thierry, Augustin, 148, 149
Thoreau, Henry David, 229
Thorpe, Earl E., 32, 346 (n. 3)
Tocqueville, Alexis de, 55, 288
To the Honorable Counsel & House of [Representa]tives for the State of Massachusetts Bay in General Court assembled, January 13, 1777, 45–46
Toussaint L'Ouverture, 63, 89, 90, 230, 246, 248, 279, 292, 322
Townsend, J. Holland, 317, 321
Townshend, Norton S., 144
Tracy, David, 21, 100, 101, 364 (n. 4)
Trumbull, Henry, 170–71
Truth, Sojourner, 114, 160, 173
Tubman, Harriet, 160, 173

Turner, Henry M., 20

Turner, Nat, 249, 279, 293; and David Walker's *Appeal*, 48; in Jacobs's *Incidents*, 200; Charles Lenox Remond on, 245; Henry Highland Garnet on, 248, 259; and effects of rebellion, 260; Amos Gerry Beman on, 316; William J. Wilson on, 327; *Confessions*, 328, 329

Underground Railroad, 322, 332
Union Missionary Society, 24
Universalist Church (New York City), 226

Van Deburg, William L., 34
Rensselaer, Thomas Van, 285, 350 (n. 1)
Vashon, George B., 140, 306, 307
Vashon, John B., 142
Vesey, Denmark, 248, 259, 279, 316
Virgil, 105
Vitzthum, Richard C., 98, 363 (n. 2)
Vogel, Todd, 280
Voltaire, 105

Wagner, Roy, 33
Wald, Priscilla, 9, 355 (n. 24)
Walker, Clarence E., 8, 10, 32, 357 (n. 35)
Walker, David, 99, 162, 213, 232, 275, 292, 316; on need for education, 40, 86; on slavery, 41, 43; on race and white supremacy, 41, 58; criticism of African Americans, 75, 358 (n. 40); on the corruption of Christianity, 86; and Robert Benjamin Lewis, 103; and William C. Nell, 133, 141; and Maria Stewart, 245; and Henry Highland Garnet, 247
—David Walker's *Appeal*, 4, 10, 19, 23, 40–41, 43, 247, 285, 314; influence of, 48–49; historical method in, 49–50; historical breadth of, 75–76; reframing of white texts in, 85–86, 291
Walker, William, 91
Ward, Samuel Ringgold, 184, 210–17, 225, 231, 232, 308, 336; *Autobiography of A Fugitive Negro*, 210–17, 376 (nn. 44, 46, 47); and problem of documenting African American history, 212; and representative identity, 212,

216; on racism and white supremacy, 213–14, 215–16; on the corruption of Christianity, 214–15
War of 1812, 80, 95, 148, 159, 279, 335
Warren, James Perrin, 378 (n. 5), 378 (n. 8)
Washington, Booker T., 116, 264
Washington, George, 140, 141, 195, 196, 248, 316, 324, 328; as representative American, 54, 191–93; compared to Toussaint, 89, 90, 246; compared to Venture Smith, 166; Maria Stewart on, 245
Washington, Madison, 213, 248, 249, 259, 279
Washington, Robert E., 82–83
Watkins, Frances Ellen. *See* Harper, Frances Ellen Watkins
Watkins, William J., 80, 84, 88, 140, 385 (n. 17)
Weekly Anglo-African, 297–98, 305
Weld, Theodore Dwight, 31, 173, 287, 289
Wesley, Dorothy Porter, 367 (n. 32)
Wesley, John, 302
Western Reserve College, 299
Weston, Caroline, 184
Wheatley, Phillis, 103, 110, 279, 316
Whipper, William, 316
White, Hayden, 46
Whitfield, James M., 140
Whitman, Walt, 30, 31, 103, 194, 339
Whittier, John G., 95, 132, 133, 140, 144
Wilberforce, William, 249
Wilberforce Society, 159
Wilkinson, James, 5–6
Williams, George Washington, 84, 331, 332
Williams, Peter, 82, 159
Wilson, David, 180
Wilson, Henry, 140
Wilson, William J., 306, 316, 386 (n. 26); "Afric-American Picture Gallery," 308, 321–28; "The Anglo-African and the African Slave Trade," 313–14
Wiltse, Charles M., 48
Winthrop, John, 137, 263, 316
Winthrop, Robert C., 140

Wolseley, Roland E., 282
Wood, Gordon S., 54
Wood, Marcus, 165, 172–73, 182, 188,
    220, 228, 376 (n. 45), 382 (n. 5)
Woodson, Lewis, 261
Woolman, John, 309
Wright, Henry C., 287, 372 (n. 21)

Wright, Richard, 132
Wright, Theodore Sedgwick, 63, 316

Yale College Divinity School, 24
Yates, William, 140

Zafar, Rafia, 370 (n. 8)